TEACHER'S HANDBOOK

Contextualized Language Instruction

Third Edition

Judith L. Shrum

Virginia Polytechnic Institute and State University

Eileen W. Glisan

Indiana University of Pennsylvania

THOMSON

HEINLE

Australia ■ Canada ■ Mexico ■ Singapore ■ Spain
United Kingdom ■ United States

THOMSON

™

HEINLE

Publisher: *Janet Dracksdorf*
Development Editor: *Heather Bradley*
Assistant Editor: *Arlinda Shtuni*
Technology Project Manager: *Maurice Albanes*
Marketing Manager: *Lindsey Richardson*
Marketing Assistant: *Rachel Bairstow*
Advertising Project Manager: *Stacey Purviance*
Editorial Production Manager: *Michael Burggren*

Senior Print Buyer: *Mary Beth Hennebury*
Permissions Editor: *Sarah Harkrader*
Production Service: *International Typesetting and Composition*
Cover Designer: *Meral Dabcovich, D/B/A Visual Perspectives*
Cover Printer: *Coral Graphics*
Text Designer/Compositor: *International Typesetting and Composition*
Printer: *Courier Corporation*

Printed in the United States of America
2 3 4 5 6 7 09 08 07 06 05

For more information about our products, contact us at:
Thomson Learning Academic Resource Center
1-800-423-0563

For permission to use material from this text or product, submit a request online at
http://www.thomsonrights.com.
Any additional questions about permissions can be submitted by email to **thomsonrights@thomson.com.**

Library of Congress Control Number: 2004112878

ISBN 1-4130-0462-8

Thomson Higher Education
25 Thomson Place
Boston, MA 02210
USA

Asia (including India)
Thomson Learning
5 Shenton Way
#01-01 UIC Building
Singapore 068808

Australia/New Zealand
Thomson Learning Australia
102 Dodds Street
Southbank, Victoria 3006
Australia

Canada
Thomson Nelson
1120 Birchmount Road
Toronto, Ontario M1K 5G4
Canada

UK/Europe/Middle East/Africa
Thomson Learning
High Holborn House
50/51 Bedford Row
London WC1R 4LR
United Kingdom

Latin America
Thomson Learning
Seneca, 53
Colonia Polanco
11560 Mexico
D.F. Mexico

Spain (includes Portugal)
Thomson Paraninfo
Calle Magallanes, 25
28015 Madrid, Spain

Contents

Acknowledgments

In this third edition, the sources of our inspiration continue to be the students and colleagues with whom we work: language learners, beginning teachers, peers, and experts. We have also found inspiration in recent changes in the visibility of our field. Key national endeavors, such as the development of standards for students and teachers, have served as a catalyst for moving language education forward in the US. Recognizing the importance of these initiatives, we have again represented real case study experiences against the backdrop of the changes in our profession, always saluting those teachers who daily commit their intellect and energy to the work of language instruction.

Again, in this edition we are grateful to Dr. Bonnie Adair-Hauck (University of Pittsburgh), Dr. Richard Donato (University of Pittsburgh), and Philomena Cumo-Johanssen (World Language Consultant, Pittsburgh, Pennsylvania) for their cutting-edge work in the area of a story-based approach for teaching grammar.

Words cannot adequately express our gratitude to Dr. Richard Donato for his expert guidance as our consultant and primary reviewer for this edition. We thank Rick for the many hours he devoted to reading and critiquing the drafts of each chapter, discussing the chapters with us in weekly conference calls, pointing us to additional sources of information, and acting as a sounding board for our ideas. We are most appreciative of his encouragement, positive feedback, sympathetic listening, patience, and never-ending willingness to take time out of his busy schedule to assist us in various ways.

In addition, we sincerely thank our principal reviewers, Frank Brooks (Florida State University), JoAnn Hammadou (University of Rhode Island), Lara Lomicka (University of South Carolina–Columbia), and Robert Terry (University of Richmond), whose insights and helpful suggestions strengthened the quality of this text. We also wish to thank the following reviewers for their input at various stages of the revision: Nancy Bell (Utah State University), Mary Brooks (Eastern Washington University), Susan Dudash (Utah State University), Robert Erickson (Brigham Young University), Elaine Fuller Carter (St. Cloud State University), Olgalucía González (Washington and Jefferson College), Sarah Gordon (Utah State University), Gail Guntermann (Arizona State University), Nancy Humbach (Miami University-Oxford), Christopher Luke (Ball State University), Martha Nyikos (Indiana University-Bloomington), Susan Ranney (University of Minnesota–Twin Cities), Evelia Romano (Evergreen State College), Brigitte Roussel (Wichita State University), Kimberly Sallee (University of Missouri-Columbia), Kathy Ulrich (University of Northern Colorado), Wynne Wong (Ohio State University). We hope that they will see their words and the results of their input throughout this third edition.

Colleagues at our respective universities and teachers and students with whom we have worked also played an important role as we wrote the book and tested concepts, providing a classroom laboratory, some of the materials, as well as reasons for reflection. We hope that they will recognize themselves in the Teach and Reflect sections, in the Discuss and Reflect case studies, and on the website.

As always, we are pleased that the book is published by Thomson Heinle and the great team of editors, under the leadership of Janet Dracksdorf as Publisher, and Heather Bradley as Senior Assistant Editor.

Finally, we wish to thank those dear to our hearts for their continuing support of our efforts. Judith thanks her Mom, Elaine Shrum, for lifelong encouragement, support, and understanding. Eileen thanks Roy Glisan for lifting all of those heavy journal boxes out of the basement on a continual basis; Nina Glisan for scanning documents and performing other complex computer tasks for Mom; and Alexander Glisan for giving up his desk and computer games so that Mommy had a place to work.

Preface

> *meaning* = "the thing one intends to convey, especially by language"
> *context* = "the interrelated conditions in which something exists or occurs"
> *(Merriam-Webster's Collegiate Dictionary*, 2003, pp. 270, 769)

Teacher's Handbook was designed with the philosophy that the purpose of language use is to convey *meaning* in a variety of *contexts*. The central theme of the text is the contextualization of language instruction. Language that is introduced and taught in meaningful contexts enables the learner to acquire competency in using language for real-world communicative purposes. Integrated language instruction allows learners to approach the learning task by combining their ability to create interpretive, interpersonal or presentational communication with their knowledge of culture and their background knowledge.

The *Standards for Foreign Language Learning in the 21ˢᵗ Century* (National Standards in Foreign Language Education Project, 1999) brought to the forefront a renewed focus on context and content, asking the question: What should students know and be able to do with another language? Each chapter of *Teacher's Handbook* assists language professionals as they develop a contextualized approach to language instruction that is based on meaningful language use, real-world communication, interaction among language learners, and learning of new information. The teaching examples and case studies offer a broad perspective of diverse teaching circumstances taken from real settings in elementary schools, middle/intermediate/junior high schools, high schools, and post-secondary settings. Further, the teaching examples are offered for various languages to show that the principles underlying contextualized instruction are constant for the many age groups represented and the languages taught.

The philosophy of *Teacher's Handbook* is that the language profession needs an openness to new ideas, research findings, and an ever expanding and emerging repertoire of practices that evolve as we discover more about teaching and learning foreign languages in today's classrooms. This philosophy is grounded in the socio-cultural environment of each individual school and classroom, recognizing the idiosyncratic influences of that environment and the roles teachers and learners perform. *Teacher's Handbook* is not simply a compendium of research on second language acquisition and foreign language teaching. Rather, its purpose is to synthesize the wealth of research for teachers, help them to understand it, and identify its implications for classroom practice. Current research undergirds *Teacher's Handbook* and serves as the backdrop for the suggestions for planning, teaching, and assessment. Since research and practice are dynamic in nature, teachers are encouraged to continuously seek new research that occurs beyond this edition and to use their own classrooms as laboratories for trying out the strategies presented here.

WHAT'S NEW IN THE THIRD EDITION?

We have remained true to our initial aim of creating a book for beginning as well as experienced teachers that they would used for reference beyond the methods course or the workshop in which they encountered it. We hoped it would find a place among the books on each teacher's desk, and that it would be well worn with dog-eared pages. Nevertheless, we also intended to bring contemporary views of language teaching to teachers, and each edition has incorporated the wide-ranging developments in our field. While the basic pedagogical support within the structure of *Teacher's Handbook* has been maintained in the third edition, there are five significant changes:

1. **New Preliminary Chapter.** A salient addition to this edition is the Preliminary Chapter, which serves as an orientation to the profession for new language teachers. It is divided into two sections: "Architecture of the Profession," which explores the various professional organizations, journals, conferences, and other supporting agencies in our field; and "Expectations for Language Teachers: A Continuum of Standards," which delineates the following sets of teacher standards that reflect shared expectations for teacher candidates, beginning teachers, and accomplished teachers:

   ■ Foreign language teacher candidates: *ACTFL/NCATE Program Standards for the Preparation of Foreign Language Teachers* (ACTFL, 2002). These standards were developed by the American Council on the Teaching of Foreign Languages and the National Foreign Language Standards Collaborative, with review, feedback, and approval by the foreign language profession at large, and approved by the National Council for Accreditation of Teacher Education (NCATE) in 2002. In each Observe and Reflect, Investigate and Reflect, Teach and Reflect, and Discuss and Reflect section of this book, the NCATE icon appears before each activity and indicates which ACTFL/NCATE standards are addressed (i.e., the specific standards to which teacher candidate evidence, produced as a result of completing the activity, can be applied; see also Preliminary Chapter).
   ■ ESL Teacher Candidates: *TESOL/NCATE Standards for P–12 Teacher Education Programs*, designed by TESOL and approved by NCATE in October 2001.
   ■ Beginning foreign language teachers: *Model Licensing Standards for Beginning Foreign Language Teachers* (INTASC, 2002), developed by the Interstate New Teacher Assessment and Support Consortium (INTASC) with support from ACTFL.
   ■ Accomplished foreign language teachers: *World Languages Other Than English Standards* (NBPTS, 2001), standards for experienced teachers, developed by the National Board for Professional Teacher Standards.
   ■ All foreign language teachers: *National Educational Technology Standards for Teachers*, developed by the International Society for Technology Education/National Educational Technology Standards Project (2003). (See Chapter 12.)

2. **New Features of the Conceptual Orientation.** The theoretical base of each chapter has been updated to include more recent research and ways to use these findings to help shape classroom instruction. These sections have been organized to facilitate student use. For example, the bulleted lists at the beginning of each chapter reflect the sequence in which topics are introduced in the chapter. In addition, each research point is interpreted in light of and with examples from language learning and teaching. Furthermore, chapters and main sections contain concluding summary comments. The focus on sociocultural theory, a key element in all editions of *Teacher's Handbook,* receives a fuller treatment throughout each chapter of the third edition. Examples are cited in more languages, such as less commonly taught languages, and English as a Second Language. In Chapter 2, the orientation to the standards includes the *ESL Standards for Pre-K-12 Students* (Teachers of English to Speakers of Other Languages [TESOL], 1997) as well as the *Standards for Foreign Language Learning in the 21st Century (National Standards for Foreign Language Education Project,* 1999).

   Several new themes have been introduced in the Conceptual Orientation: Cross Cultural Adaptability Inventory, developing advanced-level proficiency, oral conversational repair, oral and multimedia presentational communication, differentiated instruction, classroom assessment techniques (CATs), conversion of rubric scores to grades, washback effect of tests, empowering students through assessment, community-based and service learning, and issues pertinent to teaching languages in post-secondary settings. The third edition features more in-depth coverage of several themes that were introduced in the second edition, including acquisition of vocabulary, selection of textbook programs, integration and teaching of literary texts, instructional conversations (ICs), portfolios, rubric design, and integration of technology.

Chapters 8 and 9 from the second edition have been reorganized so that each focuses on one mode of communication—interpersonal and presentational, respectively. Within each chapter, the specific mode is explored in terms of both speaking and writing. In Chapter 9, presentational communication is expanded to include a discussion of multimedia presentations.

3. **New Aspects of Implementation Sections.** The Teach and Reflect and Discuss and Reflect sections of each chapter are designed to put knowledge into practice. In addition, in the Preliminary Chapter, implementation of knowledge takes the shape of an Investigate and Reflect section, and in Chapter One this section is called Observe and Reflect. Although these sections typically contain two "episodes," several chapters contain additional Teach and Reflect episodes, designed to appeal to post-secondary instructors. Discuss and Reflect sections contain case studies; sometimes the research findings are supported and sometimes the real circumstances of the classroom indicate the need for further research. Virtually all of the previous case studies have been revised or replaced with new, more engaging and illustrative cases. Some have been removed, and others have been moved to the *Teacher's Handbook* website. It bears reiterating that all case studies were inspired by real classroom scenarios, real teachers and other professionals, and real students, and as such they reflect the reality of today's foreign language classrooms.

4. **Integrated Assessment and Technology Themes.** In addition to separate chapters that deal with assessment (Chapter 11) and integration of technology (Chapter 12), the third edition features a close integration of these themes in the other chapters. Virtually every chapter now has information and ideas about assessment and technology as they relate to the particular theme of the chapter.

5. **Expanded Web Site.** For each of the chapter sections, new resources appear on the companion Web site at **http://thandbook.heinle.com.** In addition, a new implementation section has been added to the site, called View and Reflect. Here one to three video segments appear for each of the twelve chapters of the book. All of these video selections show teaching practices in real classrooms, many of which are part of the WGBH and Annenberg/CPB project "Teaching Foreign Languages K-12: A Library of Classroom Practices." Numerous links to Web sites created by teachers, as well as other online resources provided. For example, the Web site contains a video of a task-based Chinese class, a kindergarten class on a children's story about chicken pox, content-based units designed by the Center for Advanced Language Proficiency Education and Research (CALPERS), Linguafolios, WebQuests, and rubrics. Each of these resources is integrated with the appropriate chapter in the book, where an icon appears signaling that important information and extension materials can be found on the Web.

WHAT STRENGTHS OF THE FIRST EDITION HAVE BEEN MAINTAINED?

Teacher's Handbook is designed especially for the teacher who is about to start his/her career teaching foreign languages at the K–12 levels. However, professionals in higher education can make practical use of the book's suggestions related to teaching language in relation to standards for student learning, teacher performance, and program effectiveness. *Teacher's Handbook* is also suited for accomplished and experienced teachers who are searching for an update in current theory and practice, for those who are returning to the classroom after an absence from teaching, and for those who are seeking national board certification.

This text aims to enable foreign language teachers to use current theories about learning and teaching as a basis for reflection and practice. Teachers are active decision makers who use opportunities to apply theory by observing classroom interaction, designing and teaching their own lessons, and making appropriate decisions in a wide variety of situations. As developing foreign language teachers reflect upon their teaching and make decisions, they draw from many sources: competence in the second language and culture; knowledge of how the curriculum is designed and implemented; application of subject knowledge to actual teaching; application of research findings to classroom teaching; understanding of the power that technology can have in a fully articulated language program; clinical experience; and knowledge of the means by which teaching effectiveness is examined within the school context (Glisan, 2001; Glisan & Phillips, 1998; Schrier, 1993). Accordingly, *Teacher's Handbook* presents theoretical findings concerning key aspects of language teaching, as well as observational episodes, micro-teaching situations, and case studies, in order to assist beginning teachers as they develop their teaching approaches and to guide experienced teachers as they update their theoretical knowledge and teaching practices.

Teacher's Handbook assists teachers as they begin their journey toward accomplished teaching by basing their learning, teaching, and reflecting on the five propositions established by the National Board for Professional Teaching Standards:

- Teachers are committed to students and their learning.
- Teachers know the subjects they teach and how to teach those subjects to students.
- Teachers are responsible for managing and monitoring student learning.
- Teachers think systematically about their practice and learn from experience.
- Teachers are members of learning communities. (NBPTS, 1994, pp. 6–8)

The philosophy of *Teacher's Handbook* reflects Freeman's interpretist view of teaching that is founded in the daily operation of thinking and acting in context, i.e., "knowing what to do" (Freeman, 1996, p. 98). In addition, the text adopts the view that knowledge is complex and socially constructed. The teacher's sense of self is central to knowledge construction, and his/her authority and expertise are shared in the mutual construction of knowledge among peers (Baxter Magolda, 2001, p. 20). Teachers learn to interpret their worlds (e.g., their subject matter, their classroom context, and the people in it) and to use these interpretations to act and react appropriately and effectively. Knowing how to teach does not simply involve knowing how to do things in the classroom. Rather, it involves a cognitive dimension that connects thought with activity. This contextual know-how is acquired over time and its interpretations bring about effective classroom practice (Freeman, p. 99).

Accordingly, novice and experienced teachers using *Teacher's Handbook* will find structured and open-ended opportunities to observe classroom teaching and to plan and conduct micro-teaching lessons, all in light of the theory and information discussed in each chapter. A variety of case studies for K–16 describe the reality of actual teachers and learners, sometimes in support of current research findings, sometimes adding puzzling contradictions to current research, but always enriching the interpretive experience of teaching and reflecting. Related activities provide interesting opportunities to investigate and discuss effective classroom practice. Indeed, novice and experienced teachers can strengthen their individual approaches to teaching by observing, investigating, discussing ideas, teaching, and then relating these activities to one another.

In sum, according to Cochran-Smith (2004), teacher quality is "one of the most, if not *the* most, significant factor in students' achievement and educational improvement" (p. 3). It is our sincere hope that *Teacher's Handbook* impacts the quality of foreign language teachers so that language learners have successful experiences in our classrooms and are encouraged to pursue lifelong learning about other languages and cultures.

SUGGESTIONS FOR USING *TEACHER'S HANDBOOK*

We have received a substantial amount of feedback from reviewers and users of *Teacher's Handbook* that has shed light on the myriad of ways in which the text is being used. The following is a description of the key uses of the text, with selected quotes from *Handbook* users, whose names will be kept anonymous:

- *The primary methodology textbook in a methods course:* "I have two types of classes I use this text with: One is the FL methodology course, composed of undergraduates who are education majors, usually 5–8 students . . . who are getting ready to do their student teaching and graduate the following semester; and the other is made up of graduate students who are getting ready to start being FL Graduate Teaching Assistants in our department at the university and who are mixed with middle/high school FL teachers taking this as a refresher course."
- *One of several texts for preparation in ESL and World Languages:* "We use the text as one of several course texts for our initial licensure program in ESL and World Languages. It is the main source of reading that relates specifically to World Languages. . . . It is used in an integrated program that spans four courses over two semesters."
- *The primary methodology textbook divided for use in two courses:* "I teach two methods courses, Introduction to Teaching FLs and Methods of Teaching FLs. . . . I have used Chapters 1, 2, part of 3, and 10 in the first course, along with study of the *Standards for Foreign Language Learning (SFLL) in the 21st Century* (generic and language-specific) and the proficiency levels, plus some work on teaching culture (Chapter 5), teaching pronunciation, and presenting vocabulary in context. In the second course I have used Chapters 4, 5, 6, 7, 8, and 11."
- *The methodology textbook for endorsement programs, bilingual education programs, and independent studies:* "I use it . . . in my . . . upper-level interdisciplinary program, Bilingual Education and Teaching. . . . The program is preparatory for teaching careers and provides endorsement credits in foreign language and bilingual teaching. . . . I also use it extensively as the methodology textbook when working with students conducting independent studies on foreign language teaching in the elementary grades."
- *The methodology textbook for a special topics course:* "We pick and choose chapters based on what we cover but we don't go in order. I wanted to incorporate the Web site more into the course. I showed some of the digital movie clips and referred students to the online appendices."

As indicated by the above sampling of quotes by *Teacher's Handbook* users, the flexible nature of the text offers the possibility of multiple uses to serve the unique purposes and demands of specific instructional settings. In addition to the uses listed above, the text serves as a reference book and is also used as a textbook in conjunction with field experiences, including student teaching or teaching internships. The features of the third edition of *Teacher's Handbook*, including the expanded Web site, inclusion of additional topics, and applicability to more languages and levels, will undoubtedly offer methodology instructors even more possibilities for its use.

ORGANIZATION OF *TEACHER'S HANDBOOK*

Teacher's Handbook consists of twelve chapters plus a Preliminary Chapter. The first chapters present topics of a more general nature, and later chapters proceed to more specific technique-oriented issues. The Preliminary Chapter provides an introduction to the profession of language teaching. This chapter helps teachers (1) to become familiar with the professional organizations and their resources and (2) to understand the expectations of their performance in schools. Chapter 1 explores the role of contextualized input, output, and interaction in the language learning process, including a presentation of key theoretical frameworks that focus on the importance of meaning and learner engagement in acquiring language. In Chapter 1, the Observe and Reflect section helps teachers think about language learning and teaching as natural processes occurring in an environment outside of the classroom. Chapter 2 examines an integrative approach to language instruction in which language is presented and taught in meaningful contexts, consistent with the *Standards for Foreign Language Learning (SFLL) in the 21st Century* (National Standards in Foreign Language Education Project, 1999). An overview of the standards framework presented in this chapter is followed by specific ways to match activities and materials to the standards in subsequent chapters. In Chapter 3, teachers learn how to organize content and plan for integrated instruction by means of long- and short-range planning that addresses standards-based goals. Suggestions are offered for using authentic input and content to organize instruction and to engage students in the learning process.

Special attention is given in Chapters 4 and 5 to foreign/second language learners at elementary and middle school levels of instruction. The unique cognitive and maturational characteristics of learners at these two levels respond best to particular approaches and strategies. An approach utilized with older adolescents, for example, may be inappropriate for young children. However, as will be highlighted throughout the chapters, many techniques can be adapted for use across instructional levels. The information in Chapters 4 and 5 is introduced in terms of the interaction between learning and children's developmental stages, the possible effects of maturity on language learning, and the subsequent implications for teaching. Teachers explore the cognitive and maturational differences between the elementary and middle school child and the adolescent learner and develop lessons appropriate to these cognitive levels. Ways of connecting learning across disciplines and grade levels are explored as the Connections goal area is addressed in Chapter 4. In Chapter 5, the Cultures and the Comparisons goal areas are explored in terms of the products–practices–perspectives framework.

Chapters 6 through 9 offer many opportunities for teachers to focus instruction on the three modes of the Communication Standard, all within real language contexts and at various levels of instruction. Chapter 6 presents ideas for developing **interpretive communication** through the use of authentic input and building of interpretation strategies. In Chapter 7, teachers explore an approach for contextualizing grammar instruction through the use of story-based and guided participatory teaching using the PACE model. In Chapter 8, teachers learn strategies for helping students to develop oral and written **interpersonal communication** through meaningful contexts and opportunities for classroom interaction. Chapter 9 presents ideas for helping students develop oral/multimedia and written **presentational communication** through practices such as writing across the curriculum, process-oriented writing, and use of presentational software.

Chapter 10 presents ideas on how teachers might handle the diverse needs of their students that affect classroom language learning, such as learning styles, multiple intelligences, and learning disabilities. Addressing the Communities goal area, teachers explore strategies for helping students who are from a variety of cultural, ethnic, and racial backgrounds, and those who have been labeled as "at risk" or "gifted," to use language to connect with target-language communities through service learning or differentiated instruction. In Chapter 11, teachers explore many alternatives for assessing learner progress, including authentic assessment, portfolios, rubrics, and other contextualized test formats and techniques that go beyond paper-and-pencil tests, including ways to empower learners through assessment. Chapter 12 provides models and insights into the ways in which teachers can use technology to connect their students with target-language communities, while addressing the national technology standards established by the International Society on Technology Education (ISTE).

Chapter Organization

Each chapter of *Teacher's Handbook* is organized into three sections:

1. **Conceptual Orientation.** This section grounds teaching practices in a valid body of research and theoretical knowledge. It briefly describes the theoretical principles underlying the language learning observation, teaching tasks, and case studies presented later in the chapter. The section is a summary of what is known about topics in language teaching and includes references to the original research sources for additional in-depth study or review.

2. **Implementation Sections: Investigate and Reflect, Observe and Reflect, Teach and Reflect.** The Investigate and Reflect (Preliminary Chapter), Observe and Reflect (Chapter 1), and Teach and Reflect (all subsequent chapters) sections highlight practical elements of learning how to teach. In some cases, the third episode appears on the *Teacher's Handbook* Web site. The Preliminary Chapter contains Web-based tasks to engage teachers with the Web sites of their professional organizations. Chapter 1 contains guided observations, and subsequent chapters contain two or three teaching episodes. Each observation or micro-teaching situation integrates the theoretical orientation to give novice teachers an opportunity to implement pedagogically sound teaching techniques within the environment of a methods class. These micro-teaching situations can also be useful for experienced teachers attempting to learn new techniques. Discussion questions following each teaching or observation situation will help teachers integrate certain techniques into personal teaching approaches. In each Web chapter, you will find a fourth implementation section called View and Reflect, which presents opportunities to view one to three video clips of teaching scenarios and analyze them in terms of the information explored in the corresponding text chapter.

3. **Discuss and Reflect.** This section provides two or three case studies presenting non-fictitious situations actually experienced by foreign language teachers at various levels of instruction. In some chapters, the third case study appears on the *Teacher's Handbook* Web site. The case studies offer teachers the opportunity to link the theoretically grounded practices explored in the first two sections of each chapter with the reality of teaching circumstances. Every day, foreign language teachers face challenges like those presented in the case studies—challenges that may arise out of mismatches among teaching goals, learner preparedness, and academic tasks, or out of institutional goals that are inconsistent with teaching goals.

The **Discuss and Reflect** section includes two types of cases, based on real-life classroom scenarios: those that present teaching situations that support the theoretical bases featured in the chapter and those that present problematic teaching situations that are inconsistent with the theory and rationale of the chapter. The cases provide the information necessary to enable teachers to read the case and the referenced materials and to prepare a resolution of the case for class discussion. Often the cases include many details about teachers and/or teaching situations so that readers might decide which details contribute the most to resolving the case.

How to Use the Case Studies

We have been inspired by Cochran-Smith's (1999) view that "the teacher is an intellectual who generates knowledge, that teaching is a process of co-constructing knowledge and curriculum with students, and that the most promising ways of learning about teaching across the professional lifespan are based on inquiry within communities rather than training for individuals" (pp. 114–115). The case study approach was recommended by the Task Force on Teaching as a Profession (Carnegie Corporation, 1986).

A case has been defined as a descriptive document, presented in narrative form, that is based on a real-life situation or event. Cases are created for purposes of discussion and seek to elicit active analysis by users with different perspectives. Three elements are essential in a case: (1) it is real; (2) it relies on careful research and study; (3) it fosters the development of multiple perspectives by users (Merseth, 1994). Cases are not problems, though they may include problems and problem solving. In a case study, the conditions, complexity, and coping behavior of the participants are described, and the case needs to be "larger, more concrete, more engaged in its natural life, than the issues themselves [contained in the case] reveal" (Stake, 1995, p. 127).

A case study "focuses attention on a single entity, usually as it exists in its naturally occurring environment," and provides the basis for three levels of analysis and reflection (Johnson, 1992, p. 75). First, readers are given maximum guidance as they reflect upon the situations and attempt to analyze them. In the first several chapters of *Teacher's Handbook*, teachers are given a list of alternatives that represent plausible solutions to the problem or challenge presented in the teaching situation. The class discussion of each alternative assists readers in developing their own approaches to the case. In some chapters, additional information is presented, as in Chapter 3, where comparisons of block scheduling designs are given as part of the reflective practice of novice teachers facing a variety of scheduling arrangements.

Second, *Teacher's Handbook* users are encouraged to collaborate with their peers and the instructor as they discuss the alternatives and/or the development of their approaches to the situations. Sharing ideas within the classroom greatly facilitates the problem-solving process and empowers teachers in the decision-making process. Teachers are also encouraged to consult other referenced works for additional information that will assist them in formulating sound approaches to the case development. *Teacher's Handbook* users may choose from among the suggested references or consult others recommended by their instructor.

Third, as readers become increasingly familiar with case study exploration, they are asked to assume greater responsibility for developing their own solutions to the problems and challenges presented in the cases on the basis of the information provided in the chapter, the class discussions, and the previously acquired knowledge and experience. Instructors might encourage online discussions, *or completion of a professional diary or journal to include students' reflections on the cases.* Thus, the entire process leads teachers to develop their problem-solving abilities while preparing them to reflect on their teaching and classroom experiences, which are familiar and yet not completely understood.

As the case studies are designed to evoke discussion, one way to use them is to follow a jigsaw pattern, as outlined in Chapter 8, placing students in expert and novice roles and rotating them around the class, thus allowing for discussion of two or more case studies in an efficient manner.

In conclusion, we hope you will enjoy using *Teacher's Handbook* and we welcome your feedback on the third edition.

REFERENCES

American Council on the Teaching of Foreign Languages (2002). *ACTFL/NCATE program standards for the preparation of foreign language teachers.* Yonkers, NY: Author.

Baxter Magolda, M. B. (2001). *Making their own way.* Sterling, VA: Stylus.

Carnegie Corporation. (1986). *A nation prepared: Teachers for the 21st century.* New York: Carnegie Corporation.

Cochran-Smith, M. (1999). Learning to teach for social justice. In G. A. Griffith (Ed.), *The education of teachers: Ninety-eighth Yearbook of the National Society for the Study of Education* (pp. 114–44). Chicago, IL: University of Chicago Press

Cochran-Smith, M. (2004). Taking stock in 2004: Teacher education in dangerous times. *Journal of Teacher Education, 55*(1), 3–7.

Freeman, D. (1996). Redefining the relationship between research and what teachers know. In K. M. Bailey & D. Nunan (Eds.), *Voices from the language classroom: Qualitative research in second language education* (pp. 88–115). Cambridge, UK: Cambridge University Press.

Glisan, E. W. (2001). Reframing teacher education within the context of quality, standards, supply, and demand. In R. Z. Lavine (Ed.), *Beyond the boundaries: Changing contexts in language learning* (pp. 165–200). Boston: McGraw-Hill.

Glisan, E. W., & Phillips, J. K. (1998). Making the standards happen: A new vision for foreign language teacher preparation. *ACTFL Newsletter, 10*(4), 7–8, 13–14.

International Society for Technology Education/National Educational Technology Standards Project. (2003). *National Educational Technology Standards for Teachers.* Retrieved April 15, 2004, from http://cnets.iste.org/teachers/t_stands.html.

Interstate New Teacher Assessment and Support Consortium. (2002, June). *Model standards for licensing beginning foreign language teachers: A resource for state dialogue.* Washington, DC: Council of Chief State School Officers.

Johnson, D. M. (1992). *Approaches to research in second language learning.* White Plains, NY: Longman.

Merriam-Webster, Inc. (2003). *Merriam-Webster's collegiate dictionary* (11th ed). Springfield, MA: Merriam-Webster, Inc.

Merseth, K. K. (1994). *Cases, case study methods, and the professional development of educators* (Report No. EDO-SP-95-5). Washington, DC: ERIC Clearinghouse on Teaching and Teacher Education. (ERIC Document Reproduction Service No. ED401272)

National Board for Professional Teaching Standards. (1994). *What teachers should know and be able to do.* Washington, DC: Author.

National Board for Professional Teaching Standards. (2001). *World languages other than English standards.* Arlington, VA: Author.

National Standards in Foreign Language Education Project. (1999). *Standards for foreign language learning in the 21st century.* Lawrence, KS: Allen Press.

Schrier, L. L. (1993). Prospects for the professionalization of foreign language teaching. In G. Guntermann (Ed.), *Developing language teachers for a changing world, The ACTFL Foreign Language Education Series* (pp. 105-123). Lincolnwood, IL: National Textbook.

Stake, R. E. (1995). *The art of case study research.* Thousand Oaks, CA: SAGE Publications.

Teachers of English to Speakers of Other Languages. (1997). *ESL standards for pre-K-12 students.* Alexandria, VA: Author.

Teachers of English to Speakers of Other Languages. (2001). *TESOL/NCATE standards for P–12 teacher education programs.* Arlington, VA: Author.

Preliminary Chapter: Becoming Familiar with the Profession and Expectations for Language Teachers

This preliminary chapter introduces the foreign language profession by describing its structure or "architecture" and by presenting expectations for teachers in terms of standards that have been developed for teacher candidates, beginning teachers, and accomplished teachers of foreign languages. As you explore this chapter, you will want to visit the *Teacher's Handbook* Web site, where indicated, in order to access the links to professional organizations and standards documents. At the end of the chapter, you will be asked to complete a series of tasks in which you will consult these Web sites to find specific information about the organizations, conferences, and teacher standards.

In this chapter, you will be introduced to:

- key national membership organizations important to the profession
- national language-specific organizations
- organizations that provide valuable professional resources and support
- regional language conferences
- your state language association
- key professional journals
- the continuum of foreign language teacher standards: NCATE, INTASC, NBPTS

Investigate and Reflect: Learning About Your National Language-Specific Organization and Your State Language Association; Learning About Your Regional Language Conference; Familiarizing Yourself With Foreign Language Resources; Comparing Teacher Standards Across the Career Continuum

In recent years, the foreign language field has made great strides in achieving a level of professional status that enables us to play an increasingly more prominent role in educational and legislative circles. Professional organizations have collaborated with one another as never before in order to set professional goals, establish policies, and offer their constituents valuable support and assistance.[1] History will mark the past five years as a pivotal time period in foreign language education as our profession came together to articulate its expectations for language teachers in terms of standards for teacher candidates, beginning teachers, and more accomplished teachers.

ARCHITECTURE OF THE PROFESSION[2]

This section presents important information about the organizations and endeavors that constitute the architecture of our profession. The information described here is summarized from that which appears on the Web site for each organization. On the *Teacher's*

Handbook Web site, you will find links to each of these sites, which you can access to acquire additional information and updates. You will notice throughout the chapter the use of a number of acronyms. Consult our Web site for a list of key acronyms as you become familiar with the architecture of the profession.

Key National Membership Organizations

MLA.   Founded in 1883, the Modern Language Association (MLA) promotes the study and teaching of language and literature and offers opportunities for its members to share their scholarly literary findings and teaching experiences with colleagues. Comprised of over 30,000 members in 100 countries, MLA hosts an annual convention and other meetings, works with related organizations, and maintains one of the finest publishing programs in the humanities. Its involvement with foreign language teaching and learning specifically is evidenced by its role in the creation of other key organizations.

ACTFL.   The national umbrella organization for the foreign language teaching profession is the American Council on the Teaching of Foreign Languages (ACTFL), founded in 1967 by the leadership of the MLA to address issues of teacher preparation, language instruction, and curriculum development. At that time, MLA turned its focus to the promotion of foreign language study and the development of tests for use in colleges, universities, and secondary schools (Hancock & Scebold, 2000).

ACTFL is the only national organization dedicated to the improvement and expansion of the teaching and learning of all languages at all levels of instruction. The mission of ACTFL is to promote and foster the study of foreign languages and cultures as an integral component of American education and society. It is an individual membership organization of currently more than 7,000 language educators and administrators from elementary school through graduate levels of education, as well as government and industry. The organization focuses on issues that are critical to the growth of both the profession and individual teacher. ACTFL publishes the refereed journal *Foreign Language Annals*, which includes a member news section that features reports on ACTFL's activities and national news on issues of importance to foreign language educators. In addition to sponsoring an annual conference, the organization offers many professional development workshops for its members dealing with a wide range of topics, such as oral proficiency testing, standards-based instruction and curriculum development, performance-based authentic assessment, and second-language research.

ADFL.   The Association of Departments of Foreign Languages (ADFL) was established in 1969 also under the auspices of the MLA to address the professional concerns of administrators from foreign language departments at two- and four-year colleges and universities. Member departments are represented by their chairs or heads, who may in turn grant the privileges of membership to their faculty and graduate students. The ADFL puts department chairs in touch with experienced peers and provides professional development to help departmental leaders work more effectively. It provides a forum for collegial exchange about important issues through its summer seminars, Web site, and journal, the *ADFL Bulletin,* which publishes articles on scholarly and practical matters of concern to the profession and also contains news and information of interest to the profession.

State Language Associations.   Under ACTFL's umbrella are the state language associations. To obtain information about your state association, see the *Teacher's Handbook* Web site for a link to foreign language state associations.

Also working in collaboration with ACTFL are the national language-specific organizations, which include:

- American Association of Teachers of Arabic (AATA)
- American Association of Teachers of French (AATF)
- American Association of Teachers of German (AATG)
- American Association of Teachers of Italian (AATI)
- American Association of Teachers of Slavic and East European Languages (AATSEEL)
- American Association of Teachers of Spanish and Portuguese (AATSP)
- American Classical League (ACL)
- American Council of Teachers of Russian (ACTR)
- Chinese Language Association of Secondary-Elementary (CLASS) and Chinese Language Teachers Association (CLTA)
- National Council of Japanese Language Teachers (NCJLT) and Association of Teachers of Japanese (ATJ)
- American Association of Teachers of Korean (AATK)
- American Association of Teachers of Turkic Languages (AATT)
- African Languages Teachers Association (ALTA)
- Council of Teachers of Southeast Asia Languages (COTSEAL)
- North American Association for Celtic Language Teachers (NAACLT)
- International Association of Teachers of Czech (formerly the North American Association of Teachers of Czech) (IATC-NAATC)
- National Association of Professors of Hebrew (NAPH)
- Norwegian Teachers Association of North America (NORTANA)
- South Asian Language Teachers Association (SALTA)

Some of these associations also have local chapters within the states.

TESOL.   TESOL—Teachers of English to Speakers of Other Languages—is an acronym that refers to both the field itself and the professional association.[3] The field of teaching English to speakers of other languages is a professional endeavor that requires specialized training. TESOL differs from teaching English to native speakers of English, since its primary focus is on teaching non-natives to communicate in English and understand cultural practices of English-speaking communities. English as a second language (ESL) educators teach in countries where English is the dominant language, such as Australia, Canada, England, and the United States. English as a foreign language (EFL) educators teach in countries where English is spoken only as a foreign language, such as Japan and Saudi Arabia.

In English-speaking countries, ESL teachers work with immigrants and refugees at all levels of the education system, including in adult education in community colleges and community-based programs. In higher education settings, they work with international students in intensive and semi-intensive English language programs. There has been an increasing interest in the specialized area of English for specific purposes (ESP), which focuses on language skills required for academic fields (e.g., engineering, medicine, computer science) as well as business and vocational fields, and in the area of English for Academic Purposes (EAP), which prepares students to use English in their academic pursuits.

Founded in 1966, the professional organization, TESOL is headquartered in Alexandria, Virginia, and has approximately 14,000 members in over 120 countries. Its mission is to ensure excellence in English language instruction to speakers of other languages. TESOL values professionalism in language education; individual language rights; accessible, high-quality education collaboration in a global community; interaction of research and reflective practice for educational improvement; and respect for diversity and multiculturalism. TESOL's publications include a scholarly journal, *TESOL Quarterly*, and a practical magazine, *Essential Teacher*. TESOL has more than ninety worldwide affiliated organizations that represent 50,000 ESOL professionals, and its annual convention attracts 7,000–10,000 participants.

NNELL.   In 1987, the National Network for Early Language Learning (NNELL) was created to promote opportunities for all children to develop a high level of competence in at least one language in addition to their own. NNELL provides leadership, support, and service to those committed to early language learning and coordinates efforts to make language learning in programs of high quality a reality for all children. NNELL is located at Wake Forest University in Winston-Salem, NC, publishes the journal *Learning Languages*, and holds its annual meeting at ACTFL's annual conference, in addition to networking sessions at regional and state conferences.

AAAL.   Founded in 1977, the American Association for Applied Linguistics (AAAL) is a professional organization of scholars who conduct research in the field of applied linguistics. AAAL members research topics and issues related to language education, first and second language acquisition and loss, bilingualism, discourse analysis, literacy, rhetoric and stylistics, language for special purposes, psycholinguistics, second and foreign language pedagogy, language assessment, and language policy and planning. Among its many scholarly activities is its annual conference, which is recognized nationally and internationally for its in-depth symposia and workshops on key issues in applied linguistics.

NABE.   The National Association for Bilingual Education (NABE) is a nonprofit national membership organization founded in 1975 to address the educational needs of language-minority students in the U.S. and to strengthen the language competencies and multicultural understanding of all Americans. Located in Washington, DC, NABE is the only professional organization at the national level wholly devoted to representing both English language learners and bilingual education professionals. NABE supports the education of English language learners by providing professional development, collaborating with other civil rights and education organizations to ensure that the needs of language minority[4] students are met in every state, and lobbying Congress for funding for programs that serve English language learners.

CALICO.   CALICO, the Computer Assisted Language Instruction Consortium, serves members in both education and technology. With an emphasis on the role of technology in language teaching and learning, CALICO is a recognized international clearinghouse and leader in computer-assisted learning and instruction. CALICO sponsors publications, special interest groups, and annual symposia.

ASLTA.   The American Sign Language Teachers Association (ASLTA) is a national organization of professionals teaching American Sign Language (ASL) and Deaf Studies that fosters exchange of ideas among teachers on best practices at the local, state, and national levels. ASLTA was originally formed as the Sign Instructors Guidance Network (SIGN) in 1975 as a branch of the National Association of the Deaf (NAD). The mission of ASLTA is to preserve the integrity of ASL and deaf culture. The Association is committed to ensuring that teachers of ASL meet the highest level of professional competence in knowledge and skill, improving the professional status of ASL and Deaf Studies teachers, and promoting the teaching of ASL in all levels of education.

NAD.   The National Association of the Deaf (NAD) promotes, protects, and preserves the rights and quality of life of deaf and hard of hearing individuals in the United States.

With representatives from each state, the following six areas of focus have been identified for current endeavors: Civil/Legal Rights, Education/Human Services, Language and Interpreting, Multicultural/Cultural, Telecommunications/Technology, and Youth/Leadership.

RID.   Founded in 1964, the Registry for Interpreters for the Deaf (RID) works to provide training, testing, and certification for new and professional interpreters, as well as recommendations for ethical practices in interpreting. The philosophy of RID is that effective communication will be ensured by excellence in the delivery of interpretation and transliteration services among people who are deaf, or hard of hearing, and people who are hearing. Their mission is to provide international, national, regional, state, and local fora and an organizational structure for the profession of interpreting and transliterating American Sign Language and English.

NCOLCTL.   The National Council of Less Commonly Taught Languages (NCOLCTL), known as CouncilNet on the Web, addresses the issue of national capacity in the less commonly taught languages (LCTLs) by facilitating communications among member organizations and with the governmental, private, heritage, and overseas sectors of the language community. Its ultimate goal is to increase the collective impact of LCTL constituencies on America's ability to communicate with peoples from all parts of the world.

NASILP.   The National Association of Self-Instructional Language Programs (NASILP) was established to foster self-managed academic programs in the less-commonly taught languages (LCTLs). Among the languages typically offered through NASILP are American Sign Language, Haitian-Creole, Latvian, Slovak, Apache, Hebrew, Lithuanian, Slovenian, Arabic, Hindi, Mandarin (Chinese), Swahili, Armenian, Hmong, Norwegian, Swedish, Cambodian (Khmer), Hungarian, Persian, Tagalog, Cantonese, Indonesian, Polish, Telegu, Czech, Irish (Gaelic), Portuguese (Brazilian), Thai, Danish, Italian, Quechua, Turkish, Dutch, Japanese, Romanian, Ukrainian, Finnish, Kazakh, Russian, Urdu, Korean, Serbo-Croatian, Vietnamese, Lao, Siswati, Yoruba.

NCSSFL and NADSFL.   There are two national associations for foreign language administrators. The National Council of State Supervisors of Foreign Languages (NCSSFL) is an organization of education agency personnel from all states of the United States who have the responsibility of foreign language education at the state level. The National Association of District Supervisors of Foreign Languages (NADSFL) promotes excellence in foreign language education for all learners through professional development of foreign language supervisors.

Organizations/Resources Offering Valuable Professional Support

There are several organizations that provide valuable resources, professional development opportunities, and/or legislative and lobbying support for the foreign language field.

JNCL-NCLIS.   The Joint National Committee for Languages (JNCL), located in Washington, DC, was formed in 1976 as a vehicle for legislative and lobbying support for foreign languages. In the early 1980s, the National Council on Languages and International Studies (NCLIS) was created as the lobbying branch of JNCL, after which the name of the organization became JNCL-NCLIS. The organization has non-profit status and is currently comprised of over 60 organizations, united in their belief that all Americans must have the opportunity to learn and use English and at least one other language. The staff of JNCL-NCLIS monitors and influences legislation and federal programs that support many professional endeavors.

JNCL-NCLIS continues to serve as a forum that is widely recognized as a gathering place for those who govern our professional associations (Wallinger & Scebold, 2000).

CAL. The Center for Applied Linguistics (CAL) is a private, non-profit organization, headquartered in Washington, DC, and comprised of a group of scholars and educators who use the findings of linguistics and related sciences to identify and address language-related problems and issues. The mission of CAL is to promote and improve the teaching and learning of languages, identify and solve problems related to language and culture, and serve as a resource for information about language and culture. The organization conducts a wide range of activities including research, teacher education, analysis and dissemination of information, design of instructional materials, conference planning, program evaluation, and policy analysis.

NCES. The National Center for Educational Statistics (NCES) is the primary federal agency that collects and analyzes data related to education in the United States and other nations. Among its publications is the *Digest of Education Statistics*, which provides a compilation of statistical information covering the broad field of American education from pre-K through graduate school.

U.S. Department of Education. The U.S. Department of Education has awarded grants to a selected group of institutions for developing and operating "Language Resource Centers," the purpose of which is to improve the teaching and learning of foreign languages. Currently, there are fourteen Title VI Language Resource Centers nationwide:

- Brigham Young University National Middle East Language Resource Center
- University of Chicago South Asia Language Resource Center
- Duke University and UNC–Chapel Hill Slavic and East European Language Resource Center
- Georgetown University, CAL, George Washington University National Capital Language Resource Center (NCLRC)
- University of Hawaii National Foreign Language Resource Center
- Indiana University Center for Languages of the Central Asian Region
- Iowa State University National K–12 Foreign Language Resource Center (NFLRC)
- Michigan State University Center for Language Education and Research (CLEAR)
- University of Minnesota Center for Advanced Research on Language Acquisition (CARLA)
- The Ohio State University National East Asian Languages Resource Center
- University of Oregon Center for Applied Second Language Studies
- The Pennsylvania State University Center for Advanced Language Proficiency Education and Research (CALPER)
- San Diego State University Language Acquisition Resource Center (LARC)
- University of Wisconsin National African Languages Resource Center (NALRC)

FLTEACH. The Foreign Language Teaching Forum (FLTEACH) is a service for foreign language teachers that includes a WWW page, an e-mail LISTSERV Academic Discussion List, archives, and the FLNews server at the State University of New York College at Cortland. FLTEACH was launched in 1994 and operates on a computer at SUNY Buffalo. It is moderated by Jean LeLoup and Bob Ponterio, professors at SUNY Cortland. The focus of the interactive discussions is foreign language teaching methods, including school/college articulation, training of student teachers, classroom activities, curriculum, and syllabus design. Discussions are open to students in teacher preparation programs, new and experienced teachers, administrators, and other professionals interested in language teaching. Current FLTEACH membership includes colleagues from diverse institutions across the United States and around the world.

Regional Language Conferences

The foreign language profession also has regional conferences, whose mission is to conduct a yearly conference and other professional development opportunities for language teachers in the region:

- Central States Conference on the Teaching of Foreign Languages (CSC)
- Northeast Conference on the Teaching of Foreign Languages (NECTFL)
- Pacific Northwest Council on Foreign Languages (PNCFL) (meets in conjunction with a state's annual meeting)
- Southern Conference on Language Teaching (SCOLT)
- Southwest Conference on Language Teaching (SWCOLT)

As a language teacher, you should become familiar with ACTFL and/or TESOL, your national language-specific organization, your state language association, your regional language conference, and other resources that can assist you in your teaching and professional development. Your local geographical area should also have foreign language collaboratives, local chapters of the national language-specific organizations, and other language groups that offer opportunities for professional development and networking with fellow professionals.

Key Professional Journals

The following are some prominent journals in the fields of second language acquisition and/or foreign language teaching that you will find helpful as you engage in the assignments presented in *Teacher's Handbook* and as you continue your professional development as a language teacher. You have seen the names of several of these journals in the previous section "Key National Membership Organizations," as many are published by national associations. You will undoubtedly encounter other journals, particularly those that relate to the teaching of your specific language.

The Canadian Modern Language Review	*Language Learning*
Die Unterrichtspraxis	*Learning Languages*
Foreign Language Annals	*The Modern Language Journal*
French Review	*Studies in Second Language Acquisition*
Hispania	*TESOL Quarterly/Essential Teacher*

EXPECTATIONS FOR LANGUAGE TEACHERS: A CONTINUUM OF TEACHER STANDARDS

thandbook.heinle.com

For the first time in the history of our profession, there is an articulated set of expectations for language teachers at three key points across their teaching career paths: teacher education (NCATE), initial teacher licensure (INTASC), and advanced professional certification (NBPTS). These standards offer the framework for a professional development continuum— "a seamless system that takes teachers from the entry level to the accomplished level over time and acknowledges that a teacher is never really finished learning and developing as a professional" (Glisan & Phillips, 1998, p. 8; Glisan, 2001).

In October 2002, the National Council for Accreditation of Teacher Education (NCATE) approved the *ACTFL/NCATE Program Standards for the Preparation of Foreign Language Teachers*, which had been developed over a two-year period by ACTFL and the National Foreign Language Standards Collaborative, with review, feedback, and approval by the foreign language profession at large. These standards describe the *knowledge, skills*, and *dispositions* necessary for teacher candidates who are completing foreign language teacher preparation programs and earning teacher certification. NCATE is recognized by the U.S. Department of Education and the Council for Higher Education as an accrediting body for schools, colleges, and departments of education. NCATE determines which colleges of education meet rigorous national standards in preparing teachers and other classroom specialists. Foreign language teacher preparation programs seeking NCATE review and national recognition must submit program reports that address the new ACTFL/NCATE standards and provide candidate performance evidence that illustrates attainment of the standards.

In October 2001, NCATE approved the *TESOL/NCATE Standards for P–12 Teacher Education Programs*, designed by TESOL. These standards address the need for consistency throughout the United States in how teachers are prepared to teach ESL to children in pre-K–12 schools.

Simultaneous with the development of the ACTFL/NCATE Standards, the Interstate New Teacher Assessment and Support Consortium (INTASC), with support from ACTFL, developed its *Model Licensing Standards for Beginning Foreign Language Teachers* (INTASC, 2002). INTASC was created in 1987 by the Council of Chief State School Officers (CCSSO) to improve collaboration among the states as they assessed teachers for initial licensure and as they prepared and inducted new teachers into the profession. The model standards were designed to be compatible with both the ACTFL/NCATE standards for teacher preparation programs as well as with the advanced certification standards of the National Board for Professional Teaching Standards. This effort is another step toward creating a coherent approach to licensing teachers based upon shared views among the states and within the profession of what constitutes professional teaching.

In 2001, the National Board for Professional Teaching Standards (NBPTS) released its *World Languages Other Than English Standards,* which describe what accomplished teachers should know and be able to do. NBPTS hopes to raise awareness of the expertise of accomplished teachers of world languages and create greater professional respect and opportunity for the teaching community as a whole. With the NBPTS standards in place, the language profession has an articulated set of expectations for teachers from completion of a teacher preparation program to state licensing to the accomplished level. See the *Teacher's Handbook* Web site for links to these four sets of standards documents.

The International Society for Technology Education released its standards, addressing what students, teachers, and administrators should be able to do with technology in education. These standards will be fully treated in Chapter 12.

INVESTIGATE AND REFLECT

The following tasks ask you to use the Internet to find additional information concerning professional organizations and conferences and to explore the various sets of foreign language teacher standards.

TASK ONE
Learning About Your National Language-Specific Organization and Your State Language Association

Go to the *Teacher's Handbook* Web site and access the links to the Web sites of (1) your national language-specific organization (e.g., AATF, ACL, ATJ, TESOL) and (2) your state language association. Find the following information:

1. What is the mission (the goals) of each organization?
2. How do you join each organization? What is the cost of joining and what are the member benefits (e.g., publications received, discounts on conference attendance)?
3. Describe the professional development opportunities and/or other major events that each organization will sponsor in the near future (e.g., conferences, summer institutes).
4. How might your professional growth be affected by your membership and participation in one or both of these associations?

TASK TWO
Learning About Your Regional Language Conference

Go to the *Teacher's Handbook* Web site and access the link to the Web site of the regional conference in which your state is included. Your state might be included within two conferences. Find the following information:

1. What is the name of your regional conference(s) and where are the headquarters?
2. When and where will be the upcoming conference be held?
3. What services and/or resources does the conference offer to teachers (e.g., publications, teaching materials, job announcements)?
4. How might your attendance at this regional conference enable you to gain a broader perspective of the foreign language profession?

TASK THREE
Familiarizing Yourself With Foreign Language Resources

Go to the *Teacher's Handbook* Web site and visit the Web site of one of the resources listed in the chapter that most interests you (JNCL-NCLIS, CAL, one of the national language resource centers, FLTEACH, etc.). List three to five ways in which this resource can provide valuable assistance to foreign language teachers. Your instructor may ask you to share this information with fellow classmates.

TASK FOUR
Comparing Teacher Standards Across the Career Continuum

Go to the *Teacher's Handbook* Web site and access the links to the Web sites for the following three sets of foreign language teacher standards: ACTFL/NCATE or TESOL/NCATE, INTASC, NBPTS. Then find the foreign language/ESL teacher standards for the state in which you reside. You can probably access these standards through the Web site for your state organization. Compare these sets of standards in the following areas of teacher performance:

- level of oral proficiency
- cultural understanding
- instructional strategies
- implementation of performance-based assessments
- professionalism

Comment on:

1. The similarities and differences between the state standards and the NCATE standards in each of the areas above.
2. The continuum of expectations across the NCATE, INTASC, and NBPTS standards with respect to the teacher's level of oral proficiency and cultural understanding.

Your instructor might have you work in small groups on this assignment.

REFERENCES

American Council on the Teaching of Foreign Languages (2002, October). *ACTFL/NCATE program standards for the preparation of foreign language teachers*. Yonkers, NY: Author.

August, D., & Hakuta, K. (Eds.). (1997). *Improving schooling for language-minority children: A research agenda*. Washington, DC: National Academy Press.

Glisan, E. W. (2001). Reframing teacher education within the context of quality, standards, supply, and demand. In R. Z. Lavine (Ed.), *Beyond the boundaries: Changing contexts in language learning* (pp. 165–200). Boston: McGraw-Hill.

Glisan, E. W., & Phillips, J. K. (1998). Making the standards happen: A new vision for foreign language teacher preparation. *ACTFL Newsletter, 10* (4), 7–8, 13–14.

Hancock, C. R., & Scebold, C. E. (2000). Defining moments in foreign and second-language education during the last half of the twentieth century. In D. W. Birckbichler & R. M. Terry (Eds.), *Reflecting on the past to shape the future* (pp. 1–17). Lincolnwood, IL: National Textbook Company.

Interstate New Teacher Assessment and Support Consortium (2002, June). *Model standards for licensing beginning foreign language teachers: A resource for state dialogue*. Washington, DC: Council of Chief State School Officers.

National Board for Professional Teaching Standards. (2001). *World languages other than English standards*. Arlington, VA: Author.

Teachers of English to Speakers of Other Languages. (2001). *TESOL/NCATE standards for P–12 teacher education programs*. Arlington, VA: Author.

Wallinger, L.M., & Scebold, C.E. (2000). A future shaped by a united voice. In R. M. Terry (Ed.), *Agents of change in a changing world* (pp. 211–236). Lincolnwood, IL: National Textbook Company.

NOTES

1. On the *Teacher's Handbook* Web site, see the link to the New Visions in Action (NVA) Project, a national endeavor begun in 1998 by the National K–12 Foreign Language Resource Center (NFLRC) at Iowa State University and the American Council on the Teaching of Foreign Languages (ACTFL). It is a project involving Pre-K–16 foreign language educators from every state in a collaborative effort to identify and implement the actions necessary to improve the education system so that it can achieve the goal of language proficiency for all students.

2. The inspiration for this section came from the Foreign Language Methods online course developed by ACTFL/Weber State University in Ogden, UT, in 2003, with a grant from the U.S. Department of Education. This section is an expanded version of Module 2, Theme IV of the online course.

3. Professional preparation in TESOL is available throughout the world for native speakers of English and those whose first language is not English.

4. The term *language minority students* refers to individuals from homes where a language other than English is actively used and who therefore have had an opportunity to develop some level of proficiency in a language other than English. A language minority student may be of limited English proficiency, bilingual, or essentially monolingual in English (August & Hakuta, 1997, p. 15).

Understanding the Role of Contextualized Input, Output, and Interaction in Language Learning

Over the years, teachers, researchers, and theorists have attempted to answer the questions "How do people learn languages?" and "What does it mean to know a language?" Our understanding of language learning continues to develop as new research findings tell us more about this process and about how we can more effectively facilitate foreign language learning in the classroom setting. Chapter 1 presents a summary of several major theories that attempt to account for the role of contextualized input, output, and interaction in the language learning process. A framework based on socio-cultural theory is posited in an effort to acknowledge that language-learning processes are as much social as they are cognitive. Since only the key ideas concerning these theories are provided here, you may want to consult the references included at the end of the chapter in order to explore them in further detail. In Chapter 2, you will see that many of these theories served as the foundation for the development of specific approaches and methods of language teaching; see Appendix 2.1 for the chronological development of language teaching.

In this chapter, you will learn about:

- competence vs. performance
- communicative competence
- Krashen's Input Hypothesis
- input processing
- variability in performance
- Interlanguage Theory
- Long's Interaction Hypothesis
- negotiation of meaning

- Swain's Output Hypothesis
- sociocultural theory
- Vygotsky's Zone of Proximal Development
- scaffolding
- mediation
- interactional competence
- affect and motivation

Observe and Reflect: Observing a Child Interacting in His/Her Native Language (L1); Alternative Observation of a Child Interacting in His/Her Native Language (L1); Observing a Beginning Language (L2) Class

Discuss and Reflect: Creating Real Conversational Models; Using Songs to Engage Learners

In recent years, research in second language acquisition (SLA) has provided the field of language teaching with new insights into the nature of language learning (Ellis, 1997; Hall, 1997, 1999; Schulz, 1991; VanPatten & Cadierno, 1993). By studying SLA research, teachers are able to examine critically the principles upon which they base foreign language instruction. In your reading of the research, you will often encounter the term *foreign language learning* (FLL) used to refer to formal classroom instruction outside of the geographical region where it is commonly spoken, and *second language acquisition* used to refer to acquiring another language within one of the regions where the language is commonly spoken. However, in our discussion, we will use the term *language learning* to refer to the process of learning a language other than the native language in either a natural or classroom setting. The term *target language* (TL) is used to refer to the language of instruction in the classroom. The term *L1* refers to the first or native language and the term *L2* refers to the second language or TL being studied.

Much of the SLA research examines how individual language learners interface with the language, the culture, and the literature within experimental settings and classrooms. Other research views the learner as a member of a community and studies how the learner is transformed by language learning and transforms those with whom he or she interacts. This research is largely conducted in classrooms and in settings such as study abroad or in communities. To help show how our understanding of language learning has evolved over the latter part of the 20th century and the early part of the 21st century, we have divided the research themes into two categories: those that view language learning as an individual achievement and those that view language learning as a collaborative achievement within a community of learners. As you will see, each explanation of language learning generates research, new theories emerge to explain what previous theories inadequately explained, and each perspective often occurs in response to a previous one. Furthermore, each theory has implications for classroom instruction, which are suggested after each theoretical description.

Language Learning as an Individual Achievement

From Behaviorism to Cognitive Psychology: Communicative Competence

In the 1940s, a behaviorist view of language learning held that people learn by a stimulus-response habit formation pattern, and that the native language (L1) has negative interference on L2 learning. Cognitive theorists, on the other hand, believed that this explanation did not account for the ways in which humans use thought to process language. Chomsky (1965), for instance, observed that children use elements of language they know to say something they have never heard before. Chomsky proposed that humans are born with an innate "language acquisition device" (LAD) that enables them to process language. He posited that the LAD contained abstract principles of language that are universal to all languages. When children pay attention to features of the language they hear, the LAD is activated; it triggers and selects the innate rules specific to the language they hear.[1] For example, children who say "I falled down" are overgeneralizing a grammatical rule about formation of past tenses even though they have not heard that irregular form used by family, friends, and others around them; they are creating language based on what they already know. This creative use of language based on meaningful input led Chomsky to distinguish between *competence* and *performance*. Chomsky viewed *competence* as the intuitive knowledge of rules of grammar and syntax and of

FIGURE 1.1 Communicative Competence

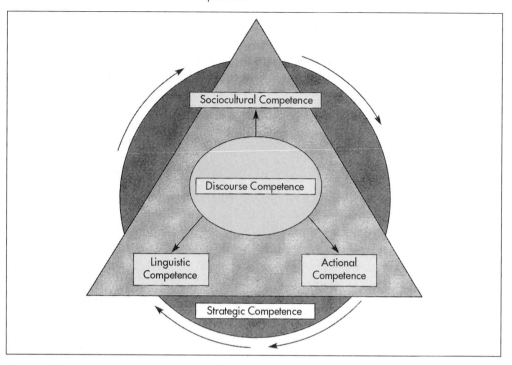

Source: Celce-Murcia, Dörnyei, and Thurrell, 1995, cf. Hall 1999, p. 20.

how the linguistic system of a language operates. *Performance*, he thought, is the individual's ability to produce language. In this view, language production results from the creative application of a learned set of linguistic rules.

Chomsky, however, was not concerned with the context in which language is learned or used. His views are considered "innatist" or "nativist" because they explain language learning capacity as being "hard-wired" into the human brain at birth. Foundational to later research was Chomsky's notion that what children hear is input, and that when they hear large amounts of language as input, children acquire language, regardless of whether it is their first or second language. An implication of Chomsky's theory for language instruction is that knowing a language is more than just stringing words together, but rather knowing how language works as a system. Other implications of his work relate to the issue of what is "innateness" to a human being; for further information on this topic, consult the research on Universal Grammar (White, 1989).

A Broader Notion of Communicative Competence: The Importance of Context

Chomsky's definition of competence was expanded to a broader notion of "communicative competence," or the ability to function in a communicative setting by using not only grammatical knowledge but also gestures and intonation, strategies for making oneself understood, and risk-taking in attempting communication (Bachman, 1990; Campbell & Wales, 1970; Canale & Swain, 1980; Hymes, 1972; Savignon, 1972). This expanded notion of competence was based upon communication within a meaningful context. The most recent model of communicative competence (Celce-Murcia, Dörnyei, & Thurrell, 1995), shown in Figure 1.1, defines the core of the concept as *discourse competence*, which refers to the way in which language elements, such as words and phrases, are arranged into utterances in order to express a coherent idea on a particular topic. Discourse competence is surrounded by sociocultural, linguistic, and actional competence. *Sociocultural competence* is knowledge about context, stylistic appropriateness, nonverbal factors, and cultural background knowledge; *linguistic competence* is the ability to make meaning when using form such as morphology, syntax, vocabulary, and spelling; and *actional competence* is the ability to match linguistic form with the speaker's intent. These components are sustained by *strategic competence*, a set of skills that enable people to communicate and compensate for deficiencies in the other competencies. For example, think of what happens when you walk into a party. Your knowledge of sociocultural competence tells you how to greet others already present in that setting with the appropriate greeting, including the most acceptable words, gestures, and body language. Actional competence helps you determine how to greet a friend you see across the room, how to ask about where another friend is, and how to express thanks for being invited to the party. Linguistic competence helps you to relate what happened to you on the way to the party by using correct tense and aspect to form past narration. Discourse competence enables you to combine multiple utterances as you talk about yourself to a new friend you meet, by using connector words such as *therefore* and *in addition*. In case you have a temporary mental block on the name of someone who greets you at the door, your strategic competence will enable you to utter a suitable greeting to buy time until you remember the name or someone else notices your discomfort and gives you the name.

An implication of communicative competence for language teachers is that students need more than grammatical or linguistic knowledge to function in a communicative setting. Of great importance, they need to be able to make meaning using grammatical forms. Also, they need knowledge of the various sociocultural factors that affect communication, knowledge of how to use language to express their ideas and intent, and knowledge of strategies for how to communicate with others and compensate for deficiencies in the other competencies.

The Role of Input

Krashen's Input Hypothesis.   Building on some of the innatist views of language learning proposed in Chomsky's work on acquisition, Krashen (1982) proposed further explanations of how language is acquired in his widely known and controversial "Monitor Model":

1. **The acquisition-learning hypothesis:** *Acquisition* is defined as a subconscious "picking up" of rules characteristic of the L1 acquisition process. *Learning*, by contrast, is a conscious focus on knowing and applying rules. Acquisition, not learning, leads to spontaneous, unplanned communication.
2. **The monitor hypothesis:** The conscious knowledge of rules prompts the internal "monitor" that checks, edits, and polishes language output and is used only when the language user has sufficient time, attends to linguistic form, and knows the rule being applied.
3. **The natural order hypothesis:** Learners acquire the rules of a language in a predictable sequence, in a way that is independent of the order in which rules may have been taught. Studies have shown that learners experience similar stages in development of linguistic structures in spite of their first languages (see, for example, VanPatten, 1993).
4. **The input hypothesis:** Acquisition occurs only when learners receive an optimal quantity of comprehensible input that is interesting, a little beyond their current level

of competence ($i + 1$), and not grammatically sequenced, but understandable using background knowledge, context, and other extralinguistic cues such as gestures and intonation. Note that the "i" refers to the current competence of the learner; the "1" represents the next level of competence that is a little beyond where the learner is now (Krashen, 1982).

5. **The affective filter hypothesis:** Language acquisition must take place in an environment where learners are "off the defensive" and the affective filter (anxiety) is low in order for the input to be noticed and reflected upon by the learner (Krashen, 1982).

Krashen's perspectives are intuitively appealing to teachers and have been influential in terms of the strong implications for classroom instruction. Among these implications are that the language classroom should provide comprehensible input at the $i + 1$ level, in a low-anxiety environment in which learners are not required to speak until they are ready to do so; input should be interesting, relevant, and not grammatically sequenced; and error correction should be minimal in the classroom since it is not useful when the goal is acquisition.

An area of language instruction that developed significantly as a result of Krashen's theory of acquisition and comprehensible input is the teaching of vocabulary. Historically, vocabulary in textbooks was presented in lists of words in the target language followed by their native language equivalents, as in the following example of events that are reported in the news in Spanish:

un terremoto	an earthquake
un incendio	a fire
una inundación	a flood
un tornado	a tornado
un robo	a robbery

This approach suggests to learners that vocabulary acquisition is a matter of memorizing target language equivalents of native language words (Lee & VanPatten, 2003). Our understanding of L1 acquisition and input illustrates that children acquire vocabulary as a result of attending to large quantities of meaningful input and by interacting with the concrete objects referred to in the input. For example, children acquire the word "milk" by hearing their caretakers say "Here's your milk" and grasping a cup of milk handed to them; or by accidentally spilling their milk on the floor and hearing someone say "Oops, you spilled your milk!"; or by watching a caretaker select a brand of milk for purchase in the grocery store. A similar process occurs in second language acquisition of vocabulary when learners are given opportunities to make connections between form (i.e., the language they hear) and meaning (i.e., the concrete objects referred to in the input)—Terrell (1986) refers to this process as *binding*:

> *Binding* is the term I propose to describe the cognitive and affective mental process of linking a meaning to a form. The concept of binding is what language teachers refer to when they insist that a new word ultimately be associated directly with its meaning and not with a translation (p. 214; cf. Lee & VanPatten, 2003, p. 39).

Binding can be facilitated during vocabulary acquisition by presenting vocabulary in meaningful groups (e.g., physical descriptions, clothing, weather), providing meaningful input in presenting vocabulary, using visuals and objects so that students can match the TL description to the concrete referents, and engaging students in demonstrating comprehension and acquisition of vocabulary before actually asking them to produce it orally or in written form. (A more detailed discussion of activities that lead to vocabulary acquisition can be found in Chapter 4.) Textbooks increasingly have moved toward using visuals to present vocabulary in order to facilitate binding, as in the example in Figure 1.2 of

FIGURE 1.2 Visual Presentation of Vocabulary to Facilitate Acquisition

Source: Glisan and Shrum, 1996, p. 204.

events that happened and were reported on in the news; compare this type of presentation to the vocabulary list you saw above.

Krashen's claims have been strongly criticized by various researchers on the grounds that (1) his theories have not been empirically tested in language learning environments; (2) concepts such as "comprehensible input" and the learning-acquisition distinction are not clearly defined or testable; and (3) his model presents far too simplistic a view of the acquisition process (McLaughlin, 1987; Munsell & Carr, 1981; Lightbown, 2004). Furthermore, use of the "acquisition-rich environment" diminishes the role of the learner in the foreign language classroom by highlighting the role of the teacher as the source of comprehensible input and by failing to recognize the function of learner-to-learner talk (Platt & Brooks, 1994). Few would deny that Krashen's model sparked a great deal of thought and discussion in the profession regarding the role of input in language learning. Nevertheless, many of his claims paint an unclear picture of the role of classroom instruction in language learning and remain to be empirically tested.

Input Processing. One application and extension of Krashen's input theory is the focus on how learners actually process input to "connect grammatical forms with their meanings" (VanPatten, 2004, p. 5). Building on Krashen's views on input, some researchers suggested that when input is simplified and tailored to the level of the learner, learners are able to make connections between form and meaning and thus convert input to intake. *Intake* is language that is comprehended and used by learners to develop a linguistic system that they then use to produce *output* in the language. VanPatten and Cadierno (1993) argue that beginning language learners need structured input activities that enable them to focus on meaning while they pay attention to form before they can use the language to produce output. Research across languages and with a variety of grammatical structures has indicated that instructional strategies that incorporate input are successful in helping learners build linguistic systems (Buck, 2000; Cheng, 2002; Farley, 2003; Wong & VanPatten, 2003).

This line of research on how learners process input led to an instructional approach called "processing instruction" (VanPatten, 2004), which is not a theory of acquisition but rather a set of principles about how languages are learned and taught, based on a primary tenet that learners pay attention to meaning before they pay attention to grammatical form. For example, one principle is that "learners process input for meaning before they process it for form"; i.e., they attempt to understand the meaning of the message before they process grammatical structures (Lee & VanPatten, 2003, p. 139). A second related principle is that "learners process content words in the input before anything else"; that is, they search for the words that offer the most clues to content, such as nouns, verbs, and adjectives (Lee & VanPatten, 2003, p. 139).[2]

In processing instruction, learners process the form or structure by means of activities that contain structured input, "input that is manipulated in particular ways to push learners to become dependent on form and structure to get meaning" (Lee & VanPatten, 2003, p. 142). Key implications of input processing theory for foreign language instruction are (1) in order to make sense of grammatical forms and be able to use them in communication, learners need to be engaged in attending to meaningful input, and (2) mechanical grammar practice is not beneficial for language acquisition (Wong & VanPatten, 2003).

Variability in Performance.   Krashen's claim that only acquisition, and not learning, leads to spontaneous communication has been criticized by researchers because it fails to account for ways in which learners use both automatic and controlled processing in communicative situations. Krashen's model also fails to account for the fact that what learners can do with language often varies within a single learner, over time, within contexts, and across different learners. In attempts to explain how and why performance varies, some researchers (Bialystok, 1981, 1982; Ellis, 1997; Tarone, 1983; McLaughlin, Rossman, & McLeod, 1983) posited that learners use automatic processes and controlled processes in a variety of combinations in their production and comprehension of the target language. When engaged in a conversation task, for example, the learner may activate automatic, unanalyzed processing as shown in this example.

Speaker 1: Hi.

Speaker 2: Hi, how are you?

Speaker 1: Fine, and you?

Speaker 2: Fine. (Gass & Selinker, 1994, p. 154)

The elements of language in this conversation become so automatized, i.e., used automatically, that we may answer "Fine" even before the question is asked. Controlled processing becomes automatic processing when learners practice regularly and what they practice becomes part of long-term memory. However, sometimes learners may be able to begin language processing with an automatized lexical item, i.e., word or expression. For instance, beginning learners on the first day of language class can ask classmates their names in Spanish without consciously thinking through the use of reflexive verbs, simply by using a lexical item of "¿Cómo te llamas?" which quickly becomes used as an automatized item. When the teacher instructs them that they must address a visiting adult guest in the classroom using the form "¿Cómo se llama?" they do so using controlled processing because they now have to consciously think about how to modify what they already know in order to use the correct phrase. According to Ellis (1994), use of these two types of processes accounts for (1) the individual variation in the language of a second language learner as different types of knowledge and processes are activated in different communicative contexts, and (2) variation in language use across language learners.

Lightbown (1985) also proposes some explanations to account for variations in learners' production of language. For example, in certain situations, learners might use a given structure that is error-free and consistent with the target language, while in subsequent situations, after new material has been presented, they might use the same structure with errors that reflect influence of the native language. Then, learners use the form correctly again, having presumably restructured their understanding of the original structure plus the new material. This is called *U-shaped behavior* because of the way it is typically mapped, as illustrated in Figure 1.3.

 Learners use automatic processes and controlled processes in a variety of combinations in their production and comprehension of the target language. ■

Research in the area of variability in performance is significant for language teachers because it indicates that an individual's performance will vary over time and that performance varies from one individual learner to the next. In addition, the evidence convincingly indicates that the ability to verbalize a language rule does not signify that the language learner can use it in communication (Lightbown, 1985).

 The ability to verbalize a language rule does not signify that the language learner can use it in communication. ■

Interlanguage Theory.   The variability in language performance that you explored in the previous section is also evident in the learner's use of the target language at any point in time. Selinker (1974) defines *interlanguage* as the "language of the learner," a system in development and not yet a totally accurate approximation of native speaker language. It is an individual linguistic system created by second language learners as a result of five cognitive processes: (1) interference from the native language; (2) effect of instruction, e.g. an instructional approach, rules provided by the teacher, classroom activities; (3) overgeneralization of target language rules, such as application of rules to contexts where they do not apply; (4) strategies involved in second language learning, such as rote memorization, use of formal rules, and guessing in context; and (5) strategies

FIGURE 1.3 U-Shaped Behavior

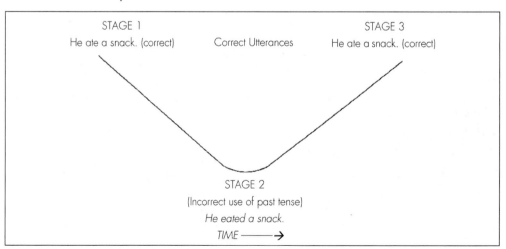

Source: Adapted from Gass and Selinker, 1994, p. 159.

involved in second language communication, such as circumlocution, use of gestures, and appeal for assistance from a conversational partner (Selinker, 1974). Current theories of L2 acquisition maintain that learners modify their interlanguage only when they integrate into their long-term memories the input that they hear or read; that is, they construct new hypotheses in order to incorporate the noticed features into the interlanguage system (Ellis, 1997; Gass, 1988).

Selinker's Interlanguage Theory helps us to understand what happens in the mind of the learner. An implication for foreign language teachers is that a learner's use of the target language reflects a system in development and therefore has errors that occur as a natural part of the acquisition process. As teachers provide good models of TL input and engage learners in attending to that input, learners alter their interlanguage to incorporate new and/or more accurate features of native speaker language.

Up to this point, you have examined the role of input in the language acquisition process and ways in which language performance is variable. As you will see in the next section, there are several ways in which input can be modified and converted to intake.

Role of Modified Input, Interaction, and Output

Long's Interaction Hypothesis.   According to Long (1983), input comes to the individual from a variety of sources, including others. Individuals make their input "comprehensible" in three ways:

- by simplifying the input, i.e., using familiar structures and vocabulary;
- by using linguistic and extralinguistic features, i.e., familiar structures, background knowledge, gestures; and
- by modifying the interactional structure of the conversation.

This third element is the basis of Long's (1981) Interaction Hypothesis, which accounts for ways in which input is modified and contributes to comprehension and acquisition. Long (1983) maintains that speakers make changes in their language as they interact or "negotiate meaning" with each other. *Negotiation of meaning* has been characterized as "exchanges between learners and their interlocuters as they attempt to resolve communication breakdown and to work toward mutual comprehension" (Pica, Holliday, Lewis, & Morgenthaler, 1989, p. 65). Speakers negotiate meaning to avoid conversational trouble or to revise language when trouble occurs. Through negotiation of meaning, interactions are changed and redirected, leading to greater comprehensibility.

What exactly does it mean to negotiate meaning?[3] Just as in a business negotiation, two parties must participate by challenging, asking questions, and changing their positions. Merely conceding is not full negotiation. In the classroom this means that both parties in a teacher-student and student-student interaction must seek clarification, check comprehension, and request confirmation that they have understood or are being understood by the other. This process is often difficult to achieve in the classroom, given the traditional roles between teachers and students. Since students are often hesitant to question or counter-question the teacher, negotiation of meaning may not occur often. Although teachers often work to provide comprehensible input through a variety of techniques (visuals, simplified input, mime, etc.), this process does not necessarily inspire or lead to the negotiation of meaning. For this type of interaction to occur, both interlocutors must have equal rights in asking for clarification and adjusting what they say.[4] Thus Long's theory implies that learners cannot simply listen to input, but that they must be active conversational participants who interact and negotiate the type of input they receive in order to acquire language.

As you have now seen, interaction also plays a role as the cognitive processes of learners interact with the input to which they pay attention. Input can become implicit, or automatic language, when learners notice specific features of it, compare these features to those of their own output, and integrate the features into their own developing language system (Gass & Selinker, 1994; White, 1987).

 Learners must be active conversational participants who interact and negotiate with the type of input they receive in order to acquire language. ∎

Swain's Output Hypothesis.   Krashen (1982) maintains that input is both a necessary and sufficient condition for language acquisition; that is, nothing else is needed for acquisition to occur. Swain (1985, 1995) argues that input is a necessary but not sufficient condition for language development. She argues that learners also need opportunities to produce output. Simply stated, learners need to speak the language to achieve higher levels of language competence. Swain's ideas derived largely from observing immersion students who, after several years of comprehensible input in immersion programs in Canada, did not show signs of language growth, specifically in the area of grammatical accuracy and sociolinguistic appropriateness. According to Swain (1995), *output*, or speaking the language for the purpose of communicating one's ideas, facilitates acquisition, as it (1) helps learners to discover that there is a gap between what they want to say and what they are able to say, (2) provides a way for learners to try out new rules and modify them accordingly, and (3) helps learners to actively reflect on what they know about the target language system. During speaking tasks, learners engage in what Swain refers to as *pushed output*, which allows them to move from what they want to say (e.g., the vocabulary they need) to how they say it (e.g., the grammar and syntax to make their meanings clear and appropriate to the context).

Additionally, by repeatedly using the target language in natural communicative situations and focusing on their output, learners eventually develop automaticity and move from analyzing what they want to say to being able to say it with ease. According to Ellis (1997), the use of linguistic knowledge becomes automatic only when learners make use of interlanguage knowledge under real conditions of communication. An example of this process occurs in a conversation in which a student who is narrating a story states "no sé" (I don't know), indicating a gap in knowledge: "Estaba en un . . . um. . . . no sé, cast . . . casto (laugh) por cinco meses" ["I was in a . . . um . . . I don't know (laugh), cast for five months"] (Liskin-Gasparro, 1993, p. 269). The student says "no sé" to signal that he's thinking about the next word he needs; he hypothesizes about a correct form based on what he already knows about cognates (casto); by laughing he shows that he is not sure of this invention and invites modification from his more capable listener; ultimately, the student succeeds in making the tale understandable to his listener. By talking through the difficulty, the student makes the story comprehensible, hypothesizes about the correct structure, attempts to apply what is already known, and reflects on the forms of language being used. Thus, as learners create output in the target language, focus on form naturally arises.

The implication of Swain's theory is that teachers need to provide opportunities for output that is meaningful, purposeful, and motivational so that students can consolidate what they know about the language and discover what they need to learn. Teachers need to provide age-appropriate and interesting topics that students can explore in discussion and collaborative writing tasks that will produce output that leads students to reflect on the forms they are using, on the appropriateness of their language, and on ways to express what they want to say using what they have learned (R. Donato, personal communication, February 25, 2004). Output activities are also an effective way to improve the use of specific communication strategies, such as circumlocution (Scullen & Jourdain, 2000). After collaborative tasks are completed, teachers may also find it useful to discuss with students how they communicated "in order to clear up unresolved language problems that the collaborative dialogues . . . revealed" (Lapkin, Swain, & Smith, 2002, p. 498).

 What factors influence an individual's ability to acquire language?

Language Learning as a Collaborative Achievement

The ability to acquire and develop a new language through input, output, and interaction is one of the goals of classroom language instruction. Much of the research explored in the previous sections focuses on how L2 input is negotiated by individual learners and made more comprehensible. Although these studies acknowledge the importance of collaborative interaction in the learning process, their focus on negotiation of L2 input offers an incomplete picture of learners' interaction in an L2 classroom setting (Antón & DiCamilla, 1998). The interactionist view has been challenged by researchers examining the nature of sociocultural theory. According to sociocultural theory, our linguistic, cognitive, and social development as members of a community is socioculturally constructed (Vygotsky, 1978; Wertsch, 1991; Wertsch & Bivens, 1992). As Wertsch states, our development "is inherently linked to the cultural, institutional and historical settings in which it occurs" (1994, p. 203). In this view, learning and development are as much social processes as cognitive processes, and occasions for instruction and learning are situated in the discursive interactions between experts and novices (Appel & Lantolf, 1994; Brooks, 1990; Lantolf, 1994; Rogoff, 1990; Wells, 1998).

 Occasions for instruction and learning are situated in the discursive interactions between experts and novices.

Vygotsky's Zone of Proximal Development

The work of Vygotsky, a social psychologist, highlights the role of social interaction in learning and development. *Learning* refers to gaining knowledge, comprehension, or skills not possible through maturation, and *development* refers to progress from earlier to later stages of maturation. Vygotsky's views on learning and development in children differ markedly from those of Piaget, for whom learning and mental development are independent processes. According to Piaget (1979), learning does not affect the course of development since maturation precedes learning. In this framework, the learner must be cognitively and developmentally ready to handle certain learning tasks. In Vygotsky's (1978) view, however, learning precedes and contributes to development, and the learner's language performance *with others* exceeds what the learner is able to do *alone.* The learner brings two levels of development to the learning task: an *actual developmental level*, representing what the learner can do without assistance, and a *potential developmental level*, representing what the learner can do with the assistance of adults or more capable peers. Through interaction with others, the learner progresses from the "actual developmental level" to the "potential developmental level." Between the two levels is the learner's Zone of Proximal Development (ZPD), which Vygotsky defined as "the distance between the actual developmental level as determined by independent problem solving and the level of potential development as determined through problem solving under adult guidance or in collaboration with more capable peers" (Vygotsky, 1978, p. 86). In this process, the potential developmental level of the learner becomes the next actual developmental level as a result of the learner's interaction with others and the expansion of cognitive abilities. In other words, what learners can do with assistance today, they will be able to do on their own tomorrow or at some future point in time.

FIGURE 1.4 The Continuous Cycle of Assistance in the Zone of Proximal Development

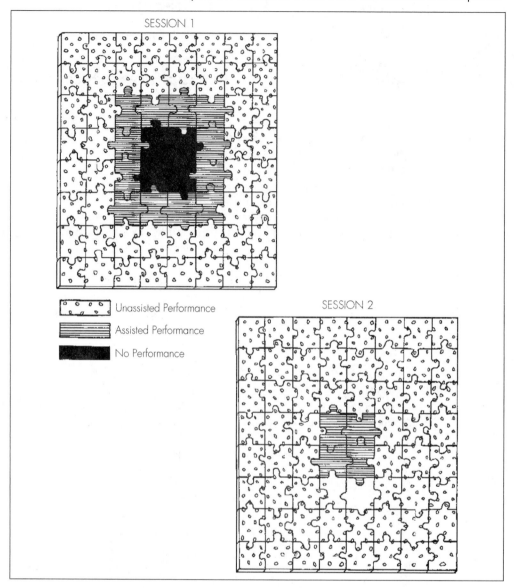

Source: Adair-Hauck, 1995.

Figure 1.4 illustrates the continuous cycle of assistance in the Zone of Proximal Development, as it occurs in the task of co-constructing a puzzle with a novice. In Session 1, or the first attempt at building a puzzle, the novice recognizes the straight edges of the perimeter and is able to put those pieces of the puzzle together alone, without assistance from the expert. When performing this task, the novice is demonstrating his/her actual developmental level. With assistance from the expert, the novice puts together pieces of the puzzle that are within the puzzle but still close to the perimeter. When performing this set of tasks, the novice is working at his/her potential developmental level; he or she is able to perform the task, but only with expert assistance. Soon the novice will be able to perform this set of tasks without assistance, hence the term *potential developmental level*. Where the learner can achieve no performance with assistance, no ZPD is created. Session 2 represents some future point in time (perhaps moments, weeks, or months later) when the novice can put more of the puzzle together on his/her own and needs assistance for only some of the puzzle. In other words, the potential developmental level of Session 1 becomes the actual developmental level of Session 2, illustrating the iterative nature of performance and assistance. In both sessions, the ZPD is depicted in the areas marked by assisted performance. Note that the ZPD gets smaller in Session 2, which is a sign of development and learning and indicates that the novice can now complete more tasks alone. In order to discover the ZPD of the novice, the expert or more capable peer enters into dialogic negotiation with the novice and offers help that is graduated, i.e., tailored to the level of the novice, and *contingent*, i.e., given only when needed and then withdrawn when the novice is able to function independently (Aljaafreh & Lantolf, 1994). The following is an example of a dialogue that might occur between an expert and a novice as they complete the task depicted in Figure 1.4, Session 1:

Expert: Let's use the picture on the box to help us put the puzzle together. Why don't we find the straight-edge pieces first?

Novice: OK. I can make the outside with the straight pieces by myself [unassisted performance].

Expert: Great, now we have the frame. Let's try to find the pieces that have the same color. Can you find the blue and white pieces?

Novice: Here are some, but I don't know how they go together.

Expert: That's OK. We'll do it together. Can we find pieces that have similar shapes?

Novice: Does this one go in this way?

Expert: Here . . . maybe if you turn it around, it'll fit. There, you got it! [assisted performance] [Let's try the other pieces that look the same].

 What learners can do with assistance today, they will be able to do on their own tomorrow or at some future point in time.

Scaffolding in the ZPD. The language of the expert or more knowledgeable peers serves as directives and moves the learner through his or her ZPD to the point where the learner is able to perform a task alone (Aljaafreh & Lantolf, 1994; Vygotsky, 1978). The interaction between the expert and novice in a problem-solving task is called *scaffolding* (Duffy & Roehler, 1986; Wood, Bruner, & Ross, 1976). In scaffolding, the expert's help is determined by what the novice is doing, and is structured so that irrelevant aspects of the task do not interfere with the learner's range of ability. The expert provides the novice with scaffolded help by enlisting the learner's interest in the task; simplifying the task; keeping the learner motivated and in pursuit of the goal; highlighting certain relevant features and pointing out discrepancies between what has been produced and the ideal solution; reducing stress and frustration during problem solving; and modeling an idealized form of the act to be performed by completing the act or by explicating the learner's partial solution (Wood, Bruner, & Ross, 1976, p. 98). The Vygotskyan concept of the ZPD suggests that language learning occurs when the learner receives appropriate types of assistance from the expert, e.g., teacher. In order to provide scaffolded assistance, it is important that the teacher know where students are in terms of their language development. Furthermore, the teacher's role is (1) to recognize that assistance is contingent on what the novice is doing, not on what the expert thinks should be done, and (2) to know when to turn the task over to the novice for solo performance (R. Donato, personal communication, February 15, 2004; VanLier, 1996). Appendix 1.1 lists the types of language-promoting assistance that reflect scaffolded help (Scarcella & Oxford, 1992).

Transformation in the ZPD.   The ZPD occurs in interactive activity where novices and experts work together to solve problems and, in the process, transform their individual knowledge of the task and understanding of each other (Newman & Holtzman, 1993). Working in the ZPD produces learning, which is reciprocal, and not just unidirectional from expert to novice. Wells (1999) points out that the results of this kind of ZPD activity enable learners to participate easily in similar communicative events and learn from them, such as when they speak with native speakers of the TL. In addition, by collaborating on a problem or task, the novice and expert transform their relationship and understanding of each other and of the task at hand.

When discussed in the context of the foreign language classroom, some view activity in the ZPD as limited to instruction on language content, such as a grammatical structure. The ZPD can be conceived of more broadly, as pointed out by Kinginger (2002), and applied to all aspects of foreign language instruction and learning, including developing discourse competence and pragmatic and cultural appropriateness. For instance, in a setting where a teacher and a small group of students are helping each other to write and edit an e-mail letter to a school in Madrid, one student might suggest "You mentioned that you went to a football game, and that your team won by an extra point at the end of the game. Will the reader understand what an extra point is in American football?" The student who wrote the letter might say, "Do you think I need to explain a little about American football?" The assistance the first student provides could then lead the teacher to another suggestion, such as, "Your audience in Madrid may not be familiar with American football since they play soccer. Let me check with their teacher in Madrid and get back to you." By working in the ZPD, this teacher and his/her learners provide mutual assistance and co-construct cultural knowledge that is available for present and future learning events. Perhaps in the future and because of this assistance, the concept of "audience" and the need to make cultural references clear will re-emerge for these students as an important aspect of the writing process. Moreover, as students make suggestions for what they want to say, they set their own learning agenda. Thus within the ZPD, teachers are informed of areas of interest to the learners and language and cultural knowledge they want to know.

When individuals work in the ZPD, scaffolding often arises. Scaffolded interactions occur when the expert, e.g., the teacher or a more knowledgeable peer, reduces the frustration level of the task. In the case of the collective e-mail letter writing, the teacher provides suggestions and tools in the form of information about the audience to reduce student frustration in trying to provide necessary details in the letter. Scaffolding also suggests that the expert identifies critical features of the task (e.g., considering the audience when writing a letter and not assuming that football is played the same way everywhere in the world). During scaffolded interactions in the ZPD, the teacher is transformed from one who provides solutions to one who facilitates the learners' search for solutions. The teacher also gains from the interaction by observing how his/her assistance is used by the students, how his/her help leads them to a potential level of development, and where his/her students might be in their letter writing ability in the future. Empirical evidence also supports the function of the ZPD as an activity through which social patterns of interaction and mutual assistance can result in learning (Donato, 1994; Ohta, 1995; Swain & Lapkin, 1998). It is important to note that the ZPD is an activity that is at the same time the tool for learning language and the result of using language with others. It is not just a tool for a result, but rather tool *and* result; e.g., a teacher uses the tool of a story and engages students in short retelling or writing, which results in the creation of the ZPD where he or she may provide scaffolding. Language use creates a ZPD so that learning can happen; this learning may be decided upon by the learners (i.e., not just by curricular objectives) and involve what they need to know in order to accomplish the activities in which they are engaged. The ZPD, therefore, is a powerful concept that offers a different view from that of the typical "delivery of instruction" model of language teaching. Donato (2004) points out that the concept of the ZPD and sociocultural aspects of interactions in second language classrooms have been largely ignored, but that they offer a rich source of understanding about how a language can be learned by learners who are actively using it in collaborative interaction.

i + 1 **is not ZPD.**   The concepts of *i* + 1 and the ZPD are intuitively appealing to teachers and are often viewed as the same concept. They are indeed very different concepts and offer differing explanations for language learning. The *i* + 1 is primarily a cognitive view that holds that language learning makes use of innate knowledge within the mind of a learner, who functions primarily as an individual in processing comprehensible input (Atkinson, 2002; Pennycook, 1997). By contrast, the ZPD posits that language learning is an activity that happens through interaction and collaboration in social settings while the learner responds to those around him/her. It is an "outside-in" (Shore, 1996) process in which learners use the language with the support of others while simultaneously learning it. The *i* + 1 is about language and input. The ZPD is about working together, participating in a community and obtaining the assistance needed to enable continued participation in that community. Thus, the ZPD is not just a tool for using and learning about language but also arises as a result of using language in meaningful and purposeful ways with others (McCafferty, 2002; Newman & Holtzman, 1993). When teachers and learners work in the ZPD, language learning cannot be separated from language use (Kinginger, 2001).

Mediation in the ZPD.   Within a sociocultural perspective, learners use tools as a means of mediating between themselves and the world, as a way of assisting and supporting their learning and making sense of the world around them, including the language classroom. Mediational tools can take the form of the textbook, visuals, classroom discourse patterns, opportunities for interaction in the second language, direct instruction, or teacher assistance (Donato & McCormick, 1994, p. 456). One type of mediational tool is the portfolio, which students can construct to reflect on language, to clarify and set goals, to select effective strategies to enhance performance, and to provide concrete evidence of strategy use (Donato & McCormick, 1994). Mediational tools assist learning, are both social and cultural, and may be determined by a variety of factors, such as distribution of educational resources. For example, in one school setting, every student might have a wireless computer, while in another setting computers may be largely inaccessible to students, e.g., there may be two computers sitting in the back of the classroom. Additionally, based largely on the instructional practices of the teacher, some students may feel that they can't learn the language unless they are given specific types of tools such as vocabulary lists and verb conjugations. In other classes, students may be more willing to use tools such as authentic documents to mediate their learning if they are provided with occasions to do so. The attitudes toward using mediational tools are often the result of social and school learning practices, since students are socialized into certain forms of mediation as a way to learn, into how to use tools to learn, and even into believing that certain types of tools contribute to learning in a valuable way.

In addition to all of the mediational tools discussed above, it is important to recognize that language itself is also an important mediational tool. Collaboration allows students to use language to mediate their language learning because in collaboration students use language to reflect on the language they are learning. It is not uncommon to hear students hypothesize about a certain way to say something in the target language when they work together on producing the language for projects, presentations, or inter-personal communication tasks. For example, learners may try out alternate ways of saying a phrase or sentence (Un piscine? Une piscine? Or Il est allé a l'école? Il a allé a l'école?). Here language itself is a tool for reflecting on the language being learned. Additionally, as one learner speaks aloud alternate forms, other learners are signaled to provide assistance. Donato's (1994) study revealed the use of this type of verbal mediation by learners of L2 French, who negotiated linguistic forms with one another in small-group work. Although no individual possessed complete knowledge of the forms produced, through their mutual assistance and collective problem-solving, the group was able to correctly construct utterances for their later presentation to the class. Thus learners can successfully acquire language through their verbalizations, which act as a way of scaffolding each other.

Sociocultural theory also maintains that learning is facilitated by the learner's use of self-talk, which serves as a mediational tool (Ellis, 1997). According to Vygotsky (1986), one of the mediational tools used by children is speech for the self, or private speech, a type of thinking aloud that helps to structure and clarify a task to be done or a problem to be solved. For example, Vygotsky cites the following example of private speech used by a child during play activity to overcome a cognitive difficulty: (Child speaking to himself/herself) "Where's the pencil? I need a blue pencil. Never mind, I'll draw with the red one and wet it with water; it will become dark and look like blue?" (Vygotsky, 1986, p. 29). Private speech is the convergence of thought and language, which acts as "an instrument of thought in the proper sense . . . as it aids the individual in seeking and planning the solution of a problem" (Vygotsky, 1986, p. 31). Adults use private speech, sometimes in the form of whispering to the self in second language learning, as they attempt to make sense of a task or reveal that they suddenly understand or have mastered a source of difficulty with some aspect of the task (Antón & DiCamilla, 1998; Brooks, Donato, & McGlone, 1997; Frawley & Lantolf, 1985; McCafferty, 1994).

Lantolf (1997) proposes that one of the functions of private speech is *language play*, the mediational tool by which learners experiment with those grammatical, phonological, and lexical features of the language being acquired. Children, for example, compare their old and new knowledge of the language by modifying language structures through strategies such as completions and substitutions, by imitating and transforming what others say, and by repeating their own utterances (Kuczaj, 1983). Children imitate parts of new utterances that are either within or slightly beyond their current level of linguistic competence. During this imitation, children also play with the language, changing it slightly or experimenting with its words. For Vygotsky, language play creates a zone of proximal development in which the child "always behaves beyond his average age, above his daily behavior" (Vygotsky, 1978, p. 102).

Some studies suggest that adolescent and adult language learners mediate learning through *mental rehearsal*, a form of language play, through activities such as mental correction of errors, silent repetition, mental practice of grammatical rules, and taking notes (de Guerrero, 1994; Reiss, 1985). Although there has been little research in the area of language play by adult learners, some evidence suggests that those who engage in these activities are more successful language learners (Ramsey, 1980) and that the value of language play in the acquisition process may decrease as the learner's proficiency in the language increases (Lantolf, 1997; Parr & Krashen, 1986). An interesting finding in Lantolf's 1997 study of the use of language play by university students studying Spanish is that learners tended to engage in language play most frequently after more meaningful activities, such as conversations, and less so after mechanical tasks, such as grammar study and pattern drills. For foreign language instruction, language play may be activated through meaningful activities and may facilitate the language learning process. In this perspective, language play is rehearsal of private speech and thus, it is part of the cognitive work of language learning.

As students acquire language, why does language play decrease?

This view of language play as rehearsal contrasts with the view of language play as fun or self-amusement known as *ludic play* (Broner & Tarone, 2001; Cook, 2000). Fun, defined as "an experience of positive affect often associated with laughter" (Broner & Tarone, p. 364) can be play with language form, including sounds, rhyme, rhythm, song, etc. It can also be play with meaning, combining semantic elements to create words that do not exist. Tarone (2000) points out that children often play with language they know or are learning for enjoyment and self-entertainment. Of importance to language teachers is that, when students invent words, create songs, or write graffiti on their notebooks in the language, they are engaging in ludic play, and are mediating learning as a result of reflecting upon language, exploring the language, and learning it. This process is very common in L1 language development. Thus, ludic language play may foster flexibility and change within the interlanguage system of the learner, resulting in its growth and development (see Larsen-Freeman, 1997).

Private speech, mental rehearsal, and language play foster flexibility and change within the interlanguage system of the learner, resulting in its growth and development.

You have seen how sociocultural theory provides the impetus for language teachers to develop a classroom setting in which learners collaborate with each other, receive scaffolded help from the teacher, work within their ZPDs, and use mediational tools in order to make sense of the target language and progress in their language development. Through a sociocultural approach to classroom instruction, teachers will become more familiar with the language levels of their students and consequently will be able to provide more effective support for their language development.

Interactional Competence

As seen in the previous section, sociocultural theory focuses on the social nature of language learning and development and the role of learners' interaction in the classroom setting. Within this framework, Mehan (1979) stresses the importance of "interactional competence," which includes the ability to manage discussions in relevant ways. Hall points out the significance of interactive practices, "recurring episodes of purposeful, goal-directed talk," in the establishment and maintenance of a community (1995, p. 38). Examples of interactive practices within the classroom community are how teachers lead discussions about texts, how they introduce or practice vocabulary, and how they promote pair/group work. Competent participation in these practices requires the development of interactional competence as learners and teachers participate in "real" conversations. Characteristics of "real" conversational models, as adapted from Hall (1995) are:

- Opening utterances establish the topic and frame the rhetorical structure: "So, how was your vacation?"
- Ellipsis—that is, not repeating information that is already known—makes clear the distinction between new and old information. As the conversational exchange continues, already established information is generally not repeated. For example, in response to a question such as "When do you leave for class today?" one might give the short answer "Ten o'clock," rather than the complete sentence "I leave for class today at ten o'clock."

- Related lexical items occur in topic-specific discourse and are linked because of their common referent. The meaning of new words is figured out by using the surrounding topically oriented words to help narrow the possible meaning choices (Clark, 1992; Halliday, 1994). For example, in a discussion about hunting, related lexical items might include these expressions: to go hunting, to shoot, gun, trap, deer, bears, turkeys, tracks, animal protectionists.
- Expressive reactions are made: "Oh my! I don't believe it!"; questions that advance the topic are asked: "What do you mean by that?"; explanations or extensions, or a transition to a new topic are made: "By the way, I wanted to ask you . . ."

In her 1995 study, Hall examined the nature of topic development and management of communication in classroom interactive practices that claimed to focus on speaking in a high school first-year Spanish classroom. She recorded classroom conversational exchanges between teacher and students and analyzed them for the characteristics of opening utterances, use of ellipses, and use of related lexical items. She found that the typical conversational exchanges that the teacher considered to be communicative showed little evidence of a real conversational topic, opening utterances, related lexical items, ellipses, or reactions. A major implication of Hall's study is that learners need truly interactive environments in the classroom if they are to develop the ability to interact effectively outside the classroom with other speakers of the target language. See Case Study 1 for examples of real-life utterances.

 How does language learning occur as a result of collaboration with others?

The Role of Affect and Motivation

Other variables that may influence the degree of success in learning another language are those pertaining to affect, such as motivation, anxiety, personality, and attitude. The Affective Filter Hypothesis, as first proposed by Dulay and Burt (1977), relates these affective factors to the second language acquisition process. Also, as seen earlier, Krashen (1982) maintains that acquisition can occur only in the presence of certain affective conditions: the learner is motivated, self-confident, and has a low level of anxiety.

Motivation has been defined as "the direction of attentional effort, the proportion of total attentional effort directed to the task (intensity), and the extent to which attentional effort toward the task is maintained over time (persistence)" (Kanfer & Ackerman, 1989, p. 661). According to Masgoret and Gardner (2003), motivation is the most influential factor in successfully learning a new language. However, it is also one of the most complex issues in SLA research.

Motivation of Individual Learners

There are many sources that motivate an individual to succeed in language learning, and it is difficult to match specific motivational factors to success. Gardner (1985) identifies two kinds of motivation: (1) instrumental, e.g., learning a language to get a better job or to fulfill an academic requirement; and (2) integrative, e.g., learning a language to fit in with people who speak the language natively. The research points to the likelihood that instrumental and integrative motivation are interrelated; that is, that they may operate in concert or that one may lead to the other (Gardner & MacIntyre, 1993). Gardner's paradigm was expanded by Oxford and Shearin (1994) to acknowledge the role of other motivational factors, including relevance of course goals to the learner, personal beliefs about success or failure, the ability of the learner to provide self-reward and self-evaluation, the nature of the teacher's feedback and assistance to the learner, and instructional features of the course; other studies have suggested similar factors (Crookes & Schmidt, 1991; Ely, 1986; Tremblay & Gardner, 1995). Furthermore, Dörnyei (1994) maintains that language learners are often motivated by the classroom experience itself: (1) course-specific factors, such as the degree to which the teaching method, materials, and learning tasks are interesting and engaging; (2) teacher-specific factors, such as the teacher's personality, teaching style, and relationship to students; and (3) group-specific factors, such as the dynamics of the learning group (p. 277).

Some researchers studied aspects of motivation known as *orientations* using a questionnaire developed by Clément and Kruidenier (1983). Among the orientations identified were integrative, instrumental, travel, friendship, knowledge, identification, sociocultural, media, whether or not the language was a requirement, ethnic heritage related, and school related (Ely, 1986; Sung & Padilla, 1998; Yang, 2003). For instance, among learners whose goal for language study was to fulfill a requirement, Reiss (1985) and Gillette (1990) found an absence of language play.

Motivation encourages greater effort from language learners and usually leads to greater success in terms of language proficiency (Gardner, 1985) and maintenance of language skills over time (Tucker, Hamayan, & Genesee, 1976).[5] Shaaban and Ghaith (2000) found that integratively motivated students worked harder with a positive attitude about language outcomes in EFL. Recent research has turned to the study of motivational factors among specific native-language groups. For instance, Yang (2003) showed that East Asian students in the United States were integratively motivated, that they were more interested in developing communication skills in listening and speaking than in reading and writing, and that female students were more integratively motivated than male students.

Personality or cognitive styles also affect language learning; these factors include the willingness to take risks, openness to social interactions, and attitude toward the target language and target language users (Wong-Fillmore, 1985; Young, 1990). Motivation and attitudes are often related to anxiety, apprehension, or fear about the language learning experience. In some cases, language activities such as speaking in front of a group can create performance anxiety, especially in the case of learners who do not enjoy interacting with others spontaneously or learners whose oral-aural skills are weaker than their visual skills (Scarcella & Oxford, 1992). Anxiety often stems from the traditional social structure of the classroom, in which the powerful teacher-centered atmosphere may inhibit interaction, or from the feeling that the learning experience is irrelevant or a waste of time (Scarcella & Oxford, 1992). Gregersen and Horwitz (2002) found that anxious learners attempted to avoid errors and were disturbed at having made them. Gregersen (2003) found that anxious learners made more errors, self-repaired and resorted to their native language more often, recognized fewer errors in a stimulated recall situation, and overestimated the number of errors they made (p. 29). Nonanxious learners, on the other hand, used their errors to learn and to communicate better.[6]

Motivation of Learners Within Tasks

The motivation of individuals, either alone or in composite groups, has been the traditional focus of motivational research. Recently, some scholars have begun to study performance on tasks as a way to explore the effects of motivation. Wen's 1997 study illustrated that expectations of the learning task and of one's own ability play a significant role in motivation and learning: When learners think that learning experiences will lead to certain meaningful results, they exert more effort. Motivation has an effect on how and when students use language learning strategies and the degree to which they take responsibility for their own progress (Oxford & Nyikos, 1989).[7] Dörnyei and Kormos (2000) also used a task-based framework to study motivation. They examined how learners addressed certain tasks and related their findings to the students' attitudes toward the L2 class, toward specific tasks, and toward achievement in the course. Findings showed motivational factors have a significant impact on the learner's engagement in a task. Students with high positive attitude toward a task were more engaged in the task and produced more language. Also, students with a low attitude toward a task still performed well if they had a positive attitude toward the course in general. For the beginning teacher, it is important to recognize that motivational factors play an important but complex role in language learning and performance in a language classroom.

The research in motivation presented here indicates that teachers can heighten the motivation of their students by (1) identifying why learners are studying a language; (2) helping shape the learners' beliefs about success and failure in L2 learning; (3) illustrating the rewards of L2 learning; (4) providing a positive classroom atmosphere where language anxiety is kept to a minimum; and (5) encouraging learners to set their own personal goals for learning and to develop their own intrinsic reward system (Oxford & Shearin, 1994, pp. 24–25). Strategies for reducing students' anxiety about language learning include providing opportunities for pair/group interaction, engaging learners in expressing their anxieties in diaries or dialogue journals, and helping learners outline performance expectations (Oxford, 1990).

 Motivational factors play an important but complex role in language learning and performance in a language classroom.

 What are some considerations you need to keep in mind about the motivation of your students?

Implications of the Research for Classroom Teaching

Throughout this chapter, you have explored key research findings and their important implications for classroom language instruction. *Teacher's Handbook* supports a sociocultural view of language instruction, whereby learners have ample opportunities to interact meaningfully with others. Within this type of instructional framework, there is NO room for mechanical practice that is devoid of meaning. Accordingly, throughout the rest of this text, you will learn more about the importance of providing the following elements in the foreign language classroom:

- comprehensible input in the target language;
- an interactive environment that models and presents a variety of social, linguistic, and cognitive tools for structuring and interpreting participation in talk;
- opportunities for learners to negotiate meaning in the target language, with assistance from the teacher and one another;
- opportunities for learners to interact communicatively with one another in the target language;
- conversations and tasks that are purposeful and meaningful to the learner and that parallel real-life situations in which they might expect to use their language skills (Met, 2004, p. 86);
- explicit instruction in strategies that facilitate language awareness, learner autonomy, and making meaning when interpreting the foreign language (Met, 2004; Pica, 2002);
- a nonthreatening environment that encourages self-expression;
- opportunities for language learners to participate in setting the agenda for what they learn.

This chapter will serve as the foundation for the topics that follow in *Teacher's Handbook*. In Appendix 1.2 (see Web site), you will find a list of "Best Practices for World Language Instruction," designed by the Pittsburgh (PA) Public Schools to identify for teachers and administrators effective instructional practices that reflect current SLA theories. It is included here to illustrate how school districts are implementing many of the practices that are presented in this text.

In some of the activities that appear in the **Observe and Reflect, Teach and Reflect, and Discuss and Reflect** sections, it is suggested that you observe a foreign language classroom. Appendix 1.3 (see Web site) contains a list of "etiquette guidelines" for observing a language classroom as a guest visitor; you may find it helpful to review these guidelines prior to making your first observation.

OBSERVE AND REFLECT

The following two activities will enable you to examine elements of language learning that occur in classrooms and in other settings.

EPISODE ONE
Observing a Child Interacting in His/Her Native Language (L1)

NC&TE_____
STANDARD
3.a.

Observe a small child between the ages of two and a half and three years old who is interacting with one or more persons (parent, older siblings, etc.) in his/her native language. Observe for at least one hour, paying particular attention to the child's use of language. Use the Observation Guide to analyze the conversation.

Alternative Observation of a Child Interacting in His/Her Native Language (L1)

If you cannot observe a small child using his/her native language, use the following transcription of a 3-year old boy named Alex talking to his mother in their native language after he returns home from preschool. Use the Observation Guide to help analyze the script as you read it.

Mother: Hi Alex! How was your day at preschool?

Alex: Good.

Mother: What did you do at preschool today?

Alex: Eated a snack.

Mother: You ate a snack? Great! What did you eat?

Alex: Cupcakes with M&Ms. It was Steven's birthday. We singed "Happy Birthday."

Mother: Really?

Alex: Yep.

Mother: Did you do anything else for Steven's birthday?

Alex: Oh, we broke a . . . a . . . pin . . . uh . . . you know . . . with a big stick.

Mother: What did you break?

Alex: A big thing. It had candy in it and went all over the floor. Can't remember what you call it . . . A pin . . .

Mother: Oh, you mean a *piñata*.

Alex: Yeah, a *piñata*. It looked like a big fish with feathers.

Mother: I'll bet that was fun, Alex.

Alex: Yep. I got a lot of candy!

Source: ACTFL / Weber State University, 2003, Foreign Language Methods Online course

EPISODE TWO
Observing a Beginning Language (L2) Class

NCATE_____
STANDARD
3.a.

Now observe a beginning language learning classroom in an elementary or secondary school. Refer to the questions presented in the Observation Guide below as you observe the students interacting in the foreign language. Then answer the questions in the guide.

OBSERVATION GUIDE
The Language of Interaction

novice = child or classroom learner
expert = caretaker, older individual, teacher

1. Why are the expert and novice speaking? What is the topic of conversation?
2. When does the novice participate in the conversation? To answer questions? To ask questions? To provide additional information? How would you characterize the nature of the novice's talk?
3. When does the expert speak? To offer information? To ask questions? What kinds of questions does the expert ask? How would you characterize the nature of the expert's talk?
4. How does the expert react to what the novice says?
5. How does the expert help the novice when the novice has trouble expressing an idea? Do you see examples of explicit talk about the language?
6. What happens when the expert and novice do not understand each other?
7. What kind of language errors do you notice?
8. What does the expert do when the novice makes a language mistake?
9. What types of assistance does the expert offer to the novice?
10. What are some examples of language play or mental rehearsal used by the novice?

As you reflect upon the classroom you visited in Episode Two (or upon any other observation you made), describe the role of input, output, meaningful interaction, and social roles and networks you observed.

Also see the *Teacher's Handbook* Web site for a link to a video of a kindergarten immersion French class for examples of emerging language use.

thandbook.heinle.com

DISCUSS AND REFLECT*

CASE STUDY ONE
Creating Real Conversational Models

NCATE_____
STANDARDS
3.a., 3.b.,
4.b.

Mr. Noonen has been teaching Spanish and French for over fifteen years in an urban middle school. He is very active in local, regional, and state organizations devoted to the teaching of foreign languages. His peers, both native and nonnative speakers of Spanish, consider him to be very proficient in his knowledge of and ability to use Spanish. He is committed to providing a Spanish language environment in which his students have many opportunities to develop their ability to use the language. He uses Spanish almost exclusively in his teaching.

---

*See *Teacher's Handbook* Web site for a third case study that deals with cooperative learning.

Dr. Lindford, professor of the foreign language teaching methods class at a local university, decided to send three Spanish Education majors to observe Mr. Noonen's class so that they could see how he manages communication in his classroom. Students were instructed to script several brief episodes of conversation between Mr. Noonen and his students. They would then analyze these scripted episodes for characteristics of real conversational models.

The next week students returned to the methods class with the scripts, one of which appears below (Hall, 1995). Students reported that the teacher began this class by telling his students that they were going to talk about different kinds of music. The teacher played a CD of Gloria Estefan singing in Spanish softly in the background as he interacted with the class.

1 Teacher: Es música ↓ no ↑ música ↓ no ↑

2 Julio: no

3 T: es música ↓ es música ↓ es música ↓

4 ahora señor te gusta ↑ te gusta la música ↑

5 Julio: no me gusta ↓

6 T: no me gusta ↓

7 Julio: no me gusta ↓

8 T: no me gusta la música ↓ te gusta la música ↑

9 no me gusta la música ↓ te gusta la música ↑

10 Several Ss: I do sí sí yeah sí

11 Rafael: aw man where you goin ↓

12 T: sí me gusta la música ↓ te gusta la música ↑

13 Andrea: sí ↓

[. . .]

31 T: [loudly] es música de Gloria Estefan ↓

32 Several Ss: [unintelligible talk]

33 [T writes on board]

34 Rafael: If you'd speak English I'd understand

35 T: sí Gloria Estefan . . . Pon Poncherelo te gusta Gloria Estefan ↑

36 Ponch: sí ↓

37 T: sí ↓

38 Julio: who's Gloria Estefan ↑

39 Ponch: me sí gusta

40 T: sí ↓ me gusta me gusta Gloria Estefan . . . sí . . . me gusta Gloria Estefan

41 Rafael: Oh, that's the person who was singing that song . . . that's the person who was singing that song

Ask yourself these questions:

1. What purpose or objective does the teacher have in mind for conducting this conversational exchange?

2. What do the responses of the students indicate about the degree to which they understand the conversation and/or are motivated to engage in discussion?

3. Does this exchange reflect "real conversation" as described by Hall in this chapter?

4. What types of language-promoting assistance, as presented in Appendix 1.1, might the teacher have used to facilitate comprehension and to encourage students to speak?

To prepare the case:

1. Read the article by Hall (1995) for more detailed information regarding the classroom script featured here and other scripts; review the types of language-promoting assistance in Appendix 1.1 that the teacher might use to keep learners engaged in topical discussion.
2. Consult these sources of information regarding interaction in the classroom: Tracy (1994) and Richards (1996).

To prepare for class discussion:

1. Analyze the script presented above for characteristics of a real conversational model using the criteria suggested by Hall (1995): opening utterance, ellipsis, use of related lexical items, and reactions.
2. Given the importance of input, how could the teacher begin this lesson by providing meaningful input and comprehension-checking activities before expecting students to speak? What do you think would happen if the teacher proposed a topic for students to talk about?
3. Teachers often require students to respond to questions in complete sentences so that they can practice various grammatical points and new vocabulary. As we saw in the script above, this teacher goal caused problems in the conversational exchange. Students need to be able to talk in sentence form, yet a question-answer format does not always lend itself to responses in complete sentences without making the conversation seem unnatural. What type of activity might you design that would more naturally elicit a discussion of likes and dislikes in the language you teach? Try to elicit sentence-length utterances.
4. See Activity A on the *Teacher's Handbook* Web site for a research study of a small group interaction task in Japanese.

thandbook.heinle.com

CASE STUDY TWO
Using Songs to Engage Learners[8]

NCATE
STANDARDS
3.a., 3.b.,
4.b., 4.c.

Mr. Kruse teaches French I and II at a suburban high school near a large Pennsylvania city. Most of his learners have had little, if any, experience with other cultures, nor have they interacted with foreigners who live in the area, except for visitors invited to the classroom. Their life experiences and their curiosity about and interest in other cultures are very limited, as evidenced in the few, mundane questions they ask when presented with a visitor from another country. While in France last summer, Mr. Kruse bought several CDs, one of which was an American Cajun recording that was then popular in France. In an attempt to stir his learners' interest and to show French influence on American culture, Mr. Kruse decided to plan a lesson using one of the songs from this recording for his French II class of 24 students. The words to this song follow, in French and in English:

"Cajun Telephone Stomp"
O bébé, j'avais essayé
De causer aujourd'hui.
'Y avait quelque chose qui est arrivé
Et moi, j'ai commencé d'être fâché.

Sur le téléphone de l'autre cîté,
'Y avait une 'tite voix mal enregistrée.
"Après le beep," c'est ça il dit,
"Laisse ton message, 'ya personne ici."

Quoi c'est ça, il dit "le beep"?
C'est pas Cadien, ni poli,
S'il n'est pas là, quoi faire sa voix?
O yé yaille, mon coeur fait mal.

"Cajun Telephone Stomp"
O baby, I tried
To talk to you on the phone today.
Something strange happened
And I started to get mad.

On the other end of the line,
There was a little voice, a bad recording
"After the beep," that's what it said,
"Leave your message, there's no one home."

What is this, it said "the beep"?
That's not Cajun, nor polite,
If no one's there, why is this voice?
O yé yaille, it makes me sad.

Après dix fois avec cette voix maudite	After hearing that darn voice ten times,
Ç'a commencé de ma faire rire,	It started to make me laugh,
J'ai oublié á qui je veux parler	I forgot who I was calling
Et enfin, j'ai accroché.	And finally, I hung up.

Source: Beausoleil *Cajun Conja.*

Mr. Kruse decided to construct his lesson in several steps. As you read his plans for the lesson, indicate which aspects of language learning you can identify based on your reading of this chapter.

1. First, he would play some of the music from the CD as students came into the class.
2. Then he would ask them what they knew about that kind of music. Had they ever heard it before? What did it remind them of? Did they know of any musicians who played it? Where did they think it came from?
3. Next, he would play the "Cajun Telephone Stomp" a second time, asking them to identify any instruments in it that they recognized; he'd play it again a third time asking students to write down words they understood; and he would play the song a fourth time asking them to use the context of the song to guess meanings of words they didn't know but that seemed to be key words.
4. Then he would show an overhead of the song in French with all of the past tense verbs removed and ask the students to fill them in as he played the song for the fifth time; he would have the students write in the words they heard and try to figure out together how to form some past tenses.
5. Next, he would ask the class as a group to write a sentence on the board summarizing what the song is about, using the past tenses contained in it, and highlighting them as they read them from the board.
6. Finally, he would ask students to role-play calling someone and leaving a message in French at the beep.
7. As homework, he would ask the students to identify four Web sites related to Cajun culture by doing Google searches. The next day he would bring some materials he had gathered from Web searches containing stories from Cajun culture and engage the students in reading activities.

To prepare the case:

1. Find a music magazine in the target language and read some articles on modern music; read a brief history of Cajun culture and music or of the music characteristic of the target cultures that you teach (see Pastorek, 1998, as an example).
2. Read the sections of Hadley (2001) that deal with the role of context in comprehension and learning.
3. Listen to current hit songs by other recording artists.

To prepare for class discussion:

1. Read the details of Appendix 1.2 (see Web site), *Best Practices for World Language Instruction*, developed by teachers in the Pittsburgh Public Schools. Which of those practices do you see evident in Mr. Kruse's lesson?
2. Describe how you might incorporate additional best practices from Appendix 1.2 into a lesson you teach using another song, as in Activity B on the *Teacher's Handbook* Web site.
3. Describe the differences and similarities you and your classmates find in songs you have heard, emphasizing the style, content, and cultural aspects of the recordings so that learners working in groups might create a song of their own.

thandbook.heinle.com

REFERENCES

ACTFL/Weber State University. (2003). Foreign Language Methods online. Course Module 4 Introduction. Ogden, UT. Funded by the U.S. Department of Education.

Adair-Hauck, B. (1995). *Exploring language and cognitive development within the Zone of Proximal Development*. Paper presented at the University of Pittsburgh.

Aljaafreh, A., & Lantolf, J. P. (1994). Negative feedback as regulation and second language learning in the zone of proximal development. *The Modern Language Journal, 78,* 465–483.

Antón, M., & DiCamilla, F. (1998). Socio-cognitive functions of L1 collaborative interaction in the L2 classroom. *The Canadian Modern Language Review, 54,* 314–342.

Appel, G., & Lantolf, J. P. (1994). Speaking as mediation: A study of L1 and L2 text recall tasks. *The Modern Language Journal, 78,* 437–452.

Atkinson, D. (2002). Toward a sociocognitive approach to second language acquisition. *The Modern Language Journal, 86,* 525–545.

Bachman, L. F. (1990). *Fundamental considerations in language testing.* Oxford, UK: Oxford University Press.

Bialystok, E. (1981). Some evidence for the integrity and interaction of two knowledge sources. In R. W. Andersen (Ed.), *New dimensions in second language acquisition research* (pp. 62–74). Rowley, MA: Newbury House.

Bialystok, E. (1982). On the relationship between knowing and using forms. *Applied Linguistics, 3,* 181–206.

Broner, M. A., & Tarone, E. E. (2001). Language play in a fifth-grade Spanish immersion classroom. *The Modern Language Journal, 85,* 363–379.

Brooks, F. B. (1990). Foreign language learning: A social interaction perspective. In B. VanPatten & J. F. Lee (Eds.), *Second language acquisition-foreign language learning* (pp. 153–169). Clevedon, UK: Multilingual Matters.

Brooks, F. B., Donato, R., & McGlone, V. (1997). When are they going to say "it" right? Understanding learner talk during pair-work activity. *Foreign Language Annals, 30,* 524–541.

Buck, M. (2000). Procesamiento del lenguaje y adquisición de una segunda lengua. Un estudio de la adquisición de un punto gramatical en inglés por hispanohablantes. Unpublished doctoral dissertation, Universidad Autónoma de México, Mexico City.

Campbell, R., & Wales, R. (1970). The study of language acquisition. In J. Lyons (Ed.), *New horizons in linguistics* (pp. 242–260). Harmondsworth, England: Penguin.

Canale, M., & Swain, M. (1980). Theoretical bases of communicative approaches to second language teaching and testing. *Applied Linguistics, 1,* 1–47.

Celce-Murcia, M., Dörnyei, Z., & Thurrell, S. (1995). Communicative competence: A pedagogically motivated model with content specifications. *Issues in Applied Linguistics, 6,* 5–35.

Cheng, A. (2002). The effects of processing instruction on the acquisition of *ser* and *estar*. *Hispania, 85,* 308–323.

Chomsky, N. (1965). *Aspects of the theory of syntax.* Cambridge, MA: MIT Press.

Clark, H. (1992). *Arenas of language use.* Chicago: University of Chicago Press.

Clément, R., & Kruidenier, B. G. (1983). Orientations in second language acquisition: I. The effects of ethnicity, milieu, and target language on their emergence. *Language Learning, 33,* 273–291.

Cook, G. (2000). *Language play, language learning.* Oxford, UK: Oxford University Press.

Crookes, R., & Schmidt, R. (1991). Motivation: Reopening the research agenda. *Language Learning, 41,* 469–512.

de Guerrero, M. C. M. (1994). Form and function of inner speech in adult second language learning. In J. P. Lantolf & G. Appel (Eds.), *Vygotskian approaches to second language research* (pp. 83–115). Norwood, NJ: Ablex.

Donato, R. (1994). Collective scaffolding. In J. Lantolf & G. Appel (Eds.), *Vygotskyan approaches to second language acquisition research* (pp. 33–56). Norwood, NJ: Ablex.

Donato, R. (2004). Aspects of collaboration in pedagogical discourse. In M. McGroarty (Ed.), *Annual Review of Applied Linguistics (vol. 24), Advances in language pedagogy* (pp. 284–302). West Nyack, NY: Cambridge University Press.

Donato, R., & McCormick, D. (1994). A sociocultural perspective on language learning strategies: The role of mediation. *The Modern Language Journal, 78,* 453–464.

Dörnyei, Z. (1994). Motivation and motivating in the foreign language classroom. *The Modern Language Journal, 78,* 273–284.

Dörnyei, Z., & Kormos, J. (2000). The role of individual and social variables in oral task performance. *Language Teacher Research, 4,* 275–300.

Duffy, G. G., & Roehler, L. R. (1986). The subtleties of instructional mediation. *Educational Leadership, 43,* 23–27.

Dulay, H., & Burt, M. (1977). Remarks on creativity in language acquisition. In M. Burt, H. Dulay, & M. Finnochiaro (Eds.), *Viewpoints on English as a second language* (pp. 95–126). New York: Regents.

Ellis, R. (1994). *The study of second language acquisition.* Oxford, UK: Oxford University Press.

Ellis, R. (1997). *SLA research and language teaching.* Oxford, UK: Oxford University Press.

Ely, C. M. (1986). Language learning motivation: A descriptive and causal analysis. *The Modern Language Journal, 70,* 28–35.

Farley, A. P. (2003). Authentic processing instruction and the Spanish subjunctive. *Hispania, 84,* 289–299.

Frawley, W., & Lantolf, J. P. (1985). Second-language discourse: A Vygotskyan perspective. *Applied Linguistics, 6,* 19–44.

Gardner, R. C. (1985). *Social psychology and second language learning: The role of attitudes and motivation.* London, Ontario, Canada: Edward Arnold.

Gardner, R. C., & MacIntyre, P. (1993). A student's contributions to second-language learning. Part II: Affective variables. *Language Teaching, 26,* 1–11.

Gass, S. (1988). Integrating research areas: A framework for second language studies. *Applied Linguistics, 9,* 198–217.

Gass, S., & Selinker, L. (1994). *Second language acquisition.* Hillsdale, NJ: Lawrence Erlbaum.

Gillette, B. (1990). *Beyond learning strategies: A whole-person approach to second language acquisition.* Unpublished doctoral dissertation, University of Delaware, Newark, DE.

Glisan, E. W., & Shrum, J. L. (1996). *Enlaces.* Boston: Heinle & Heinle.

Gregersen, T. S. (2003). To err is human: A reminder to teachers of language-anxious students. *Foreign Language Annals, 36,* 25–32.

Gregersen, T. S., & Horwitz, E. K. (2002). Language learning and perfectionism: Anxious and non-anxious language learners' reactions to their own oral performance. *The Modern Language Journal, 86,* 562–570.

Hadley, A. O. (2001). *Teaching language in context.* Boston: Heinle & Heinle.

Hall, J. K. (1995). "Aw, man, where we goin'?": Classroom interaction and the development of L2 interactional competence. *Issues in Applied Linguistics, 6,* 37–62.

Hall, J. K. (1997). A consideration of SLA as a theory of practice: A response to Firth and Wagner. *The Modern Language Journal, 81,* 301–306.

Hall, J. K. (1999). The communication standards. In J. K. Phillips & R. M. Terry. *Foreign language standards: Linking research, theories, and practices* (pp. 15–56). Lincolnwood, IL: NTC/Contemporary Publishing Group.

Halliday, M. A. K. (1994). *An introduction to functional grammar.* London, Ontario, Canada: Edward Arnold.

Hymes, D. (1972). On communicative competence. In J. P. Pride & J. Holmes (Eds.), *Sociolinguistics* (pp. 269–293). Harmondsworth, UK: Penguin.

Johnson, K. (1988). Mistake correction. *ELT Journal, 42,* 89–101.

Kanfer, R., & Ackerman, P. L. (1989). Motivation and cognitive abilities: An integrative/aptitude-treatment interaction approach to skill acquisition. *Journal of Applied Psychology Monograph, 74,* 657–690.

Kinginger, C. (2001). *i* +1 ≠ ZPD. *Foreign Language Annals, 34,* 417–425.

Kinginger, C. (2002). Defining the zone of proximal development in U.S. foreign language education. *Applied Linguistics, 23,* 240–261.

Krashen, S. (1982). *Principles and practice in second language acquisition.* Oxford, UK: Pergamon Press.

Kuczaj, S. A., II. (1983). *Crib speech and language play.* New York: Springer-Verlag.

Lantolf, J. P. (1994). Sociocultural theory and second language learning. *The Modern Language Journal, 78,* 418–420.

Lantolf, J. P. (1997). The function of language play in the acquisition of L2 Spanish. In W. R. Glass & A. T. Pérez-Leroux (Eds.), *Contemporary perspectives on the acquisition of Spanish* (pp. 3–24). Somerville, MA: Cascadilla Press.

Lapkin, S., Swain, M., & Smith, M. (2002). Reformulation and the learning of French pronominal verbs in a Canadian French immersion context. *The Modern Language Journal, 86,* 485–507.

Larsen-Freeman, D. (1997). Chaos/complexity science and second language acquisition. *Applied Linguistics, 18,* 141–165.

Lee, J. F., & VanPatten, B. (2003). *Making communicative language teaching happen.* San Francisco: McGraw-Hill.

Lightbown, P. (1985). Great expectations: Second-language acquisition research and classroom teaching. *Applied Linguistics, 6,* 173–189.

Lightbown, P. (2004). Commentary: What to teach? How to Teach? In B. VanPatten (Ed.), *Processing instruction* (pp. 65–78). Mahweh, NJ: Erlbaum.

Lightbown, P., & Spada, N. (2003). *How languages are learned.* Oxford UK: Oxford University Press.

Liskin-Gasparro, J. (1993). Talking about the past: An analysis of the discourse of intermediate high and advanced level speakers of Spanish. *Dissertation Abstracts International, 54,* 12(A), 4380. (UMI No. AAG9413541).

Long, M. H. (1981). Input, interaction and second language acquisition. In H. Winitz (Ed.), Native language and foreign language acquisition (pp. 259–278). *Annals of the New York Academy of Sciences 379.* New York: Academy of Sciences.

Long, M. H. (1983). Native speaker/non-native speaker conversation in the second language classroom. In M. A. Clarke & J. Handscomb (Eds.), *On TESOL '82: Pacific perspectives on language learning and teaching* (pp. 207–225). Washington, DC: TESOL.

Masgoret, A.-M., & Gardner, R. C. (2003). Attitudes, motivation, and second language learning: A meta-analysis of studies conducted by Gardner and Associates. *Language Learning, 53,* 123–163.

McCafferty, S. G. (1994). Adult second language learners' use of private speech: A review of studies. *The Modern Language Journal, 78,* 421–436.

McCafferty, S. G. (2002). Gesture and creating zones of proximal development for second language learning. *The Modern Language Journal, 86,* 192–203.

McLaughlin, B. (1987). Theories of second-language learning. London, Ontario, Canada: Edward Arnold.

McLaughlin, B., Rossman, T., & McLeod, B. (1983). Second language learning: An information processing perspective. *Language Learning, 33,* 135–158.

Mehan, H. (1979). What time is it, Denise: Asking known information questions in classroom discourse. *Theory Into Practice, 28*(4), 285–294.

Met, M. (2004). Foreign language. In Cawelti, G. (Ed.), *Handbook of research on improving student achievement* (pp. 86–87). Arlington, VA: Educational Research Service.

Munsell, P., & Carr, T. (1981). Monitoring the monitor: A review of second-language acquisition and second language learning. *Language Learning, 31,* 493–502.

Murphy, J. M. (1992). An etiquette for the nonsupervisory observation of L2 classrooms. *Foreign Language Annals, 25,* 223–225.

Newman, F., & Holtzman, L. (1993). *Lev Vygotsky: Revolutionary scientist.* New York: Routledge.

Ohta, A. S. (1995). Applying sociocultural theory to an analysis of learner discourse: Leaner-learner collaborative interaction in the zone of proximal development. *Issues in Applied Linguistics, 6,* 93–122.

Oxford, R. (1990). *Language learning strategies: What every teacher should know.* Boston: Heinle & Heinle.

Oxford, R., & Nyikos, M. (1989). Variables affecting choice of language learning strategies by university students. *The Modern Language Journal, 73,* 291–300.

Oxford, R., & Shearin, J. (1994). Language learning motivation: Expanding the theoretical framework. *The Modern Language Journal, 78,* 12–28.

Parr, P. C., & Krashen, S. D. (1986). Involuntary rehearsal of second language in beginning and advanced performers. *System, 14,* 275–278.

Pastorek, M. (1998). How about a bit of Cajun culture in the classroom? *Northeast Conference on the Teaching of Foreign Languages Newsletter, 44,* 46–48.

Pennycook, A. (1997). Cultural alternatives and autonomy. In P. Benson & P. Voller (Eds.), *Autonomy and independence in language learning* (pp. 35–53). London: Longman.

Piaget, J. (1979). *The development of thought.* New York: Viking.

Pica, T. (2002). Subject-matter content: How does it assist the interactional and linguistic needs of classroom language learners? *The Modern Language Journal, 86,* 1–19.

Pica, T., Holliday, L., Lewis, N., & Morgenthaler, L. (1989). Comprehensible output as an outcome of linguistic demands on the learner. *Studies in Second Language Acquisition, 11,* 63–90.

Platt, E., & Brooks, F. B. (1994). The "acquisition-rich environment" revisited. *The Modern Language Journal, 78,* 497–511.

Ramsey, R. (1980). Learning-learning approach styles of adult multilinguals and successful language learners. *Annals of the New York Academy of Sciences, 345,* 73–96.

Reiss, M. (1985). The "good" language learner: Another look. *The Canadian Modern Language Review, 41,* 511–523.

Richards, J. C. (1996). Teachers' maxims in language teaching. *TESOL Quarterly, 30,* 281–296.

Rogoff, B. (1990). *Apprenticeship in thinking, cognitive development in social context.* New York: Oxford University Press.

Savignon, S. J. (1972). *Communicative competence: An experiment in foreign language teaching.* Philadelphia: Center for Curriculum Development.

Scarcella, R. C., & Oxford, R. L. (1992). *The tapestry of language learning.* Boston: Heinle & Heinle.

Schulz, R. A. (1991). Second language acquisition theories and teaching practice: How do they fit? *The Modern Language Journal, 5,* 17–26.

Scullen, M. E., & Jourdain, S. (2000). The effect of explicit training on successful circumlocution: A classroom study. In J. F. Lee & A. Valdman (Eds.), *Form and meaning: Multiple perspectives* (pp. 231–253). Boston: Heinle & Heinle.

Selinker, L. (1974). Interlanguage. In J. H. Schumann & N. Stenson (Eds.), *New frontiers in second-language learning* (pp. 114–136). Rowley, MA: Newbury House.

Shaaban, K. A., & Ghaith, G. (2000). Student motivation to learn English as a foreign language. *Foreign Language Annals, 33,* 632–644.

Shore, B. (1996). *Culture in mind: Cognition, culture, and the problem of meaning.* New York: Oxford University Press.

Sung, H., & Padilla, A. M. (1998). Student motivation, parental attitudes, and involvement in the learning of Asian languages in elementary and secondary schools. *The Modern Language Journal, 82,* 205–216.

Swain, M. (1985). Communicative competence: Some roles of comprehensible input and comprehensible output in its development. In S. Gass & C. Madden (Eds.), *Input in second language acquisition* (pp. 235–253). Rowley, MA: Newbury House.

Swain, M. (1995). Three functions of output in second language learning. In G. Cook & B. Seidlhofer (Eds.), *Principle and practice in applied linguistics: Studies in honour of H. G. Widdowson* (pp. 125–144). Oxford, UK: Oxford University Press.

Swain, M., & Lapkin, S. (1998). Interaction and second language learning: Two adolescent French immersion students working together. *The Modern Language Journal, 82,* 320–337.

Tarone, E. (1983). On the variability of interlanguage systems. *Applied Linguistics, 4,* 142–163.

Tarone, E. (2000). Getting serious about language play: Language play, interlanguage variation, and SLA. In B. Swierzbin, F. Morris, M. Anderson, C. Klee, & E. Tarone (Eds.), *Interaction of social and cognitive forces in SLA: Proceedings of the 1999 Second Language Research Forum* (pp. 31–53). Somerville, MA: Cascadilla Press.

Terrell, T. D. (1986). Acquisition in the natural approach: The binding/access framework. *The Modern Language Journal, 70,* 213–227.

Tracy, K. (1994). Staying on topic: An explication of conversational relevance. *Discourse Processes, 7*, 447–464.

Tremblay, P. F., & Gardner, R. C. (1995). Expanding the motivation construct in language learning. *The Modern Language Journal, 79*, 505–518.

Tucker, G. R., Hamayan, E., & Genesee, F. H. (1976). Affective, cognitive, and social factors in second language acquisition. *The Canadian Modern Language Review, 32*, 214–226.

VanLier, L. (1996). *Interaction in the language classroom.* New York: Longman.

VanPatten, B. (1993). Grammar teaching for the acquisition-rich classroom. *Foreign Language Annals, 26*, 435–450.

VanPatten. B. (Ed.). (2004). *Processing instruction.* Mahwah, NJ: Erlbaum.

VanPatten, B., & Cadierno, T. (1993). Input processing and second language acquisition: A role for instruction. *The Modern Language Journal, 77*, 45–57.

Vygotsky, L. S. (1978). *Mind in society: The development of higher psychological processes.* Cambridge, MA: Harvard University Press.

Vygotsky, L. S. (1986). *Thought and language.* Cambridge, MA: MIT Press.

Wells, G. (1998). Using L1 to master L2: A response to Antón and DiCamilla's "Socio-cognitive functions of L1 collaborative interaction in the L2 classroom." *The Canadian Modern Language Review, 54*, 343–353.

Wells, G. (1999). *Dialogic inquiry: Toward a sociocultural practice and theory of education.* Cambridge, UK: Cambridge University Press.

Wen, X. (1997). Motivation and language learning with students of Chinese. *Foreign Language Annals, 30*, 235–251.

Wertsch, J. V. (1991). *Voices of the mind: A sociocultural approach to mediated action.* Cambridge, MA: Harvard University Press.

Wertsch, J. V. (1994). The primacy of mediated action in sociocultural studies. *Mind, Culture, and Activity, 1*, 202–208.

Wertsch, J. V., & Bivens, J. (1992). The social origins of individual mental functioning: Alternatives and perspectives. *Quarterly Newsletter of the Laboratory of Comparative Human Cognition, 14*, 35–44.

White, L. (1987). Against comprehensible input: The input hypothesis and the development of second language competence. *Applied Linguistics, 12*, 121–134.

White, L. (1989). Universal grammar and second language acquisition. Amsterdam: John Benjamins.

Wong, W., & VanPatten, B. (2003). The evidence is IN: Drills are OUT. *Foreign Language Annals, 36*, 403–424.

Wong-Fillmore, L. (1985). Second language learning in children: A proposed model. Proceedings of Conference on Issues in English Language Development for Minority Language Education. Arlington, VA, July 24. (ERIC Document Reproduction Service No. ED273149)

Wood, D., Bruner, J. S., & Ross, G. (1976). The role of tutoring in problem solving. *Journal of Child Psychology and Psychiatry, 17*, 89–100.

Yang, J. S. R. (2003). Motivational orientations and selected learner variables of East Asian language learners in the United States. *Foreign Language Annals, 36*, 44–56.

Young, D. J. (1990). An investigation of students' perspectives on anxiety and speaking. *Foreign Language Annals, 23*, 539–553.

NOTES

1. In more recent research, the innate set of universal principles is referred to as *Universal Grammar* (White, 1989).

2. See VanPatten (2004) for a full description of the principles of Processing Instruction and Lee and VanPatten (2003) for a listing (p. 139). For examples of structured input activities, see pp. 142–146 of Lee and VanPatten (2003).

3. Thanks to Dr. Rick Donato, University of Pittsburgh, for the insights here concerning negotiation of meaning. If students learn explicitly through instruction or implicitly through a teacher model and understand that their signals of noncomprehension are welcomed and are good for language learning, then classrooms can provide the context for negotiation of meaning. If learners are merely passive receivers of comprehensible input, or the beneficiaries of teacher reformulations, then we cannot claim that the classroom is providing opportunities for students to negotiate meaning.

4. Refer to Chapter 8 for a discussion of how learners use various types of "talk" during pair-work activities in order to understand the tasks more fully and ultimately to complete them more successfully.

5. See Dörnyei (1994) for a list of thirty strategies for motivating L2 learners according to language level, learner level, course content and activities, teacher-specific factors, and group-specific factors.

6. See Chapter 8 for a more extended discussion of error correction and repair.

7. See Chapter 10 for a discussion of learning strategies.

8. We would like to thank Dr. Bonnie Adair-Hauck, Dr. Rick Donato, and Philomena Cumo-Johanssen for their design of the original version of this case study.

CHAPTER 2

Contextualizing Language Instruction to Address Goals of the Standards for Foreign Language Learning

In this chapter, you will learn about:

- the chronological development of language teaching
- context
- proficiency
- *Standards for Foreign Language Learning in the 21st Century* (philosophy, development, goal areas, content standard, progress indicator, learning scenario)

- *ESL Standards for Pre-K–12 Students*
- bottom-up/top-down approaches to teaching
- textbook evaluation

Teach and Reflect: Developing a Learning Scenario; Contextualizing the Teaching of a Past Tense Grammar Point; Applying the Standards to the Post-Secondary Level

Discuss and Reflect: Textbook Evaluation: A Look at the Use of Context in Exercises; Developing a Top-Down ESL Lesson

CONCEPTUAL ORIENTATION

For decades, elementary school teachers have been combining language and academic content through techniques such as storytelling, games, role playing, and, more recently, integration of subject areas such as mathematics and geography. However, at middle and high school levels of instruction, we have had a tradition of separating linguistic form from academic content and culture as students in higher language levels become cognitively able to analyze linguistic forms. Furthermore, various methods of language instruction (see Appendix 2.1) advocate separation of skills and a discrete-point approach to the teaching of grammar. Many teachers still allow their instruction to be driven by a textbook that is organized around a grammatical syllabus and devoid of stimulating content. Fortunately, the implementation of student standards, the vision of foreign language as a subject area that can be related to other disciplines and to the world at large, current research that advocates a sociocultural approach to language learning and teaching, and the advances in modern technology continue to serve as catalysts in placing context, or meaning, into the forefront of language teaching. In this chapter, you will see the role that the theories presented in Chapter 1 play in setting goals for and implementing language instruction.

A Historical View of Context in Foreign Language Instruction

Appendix 2.1 presents a chart that illustrates the chronological development of language teaching in terms of key time periods when particular approaches and/or methods were used. You may find it helpful to review the chart, explore the role of context in each method, and associate the theories you learned in Chapter 1 with these approaches. The term *context* here refers to the degree to which meaning and situations from the world outside the classroom are present in an instructional approach, method, or classroom activity.

This section presents a brief discussion of the key methods featured in Appendix 2.1, in terms of their impact on the development of foreign language teaching. The earliest method, used in the teaching of Latin and Greek, was the Grammar-Translation (G-T) method, which focused on translation of printed texts, learning of grammatical rules, and memorization of bilingual word lists. The Direct Method appeared in reaction to G-T and its emphasis was on teaching speaking through visuals, exclusive use of the TL, and inductive teaching (i.e., students subconsciously "pick up" grammar rules and guess meaning within context). The Audiolingual Method (ALM), which brought a new emphasis to listening and speaking, advocated teaching the oral skills by means of stimulus-response learning: repetition, dialogue memorization, and manipulation of grammatical pattern drills (Lado, 1964). Therefore, speaking in the ALM mode usually meant repeating after the teacher, reciting a memorized dialogue, or responding to a mechanical drill, as in the following example of a person-number substitution drill taken from a 1969 French I ALM textbook (English translations appear here in parentheses):

Teacher:	Vous travaillez tout le temps.	(You [plural] work all the time.)
	Nous . . .	(We . . .)
Student:	Nous travaillons tout le temps.	(We work all the time.)
Teacher:	Je . . .	(I . . .)
Student:	Je travaille tout le temps.	(I work all the time.)
Teacher:	Michel . . .	(Michel . . .)
Student:	Michel travaille tout le temps.	(Michel works all the time.)
Teacher:	Ils . . .	(They . . .)
Student:	Ils travaillent tout le temps.	(They work all the time.)

(Ray & Lutz, 1969, p. 15).

You will notice the lack of context in such a drill—there is little apparent meaning nor a situation in the world outside the classroom where one would interact in this way. In fact, students can complete a mechanical drill successfully by simply following the pattern, without even knowing the meaning of what is being said. With the ALM method, unfortunately, learners were seldom exposed to meaningful, contextualized input and were unable to transfer the memorized material into spontaneous communication.

The cognitive approaches, first proposed in the 1960s, promoted more meaningful language use and creativity (Ausubel, 1968). This cognitive view was based largely on Chomsky's (1965) claims that an individual's linguistic knowledge does not reflect conditioned behavior but rather the ability to create an infinite number of novel responses. In this theoretical framework, learners must understand the rules of the language before they can be expected to perform or use the language. However, although the cognitive approaches advocate *creative* language practice, extensive discussion about grammar rules (in either a deductive or an inductive mode) and mechanical practice often leave little time for communicative language use in real-world contexts.

How did Chomsky define "competence" and "performance"? See Chapter 1.   ▪

How did Canale and Swain (1980) expand upon the definition of communicative competence? See Chapter 1.   ▪

In the 1970s, greater attention was given to developing a more communicative approach to teaching language, focusing on the needs of learners and on the nature of communication. In a recent commentary on the work of the 1970s, Savignon supports the communicative approach, stating that "the development of the learner's communicative abilities is seen to depend not so much on the time they spend rehearsing grammatical patterns as on the opportunities they are given to interpret, to express, and to negotiate meaning in real-life situations" (Savignon, 1997, p. xi). She further suggests the development of a communicative approach that includes appealing topics, a functional treatment of grammar, and emphasis on communication rather than on formal accuracy in the beginning stages.

Several methods for teaching language that were developed since the late 1970s reflect many of Savignon's ideas for a communicative approach. The Natural Approach, a modern-day version of the Direct Method, was Terrell's (1982) attempt to operationalize Krashen's theories in the classroom. Anchored in the philosophy that L2 learning occurs in the same way as L1 acquisition, the Natural Approach stresses the importance of authentic language input in real-world contexts, comprehension before production, and self-expression early on, and de-emphasizes the need for grammatical perfection in the beginning stages of language learning. Based on the same philosophy, the Total Physical Response Method (TPR) (Asher, Kusudo, & de la Torre, 1974) uses activities directed at the learner's kinesthetic-sensory system (body movements). Learners initially hear commands in the foreign language, respond physically to the commands (e.g., run, jump, turn around, walk to the door), and later produce the commands orally and in writing. TPR is based on the way in which children acquire vocabulary naturally in their native language. This method, which is often used as one instructional strategy for teaching vocabulary, has been shown to be very effective in enabling learners to acquire large amounts of concrete vocabulary and retain them over time (Asher, Kusudo, & de la Torre, 1974).[1] You will learn more about TPR and the teaching of vocabulary in Chapter 4.

Among the various humanistic or affective approaches to language instruction that place a top priority on the emotions or the affect of the learner are the Silent Way (Gattegno, 1976), Community Language Learning (Curran, 1976), and Suggestopedia (Lozanov, 1978). In many affective approaches, learners determine the content of what they are learning and are encouraged to express themselves from the start.

The Role of Context in Proficiency-Oriented Instruction

The definitions of communicative competence of the 1970s prompted new insights into the various aspects of language ability that needed to be developed in order for an individual to know a language well enough to use it. Early approaches to language instruction failed to specify levels of competence so that learners' progress could be measured or program goals could be articulated. Furthermore, there was a growing realization in the profession that perhaps rather than searching for one perfect method, we needed an "organizing principle" about the nature of language proficiency that could facilitate the development of goals and objectives of language teaching (Higgs, 1984).

With World War II came the realization that the United States needed a citizenry who could communicate with people from other countries. Consequently, by the end of the 1970s, it was clear that a nationally recognized procedure for assessing language proficiency was needed, as was some consensus on defining proficiency goals for second language programs. This need for goals and assessment in the area of foreign languages was later brought to the public's attention by Senator Paul Simon of Illinois and other legislators, whose efforts led to the creation of the President's Commission on Foreign Language and International Studies in 1978, with the support of President Jimmy Carter. In 1979, the Commission published the report *Strength Through Wisdom*, which recommended that the profession develop foreign language proficiency tests to assess language learning and teaching in the United States. This report, together with recommendations by the Modern Language Association-American Council on Language Studies (MLA-ACLS) Task Force and the work of the Educational Testing Service (ETS), initiated a project whereby a proficiency scale and oral interview procedure developed in the 1950s by the Foreign Service Institute (FSI) of the U.S. Department of State would be adapted for use in academic contexts. In what came to be known as the Common Yardstick Project of the 1970s, ETS cooperated with organizations in Great Britain and Germany, representatives of the U.S. government, and business and academic groups to adapt the government FSI scale, currently known as the Interagency Language Roundtable (ILR) scale, and interview procedure for academic use (Liskin-Gasparro, 1984). This work, which was continued in 1981 by the American Council on the Teaching of Foreign Languages (ACTFL), in consultation with MLA, ETS, and other professional organizations, ultimately led to the development of the *ACTFL Provisional Proficiency Guidelines* in 1982.

These guidelines define what language users should be able to do with the language in speaking, listening, reading, and writing, at various levels of performance. The speaking guidelines were revised in 1999, the writing guidelines were revised in 2001, and the listening and reading guidelines are presently under revision. These guidelines, which marked a shift from a focus on methodology to a focus on outcomes and assessment, continue to have a great impact on language instruction. Although neither a curricular outline nor a prescribed syllabus or sequence of instruction in and of themselves, the guidelines have implications for instructional strategies, the setting of performance expectations, and performance-based assessment (see Chapters 3, 8, and 11). See Appendix 2.2 for a historical overview of the development of the proficiency concept and Appendix 2.3 (see Web site) for the listening and reading guidelines themselves. See the *Teacher's Handbook* Web site for the link to the speaking guidelines, revised in 1999, and the writing guidelines, revised in 2001.

thandbook.heinle.com

The proficiency framework assesses language ability in terms of four interrelated criteria: (1) **global tasks or functions:** linguistic tasks, such as asking for information, narrating and describing past events, and expressing opinions; (2) **contexts/content areas:** the sets of circumstances, linguistic or situational, in which these tasks are performed and the topics that relate to these contexts (e.g., context—in a restaurant in Mexico; content—ordering a meal); (3) the **accuracy** with which the tasks are performed: the grammar, vocabulary, pronunciation, fluency, sociolinguistic appropriateness or acceptability of what is being said within a certain setting, and the use of appropriate strategies for discourse management; and (4) the **oral text type** that results from the performance of the tasks: discrete words and phrases, sentences, paragraphs, or extended discourse (Swender, 1999, p. 2).

Language practice that is contextualized and reflects real-world use forms the foundation for an approach that seeks to develop proficiency.[2]

 The proficiency framework assesses language ability in terms of global tasks or functions, contexts/content areas, accuracy, and oral text type. ∎

An Introduction to the Standards for Foreign Language Learning in the 21st Century (*SFLL*)

The Developmental Process

An interest in standards in the academic disciplines was sparked by an initiative of the George H. W. Bush administration and was continued under the Goals 2000 initiative of the Clinton administration. Visionary Goals 2000 (1994) described the competence that all students should demonstrate in challenging subject matter in grades four, eight, and twelve in seven subject areas, including foreign language. With its inclusion in Goals 2000, foreign language was recognized as part of the K–12 core curriculum in the United States (Phillips & Lafayette, 1996).

The National Standards in Foreign Language Education Project (NSFLEP, 1996) was a collaborative effort of ACTFL, the American Association of Teachers of French (AATF), the American Association of Teachers of German (AATG), and the American Association of Teachers of Spanish and Portuguese (AATSP). The standards framework was drafted by an eleven-member task force that represented a variety of languages, levels of instruction, program models, and geographic regions. The task force shared each phase of its work with the profession as a whole, disseminating the drafts and seeking written comments, which were then considered as subsequent revisions were made. The final draft, called *Standards for Foreign Language Learning: Preparing for the 21st Century,* was published in 1996 and made available to members of the profession. In 1999, it was expanded and renamed *Standards for Foreign Language Learning in the 21st Century,* to include standards for the post-secondary level (K–16) as well as language-specific versions of the standards created by the professional organizations in Chinese, classical languages, French, German, Italian, Japanese, Portuguese, Russian, and Spanish. The vast majority of states have developed student standards based entirely or in large part on the national standards, abbreviated as *SFLL* in this text.

 To what degree are the foreign language student standards in your state based upon the *Standards for Foreign Language Learning in the 21st Century?* Consult the Web site of your state language association or your state department of education to access your state's foreign language student standards. ∎

Organizing Principles: Philosophy, Goal Areas, Standards

The work on proficiency during the past two decades has placed the profession in an excellent position to define what students should know and be able to do with a foreign language they learn. Although influenced by the proficiency guidelines, the standards do not represent communication as four separate skill areas of listening, speaking, reading, and writing. Standards define the central role of foreign language in the learning experiences of all learners, and they have the potential for a lasting impact in the future by placing content (i.e., gaining access to information in a range of areas of inquiry and human activity)

FIGURE 2.1 The Five C's of Foreign Language Study

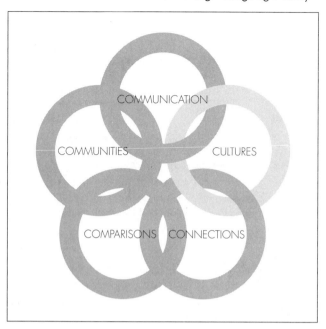

Source: NSFLEP, 1999, p. 32.

as the central focus for instruction (NSFLEP, 1999, p. 14). As it began its work, the NSFLEP task force developed a Statement of Philosophy that served as the foundation for the development of standards. This statement, which appears in Appendix 2.4 (see Web site), describes key assumptions that enabled the task force to identify five goal areas that reflect a rationale for foreign language education. These goals are known as the "5 Cs of foreign language education": Communication, Cultures, Connections, Comparisons, Communities.

 The Five Cs of foreign language education are Communication, Cultures, Connections, Comparisons, Communities. ■

As Figure 2.1 illustrates, these five goals interconnect to suggest the richness of human language; no one goal can be separated from the other, nor is any one goal more important than another. Each goal area contains two to three content standards that describe the knowledge and abilities that all students should acquire by the end of their high school education in order to achieve the goals. Figure 2.2 illustrates the five goals and eleven standards. Each goal area and standards, as they relate to topics in *Teacher's Handbook*, will be explored in depth in subsequent chapters. The research base, theories, and instructional models related to each goal area will also be presented.

 Content standard = what students should know and be able to do ■

It is important to note that these 11 standards are *content standards*, which describe what students should know and be able to do. They are not *performance standards*, which address the issue of *how well* students demonstrate competency in subject matter (e.g., the *ACTFL Proficiency Guidelines*). Individual states and school districts are responsible for determining performance standards for their students and for answering the question, "How good is good enough?" However, in order to assist states and districts in this task, the standards document includes sample progress indicators for grades four,

FIGURE 2.2 Standards for Foreign Language Learning

STANDARDS FOR FOREIGN LANGUAGE LEARNING

COMMUNICATION
Communicate in Languages Other Than English

Standard 1.1: Students engage in conversations, provide and obtain Information, express feelings and emotions, and exchange opinions.

Standard 1.2: Students understand and interpret written and spoken language on a variety of topics.

Standard 1.3: Students present information, concepts, and ideas to an audience of listeners or readers on a variety of topics.

CULTURES
Gain Knowledge and Understanding of Other Cultures

Standard 2.1: Students demonstrate an understanding of the relationship between the practices and perspectives of the culture studied.

Standard 2.2: Students demonstrate an understanding of the relationship between the products and perspectives of the culture studied.

CONNECTIONS
Connect with Other Disciplines and Acquire Information

Standard 3.1: Students reinforce and further their knowledge of other disciplines through the foreign language.

Standard 3.2: Students acquire information and recognize the distinctive viewpoints that are only available through the foreign language and its cultures.

COMPARISONS
Develop Insight into the Nature of Language and Culture

Standard 4.1: Students demonstrate understanding of the nature of language through comparisons of the language studied and their own.

Standard 4.2: Students demonstrate understanding of the concept of culture through comparisons of the cultures studied and their own.

COMMUNITIES
Participate in Multilingual Communities at Home and Around the World

Standard 5.1: Students use the language both within and beyond the school setting.

Standard 5.2: Students show evidence of becoming life-long learners by using the language for personal enjoyment and enrichment.

Source: NSFLEP, 1999, p. 9.

eight, and twelve that define student progress in meeting the standards but are not themselves standards. They apply to many languages, can be realistically achieved at some level by all students, provide many instructional possibilities, are assessable in numerous ways, and are designed for use by states and districts to establish acceptable performance levels for their students. The following is an example of these progress indicators:

Goal area: Cultures

Standard: Students demonstrate an understanding of the relationship between the practices and perspectives of the cultures studied.

Sample progress indicators:

Grade 4: Students use appropriate gestures and oral expressions for greetings, leave takings, and common classroom interactions.

Grade 8: Students observe, analyze, and discuss patterns of behavior typical of their peer group.

Grade 12: Students identify, examine, and discuss connections between cultural perspectives and socially approved behavioral patterns. (NSFLEP, 1999, pp. 50–51)

Sample progress indicator = defines student progress in meeting standards ▪

To assist teachers in applying the standards to their classroom instruction, the standards document includes various examples of learning scenarios, each of which is a series of learner-centered activities based on a specific theme or unit of instruction and integrated so that one activity is the basis for the subsequent activity (e.g., a listening activity provides the content for a small-group discussion). See Teach and Reflect, Episode One of this chapter for a sample learning scenario.

 Learning scenario = series of learner-centered activities based on a specific theme and integrated so that one activity is the basis for the next ▪

In order to address expectations of what learners should be able to do in terms of both proficiency and key areas of the standards, ACTFL published its *ACTFL Performance Guidelines for K–12 Learners* (1998). The guidelines take into account the various sequences of language instruction that typically exist in American schools and outline language performance expectations, depending on the length and nature of students' learning experiences. These guidelines (see Appendix 2.5 on the Web site) describe language performance evidenced by K–12 students at the benchmarks of language development labeled Novice Range, Intermediate Range, and Pre-advanced Range. Each of these learner ranges defines the following areas of student performance within the three modes of communication (Interpersonal, Interpretive, Presentational):

- Comprehensibility: How well are they understood?
- Comprehension: How well do they understand?
- Language Control: How accurate is their language?
- Vocabulary Use: How extensive and applicable is their vocabulary?
- Communication Strategies: How do they maintain communication?
- Cultural Awareness: How is their cultural understanding reflected in their communication?

The language performance descriptions featured in these guidelines are designed to help teachers understand how well students demonstrate language ability at various points along the language learning continuum, according to the length and nature of their language learning experiences *(ACTFL,* 1998).

Focus on Context: The "Weave" of Curricular Elements

The *Standards for Foreign Language Learning in the 21st Century* broaden the definition of the content of the language curriculum. Figure 2.3 depicts the elements that should be "woven" into language learning: language system, cultural traits and concepts, communication strategies, critical thinking skills, and learning strategies. In addition, other subject areas and technology are also important elements in a standards-driven curriculum.

The language system goes beyond grammar rules and vocabulary; it also includes sociolinguistic elements of gestures and other forms of nonverbal communication, discourse style, and "learning what to say to whom and when" (NSFLEP, 1999, p. 33). In addition to being able to use the language system, learners must be able to identify key cultural concepts that will facilitate sensitive and meaningful interaction. Communication strategies such as circumlocution, guessing intelligently, making hypotheses, asking for clarification, and making inferences will empower learners in their attempts to interact. In learning a foreign language, students use critical thinking skills as they apply their existing knowledge to new tasks, incorporate new knowledge, and identify and analyze issues

FIGURE 2.3 The "Weave" of Curricular Elements

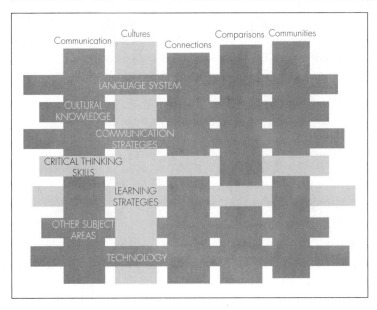

Source: NSFLEP, 1999, p. 33.

in order to arrive at informed decisions and to propose solutions to problems. In assuming greater responsibility for their own learning, students use learning strategies such as organizing their learning, previewing new tasks, summarizing, using questioning strategies, and inferring information from a text. By exploring interesting and challenging content and topics, students can enhance their learning of the language while expanding their knowledge of other subject areas. Additionally, increased access to a wide range of forms of technology, such as the World Wide Web, e-mail, CD-ROMs, and interactive video, will enable learners to use their linguistic skills to establish interactions with peers and to learn about the contemporary culture of the target country.

ESL STANDARDS FOR PRE-K–12 STUDENTS

In 1997, TESOL published *ESL Standards for Pre-K–12 Students,* informed in part by the work that was underway at that time to develop foreign language standards. Some English language learners in U.S. schools are recent immigrants, others are seeking refuge from political unrest in their homelands, and others are in the United States with their families for professional reasons.[3] Their levels of education vary as does their language proficiency in English. You may find some English language learners in your foreign languages classes.

The *ESL Standards* are undergirded by these important perspectives:

- language as communication;
- language learning through meaningful and significant use;
- the individual and societal value of bi- and multilingualism;
- the role of ESOL students' native languages in their English language and general academic development;
- cultural, social, and cognitive processes in language and academic development; assessment that respects language and cultural diversity (p. 2).

The *ESL Standards* delineate what students learning English as a second or additional language should know and be able to do with English. The ESL standards are framed around three goals, which reflect three overarching areas in which students need to develop competence in English: social language, academic language, and sociocultural knowledge. Each goal is supported by three standards, for a total of nine standards. Each standard is further illustrated by descriptors, sample progress indicators, and classroom vignettes with discussions. The standards are organized into grade-level clusters: pre-K–3, 4–8, and 9–12. Each cluster's goals and standards are aligned with descriptors, progress indicators, and vignettes specific to that grade range. This organization helps build foundational knowledge and increases the sophistication of language use as students move up through the grades and become older. In other words, older students are held to higher expectations for demonstrating English proficiency: The descriptors remain the same across the clusters, but more progress indicators are added at each cluster (TESOL, 1997, p. 19).

The three goals and nine standards are:

Goal 1: To use English to communicate in social settings
    Standard 1: Students will use English to participate in social interactions.
    Standard 2: Students will interact in, through, and with spoken and written English for personal expression and enjoyment.
    Standard 3: Students will use learning strategies to extend their communicative competence.

Goal 2: To use English to achieve academically in all content areas
    Standard 1: Students will use English to interact in the classroom.
    Standard 2: Students will use English to obtain, process, construct, and provide subject matter information in spoken and written form.
    Standard 3: Students will use appropriate learning strategies to construct and apply academic knowledge.

Goal 3: To use English in socially and culturally appropriate ways
    Standard 1: Students will use the appropriate language variety, register, and genre according to audience, purpose, and setting.
    Standard 2: Students will use nonverbal communication appropriate to audience, purpose, setting.
    Standard 3: Students will use appropriate learning strategies to extend their sociolinguistic and sociocultural competence (TESOL, 1997, pp. 31–39, 45–52, 57–65).

thandbook.heinle.com

See the *Teacher's Handbook* Web site link for the full text of the *ESL Standards*.

Role of the SFLL in Curricular Planning, Instruction, and Assessment

The authors of the *Standards for Foreign Language Learning in the 21st Century* caution educators of what the standards are NOT intended to be:

- They do not describe the current state of foreign language education in this country nor do they describe what is being accomplished by the majority of foreign language students.
- They are not a curriculum guide inasmuch as they do not prescribe specific course content nor a recommended scope and sequence.

FIGURE 2.4 Standards: Where We Are Now and Where the Standards Take Us

WHERE WE ARE NOW (adapted from Met, 2000, p. 52)	WHERE THE STANDARDS TAKE US (Shrum & Glisan, 2005, original material)
Concept of proficiency in listening, speaking, reading, writing	Communication in three modes to emphasize content and purpose of communication
Student pair and group work	Tasks that provide opportunities for students to negotiate meaning and develop interactional competence (e.g., ability to manage discussions)
Oral teacher-to-student exchanges that are communicative in nature	Classroom interaction that is intellectually meaningful and stimulating (i.e., encourages students to ask questions, expand on their talk, take multiple turns in conversations)
Grammar as a component of communication rather than an end itself	Grammar that serves communication needs
Use of authentic[4] materials and commercially produced materials organized around communicative topics or situations	A central focus on the development of interpretation skills, which are pivotal to acquiring new information, cultural knowledge, and connections to other disciplines and target-language communities
Classroom activities that are meaningful and purposeful	A more central role for inquiry-based activities, such as cultural investigations, authentic text exploration, and research- and technology-based projects—previously considered unit add-ons or supplemental
Classroom environment that focuses on meaningful communication	Classroom environment that fosters a sociocultural community of learners engaged in meaning making and acquiring knowledge through the foreign language
Integration of various aspects of culture into language learning	Approach to culture that emphasizes the connection of cultural products and practices to their philosophical perspectives, enabling learners to develop more relevant cultural insights into the target culture and their own
Ways of measuring student learning that focus on performance, on knowledge in use	Performance assessments that go beyond paper-and-pencil tests, have an expanded role in determining student progress in meeting the standards, and offer a more useful link between teaching and learning

■ They do not represent a stand-alone document, but should be used with state and local frameworks and standards to determine the best approaches and responsible expectations for students (NSFLEP, 1999, p. 28).

For what purposes are the standards intended to be used? Since they describe the ideal best practices, the standards provide a gauge against which to measure improvement in foreign language education. They are visionary in describing what language learners should be able to attain as a result of foreign language study. In addition, the standards support the ideal of extended sequences of language study and suggest the kinds of content and curricular experiences that will enable learners to attain the standards. Finally, the document has the potential to inform and influence teachers, parents, administrators, and others to ensure that all students have opportunities to acquire the knowledge and skills necessary to enable them to function successfully in our multicultural society (NSFLEP, 1999, p. 28).

According to Met (2000), the standards built upon a number of instructional practices that were previously found to be effective in realizing communicative and proficiency-based learner goals. However, the standards have also introduced instructional implications that are new for the majority of foreign language teachers. The initial release of the standards in 1996 spawned a steady stream of studies that have examined the standards through the lens of both current research and classroom practice (see, for example, Phillips, 1997). (These studies will be presented as each goal area is explored in subsequent chapters.) Figure 2.4 illustrates the areas of current classroom practice and the ways in which the standards can provide direction in refining these areas, as teachers work to address them in curricular design, instruction, and assessment. These refinements will undoubtedly spark much more research as the field continues to explore ways to implement the standards.

Using the Standards Framework to "Contextualize" the Curriculum

The standards framework and implications, as discussed in the previous section, present various possibilities to language teachers as they strive to strengthen their curricula and instruction. The specific ways in which the standards may be embraced by teachers depend largely on teachers' philosophies of and approaches to language instruction. The methods of instruction presented earlier in this chapter can be categorized into one of two broader approaches to language teaching, based on one's theoretical understanding of how learners best learn a second language: the bottom-up approach and top-down approach. The standards framework has something to offer to each of these approaches in view of the role of context that can be brought to the learning experience. Furthermore, the standards have implications for foreign language textbooks, which still often drive the curriculum and instruction and influence the teacher's approach.

The Traditional Bottom-Up Approach: Skill-Based Approaches

Historically, foreign languages have been taught in the United States by means of a bottom-up approach: Students analyze and learn grammar rules and vocabulary, and then later practice using them in communication. Rivers (1983) used the terms *skill getting* and *skill using* to characterize this dichotomy. *Skill getting* refers to the type of practice that helps students "learn" grammatical structures, while in *skill-using*, students use the learned structures in communicative activities designed to focus their attention on meaningful interaction. A decade earlier, Paulston (1972) classified three categories of drills: (1) mechanical—complete control of the response and only one correct way of responding; (2) meaningful—still control of the response, may be more than one way to respond, learner must understand the stimulus; (3) communicative-learner provides new information, no right or wrong response except in terms of grammatical correctness.[5]

Similarly, Littlewood (1980) suggested that classroom practice activities be sequenced so that meaning increasingly receives more focus. In his model, activities progress through the following stages: (1) primary focus on form; (2) focus on form, plus meaning; (3) focus on meaning, plus form; and (4) primary focus on meaning (cf. Hadley, 2001, p. 143). Despite the emphasis on more meaningful and communicative activities in recent years, decontextualized mechanical practice has remained pervasive over the course of decades in the language approaches used by teachers. However, the usefulness of rote practice for the language learner has repeatedly been called into question, particularly in light of the key role that meaning-making and social interaction play in language acquisition (see Chapter 1). Furthermore, a recent study that examined the utility of mechanical drills boldly concluded that these exercises "are not beneficial for foreign language acquisition or the development of fluency and should be discarded from instructional practice" (Wong & VanPatten, 2003, p. 403). See Chapter 7 for additional discussion of the focus on form vs. focus on meaning controversy and the teaching of grammar.

It should be noted that students require copious amounts of practice in using the target language, but this practice must be meaningful and engaging for students. In *Teacher's Handbook,* whenever we advocate practice, we are referring only to practice that has meaning and is purposeful.

 What theories from Chapter 1 support the key role of meaning-making and social interaction in facilitating language acquisition?

The *Standards for Foreign Language Learning in the 21st Century* can help the teacher to incorporate more engaging content in a bottom-up approach. While maintaining a familiar sequence of instruction that is often organized around the textbook, the teacher might:

- include additional information, practice, and activities related to the standards as each chapter or unit is explored (e.g., for practice of numbers, students listen to and interpret an authentic radio advertisement announcing a sale at a local department store);
- incorporate an increasing number of "synthesis" activities that integrate more than one mode of communication and address a particular goal area/standard (e.g., students send an e-mail message to a key pal abroad in order to find out information about peers in the target country);
- limit the number of mechanical, decontextualized textbook exercises and replace or revise them to bring meaning to the tasks as well as opportunities for student interaction and negotiation of meaning; and
- use some resources beyond the text to accommodate the gaps in context (e.g., video, Internet, visuals, stories).[6]

A Top-Down Approach

A top-down approach to language instruction resists reducing language to word lists, verb conjugations, discrete grammar points, or isolated linguistic elements (Adair-Hauck & Cumo-Johanssen, 1997). In this approach, learners are presented with a "whole" text (e.g., story, poem, song, tape-recorded listening selection), are guided through comprehending its main ideas, explore these ideas through interaction with others, and then focus on specific details and/or linguistic structures (e.g., vocabulary, grammar). Learners manipulate language to communicate thoughts using higher-level skills (e.g., relating knowledge from several areas, using known ideas to create new ones, generalizing from facts, predicting, drawing conclusions) before attending to discrete language structures with the use of lower-level skills (e.g., recognizing, identifying, recalling, explaining, observing, interpreting). By means of activities such as negotiation of meaning and joint problem solving *with* the teacher and classmates, learners demonstrate performance before competence; that is, they participate in a more complex task than they are capable of completing without assistance (Rogoff, 1990). You will learn in a later chapter the specific implications of this approach for the teaching of grammar.

The purpose of top-down learning is to give the student a clear and whole picture of how the words and structures they must learn are contained in a context that makes these elements meaningful through the overall message. This, in turn, allows for strategic guessing, similar to the process one uses to identify unfamiliar elements in L1. In this type of learning, meaning is constructed from the whole and does not represent a linear process.[7] An example of this kind of human learning in another field is the way in which novice golfers might approach playing golf for the first time. They may have observed other golfers on the golf course or watched golf tournaments on television. Consequently, they may use this background knowledge to approach the sport in a top-down fashion initially by just grasping their golf clubs and swinging to see if they can even hit the ball. They may keep practicing by trying out different strategies and imitating what they see fellow golfers do. In this way, novice golfers get a feel for what it is like to play golf—i.e., the focus is on the "whole picture" of golfing. However, novice golfers may revert to a bottom-up approach if, for example, they want to improve their golf swing. They may take private golf lessons to focus on the way to properly grip the clubs, align themselves with the ball, and swing correctly. This bottom-up approach involves a linear, step-by-step process of focusing on one aspect of the golf game at a time.

 The purpose of top-down learning is to give the student a clear and whole picture of how the words and structures they must learn are contained in a context that makes these elements meaningful through the overall message. ▪

How does one implement a top-down approach? Within the thematic unit being taught, the teacher might present a "text" to the class for the purpose of helping learners understand its meaning while discussing it. This "text" can be a story, an authentic taped conversation or short reading, a piece of *realia* (an object from the target culture such as a postcard, a letter, an invitation, etc.), or any verbal input given by the teacher. For example, in a chapter dealing with travel, learners might (1) listen to a public service announcement that gives advice to travelers, (2) read an advertisement for taking a cruise, or (3) listen to their teacher tell a story about a family vacation. If the vocabulary and grammar have been appropriately matched to the theme, then these initial authentic contexts contain examples of structures and words used naturally. In a Spanish version of the contexts given above, appropriate grammatical structures might include the future tense, the prepositions *por* and *para*, and the subjunctive used with adverbial expressions.

As students attend to the initial context, they are given tasks for demonstrating understanding of main ideas and/or particular details, such as selecting the main idea from a list of alternatives, creating a possible title for the text, responding to true-false statements, and finding specific pieces of information. The teacher leads the class in discussion for the purpose of relating new information to previously learned information, for heightening understanding of the text, or, in the case of a story, for recreating the text. While the text may contain new vocabulary and grammatical structures, students cope with the unknown by negotiating meaning with the teacher by asking questions, requesting clarification, and gleaning meaning from the context itself. Through exploration of the text, students indirectly learn vocabulary and grammar that can later become the focus of more directed and personalized practice. Students may actively use grammatical forms that are contained in the text prior to actually being taught the forms explicitly. Students can also use technology to access additional authentic sources of information in order to explore cultural products, practices, and perspectives related to the theme. Within a top-down approach, the *Standards for Foreign Language Learning in the 21st Century* can serve as the organizing principle, focusing on meaningful and motivating content through which students develop language abilities, rather than allowing a textbook or teacher-controlled grammatical content to drive the curriculum (Sandrock, 2000). Thus a standards-based unit/chapter plan that is top-down in nature might feature the following sequence of learner activity:

Level of Instruction: Intermediate high school/college Spanish

Context: Travel

Language functions: Making travel plans, getting a hotel room, discussing means of transportation, investigating a *parador* (historical site such as a castle or convent turned into a place to stay) on the Internet, communicating with a key pal by e-mail, understanding main ideas of authentic conversations dealing with lodging and travel arrangements, interpreting an authentic travel advertisement, interacting in role play situations dealing with travel.

1. Students listen to an authentic conversation between an airline employee and a traveler. Students explore main ideas through discussion and check-off lists. They acquire and practice using new vocabulary from the conversation through Total Physical Response activities, role play, and contextual guessing.
2. Students read an authentic advertisement on vacation packages. They explore main ideas and offer their opinions.
3. Students listen to the teacher introduce the concept of a *parador* while looking at a map of Spain and finding areas in which *paradores* are located. Students read an authentic article from a travel magazine that presents three types of *paradores* (the reading includes pictures, symbols that illustrate the amenities included in each *parador*, and a key to understanding the symbols). Working in groups, students read about one of the *paradores* and interpret the symbols. Each group presents its *parador* to the class by describing its location on the map, type of construction, rooms, and amenities.
4. Students listen to an authentic conversation between a hotel clerk and a guest. They explore main ideas and some details and use this as a context for discussion and role play.
5. Students engage in discovery learning of new grammatical structures (future tense, *por/para*, present subjunctive with adverbial clauses) that were seeded in the initial authentic oral and printed texts. They complete several PACE grammar lessons (more on this in Chapter 7) and co-construct grammatical structures. Grammar is practiced in context by means of guided and open-ended activities and self-expression.
6. Students find other *paradores* on the Internet and acquire additional information about historical sites, geography, and travel.
7. Students communicate with key pals in Spain via e-mail in order to acquire information about daily life that would be important to know as a traveler. Once they receive responses from their key pals, they discuss cultural comparisons with their classmates.
8. Students are assessed on their ability to make travel plans through tasks such as:

   ■ an oral role play situation in which they interact with a hotel clerk or airline employee;
   ■ reading a written text found on the Internet that deals with a *parador* and summarizing key points about it, including whether or not they might want to stay there on a trip;
   ■ responding by e-mail to a Spanish-speaking key pal, in which they discuss suggestions for travelers and explore cultural products, practices, and perspectives that would be important information for someone traveling to a Spanish-speaking country.[8]

While top-down processing is still a new area of research, preliminary studies point to the likelihood that students of a top-down or whole-language approach may be able to acquire language at a higher and more successful rate than through the traditional bottom-up approach (Adair-Hauck & Cumo-Johanssen, 1997). One of the reasons for this may be that a bottom-up approach often allows little time in the unit for contextualized practice, since most of the time is spent analyzing small segments of language.

The Role of the Foreign Language Textbook

Historically, the foreign language textbook has been at the center of the foreign language curriculum, used by teachers—especially those who use a bottom-up approach—as the framework for organizing instruction and the primary source of exercises and activities. The student standards and the goal of contextualizing language instruction prompt several observations concerning the role of the language textbook. On the one hand, more attention to context is evident in some textbook series published in the last several years, since many of them have begun to integrate connections to other disciplines, exploration of cultural perspectives, and interaction with target-language communities. On the other hand, despite the wealth of research in second language learning that supports the notion that language learners require opportunities for meaningful interaction (see Chapter 1), foreign language textbooks have continued to depend heavily on bottom-up, drill, and form-focused activities that lack context or meaning (Aski, 2003). This finding has been corroborated by studies that have examined textbooks in French (Lally, 1998), Italian (Aski), Japanese (Takenoya, 1995), and Spanish (Frantzen, 1998).

Foreign language publishers recently pointed out that, despite the major initiatives undertaken by the profession (e.g., proficiency and standards) to develop national *policies*, the world of *practice* has reflected less change in materials and teaching than the field realizes (Dorwick & Glass, 2003). In their experience, what changes most notably in textbooks are the prefaces and names of "features," usually in response to the latest trends or policies (Dorwick & Glass, p. 593). Bragger and Rice (2000) surveyed teachers regarding their willingness to accept change in instructional materials. Respondents reported that materials change slowly due to factors such as the conservative nature of the profession, resistance to or fear of change, the teacher/publisher tension, lack of time to make changes, and budgets (pp. 124–125). Aski (2003) echoes the view of Dorwick and Glass when she concludes that textbook publishers only produce the materials requested by their audience—foreign language instructors—and that the change will occur only when instructors embrace SLA research and indicate a preference for materials that reflect this research.[9]

In his review of textbook exercise formats, Walz (1989) found that, in the mid- to late-1980s, textbook authors and publishers responded to the focus on communicative language teaching by "contextualizing" mechanical or skill-getting exercises in a wide variety of ways, such as by (1) connecting exercise sentences with the same situation or theme; (2) providing a context for the exercise in the form of information concerning people, activities, or descriptions; and (3) combining cultural aspects with language practice within the exercise (p. 161). As noted by both Frantzen (1998) and Walz (1989), textbook authors have different ideas about what "contextualization" of an exercise means. "Contextualization, especially with respect to mechanical drills, does not seem to be the same as creating a context, which is the topic and situation of a communicative act that are necessary for understanding" (Walz, 1989, p. 162). Frantzen cautions that the contextualization of mechanical drills may trick students and teachers into believing that meaningful discourse is being fostered.

FIGURE 2.5 Textbook Evaluation Criteria

Rate each criterion on the following scale: 3 = Excellent 2 = Satisfactory 1 = Poor

1. Features an organization based on interesting topics and cultural contexts
2. Provides activities in which students talk to each other, share information and opinions, ask questions, and express feelings
3. Encourages students to negotiate meaning with one another
4. Provides authentic oral input (audio tapes, videotapes, CD-ROM programs) that features engaging content and tasks
5. Provides authentic printed texts (newspaper/magazine articles, ads, poems, short stories) that have engaging content and tasks
6. Suggests strategies for comprehending and interpreting oral and written texts
7. Includes pre-listening/pre-viewing/pre-reading tasks
8. Includes tasks in which students speak and write to an audience of listeners/readers
9. Provides contextualized and meaningful activities
10. Presents clear, concise grammar explanations that are necessary for communication
11. Presents vocabulary thematically, in context, and with the use of visuals and authentic realia
12. Provides for integrated practice of the three modes of communication
13. Presents an accurate view of the cultures in which the target language is spoken
14. Includes visuals for presenting vocabulary and illustrating cultural aspects (overhead transparencies, pictures, slides, realia)
15. Provides opportunities for students to explore the products of the culture and their relationship to cultural perspectives
16. Provides opportunities for students to explore the practices of the culture and their relationship to cultural perspectives
17. Provides opportunities for students to use the target language to learn about other subject areas
18. Engages students in using the target language to acquire new information on topics of interest
19. Provides opportunities for students to compare key features of the native and target languages in interesting ways
20. Provides opportunities for students to compare products, practices, and perspectives of the native culture and target cultures in interesting ways
21. Includes activities in which students use the target language with peers in other communities and target language regions (e-mail, World Wide Web, interactive video, field trips)
22. Provides opportunities for students to select authentic texts to explore for enjoyment and learning
23. Provides contextualized, performance-based achievement tests with scoring rubrics[10]
24. Suggests strategies for assessing student progress in attaining standards
25. Integrates technology into instruction effectively (audiotapes, videotapes, interactive video, CD-ROM, World Wide Web, e-mail)

The evaluator/teacher may choose to add additional criteria of importance to specific language programs.

Source: Shrum and Glisan, 2005, original material.

Unfortunately, many school districts use the same textbook series for seven to ten years or even longer. Teachers who seek to address the *Standards for Foreign Language Learning in the 21st Century* may be faced with using an old textbook that is filled with drills and/or decontextualized exercises. In this case, teachers might consider adapting the more promising exercises by:

- attaching a real-world context, such as a cultural one, that students must understand in order to communicate (Frantzen, 1998);
- providing opportunities in the exercises for students to acquire new information, such as from other disciplines;

- eliminating fictitious characters and personalizing the exercises to the lives of students;
- allowing for divergent responses rather than one correct answer.

See Case Study One in this chapter for sample textbook exercises.

Teachers in a position to select a new textbook should consider the degree to which the textbook is aligned with the 5 Cs and standards as well as with proficiency and current SLA research implications for foreign language teaching. In a standards-based language curriculum that focuses on the development of real-world communication, the components of a textbook that are labeled "supplementary materials" are often just as important as or even more important than, the textbook itself, for they provide contextual, visual, cultural, and interdisciplinary support that is at the heart of meaningful, contextualized language instruction. Figure 2.5 presents sample criteria that teachers might use as they evaluate and select new language textbooks.

In summary, the *Standards for Foreign Language Learning in the 21st Century* offer a description of what language learners should be able to attain as a result of foreign language study, a framework for contextualizing language instruction, and a gauge against which to measure improvement in foreign language education. Additionally, the standards present a future research agenda and challenges as we find new ways to provide language learning experiences that meaningfully relate to real-world communication, the interests of learners, the content of other disciplines, and target culture communities.

TEACH AND REFLECT

NCATE
STANDARD
4.a.

EPISODE ONE
Developing a Learning Scenario

Part One: Read the following learning scenario (NSFLEP, 1999, p. 185) and then identify which goal areas and standards are addressed and how you can tell.

A Roman Election

Mrs. Robinson's eighth grade Latin students at Harbor Day School in Corona del Mar stage an election while they are studying the Roman Republican Period. Students read a variety of original and adapted texts on the topic, including passages from Cicero, Catullus, and Pompeian campaign graffiti.

Students discuss thoroughly the Roman political system, how elections were held, and what political campaigns were like. Students then prepare to reenact the election of 63 B.C. Cicero presided over this election, and one of the two consular seats was hotly contested by the lawyer Sulpicius and the general Murena. Students discuss the different personalities and qualifications of these two men and the general state of affairs in the Roman world, and they compare them to modern American elections, campaigns, and candidates.

Students receive instruction on Latin commands, greetings, questions, and responses. Simple sentence constructions are reviewed. Then every student receives a personal "voter profile" with name, occupation, family background, ties to candidates, and other pertinent information. Two students, chosen by the teacher to portray the candidates, write campaign speeches and learn how to respond in character to questions from the voters. The remaining students work in groups to produce Latin campaign posters to decorate the room and hall on election day. Latin slogans are checked for historical and linguistic accuracy. Election events can last one to three hours (longer versions include Roman lunch and victory games sponsored by the winner). Students dress in Roman attire. "Cicero" conducts the opening ceremonies.

After the candidates are introduced, they give their speeches, answer questions from the voters, give rebuttals, and mill among voters for a little handshaking. Finally, after all voters file past the voting boxes and cast their tokens, Cicero congratulates the winner who is acclaimed by the "voters."

NCATE_____
STANDARDS
4.a., 4.b.

Part Two: Choose one of the following themes and develop a learning scenario for the foreign language you teach. Remember to build the scenario around an interesting context and to integrate at least two of the modes of communication and culture. Identify the standards addressed in the scenario (be sure that at least one standard in each of three goal areas is addressed). How much class time do you think it might take to complete this scenario?

Suggested themes: education, celebrations, work and leisure time, life in the city, health and medicine, the environment, fine arts, tourism

(You might want to keep this learning scenario for Teach and Reflect activities in later chapters.)

EPISODE TWO
Contextualizing the Teaching of a Past Tense Grammar Point

NCATE_____
STANDARDS
3.a., 4.c.

You are beginning a new unit/chapter that introduces a past tense in your target language. Unfortunately, your textbook is outdated, organized around grammar points with little contextual support. Vocabulary is included for leisure-time activities. Your task, as you plan, is the following:

1. Find a theme or context in which the past tense can logically be studied (e.g., school, work, shopping, diversion, travel). You might build on the theme of the given vocabulary.
2. Identify what you would like students to be able to do by the end of the chapter/unit in terms of language functions (e.g., ask for directions, tell a story, share opinions, interview a classmate). Be sure to address the integration of modes and the culture paradigm.
3. Describe a possible authentic oral text (e.g., news report, talk show segment, conversation) and a possible authentic printed text (e.g., newspaper or magazine article, short story) that you might find to present in this unit in a top-down fashion, keeping in mind your unit theme, the language level, and the interest level of your students. Your instructor may ask you to actually select these texts. How would students explore these texts?
4. What other vocabulary and grammar would you need to integrate into this unit in addition to the past tense, given the theme and your language functions?

EPISODE THREE
Applying the Standards to the Post-Secondary Level

NCATE_____
STANDARDS
4.a., 4.b.,
6.b.

If you are preparing to teach or are already teaching at the post-secondary level (beyond K–12), this task is designed to engage you in reflecting upon the implications of the standards for foreign language program development, instruction, and assessment at the college and university levels. Go to the ACTFL Web site (**http://www.actfl.org**), click on "Publications," "Download Library," and then on Dorothy James' white paper: "The Impact on Higher Education of *Standards for Foreign Language Learning: Preparing for the 21st Century.*" Read the paper and then respond to the following:

1. Explain Paul Sandrock's statement that is cited in the article: "Curriculum really bubbles up: it does not get directed from the highest level down."

2. According to James, the publication of the standards "signals the end of business as usual in departments of national languages and literature in our colleges and universities." Give several examples to explain what this statement means.

3. Explain several reasons why the standards might not be fully embraced at the higher education levels.

4. In what areas do you envision the standards having a positive impact at the post-secondary level?[11]

DISCUSS AND REFLECT

NCATE
STANDARD
4.c.

CASE STUDY ONE
Textbook Evaluation: A Look at the Use of Context in Exercises

The Sharpsburg Community School District adopts new textbooks every seven years. This year, textbooks will be ordered for the Spanish program. Two of the five Spanish teachers, Mr. Lynch and Ms. Raible, were given the task of examining new textbook series for Spanish I–II. In their initial meeting about textbook selection, the two teachers agreed that one of the most important criteria for them is that the textbook program be highly contextualized, since their current text lacks interesting content.

As they examine each first-year textbook, Mr. Lynch and Ms. Raible discover that there is a wide variety in the types of "contextualized" practice exercises presented in today's textbooks. They decide to more closely analyze the contexts of the oral grammar exercises in the text that they tentatively selected as their top choice. They examine the language function of "talking about your daily routine" found in Lesson 14. Three exercises for this function follow.

D. En casa de Ramón y Ana Mari.

Parte 1. Ana Mari describe la rutina diaria de su familia. Conjuga los verbos para formar frases completas y haz los cambios necesarios.
En mi casa:

1 mis padres/levantarse/antes que todos

2 a mí/me/gustar/acostarse temprano

3 por eso/(yo) bañarse/por la noche

4 mis hermanos/preferir/bañarse/por la mañana

5 mi mamá/pintarse/mientras que mi papá/preparar/el desayuno

6 a las ocho/todos (nosotros)/desayunar/juntos

7 luego/todos irse/al trabajo o a la escuela

English translation
D. At Ramón and Ana Mari's House

Part 1. Ana Mari describes the daily routine of her family. Conjugate the verbs in order to form complete sentences and make the necessary changes.

1. my parents/to get up/before everyone

2. to me (I)/to like to/to go to bed early

3. therefore/(I) to take a bath/at night

4. my brothers and sisters/to prefer/to take a bath/in the morning

5. my mother/to put on makeup/while my father/to prepare/breakfast

6. at 8:00/all of us/to have breakfast/together

7. then/everyone/to leave/for work or school

Parte 2. Ahora contesta las preguntas.

1 ¿Quién se levanta primero en casa de Ramón y Ana Mari? ¿Y en tu casa?

2 ¿Quién se baña por la noche? Y tú, ¿cuándo te bañas?

3 ¿Quién prepara el desayuno? ¿Y en tu casa?

English translation
Part 2. Now answer the questions.

1. Who gets up first at Ramón and Ana Mari's house? And at your house?

2. Who takes a bath at night? And you, when do you take a bath?

3. Who prepares breakfast? And at your house?

G. ¡A hablar! En grupos de cuatro, hablen de sus rutinas por la mañana y por la noche, para encontrar quién en el grupo es el/la madrugador(a) *(early bird)*, quién es el/la más elegante, quién se acuesta más temprano y quién es el/la parrandero/a *(night owl)*.

English translation
G. Let's talk! In groups of four, talk about your morning and evening routines, in order to find out who in the group is the early bird, who is the most elegant, who goes to bed earliest, and who is the night owl.

Source: Alonso-Lyrintzis, Alonso, & Zaslow, 2004, pp. 352–353.

Ask yourself these questions:

1. What comments might Mr. Lynch and Ms. Raible make as they discuss whether these exercises are "contextualized"?

2. How would you classify each of these three exercises according to Littlewood's categorization of activities presented on page 51 of this chapter? Explain your rationale.

3. How does the use of "contextualization" in each exercise address the suggestions offered by Walz (1989), as described earlier in this chapter?

4. Create another activity in which you would have students engage in the function of describing their daily routines. Be sure that the activity is interesting and integrates one of the Cultures or Connections standards.

To prepare the case:

1. Review the *Standards for Foreign Language Learning in the 21st Century* (1999) presented earlier in this chapter and reflect on the implications they have for textbook evaluation.

2. Read Aski (2003) for an in-depth review of foreign language textbook activities as they relate to SLA research and Dorwick & Glass (2003) for a publisher's view of foreign language policy vs. instructional practice and material design.

3. Find a textbook written in the 1960s, one written in the early 1980s, one written in the 1990s, and one written in the past two years. Compare the four on these points:

- integration of the 5 Cs for foreign language learning
- meaningful contexts for presentation of language
- sequencing of oral exercises
- strategies to help students interact with and use the language presented

Describe the differences and similarities you find. Trace the changes in our understanding of how people learn languages, and show how these changes are reflected in the four textbooks you examined.

To prepare for class discussion:

1. Review the three exercises that present practice of the function "describing your daily routine." How might this function be taught in a top-down fashion in your target language? Use the suggestions provided earlier in this chapter and your own ideas to develop a plan.
2. Evaluate a textbook for use in a standards-based curriculum. Select a first-year textbook program for the foreign language you teach. Evaluate the program using the criteria presented in this chapter. Would you choose this text for your standards-based language program? Provide a rationale to convince your colleagues.

CASE STUDY TWO
Developing a Top-Down ESL Lesson

NCATE
STANDARDS
3.a., 4.b.

Ms. Cravener teaches an advanced class of English as a Second Language (ESL) for the English Language Institute in a northeastern state. Learners in her class speak Portuguese and Arabic. For the most part, they earn their living from commercial fishing, working in restaurants, or helping to develop computer software.

When the class began, the students told Ms. Cravener that their biggest problem was listening to and understanding English as it was spoken to them by local native speakers and in the media. Ms. Cravener decided to use taped segments from radio and television and recorded conversations of people in the community to help her students develop the necessary skills for listening in context.

As Ms. Cravener planned the unit that presented the language function/context of "ordering a meal," she decided to use a top-down approach and begin with an authentic conversation. She obtained permission from a restaurant owner and clients to record the conversational exchanges between a waitress and two college students having dinner. A transcript of the taped segment appears below. Ms. Cravener now needs to plan how she will use the conversation as a basis for developing a lesson.

[Transcript of the taped conversation at the restaurant]

WAITRESS: Good evening, and welcome to the The Atrium Restaurant. May I bring you something to drink?

CLAUDIA: Just water please.

WAITRESS: Tap water or Perrier?

CLAUDIA: Perrier, please.

HEATHER: Um . . . Diet Coke, please.

WAITRESS: Diet Pepsi ok?

HEATHER: Sure.

WAITRESS: I'll be right back with your drinks. Here are the menus.

CLAUDIA: Gee, there's quite a variety here! Some of these entrees are sure tempting, but I have been trying to cut back on carbs. Plus I've been exercising like crazy to get into shape!

HEATHER: I know what you mean. But, look, they do have a section on the menu that features items that are high in protein and low in carbohydrates. They look pretty appetizing.

WAITRESS: Here's your Perrier and your Diet Pepsi. Also some of our fresh breads. Uh . . . let me tell you about our specials for today. Our catch of the day is golden trout, served with a butter sauce. Let's see . . . the second special is fresh lobster, served with rice. We also have a baked chicken breast with a white wine and mushroom sauce. One more . . . baked lasagna with a garden salad.

CLAUDIA: The chicken breast sounds great to me. Does that come with a garden salad?

WAITRESS: You can order the salad separately. We have a garden salad and Caesar salad.

CLAUDIA: I'll have the garden salad with light Italian dressing on the side please.

HEATHER: I'd like the lobster, but may I substitute a vegetable for the rice? And I'd also like a garden salad, but with French dressing on the side.

WAITRESS: Sure. Today's vegetable is steamed broccoli. Will that be okay?

HEATHER: Sounds great.

CLAUDIA: I'm so hungry tonight. These breads sure look great, but I've been trying to eat only wheat bread on this new diet.

HEATHER: Why don't we skip the bread and split a dessert later? Maybe we can reward ourselves for all the exercising we've been doing!

CLAUDIA: We do deserve it, don't we? As long as it's something chocolate, you have a deal!

Ask yourself these questions:

1. What types of background knowledge might students need to understand the conversation?
2. What type of pre-listening work might be done in order to prepare students for the listening task?
3. What kinds of vocabulary and common grammatical structures are found in the conversation? Which words and structures might be most important in this context?
4. What types of cultural products, practices, and perspectives would students learn from this conversation?
5. How might comprehension be checked?
6. How might students be engaged in oral and written communication as a follow-up to listening?
7. What types of printed texts might Ms. Cravener select as the unit is continued?
8. What types of synthesis activities might be used in order to integrate the three modes of communication and several goal areas? What specific standards would be addressed in these activities?

To prepare the case:

1. Read pages 177–189 in the chapter by Williams, Lively, and Harper (1998) on designing theme-based activities.
2. Read Hall (1999) for a discussion of how to address the Communication goal area in classroom instruction and assessment.
3. Read Chapter 5 in Galloway and Herron (1995) on listening.
4. Find a first-year textbook that presents lessons with an initial listening or reading segment and examine the manner in which grammar and vocabulary are taught.

To prepare for class discussion:

1. Write a brief introduction for Ms. Cravener's restaurant conversation in which you set the scene so that students will understand the context in which the conversation takes place. Which ESL standards could be addressed?

2. Select a grammar point from a textbook for beginning, intermediate, or advanced learners of the foreign language you teach. Describe how the grammar is contextualized in terms of functions, tasks, and the five goal areas of the standards. Grammar may or may not be contextualized effectively. Offer additional ideas on how you might contextualize this particular grammar point–for example, by means of an initial taped segment, other functions and/or contexts, personalized activities, and so forth.

REFERENCES

Adair-Hauck, B., & Cumo-Johanssen, P. (1997). Communication goal: Meaning making through a whole language approach. In J. K. Phillips (Ed.), *Collaborations: Meeting new goals, new realities, Northeast Conference Reports* (pp. 35–96). Lincolnwood, IL: NTC/Contemporary Publishing Group.

Alonso-Lyrintzis, D., Alonso, E., & Zaslow, B. (2004). *Invitaciones: An interactive worktext for beginning students.* Boston: Vista Higher Learning.

American Council on the Teaching of Foreign Languages. *ACTFL performance guidelines for K–12 learners.* (1998). Yonkers, NY: Author.

American Council on the Teaching of Foreign Languages. *ACTFL provisional proficiency guidelines.* (1982). Hastings-on-Hudson, NY: Author

American Council on the Teaching of Foreign Languages. *ACTFL proficiency guidelines—Speaking.* (1999). Yonkers, NY: Author

American Council on the Teaching of Foreign Languages. *ACTFL proficiency guidelines—Writing.* (2001). Yonkers, NY: Author

Anthony, E. M. (1963). Approach, method, and technique. *English Language Teaching, 17,* 63–67.

Asher, J., Kusudo, J., & de la Torre, R. (1974). Learning a second language through commands: The second field test. *The Modern Language Journal, 58,* 24–32.

Aski, J. M. (2003). Foreign language textbook activities: Keeping pace with second language acquisition research. *Foreign Language Annals, 36,* 57–65.

Ausubel, D. (1968). *Educational psychology: A cognitive view.* New York: Holt, Rinehart and Winston.

Bragger, J. D., & Rice, D. B. (2000). Foreign language materials: Yesterday, today, and tomorrow. In R. M. Terry (Ed.), *Agents of change in a changing age* (pp. 107–140). Lincolnwood, IL: National Textbook Company.

Canale, M., & Swain, M. (1980). Theoretical bases of communicative approaches to second language teaching and testing. *Applied Linguistics, 1,* 1–47.

Chastain, K. C. (1988). *Developing second-language skills: Theory and practice.* San Diego: Harcourt Brace Jovanovich.

Chomsky, N. (1965). *Aspects of the theory of syntax.* Cambridge, MA: MIT Press.

Curran, C. (1976). *Counseling-learning in second languages.* Apple River, IL: Apple River Press.

Dorwick, T., & Glass, W. R. (2003). Language education policies: One publisher's perspective. *The Modern Language Journal, 87,* 592–594.

Frantzen, D. (1998). Focusing on form while conveying a cultural message. *Hispania, 81,* 134–145.

Galloway, V. (1998). Constructing cultural realities: "Facts" and frameworks of association. In J. Harper, M. Lively, & M. Williams (Eds.), *The coming of age of the profession* (pp. 129–140). Boston: Heinle & Heinle.

Galloway, V., & Herron, C. (Eds.). (1995). *Research within reach II.* Southern Conference on Language Teaching. Valdosta, GA: Valdosta State University.

Gattegno, C. (1976). *The common sense of foreign language teaching.* New York: Educational Solutions.

Glisan, E. W. (1986). Total physical response: A technique for teaching all skills in Spanish. *Foreign Language Annals, 19,* 419–427.

Glisan, E. W. (1999). The impact of *Standards* on higher education: For more than just the sake of "continuity." *ADFL Bulletin, 31,* 75–78.

Glisan, E. W., & Phillips, J. K. (1998). Making the standards happen: A new vision for foreign language teacher preparation. *ACTFL Newsletter, X*(4), 7–8, 13–14.

Goals 2000: World-class education for every child. (1994). Washington, DC: U.S. Government Printing Office.

Hadley, A. O. (2001). *Teaching language in context.* Boston: Heinle & Heinle.

Hall, J. K. (1999). The communication standards. In J. K. Phillips & R. M. Terry (Eds.), *Foreign language standards: Linking research, theories, and practices* (pp. 15–56). Lincolnwood, IL: National Textbook Company.

Higgs, T. V. (Ed.). (1984). *Teaching for proficiency; the organizing principle.* The ACTFL Foreign Language Education Series. Lincolnwood, IL: NTC/Contemporary Publishing Group.

James, D. (1998, Fall). The impact on higher education of standards for foreign language learning: Preparing for the 21st century. *ACTFL Newsletter,* pp. 11–14.

Lado, R. (1964). *Language teaching.* New York: McGraw-Hill.

Lally, C. (1998). Back to the future: A look at present textbooks and past recommendations. *Foreign Language Annals, 31,* 307–314.

Liskin-Gasparro, J. E. (1984). The ACTFL Proficiency Guidelines: A historical perspective. In T. V. Higgs (Ed.), *Teaching for proficiency: The organizing principle*. The ACTFL Foreign Language Education Series (pp. 11–42). Lincolnwood, IL: NTC/Contemporary Publishing Group.

Littlewood, W. T. (1980). Form and meaning in language teaching methodology. *The Modern Language Journal, 64*, 441–445.

Lozanov, G. (1978). *Suggestology and outlines of suggestopedy*. New York: Gordon and Breach.

Met, M. (2000). Instruction: Linking curriculum and assessment to the standards. In G. Guntermann (Ed.), *Teaching Spanish with the five C's: A blueprint for success* (pp. 49–69). Fort Worth, TX: Harcourt College.

National Standards in Foreign Language Education Project. (1996). *National standards for foreign language learning: Preparing for the 21st century*. Lawrence, KS: Allen Press.

National Standards in Foreign Language Education Project. (1999). *Standards for foreign language learning in the 21st century*. Lawrence, KS: Allen Press.

Paulston, C. B. (1972). Structural pattern drills: A classification. In H. Allen & R. Campell (Eds.), *Teaching English as a second language* (pp. 129–138). New York: McGraw-Hill.

Paulston, C. B., & Bruder, M. N. (1976). *Teaching English as a second language: Techniques and procedures*. Cambridge, MA: Winthrop.

Phillips, J. (Ed.). (1997). *Collaborations: Meeting new goals, new realities*. Lincolnwood, IL: National Textbook Company.

Phillips, J. K., & Lafayette, R. C. (1996). Reactions to the catalyst: Implications for our professional structure. In R. C. Lafayette (Ed.), *National standards: A catalyst for reform* (pp. 197–209). Foreign Language Education Series. Lincolnwood, IL: National Textbook Company.

Rassias, J. A. (1983). New dimensions in language training: The Dartmouth College experiment. In J. W. Oller, Jr. & P. A. Richard-Amato (Eds.), *Methods that work: A smorgasbord of ideas for language teachers* (pp. 363–374). Rowley, MA: Newbury House.

Ray, M., & Lutz, K. B. (1969). *A-LM French: Level One*. New York: Harcourt, Brace & World.

Rivers, W. (1983). *Communicating naturally in a second language*. Chicago, IL: University of Chicago Press.

Rogoff, B. (1990). *Apprenticeship in thinking*. New York: Oxford University Press.

Sandrock, P. (2000). Creating a standards-based curriculum. In G. Guntermann (Ed.), *Teaching Spanish with the Five C's: A blueprint for success (volume 2)*. Orlando, FL: Harcourt, AATSP.

Savignon, S. J. (1997). *Communicative competence: Theory and practice*. New York: McGraw-Hill.

Shrum, J. L., & Glisan, E. W. (1994). *Teacher's handbook: Contextualized language instruction*. Boston: Heinle & Heinle.

Strength through wisdom: A critique of U.S. capability. (1979). A report to the President from the President's Commission on Foreign Languages and International Studies. Washington, DC: U.S. Government Printing Office.

Swender, E. (1999). *ACTFL oral proficiency interview tester training manual*. Yonkers, NY: American Council on the Teaching of Foreign Languages.

Takenoya, M. (1995). Acquisition or pragmatic rules: The gap between what the language textbooks present and how learners perform. In M. A. Haggstrom, L. Z. Morgan, & J. A. Wieczorek (Eds.), *The foreign language classroom: Bridging theory and practice* (pp. 149–164). New York: Garland.

Terrell, T. (1982). The natural approach to language teaching: An update. *The Modern Language Journal, 66*, 121–132.

Teachers of English to Speakers of Other Languages. (1997). *ESL standards for pre-K-12 students*. Alexandria, VA: Author.

Walz, J. (1989). Context and contextualized language practice in foreign language teaching. *The Modern Language Journal, 73*, 160–168.

Williams, M. K., Lively, M. G., & Harper, J. (1998). Designing theme-based activities: Bringing ideas to speech. In J. Harper, M. Lively, & M. Williams (Eds.), *The coming of age of the profession* (pp. 177–189). Boston: Heinle & Heinle.

Wong, W., & VanPatten, B. (2003). The evidence is IN: Drills are OUT. *Foreign Language Annals, 36*, 403–423.

NOTES

1. For additional ideas for using TPR as a strategy in teaching all skills, see Glisan (1986).

2. The ACTFL Proficiency Scale will be described in detail in Chapter 8, and the oral proficiency interview procedure will be presented in Chapter 11.

3. The acronym *ESL* is used to refer to the field of English as a second language and the standards themselves. Those students who are learning English are called English language learners (ELL). The *ESL Standards* (TESOL, 1997) also use the term *English-to-Speakers-of Other-Languages (ESOL) students*. The term *LEP* (Limited English Proficient) is used in most federal legislation.

4. *Authentic materials* are "those written and oral communications produced *by* members of a language and culture group *for* members of the same language and culture group" (Galloway, 1998, p. 133). See Chapter 3 for a more detailed discussion.

5. Examples of drill types (Paulston & Bruder, 1976, pp. 8, 18, 42):

1. Mechanical single slot substitution drill: Negative modal

   Repeat: T: I might not go to class today.

   Substitute: go shopping   S: I might not go shopping today.

                 do the laundry   S: I might not do the laundry today.

                 finish the lesson, etc.

2. Meaningful:
   T: Which boy is in your class?   S: The thin boy with long sideburns.
                                           S: The handsome boy with black hair.

3. Communicative:
   T: Describe the weather in your country.   S: It's beautiful.
                                               S: It's wonderful.

6. These ideas were adapted from the four options for implementing the K–12 Standards for Foreign Language Learning, developed by Tom Welch, Jessamine County Public Schools, Kentucky.

7. Thanks to an anonymous reviewer for this explanation of top-down learning.

8. For an in-depth description of a standards-based daily lesson based on travel plans featuring these student activities, see Glisan & Phillips (1998).

9. See Bragger and Rice (2000), pp. 127–128, for a description of what the classroom and materials of the future might look like.

10. See Chapter 11 for an explanation of performance-based assessment and rubrics.

11. You might also read Glisan (1999) for other ideas concerning ways in which *SFLL* can impact post-secondary language instruction.

Organizing Content and Planning for Integrated Language Instruction

In this chapter, you will learn about:

- a new paradigm for instructional planning
- L2 input and teacher talk
- classroom discourse: IRE vs. IRF
- Oller's Episode Hypothesis
- unauthentic vs. authentic oral texts

- content-based instruction (CBI)
- state frameworks
- thematic unit planning
- lesson objectives
- Bloom's Taxonomy of Thinking
- advance organizers

Teach and Reflect: Planning for Instruction: Writing Daily Lesson Objectives, Creating a Daily Lesson Plan, and Designing a Unit of Instruction; Developing a Content-Based Level 5 Foreign Language Class; Comparing State Framework and Curriculum Documents

Discuss and Reflect: The Effect of Class Scheduling on Planning for Instruction; Analyzing the Use of Content and Context in a Japanese Lesson

CONCEPTUAL ORIENTATION

The initial purpose of Goals 2000 (1994) was to provide a broad-based structure of goals that would prompt states and local school districts to rethink and redesign curriculum in ways pertinent to their local situations. State frameworks focus on national standards and specify benchmark tasks, and local school districts design a curriculum specific to their needs (Bartz & Singer, 1996). The national standards document depicts the relationship between the national, state, and local systems as shown in Figure 3.1. The set of documents at each level informs the others: "standards" at the national level provide the basis for "frameworks" at the state level, for "district curricula" at the school district level, and for "lesson/unit plans" at the classroom level. More states are using the *SFLL* as the basis for the creation of state frameworks or standards, and school districts are using state frameworks to specify curricular goals and objectives.

Beginning teachers usually receive a written foreign language curriculum guide that outlines the content students are expected to learn by the end of the year while remaining consistent with the general purposes described for the entire school system and for the statewide framework. Curriculum guides are generally optional, although some states monitor their implementation more than others. Historically, curriculum guides have been nothing more than a list of the textbook's table of contents, consisting of a series of grammar

FIGURE 3.1 The Relationships Among National, State, and Local Standards Documents

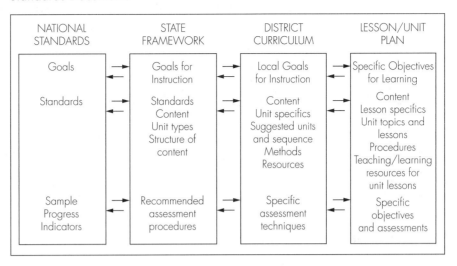

NATIONAL STANDARDS	STATE FRAMEWORK	DISTRICT CURRICULUM	LESSON/UNIT PLAN
Goals	Goals for Instruction	Local Goals for Instruction	Specific Objectives for Learning
Standards	Standards Content Unit types Structure of content	Content Unit specifics Suggested units and sequence Methods Resources	Content Lesson specifics Unit topics and lessons Procedures Teaching/learning resources for unit lessons
Sample Progress Indicators	Recommended assessment procedures	Specific assessment techniques	Specific objectives and assessments

Source: NSFLEP, 1999, p. 28.

points and sometimes including vocabulary themes such as weather expressions, numbers, kinship terms, and so on. However, more recently, curriculum design has been changing to reflect the content standards students should achieve at each level of instruction. Teachers regularly use curriculum guides as they organize the content of the year-long course into unit and daily lesson plans.

In this chapter, we will use the following terms as they relate to organizing content and planning for instruction:

- *Goal:* an aim or purpose of instruction, often stated in broad terms, as in the five goal areas of the *SFLL*; for example, "to gain knowledge of another culture";
- *Objective:* what the learner will be able to do with the language as a result of instruction, defined in terms of observable behavior; for example, "The learner will be able to invite a friend to go to a social event"; sometimes the term *outcome* is used to refer to an objective;
- *Framework:* state document that describes goals and standards to be met by language programs.

New Paradigm for Instructional Planning

A recent paradigm shift in curricular and daily lesson planning results from an increasing focus on standards-based goals and integrated language instruction. Figure 3.2 illustrates the old and new paradigms in instructional planning. Objectives are designed to reflect the content standards—that is, what students should know and be able to do with the language rather than the table of contents in the textbook. Interdisciplinary content and culture are no longer ancillary but rather the core of standards-driven curricula. The three modes of communication are integrated into lesson design by means of tasks that build on one another. The learner is given more responsibility for learning and is encouraged

FIGURE 3.2 Paradigm Shift in Instructional Planning

	OLD PARADIGM	**NEW PARADIGM**
Objectives	Stated in terms of grammatical knowledge as provided in textbook	Stated in terms of what learners should know and be able to do with the language
Content/Culture	Content limited to bits and pieces of cultural information included in textbook; connections to other disciplines absent	Interdisciplinary and cultural connections; integration of cultural and academic content; culture explored by means of products, practices, and perspectives
Skills	Practice of individual skills: listening, speaking, reading, writing	Integrated practice of three modes of communication, which build on one another
The Learner	Mostly passive and learns the material presented by the teacher	Actively engaged in learning and has opportunities to explore personal interests
The Teacher	The center of instruction and the audience for learners; students work to impress the teacher	Facilitates instruction and guides student learning; designs opportunities for cooperative learning; audience includes peers and community
Materials	Textbook as primary material	Textbook as one of many tools; others include authentic materials (tape recordings, videos, magazines, short stories, folklore), World Wide Web, visuals, realia
Assessment	To evaluate student achievement; focus on discrete-point grammar items, often out of context; primarily paper-and-pencil testing; learners provide one right answer	To assess progress in meeting standards and to improve instruction; assessment strategies include integration of modes for meaningful purposes, exploration of content, completion of real-world tasks, self-assessment by learners

Source: Adapted from Bragger & Rice, 1998.

to use the foreign language to acquire new knowledge about topics of personal interest. The teacher assumes the role of a facilitator who guides instruction without being the sole source or expert transmitter of knowledge. This approach helps to dispel what Lee and VanPatten (2003) refer to as the "Atlas Complex," through which the teacher provides all information and students receive it.

Planning in the new paradigm assumes (1) the use of a wide variety of materials and tools that extend beyond the capabilities of a textbook, and (2) ongoing assessment of student progress toward addressing the standards through strategies such as completion of real-world tasks, exploration of content, and self-assessment.

The new paradigm for planning assumes the use of a variety of materials beyond the textbook and ongoing performance assessments of student progress toward meeting the standards. ■

Considerations in Providing Input and Selecting Content

Devising a lesson plan involves more than just completing a form. Planning for language instruction in the new paradigm requires maximum use of the target language, meaningful teacher feedback, integration of oral and printed authentic texts, and use of content-based learning. Attention to these elements enables the foreign language teacher to develop interesting topics and contexts in which to communicate, which leads to engagement of students and increased interest in language learning. Teachers make decisions as they plan that will influence student learning. This section of the chapter provides a discussion of the elements identified above in order to help you answer some questions you will probably ask yourself as you approach unit and lesson planning:

- What characteristics should my teacher talk or L2 input have?
- How should I respond to students' utterances?
- What types of oral and printed texts will lend interesting content to my lessons?
- How can I help my students connect the foreign language they are learning in my class with what they are learning in their study of other subject areas?

L2 Input and Teacher Talk

In Chapter 1, you learned about the key role of comprehensible input in the acquisition process (Krashen, 1982). If students are to acquire a foreign language, they must have maximum opportunities to hear the target language at a level a little beyond their current range of competence, but understandable through strategies such as their use of background knowledge, context, and other extralinguistic cues. In order for language teachers to provide a classroom environment that is rich in target language input, their own level of proficiency must be high enough to allow them to speak in an unscripted, spontaneous manner and to tailor their speech so that it is comprehensible to students.

However, recent studies have shown that teacher talk must have other characteristics in addition to being in the target language. As part of her research on classroom interaction, Hall (1995) studied the discourse of a high school Spanish classroom (see Case Study 1 in Chapter 1). The term *discourse* refers to a back-and-forth communication of thought by means of a connected series of utterances shared through social interaction and collaboration. According to Wells (1999), "Discourse builds on understanding which has come to be over time and various situations with both the students and the teachers acting as speakers and listeners throughout communication" (p. 68, cf. Mantero, 2002, p. 440). In examining classroom discourse, Hall (1995) found that although the teacher's talk contained features of comprehensible input, such as simple syntax and multiple re-phrasings, it lacked topic development and provided no foundation upon which students could add to and extend the talk in a meaningful way. According to Hall (1995), classroom discourse was limited to "lexical chaining," the "linking of utterances through the use of the same or similar words that had no connection to any larger topically related goal" (p. 34).

Similarly, in his study of a university Spanish classroom, Toth (1997) found that teacher talk negatively affected learners' ability to participate in the conversation activity because it did not contribute to a larger topic or goal-directed agenda. Toth (2004) suggests that during discussions that focus on the teacher's grammatical agenda, students need more time to respond because they have to focus simultaneously on what they want to say while satisfying the grammatical goals of the teacher. In these types of exchanges, students report being confused and frustrated in their attempts to understand the teacher's motivation for the questions asked. On the other hand, when exchanges are organized in terms of meaningful, natural conversations, students are able to process the content of an utterance without having to figure out the grammar-focused agenda of each question.

These studies illustrate that in order to facilitate students' communicative development, teacher talk must not only be in the target language, but it must also contribute to the development of a topic and a larger, activity-based communicative goal (Hall, 1999). In addition, for collaborative talk to occur, participants need to share conversational goals, recognize these goals as being legitimate, and understand how each participant's actions move the interaction forward (Donato, 2004).

Classroom Discourse: Teacher Feedback vs. Evaluation

Another aspect of teacher talk is the nature of the teacher's responses to learners' utterances. Planning meaningful and helpful responses is important in addressing the communicative goals of a standards-based curriculum. In Chapter 1, you explored the importance of developing learners' interactional competence so that they are able to manage discussions in relevant ways. As Hall (1999, 1995) points out, the rhetorical structure of most classroom talk is "IRE":

- The teacher *initiates* an assertion or asks a question.
- The student *responds*.
- The teacher *evaluates*, by giving an evaluative statement such as "very good" or by asking the same or similar question of another student (Mehan, 1979).

The purpose of this type of questioning is for the teacher to find out whether the student has learned specific material (a grammatical structure or set of vocabulary). For example, in order to find out whether students can tell time in the foreign language, the teacher might use a cardboard clock with movable hands, ask students to tell what time is displayed on it, and then provide feedback to indicate whether the response was correct or not (e.g., "That's it," or "No, that's not right). In this type of oral exchange, the teacher often asks *assessing* questions (i.e., questions that usually have one right answer or a predictable set of responses) and offers an evaluative response such as "very good," "right," "excellent" (Tharp & Gallimore, 1991). While IRE may be useful for the teacher in assessing achievement of material taught in a particular unit or lesson, it leads to mechanical, topically disjointed talk and limited student involvement (Hall, 1999). Moreover, it does not lead to use of the target language for interpersonal communication as defined in Standard 1.1.

 Reread the scripted classroom discourse sample that appears in Case Study 1 in Chapter 1. What are some examples of IRE in this script? ■

 IRE = teacher initiation ⇒ student response ⇒ teacher evaluation (assessing questions) ■

As discussed earlier in this chapter, teacher talk must be more than "comprehensible" target language input, and from the perspective of "talk-as-discursive-practice," should be expanded to include the aspects of topic development and management (Hall, 1995). If learners are to acquire the skills necessary to be able to participate in conversations outside the classroom, then they must participate in more than just the typical IRE sequences that occur in most classrooms. Wells (1993) contrasts "IRE" with "IRF," which he defines as the type of classroom communication that focuses on making meaning and extending discourse, not on evaluating responses:

- The teacher *initiates* an assertion or asks a question.
- The student *responds*.
- The teacher provides *feedback* in order to encourage students to think and to perform at higher levels (e.g., "Tell me more! Are you saying that . . . ?").

In this discourse model, teachers use *assisting* questions, which encourage learners to think, push learners to perform at higher levels, and integrate content and topics (Tharp & Gallimore, 1991). Examples of assisting questions are: "What do you mean by that?" and "That's incredible! Could you explain that a little more?"

Furthermore, students need experience in using turn taking, which Hall (1996) notes is a primary communicative resource in speech-based instructional practices and a crucial part of the development of sociality. In classrooms dominated by IRE, learners do not have real opportunities to engage in turn taking, as the teacher controls who will speak and when. The implications of Hall's research is that, when planning for instruction, the teacher should simulate real conversations in the classroom and thereby help learners develop interactional strategies, such as turn taking. This means that students would benefit from opportunities during which they assume the responsibility for taking a conversational turn rather than raise a hand and wait to be called upon by the teacher.

    IRF = teacher initiation ⇒ student response ⇒ teacher feedback (assisting questions)

How might teachers plan to incorporate more IRF and interpersonal communication into their teaching?

- They can plan curriculum around interesting topics and contexts in which to anchor interpersonal communication.
- They can incorporate tasks that provide opportunities for engaging students in meaningful interaction and for asking assisting questions to move discussions forward.
- They can change the way in which the traditional warm-up is done at the beginning of class. Instead of asking each student a question that has little communicative value (e.g., "What's the weather like today?" or "What time is it?"), they can introduce an interesting and/or personalized topic (e.g., an upcoming dance or championship game) and engage only a few students in discussion so that they are able to take multiple turns. If time does not permit participation by the whole class, those who don't speak on a particular day will benefit from observing a meaningful conversation and will have opportunities to participate on another day.
- They can plan opportunities for students to acquire new information and/or engage in activities in which there is an information gap with the teacher and/or peers on a topic important to them.
- They can seek students' input regarding the types of topics that they would be interested in discussing in an open discussion format where divergent answers, opinions, and IRF have a role and students are instructed in how to make feedback moves during an interpersonal exchange.

See Chapter 8 for additional ideas about developing oral interpersonal communication.

 How might teachers plan to incorporate more IRF and interpersonal communication into their teaching?

Now examine the following script of classroom discourse. What examples of IRF are there? How does this script differ from the one you analyzed in Chapter 1?

Note: This is a transcript and an English translation of a discussion that takes place in a French I high school class. The prelude for this discussion is a question posed by the teacher: "What plans do you have for Thanksgiving vacation?" A student responds that he is going hunting. The teacher, who is a native of France and unfamiliar with the concept of hunting, asks him for additional information.

> T: Tu vas chasser... pour... une personne?
>
> Ss: *[Rires...]*
>
> S1: Non... quelque... chose!
>
> T: Tu veux dire un animal?
>
> S1: Oui!
>
> T: Hum... chasser *[she writes the verb* chasser *on the board]*
>
> S1: Chasser. Euh... je... vais... euh... chasser... euh... dinde.
>
> T: Ah! Tu vas chasser la dinde?
>
> S1: Oui.
>
> S2: *[In English]* Shoot a turkey . . . that's not nice.
>
> Ss: *[Rires...]*
>
> T: Non, mais c'est bon la dinde! Et puis, c'est un sport la chasse, n'est-ce pas?
>
> S1: Oui, un sport.
>
> T: *[Looking at the class]* Vous ne chassez pas?
>
> Ss: NON!!!
>
> T: Oh! Vous êtes protecteurs des animaux?
>
> Ss: Non! *[Rires...]*
>
> T: Vous mangez les animaux, non? Oui, on mange les animaux! En plus, c'est stupide une dinde, non?
>
> S1: Hum... la dinde domestique... euh... *domesticated turkeys*... c'est stupide!
>
> T: Ah? Mais la dinde sauvage est intelligente?
>
> S1: ... oui... très intelligente. *[Rires...]*

[English translation]

> T: You're going hunting . . . for . . . a person?
>
> Ss: *[Laughter . . .]*
>
> S1: No . . . some . . . thing!
>
> T: You mean an animal!
>
> S1: Yes!
>
> T: Hum . . . to hunt *[she writes the verb* chasser *on the board]*
>
> S1: To hunt. Eh . . . I'm . . . going . . . uh . . . to hunt . . . uh . . . turkey.

T:	Ah! You're going to hunt turkey?
S1:	Yes.
S2:	*[In English]* Shoot a turkey . . . that's not nice.
Ss:	*[Laughter . . .]*
T:	No, but turkeys are nice! So . . . hunting is a sport, right?
S1:	Yes, a sport.
T:	*[Looking at the class]* The rest of you don't hunt?
Ss:	NO!!!
T:	Oh! You are animal protectors?
Ss:	No! *[Laughter . . .]*
T:	You eat animals, right? Yes, we eat animals! Besides, turkeys are dumb, aren't they?
S1:	Hum . . . domesticated turkeys . . . uh . . . *domesticated turkeys* . . . are dumb!
T:	Oh? But wild turkeys are intelligent?
S1:	Yes, very intelligent. *[Laughter . . .]*

Source: R. Donato, personal communication, June 3, 1998.

Integration of Authentic Oral and Printed Texts[1]

As you have seen, the teacher's use of meaningful target language input and IRF can only occur in the presence of communicative contexts and interesting topics. In Chapter 2, you learned that a top-down approach uses an initial oral or printed text that provides the context, theme, or topic featured in the unit. Of critical importance is selecting texts that reflect natural language use and bring content and interest to learning tasks. As early as 1983, Oller maintained that certain kinds of texts are more easily internalized than others. According to Oller's Episode Hypothesis, "Text (i.e., discourse in any form) will be easier to reproduce, understand, and recall, to the extent that it is motivated and structured episodically" (Oller, 1983, p. 12). Episodic organization has two aspects: "motivation," or affect, and logical structure. According to Oller, a text that has "motivation" has an apparent purpose, holds the attention and interest of the listener or reader, introduces a conflict of some sort, and is not dull and boring. A text that is logically organized has the characteristics of a good story and connects meaningfully to our experience in the world (Oller, 1983).

Carrell also found that text organization is an important factor in comprehension. Her research revealed that readers comprehend most effectively texts that feature the typical "problem-solution" type of organization (1984). In discussing the implications of the Episode Hypothesis for language teaching, Oller states that "perhaps second language teaching would be more successful if it incorporated principles of good storywriting along with the benefits of sound linguistic analysis" (1984, p. 12). Unfortunately, language textbooks often still contain boring texts and dialogues that do not reflect real-world language or situations, although they usually contain multiple examples of the grammar being presented.

 "Text (i.e., discourse in any form) will be easier to reproduce, understand, and recall, to the extent that it is motivated and structured episodically."

In addition to episodic organization, another key characteristic of texts in bringing meaningful content to the classroom is the degree to which they are *authentic*. Remember from Chapter 2 that Galloway defined *authentic texts* as "those written and oral communications produced *by* members of a language and culture group *for* members of the same language and culture group" (Galloway, 1998, p. 133). According to Villegas Rogers and Medley, authentic materials reflect a "naturalness of form and an appropriateness of cultural and situational context" found in the language as used by native speakers (1988, p. 468). Authentic texts include realia, magazine and newspaper articles, literary excerpts, poems, audio recordings, videotapes, satellite broadcasts, radio programs, and so forth. Through exploring these materials, students have the opportunity to see and hear real language that serves a purpose. Another convincing reason to use authentic samples is for their richness in cultural content. Because these texts are prepared for native speakers, they reflect the details of everyday life in a culture as well as its societal values. Galloway (1998) suggests that "authentic texts, as total communicative events, invite observation of a culture talking to itself, not to outsiders; in its own context; through its own language; where forms are referenced to its own people, who mean through their own framework of associations; and whose voices show dynamic interplay of individuals and groupings of individuals within the loose general consensus that is the culture's reality" (p. 133).

 Authentic texts = "those written and oral communications produced *by* members of a language and culture group *for* members of the same language and culture group" ◼

The types of texts used for listening and viewing can be classified along a continuum as *unauthentic scripted, semiscripted,* and *authentic. Unauthentic scripted* texts are prepared, scripted out, and recorded by speakers of the TL onto an audio tape, CD, or video. Since these texts are not prepared by and for speakers of the target culture, but rather to accompany textbook chapters, they are considered unauthentic. They typically contain multiple examples of grammatical structures and vocabulary presented in the chapter, their context is often artificial, and since they are read aloud, they usually sound stilted and unnatural (i.e., pronunciation is deliberate and exaggerated, there are few or no natural pauses and/or repetition, and the rate of speech is abnormally slow). At the other end of the continuum are *authentic* segments, which are prepared by and for native speakers of the target culture, and NOT for language learning purposes. They may also be scripted (e.g., radio/television commercials, news/weather broadcasts, public service announcements) or unscripted (e.g., face-to-face or telephone conversations that are tape recorded, interviews, talk show segments) (Galloway, 1998; Villegas Rogers & Medley, 1988). In between unauthentic scripted and authentic texts are *semiscripted* segments, which are recorded by native speakers who speak spontaneously within a situation that they are given (similar to a role-play activity). Although semiscripted segments are not authentic, they have many features of authentic language, such as natural pauses, repetition, normal rate of speech and pronunciation, and negotiation of meaning (Geddes & White, 1978). Some newer textbook programs include semiscripted segments, which offer better examples of natural language use and contexts than do their unauthentic scripted counterparts.

 Visit the *Teacher's Handbook* Web site to listen to the following example of a dialogue from a beginning-level Spanish textbook program (Terrell, Andrade, Egasse, & Muñoz, 2002, p. 2). Is it episodically organized? That is, does it reflect logical organization and motivation, according to Oller's definition? Does it captivate the interest of the reader? Does it have a real-world context? Is there an exchange of information that isn't already obvious to the speakers? Is it unauthentic scripted, semiscripted, or authentic?

thandbook.heinle.com

Oral Text Sample A:

Nora y Esteban hablan de la ropa que llevan los estudiantes y la profesora.

Nora: Esteban, la blusa rosada de Lan es bonita, ¿no?

Esteban: Sí, es muy bonita, pero... ¿es rosada o roja?

Nora: ¡Es rosada, Esteban!

Esteban: ¿De qué color son los pantalones de Alberto?

Nora: Son grises. Y su camisa es anaranjada.

Esteban: *[Disgusted]* El color gris con el color anaranjado... ¡yuck!

Nora: ¿Es morada la chaqueta de Luis?

Esteban: *[Unsure]* Eh... hummm... es azul... ¿no?

Nora: Sí, Esteban. La chaqueta de Luis es azul.

Esteban: Pero el abrigo de la profesora Martínez es morado, *right?*

Nora: ¡Correcto! ¡Y es muy elegante!

Esteban: *[Unconvinced]* ¿Elegante? Bueno, sí, un poquito...

[English translation]

Nora and Esteban talk about the clothing that the students and professor are wearing.

Nora: Esteban, Lan's pink blouse is pretty, isn't it?

Esteban: Yes, it's very pretty, but . . . is it pink or red?

Nora: It's red, Esteban!

Esteban: What color are Alberto's pants?

Nora: They are gray. And his shirt is orange.

Esteban *[Disgusted]* The color grey with the color orange . . . yuck!

Nora: Is Luis's jacket purple?

Esteban: *[Unsure]* Uh . . . hmmm . . . it's blue . . . right?

Nora: Yes, Esteban. Luis's jacket is blue.

Esteban: But Professor Martínez's coat is purple, right?

Nora: Right! And it's very elegant!

Esteban: *[Unconvinced]* Elegant? Well, yes, a little . . .

---

thandbook.heinle.com

Visit the *Teacher's Handbook* Web site and listen to the following conversation (Glisan & Shrum, 1996, p. 1), then compare it to the dialogue that you heard previously. How does this conversation reflect the typical organization of a conversation that is not intended to teach grammar and vocabulary? Is the conversation "motivated"? Does it leave the listener wondering about anything at the end of the conversation? How would you classify this segment along the authenticity continuum?

Oral Text Sample B:

Ud. va a escuchar una conversación breve entre Memo y Maite, dos estudiantes que acaban de conocerse. Ellos están en la residencia estudiantil.

Memo: ¡Hola! ¿Qué tal? Mira, no conozco a mucha gente, pero si me permites me presento. Me llamo Guillermo, pero mis padres me dicen Memo. Tú, ¿cómo te llamas?

Maite: Hola, Memo. Yo me llamo Maite y aunque nací en los EE.UU., mis padres son de España.

Memo: ¡Ah sí!

Maite: Mmmm.

Memo: ¿De qué parte de España?

Maite:	Bueno, mi padre es del País Vasco, y mi madre es de Galicia.
Memo:	Ah, de Galicia ... y dime, ¿llevan mucho tiempo aquí?
Maite:	Mmmm ... aproximadamente unos treinta años, o algo así. Pero yo estoy muy contenta de haber nacido aquí.
Memo:	Mmm. Ya...
Maite:	Dime una cosa, ¿dónde vives tú? ¿Eres nuevo aquí en la universidad?
Memo:	Sí, éste es mi primer año. Estoy recién llegado de Chile y mi casa, bueno ... vivo en un ... vivo en un apartamento aquí como a dos cuadras en la calle Tremont. Creo que es el 791. Apenas llegué ayer, así que no me sé la dirección muy bien.
Maite:	Mmm, ¡qué coincidencia! Yo también vivo muy cerca de donde vives tú. Yo vivo en el 721 de la Tremont, ¡mmmm!
Memo:	Ah, ¡qué bien! Y dime ... ¿qué vas a ... qué vas a estudiar tú aquí?
Maite:	Bueno, me interesa mucho el periodismo.
Memo:	¡Ajá!
Maite:	Bueno. Mucho, mucho, pero pues, no sé, todavía no estoy muy segura. Y tú, ¿qué es lo que quieres estudiar?
Memo:	Bueno, yo soy músico y quiero especializarme en música. Dime, ¿tú estás casada?
Maite:	No, soy soltera. ¿Y tú?
Memo:	También soltero, soltero, y estoy tratando de conocer gente porque...
Maite:	Mira, me tengo que ir porque me quedé en ver con una persona en biblioteca, ¿OK?
Memo:	OK, entonces, nos vemos luego.
Maite:	Mmmm ... Hasta pronto.
Memo:	Chao.
Maite:	Chao.

(Source: Glisan and Shrum, 1996)

[English translation]

Memo:	Hi! How are you? Listen, I don't know a lot of people, but if you'll let me, I'll introduce myself. I'm Guillermo, but my parents call me Memo. And you, what's your name?
Maite:	Hi, Memo. I'm Maite and, although I was born in the U.S., my parents are from Spain.
Memo:	Oh yes!
Maite:	Mmmm.
Memo:	From what part of Spain?
Maite:	Well, my father is from the Basque Country, and my mother is from Galicia.
Memo:	Oh, from Galicia . . . and tell me, have they been here a long time?
Maite:	Mmmm . . . approximately thirty years, or something like that. But I'm very happy to have been born here.
Memo:	Mmm. So . . .
Maite:	Tell me something, where do you live? Are you new at the university?

Memo:	Yes, this is my first year. I have recently arrived from Chile and my house, well . . . I live in . . . I live in an apartment about two blocks from here on Tremont Street. I think it's number 791. I just got here yesterday, so I don't know the address very well.
Maite:	Mmm, what a coincidence! I also live very close to where you live. I live at number 721 on Tremont, mmm!
Memo:	Oh, great! And tell me . . . what are you going to . . . what are you going to study here?
Maite:	Well, I'm interested a lot in journalism.
Memo:	Oh!
Maite:	Well, a lot, a lot, but well, I don't know; I'm still not very sure. And you, what do you want to study?
Memo:	Well, I'm a musician and I want to major in music. Tell me, are you married?
Maite:	No, I'm single. And you?
Memo:	I'm also single, single, and I'm trying to meet people because . . .
Maite:	Listen, I have to go because I have to see someone in the library, OK?
Memo:	OK, then, see you later.
Maite:	Mmmm . . . See you soon.
Memo:	Bye.
Maite:	Bye.

thandbook.heinle.com

See the *Teacher's Handbook* Web site for other sample tape-recorded segments in English, French, German, and Spanish.

In recent years, particularly with the publication of *SFLL* (NSFLEP, 1999) and the availability of technology, there has been an increasing impetus for using authentic materials in language instruction. One of the challenges teachers often describe when using authentic texts is that these materials contain linguistic structures and vocabulary that students may not have already learned. Although a text may have varying levels of sophistication or complexity, its difficulty is determined by what learners are asked to do with it. Thus, the difficulty level lies within the tasks that learners are asked to complete based on that material, and not within the text itself (Terry, 1998). The suggestion "Edit the task, not the text" has become a well-known instructional guideline for teachers as they design activities around an authentic text. Because of the richness of these materials, the teacher might use a particular text for the first time and ask students simply to identify certain pieces of information; he or she might present the same text at a later time and ask students to explore it in more depth. As Pusack and Otto (1996) point out, without early exposure to authentic texts, learners are ill-prepared to interpret them when they are suddenly presented at a later stage in language study. In Chapters 5 and 6, you will learn more about how to integrate authentic materials as a strategy for addressing the Cultures and Communication goal areas and how to guide students through authentic texts.

Making Connections: Integrating Language and Content Learning[2]

You have seen that the absence of meaningful contexts and topics in the classroom often results in the use of IRE and a focus on grammatical accuracy in a void. The previous section presented one avenue for bringing context to language teaching, through the use of authentic texts. Another interesting option for contextualizing language instruction is to merge language learning with content from other subject areas, disciplines, or cultures.

FIGURE 3.3 Content-Based Language Teaching: A Continuum of Content and Language Integration

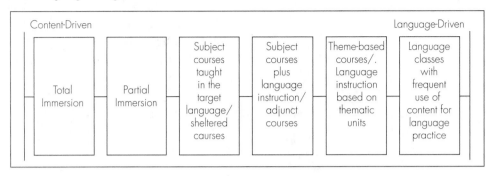

Source: Met, 1999, p. 144.

This merging of language and content is at the heart of the Connections and Cultures *SFLL* goal areas and planning for standards-oriented instruction. In recent years, there has been increasing interest in *content-based, content-related, content-enriched,* and *theme-based* approaches, all of which propose interweaving content to varying degrees with language instruction. The range of programs that integrate language and content learning are depicted in Met's (1999) continuum of programmatic possibilities, shown in Figure 3.3. One end of the continuum illustrates the most content-based or content-driven language programs while the other shows those that are primarily language-driven but use content as the vehicle for communicative language use.

Content-based instruction (CBI) has historically received a great deal of attention, as it has been widely implemented in FLES (Foreign Language in the Elementary School) and ESL (English as a Second Language) programs. CBI became the foundation of immersion and foreign language programs for K–12 students as early as the 1960s, and its success in immersion programs in Canada has been widely documented (Lambert, 1984). Research from foreign/second language immersion programs confirms that content-based approaches promote L2 proficiency and facilitate skill learning in relevant ways for second-language learners (Pica, 2002; Genessee, 1998; Johnson & Swain, 1997). CBI uses the content, learning objectives, and activities from the school curriculum as the vehicle for teaching language skills, and it has been shown to result in enhanced motivation, self-confidence, language proficiency, and cultural literacy (Leaver & Stryker, 1989; Met, 1999, 1991; Snow & Brinton, 1997).

Although historically CBI has been implemented primarily at the elementary school level, its potential positive impact on secondary and post-secondary language instruction has been acknowledged (Glisan & Fall, 1991; Lafayette & Buscaglia, 1985). Glisan and Fall note that "the content-based instruction found in elementary immersion programs utilizes a key educational principle that advances all learning—increased time on task" (p. 11). Curtain and Dahlberg (2004) distinguish between *content-based* programs and *content-related* programs. *Content-based programs* take responsibility for teaching a specific portion of the regular school curriculum for that grade level in the target language (e.g., math or social studies classes). *Content-related programs* use some of the concepts or topics from the regular curriculum as the vehicle for integrating content (e.g., integrating geography and map skills while exploring target language regions). Any standards-based program that teaches language through theme-based or thematic units can be described as content-related.

 CBI uses the content, learning objectives, and activities from the school curriculum as the vehicle for teaching language skills.

Regardless of the degree to which language and content are integrated, several important factors to consider when planning connections with content are:

- the content-area skills and concepts that can interrelate most effectively with the language goals
- the language competencies needed to work with the content selected
- the cognitive skills necessary to perform the tasks in the lesson
- the potential for integration with cultural concepts and goals (Curtain & Dahlberg, 2004, p. 268).

The challenge is to blend content and language in such a way that learners acquire new subject-matter material while progressing in their language development. Bragger and Rice (1998) proposed a developmental model for content-oriented instruction that recognizes that in order for learning to occur, "there must be familiarity with *either* the language needed to deal with the content *or* the content itself" (pp. 200–201):

Stage 1: Preparing for Content Connections: The academic content is usually familiar to learners while the language may be one step beyond their productive proficiency skills. The focus is on helping learners to understand content while listening and reading in the target language. Example: Students are given mathematical word problems that combine numbers with reading comprehension.

Stage 2: Developing the Content Orientation (Familiar Material): The content is familiar while the language is a step beyond the learner and must be made comprehensible. Since students are expected not only to understand the content but also to discuss it in the foreign language, they benefit from guided assistance from the teacher and peers. Example 1: Students perform a science experiment, explain it orally in the foreign language, and write a composition to further analyze it. Example 2: Students read an authentic text written in the target language on a topic for and about young people and one that students are familiar with (e.g., peer pressure). They receive guided assistance in interpreting the text and then talk and write in the target language about the basic story line and theme.

Stage 3: Developing the Content Orientation (Less Familiar Material): The language is at the level of the learner but the content may be unfamiliar. Students work collaboratively with peers to research cultural and subject-content topics and engage in presentational tasks. Example: Students may have the language necessary for talking about geography, but the theme of geography of the region of a target culture and its effects on the target population may be less familiar.

Stage 4: Expanding the Content Orientation (Unfamiliar Material): Learners stretch linguistic skills and explore unfamiliar content. Learners' language skills and comprehension strategies are at a level that enables them to work with a text that contains unfamiliar vocabulary and/or structures. The challenge for the teacher is to set expectations so that students' linguistic and content skills progress in a continuous way. Example: Students read and interpret authentic literature and engage in a variety of oral and written interpersonal and presentational tasks to explore the main ideas and themes contained therein (pp. 202–215).

 What role can sociocultural theory play in the implementation of content-based instruction?

While there is considerable recognition of the benefits of CBI in bringing interest and relevance to L2 learning, Pica (2002) has pointed out a concern in SLA research that classroom experiences with subject-matter content might not provide sufficient attention to the kinds of L2 input, feedback, and output that are critical to interlanguage development. In her study of two content-based ESL classes, Pica found that the strategy used most often by instructors was "discussion" involving subject-matter content, but that these discussions featured very limited use of negotiation of meaning and attention to form-focused intervention or instruction. That is, instructors focused on students' comprehension of lengthy texts and on their discussions of subject-content but paid little attention to the development of their L2 linguistic skills. A similar finding occurred in a recent study that examined the extent to which advanced undergraduate literature courses provide discourse opportunities for students to develop advanced-level language functions (Donato & Brooks, 2004). See Chapter 8 for a more detailed discussion.

Pica (2002) offers two approaches that teachers might take to promote L2 learning through content. First, she suggests that they modify their responses to students' utterances in ways that will generate more input, feedback, and production of student output. For example, teachers can provide comments and assisting questions that will prompt students to expand their utterances, and they can call students' attention to issues of form through feedback strategies such as elicitation and clarification requests. See Chapter 8 for a fuller discussion of feedback strategies.

The second approach is to use the "discussion" strategy as an initial activity to introduce or review subject-matter content and then implement interactive form-focusing tasks that elicit more targeted input, feedback, and student production of modified output. For example, Pica (2002) suggests that students might reconstruct a scene from a film or story by taking notes on it and then using the notes to collaboratively reconstruct the scene. As students collaborate on reconstruction tasks, they provide each other with feedback that focuses on grammar and edits discourse, and they can then use this input as a basis for modifying their output (Swain, 1995). An additional related strategy is to engage students in writing journal entries as a way to enable them to explore subject-matter content and focus on their linguistic output.

In sum, in planning for standards-based instruction, the teacher should consider:

1. ways to provide maximum opportunities for students to hear meaningful teacher talk in the target language;
2. ways in which optimal amounts of IRF can be incorporated to promote meaningful discourse in the classroom;
3. the nature of oral and printed texts to be integrated (according to episodic organization and degree of authenticity); and
4. strategies for bringing context into the learning experience by integrating language and subject-matter content.

Long-Term Planning for Instruction

From State Framework to Year-Long Planning

Appendix 3.1 presents an excerpt from Nebraska's framework that is based on the national standards (Nebraska Department of Education, 2004a). You will note that the framework describes what learners are able to do at three levels of ability: beginning, developing, and expanding. School districts use such state frameworks as the basis for program and course development.

At some point in your teaching career, you will be involved in writing curriculum for a language program. Recent methods for designing standards- or performance-based curricula use an approach often referred to as "backward-design," "design-down," or "top-down," since the process begins with a focus on the **end results** that are desired, whether they are for the entire program, a particular level of study, a unit of study, or daily lesson plans. As illustrated in Figure 3.4, curriculum planning might begin with the question: What should students know and be able to do . . .

- **at the end of** the entire language program?
- **at the end of** the individual language program (if each program is planned separately)?
- **at the end of** the course (course structures vary across districts: some are organized by courses, some by levels, others by semesters or years)?
- **at the end of** the unit (a series of units is offered within each course)?
- **at the end of** the concept lessons (these vary by district; lessons on essential skills and knowledge)?
- **at the end of** daily lessons? (Nebraska Deptartment of Education, 2004b, pp. 199–200)

In backward-design planning, the desired end result drives the creation of unit and lesson plans and assessment.

 What is the connection between the national standards and the state framework in Appendix 3.1? ■

Since long-term objectives must be valid regardless of which textbook is used, teachers should write a curriculum for any given level without reference to a particular textbook. The text should then be adapted to reflect the objectives rather than vice versa.

Appendix 3.2 is an example of an excerpt from a year planner for a Level 1 language class from the state of Nebraska (Nebraska Department of Education, 2004b).

 What is the relationship between the year planner in Appendix 3.2 and the state framework in Appendix 3.1? ■

Thematic Unit Planning

The next task in planning is to divide the long-term plan into teachable chunks, called *units of instruction*. In recent years, teachers have focused on creating *thematic units*, a series of related lessons around a topic (e.g., travel), a particular context (e.g., a story), or a particular subject-content theme (e.g., the effect of geography on daily living). While thematic units may correspond to unit divisions in the textbook, they often include objectives, activities, and materials that are not part of the textbook. The following are some steps that teachers might follow in designing a unit plan. Note the same type of backward design presented in the discussion of year-long curriculum planning.

1. Standards as a Mind-Set: Identify the goal areas (the 5 Cs) and specific standards to be addressed.
2. Unit Theme/Context: Identify the theme or functional context of the unit.
3. Objectives/Progress Indicators: Describe what students will be able to do by the end of the unit. Progress indicators from national or state standards might be used or adapted when setting these objectives.
4. Performance Assessments: Design performance assessments through which students will demonstrate that they have achieved the unit objectives and attained the targeted standards. These assessments should integrate the three modes of communication and other goal areas addressed in the unit.
5. Essential Skills/Knowledge: Identify the key elements from the *ACTFL Performance Guidelines for K–12 Learners* that learners should demonstrate in order to achieve unit

FIGURE 3.4 Backward-Design Planning

Curriculum Planning—Where Do You Begin?

Program
Are all languages offered in one program?
Examples: Exploratory + 1st–5th year; 1st–2nd year;
4th–6th grade + 1st–5th year

Language-Specific Program
Is each language program planned separately?
Examples: Spanish: 1st–4th year;
German 1st–2nd year

Course/Level/Semester/Year
Does your district go by courses? Levels? Is the time period in
semesters or years?
Examples: Spanish 1 (one year); French 7–8 (one year);
German 2 (one semester)

Units
What units are offered within the course?
Examples: Shopping at the market;
Functioning at social gatherings

Concept Lessons
What specific skills/knowledge are needed to achieve the
progress indicators, context/outcomes, and standards?
Examples: Food customs and vocabulary and phrases,
use of adjectives, expressing preferences

Daily Lessons
What concepts (skills/knowledge) are interwoven each day to
achieve the standards and progress indicators?
Examples: Pairs practice expressing the food preferences;
video/group discussions of the customs of shopping
at market to buy food; review adjective use as
it applies to describing food; practice a situation
where students shop at a market

Source: Nebraska Department of Education, 2004b, http://www.nde.state.ne.us/FORLG/Frameworks/FLFCurric.pdf, p. 201.

objectives—e.g., language control: grammar/pronunciation, vocabulary use, communication strategies, cultural awareness.

6. **Instructional Strategies:** Select and/or design appropriate instructional strategies that will form the best approach to teach the lessons contained in the unit.

7. **Resources:** Select and/or design appropriate resources that will enhance student learning in the unit. Remember that the textbook is only one resource of many! (Adapted from the Nebraska K–12 Foreign Language Frameworks documents, 2004, and the Wisconsin Department of Public Instruction's Planning Curriculum for Learning World Languages, 2002)

Figure 3.5 summarizes the steps described above in planning units of instruction. Note that the steps involving assessments, essential skills/knowledge, and instructional strategies (steps 4, 5, 6) are recursive and that each element informs and improves the other. Appendix 3.3 illustrates a sample unit plan for a unit on "Shopping at the Market," which integrates the five goal areas (Nebraska Department of Education, 2004b). Note that some units, depending on their themes and objectives, may integrate only three or four goal areas. The "progress indicators" listed in this sample refer back to the Nebraska K–12 Foreign Language Frameworks. As you use this template, you may find it more helpful to list the specific performance objectives that relate to your unit theme and which would also appear on daily lesson plans for the unit (e.g., Students will be able to . . . ask a sales clerk questions about prices, sizes, etc., . . . identify the key details regarding a department store sale advertised in the newspaper . . . express likes and dislikes about clothing on sale at a market/department store).

FIGURE 3.5 The Relationship of Curriculum-Planning Elements

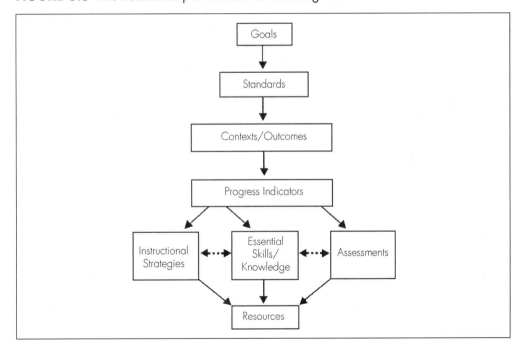

Source: Nebraska Department of Education, 2004b, http://www.nde.state.ne.us/FORLG/Framewoks/FLFCurric.pdf, p. 210.

A *thematic unit* is a series of related lessons around a topic, a particular context, or a particular subject-content theme.

Daily Lesson Planning

Writing Objectives

Working from the broader thematic unit plans, language teachers organize the material to be presented in daily lessons. One of the most important aspects of planning a daily lesson is to identify the objective(s) that you want to achieve by the end of the class period. Effective objectives are measurable and describe what learners will be able to do in and with the target language in terms of meaningful language use, such as that which is described by the *SFLL*. For example, the objective may focus on learners' ability to accomplish some language function—to communicate real information. Examples of good objectives are: learners will be able to describe their daily routine; learners will be able to identify prices of clothing given in a radio commercial; learners will be able to compare the educational systems of the United States and target cultures; learners will be able to write an e-mail message to a key pal from a target country. Objectives use action verbs that represent desired student behavior. Verbs such as "learn" or "understand" are too vague for use in objectives.

Objectives should also contain an indication of the realistic context in which students will be able to use the target language that they learn. Objectives should not consist of a listing of textbook exercises or grammar points, although these may be a part of the instructional strategies. In planning lessons and writing objectives, you may find it helpful to refer to Appendix 3.4 for Bloom's Taxonomy of Thinking, which is a model that depicts six levels of thinking arranged in order of complexity of thinking processes.[3] *Knowledge* and *comprehension* are the lower or more concrete levels of thinking, while *analysis, evaluation,* and *synthesis* represent higher or more complex levels of thinking. The *application* level, which falls in between the lower and higher levels, can be very concrete or very complex depending on the task (Nebraska Department of Education, 2004c).

Bloom's Taxonomy can be useful for language teachers in at least two ways. First of all, you will notice that the chart contains a list of action verbs in the "Instructional Strategies" column that can be used in writing objectives. Secondly, the taxonomy illustrates the level of thinking required by specific learning activities. Examples of activities that use lower-level thinking include naming objects in the foreign language, matching visuals to words, identifying objects in a TPR activity, and summarizing the gist of an authentic magazine article. Higher-level thinking, also called *higher-order thinking* or *critical thinking*, is exemplified in activities such as predicting the ending of a story, enacting a spontaneous role-play, comparing two cultural practices, analyzing an authentic short story for the plot and characters, and debating an issue. As teachers design learning experiences, they should be aware of what level of thinking they are requiring students to perform. Thinking should not be limited to the knowledge and comprehension levels, and teachers might use Bloom's Taxonomy for ideas on how to move students toward higher-level thinking. You may also find Appendix 3.5 [see Web site] helpful, as it contains Bloom's Taxonomy applied to the *Nebraska K–12 Foreign Language Frameworks* progress indicators.

thandbook.heinle.com

As you think about how to write lesson objectives, examine the list below.

Which of the following are appropriate functional lesson objectives and why? Which lead to critical or higher-level thinking skills?

1. The student will learn about typical dinner foods in the target culture.
2. The teacher will present ways to tell time.
3. The student will describe his or her family.
4. The student will understand how to form the future tense.
5. The student will compare and contrast daily teenage life in the native and target cultures.

6. The student will identify numbers given in a taped airline announcement.
7. The student will create a magazine feature article about a popular singer from the target culture.
8. The student will summarize the main ideas of an authentic news report.

An objective describes what learners will be able to do in/with the target language in terms of meaningful language use.

The *ACTFL Proficiency Guidelines* and Design of Objectives

The teacher might use the *ACTFL Proficiency Guidelines—Speaking* (1999) to design objectives in two ways. First, the guidelines can be used to establish a performance level to be attained by the end of a given program. For example, teachers might establish Intermediate-Mid as the minimal speaking performance level to be attained by the end of a four-year high school sequence of study. In this case, the ACTFL guidelines would be used to develop broader objectives or outcomes that describe Intermediate-Mid proficiency. For example, these proficiency-based objectives describe what the student should be able to do at this level:

- ask and answer questions related to personal needs and familiar topics;
- participate in short conversations and express basic courtesy;
- successfully handle a number of uncomplicated situations necessary for survival in the target culture.

It is important to note that while the proficiency guidelines can be helpful in establishing performance expectations, they are not curriculum and cannot be used verbatim as objectives since they are written as assessment descriptors for testers. However, they can be helpful in setting expectations of learner performance. Second, teachers might use proficiency principles for both unit and daily planning. Expected learner outcomes can be defined in terms of the functions learners can perform (lesson objectives), the specific contexts in which they can use the language, and the accuracy of their language (Swender, 1999).

How were the terms *function, context/content areas, accuracy*, and *oral text type* defined in Chapter 2?

Designing a Daily Lesson Plan

Freeman (1996) points out the results of research that examined how teachers actually plan lessons—that is, what they thought about ahead of time for the lesson and what they were thinking about as they taught (Nunan, 1992). Teachers do informal planning first by assessing what their students already know or bring to the learning task and then figuring out what they need to teach them to get them to the appropriate objective. They tend to visualize lessons as clusters or sequences of activity and to blend content with activity (Clark & Peterson, 1986; Freeman, 1996).

Next, teachers plan more formally by creating a written daily lesson plan, such as the one that appears on pages 86–87. This format illustrates the process the teacher follows during the planning phase, teaching phase, and reflective phase. Under the *Activities* section (Part IV in the outline) of the teaching phase, possible segments of the lesson are listed. This approach is adapted from the one suggested by Ballman (1998, 1996).[4] The purpose of the *Setting the Stage* segment (Part IV.A.) is to capture students' attention on the lesson context, to activate students' background knowledge, and to prepare students for the learning process. Ausubel, Novak, and Hanesian recommend the use of *advance organizers*, that is, "appropriately relevant and inclusive introductory materials that are maximally clear and stable . . . introduced in advance of the learning material itself, used to facilitate establishing a meaningful learning set" (1978, pp. 170–171). Advance organizers, such as visuals and pre-listening/pre-reading activities, can be used to activate students' existing knowledge and facilitate meaningful learning.

The *Providing Input/Engaging Learners* segment (Part IV.B.) consists of presenting oral language in context; using visual support in the form of drawings, photos, and other visuals and/or written language; and incorporating comprehension check techniques to ensure comprehension. It also provides opportunities for learners to be actively involved in attending to the input and interacting with the teacher. *Guided Participation* (Part IV.C.) is used here within a Vygotskyan framework to refer to the scaffolded assistance offered to the learner (novice) by the teacher and/or more capable peers (experts) in helping the learner to solve a problem or perform a task. The *Extension* segment (Part IV.D.) denotes the opportunities for pairs/groups of students to participate in culminating activities that integrate multiple skills and standards.

The teacher conducts *Informal Assessment* (Part IV.E.) as students perform throughout the lesson, gauging how well students have achieved the objectives of the lesson. Informal assessment does not necessarily require an additional step in the lesson plan but rather can be done as students are performing activities throughout the lesson. Some of the informal assessments may guide the teacher to redesign activities or develop additional ones. More formal assessments, such as a short quiz, may also be recorded for a grade. (See Chapter 12 for further explanation and examples of informal and formal assessments.)

During the *Closure* segment (Part IV.F.), the teacher brings the lesson to a close by asking students to recall what they learned and/or by describing how the current lesson will be used as the basis for the next lesson. Note that every lesson may not feature all of the components. For example, on a day when the teacher is presenting a story or a tape-recorded authentic segment, he or she may need more time to provide input. On the following day, the teacher may give much less input, as students are engaged in activities.

PLANNING PHASE

  I. CONTENT
    A. Context/Theme/Topic:
    B. Objectives: Learners will be able to. . .
    C. Grammar/Vocabulary Addressed:
    D. Goal Areas/Standards addressed:
  II. LEARNERS: What do I need to know about the learners in order to plan instruction? What background knowledge do they need? What experiences, if any, have they had with this content? What special needs of my students need to be addressed in instruction?
  III. MATERIALS

TEACHING PHASE

  IV. ACTIVITIES: What are the learners doing? What am I doing? (Possible instructional sequence; these will vary according to the specific lesson:)
    A. Setting the Stage
    B. Providing Input/Engaging Learners
    C. Guided Participation
    D. Extension

E. Informal or Formal Assessment

F. Closure

REFLECTION PHASE

thandbook.heinle.com

V. ADAPTATIONS TO LESSON: What changes did I have to make as I taught the lesson? Explain.

VI. SELF-REFLECTION ON LESSON EFFECTIVENESS: Did I achieve my lesson objectives? How do I know? What worked especially well and why? What would I change if I were to teach this lesson again?

TEACH AND REFLECT

EPISODE ONE

Planning for Instruction

Task A: Writing Daily Lesson Objectives

NCATE_____
STANDARD
4.a.

Use the Nebraska Foreign Language Frameworks Unit Planner in Appendix 3.3. Imagine that you are beginning the "Shopping at the Market" unit in your Level 1 language class. Design Part I (Content) of the lesson plan outline presented earlier for the first two days of this unit. Describe the context/theme, the objectives (what learners will be able to do), grammar/vocabulary addressed, and the goal areas/standards addressed.

Task B: Creating a Daily Lesson Plan

NCATE_____
STANDARD
4.a.

Now use Part I of the lesson plan that you designed for Day 1 of the unit and create Parts II, III, and IV for a typical forty-two-minute class period. Your instructor may ask you to present this lesson to your classmates.

Task C: Designing a Unit of Instruction

NCATE_____
STANDARD
4.a.

Using the Year Planner in Appendix 3.2 and the Unit Planner in Appendix 3.3, design another unit of instruction for a Level 1 language class that reflects the goals of the Year Planner. Follow the steps provided earlier in this chapter for creating a unit plan. Be sure to structure your lesson around authentic materials, and use the textbook only as a secondary source.

EPISODE TWO

Developing a Content-Based Level 5 Foreign Language Class

NCATE_____
STANDARDS
2.c., 4.a.

You are a high school foreign language teacher whose teaching assignment for next year includes a Level 5 class. This is the first time that your program has had enough students for Level 5, and you want to make the course a valuable experience that will motivate other students to take it in the future. You would like to design a content-based course instead of a skills-based one. What are some possibilities for incorporating subject-matter and cultural content at this level in the high school curriculum? Identify four or five strategies that you might want to incorporate into your teaching in order to address current issues concerning integration of language and content. Your instructor may ask you to work with one or two classmates on this assignment.

Note: If you are preparing to teach at the post-secondary level, you might design an advanced-level course that focuses on specific subject matter, culture, or literature.

EPISODE THREE
Comparing State Framework and Curriculum Documents

NCATE___
STANDARD
4.a.

States have different ways of designing their state frameworks and curricular plans. The purpose of this assignment is to engage you in comparing model standards documents from several states. Even though they are organized differently, each represents an effective approach for the design of standards and curriculum. Choose two of the tasks below, or your instructor might assign you specific tasks from the list. To access the frameworks listed, go to the *Teacher's Handbook* Web site, where you will find links to documents and/or the documents themselves, e.g., Appendix 3.6 (Web site), which is a sample thematic unit on careers/work for grade 8.

1. Compare the Connecticut Standards Frameworks with the Nebraska Standards Frameworks. Describe the similarities and differences. What are Connecticut's "Curriculum Trace Maps" and what purpose do they serve?
2. Compare the Wisconsin thematic unit sample (Appendix 3.6 on the Web site) with the unit plan from Nebraska (Appendix 3.3 of text). How does the organization of these two units differ? What role do the three modes of communication play in the Wisconsin thematic unit plan format?
3. Compare New Jersey's learning scenarios with Nebraska's curricular units. What similarities and differences do you find?
4. Look at the American Sign Language (ASL) standards in the Texas Frameworks. What differences do you see between these standards and those of other foreign languages?

Your instructor may ask you to compare the frameworks for your state with those of Connecticut, Nebraska, New Jersey, Texas, and/or Wisconsin. See the *Teacher's Handbook* Web site for a link to state frameworks.

DISCUSS AND REFLECT*

thandbook.heinle.com

NCATE___
STANDARD
4.a.

CASE STUDY ONE
The Effect of Class Scheduling on Planning for Instruction

(Note: The previous edition of *Teacher's Handbook* presented a case study that explored the advantages and disadvantages of block scheduling. Although some debate continues over the educational benefits of this type of class scheduling, the current focus is on ways in which the instructor may plan and teach effectively on the block, given that this is now a reality in many schools.)

Jesús and Emily recently graduated from the same university and enrolled in the Foreign Language Teacher Preparation Program together. Shortly after graduation, they each accepted teaching jobs in different school districts, Jesús teaching Spanish at Grand Forks High School, and Emily teaching German and ESL at Widdowdale Middle School. Much to his surprise, Jesús was assigned to teach a Spanish I class on a regular schedule of forty-two minutes a day plus two Spanish III classes on a straight block schedule, meeting ninety minutes every day. He contacted Emily to find out what her teaching schedule was and discovered that she also was assigned to teach German II and ESL on a block schedule, but it

---

*See the *Teacher's Handbook* Web site for a third case study that deals with an ESL teacher in a factory on a Native American reservation and the ways in which she addresses the needs of her learners in planning instruction.

was the rotating block in which the classes are scheduled on the alternating "A" day/"B" day schedule.

Jesús and Emily decided to meet to help one another to plan for their block classes. They recalled that they had learned the following information about block scheduling from their foreign language methods class:

In the straight block, also known as the 4 x 4 model, students take four ninety-minute classes a day, five days a week. Courses that were previously taught for a full year of 40–50 minute classes are scheduled for half year of 90-minute classes. Students may now take eight courses each year for a total of thirty-two courses over four high school years, as compared with twenty-four in the traditional scheduling model. The following is a schematic for the straight-block model, also known as the 4 x 4 model or the four-block model:

FIGURE 3.6 4 x 4 Block Schedule

FIRST SEMESTER						
Course 1 (90 min.)	Passing (5–15 min.)	Course 2 (90 min.)	Lunch	Course 3 (90 min.)	Passing (5–15 min.)	Course 4 (90 min.)
SECOND SEMESTER						
Course 5 (90 min.)	Passing (5–15 min.)	Course 6 (90 min.)	Lunch	Course 7 (90 min.)	Passing (5–15 min.)	Course 8 (90 min.)

Source: ACTFL Professional Issues Report, 1996.

In the rotating block model, students take four 90-minute classes Monday, Wednesday, and Friday, and four different 90-minute classes on Tuesday and Thursday. Each course runs for the entire school year, and so students on this schedule also may complete eight courses during a school year, or 32 courses during four high school years.

The following schematic is a sample of a rotating block schedule:

FIGURE 3.7 Rotating Block Schedule

BLOCK A	BLOCK B
Course 1 Course 2 Lunch Course 3 Course 4	Course 5 Course 6 Lunch Course 7 Course 8
Week 1: Mon./Block A Tues./Block B Wed./Block A Thurs./Block B Fri./Block A	Week 1: Mon./Block B Tues./Block A Wed./Block B Thurs./Block A Fri./Block B

Source: ACTFL Professional Issues Report, 1996.

Jesús and Emily also recall learning that now that foreign language teachers have had some time to work with block scheduling, they report that the additional instructional time afforded by the ninety-minute period is beneficial in helping them to (1) vary their instructional strategies, (2) address the various learning styles of their students, (3) integrate instructional technology, (4) teach the curriculum in more depth, (5) work individually with their students, (6) use a variety of assessment techniques, (7) plan for instruction, (8) meet the needs of special education students, and (9) reduce stress (Fairfax County Public Schools, 1997, cf. Wallinger, 2000, p. 38). This type of scheduling also provides for more time on task for students to internalize the language and increased opportunities for students to take more language courses. On the other hand, concerns about block scheduling include the sequencing of language courses (i.e., students may not have language courses in back-to-back semesters), the ability of students to remain attentive during the longer class period and to retain the material, avoiding the tendency to lower standards or water down the material, and the challenge of helping students to make up work after class absences (Wallinger, 2000; Schoenstein, 1994; Steen, 1992).[5]

In their methods class, Jesús and Emily had explored strategies for planning lessons on the block. They recalled the following suggestions: (1) Link activities together with a common theme or context, and avoid jumping from one topic to another; (2) Plan for a variety of activities, addressing factors such as different learning styles and multiple intelligences (see Chapter 10); (3) Address the three modes of communication and integrate technology; (4) Integrate various types of groupings (pairs, large group, quartets) and multimedia to maintain student attention; (5) Design learning "centers" around the classroom for focused learning tasks that can be done individually or in pairs (see Chapter 4); (6) Intersperse opportunities for students to work independently on written assignments with other activities throughout the class period instead of allowing an extended period of time to complete homework at the end of the class; (7) Include closure activities so that students can recall and review what was learned during the ninety minutes; (8) Collaborate with other teachers and take advantage of staff development opportunities that your school may provide to help with teaching on a block schedule (adapted from Espitia, 1998).

Ask yourself these questions:

1. How does the block scheduling concept support some of the language learning theories that you learned about in Chapter 1?
2. How would teaching on a block schedule affect your approach to unit and lesson planning?
3. What differences might Jesús and Emily have in their planning since they have two different types of block schedules?
4. What reactions might the learner have to experiencing foreign language learning in a class that is block scheduled?

To prepare the case:

1. Read Wallinger (2000) and ACTFL's Professional Issues Report (1996), "Block Scheduling and Second-Language Instruction."
2. Read Espitia (1998) for practical ideas on how to make block scheduling work.
3. Interview a teacher who teaches on a block schedule.
4. Summarize the information and comments you collect and compare them with those of your classmates.

To prepare for class discussion:

1. Return to the daily lesson plan that you designed in this chapter's Teach and Reflect, Task B. Expand this plan for use in a ninety-minute block class. What principles for instructional design will you need to keep in mind? Use the daily lesson plan format presented in this chapter.
2. Your school principal has asked you for your opinion about switching from a traditional forty-two-minute period to a ninety-minute block schedule. Specifically, he or she would like to know about the effect of block scheduling on foreign language learning. Use research findings and other information that you have acquired in order to make a case either for or against block scheduling.

CASE STUDY TWO
Analyzing the Use of Content and Context in a Japanese Lesson

Sensei Hiroshi has been teaching Japanese for ten years at Rifton City High School, where he is the only Japanese teacher and teaches Levels I, II, and III. He is a popular foreign language teacher who has built a strong Japanese program at this school. Although his initial preparation as a language teacher was traditional in nature, Mr. Hiroshi has regularly attended conferences and workshops and learned about current approaches to language instruction. Language teachers in Mr. Hiroshi's school district are observed at least once a year by the district foreign language supervisor, Dr. Bonnie Herbert, who is knowledgeable about the current state of the art in language teaching and always offers helpful guidance.

Today Dr. Herbert is observing Mr. Hiroshi's Japanese I class during the traditional forty-two minute period. Mr. Hiroshi greets students in Japanese as they enter the classroom and begins today's class with several warm-up questions in Japanese dealing with today's date, weather, and time of day, and the clothing and colors students are wearing. As students answer in Japanese, he provides IRE responses to offer praise and indicate whether the answers were accurate; this activity lasts for ten minutes. Next Mr. Hiroshi continues the lesson on food that he began the previous day by distributing plastic food items and having students, as a whole class, name them and answer questions about their colors and food group connections. Students seem to enjoy this activity, which takes twelve minutes. Then Mr. Hiroshi presents a new grammatical concept in English: use of the particle "o" after direct objects. He explains in English the new pattern, writes examples on the board, and asks students to analyze similar examples in the textbook; this lasts for ten minutes. For the last ten minutes, students complete mechanical workbook exercises on the new grammar point, in which they fill in blanks and answer questions using the particle. After the lesson, Dr. Herbert and Mr. Hiroshi meet for a post-observation conference.

Ask yourself these questions:

1. Based upon what you have learned about language acquisition and instruction in Chapters 1, 2, and 3, which instructional strategies in this lesson are effective and why? Which strategies could be improved and how?
2. How would you characterize the use of content and/or contexts in this lesson?
3. How would you characterize Mr. Hiroshi's use of Japanese in this lesson in terms of meaningful target language use, IRE, and IRF?
4. What might be some student reactions to the different parts of the lesson?

thandbook.heinle.com

To prepare the case:

1. Read the Pittsburgh Public School's *7 Best Practices for World Languages Instruction* (2003) that appears on the *Teacher's Handbook* Web site (Chapter 1).
2. Consult Met's (1999) chapter for ideas on integrating connections into language teaching.
3. Read Toth (2004) for a discussion of target language use and classroom discourse.
4. Review Hall (1999) for a discussion of IRE.

To prepare for class discussion:

1. Imagine that you are Dr. Herbert, have observed Mr. Hiroshi's class, and must now have a conference with him. What specific suggestions would you make regarding the role of context in his teaching, his use of Japanese, and the responses he gives to students' utterances? Use the document *7 Best Practices for World Languages Instruction* (Pittsburgh Public Schools, 2003), which is also used in Mr. Hiroshi's school district, to support your suggestions.

2. Imagine that you are Mr. Hiroshi and have been given several suggestions by your supervisor regarding ways to integrate more content and contexts into your teaching. How might you obtain the knowledge and skills that you need in order to make these changes? You might refer back to the Preliminary Chapter for some ideas on how your professional organizations might be of assistance.

REFERENCES

American Council on Teaching of Foreign Languages. (1996). Block scheduling and second-language instruction. ACTFL Professional Issues Report. *ACTFL Newsletter, 6* (2): 11–15. Yonkers, NY: Author.

American Council on Teaching of Foreign Languages. (1998). *ACTFL performance guidelines for K-12 learners.* Yonkers, NY: Author.

American Council on Teaching of Foreign Languages. *ACTFL proficiency guidelines—Speaking.* (1999). Yonkers, NY: Author.

Ausubel, D. P., Novak, J. D., & Hanesian, H. (1978). *Educational psychology: A cognitive view.* New York: Holt, Rinehart and Winston.

Ballman, T. L. (1996). Integrating vocabulary, grammar, and culture: A model five-day communicative lesson plan. *Foreign Language Annals, 29,* 37–44.

Ballman, T. L. (1998). From teacher-centered to learner-centered: Guidelines for sequencing and presenting the elements of a foreign language class. In J. Harper, M. Lively, & M. Williams (Eds.), *The coming of age of the profession* (pp. 97–111). Boston: Heinle & Heinle.

Bartz, W. H., & Singer, M. K. (1996). The programmatic implications of foreign language standards. In R. C. Lafayette (Ed.), *National standards: A catalyst for reform. The ACTFL Foreign Language Education Series* (pp. 139–167). Lincolnwood, IL: NTC/Contemporary Publishing Group.

Bragger, J. D., & Rice, D. B. (1998). Connections: The national standards and a new paradigm for content-oriented materials and instruction. In J. Harper, M. Lively, & M. Williams (Eds.), *The coming of age of the profession* (pp. 191–217). Boston: Heinle & Heinle.

Carrell, P. L. (1984). The effects of rhetorical organization on ESL readers. *TESOL Quarterly, 18,* 441–469.

Clark, C., & Peterson, P. (1986). Teachers' thought processes. In M. Wittrock (Ed.), *Handbook of research on teaching* (3rd ed.) (pp. 255–296). New York: Macmillan.

Curtain, H. A., & Dahlberg, C. A. (2004). *Languages and children—Making the match* (3rd ed.). Boston: Pearson.

Donato, R. (2004). Aspects of collaboration in pedagogical discourse. In M. McGroarty (Ed.), *Annual Review of Applied Linguistics (Vol. 24): Advances in language pedagogy* (pp. 284–302). West Nyack, NY: Cambridge University Press.

Donato, R., & Brooks, F. B. (2004) Literary discussions and advanced speaking functions: Researching the (dis)connection. *Foreign Language Annals, 37,* 183–199.

Espitia, D. (1998). Making the block work for you! *Northeast Conference Newsletter, 43,* 45–53.

Fairfax County (VA) Public Schools. (1997, Jan.). *A status report on the implementation of block scheduling in nine high schools.* Falls Church, VA: Author.

Freeman, D. (1996). Redefining the relationship between research and what teachers know. In K. M. Bailey & D. Nunan (Eds.), *Voices from the language classroom* (pp. 88–115). Cambridge, UK: Cambridge University Press.

Galloway, V. (1998). Constructing cultural realities: "Facts" and frameworks of association. In J. Harper, M. Lively, & M. Williams (Eds.), *The coming of age of the profession* (pp. 129–140). Boston: Heinle & Heinle.

Geddes, M., & White, R. (1978). The use of semi-scripted simulated authentic speech in listening comprehension. *Audiovisual Language Journal, 16,* 137–145.

Genessee, F. (1998). Content-based language instruction. In M. Met (Ed.), *Critical issues in early second language learning* (pp. 103–105). Glenview, IL: Scott Foresman-Addison Wesley.

Glisan, E. W., & Fall, T. F. (1991). Adapting an elementary immersion approach to secondary and postsecondary language teaching: The methodological connection. In J. K. Phillips (Ed.), *Building bridges and making connections* (pp. 1–29). Burlington, VT: Northeast Conference on the Teaching of Foreign Languages.

Glisan, E. W., & Shrum, J. L. (1996). *Enlaces. Text tapescript.* Boston: Heinle & Heinle.

Goals 2000: Educate America Act. (1994). Washington, DC: Department of Education.

Hall, J. K. (1995). "'Aw, man, where we goin'?": Classroom interaction and the development of L2 interactional competence. *Issues in Applied Linguistics, 6,* 37–62.

Hall, J. K. (1996). The discursive formation of Spanish as a foreign language classroom community. Paper presented at AILA 1996, 11th World Congress of Applied Linguistics Symposium.

Hall, J. K. (1999). The communication standards. In J. K. Phillips & R. M. Terry (Eds.), *Foreign language standards: Linking research, theories, and practices* (pp. 15–56). Lincolnwood, IL: National Textbook Company.

Johnson, K., & Swain, M. (1997). *Immersion education: International perspectives.* New York: Cambridge University Press.

Krashen, S. (1982). *Principles and practice in second language acquisition.* Oxford, UK: Pergamon Press.

Lafayette, R., & Buscaglia, M. (1985). Students learn language via a civilization course: A comparison of second language classroom environments. *Studies in Second Language Acquisition, 7,* 323–342.

Lambert, W. E. (1984) (Ed.). An overview of issues in immersion education. In *Studies on immersion education: A collection for United States educators.* Sacramento, CA: California State Department of Education.

Lapkin, S., Harley, B., & Hart, D. (1997). Block scheduling for language study in the middle grades: A summary of the Carleton case study. *Learning Languages, 2* (3), 4–8.

Leaver, B. L., & Stryker, S. B. (1989). Content-based instruction for foreign language classrooms. *Foreign Language Annals, 22,* 269–275.

Lee, J. F., & VanPatten, B. (2003). *Making communicative language teaching happen.* (2nd ed.). New York: McGraw-Hill.

Mantero, M. (2002). Bridging the gap: Discourse in text-based foreign language classrooms. *Foreign Language Annals, 35,* 437–455.

Mehan, H. (1979). What time is it, Denise? Asking known information questions in classroom discourse. *Theory Into Practice, 28* (4), 285–294.

Met, M. (1991). Learning language through content; learning content through language. *Foreign Language Annals, 24* (4), 281–295.

Met, M. (1999). Making connections. In J. K. Phillips & R. M. Terry (Eds.), *Foreign language standards: Linking research, theories, and practices* (pp. 137–164).

National Standards in Foreign Language Education Project. (1999). *Standards for foreign language learning in the 21st century.* Lawrence, KS: Allen Press.

Nebraska Department of Education. (2004a). *Nebraska K–12 foreign language frameworks.* Retrieved on February 7, 2004, from http://www.nde.state.ne.us/FORLG/Frameworks/Frameworks.pdf.

Nebraska Department of Education. (2004b). *Nebraska K–12 foreign language frameworks.* Retrieved on February 7, 2004, from http://www.nde.state.ne.us/FORLG/Frameworks/FLFCurric.pdf.

Nebraska Department of Education. (2004c). *Nebraska K–12 foreign language frameworks.* Retrieved on February 7, 2004, from http://www.nde.state.ne.us/FORLG/Frameworks/FrameworksMain.htm.

Nebraska Department of Education. (2004d). *Nebraska K–12 foreign language frameworks.* Retrieved on February 7, 2004, from http://www.nde.state.ne.us/FORLG/Frameworks/FLFDiv.pdf.

Nunan, D. (1992). The teacher as decision-maker. In J. Flowerdew, M. Brock, & S. Hsia (Eds.), *Perspectives on second language teacher education* (pp. 135–165). Hong Kong: City Polytechnic of Hong Kong.

Oller, J., Jr. (1983). Some working ideas for language teaching. In J. Oller, Jr., & P. A. Richard-Amato (Eds.), *Methods that work* (pp. 3–19). Rowley, MA: Newbury House.

Pica, T. (2002). Subject-matter content: How does it assist the interactional and linguistic needs of classroom language learners? *The Modern Language Journal, 86,* 1–19.

Pittsburgh Public Schools. (2003). *7 best practices for world languages instruction.* Pittsburgh, PA: Author.

Pusack, J. P., & Otto, S. K. (1996). Taking control of multimedia. In M. D. Bush (Ed.), *Technology-enhanced language learning. The ACTFL Foreign Language Education Series* (pp. 1–46). Lincolnwood, IL: NTC/Contemporary Publishing Group.

Schoenstein, R. (1994). Block schedules: Building the high schools of the future? *Virginia Journal of Education, 88* (3), 7–12.

Snow, M. A., & Brinton, D. M. (1997). *The content-based classroom: Perspectives on integrating language and content.* New York: Addison Wesley Longman.

Steen, M. S. (1992). Teaching foreign language on the block. Unpublished response to request for information by Yorktown H.S., Arlington, VA.

Sternberg, R. J. (1999). Successful intelligence: Finding a balance. *Trends in Cognitive Science, 3,* 436–442.

Swain, M. (1995). Three functions of output in second language learning. In G. Cook & B. Seidlhofer (Eds.), *For H. G. Widdowson: Principles and practice in the study of language* (pp. 125–144). Oxford, UK: Oxford University Press.

Swender, E. (1999). (Ed.) *The ACTFL oral proficiency interview tester training manual.* Yonkers, NY: ACTFL.

Terrell, T., Andrade, M., & Egasse, J., & Muñoz, J. (2002). *Audioscript to accompany Dos Mundos* (5th ed.). Columbus, OH: McGraw-Hill.

Terry, R. M. (1998). Authentic tasks and materials for testing in the foreign language classroom. In J. Harper, M. Lively, & M. Williams (Eds.), *The coming of age of the profession* (pp. 277–290). Boston: Heinle & Heinle.

Tharp, R. G., & Gallimore, R. (1991). *The instructional conversation: Teaching and learning in social activity.* Washington, DC: National Center for Research on Cultural Diversity and Second Language Learning.

Toth, P. (1997). The pragmatics of foreign language communities. Paper presented at the 1997 meeting of the American Association of Applied Linguistics, Orlando, FL.

Toth, P. (2004). When grammar instruction undermines cohesion in L2 Spanish classroom discourse. *The Modern Language Journal, 88,* 14–30.

Villegas Rogers, C., & Medley, F. W., Jr. (1988). Language with a purpose: Using authentic materials in the foreign language classroom. *Foreign Language Annals, 21,* 467–478.

Wallinger, L. M. (2000). The effect of block scheduling on foreign language learning. *Foreign Language Annals, 33,* 36–50.

Wells, G. (1993). Reevaluating the IRF sequence. *Linguistics and Education,* 5, 1–38.

Wells, G. (1999). *Dialogic inquiry: Toward a sociocultural practice and theory of education.* Cambridge, UK: Cambridge University Press.

Winebrenner, S. (1992). *Teaching gifted kids in the regular classroom.* Minneapolis: Free Spirit Publishing.

Wisconsin Department of Public Instruction. (2002). *Planning curriculum for learning world languages.* Milwaukee, WI: Author.

NOTES

1. The focus of this section is to explore the nature of oral and printed texts used in language teaching in terms of their episodic organization and authenticity. Other characteristics of texts, as well as instructional strategies for guiding students through them, will be discussed in Chapter 6.

2. This chapter presents some options for merging language and content teaching and key issues as they relate to the development of language skills and learning of content. In Chapter 4, you will explore content-based instruction as it relates to the Connections goal area of the standards and to specific strategies for subject-content teaching at the elementary school level.

3. Levels of thinking may be described in a variety of ways. For example, Sternberg (1999) describes three kinds of thinking—*analytical, creative,* and *practical*—that enable learners to think in ways characteristic of experts in a variety of disciplines. Learners use *creative* thinking to generate ideas, *analytical* thinking to evaluate those ideas, and *practical* thinking to implement the ideas and convince others of their value.

4. See Ballman, 1996, for a "Model Five-Day Communicative Lesson Plan."

5. As of this writing, several studies that have compared block vs. traditional scheduling have found no significant differences between the two in terms of their effect on foreign language learning; see Wallinger, 2000; Lapkin, Harley, and Hart, 1997; *ACTFL Professional Issues Report,* 1996.

CHAPTER 4

Connecting Language Learning to the Elementary School Curriculum

In this chapter, you will learn about:

- role of age in language acquisition
- characteristics of elementary school learners
- mythic stage of development
- program models: FLES, FLEX, immersion
- content-based/content-related (content-enriched) FLES
- thematic planning webs
- content-obligatory/content-compatible language
- graphic organizers

- semantic maps
- Venn diagrams
- Total Physical Response
- storytelling
- language experience chart approach
- story maps
- learning centers
- cooperative learning
- global units
- performance assessment strategies
- Connections Goal area

Teach and Reflect: Designing a Content-Based Elementary School Lesson; Developing a Storytelling Lesson

Discuss and Reflect: Teaching Fourth-Grade Content in French; Implementing an Elementary School Language Program

CONCEPTUAL ORIENTATION

In recent years, increasing attention has been given to introducing language instruction to students in the elementary grades. An early start provides increased time for learning and the opportunity to attain a functional level of language proficiency (Carroll, 1975). Much of the research in early language learning has focused on the outcomes of early language learning as compared to those of later language learning. This continues to be a key area of investigation as we seek to provide language learning experiences at optimal times during learners' cognitive and social development. It is important to note that, until recently, the vast majority of studies in early language acquisition had been done in immersion settings or with immigrant children arriving in the United States at a young age. As you will see later, only since the mid-1990s have we examined the performance of younger language learners in elementary school foreign language classrooms.[1]

In this chapter, you will encounter the following terms that relate to language programs in the elementary/middle school:

- *FLES*: Foreign Language in the Elementary School
- *FLEX*: Foreign Language Exploratory or Experience

These program models will be described later in the chapter.

 An early start provides increased time for learning and the opportunity to attain a functional level of language proficiency. ■

An Optimum Age for Language Acquisition?

The Factor of Age

Much of the research in early language acquisition has examined the same question: Is there a *critical* (or *sensitive*) period for language acquisition, "a time in human development when the brain is predisposed for success in language learning"? (Lightbown & Spada, 2003, p. 60). According to the Critical Period Hypothesis, neuropsychological functioning of the brain in the early childhood years may facilitate first- or second-language acquisition up until the time of puberty or even earlier. Studies in neuropsychology claim that the brain of a younger learner is malleable and is shaped by its own activity, while the brain of an older learner is stable and is not as equipped to reorganize itself. Therefore, "the old brain encountering a new task must make do with the brain structure that has already been set" (Hoff-Ginsberg, 1998, p. 35). In this view, as one matures, more of the brain is used for new functions, and there is less uncommitted capacity to access. One of the claims of the Critical Period Hypothesis that has been widely corroborated in research studies is the role of age in the acquisition of pronunciation and "accent." The work of Scovel (1999) and others (Long, 1990; Thompson, 1991) has confirmed that language learners who begin as children are able to achieve a more native-like accent than those who begin as adolescents or adults. The critical age for pronunciation has been identified as being between six years (Long, 1990) and ten years (Thompson, 1991).

However, the research has called into debate claims that age has a significant effect on aspects of language acquisition other than pronunciation. Marinova-Todd, Marshall, and Snow (2000) criticize the research that supports the Critical Age Hypothesis. They claim that:

- people have misinterpreted the success of children in second language study to mean that younger children have a higher rate of success than older learners;
- results of brain study research have been inaccurately used to justify poorer performance of older language learners; and
- too much emphasis has been placed on unsuccessful adult second language learners while older learners who do attain a native-like second language proficiency have been ignored.

Beyond the issue of a critical period for pronunciation, the research seems to support the notion of multiple "critical (or sensitive) periods" for other aspects of language, particularly within informal learning environments:

- Competency in Syntax/Grammar: Evidence indicates that children may also be more likely to acquire a higher level of competence in syntax, morphology, and grammar than older learners (Harley & Wang, 1997; Johnson & Newport, 1989).

The critical age for syntactical/grammatical accuracy is likely to be later than for pronunciation—around age fifteen (Patkowski, 1990). Adult learners, however, may reach native levels of grammatical accuracy in speech and writing (Ellis, 1994).

■ Language Proficiency: Evidence indicates that younger learners may reach higher levels of functional proficiency than those who begin language learning at a later age. Cummins (1981a) found that younger learners perform better on communicative tasks measuring interpersonal skills such as oral fluency and phonology. Evidence indicates that younger learners may make more uniform gains as a group than older learners do (Tucker, Donato, & Antonek, 1996).

■ Rate of Language Acquisition: Adult language learners may have a greater advantage than younger learners where the rate of acquisition of language is concerned. Several studies have revealed that older learners may acquire language faster and make more rapid progress than younger learners (Krashen, Long, & Scarcella, 1979; Snow & Hoefnagel-Höhle, 1978). This phenomenon is probably due to the fact that older learners experience more negotiation of meaning and possess more fully developed cognitive skills, which equip them for the language learning task (Ellis, 1994).

Benefits of An Early Start

There may be other reasons to justify an early start to language learning that transcend the issue of age. Studies of bilingualism and cognition reveal that children who begin to study a second language in the early years reap cognitive, academic, and attitudinal benefits (Robinson, 1998). As supported by Vygotsky's theory of language as a mediator that guides thought and shapes social development (see Chapter 1), bilingual children develop a diversified set of abilities as they work to perceive, process, store, and recall information (Lapkin, Swain, & Shapson, 1990; Vygotsky, 1962). Accordingly, evidence indicates that immersion students perform better than their nonimmersion counterparts in metacognitive processing, analysis, synthesis, and evaluation (Foster & Reeves, 1989). It has also been found that children who have studied a foreign language score higher on standardized tests and tests of basic skills in English, math, and social studies than those who have not experienced language study (Rosenbusch, 1995; Rafferty, 1986).

Additionally, according to Lambert and Klineberg (1967), the age of ten seems to be a crucial time in developing attitudes toward nations and groups perceived as "other." Children who are ten years of age appear to be more open toward people who are different from themselves than are fourteen-year-olds. Since they are in the process of proceeding from egocentricity to reciprocity, they are open to new information introduced during this time (Lambert & Klineberg; c.f. Robinson, 1998). Children between the ages of seven and twelve also demonstrate role-taking ability and seem to be the most open to learning about people from other cultures (Muuss, 1982). This research, most of which has been conducted with immersion students, confirms various benefits of language study for younger learners that include a heightened level of oral proficiency, more complex cognitive processing, higher performance on standardized tests and tests of basic skills, and a greater openness to other cultures.

Until recently, there have been few empirical studies that have investigated the specific accomplishments of students in a traditional FLES setting that would serve to shed light on the possible benefits of an early start to language learning. Donato, Tucker, Wudthayagorn, and Igarashi (2000) reported on a longitudinal study of program ambiance and learner achievement in early language learning. The study tracked progress of North American students who studied Japanese for five or six consecutive years (i.e., since kindergarten) in a FLES program by means of fifteen-minute daily lessons, five days per week.[2]

The measures that were administered included (1) student language and culture questionnaires; (2) parent, teacher, and administrator attitude surveys; (3) individual prochievement[3] oral interviews with the children, using an adaptation of the ACTFL Oral Proficiency Interview and proficiency rating scale, with ratings of these oral samples and classroom performance according to the criteria of comprehension, fluency, vocabulary, pronunciation, and grammar; (4) a student end-of-year self-assessment; and (5) weekly observations of classes for analysis. At the mid-point in this study (after the third year of Japanese study), results indicated that children in grades 3–5 performed better than those in K–2 in comprehension, fluency, vocabulary, and grammar, but not in pronunciation, which supports previous research findings dealing with the effect of age on development of pronunciation. Of importance is that there was less variability among scores in the K–2 group; that is, the older learners exhibited a wider range of abilities, while the younger children made more uniform progress overall. At the end of both the first and second years of instruction, children scored highest in pronunciation and lowest in grammar.

In the second phase of the study (after five or six years of Japanese study), findings revealed that students who had been in the program longer expressed more positive attitudes about learning Japanese, students with more positive attitudes were able to assess themselves more positively (i.e., they assessed themselves in terms of what they *could* do and their assessments were accurate), and students with positive self-assessments also performed better on the oral interview. Thus "time on task, attitude, and self-assessment relate closely to individual achievement" (Donato, Tucker, Wudthayagorn, & Igarashi, 2000, p. 386). The study also showed that students' oral proficiency had progressed over the six-year period, and that learners require a good deal of time on task to progress through the various stages of proficiency.

This longitudinal study revealed that learners progressed in their language development in a differentiated manner; that is, some children made more progress in fluency, some more in vocabulary, and others more in pronunciation. Thus language acquisition did not develop in exactly the same way for all young learners (Donato, Antonek, & Tucker, 1996). This same finding was echoed in a study that charted the proficiency-based achievement of fourth graders enrolled in a Spanish FLES program (Montás, 2003). These studies provide further support to the claim that young language learners demonstrate differentiated achievement—that is, they progress in varied ways and at different rates.

Early language study also enables learners to begin literacy development in foreign language in the early grades. The fourth grade Spanish students in the study described by Montás (2003) made significant gains in their ability to interpret written Spanish. The Japanese study documented by Donato et al. (2000) revealed that middle school students of Japanese showed signs of emerging literacy skills through their sensitivity to the meanings and shapes of *kanji* characters (Chinen, Donato, Igarashi, & Tucker, 2003). Furthermore, this study found evidence that elementary school language learners are able to go beyond literal comprehension and interpret printed texts; they are able to anticipate what is coming next in a story, they are willing to hypothesize about what is happening or may happen, and they are often eager to share their opinions of what the story's message might be (R. Donato, personal communication, February 25, 2004).

The role of attitude and language learning in FLES programs was also examined in a study that compared attitudinal differences between K–5 FLES students and their peers who were not exposed to language learning (Kennedy, Nelson, Odell, & Austin, 2000). Results revealed that the FLES group had significantly more positive attitudes toward school, beliefs about being able to learn a foreign language, motivation for learning a second language, foreign people and cultures, and self-confidence. The researchers concluded that FLES programs motivate students to participate, persist, and succeed in second language study.

The results obtained through all of these empirical studies reveal the following about the effects of early language learning experiences in traditional classroom settings: (1) elementary school language learners make significant gains in pronunciation; (2) children in grades K–6 are able to demonstrate notable progress in developing oral proficiency over a six-year period of instruction; (3) since younger learners can generally keep up with older learners in the language learning process, being older may not be a distinct advantage for learning a language; (4) some evidence suggests that an early start in language learning may result in more uniform gains for the majority of learners, although this remains to be researched further by means of additional longitudinal studies; (5) young learners generally form a positive attitude toward language study, which may affect their ability to self-assess accurately and perform successfully in the target language; (6) literacy can be introduced from the beginning of language instruction and young learners demonstrate gains in this area; (7) young learners demonstrate progress in language acquisition in differentiated ways; and (8) young learners require significant time on task to show progress in moving up the proficiency scale (Donato et al., 2000; Donato, Antonek, & Tucker, 1994, 1996; Tucker, Donato, & Antonek, 1996). This last finding is especially significant in terms of understanding that language acquisition takes a great deal of time and that learners' language develops in varied ways. However, as we will see in a later section in this chapter, time alone is not sufficient to develop language proficiency in extended sequences of instruction; instructional approaches must also maintain the interest and motivation of students (Chinen et al., 2003).

The Elementary School Learner

Curtain and Dahlberg (2004) defined the following key characteristics of elementary and middle school learners:

- Preschool students (ages 2–4): absorb languages effortlessly and imitate speech sounds well; are self-centered and do not work well in groups; respond best to activities relating to their own interests; have a short attention span; respond best to concrete experiences and to large-motor involvement.
- Primary students (ages 5–7; kindergarten, grades 1 and 2): learn best through concrete experiences and immediate goals; are imaginative and respond well to stories of fantasy and dramatic play; learn through oral language and can develop solid oral skills, pronunciation, and intonation when they have a good model; learn well through dramatic play, role play, and use of stories; have a short attention span and require large-muscle activity; need structured and specific directions and regular routines.
- Intermediate students (ages 8–10; grades 3–5): are at their peak for being open to people different from themselves; benefit from a global emphasis in language study; begin to understand cause and effect; work well in groups; continue to need concrete learning experiences; often dislike working with classmates of the opposite sex; learn well from imagination and stories that feature binary opposites (e.g., good vs. evil) and real-life heroes and heroines.
- Early adolescent students (ages 11–14; grades 6–8): experience more dramatic developmental changes than at any other time in life; reach a cognitive plateau for a time; have multiplying and rapidly changing interests; feel a need to assert their independence, develop their own self-image, and become members of a peer group; benefit from the encouragement of positive relationships and a positive self-image; respond well to opportunities to learn about subjects of interest to them and to learning experiences with a strong affective component (pp. 16–20).

What implications for instruction are suggested by the characteristics of elementary and middle-school learners?

Egan (1979) described the "mythic" stage of development in which children ages four/five to nine/ten make sense of the world by responding in terms of emotional categories, such as love, hate, fear, and joy, and morals, such as good or bad. They want to know how to *feel* about whatever they are learning, and they perceive the world as feeling and thinking like the child. In order to plan effective learning experiences for children in the mythic stage, Egan suggests experiences that enable students (1) to interpret what they are learning in terms of their emotions and broad moral categories; (2) initially to build new information in terms of contrasting qualities, such as big/little and good/bad; and (3) to illustrate clear, unambiguous meaning, such as good or evil. Since children in the mythic stage are open to imagination and make-believe, Egan suggests the story form as the most powerful vehicle for instruction. The use of this technique will be discussed later in the chapter.

Children in the mythic stage (ages four/five to nine/ten) make sense of the world by responding in terms of emotional categories, such as love, hate, fear, and joy, and morals, such as good or bad.

In sum, it is important for language teachers to be familiar with the characteristics of young learners so that they are equipped to plan instruction that maximizes the learning potential of these learners and addresses their cognitive and social needs.

Program Models

FLES, FLEX, and Immersion Models

As school districts across the nation examine ways to expand language programs by introducing instruction at the elementary school level, they are faced with the need to choose from several different program models. There are three basic program models for early foreign language learning: FLES,[4] FLEX, and immersion. Figure 4.1 presents the types of elementary school foreign language programs and the goals and percent of class time spent in the foreign language per week.

The term *FLES* is sometimes used to describe all programs at the elementary school level for Languages Other Than English (LOTE). However, FLES usually describes an elementary school language program that is taught three to five times per week for class periods of twenty minutes to an hour or more, the goals of which are:

- to develop functional proficiency in the second language (not as high as in immersion programs);
- to provide a meaningful context for teaching listening and speaking, with some reading and writing; and
- to build understanding and appreciation of the target cultures (Curtain & Dahlberg, 2004, pp. 423–424).

The following are the minimum criteria for a FLES program (Rosenbusch, 1992a):

- A FLES program is a presecondary program that is articulated vertically throughout the entire program sequence.

FIGURE 4.1 Elementary School Foreign Language Program Goals

Programs That Are Continuous • Cumulative • Sequential • Proficiency-Oriented • That Are Part of an Integrated K–12 Sequence

Program Type	Percent of Class Time Spent in FL per Week	Goals
Total Immersion Grades K–6	50–100% (Time is spent learning *subject matter* taught in FL: language learning *per se* incorporated as necessary throughout curriculum)	To become functionally proficient in the new language To master subject content taught in the foreign language To acquire an understanding of and appreciation for other cultures
Two-Way Immersion Grades K–6 *Also called Two-Way Bilingual, Dual Language and Developmental Bilingual Education*	at least 50% (Time is spent learning *subject matter* taught in FL: language learning *per se* incorporated as necessary throughout curriculum) Student population is both native speakers of English and of the target language	To become functionally proficient in the language that is new to the student To master subject content taught in the new language To acquire an understanding of and appreciation for other cultures
Partial Immersion Grades K–6	approx 50% (Time is spent learning *subject matter* taught in FL: language learning *per se* incorporated as necessary throughout curriculum)	To become functionally proficient in the new language (although to a lesser extent than is possible in total immersion) To master subject content taught in the foreign language To acquire as understanding of and appreciation for other cultures
Content-Based FLES Grades K–6	15–50% (More scheduled time than FLES, less than partial immersion.) Time is spent learning language *per se* as well as subject matter to the FL	To acquire proficiency in listening, speaking, reading, and writing the new language To use subject content as a vehicle for acquiring foreign language skills To acquire an understanding of and appreciation for other cultures
FLES Grades K–6	5–15% (minimum 30–50 minutes per class, at least 3–5 days per week) Time is spent learning language *per se;* optical language curriculum integrates language, subject matter, and culture.	To acquire proficiency in listening and speaking (degree of proficiency varies with the program) To acquire an understanding of and appreciation for other cultures To acquire some proficiency in reading and writing (emphasis varies with the program)

(Continued)

FIGURE 4.1 (Continued)

**Non-Continuous Programs
Not Usually Part of an Integrated K–12 Sequence**

Program Type	Percent of Class Time Spent in FL per Week	Goals
Exploratory Grades K–6 Frequent and regular sessions over a short period of time -OR- Short and/or infrequent sessions over an extended period of time	1–5% (Time spent sampling one or more languages and/or learning *about* language—sometimes taught mostly in English)	To develop an interest in new languages for future language study To learn basic words and phrases in one or more new languages To develop careful listening skills To develop cultural awareness To develop linguistic awareness

Source: Rhodes, 1985; adapted and revised by Curtain & Dahlberg, 1992. Cf. Curtain & Dahlberg, 2004, pp. 420–421.

- In a FLES program, a student studies a single language throughout the program sequence. This does not imply that only one language is offered throughout the school district.
- A FLES program results in language proficiency outcomes that involve the production and comprehension of meaningful messages in a communicative setting.
- Teachers in a FLES program have both language proficiency and the professional knowledge and skills necessary for effective foreign language instruction at the elementary school level.
- Classes meet within the school day, throughout the entire school year (cf. Curtain & Dahlberg, 2004, p. 423).

As you learned in Chapter 3, FLES programs can be either *content-based,* in which the foreign language teacher teaches certain parts of the regular elementary school curriculum through the foreign language, or *content-related* (also called *content-enriched*), in which the foreign language teacher uses concepts from the regular elementary school curriculum to enrich the language program with academic content (Curtain & Dahlberg, 2004).

 There are three basic program models for early foreign language learning: FLES, FLEX, and immersion.

FLEX programs are designed to introduce learners to one or several languages and cultures at either the elementary or middle school levels. A minimal amount of instruction is provided, as little as once a week, for six to nine weeks a year (Hoch, 1998). Most FLEX programs address the following goals:

- introduction to language learning
- awareness and appreciation of foreign culture
- appreciation of the value of communicating in another language
- enhanced understanding of English
- motivation to further language study (Curtain & Dahlberg, 2004, p. 426).

You will learn more about exploratory programs in Chapter 5.

In immersion programs, the foreign language is the vehicle for teaching academic content in the regular elementary school curriculum (e.g., mathematics, science, art) rather than the subject of instruction itself. In total immersion, all instruction is conducted in the foreign language; students learn to read in the foreign language first, then in English. In partial immersion programs, students receive instruction in the foreign language for up to fifty percent of the school day; reading and language arts are taught in English (Hoch, 1998). Curtain and Dahlberg (2004) identified the following goals common to immersion programs:

- functional proficiency in the second language, with children able to communicate in the second language on topics appropriate to their age level
- mastery of subject content material of the school district curriculum
- cross-cultural understanding
- achievement in English language arts comparable to or surpassing that of students in English-only programs (p. 421).

thandbook.heinle.com

In immersion teaching, although language is simplified, it is not grammatically sequenced. Language reflects the themes and concepts of the elementary curriculum and the communicative and conceptual needs of the students. Reading instruction is based on previously mastered oral language. See Appendix 4.1 (see the *Teacher's Handbook* Web site) for a description of total or full immersion, partial immersion, early immersion, late immersion, continuing immersion, and two-way immersion programs.

In immersion programs, the foreign language is the vehicle for teaching academic content in the regular elementary school curriculum rather than the subject of instruction itself.

Other Instructional Models

Other instructional models that have gained increasing attention are *media-based programs* and *distance learning*, which provide alternatives to the programs described above, particularly in the face of challenges such as budgetary considerations or difficulty in finding teachers. *Media-based programs* feature the use of a particular type of media, such as videotape, interactive television, CDs, audiotapes, or computers, with follow-up by the classroom teacher or traveling specialist. The key to the success of these programs is the quality of the follow-up, since in the past programs that have not been staffed by a qualified teacher have not produced effective results (Curtain & Dahlberg, 2004). Another instructional model uses interactive television as a vehicle for *distance learning*, where the language teacher is located at a base site with a group of students, and one or more groups of students are located at a remote site or sites. Communication occurs by means of interactive teleconferences via computer, audio, or video networks, offering opportunities for interaction between the learner and instructor (Moore & Thompson, 1997).

Although few empirical studies have been conducted in the area of distance learning, the existing research points to the possibility that students in distance learning programs may achieve as well as or even better than those taking traditional courses (Martin & Rainey, 1993). In one study examining the effectiveness of videoconferencing technology in a K–3 Spanish program, students at the remote site performed higher on achievement tests than students at the base site (Glisan, Dudt, & Howe, 1998). The researchers attribute this difference to the role of the facilitators at the remote site and the review sessions that they voluntarily conducted between class sessions. An additional interesting finding of this study was that sixty-five percent of the students who participated in this project reported having used Spanish

thandbook.heinle.com

outside the classroom, either with friends or to teach family members Spanish words (Glisan, et al.). This illustrates the enthusiasm of elementary school learners toward language study and may lend further support for an early start to language learning. Although much more research is needed in this area, distance learning may hold promise for the future as one way for school districts to provide language learning opportunities to *all* students. Appendix 4.2 (Web site) presents the guidelines for distance learning programs published by the National Council of State Supervisors of Foreign Languages (NCSSFL, 2002).

Factors to Consider When Selecting a Program Model

Selecting a program model may be based on one or more of the following factors (adapted from Hoch, 1998):

1. Desired level of proficiency: As Curtain and Dahlberg (2004) state, "Language proficiency outcomes are directly proportional to the amount of time spent by students in meaningful communication in the target language. The more time students spend working communicatively with the target language, under the guidance of a skilled and fluent teacher, the greater will be the level of language proficiency that they acquire" (p. 419). Immersion programs enable students to attain the greatest amount of proficiency over time, FLES programs lead to some functional proficiency depending on the amount of instructional time, and FLEX programs are not designed with functional proficiency goals in mind because of the minimal amount of instructional time.

2. Length of sequence: Immersion programs require a commitment by the school district to invest in an uninterrupted sequence of language courses. Successful FLES programs are part of a sequential, well-articulated program that continues beyond the elementary grades to enable students to build on and strengthen the skills they developed earlier. There is a caveat with long-term sequences of instruction, however: Instructional strategies and learning experiences must be varied from year to year, or else students may lose interest in the face of language experiences that become routinized and dull (Chinen, Donato, Igarashi, & Tucker, 2003). If school districts are unable to invest in long sequences of study, the FLEX model may be the best option as it offers a language experience without the same level of commitment in terms of sequence of courses.

3. Student population: FLES and FLEX models are generally chosen by districts that seek to provide language instruction to all children, as more students can be taught with fewer foreign language teachers. Immersion models require more resources and specialized language personnel. Immersion programs may not be desired by parents who are not convinced that their children can learn as much subject content in a second language as in their own.

4. Availability of resources: In order to be effective, all of the program models require qualified foreign language teachers. According to Met. "Immersion requires teachers who are elementary trained and experienced in the grade level to be taught, who have near native proficiency in oral and written forms of the language, and who have a knowledge of the culture" (1993, p. 3). Trained immersion teachers are usually not plentiful, and districts may need to hire teachers from other countries and must be willing to provide ongoing in-service training. In addition, immersion programs often require additional tasks, including accurately assessing target language skills of prospective teachers, developing and identifying effective textbooks and materials, and designing appropriate in-service education (Fortune & Jorstad, 1996). FLES programs require specialists with functional proficiency in the target language, an understanding of the nature of first- and second-language acquisition, and the ability to create their own instructional materials.

5. Community and parental support: For immersion programs to be successful, the parents and community must believe in the possibility that students can learn skills and subject content in a second language. In FLES programs, it is important that the regular classroom teachers view language as an important component of the curriculum rather than as a frill. Faculty, parents, and administrators need to provide feedback about scheduling so that they are not concerned about time for language being "taken away" from the other subject areas. Although FLEX programs may not require the same degree of community support, it is necessary for everyone to acknowledge their educational value. As indicated in the FLES study by Donato, Tucker, Wudthayagorn, and Igarashi (2000), parental attitudes may not always be in consonance with the goals of an early language program. In their study, parents reported that their top two goals for their children's study of Japanese were to enjoy language learning and acquire cultural knowledge, with the development of fluency not a high priority.

An issue that often poses a challenge is deciding which language(s) to offer in an early language program. Factors that should be taken into consideration include community interest, which can be ascertained by means of a survey; availability of materials and staff; and potential for articulation and continuation of the language at higher levels of instruction (Curtain & Dahlberg, 2004). Presently it is desirable to introduce into the elementary school the less commonly taught languages, such as Arabic, Chinese, Japanese, and Russian, in view of their critical importance to our national agenda (Curtain & Dahlberg, 2004).

Additional factors that play a role in program selection and design are budgetary issues, professional development of teachers, scheduling of language classes, integration of the language program into the total school curriculum, program assessment, and building of public relations. In their description of model early language programs, Gilzow and Branaman (2000) identified the following ten critical program elements: (1) implementation of national standards into the curriculum; (2) a focus on content, (3) articulation and alignment across grade and language levels; (4) use of a variety of communicative, interactive, and age-appropriate teaching methods; (5) use of technology to enhance instruction; (6) program evaluation; (7) interesting and useful student assessment strategies; (8) support from grant funding; (9) professional development opportunities for teachers; and (10) advocacy within the community (cf. Curtain & Dahlberg, 2004, p. 461).

FLES Programs of the Past and Present

While elementary school language programs are being developed at an increasing rate, the profession is trying to avoid the problems experienced by the FLES programs of the 1960s. The heyday of audiolingualism brought with it a burst of enthusiasm, albeit short-lived, for elementary school language instruction. Unfortunately, despite government funding and public support, the new elementary school programs declined rapidly after 1964. Rosenbusch (1995) cites seven primary reasons for the demise of the FLES programs of the 1960s:

1. FLES teachers often lacked linguistic proficiency and skill in teaching young children. In 1961, a survey by Alkonis and Brophy indicated that in sixty-two elementary school language programs, the majority of teachers had no foreign language background.
2. FLES programs were begun quickly without sufficient coordination and planning.
3. Program goals were unrealistic or inappropriate and promised too much linguistic fluency in too short a time.
4. Few programs had a coordinator to provide supervision and articulation across levels.

5. FLES programs featured inappropriate methodologies as they relied on memorization and pattern drills, often with little real communication.
6. Programs lacked adequate instructional materials.
7. Many schools made no attempt to assess student progress (pp. 2–3).

Caveats for Present and Future FLES Programs

The programs of today and tomorrow must be careful not to repeat the mistakes of the past. On the positive side, the revolution in language teaching over more than two decades has affirmed the importance of communicative language teaching. FLES programs are being planned and organized to match the age of the learners. New programs are emphasizing content-based learning that provides an integrated place for language in the elementary school curriculum. Culture and global connections are becoming integral components of the foreign language curriculum. New teacher training programs are enabling elementary school teachers to acquire proficiency in a foreign language and expertise in integrating language instruction into their curricula. (See Appendix 4.3 for an observation guide to assess the effectiveness of the elementary and middle school foreign language teacher, and Appendix 4.4 on the Web site for a guide to assess the effectiveness of the immersion teacher.) More effective teaching materials that contextualize language instruction continue to appear on the market.

thandbook.heinle.com

Program developers must be careful to set realistic expectations of what students are able to achieve as a result of elementary school language study. Clearly much more research is needed in this area. The FLES study reported on by Montás (2003) illustrates the effectiveness of using a meaningful, context-centered curriculum in order to develop learners' language proficiency, especially when teaching with limited instructional time. However, the study of a Japanese FLES program by Donato et al. (2000) found that after five or six years of consecutive years of language study, students' proficiency was still rated in the novice level. Students rarely demonstrated the ability to engage in unplanned, interpersonal communication, they were unable to narrate stories orally, and they were unable to produce language beyond isolated words and sentences (Donato, Tucker, Wudthayagorn, & Igarashi, 2000).

These findings echo a concern that has arisen in other investigations, which is that early language learners, whether in FLES or immersion programs, may not become independent language users (Igarashi, 1997). Current research seems to point to the possibility that (1) contextualization and culture do not necessarily lead to language creativity and (2) interaction between students and teachers does not automatically promote interpersonal communication skills and negotiation of meaning (Donato, Tucker, Wudthayagorn, & Igarashi, 2000, p. 388). These claims imply that teachers must carefully design opportunities for learners to create with the language and communicate with one another within the context of the lesson or thematic unit.

Such claims and implications are significant as we consider the development of FLES programs in the future because:

1. They lend support for extended sequences of instruction given the fact that children advance slowly through novice performance and only reach intermediate levels after a significant period of time following the start of language study.
2. They illustrate the key role of instructional practices in influencing what children can and cannot do with the foreign language. If we want children to speak in sentences, engage in interpersonal communication, and narrate stories, then teachers must provide these types of opportunities in class and must assess students' progress in achieving these skills over time.

3. They stress the benefits of a literacy-rich classroom environment in which learners are engaged in exploring printed materials and in interpreting them.
4. They indicate an important need for additional research by means of longitudinal studies of learners' accomplishments in elementary school programs.

Strategies for Teaching Language to Elementary School Learners

Elementary school foreign language instruction involves careful planning and the use of a wide variety of approaches and techniques designed to involve students actively in language use. In the sections that follow, you will be introduced to several instructional strategies within the *SFLL* framework that are considered to be key in teaching languages to children. Since space permits the description of only a few of the most salient techniques, you may find it helpful to consult one or more of the references listed at the end of this chapter in order to explore other strategies in greater detail. Note that all of these techniques can be adapted and used effectively in secondary classrooms as well. Subsequent chapters will also address implications for teaching at the elementary school level as they relate to the topics presented in those chapters.

It is important to note the pivotal role of *context* and *attention to integration of meaning* in all activities that take place in the elementary school setting. As Curtain & Dahlberg (2004) point out, FLES programs have historically had (1) an emphasis on recitation (lists; labels; memorized patterns and dialogues, usually cued by a teacher question; songs, often not integrated into the rest of the language curriculum; games, used for a change of pace or for grammar practice; rhymes and poems chosen at random; and reading for recitation or reading aloud), and (2) pervasive use of English for discipline, giving directions, clarifying the target language, checking comprehension, and teaching culture (p. 26). These types of strategies strip language of meaning, affect students' attitudes about language learning in a negative way, and contribute to the deterioration of FLES programs.

Thematic Unit and Lesson Planning

The focus of planning for elementary school foreign language instruction is usually the *thematic unit*, to which you were introduced in Chapter 3. Curtain and Dahlberg (2004) emphasize that at the elementary school level, thematic planning (1) makes instruction more comprehensible, because the theme creates a meaningful context; (2) changes the instructional focus from the language itself to the use of language to achieve meaningful goals; (3) provides a rich context for standards-based instruction; (4) offers a natural setting for narrative structure and task-based organization of content; (5) involves students in real language use in a variety of situations, modes, and text types; (6) involves activities or tasks that engage learners in complex thinking and more sophisticated use of language; (7) avoids the use of isolated exercises with grammatical structures, practiced out of context, that tend to fragment language at the word or sentence level and neglect the discourse level; and (8) connects content, language, and culture goals to a "big idea" (pp. 131–133). At the center of this framework for curriculum development is the *thematic center*, which includes the theme, targeted standards, broad unit outcomes, and a culminating performance assessment, as illustrated in Figure 4.2 (Pesola, 1995). This framework reflects the principles of backward curricular design described in Chapter 3.

FIGURE 4.2 A Framework for Curriculum Development for FLES Programs

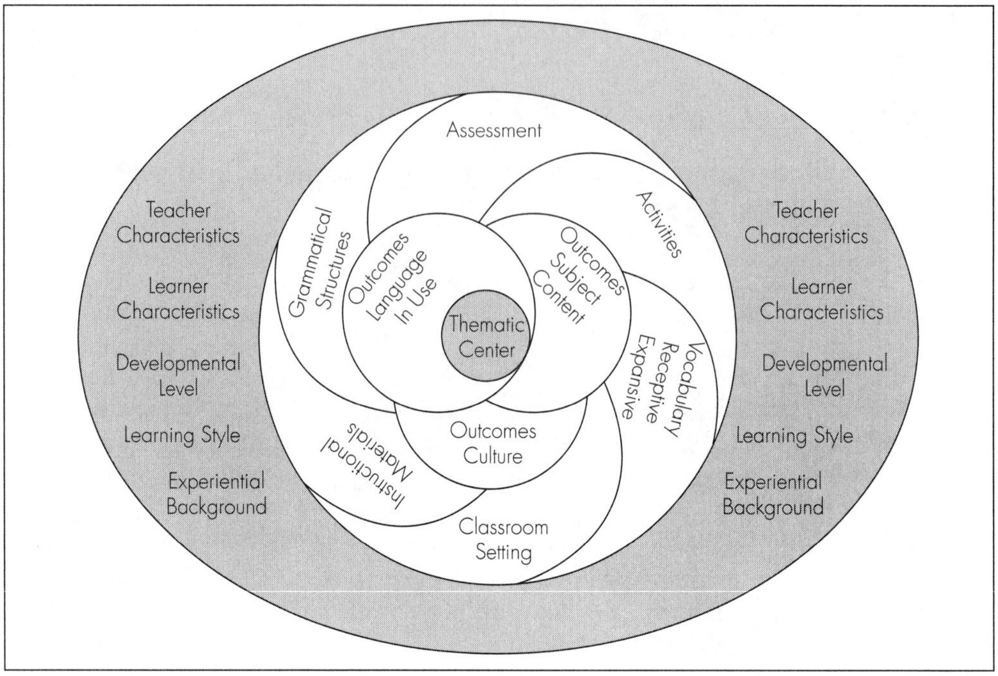

Source: Pesola, 1995; cf. Curtain & Dahlberg, 2004, p. 135.

Selection of a thematic center is based on the interests of the learners and teacher, relationship to curricular goals, potential for integration with culture, and potential for developing appropriate language functions and modes of communication. The focus of the thematic center could be a topic from the general school curriculum or one taken from the culture or literature of the target language; a "generative" theme around a question such as "How do we grow?"; a story or book; a work of art, or an artist; or music, or a composer (Curtain & Dahlberg, 2004). The topic might be a broad one (e.g., "the environment") that lasts for several weeks or might be developed into a more focused theme (e.g., a single story) that would last for a week. Once a topic or theme has been selected, the teacher might engage in a brainstorming process designed to develop the theme into meaningful categories and extend it in various directions (Pappas, Kiefer, & Levstik, 1990). Useful in this brainstorming is a *thematic planning web*, a cognitive organizer that illustrates a visual representation of concepts and their relationships (see Appendix 4.5 for an example). It is important to note that not every element in the web may be included in the unit, and the information organized in the web may be included in future planning. The selected ideas from the planning web can then be used to design the unit plan and lessons plans according to the models presented in Chapter 3.

Content-Based Instruction

In Chapter 3, you learned about the general concept of content-based instruction (CBI). CBI is, of course, an integral component of immersion instruction. However, content-based lessons can also be designed in FLES or content-related (content-enriched) FLES programs.

These lessons provide the means for contextualizing instruction and for integrating foreign language and elementary subject-content. Met (1999) emphasizes that the "content" in content-based programs "represents material that is cognitively engaging and demanding for the learner, and it is material that extends beyond the target language or target culture" (p. 150). Integrating CBI into language instruction requires planning and considerations about the nature of subject-content tasks that learners are asked to perform.

According to Cummins (1981b), communicative activities should be developed keeping in mind the *degree of contextual support* that is available as well as the *degree of cognitive involvement*, or the amount of information a learner must process simultaneously in order to complete a task. *Context-embedded language* is supported by a range of clues (eg., illustrations, physical gestures, realia), while *context-reduced language* offers little extra support, which means that learners must rely on the language itself for meaning (e.g., telephone conversations, explanations without diagrams or examples). Figure 4.3 illustrates the way in which language/subject-content tasks can be classified into four categories according to the degree of contextual support provided and cognitive involvement required.

One implication of Cummins' classification is that language teachers might make new concepts less language dependent by incorporating more visuals and realia, meaningful contexts, hands-on learning, vivid examples and analogies, learners' background knowledge and past experiences, and rephrasing and natural repetition. Another implication is that language tasks can be made more cognitively engaging by integrating language and concepts in the general school curriculum; involving students in higher-order thinking skills such as classifying, categorizing, predicting, comparing, imagining, evaluating, debating, etc., even when the language itself might be simple; and providing opportunities for learners to practice new language in problem-solving situations, rather than relying on imitation and rote learning (Curtain & Dahlberg, 2004).

FIGURE 4.3 Range of Contextual Support and Degree of Cognitive Involvement in Communicative Activities

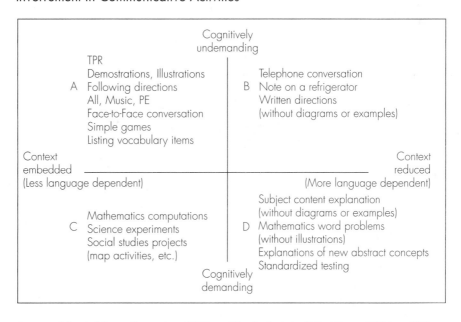

Source: Adapted from Cummins, 2000, p. 68; cf. Curtain & Dahlberg, 2004, p. 259.

The "content" in content-based programs "represents material that is cognitively engaging and demanding for the learner, and it is material that extends beyond the target language or target culture."

The following are some steps that the teacher might follow in planning for CBI:

1. Identify possible concepts from the subject-content curriculum. Sources of these concepts include school district curriculum documents, state department of education standards for instruction, the *Standards for Foreign Language Learning in the 21st Century,* and the *ESL Standards for Pre-K-12 Students.*
2. Select concepts that lend themselves to concrete, hands-on learning that is characteristic of the language classroom. A key issue to consider is whether or not the concepts can be taught using the language of learners at a particular level (e.g., novice, intermediate) or whether they require more abstract, sophisticated language.
3. Identify the language needed in terms of both content vocabulary for the subject area and new language necessary for students to understand the lesson. *Content-obligatory language* is the language (concept vocabulary, grammar, language functions) that must be taught in order to teach the subject-content concept. *Content-compatible language* is the language that may be integrated logically into the curriculum concept, although it is not required for comprehension or mastery of the subject-content concept (Lorenz & Met, 1989). In Appendix 4.6, you will find a partial lesson plan for a grade 1 mathematics lesson with these two kinds of objectives illustrated.
4. Locate, adapt, and/or create the instructional materials to be used in the lesson.
5. Create integrated, contextualized, hands-on instructional activities for teaching and practice of the new concept.
6. Provide for multiple opportunities for assessing student progress (adapted by Curtain & Dahlberg, 2004, pp. 269–271).

In sum, content-based instruction offers interesting possibilities for providing students with engaging content that they can explore using the foreign language. It offers ways to teach language as a means of acquiring new information and perspectives instead of as an end in and of itself.

 Content-obligatory language is the language (concept vocabulary, grammar, language functions) that must be taught in order to teach the subject-content concept.

 Content-compatible language is the language that may be integrated logically into the curriculum concept, although it is not required for comprehension or mastery of the subject-content concept.

Helping Students to Organize and Explore Content

Graphic organizers, such as semantic maps and Venn diagrams, are visuals that display words or concepts in categories to illustrate how they relate to one another (Curtain & Dahlberg, 2004). They can be an effective means of helping students organize subject-content topics and concepts. *Semantic maps* depict words or concepts in categories and show how they relate to each other. A key word or question is placed at the center or top of the map; students and teacher create the map together. In this way, students organize what they are learning and are able to see how it fits with the language and information previously learned (Curtain & Dahlberg). Appendices 4.7 and 4.8 illustrate two different types of semantic maps.

thandbook.heinle.com

Venn diagrams can be used for making comparisons and contrasts; they consist of two or more intersecting circles that depict relationships among concepts (see Appendix 4.9 on the Web site).

Graphic organizers are visuals that display words or concepts in categories to illustrate how they relate to one another.

Acquisition of Vocabulary

In Chapter 1, you learned that children acquire vocabulary as a result of attending to large quantities of meaningful input and by interacting with the concrete objects referred to in the input through a process referred to as *binding* (Terrell, 1986). You were also introduced to some ways in which binding can be facilitated in the classroom, such as presenting vocabulary in thematic groups, providing meaningful input, using visuals and objects, and using Total Physical Response (TPR) to actively engage students in connecting the vocabulary they hear to actions they perform or objects that they manipulate.

In TPR (Asher, 1986), the teacher gives a series of oral commands in the target language, and students demonstrate comprehension by responding physically. At first, students imitate the teacher performing the commands; later, they perform the commands without the teacher's assistance. The following is a typical series of commands that the teacher might give early in the language learning experience (these would be given in the target language):

> *Stand up. Sit down. Stand up. Sit down. Stand up. Walk to the door. Stop. Turn around. Walk to the blackboard. Stop. Turn around. Jump up and down! Stop. Turn around. Walk to the door. Stop. Turn around. Walk to your seats. Sit down.*

At first, the teacher performs the commands along with students until they begin to bind the oral command forms to the physical activities; then the teacher gives the commands and students respond without seeing the teacher's physical responses first. Note that the series of commands is repetitive in nature because students need to hear the input multiple times in order for binding to occur. At some point after students have acquired the forms, the teacher may move beyond the comprehension stage by having students produce the commands themselves and asking their classmates to respond physically.

TPR can be used effectively to teach concrete vocabulary words, with the use of oral input and visuals or objects. In addition to physical responses, students can give yes-no answers, choose the correct word, or manipulate visuals while listening to input. For example, the teacher might teach vocabulary for food by showing plastic or real food items, presenting the items one at a time, and providing comprehensible input that also builds on students' background knowledge in the target language, as in the following example (substitute your target language for the English version that appears below):

> Class, we're going to talk about some fruits and vegetables today in preparation for the recipe that we will be making later this week. *[Teacher holds up a shopping bag full of groceries.]* I went shopping early this morning and bought several things for our recipe. What do I have in the bag? Let's see. *[Teacher lifts an object out of the bag.]* Oh, I have here an apple, an apple. What color is the apple? *[A student responds "red."]* Yes, it's red, and delicious, too. Some apples are green but this one is red. Apples are good for our health. How many of you like apples? *[Teacher asks for a show of hands or takes individual responses.]* OK. I usually bring an apple in my lunch once or twice a week. *[Teacher lifts another item out of the bag.]* Class, is this an apple—yes or no? *[Class responds "no."]* No, it's not an apple, but it is a type of fruit. It's an orange. What color is it? *[A student responds "orange."]* Yes, it's orange and the apple is.... *[Class responds "red."]*

Oranges are also good for you; they have a lot of vitamin C. *[Teacher holds the apple in one hand and the orange in the other.]* I like to snack on oranges at home. Point to the apple. Now point to the orange. *[The teacher goes up to several students and has them point to the fruit.]* Which is this, the apple or the orange? *[Students identify the name of the fruit.]* . . .

?   What makes the input comprehensible in this TPR example?   ▬

This type of discussion continues with the remainder of the items in the bag until students have demonstrated some degree of acquisition and the ability to name the items in the target language. During a TPR lesson, it is important for the teacher to present the items one at a time and return to the previous items presented so that students can gradually acquire the words. If the teacher rushes through the presentation without proper "build-up," students will not be able to remember the words.

At the conclusion of the lesson, the teacher might show students the written names of the items so that they can associate the oral language they acquired with the written representations. They might copy the words from the board or overhead projector into their notebooks. It is important that the teacher not show students the written words before or during the TPR lesson so that acquisition of oral language may occur. If students see the words first, they will tend not to acquire the oral forms but rather just read the written forms. Students will pronounce new words more accurately if they acquire them orally first, since they will acquire what they hear—which will minimize the likelihood that they will project their L1 pronunciation onto L2 words that they read.

The teacher might also engage students in the following activities to further facilitate acquisition of the new words:

- numbering drawings of foods according to the order in which the teacher says them
- drawing and labeling their favorite foods
- matching labels of the words to visual representations of the foods
- coloring drawings of the foods according to the teacher's verbal instructions
- playing games that incorporate the food vocabulary
- singing songs that incorporate the food vocabulary
- identifying pictures of the foods in an authentic TL advertisement (with prices)
- making lists of food items that need to be purchased for a party, meal, etc.
- conducting surveys of which foods their classmates like/don't like, eat regularly, etc.
- making posters with labeled drawing of the food pyramid, authentic dishes from the target cultures, etc.

The important point about teaching vocabulary is that, in order for acquisition to occur, students must hear it in meaningful contexts and must actively use it for meaningful purposes.

Interpretive Listening and Reading

At the elementary school level, interpretive listening is used as the vehicle through which students first begin to acquire language. Many studies show the benefits of providing an initial period of instruction in which students listen to input without being forced to respond in the target language, through strategies such as TPR (Postovsky, 1974; Winitz & Reeds, 1973). Such a "comprehension before production" stage allows students to mentally associate input with meaning and instills the self-confidence necessary for producing language (Terrell, 1986). However, younger learners need to move quickly beyond this comprehension stage and begin to produce output within meaningful tasks and contexts.

In Chapter 2, you learned ways to contextualize language instruction by presenting an initial authentic oral or written segment. At the elementary school level, teachers use children's stories within age-appropriate contexts to provide an integrated-skills approach to acquisition. Storytelling can develop interpretive abilities, even at very early stages of acquisition, especially when the story (1) is highly predictable or familiar to children from their native language, (2) is repetitive, (3) lends itself to dramatization and pantomime, and (4) lends itself to use of visuals and realia to illustrate meaning (Curtain & Dahlberg, 2004, p. 63). The teacher tells the story a number of times over an extended period of time (without resorting to English), while also showing pictures and using gestures and mime to demonstrate meaning. After students hear the story numerous times, they are then involved through TPR and acting out story parts. Story mapping may be used to help students recall and visually organize the central theme and main components of a story setting, as well as the problem, characters, events, solution, and ending (Heimlich & Pittelman, 1986). See Appendix 4.10 on the Web site for a sample story map.

thandbook.heinle.com

Children's literature from the countries where the target language is spoken serves as an excellent source for story texts and provides another avenue for integrating culture into the program. In addition to helping students experience culture, authentic literature can serve as the foundation for a whole-language curriculum and appeals to children in Egan's (1979) mythic stage of learning, as described earlier. Pesola (1991) suggests the use of both folktales and contemporary children's literature in the elementary school classroom. Folktales, which present cultural information and describe solutions to human challenges, make effective stories since they come from a culture's oral tradition. Contemporary children's literature lets young students identify with the feelings and moral challenges faced by story characters (Pesola, 1991).[5]

How might Oller's Episode Hypothesis assist a teacher in selecting an appropriate literary text?

Egan (1992 as cited in Curtain & Dahlberg, 2004) suggests teachers use the following framework as they plan to use stories with children in the primary school years:

1. *Identifying importance.* What is most important about this story's topic? Why should it matter to children? How is it affectively engaging?
2. *Finding binary opposites.* What powerful binary opposites best catch the importance of the topic (e.g., sad/happy, good/bad, threatened/secure)?
3. *Organizing content in story form.*
   3.1. What content most dramatically embodies the binary opposites in order to provide access to the topic?
   3.2. What content best articulates the topic into a developing story format?
4. *Conclusion.* What is the best way to resolve the dramatic conflict inherent in these binary opposites? What degree of mediation of these opposites is it appropriate to seek?
5. *Evaluation.* How can one know whether the topic has been understood, whether its importance has been grasped, and whether the content was learned? (Curtain & Dahlberg, 2004, p. 141).

One of the ways in which the transition to reading from hearing a story or attending to other oral input is made is through the use of the *language experience chart approach.* This technique uses previously learned oral language as the basis for practicing reading and writing skills. The context is an experience that is shared by the class, such as a field trip, story, film, or cultural experience. This approach features the following steps: (1) the teacher provides target language input that describes the shared experience, in a top-down fashion as described in Chapter 2; (2) the teacher checks comprehension through TPR and questions requiring one-word and then longer responses; (3) students retell the story or experience with the teacher's help as the teacher writes their account on large "language experience chart" paper (lined paper on an easel); (4) students copy this version into their notebooks; and (5) this permanent record is used for a variety of reading and writing tasks (Allen, 1970; Hall, 1970; Hansen-Krening, 1982).

The language experience chart approach exemplifies the ZPD since it is an activity in which the expert allows novices to set their own learning agendas, and it fosters reciprocal learning in which novices work toward their potential developmental level by interacting with the teacher and more capable peers. The technique has been used with success by both first- and second-language learners (Dixon & Nessel, 1983). It is particularly helpful to poor readers, who benefit from the progression from listening and speaking (while experiencing) to reading and writing.

Another strategy for engaging students in interpretive activities is the use of the *learning center*, a designated area of the classroom that contains materials and directions for a specific learning task, such as a game, an interpretive listening activity, or an interpretive reading task. It may be a desk or group of desks, bulletin board, or computer center, but it always attracts attention because of its bright colors or attractive use of shapes and pictures (Glisan & Fall, 1991). The learning center should be thematically arranged, contain instructions for self-pacing, and allow for a range of student ability and interest levels. Learning centers may be effectively used for both individual and small-group activities and for differentiating instruction; i.e., engaging learners in activities designed to meet their individual learning needs.

Interpersonal Communication: Cooperative Learning

It is important to recall that interpersonal communication is two-way communication while presentational communication is one-way communication to an audience of listeners or readers. The elementary school teacher uses a repertoire of techniques for actively involving children in communicating with one another. Through cooperative learning, in which students interact with one another in pairs and small groups in order to accomplish a task together, opportunities for using the target language are significantly increased. Research on cooperative learning by Johnson and Johnson (1987) suggests that the benefits of group and pair work include higher retention and achievement, development of interpersonal skills and responsibility, and heightened self-esteem and creativity. Cooperative learning is most successful when students depend on one another, participate in face-to-face interaction, take responsibility for the skills being learned by the group, use appropriate social skills (following directions, asking for help, taking turns), and analyze what is working and not working in the group activity. Curtain & Dahlberg (2004) suggest that students assume roles such as the following when participating in a cooperative learning activity:

- *Encourager/Praiser* ensures that group members perform well and stay on task.
- *Manager/Timekeeper/Supervisor/Checker* organizes the group, keeps the group on task, makes sure everyone contributes.
- *Recorder/Secretary* records group answers.
- *Spokesperson/Speaker/Reporter* reports back to the whole class (p. 100).

 Through cooperative learning, students interact with one another in pairs and small groups in order to accomplish a task together. ■

Examples of cooperative learning activities that promote interpersonal communication are paired interviews, information-gap activities, jigsaw activities, and interviews or surveys (see Chapter 8 for explanations of these activities and examples). In planning for cooperative learning tasks, the teacher should consider the following: (1) the source of the message(s) to be exchanged (Is there an information gap or reason for students to want to know the information?); (2) the appropriate target language vocabulary and grammar required to complete the activity; (3) the product that results from the activity and how it will be shared or evaluated; (4) how the language will be guided, controlled, or scaffolded; (5) how partners or group members will take turns; (6) how students will find out whether they have been successful; (7) how the teacher will follow up on the activity in a communicative way; (8) how the activity can be extended for groups that finish early; and (9) the plan for a student who does not have a partner (Curtain & Dahlberg, 2004, pp. 106–108). See Chapter 8 for more information regarding group/pair activities as well as the role of collaboration in cooperative learning. See Curtain & Dahlberg (2004) and Lipton (1998) for numerous examples of cooperative learning activities as well as other strategies used to promote oral interpersonal communication and hands-on learning, such as the use of games, finger plays, puppets, and role play.

Presentational Speaking

Detailed information about presentational speaking and writing is featured in Chapters 8 and 9, together with specific strategies for integrating presentational communication into instruction. An effective avenue for encouraging presentational speaking at the elementary school level is through the performance of skits and dramatic songs. Presentations and performances are often used as culminating activities for a thematic unit. Examples include plays; performances of authentic songs, accompanied by culturally appropriate instruments; small-group presentations of scenes from an authentic story; puppet plays; PowerPoint presentations; short skits; and videotaped productions of "how-to" shows. Student interest in presentations is greatly heightened if students can perform for an audience. Students might perform for other classes, school assemblies, special classroom programs, and parent-teacher organization meetings (Curtain & Dahlberg, 2004, pp. 72–73).

Learning Through Culture

Culture is a key component in a content-based elementary school language program, since it is integrated with all subjects in the curriculum. The next chapter introduces the Cultures goal area of the national standards and presents some strategies for engaging students, including those in elementary school, in exploring the products, practices, and perspectives of the target cultures. Pesola (1991) suggests that students explore cultural perspectives through the study of (1) cultural products such as traditional stories and legends, folk arts, visual arts and artists, musical arts and composers, and realia such as currency, coins, and stamps; and (2) cultural practices such as forms of greeting, use of gestures, recreational activities, home and school life, types of pets and attitudes toward pets, and how children and families move from place to place.

As described earlier in this chapter, the use of authentic literature can be an effective way to introduce many elements of cultural heritage in the classroom. The teaching of thematic units such as "Nutrition" or "Holidays" also provides the opportunity to present visual materials that show certain characteristics of the target culture—photographs, magazine pictures, and realia obtained from the target culture are rich in cultural information. Pesola (1991) suggests the following activities for integrating culture within the elementary school content areas:

- Social Studies: For display create banners or other items that reflect symbols used for the target city; celebrate an important holiday in the target city, preferably one that is not celebrated locally, or at least not celebrated in the same way.

- Mathematics and Science: Apply the concepts of shapes and symmetry to the folk arts and other visual arts from the target culture; use catalogs from the target culture for problem-solving mathematics activities involving budgeting and shopping.
- Art and Music: Replicate authentic crafts from the target culture in classroom art activities; incorporate typical rhythms from the target culture in the development of chants and rhymes to reinforce new vocabulary and concepts (pp. 341–343).

See Pesola (1991) for other ideas on ways to integrate culture with these content areas.

Just as acquiring a language means more than knowing about its linguistic system, understanding another culture involves more than learning facts about it. Rosenbusch (1992b) suggests the development of *global units* to help elementary school students develop a global perspective and deeper awareness of key issues in the target culture. For example, she describes a global unit called "Housing," in which students compare housing in the native and target cultures through activities such as viewing and discussing slide presentations and making drawings, graphs, and housing models to illustrate similarities and differences.

Students can also gain a deeper awareness of the target culture by role playing authentic situations or participating in "fantasy experiences" (Curtain & Dahlberg, 2004). For example, Curtain and Dahlberg describe an airplane fantasy experience in which children pretend that they are taking a trip, acting out each phase from checking baggage to finding their seats to landing (p. 237). A truly integrated elementary school program carefully connects language and culture and provides many opportunities for students to learn about the culture through contextualized instruction and meaningful interaction.

 Global units help elementary school students develop a global perspective and deeper awareness of key issues in the target culture. ▪

Contextualized Performance Assessment

Current approaches to assessment emphasize standards-based, contextualized, and performance-based assessment and the development of multiple forms of assessment administered in an ongoing manner (see Chapter 11 for further discussion). In performance-based assessments, learners use their repertoire of knowledge and skills to create a product or a response, either individually or collaboratively (Liskin-Gasparro, 1996). The focus on performance is one which relates well with the hands-on nature of the elementary school language program. Wiggins (1992) offers the following suggestions concerning the design of performance assessment tasks:

- Contextualize the task. Provide rich contextual detail.
- Aim to design "meaningful" tasks that are interesting to the learner and relevant/ practical.
- Design performances, not drills. Performance is not about desired bits of knowledge, but about "putting it all together."
- Refine the tasks you design by building them backwards from the models and scoring criteria. Students should know the target and the standard in advance. (Wiggins [1992] cf. and adapted from Curtain & Dahlberg [2004], pp. 163–164).

In addition, when assessing students' achievement of material covered, it is a good idea to test what has been taught in the way it has been taught and to use the test primarily as a vehicle for discovering what children *know* and *can do*, as opposed to what they don't know and can't do (Curtain & Dahlberg, 2004).

The elementary school language curriculum uses both *formative assessments* (e.g., those that are administered throughout the year, are integrated into the teaching and learning process, and serve to inform and change instructional practices), and *summative assessments* (e.g., those that occur at the end of a course or at instructional benchmarks, such as after the first three years of instruction, in order to determine what the learner can do with language at a specific point in the language program). Both types of assessments should play a key role in the elementary program in order to verify achievement in an ongoing manner, provide feedback to students and parents, track long-term progress in terms of proficiency goals, provide information to teachers so that improvements in instruction can be made, and obtain data that can be used to evaluate the program.

A team of French teachers in Canada has developed a series of prototype *formative evaluation instruments* for novice students of French in grades four to six. The following are four of the team's sample prototype instruments: (1) a teacher checklist and peer evaluation form designed for use with a short oral presentation to the class (e.g., introducing one's family with the help of pictures); (2) a listening comprehension activity sheet and self-evaluation form (the task requires students to use thematic vocabulary and background knowledge to predict answers prior to listening to a segment, then listen to the segment, obtain specific information to complete the task, and self-assess their performance and their use of comprehension strategies); (3) a performance checklist that guides students in the preparation of a simple letter to a pen pal; and (4) a teacher observation checklist that allows teachers to monitor students' class participation and use of communicative strategies (Vandergrift, 2000). Findings of this project revealed that, as a result of these formative evaluation tasks and instruments, students reported a greater sense of involvement and empowerment in their learning, a heightened motivation for studying French, and a greater awareness of the language learning process and how to become more autonomous language learners (Vandergrift, 2000).

Below are some additional examples of formative assessments, which may easily integrate culture and/or content in an effort to assess within meaningful contexts.

Interpretive Listening and Reading:

- Students respond to TPR commands.
- Students select a visual or object to match an oral or written description.
- Students listen to or read a narrative and number pictures or put them in order.
- Students complete true-false, matching, fill-in-the blank, or short response items to demonstrate comprehension of an oral or printed text.
- Students create short oral or written summaries of stories heard or texts read.

Interpersonal Speaking:

- Students enact spontaneous role plays in pairs.
- Students discuss a familiar topic or a cultural/subject-content concept with the teacher and/or with one another.
- Students ask classmates questions about familiar topics and respond to their classmates' questions, taking multiple turns to do so in order for negotiation of meaning to be possible.

Presentational Speaking and Writing:

- Students create and present skits, plays, or puppet shows to an audience.
- Students describe a picture, objects, realia, etc. in oral or written form.

- Students give an oral or written monologue or narration.
- Students write short compositions, friendly letters, or notes on a familiar topic.

Note that *rubrics* may be used effectively to assess many of the tasks described above. They will be discussed in Chapter 11.

The following are three examples of summative assessments, which use the criteria of the *ACTFL Performance Guidelines for K–12 Learners* (1998) and the *ACTFL Proficiency Guidelines* (1982, 1999, 2001) to assess students' performance holistically.

- Student Oral Proficiency Assessment (SOPA)[6]: The SOPA is an oral assessment interview developed by the Center for Applied Linguistics, originally developed in 1991 for use in immersion programs and adapted in 1996 for use in other types of elementary foreign language programs. The SOPA interview is designed to assess the oral fluency, grammar, vocabulary, and listening comprehension of students in grades three through five who have had at least four years of language instruction. It is a 15–20 interview in which students participate in pairs, and there are two testers, one to conduct the interview and the other to rate it. The phases of the interview include a warm-up; tasks that focus on listening skills, using manipulatives (e.g., plastic fruits, stuffed animals); simple questions about colors, numbers, etc.; tasks that require interaction between students; higher level tasks (for students at higher levels) for giving descriptions and telling stories; and a wind-down.
- Early Language Listening and Oral Proficiency Assessment (ELLOPA): The ELLOPA was developed by the Center for Applied Linguistics (2001) during the SOPA validation project, when it became clear that a different assessment was necessary to capture the more subtle progress of children in prekindergarten through grade two. This assessment focuses primarily on listening skills and only secondarily on speaking skills. It consists of a series of game-like activities in which students interact with a cow puppet who speaks only the target language. Student performance is rated holistically on a scale that measures listening comprehension, fluency, vocabulary, language control (grammar), communication strategies, and cultural awareness (Curtain & Dahlberg, 2004, p. 191).
- Integrated Performance Assessment (IPA)[7]: The IPA (Glisan, Adair-Hauck, Koda, Sandrock, & Swender, 2003) is designed to measure student progress in attaining the competencies described in *SFLL* and the *ACTFL Performance Guidelines for K–12 Learners*. The IPA provides opportunities for students to demonstrate the ability to communicate within a specific content area or context (e.g., "Famous Person" or "Your Health") across the three modes of communication. It is structured so that students first complete an interpretive task, then use the information learned to perform an oral interpersonal task, and finally use the information from both tasks to complete a presentational activity (either oral or written). Rubrics guide the students' task completion as well as how to score the performance. (See Chapter 11 for a more detailed discussion of the IPA.)

In this section, you have explored ways to use the theoretical concepts about early language learning in order to plan thematic units and lessons; integrate content-based instruction; help students to organize content; facilitate vocabulary acquisition; develop interpretive listening and reading, interpersonal communication, and presentational speaking; help students to learn through cultural exploration; and assess students' performance. In the next section, you will see how the Connections goal area and standards of *SFLL* might serve as the impetus for enabling students to acquire new information from other disciplines in the target language.

STANDARDS HIGHLIGHT: Making CONNECTIONS Between Language and the Elementary School Curriculum

The Connections Goal Area

The benefits of linking language and content have been explored in Chapter 3 and earlier in this chapter. The Connections goal area of the standards states that students should be able to "connect with other disciplines and acquire information" (NSFLEP, 1999, p. 53). The two Connections standards are the following:

- Students reinforce and further their knowledge of other disciplines through the foreign language.
- Students acquire information and recognize the distinctive viewpoints that are only available through the foreign language and its cultures (NSFLEP, 1999, pp. 54, 56).

When combined with other disciplines, knowledge of another language and culture shifts the focus from language acquisition alone to broader learning experiences. Students deepen their understanding of other subjects while they enhance their communicative skills and cultural awareness. Furthermore, as students learn a foreign language, they gain greater access to sources of information and a "new window on the world" (NSFLEP, 1999, p. 56). The foreign language can be used as the vehicle for acquiring new knowledge.

 Connections enable students to further their knowledge of other disciplines, acquire new information, and recognize the distinctive viewpoints that are available only through the foreign language and its cultures. ■

Implications of the Connections Standards on Instruction

Teachers who begin to experiment with making connections with other areas of the curriculum should start with a simple connection, such as addressing one small content piece of another subject (e.g., art, music, social studies, math). In lower levels of instruction, the foreign language teacher might *continue* the presentation of content introduced in science, mathematics, and social studies. For example, students in a science class might continue to explore weather, seasons, and temperatures in the foreign language class (NSFLEP, 1999, p. 54). At various levels of instruction, students might read authentic documentation in the foreign language to support topics being explored (e.g., autobiographical accounts of historical figures, achievements of artists and musicians). These types of connections can be made by means of the thematic or interdisciplinary unit. In addition, the teacher might team teach a language course or a portion of it with a teacher from another subject area (e.g., history and foreign language). Also, individuals with language expertise who reside in the community might be invited to give presentations on certain content areas (e.g., art, music).

A recent endeavor that addresses the Connections standards is Global Learning and Observations to Benefit the Environment (GLOBE), a worldwide network of students and teachers representing over 6,500 schools in more than seventy-five countries. GLOBE students collect atmospheric, hydrologic, geologic, and biometric data from their schools' study site and report their scientific data to GLOBE and NASA/NOAA scientists via the Internet (Kennedy, 1999, p. 23). This program provides an excellent foundation for interdisciplinary and content-based study and a vehicle for learning a foreign language while studying science, mathematics, social studies, and technology.

Since GLOBE manuals and materials are available in various foreign languages, language teachers have access to content curriculum that can be easily incorporated in their classrooms.[8]

As students become more proficient in the target language, they can be expected to take more responsibility for acquisition of knowledge in areas of interest to them. They can find materials of interest, analyze the content, compare it to information available in their own language, and compare the linguistic and cultural characteristics (NSFLEP, 1999, p. 56). For example, students might research fashion, cars, music, art, and other topics of meaning and interest to them. As was mentioned in Chapter 3, the foreign language teacher does not need to be an expert in a subject-content area in order to engage students in exploration of it. Rather, teachers and students can be co-investigators, acquiring new information together. The teacher acts as a coach, helping students to select materials and to interpret language appropriately; students become the content experts.

As you have seen in this chapter, there are many reasons to begin foreign language study in the elementary grades. Younger learners bring a unique learning capacity and enthusiasm to the language classroom. Beginning language learning in the elementary grades ensures a long sequence of instruction, which is extremely important in developing language proficiency and cultural understanding. This chapter has presented a variety of strategies for addressing the standards in instruction in the elementary grades and for developing a hands-on approach in which young learners are actively involved in and excited about learning another language.

TEACH AND REFLECT

EPISODE ONE
Designing a Content-Based Elementary School Lesson

NCATE_____
STANDARDS
2.c., 4.b.

Design a content-based lesson that addresses a subject-content learning objective for grade 1. You may choose ONE of the following learning objectives or design your own:

- Grade 1 Mathematics: The student will identify halves, thirds, and fourths of a region or set.
- Grade 1 Science: The student will classify objects by size, shape, and color.
- Grade 1 Science: The student will make accurate observations using the senses.

(Adapted from Curtain and Dahlberg, 1994, pp. 407–419)

Assume that your lesson is thirty minutes in length and that this is the first day spent on this topic. Use a lesson plan format presented in this chapter or the one that appears in Chapter 3, being sure to include both content-obligatory and content-compatible language objectives, as described earlier in this chapter and as exemplified in Appendix 4.6. Plan your presentation and two or three student activities. As you plan the lesson, keep in mind the following guidelines:

- Design a lesson that is appropriate, given the developmental characteristics of your students.
- Present oral (not written) language.
- Involve students in hands-on activities from the start of the lesson.
- Do not lecture or overwhelm students with information they do not understand. They learn by being involved actively.
- Use the target language. Make yourself understood by using realia, gestures, and mime.
- Check comprehension often through TPR or short-response questions.

Your instructor may ask you to present part of this lesson to the class.

Next, write a paragraph explaining how you would adapt this grade 1 lesson for a grade four class. You might find it helpful to refer back to the description of intermediate students on page 99.

NC&TE____
STANDARDS
2.b., 3.a.

EPISODE TWO
Developing a Storytelling Lesson

Design a ten-minute storytelling lesson in which you present a story that is familiar to the children from their native culture (such as "Goldilocks and the Three Bears") or a simple, authentic children's story or folktale. Prepare visuals and realia as necessary for depicting meaning. Follow Egan's (1992) story framework planning guide and the suggestions given in this chapter for presenting the story orally and incorporating student involvement. Prepare a lesson plan, remembering that this is the first day using the story. Your instructor may ask you to present all or part of your story to the class. Be prepared to discuss how you would use the language experience chart approach to progress to reading after spending sufficient time working with the oral version of the story.

DISCUSS AND REFLECT

NC&TE____
STANDARDS
2.c., 3.a.,
4.b.

CASE STUDY ONE
Teaching Fourth-Grade Content in French

Amy Guilderson and Georges Arnault have been teaching fourth grade at the elementary school in Milford City for two years, ever since they began their teaching careers. Georges is of French descent and grew up speaking French at home. Amy studied French in college and completed a semester-long study abroad experience in France before graduating. She also had a minor in History. Amy enjoys the opportunity to speak French with Georges.

While having lunch together one day, they began talking about integrating some French instruction into their teaching, although their school did not have a French program. Georges had been reading some recent journal articles that presented the idea of combining foreign language and subject-content instruction. They wondered if they could develop a social studies unit that incorporated French. Much to their surprise, when they consulted *SFLL* (NFSLEP, 1999), they found the following learning scenario that integrates a social studies concept into a fourth-grade French lesson. Since this fit in perfectly with an upcoming social studies unit in their school district curriculum, they decide to try the unit and introduce the teaching of French.

Les Voyageurs: The French *Voyageurs* (elementary)

A study of the colorful and demanding life of the French *voyageurs* and their role in the fur trade provides an excellent complement to the elementary school social studies curriculum. The teacher can introduce the topic in French via videotape (for example, *Les Voyageurs* from the French Canadian Film Society), by reading the French coloring book about the *voyageurs* from the Minnesota Historical Society, or by playing the role of a *voyageur* himself/herself. Students then learn to describe the clothing worn by the *voyageurs*, discovering as they do which items are European in origin and which are adapted from Native American dress. They also make red *toques*, the woolen caps so readily identified with the *voyageurs*. The students dramatize each facet of the life of the *voyageurs*, including loading the canoe, paddling and singing, portaging, resting, eating pea soup, trading with Native Americans, and dancing at a *rendez-vous*. They also learn to identify and describe the animals hunted for their fur, and they make a map showing the itinerary of the *voyageurs'* travels. Students may also perform a reenactment of the life of the *voyageurs*, including songs and dances, in a presentation for students in other classes and/or for parents (p. 239–240).

Ask yourself these questions:

1. What are some dos and don'ts Amy and Georges should keep in mind as they teach their students this social studies unit?
2. What specific standards are addressed in the learning scenario?
3. How are the three modes of communication integrated into the activities described in the scenario?
4. What are the academic and social benefits of this type of interdisciplinary instruction for fourth graders?

To prepare the case:

1. Talk with an elementary school teacher to find out how this particular type of social studies unit is generally taught to fourth graders.
2. Read Brumen (2000) for examples of effective strategies for content-based language learning.
3. Read Met (1999) for ideas about connecting language and social studies.

To prepare for class discussion:

1. Imagine that you are Georges or Amy and are planning your first lesson in this social studies unit. What is the content-obligatory language students will need to know? What is the content-compatible language you have selected?
2. How might Georges and Amy expand this project so that students receive more content-based instruction in French? How would parents and school administrators be convinced that this plan is both beneficial academically and cost-effective?

CASE STUDY TWO
Implementing an Elementary School Language Program

NCATE
STANDARDS
3.b., 4.a.

The Pinecreek School District is a growing suburban school district that is quickly becoming well known for its innovative educational programs. It recently began to address the national standards for the various content areas in an attempt to provide effective, cutting-edge instruction for the increasing numbers of youngsters moving into the area. Three years ago the district redesigned its foreign language program, instituting a fifth-grade exploratory program and updating its sequential program beginning in grade 6.

This year, the district began to investigate the merit of starting language instruction in first grade and continuing it through the elementary grades. A special task force comprised of teachers, parents, and administrators was appointed to research this issue and made positive recommendations to the school board. Subsequently, in an effort to pilot instruction in the early grades, the district followed the task force's suggestion and hired Ms. Marianne Howe, a teacher certified in both Spanish (K–12) and elementary education. Ms. Howe was hired as an itinerant teacher who traveled among four elementary schools, providing thirty-minute Spanish lessons to the 200 students in grades 1–4. The objective of the FLES pilot program was to develop students' functional oral proficiency and to build cultural awareness. Ms. Howe's expertise in teaching Spanish and in working with young learners enabled her lessons to be very effective and well received by the students. In light of the success of the Spanish pilot program, the task force made the following recommendations to the school board regarding the implementation of a language program in the elementary grades:

1. Design a Spanish program for first grade to be implemented in Year One and assign Ms. Howe to that grade level.
2. During Year Two, add Japanese as an offering beginning in first grade. Hire one Japanese teacher certified in Japanese (K–12) and elementary education. During Year Three, add French as an offering beginning in first grade. Hire one French teacher certified in French (K–12) and elementary education.
3. Since the program must be cost-effective, ask for volunteers from the regular elementary school faculty to learn enough Spanish, Japanese, or French so that they could begin to deliver language instruction in subsequent years (grades 2, 3, and 4). This group should also observe Ms. Howe in order to acquire strategies for teaching a foreign language. Using already employed elementary teachers will save funds that can then be used for materials and in-service training.
4. In each subsequent year of the project, continue instruction in the foreign language(s) at the next grade level so that the program is developed gradually from the bottom up.
5. Employ the services of experts in the area of elementary school language instruction to assess the program's effectiveness as it is being developed.

Ask yourself these questions:

1. What factors did the task force probably consider as they designed their proposal for an elementary school language program?
2. What elements of their proposal are effective, given the information presented in this chapter?
3. Considering the reasons for the decline in FLES programs of the 1960s, what aspects of the proposal might merit reconsideration?

To prepare the case:

1. Review the section of this chapter dealing with problems with FLES programs of the past; read Chapter 18 of Curtain and Dahlberg (2004), which deals with selecting and staffing an elementary school language program model.
2. Interview an elementary school language teacher and/or an administrator in a district that has an effective language program in the early grades. Find out their views on what makes such a program successful.
3. Read Chapter 6 of Lipton (1998), which deals with planning effective FLES programs.
4. Refer to Chapter 12 of this text to explore the use of distance education programs as a cost-effective means of providing language instruction in the elementary grades.

To prepare for class discussion:

1. Prepare a written justification for an elementary school foreign language program that could be presented to the school board and the tax-paying public. You might reference the *Statement of Philosophy* from the *Standards for Foreign Language Learning in the 21st Century* (see Appendix 2.4) for some ideas as you formulate your argument.
2. What background information would you offer the task force concerning the qualifications of elementary school foreign language teachers? How would you address the issue of cost effectiveness in employing new personnel?
3. Create written testimony for the school board regarding your views of the proposal submitted by the task force. Support your views with research findings and other information you have read. Be prepared to answer questions.

REFERENCES

Alkonis, N. V., & Brophy, M. A. (1961). A survey of FLES practice. *Reports and studies in the teaching of modern foreign languages, 1959–1961* (pp. 213–217). New York: The Modern Language Association of America.

Allen, R. V. (1970). *Language experience in reading.* Chicago: Encyclopaedia Britannica Press.

American Council on the Teaching of Foreign Languages. *ACTFL performance guidelines for K–12 learners.* (1998). Yonkers, NY: Author.

American Council on the Teaching of Foreign Languages. *ACTFL provisional proficiency guidelines.* (1982). Hastings-on-Hudson, NY: Author.

American Council on the Teaching of Foreign Languages. *ACTFL proficiency guidelines—Speaking.* (1999). Yonkers, NY: Author.

American Council on the Teaching of Foreign Languages. *ACTFL proficiency guidelines—Writing.* (2001). Yonkers, NY: Author.

Asher, J. J. (1986). *Learning another language through actions: The complete teachers' guidebook.* Los Gatos, CA: Sky Oaks Publications.

Brumen, M. (2000). Content-based language learning—Why and how? *Learning Languages, 5,* 10–16.

Campbell, R. N., Gray, T. C., Rhodes, N. C., & Snow, M. A. (1985). Foreign language learning in the elementary schools: A comparison of three language programs. *The Modern Language Journal, 69,* 44–54.

Carroll, J. B. (1975). *The teaching of French as a foreign language in eight countries.* New York: John Wiley.

Center for Applied Linguistics (1992). *Student oral proficiency assessment (SOPA).* Washington, DC: Center for Applied Linguistics.

Center for Applied Linguistics (2001). *Early language listening and oral proficiency assessment (ELLOPA).* Washington, DC: Center for Applied Linguistics.

Chinen, K., Donato, R., Igarashi, K., & Tucker, G. R. (2003). Looking across time: Documenting middle school Japanese FLES students' attitudes, literacy and oral proficiency. *Learning Languages, 8,* 4–10.

Clyne, M. (Ed.). (1986). *An early start: Second language at primary school.* Melbourne, Australia: River Seine Publications.

Cummins, J. (1981a). Age on arrival and immigrant second language learning in Canada: A reassessment. *Applied Linguistics, 2,* 132–149.

Cummins, J. (1981b). The role of primary language development in promoting educational success for language minority students. In *Schooling and language minority students: A theoretical framework.* Los Angeles: Evaluation, Dissemination, and Assessment Center, California State University.

Cummins, J. (2000). *Language, power and pedagogy: Bilingual children caught in the crossfire.* Clevedon, UK: Multilingual Matters.

Curtain, H. A., & Dahlberg, C. A. (2004). *Languages and children—Making the match* (3rd ed.). Boston: Pearson Education.

Curtain, H. A., & Pesola, C. A. (1994). *Languages and children—Making the match* (2nd ed.). White Plains, NY: Longman.

Dixon, C., & Nessel, D. (1983). *Language experience approach to reading (and writing): Language experience reading for second language learners.* Hayward, CA: Alemany Press.

Donato, R., Antonek, J. L., & Tucker, G. R. (1994). A multiple perspectives analysis of a Japanese FLES program. *Foreign Language Annals, 27,* 365–378.

Donato, R., Antonek, J. L., & Tucker, G. R. (1996). Documenting a Japanese FLES program: Ambiance and achievement. *Language Learning, 46,* 497–528.

Donato, R., Tucker, G. R., Wudthayagorn, J., & Igarashi, K. (2000). Converging evidence: Attitudes, achievements, and instruction in the later years of FLES. *Foreign Language Annals, 33,* 377–393.

Egan, K. (1979). *Educational development.* New York: Oxford University Press.

Egan, K. (1992). *Imagination in teaching and learning: The middle school years.* Chicago: University of Chicago Press.

Ellis, R. (1994). *The study of second language acquisition.* Oxford, UK: Oxford University Press.

Fortune, T., & Jorstad, H. L. (1996). U.S. immersion programs: A national survey. *Foreign Language Annals, 27,* 163–90.

Foster, K., & Reeves, C. (1989). FLES improves cognitive skills. *FLES News, 2*(3), 4.

Gilzow, D. F., & Branaman, L. E. (2000). *Lessons learned: Model early foreign language programs.* McHenry, IL: Center for Applied Linguistics and Delta Systems.

Glisan, E. W., Adair-Hauck, B., Koda, K., Sandrock, S. P., & Swender, E. (2003). *ACTFL integrated performance assessment.* Yonkers, NY: ACTFL.

Glisan, E. W., Dudt, K. P., & Howe, M. S. (1998). Teaching Spanish through distance education: Implications of a pilot study. *Foreign Language Annals, 31,* 48–66.

Glisan, E. W., & Fall, T. F. (1991). Adapting an immersion approach to secondary and postsecondary language teaching: The methodological connection. In J. K. Phillips (Ed.), *Building bridges and making connections,* Northeast Conference Reports (pp. 1–29). Burlington, VT: Northeast Conference on the Teaching of Foreign Languages.

Hall, M. A. (1970). *Teaching reading as a language experience.* Columbus, OH: Merrill.

Hansen-Krening, N. (1982). *Language experiences for all students.* Reading, MA: Addison-Wesley.

Harley, B., & Wang, W. (1997). The critical period hypothesis: Where are we now? In A. M. B. de Groot & J. F.

Kross (Eds.), *Tutorials in bilingualism: Psycholinguistic perspectives* (pp. 19–51). Hillsdale, NJ: Lawrence Erlbaum.

Heimlich, J. E., & Pittelman, S. D. (1986). *Semantic mapping: Classroom applications*. Newark, DE: International Reading Association.

Hoch, F. S. (1998). A view from the state level. In M. Met (Ed.), *Critical issues in early second language learning: Building for our children's future* (pp. 5–10). Glenview, IL: Addison-Wesley.

Hoff-Ginsberg, E. (1998). Is there a critical period for language acquisition? In M. Met (Ed.), *Critical issues in early second language learning: Building for our children's future* (pp. 31–36). Glenview, IL: Addison-Wesley.

Igarashi, K. (1997). *Early oral production of child second language learners in a Japanese immersion kindergarten*. Unpublished master's thesis, University of Oregon, Eugene.

Johnson, D., & Johnson, R. (1987). *Learning together and alone: Cooperation, competition, and individualization*. Englewood Cliffs, NJ: Prentice Hall.

Johnson, J., & Newport, E. (1989). Critical period effects in second language learning: The influence of maturational state on the acquisition of English as a second language. *Cognitive Psychology, 21,* 60–99.

Kennedy, T. J. (1999). GLOBE integrates mathematics, science, social studies, and technology into the foreign language classroom. *Learning Languages, 4,* 23–25.

Kennedy, T. J., Nelson, J. K., Odell, M. R. L., & Austin, L. K. (2000). The FLES attitudinal inventory. *Foreign Language Annals, 33,* 278–287.

Krashen, S. D., Long, M. A., & Scarcella, R. C. (1979). Age, rate and eventual attainment in second language acquisition. *TESOL Quarterly, 13,* 573–582.

Lambert, W. E., & Klineberg, O. (1967). *Children's views of foreign people*. New York: Appleton-Century-Crofts.

Lapkin, S., Swain, M., & Shapson, S. (1990). French immersion research agenda for the '90s. *Canadian Modern Language Review, 4,* 638–674.

Lightbown, P. M., & Spada, N. (2003). *How languages are learned*. Oxford: Oxford University Press.

Lipton, G. C. (1998). *Practical handbook to elementary foreign language programs (FLES*)* (3rd ed.). Lincolnwood, IL: NTC/Contemporary Publishing Group.

Liskin-Gasparro, J. E. (1996). Assessment: From content standards to student performance. In R. C. Lafayette (Ed.), *National standards: A catalyst for reform*. The ACTFL Foreign Language Education Series (pp. 169–196). Lincolnwood, IL: NTC/Contemporary Publishing Group.

Long, M. (1990). *Input, interaction and second language acquisition*. Unpublished doctoral dissertation. University of California at Los Angeles.

Lorenz, E. B., & Met, M. (1989). *Planning for instruction in the immersion classroom*. Rockville, MD: Montgomery County Public Schools.

Marinova-Todd, S. H., Marshall, D. B., & Snow, C. E. (2000). Three misconceptions about age and L2 learning. *TESOL Quarterly, 34,* 9–34.

Martin, E., & Rainey, L. (1993). Student achievement and attitude in a satellite delivered high school science course. *The American Journal of Distance Education, 7,* 54–61.

Met, M. (1993). *Foreign language immersion programs*. Washington, DC: Center for Applied Linguistics. (ERIC Document Reproduction Service No. ED 363-141)

Met, M. (1999). Making connections. In J. K. Phillips & R. M. Terry (Eds.), *Foreign language standards: Linking research, theories, and practice* (pp. 137–164). Lincolnwood, IL: National Textbook Company.

Montás, M. (2003). Observing progress and achievement of beginning students in a fourth-grade Spanish FLES program. *Learning Languages, 9,* 8–20.

Moore, M., & Thompson, M. (1997). The effects of distance learning. American Center for the Study of Distance Education. *Research Monograph*, 15.

Muuss, R. (1982). Social cognition: Robert Selman's theory of role taking. *Adolescence, 17*(65), 499–525.

National Council of State Supervisors of Foreign Languages (NCSSFL). (2002). NCSSFL position statement on distance learning in foreign languages. Retrieved on February 7, 2004, from http://www.ncssfl.org/distancelearning.htm.

National Standards in Foreign Language Education Project (NSFLEP). (1999). *Standards for foreign language learning in the 21st century*. Lawrence, KS: Allen Press.

Pappas, C. C., Kiefer, B. Z., & Levstik, L. S. (1990). *An integrated language perspective in the elementary school*. New York: Longman.

Patkowski, M. (1990). Age and accent in a second language: A reply to James Emir Flege. *Applied Linguistics, 11,* 73–89.

Peregoy, S. F., & Boyle, O. F. (2001). *Reading, writing, and learning in ESL: A resource book for K–12 teachers*. New York: Longman.

Pesola, C. A. (1991). Culture in the elementary school foreign language classroom. *Foreign Language Annals, 24,* 331–346.

Pesola, C. A. (1995). *Background, design, and evaluation of a conceptual framework for FLES curriculum*. Unpublished Ph.D. dissertation, University of Minnesota, Minneapolis, MN.

Postovsky, V. (1974). Effects of delay in oral practice at the beginning of second language learning. *The Modern Language Journal, 58,* 5–6.

Rafferty, E. (1986). *Second language study and basic skills in Louisiana*. Baton Rouge, LA: Louisiana Department of Education.

Rhodes, N. (1985). Elementary School Foreign Language Program Goals. Washington, DC: Center for Applied Linguistics.

Robinson, D. W. (1998). The cognitive, academic, and attitudinal benefits of early language learning. In M. Met (Ed.), *Critical issues in early second language learning: Building for our children's future* (pp. 37–43). Glenview, IL: Addison-Wesley.

Rosenbusch, M. H. (1992a). *Colloquium on foreign languages in the elementary school curriculum. Proceedings 1991.* Munich: Goethe Institut.

Rosenbusch, M. H. (1992b). Is knowledge of cultural diversity enough? Global education in the elementary school foreign language program. *Foreign Language Annals, 25,* 129–136.

Rosenbusch, M. H. (1995). Language learners in the elementary school: Investing in the future. In R. Donato, & R. M. Terry (Eds.), *Foreign language learning: The journey of a lifetime.* The ACTFL Foreign Language Education Series (pp. 1–36). Lincolnwood, IL: NTC/Contemporary Publishing Group.

Scovel, T. (1999). 'The younger the better' myth and bilingual education. In Gonzalez, Rosenn, & Melis, I. (Eds.). *Language ideologies: Critical perspectives on the English only movement.* Urbana, IL: National Council of Teachers of English.

Snow, C., & Hoefnagel-Höhle, M. (1978). The critical age for language acquisition: Evidence from second language learning. *Child Development, 49,* 1114–1128.

Terrell, T. D. (1986). Recent trends in research and practice: Teaching Spanish. *Hispania, 68,* 193–202.

Thompson, E. (1991). Foreign accents revisited: The English pronunciation of Russian immigrants. *Language Learning, 41,* 177–204.

Tucker, G. R., Donato, R., & Antonek, J. L. (1996). Documenting growth in a Japanese FLES program. *Foreign Language Annals, 29,* 539–550.

Vandergrift, L. (2000). Setting students up for success: Formative evaluation and FLES. *Foreign Language Annals, 33,* 290–303.

Vygotsky, L. (1962). *Thought and language.* Cambridge, MA: MIT Press.

Wiggins, G. (1992). Creating tests worth taking. *Educational Leadership, 49,* 26–33.

Winitz, H., & Reeds, J. (1973). Rapid acquisition of a foreign language by the avoidance of speaking. *International Review of Applied Linguistics, 11,* 295–317.

NOTES

1. For two exceptions, see Campbell, Gray, Rhodes, & Snow (1985) and Clyne (1986).

2. See Donato, Antonek, & Tucker (1994, 1996) and Tucker, Donato, & Antonek (1996) for earlier reports on this study.

3. For a description of prochievement testing, see Chapter 11.

4. Lipton (1998) uses the term *FLES** to refer in general to any type of foreign language instruction in elementary and middle schools.

5. See Chapter 5 for the use of children's literature in a middle school setting.

6. SOPA training is available through the Center for Applied Linguistics (http://cal.org). It is also offered at language conferences and available to school districts upon request.

7. IPA training and manuals are available upon request from ACTFL.

8. See Kennedy (1999) for a description of a model GLOBE foreign language program in Idaho.

CHAPTER 5 Integrating Language Study in the Middle School Curriculum

In this chapter, you will learn about:

- the definition of middle school
- the middle level learner
- middle level programs
- sequential vs. exploratory language programs
- classroom management
- Cultures and Comparisons standards

- The three Ps: practices, products, perspectives
- Kluckhohn Method
- Cross-Cultural Adaptability Inventory
- cultural simulators
- sample thematic units
- assessment of middle school performance

Teach and Reflect: Developing Culture-Specific Examples of the Three Ps; Unit and Lesson Design Around a Story, Myth, or Folktale; Analyzing Lesson Plans for the Three Ps

Discuss and Reflect: Exploratory vs. Sequential Middle School Programs; It's McLicious! Staying in the Target Language

CONCEPTUAL ORIENTATION

Current emphasis on teaching language at this level is due in part to two factors: (1) a growing change in approach to teaching eleven- to fourteen-year-old learners, and (2) an attempt to begin language learning experiences as early as possible so that students benefit from a longer, uninterrupted period of language study. By 1993, a variety of configurations between grades 5 and 9 had been defined by these perspectives:

- Purpose: Developmentally responsive to the needs of young adolescents;
- Uniqueness: A unique autonomous unit, separate from the elementary school and the high school;
- Organization: Includes the grade levels with the largest number of students who are becoming adolescents;
- Curriculum and instruction: Content is connected to everyday lives of students and instruction actively involves them in learning (adapted from Clark & Clark, 1994).

Currently, the most popular grade-level configuration includes grades 6–8, but other models do exist. Research shows that grade level configuration does not determine effectiveness (Johnston, 1984; National Middle School Association, 2003). What is most important is the quality of the middle level program in providing opportunities for learners to explore not only many subjects, but also many approaches within a subject (Melton, 1984). According to Nerenz, "Good middle level education allows students to experience old things in new ways and entirely new fields of learning in varied ways" (1990, p. 95).

A middle school concept generally presumes the presence of five components that have been empirically recognized as beneficial to middle level learners by educators, associations, foundations, state boards of education, and researchers:

1. interdisciplinary teaming, consisting of two to five team members in two, three, or four subject areas whose schedules allow them to plan and collaborate on interdisciplinary lessons;
2. advisory programs that consist of a small group of students (usually 20 or fewer) assigned to a teacher, administrator, or other staff member for a regularly scheduled meeting to discuss topics of concern to students;
3. varied instruction integrating learning experiences, addressing students' own questions, focusing upon real-life issues relevant to the student; actively engaging students in problem solving and accommodating individual differences; emphasizing collaboration, cooperation, and community; seeking to develop good people, caring for others, democratic values, and moral sensitivity;
4. programs that capitalize on the innate curiosity of young adolescents, exposing them to a range of academic, vocational, and recreational subjects for career options, community service, enrichment, and enjoyment;
5. transition programs that focus on creating a smooth change of schools for the young adolescent (adapted from National Middle School Association, 2003).

 "Good middle level education allows students to experience old things in new ways and entirely new fields of learning in varied ways." ▪

The Middle Level Learner

Social Aspects

Eichhorn (1966) termed learners ages 11 to 14 as "transescents." Middle school children are different from elementary and high school learners because of the many physical, cognitive, and emotional changes that happen to them within a short period of time. Middle school learners are a diverse student group. As Mead maintains, they are "more unlike each other than they have ever been before or ever will be again in the course of their lives" (1965, p. 10). Rapidly occurring physical changes often accompany periods of restlessness and variable attention span (Nerenz, 1990). As Martin states, "Young adolescent students may have alternating periods of high energy and listlessness. They may need to squirm and move around, and may need to vent energy through physical exercise" (1993, pp. S-24). Middle level learners are aware of their physiological changes and become preoccupied with self-image. Nerenz suggests that these feelings often make students sensitive to typical classroom discussions concerning physical descriptions, daily routines with reflexive verbs, comparisons of clothing sizes, and other similar topics that refer to appearance.

Egan (1979) characterizes middle school students as "romantic learners" who enjoy knowledge for its own sake, bringing a great deal of curiosity to the classroom. They have begun to notice "otherness" and the world apart from their inner selves. They seek out the "limits" of the real world, exploring its challenges that are beyond daily living, such as nobility, courage, genius, energy, or creativity (Curtain & Dahlberg, 2004). Though they are curious about this new world beyond themselves, it is nevertheless a potentially threatening and alien world. Emotional and physical safety of their students is a concern of all middle schools (National Middle School Association, 2003).

The research of Andis (1981), Egan (1979), Johnston (1984), Lipsitz (1980), and Wiseman, Hunt, and Bedwell (1986) reveals that the middle level learner views issues as either right or wrong, demonstrates a strong sense of justice and will work conscientiously for an important cause, is fascinated with the extremes of what exists and what is known, is able to memorize and retain massive amounts of detail, strives for individual definition of self, and gains identity by becoming part of a group. Being a member of a group and conforming to its values provides security and protection against the overwhelming sentimentality that most middle school students feel (Curtain & Dahlberg, 2004, p. 14).

Middle school learners need to see a connection between language learning and their real lives and interests in order to be motivated to learn. Since these learners place much importance on peer norms, they are less accepting of differences and are susceptible to developing negative stereotypes of individuals from other cultures (Met, 1994). However, they do tend to have more positive feelings toward people unlike themselves when they know more about them and when they understand more about the "way other people think and feel" (Robinson, 1981, p. 106).

Cognitive Aspects

We now know more about the ways in which the brains of middle school learners function as a result of recent advances in brain research, which shows that the brain changes its structure in response to external experiences (Diamond & Hopson, 1998; Wolfe & Brandt, 1998); that the search for meaning is innate (Caine & Caine, 1997; cf. Curtain & Dahlberg, 2004); that the brain seeks meaning by looking for patterns in the information it receives (Curtain & Dahlberg, 2004); and that emotions drive attention to meaning and remembering (Caskey & Ruben, 2003; Jensen, 1998, 2000). Research by Epstein and Toepfer (1978) indicates that children between the ages of eleven and thirteen and a half experience a progressively slower period of brain growth, which may make them less able to acquire new cognitive skills and handle complex thinking processes. Thus the difficulty many middle school learners experience in understanding abstract grammatical concepts, such as verb conjugation, may be a reflection of cognitive maturity (Met, 1994).

Cognitively, middle school learners demonstrate a wide diversity of skills and abilities. Sociocultural theory provides teachers with a way to tap the wide range of Zones of Proximal Development among this group of learners. Teachers should be aware that the range of abilities across learners in this group is wider than among other learners (Mead, 1965), and that the difference between the actual and the potential ZPD for each learner offers a rich environment for learning.

Language Instruction in the Middle School

The *Standards for Foreign Language Learning in the 21st Century* (NSFLEP, 1999) call for language instruction for all students in grades K–12. Attainment of the standards requires an early start and an extended, uninterrupted sequence of foreign language learning. In the 1990s, school districts with high school language programs responded to the emphasis on middle education and expanded instruction into the middle school in an effort to pique students' interest in other languages and cultures, provide students with more time to study a language, and enable students to reach specific levels of oral proficiency (Adair-Hauck, 1992). However, the effects of the Elementary and Secondary Education Act of 2001, known as No Child Left Behind, has focused attention on math, science, and reading, threatening instructional time in foreign language programs in schools. A study conducted by the Council for Basic Education (2004) surveyed 956 principals in grades K–5 and 6–12 in Illinois, Maryland, New Mexico and New York and conducted focus groups with principals from across the US. Only 9% of principals reported that they anticipated an increase in foreign language programs while 19% anticipated decreases in the period 2004–2006. In high-minority schools, even more principals (29%) anticipated decreases in foreign language instructional time and professional development for teachers, and more than half of these principals expected the decreases to be large. Although the report acknowledges that inclusion of foreign language in the entire K–12 curriculum enhances student learning in other areas because it develops critical thinking, supports cognitive development, and improves native language reading and writing skills, financial limitations often restrict the extent to which fully articulated programs across grade levels can be implemented.

Verkler (1994) examined the language competency and attitudes toward language study of middle school and high school students, all enrolled in Spanish I. Middle school students demonstrated higher competencies in all four language skills (listening, speaking, reading and writing) than did their high school counterparts, and their attitude toward the foreign language learning experience was significantly more favorable. Verkler attributes these findings to the positive climate of middle school, which fosters students' social, emotional, and academic needs, and to the tenets of second language acquisition, which stress the key role of a positive and meaningful learning environment. Because of their unique openness and curiosity about challenges in the world around them, middle level learners can benefit from opportunities for language learning.

Middle schools are often organized around interdisciplinary teams, which consist of four to five teachers who serve approximately 100 to 120 students (Met, 1995). These teams meet often and regularly to plan jointly and to deliver instruction that integrates content from various subject areas. Teams develop thematic units that integrate content and skills around a specific theme, establish interdisciplinary connections, and provide opportunities for students to use critical thinking skills. Although teams have usually been comprised of teachers of mathematics, science, social studies, and English/reading/language arts, more innovative middle schools now include foreign language teachers. Being part of a team enables foreign language teachers to integrate language instruction into the regular curriculum and helps teachers of other subject areas understand the role of language study.

 How does middle school structure and organization match the characteristics of middle school learners?

Middle School Language Program Design[1]

Until recently, there has been little consistency in the type of language program developed for the middle school, due in part to the lack of consensus regarding the goal of language instruction at this level. Is the goal to offer exploration of languages and cultures or to begin to develop proficiency in a language? Accordingly, there is a divided opinion in the profession about whether middle school programs should be "exploratory" or "sequential."[2] Many middle school programs have been exploratory, based on the middle school philosophy that students should have opportunities to explore a wide range of subjects. The term *exploratory*, however, has been interpreted in a variety of ways as indicated by the range of foreign language exploratory or foreign language experience (FLEX) programs: (1) language readiness courses that introduce students to how language works (vocabulary roots, grammar, syntax, etc.) (Adair-Hauck, 1992); (2) multiple minicourses in language or potpourri courses that expose students to several languages and focus on cultural awareness and limited survival skills; (3) interdisciplinary courses that focus on topics from the perspective of more than one content area, such as foreign language plus geography, social studies, history, and/or literature, enabling students to explore ideas from a new point of view (Nerenz, 1990); and (4) auxiliary or noncurricular language programs that take place outside of the school day and include before- and after-school programs, summer camps, immersion weekends, summer day programs, and ethnic Saturday or day schools (Curtain & Pesola, 1994).

Kennedy and DeLorenzo (1994) argue that exploratory programs offer middle school learners a "learner-friendly" way of beginning language study. In their view, effective exploratory courses include an introduction to linguistics, an option to explore several languages, development of survival language skills, fostering of strategies for language learning and readiness for language study, connections of other languages to English, exploration of cultures related to the languages being learned, and connections between languages and career paths (p. 70).[3]

By contrast, Knop and Sandrock (1994) maintain that many of the goals of exploratory programs can be achieved just as well, if not better, by sequential language programs, which are more likely to enable students to acquire functional language ability in a cultural context, rather than talking in English about language and culture. They identify the following limitations of traditional exploratory programs: students have a superficial exposure to many languages; students often do not advance beyond rote memorization of vocabulary and sentences; the same vocabulary is often taught in all of the languages, resulting in student boredom; courses are frequently taught in English, particularly when cultural knowledge is the primary goal; language potpourri courses are taught by teachers who may be less qualified in one language than another; and students' choice of which language to study in a sequential course is an uninformed one, often based on the exploratory teacher's popularity or personality (pp. 78–79).

In a position paper for the National Council of State Supervisors of Foreign Languages (NCSSFL), Sandrock & Webb (2003) point out that language programs in middle schools should be available for all learners, provide interdisciplinary connections, connect courses from one level to the next, and strive for the proficiency levels required for the workplace. Like all standards-based programs, effective programs for middle school learners incorporate the following goals into curriculum and instruction:

- develop students' ability to communicate effectively in real-life situations
- broaden students' educational background through language development and cross-cultural awareness
- foster healthy attitudes about people of other cultures through the interdisciplinary study of language and culture
- provide motivation for continued language study so that students can achieve higher levels of proficiency in the language (p. 6).

Additionally, Sandrock & Webb (2003) recommend that the longest possible sequence of language learning be provided, beginning with exploratory programs in the elementary school, followed by middle school courses in a single language with multiple levels of instruction to allow for entry points for new and transfer students. They also advocate opportunities to add another language later in middle school, followed by continuing courses in two or three languages in high school (p. 9). Sandrock and Webb caution that some practices common to exploratory programs should be avoided in sequential programs, such as talking about languages in English; learning about cultures in English; learning only grammar rules until students are ready to speak; learning vocabulary in isolation; focusing on abstract data and facts unrelated to students' lives; and relying solely on the textbook as a teaching resource (p. 6).

 The longest possible sequence of language learning should be provided, beginning with exploratory programs in the elementary school, followed by middle school courses in a single language with multiple levels of instruction to allow for entry points for new and transfer students. Additionally, opportunities should be provided to add another language later in middle school, followed by continuing courses in two or three languages in high school. ■

Principles for Middle School Language Instruction

What is the ideal middle school environment? According to Beane (1986), it is one in which the adults are "nice"; that is, they know students' names and are interested in them as individuals. The curriculum should be lively and contain activities that vitalize ideas through doing, creating, building, and dramatizing. Learners should have frequent opportunities to work together in pairs or in small groups. In their summary of the research on characteristics of effective middle school teachers, Johnston and Markle (1979) noted that, among other qualities, these teachers have a positive self-concept; demonstrate warmth; are optimistic, enthusiastic, flexible, and spontaneous; accept students; demonstrate awareness of developmental levels; use a variety of instructional activities and materials; use concrete materials and focused learning strategies; and incorporate indirectness and "success-building" behavior in teaching.

 The middle school language curriculum should be lively and should contain activities that vitalize ideas through doing, creating, building, and dramatizing. ■

It is the philosophy of this textbook that the ideal characteristics of the middle school environment, curriculum, and teachers, as presented above, are applicable to all levels of instruction. Regardless of the instructional level, the curriculum should be learner-centered; organized around the social, cultural, and communicative use of language; and driven by what learners will know and be able to do with language rather than the grammatical concepts they can recite. A Vygotskyan approach (see Chapter 1) engages learners so that they can derive meaning and use the language by means of guided participation, scaffolding, and assisted problem solving. Curriculum should encourage the negotiation of meaning for expression of ideas, engaging learners in tasks that are of interest to them and related to the real world. These principles are key to language instruction at all levels of instruction, including the middle school level.

At the middle school level, the curriculum uses a spiral approach in which previously taught material is recycled and new expressions and more complex language are integrated within a familiar framework. As is the case with language teaching at all levels, a variety of classroom techniques and multimedia presentations should be used in the middle school language class. Since middle school learners are concerned with their self-image and the opinions of their peers, topics for thematic units and discussions should be selected with care (e.g., again, middle school learners may be uncomfortable describing the physical appearance of themselves and others). To appeal to students' curiosity and fascination with adventure and drama, a top-down approach as shown in Chapter 7 might be implemented, in which culturally appropriate myths, folktales, science fiction, and adventure stories are presented (Adair-Hauck, 1992).

 How is second language instruction in middle school consistent with goals for middle school learning? What aspects of second language learning add uniqueness to the middle school program?

Managing a Middle School Classroom

Teaching middle level learners can be a thrilling experience. They are energetic, enthusiastic, and ready to explore. In the words of middle school teachers, they

- want to know about "stories from real life, real people";
- want to know the "weirdities" in their own culture as well as in others;
- love to compare and contrast;
- are more concerned with getting their point across (although accuracy is beginning to develop);
- want to explore beyond their "safe" world;
- need to feel grown up;
- still need structure (Curtain & Dahlberg, 2004, pp. 20–22).

A number of factors beyond the teacher's control can affect how the students perform in class. For example, middle school learners are often sleepy early in the morning, while at midday they are hungry and watching the clock for lunch; in the afternoon they are eager to move around. Sometimes the language class is held in an auditorium, or in another teacher's classroom.[4]

Regardless of the circumstances in which they teach, however, the most successful middle school second language teachers find these tips useful:

- Plan your lesson thoroughly to engage learners every single moment—and beyond.
- Establish clear procedures that are observable, enforceable, in the target language, non-judgmental, and important to you so that you can teach effectively.
- Establish the connection between behavior and consequences.
- Establish routines for opening the class, ending the class, and other regularly occurring events.
- Involve parents and the community (adapted from Curtain & Dahlberg, 2004).

Observing a talented middle school teacher will provide you with many strategies for keeping the focus on learning in a student-centered classroom. See Appendix 5.1 on the Web site for suggestions to use when observing a middle school class.

 STANDARDS HIGHLIGHT: Integrating CULTURES and COMPARISONS into Middle School Language Instruction

Earlier in the chapter we saw that middle school learners have begun to notice "otherness," are curious about the world beyond themselves, and tend to have more positive feelings toward people unlike themselves when they know more about them. In this chapter, we present the Cultures and Comparisons goal areas and standards because the middle school is an ideal level for exploring target cultures and comparing the target cultures with their own. These goal areas should also be an integral part of language instruction at other levels of instruction as well.

The Cultures Goal Area

Middle school language instruction should emphasize the acceptance of diversity, developing students' sensitivity to the differences they encounter in others, both within and beyond their classrooms, thus providing support for students' self-esteem (Met, 1995). The foreign language program is in a unique position to address the issue of diversity by exposing students to the cultures in which the foreign language is spoken. The Cultures goal area of the national standards states that students should be able to "gain knowledge and understanding of other cultures" (NSFLEP, 1999, p. 47). The two Cultures standards are:

- Students demonstrate an understanding of the relationship between the practices and perspectives of the cultures studied.
- Students demonstrate an understanding of the relationship between the products and perspectives of the cultures studied (pp. 50–51).

Practices are the patterns of behavior accepted by a society; they represent knowledge of "what to do when and where" (e.g., how individuals address one another, the social "pecking order," the use of space, gestures, mealtime etiquette). *Products* refer to things created by members of the culture, both tangible (e.g., a house, an eating utensil, a painting, a piece of literature) and intangible (e.g., a system of education, a ritual, an oral tale, a dance). Practices and products are derived from the *perspectives* of the culture, that is, traditional ideas, attitudes, meanings, and values (NSFLEP, 1999, pp. 47–49). For example, in some Asian cultures, social hierarchy (a perspective) is very important and is based on age, education, and social status. In those cultures, people often exchange business cards (a product), which facilitate social interaction and are treated with respect (one should not scribble another name or phone number on the business card). The information on the business card thereby affects the nonverbal behavior of those involved in communication (a practice) (p. 50). It is important to note that (1) not every product or practice has a perspective that is easily identifiable, and (2) sometimes the perspective has lost its historical significance and is no longer a perspective embraced by the contemporary culture.[5] Language teachers should be careful not to make up possible perspectives, but rather they should engage in cultural investigations with students to try to discover perspectives or confirm that perspectives have been lost or are unknown.

Figure 5.1 illustrates how practices and products reflect the philosophical perspectives that form the world view of a cultural group, and it depicts the interrelatedness of these three cultural components. This model reflects the sociocultural framework posited by Fantini (1997), which consists of *sociofacts* (how people come together and for what purpose—practices), *artifacts* (things people make—products), and *mentifacts* (what people think or believe—perspectives). Since language is used to express cultural perspectives and to participate in social practices, language study offers students insights into a culture that are available in no other way. Although some cultural knowledge can be obtained from other kinds of courses, "only second language study empowers learners to engage successfully in meaningful, direct interaction, both orally and in writing, with members of other cultures" (NSFLEP, 1999, p. 49).

 Practices are the patterns of behavior accepted by a society; they represent knowledge of "what to do when and where." ■

 Products refer to things created by members of the culture, both tangible and intangible. ■

 Perspectives of the culture are the traditional ideas, attitudes, meanings, and values of members of that society. ■

FIGURE 5.1 The Culture Paradigm

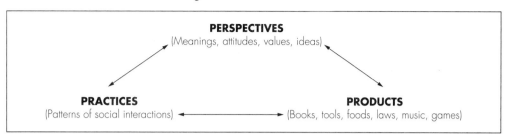

Source: NSFLEP, 1999, p. 47.

"Only language study empowers learners to engage in direct interaction with members of other cultures."

To help her students analyze cultural practices, products, and perspectives, a Japanese instructor asked them to brainstorm what they had learned about Japanese culture in a thematic unit they were studying (Curtain & Dahlberg, 2004). The teacher renamed the three Ps with more "child-friendly" terms and the students categorized the recalled information as shown in the culture paradigm in Figure 5.2. Products are things the Japanese make, such as Pokemon and origami; practices are what they do, such as sumo wrestling or serving lunch; and perspectives are how they think, such as liking to keep indoors clean.

The culture paradigm, with its anthropological approach to representing culture, lends itself to a *constructivist approach* to learning about culture, in which learners construct their views of culture through social interaction and interpersonal communication. Such an approach emphasizes the use of (1) a constructive process to understand the three Ps and their interrelatedness, and (2) connections, associations, and linkages between new and existing knowledge (Poplin & Stone, 1992)—what Wright (2000) refers to as "intersubjectivity." That is, learners construct their understandings of a culture by

FIGURE 5.2 Products, Practices and Perspectives in a Japanese Fifth Grade Class

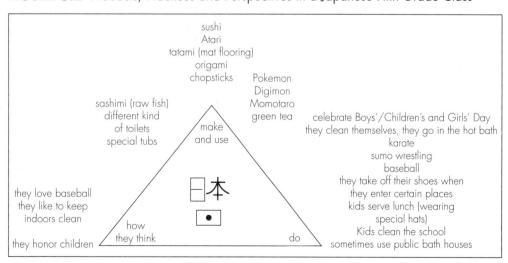

Source: Curtain and Dahlberg, 2004, p. 228.

examining the relationships between products, practices, and perspectives, and by focusing initially on their own values and sense of self that evolve out of their respective native cultural perspectives (Wright). This approach contrasts with an *information-acquisition approach* through which students learn information and facts about the target culture as provided by the teacher.

Wright (2000) compared the effect of these two approaches on the development of cultural receptivity of beginning college-level German students, as measured on the Cross-Cultural Adaptability Inventory (CCAI), a test of cross-culture adaptability (Kelley & Meyers, 1995). You will learn more about the CCAI later in this chapter. Over a fifteen-week period, the control group received traditional instruction, in which cultural information was presented in terms of factual knowledge and discussions that referred to the information in or claims made by the textbook. In addition, they were given five lessons on language learning strategies and designed a strategy portfolio. The experimental group, i.e. the one using a constructivist approach, received not only the same factual information, but they also participated in five lessons on cross-cultural awareness and designed a culture portfolio. See Appendix 5.2 on the Web site for instructions on how to design the culture portfolio.[6] The cross-cultural awareness lessons had five goals: (1) to pose authentic problems/topics that lead to a mild sense of confusion; (2) to encourage students to try to address the problems in their own way while the teacher acts only as mediator; (3) to help students put their own reasoning into words by sharing opinions, solutions, and strategies with the teacher and other students; (4) to use probing questions and allow enough wait time for students to think about answers; and (5) to give students an opportunity to reflect on the topic at hand in relationship to their own personal goals of second language and culture learning (Wright, 2000, p. 334).

Findings of the study revealed that students who experienced the constructivist approach showed statistically significant gains in flexibility, openness, personal autonomy, and on the overall composite score on the CCAI (Kelley & Meyers, 1995). This means that students who experienced a constructivist standards-based approach were able to separate facts from cultural assumptions and beliefs about those facts; they could shift their perspectives about culture, language, and people; they could differentiate between personal discomfort and intellectual disagreement; and they would be likely to function better in a culture unlike their own (Wright, 2000, pp. 335–336). The author of the study believes that the constructivist group rated themselves as *comfortable with cultural diversity* on the CCAI because the culture lessons and the culture portfolio had enhanced students' sense of empowerment.

In a follow-up study, Abrams (2002) used the same cultural portfolio as Wright (2000) to study how learners' use of the internet shaped their views of culture, specifically with regard to stereotypes and use of the internet to investigate them. In her study the students who used the culture portfolio (1) were better able to perceive culture from an *emic*, or "insider's" perspective, (2) reflected a developing sensitivity to diversity within the cultures of the German-speaking countries, and (3) demonstrated an awareness of the idea that political boundaries are not adequate for determining memberships in cultural groups (p. 151).

These studies (Abrams, 2002; Wright, 2000) provide empirical evidence that an information-acquisition approach to culture "may lack essential dimensions that help students to comprehend, internalize, and feel comfortable with unfamiliar social demands" (p. 337). It lends support for a process-oriented constructivist approach to culture, which provides learners with the experiences they need to approach, appreciate, and bond with people from other cultures.

 A process-oriented constructivist approach to culture provides learners with the experiences they need to approach, appreciate, and bond with people from other cultures. ■

The Comparisons Goal Area

The Comparisons goal area is presented here with the Cultures goal area because a deeper understanding of one's own culture comes about as a result of understanding another. The Comparisons goal area of the national standards states that students "develop insight into the nature of language and culture" (NSFLEP, 1999, p. 57). The two Comparisons standards are:

- Students demonstrate understanding of nature of language through comparisons of the language studied and their own.
- Students demonstrate understanding of the concept of culture through comparisons of the cultures studied and their own (pp. 58, 60).

The second Comparisons standard can be addressed effectively with the Cultures standards as students analyze cultural products, practices, and perspectives between the target and native cultures. For example, as part of a thematic unit on family and celebrations, middle school students studying French explore how different cultures celebrate the birth of a baby. Students might imagine that their family receives two birth announcements, like those shown in Figure 5.3. Students compare the two birth announcements, and through analysis and discussion, they discover that the North American announcement focuses on the infant as an individual who announces her/his own birth, and places the parents' names last. In the French announcement, the focus is more on family lineage, with parents' names first, clear delineation of the mother's maiden name, and names of siblings who actually announce the birth of the newcomer. Students might also note that the French announcement includes notice of the baby's baptism, a feature absent from the North American announcement.

As you consider using the three Ps of the Culture goal area coupled with the Comparisons standard, keep in mind that there can be multiple perspectives related to a single product or practice, that it is impossible to know all of the perspectives of your own culture and the target culture, and that your openness to learning new aspects of cultures will contribute greatly to your students' development of cultural perspectives. One way to think about your own culture and to help your students understand it as well is to make cross-cultural comparisons using the Kluckhohn Values Orientation Method (Kluckhohn & Strodtbeck, 1961; Ortuño, 1991). The method categorizes five basic concerns common to all human beings: (1) What is a person's assessment of innate human nature (perception of self and others)?; (2) What is a person's relation to nature (world view)?; (3) What is the person's temporal focus of life (temporal orientation)?; (4) What is the principal model of activity (forms of activity) for a person, or the group to which he or she belongs?; (5) What is the modality of the person's or the group's relationships to others (social relations)? (adapted from Ortuño, p. 450).

Figure 5.4 depicts the range of variations that exist across cultures within each of these value orientations. Students might use this framework for understanding their own culture and for comparing it to that of the target culture. For example, the dominant mode of activity in North American society is "doing," as individuals are judged primarily by what they can accomplish. In the non-Western world, the emphasis is on who and what a person *is* rather than what he or she does. Ortuño (1991) cautions that a given culture cannot necessarily be classified on one side of the continuum in all five areas, although it might be plotted more on one than the other. Also, the Kluckhohn method is not designed to make sweeping cultural generalizations, since much variation may also exist within a specific culture, but rather to account for dominant cultural patterns and perspectives.

FIGURE 5.3 Birth Announcements (English and French)

... but I'm already big news!

Name _____

Date _____

Weight _____

Born to _____

I may be little now ...

Monsieur Christian LeBlanc et Madame
née Françoise Durant,
laissent à Joffrey, Marie et Michel
la joie de vous annoncer la naissance
et le baptême de leur petite sœur
Anne
les 4 et 14 Juin 1999

68, boulevard Arago
75013 Paris
01-42 53 27 60

Source: Kaplan, 1997.

In another attempt to measure and extend the levels of cultural understanding that individuals demonstrate, Kelley and Meyers (1995) developed the Cross-Cultural Adaptability Inventory (CCAI), a fifty-item self-scoring tool that helps individuals understand how they respond in cross-cultural situations. As a result of their responses to questions on the CCAI, individuals receive a score on the diagram shown in Figure 5.5. This mapping helps inform individuals about their effectiveness in each of these perspectives:

- flexibility and openness: ability to adapt to different ways of thinking and behaving that are encountered in cross-cultural experiences
- perceptual acuity: ability to pay attention and to accurately perceive various aspect of their surroundings
- emotional resilience: ability to rebound and react positively to new experiences
- personal autonomy: whether a person has developed a system of values and beliefs and at the same time respects others and their value systems (adapted from Wright, 2003, p. 37)

A number of simulations have been devised to increase cross-cultural awareness among professionals, such as police officers, medical personnel, coaches, etc., who often

FIGURE 5.4 Kluckhohn Values Orientation Method

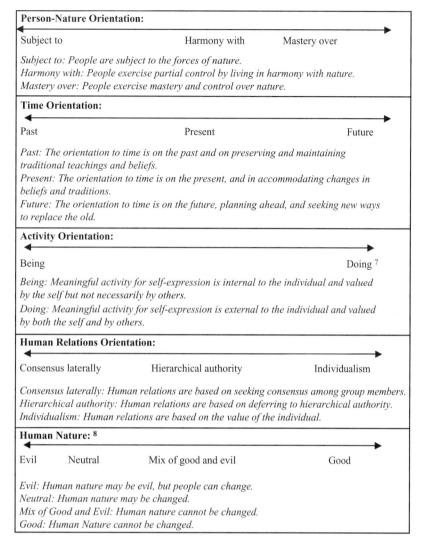

Person-Nature Orientation:

Subject to   Harmony with   Mastery over

Subject to: People are subject to the forces of nature.
Harmony with: People exercise partial control by living in harmony with nature.
Mastery over: People exercise mastery and control over nature.

Time Orientation:

Past   Present   Future

Past: The orientation to time is on the past and on preserving and maintaining traditional teachings and beliefs.
Present: The orientation to time is on the present, and in accommodating changes in beliefs and traditions.
Future: The orientation to time is on the future, planning ahead, and seeking new ways to replace the old.

Activity Orientation:

Being   Doing [7]

Being: Meaningful activity for self-expression is internal to the individual and valued by the self but not necessarily by others.
Doing: Meaningful activity for self-expression is external to the individual and valued by both the self and by others.

Human Relations Orientation:

Consensus laterally   Hierarchical authority   Individualism

Consensus laterally: Human relations are based on seeking consensus among group members.
Hierarchical authority: Human relations are based on deferring to hierarchical authority.
Individualism: Human relations are based on the value of the individual.

Human Nature: [8]

Evil   Neutral   Mix of good and evil   Good

Evil: Human nature may be evil, but people can change.
Neutral: Human nature may be changed.
Mix of Good and Evil: Human nature cannot be changed.
Good: Human Nature cannot be changed.

Source: Adapted from Kluckhohn & Strodbeck, 1961.

face cross-cultural situations.[9] Adaptation of simulations such as *Barnga* (Thiagarajan, 1994) and *Rafá Rafá* (Shirts, 2001b) for students in grades 5–8 and *Bafá Bafá* (Shirts, 2000a) for high school students can help learners understand their native culture and the target culture (Wright, 2003). Use of simulations coupled with reflection on standards of the Cultures and Comparisons goal areas can be especially useful for middle school learners as they form a sense of "otherness," as they explore a potentially threatening outside world, and as they seek the limits of the real world. See Appendix 5.3 on the *Teacher's Handbook* website for a description of the use of *Barnga* in a second language class. See Appendix 5.4 on the Web site for a scenario in which a teacher helps learners to perceive and compare the impact of the idioms in use around them.

thandbook.heinle.com

In addition to understanding one's willingness to adapt to other cultures, it is important that students learn how to use language to bridge the gaps between C1 (native culture) and C2 (target culture). Savignon and Sysoyev (2002) explored the use of

FIGURE 5.5 Cross Cultural Adaptability Inventory (CCAI)

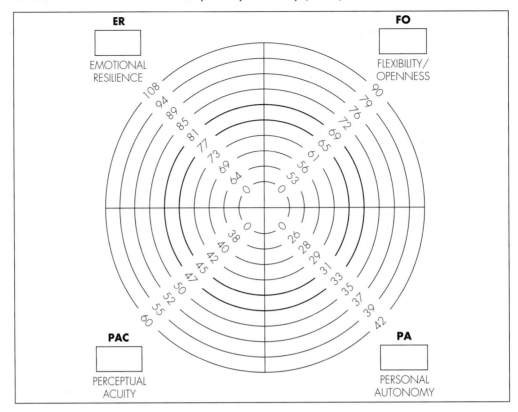

Source: Kelley & Meyers, 1995; cf. Wright, 2003, p. 37.

sociocultural strategies to make the connection between language and cultural understanding. They developed four strategies learners could use to initiate and sustain contact with people from other cultures (strategies 1–4 below) and four strategies learners could use to create accurate portraits of a C2 (strategies 5–8 below).

1. Initiate and maintain intercultural contact to learn about values, norms, spiritual heritage, etc. of the C2 and to represent the C1, e.g., US students use English (L2 for Russian students learning ESL) to explain why certain activities are associated with a national holiday in the US culture.
2. Anticipate sociocultural gaps that can result in misunderstandings or false stereotypes, e.g. examining a situation in which a member of C1 misinterprets a cultural norm from C2, such as arriving late to class.
3. Avoid misunderstandings, explaining C1 and asking for explanations of C2, e.g., apologizing in L2 for not removing shoes because in C1 there is not much mud and shoe removal is not necessary when entering a home.
4. Use diplomacy to redirect conversation to more neutral topics, or to dissimulate personal views and thus avoid conflict, e.g., see Alex's conversation on p. 141.
5. Compare the facts and realities of C1 and C2 using analogies, oppositions, and generalizations, e.g., after studying a reading selection on "Family Life in Britain," L2 learners prepared a similar report on family life in their own culture.
6. Identify and interpret unfamiliar features of C2; e.g. viewing authentic video multiple times to focus on cultural patterns of greetings, dress, and social interaction after meaning and story line have been understood.

7. Classify, compile and generalize sociocultural information from mass media, the Internet and other sources of information, e.g. compiling a written report or oral presentation on environmental protection issues in the C2.
8. Review authentic cultural material, e.g., write a review of an authentic article or brochure published in the L2 for C2 users on a topic such as acid rain or other environmental issues (adapted from Savignon & Sysoyev, 2002, pp. 513–518).

Savignon and Sysoyev then helped students in eleventh grade English (EFL) classes in Russia as they collaborated in groups to develop sample interactive cultural conversations in which these strategies were used. For instance, for Strategy 4, groups of students were given the following situation and asked to construct a dialogue, using diplomacy to avoid cross-cultural conflict by changing the topic of discussion.[10]

Situation: Pavel, Misha, and Tom are university students majoring in music. They play the piano, violin, and flute. They consider themselves to be musicians with a capital "M" and they cannot stand modern popular music. Another student, Alex, becomes involved in a conversation that turns against pop music/musicians and has to find a way out of the situation.

Misha: I cannot stand that music. It drives me crazy.

Pavel: Right. You don't need to know anything about music to play like that.

Misha: And those people who come to their concerts. They are idiots. They can't understand that music like that is not art. It kills their minds and pollutes their souls.

Pavel: Yeah, those fans are so dumb. What do you think, Alex?

Alex: Well, I don't know.

Tom: You mean to say that you like that pop junk?

Alex: I would say that sometimes people do things that don't make any sense. And you guys, you sound like professionals. How long have you been playing musical instruments? (adapted from Savignon & Syosyev, 2002, p. 517)

Notice how Alex uses diplomatic language to change the topic and redirect the focus of the conversation to the expertise of the musicians. Results of the research conducted by Savignon and Sysoyev (2002) showed that students were able to use the strategies in spontaneous communication beyond the classroom.

The following sections of this chapter will help you design instruction to enable your students to use language to communicate effectively in C2.

Implications of the Cultures and Comparisons Standards for Instruction

For decades, culture has been divided into two areas: "big C" (formal) culture—arts, literature, music, history; and "little c" (daily life) culture—anthropological and sociological aspects, such as social behavior, beliefs, housing, food, and transportation (Brooks, 1975). Culture has been treated traditionally in the classroom in terms of imparting facts and information, as teachers often lack sufficient cultural experiences themselves and have difficulty integrating culture into the linguistic component of the language program. Galloway (1985) characterized four common approaches to teaching culture:

- The Frankenstein Approach: a taco from here, a flamenco dancer from there, a gaucho from here, a bullfight from there
- The 4-F Approach: folk dances, festivals, fairs, and food
- The Tour Guide Approach: identification of monuments, rivers, and cities
- The "By-the-Way" Approach: sporadic lectures or bits of behavior selected indiscriminantly to emphasize sharp differences (cf. Hadley, 2001, p. 348–349)

Making culture an integral part of language learning is a challenging task for teachers, and learners sometimes do not understand the relationship of culture to language. In a constructivist view, culture is something that people construct in the living of their daily lives, and language is the primary means by which they make their culture vibrant (Roberts, Byram, Barro, Jordan, & Street, 2001). In this sense, working through the ZPD, teachers can assist learners in shaping their views of their own culture and their understanding of the target culture. As shown earlier in this chapter (Wright, 2000), a constructivist approach to culture learning enables students to exhibit cross-cultural adaptability, while cultural understanding is likely to be inhibited if the teaching approach has an information-only, factual base.

Lange (1999) suggests that, in planning for and using the Cultures standards, teachers help students to develop cultural understandings by activating their multiple intelligences, that is, their brain functions that consist of skills for "resolving genuine problems or difficulties" and for "finding or creating problems" (Gardner, 1993, p. 61). You will learn more about multiple intelligences in Chapter 10. Acquiring this cultural competence involves both *cognitive learning* (e.g., recalling, comprehending, applying, analyzing, synthesizing, and evaluating knowledge) as well as *affective learning* (e.g., receiving knowledge and attending to it, responding to knowledge with satisfaction, valuing difference, organizing values into a value system, respecting differences in dealing with other cultures, showing a willingness to revise attitudes) (Lange, 1999). Lange recommends that teachers help students to develop sensitivity to other cultures by engaging them in activities that tap their multiple intelligences and involve them in both cognitive and affective learning. He argues that "the avoidance of affective learning could be detrimental to culture learning" (p. 65).

The Cultures Paradigm Across the Continuum of Learning. The Cultures paradigm can be effectively used to establish goals for culture learning across instructional levels, particularly when instruction is standards-based. Figure 5.6 shows how one state addressed the Culture Standard 2.2 in World Languages (WL) across grade levels (Kentucky Department of Education, 2004b). If a student enters the school system at the primary school level (pre-K or K), note that the first column describes three ways in which the standard is addressed at the Beginning (B) level. The second column describes one way in which the standard is addressed as students study the beliefs of the culture as reflected in its products (e.g. Ojo de Dios). The third column describes how the standard is addressed at the Developing (D) level of competency in Primary through Middle school (PM), and the last column describes how the standard is addressed as student competency reaches the levels of Expanding (E) and Refining (R) in grade levels from primary through high school (PH). You can see how the expectation for students to demonstrate their understanding of the relationship between products and perspectives of the target culture is developed over the grade levels. For instance, if students begin language study at the primary level, an expectation is that they will develop an ability to identify some common products of the target culture, such as coins or costumes (WL-P-2.2.B1). In the intermediate grades, they begin to recognize and identify contributions and beliefs of the target culture. At the middle school level, they should be able to explain images and symbols of the target culture and identify the economic and social impact of products. Finally, at the high school level, it is expected that students would be able to demonstrate cultural competencies such as analyze relationships between cultural perspectives and products and evaluate the effects of cultures' contributions on other societies.

A Thematic Unit for Beginning and Intermediate Middle School Learners.
You learned about ways to use children's literature and storytelling in Chapter 4. You also learned about the development of thematic units, thematic planning, and thematic planning

FIGURE 5.6 A Cultures Standard Across the Grade Levels

ENTRY POINT: **PRIMARY P1 OR P2** 	WL-P-2.2.B1 Identify some common products (e.g., coins, costumes) of large culture(s). WL-P-2.2.B2 Identify some expressive forms (e.g., dance, artwork, songs) and contributions of target culture(s). WL-P-2.2.B3 Identify some objects, images and symbols of target culture(s) (e.g., Aztec calendar, lederhosen).	WL-PI-2.2.B4 Recognize and identify contributions and beliefs as reflected in products and contributions of target culture(s) (e.g. Ojo de Dios).	WL-PM-2.2.D1 Explain objects, images and symbols of target culture(s) (e.g., the Mexican flag). WL-PM-2.2.D2 Identify economic and social impact of products (e.g., music, soccer) on world markets. WL-PM-2.2.D3 Describe expressive forms of culture (e.g., art, literature, music, drama, dance).	WL-PH-2.2.E1 Discuss and explain external factors that impact products and contributions (e.g., effects of colonialization). WL-PH-2.2.E2 Identify and describe contributions of diverse groups within target culture(s) (e.g., Basque contribution to Spanish music). WL-PH-2.2.E3 Analyze relationships between cultural perspectives and products (as represented in expressive forms) [e.g., musical instruments, dances]. WL-PH-2.2.R1 Assess the significance of objects, images and symbols of other cultures. WL-PH-2.1.R2 Evaluate effects of cultures' contributions on other societies. WL-PH-2.1.R3 Assess economic and social impact of products on world market.

Source: Kentucky Department of Education, 2004.

webs to increase literacy among young language learners at the elementary level. In Chapter 3, you learned about backward planning design. All of these practices are also good educational practices recommended for use at the middle school and high school levels with age- and interest-appropriate adjustments. This knowledge will be helpful as you read about the following example that includes children's literature in a middle school foreign language program, designed by five French teachers at the National K–12 Foreign Language Resource Center Summer Workshop (Coblin, Huss, Kirk, Lonneman, & Melville, 1998).

Crictor, written in French for French children by Tomi Ungerer (1980), is the tale of a boa constrictor named Crictor, who was sent from Africa to Madame Bodot, a school teacher in a small village in France. The village experiences a crisis, and Crictor uses his unusual talents, saves the day, and is decorated as a hero for his bravery. Figure 5.7 shows a thematic web of the entire story and the lessons associated with it over several class lessons. You can see in the web how the teacher will integrate content of the book, culture, and language to enable students to explore mathematics, science, history, education, traditions, and literacy. The thematic planning web shows products and practices; as the teacher and students discover perspectives while working through the lesson, the web can be modified to place perspectives in the appropriate locations relative to products and practices. The story of Crictor is especially appealing to early middle level learners who are still somewhat tied to the fantasy and mythic worlds of their childhood but who are seeking heroes dealing with realistic problems (Egan, 1979).

thandbook.heinle.com

In Appendix 5.5 (see the Web site), notice how the teacher structures the language, content, and culture to incorporate the products, practices and perspectives of the Culture and Comparisons standards. Use of a Venn diagram provides a visual of the French village in the past that can then be compared to a French village of today, or to a small town in

FIGURE 5.7 Thematic Planning Web for "Crictor"

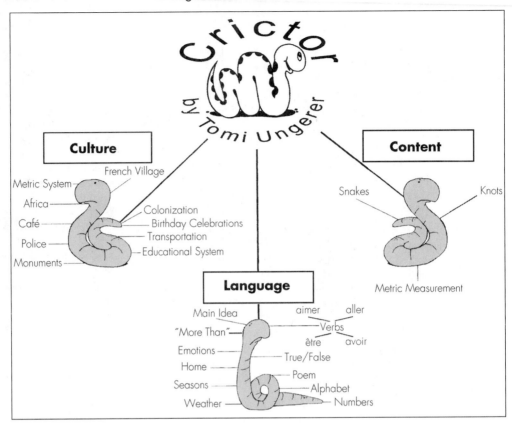

Source: Coblin, Huss, Kirk, Lonneman, & Melville, 1998, p. 2, used with permission of Marcia Harmon Rosenbusch. Director. National K–12 Foreign Language Resource Center, Iowa State University.

thandbook.heinle.com

the students' country.[11] For additional activities in this thematic unit, see Appendix 5.6 (on the Web site), a thematic unit activity for "Sauter à la corde (Jumprope)." Additional standards-based lessons for middle school language classrooms are available in Redmond and Lorenz's, *Teacher to Teacher: Model Lessons for K–8 Foreign Language* (1999). These lessons, endorsed by the National Network for Early Language Learning (NNELL) are available in Chinese, German, Latin, Japanese, and Spanish.

Strategies for Integrating Language and Culture.   At the heart of the cultural framework posited by the national standards is the importance of helping students to relate cultural practices and products to each other and to their cultural perspectives. The following are a few examples of instructional strategies for integrating culture instruction at the middle and high school levels. Because *Teacher's Handbook* advocates integration of culture into the teaching of the other standards and skills, additional instructional strategies will be addressed within each of the subsequent chapters.

- Visual literacy: Students look at a scene from the target culture (e.g., a street scene with traffic lights) or an authentic magazine advertisement and discuss the possible practices and products depicted and the perspectives to which they relate.
- Integration of language and culture: As students learn vocabulary, they see and discuss culturally authentic visuals/realia[12] so that they acquire both language and cultural concepts. For example, in a lesson on housing, students look at photos of

various types of housing from the target cultures, name features of each building type, and compare and contrast the housing types with each other and with housing from their own cultures.

thandbook.heinle.com

- Semantic mapping: As presented in Chapter 4, semantic maps can be used to associate word clusters graphically around an idea, key word, or concept. Words can be grouped thematically according to cultural practices and products. See Appendix 4.5 (on the Web site) for a sample semantic map based on the study of a river system.

- Use of authentic documents: Students discover information dealing with practices and products by analyzing authentic documents, such as movie listings, restaurant ads, bus/subway schedules, invitations, and so on. For example, students might read a restaurant ad from a Spanish-speaking country and discuss why the restaurant's hours are different from the hours of a North American restaurant (cultural perspectives and comparisons).

- Investigation of cultural truths: students communicate with target language counterparts via e-mail; gather information about their daily routines, school, and interests; and compare these data to their own responses.

Conducting interviews with native speakers or recent immigrants enables learners to understand the lives of the interviewees. Bateman (2002) reports that her students conducted such interviews and came to understand that "as Americans we lack knowledge about other cultures;" that they "can carry on a conversation with a native speaker;" that they have stereotypes that need to change; and that realistically their language is very limited (p. 326).

ASSESSMENT AND EVALUATION OF MIDDLE SCHOOL PERFORMANCE

In Chapter 4, you learned about contextualized performance assessment; in Chapter 11 you will see a more elaborated explanation of assessment in general. In middle level education as well as in elementary education, successful assessment improves learning, instruction, and program effectiveness (Donald, 1997). Consistent with the middle learner's interest in the real world, authentic assessment that makes use of real-life tasks and real audiences is recommended. Examples of types of assessment are performance tasks, portfolios, student self-assessment surveys and probes, peer assessments, journals, logs, products, and projects. As pointed out in Chapter 4, assessment is an essential part of teaching, and what is measured should reflect what is taught (Shrenko, 1994; Shrum, 1991).

For middle level learners who want to know how things work in the real world, it is important that they participate in assessment and evaluation, help set individual and group goals, help identify ways to measure progress, and evaluate their own accomplishments. Student self-evaluation is an important means of developing a fair and realistic self-concept (NMSA, 2003). Since early adolescence is a crucial period for establishing a clear self-concept and positive self-esteem, all assessment and evaluation should emphasize individual progress instead of comparison with other students. The goal is to help students discover and understand their strengths, weaknesses, interests, values, and personalities.

As you saw earlier in this chapter with the cultural portfolio used by Wright (2000), portfolios are an excellent way for middle level learners to accumulate examples of their work that show their progress. Portfolios allow for self-selection of items to be included and provide for reflection on the learning process. Portfolios as a recommended form of authentic assessment will be examined more completely in Chapter 11. One example of a portfolio that is especially useful for elementary and middle school learners is LinguaFolio Kentucky! Using the model of a European language portfolio developed by the Council of Europe (2000),

thandbook.heinle.com

Van Houten & Fulkerson (2004) created *LinguaFolio Kentucky!*, which appears in Appendix 5.7 on the Website. This record of learners' language capabilities is built over the early years of language learning and has three parts: a biography, a passport, and a dossier. The biography describes the learners' language background, what they can do with the languages and cultures they study and have experienced, and shows that they are learning more and more. The passport section is a short document that shows what learners know and can do in the languages they study, and the dossier contains samples of their work the learners have selected, e.g. sample recordings, poems, or papers they have written.

Teachers and school administrators often wonder how they will manage the collection of data that accumulates if they use portfolios over more than one year. One portfolio management system recommended by the National Middle School Association is the Grady Profile (Aurbach & Associates, 1998). This software allows students and teachers to construct and manage portfolios as alternative assessments.[13] It organizes portfolios with dates and titles; compares samples of work over time; holds many examples in any digital format, e.g. sound, video, etc.; prints reports in several formats to accommodate needs; provides a place for students to self-assess and reflect; and, tailors its feedback to department, school, district, state, and national standards.

To summarize, you have seen in this chapter that the concept of middle school education revolves around the special characteristics of learners ages 10–14. Language and cultural learning are especially suited to their needs and interests, matching up well with the *SFLL* Cultures and Comparisons goal areas. You saw ways to measure cultural adaptability, and you explored constructivist models of how to help learners demonstrate their understanding of the relationships between the products, practices, and perspectives of another culture. You saw some ways to manage a middle level classroom and some forms of assessment for learning accomplished at this level. As the profession strives to provide language instruction for all students and at all levels, increasing attention will need to be given to the unique needs of the middle level learner. Furthermore, clear goals will need to be articulated for this level of language instruction so that there is a smooth transition from elementary to middle to high school language courses and so that one level builds effectively on the next.

TEACH AND REFLECT

NCATE_____
STANDARDS
2.a., 4.a.,
4.b.

thandbook.heinle.com

VIEW AND
REFLECT

EPISODE ONE
Developing Culture-Specific Examples of the Three Ps

Create three age-appropriate examples of products, practices, and perspectives for the cultures of the foreign language you are preparing to teach. For the first example, begin with the product and match a practice and perspective to it. For the second example, begin with the practice and match a product and perspective to it. For the third example, begin with the perspective and match a product and practice to it. Into what types of middle school lessons might these examples be integrated? How do these examples relate to the Kluckhohn Values Orientation Method, or to the four major concepts underlying the Cross-Cultural Adaptability Inventory? See Activity A in the View and Reflect section of the *Teacher's Handbook* Web site for an example lesson that integrates the three Ps around Cajun folktales and Zydeco music.

NCATE_____
STANDARDS
2.b., 3.a.,
4.a., 4.b.

EPISODE TWO
Unit and Lesson Design Around a Story, Myth, or Folktale

In Chapter 4, you designed a storytelling lesson appropriate for elementary school students. Now select a culturally authentic story, myth, or folktale that you will present to a middle school class in your target language. First, design a unit plan built around the story you select (use the unit plan model presented in Chapter 3.) Second, design a lesson plan for the first day devoted to this story. Follow the lesson plan format presented in Chapter 3. Be sure to include your objectives for the lesson and connections with the Cultures and Comparisons standards. Prepare visuals and realia to help demonstrate meaning. Your instructor may ask you to present part of your lesson to the class.

EPISODE THREE
Analyzing Lesson Plans for the Three Ps

NC&TE
STANDARDS
2.a., 3.a.,
4.a., 4.b.

Consult the sample lesson plan in Appendix 5.8, "Skinhead Culture" by Jill Dunn and in Appendix 5.9 (on the Web site), "Hotels in Spain" by Merle Wilder (Allen, 2000). Identify the products, practices, and perspectives you see in these sample lesson plans. Modify the plans, which were originally created for high school students, to make them suitable for middle school students. What aspects of the romantic learner (Egan, 1979) will you need to consider as you make these adjustments?

DISCUSS AND REFLECT

CASE STUDY ONE
Exploratory vs. Sequential Middle School Programs

NC&TE
STANDARD
3.c., 4.b.,
4.c., 5.b.,
6.b.

Mr. Freeman is chair of the World Languages Department in the Stonecrest Area School District. His district currently offers an exploratory language potpourri course in the sixth grade, in which students experience nine weeks of "Phenomenon of Language," nine weeks of French, nine weeks of German, and nine weeks of Spanish. In seventh grade, students choose one language and take what the district calls an "exploratory" course, which is really a shortened version of Level 1. Instruction is given on a six-day rotation—students take language on days one, two, and three and have other classes on days four, five, and six. In eighth grade, students take the traditional Level 1 class and continue the sequence in grades nine through twelve.

The language teachers in Mr. Freeman's department have complained about the curriculum design for the following reasons:

- In the sixth grade language potpourri exploratory course, teachers are often expected to teach languages they don't know themselves; for example, Ms. Alvarez had to teach not only Spanish, in which she is certified, but also French and German, languages in which she has no expertise.
- In the seventh grade exploratory program, teachers feel that students are without language instruction for too many days in a row (sometimes a week) on the six-day rotation schedule. Also, they feel that the goals of this program are poorly defined, as students end up being exposed to the same material (in a less abbreviated form) in eighth grade.
- In the eighth grade Level 1 program, teachers say that some students are bored since they have already learned a lot of the vocabulary in seventh grade, while others demonstrate little mastery over the material taught in seventh grade.
- Teachers at the high school wonder why the exploratory program does not include Latin, since it is available in grades 9–12.

In addition, parents in the district have been pushing for language instruction to be introduced in the fifth grade, and Mr. Freeman and his faculty have been asked to present a proposal to the school board for both redesigning the existing program and for implementing the starting point in the fifth grade.

Ask yourself these questions:

1. Why do you think that teachers are being asked to teach languages in which they lack competence?
2. What are the benefits of an exploratory potpourri language course? What might be some shortcomings?
3. Why do you think programs might be designed around a six-day rotation schedule?

To prepare the case:

thandbook.heinle.com

1. Read about ways to expand middle school instruction in Adair-Hauck (1992).
2. Use Appendix 5.1 (see the Web site) to observe an exploratory middle school language class and interview the teacher to find out his/her views concerning the program's effectiveness.
3. Read the published debate concerning exploratory vs. sequential language programs in the special middle school edition of *Foreign Language Annals, 27*, 1994 (pp. 69–88).
4. Read Curtain and Dahlberg (2004, pp. 437–464) for information about how to build a middle school language program.
5. Read DiRocco (1998–1999) to learn how an alternating day schedule can empower teachers.

To prepare for class discussion:

1. Design one program option that introduces language in grade 5 and begins with a year of exploratory study. Define *exploratory* so that it addresses the possible shortcomings of the traditional exploratory course as presented in this chapter.
2. Design another program option that features sequential language courses beginning in grade 5.
3. Prepare a written report to the school board in which you justify offering foreign languages beginning in grade 5. Describe how this will affect the rest of the language curriculum. Address the following issues:

   - rationale for foreign languages in grades five and six
   - expected outcomes/goals of language study in the middle school
   - fitting foreign languages into the existing curriculum
   - fitting foreign languages into the school day
   - time allotment

CASE STUDY TWO
It's McLicious! Staying in the Target Language

NC&TE_____
STANDARDS
1.c., 2.a.,
2.c., 3.b.,
4.a., 4.b.,
4.c., 5.a.

Having completed his degree in German with licensure to teach, Greg secured his first teaching job at a middle school in Kentucky. As he began to plan his lessons for the year, he was delighted to find this learning scenario for his state on the Web (see Figure 5.8). He read through the scenario, noting its interdisciplinary nature, the use of the Cultures and Comparisons goal areas, and the appropriateness of the activities of the scenario for middle school learners. However, Greg found himself unsure of how to implement the scenario in his lessons because the words "TAUGHT IN THE TARGET LANGUAGE" seemed to present an almost impossible task to him.

He called his mentor teacher, Mr. Poff, who teaches French, and asked him how he would carry out the scenario in the target language. Mr. Poff was very helpful and gave Greg some tips such as wearing a button that says "Speak French" and posting key vocabulary from the scenario around the room with colorful photos and pictures.

FIGURE 5.8 Kentucky World Language Learning Scenario

It's McLicious! (C'est McLicieux! ¡Es McLicioso! Es ist McLecker!)

Intended Level: Middle School, Developing (Can be adapted to High School.)

Guiding Question: How do cultural differences affect the marketing of products?

Activity Summary: McDonald's restaurants can be found in countries around the world, but we are often surprised at the differences we find there. Students will compare/contrast McDonald's in their regions to at least one in the target culture and explore the effects of culture and resources on business practices and products.

Task: Individually or in pairs, students will prepare an advertisement **in the target language** in the medium of their choice for the opening of a new McDonald's or other fast food restaurant in their target country/culture.

Kentucky World Language Content:

WL-PM-1.3.D4 Interpret and present information from authentic material to audience.

WL-PM-2.2.D2 Identify economic and social impact of products on world markets.

WL-PM-4.2.XX Analyze the differences between target culture(s) and students' own cultures.

Kentucky Core Content for Assessment:

SS-M-3.4.1 Basic economic issues addressed by producers are production, distribution, and consumption of goods and services.

SS-M-3.4.2 Productivity can be improved by specialization, new knowledge, and technology/tools.

SS-M-3.4.3 Personal, national, and international activities are interdependent.

PL-M-3.1.4 There are positive and negative aspects of advertising strategies (e.g., providing accurate or misleading information, gimmicks).

PL-M-1.4.2 Using dietary guidelines, food guide pyramid, and other nutritional resources (e.g., food tables) helps make daily food choices.

Steps for Planning and Implementing TAUGHT IN THE TARGET LANGUAGE

1. Teacher uses TPR, visuals, manipulatives, and other communicative approaches to present food vocabulary and appropriate grammatical structures (e.g., imperatives, courtesies).
2. Teacher highlights cultural considerations as they relate to food in the target culture(s) (e.g., dietary staples, food guide pyramid).
3. Students use websites to investigate McDonald's restaurants in target language culture(s) by:

   ▪ preparing and sharing Venn diagrams that compare/contrast local and target-culture McDonald's menus;
   ▪ completing a list of common phrases or expressions found throughout the websites;
   ▪ preparing and sharing charts that examine marketing techniques (e.g., use of technology, toys, slogans, other icons).

4. Students role play ordering at a McDonald's counter in the target culture(s).
5. Performance* Task: Individually or in pairs, students prepare an advertisement in the medium of their choice for the opening of a new McDonald's or other fast food restaurant in their target country/culture.

(Resource URLs: http://www.nal.usda.gov; http://www.mcdonalds.com; http://www.mcdonalds.fr; http://www.mcdonalds.es; http://www.mcdonalds.de; http://monarch.gsu.edu/nutrition/Spanish2.htm)

Source: Kentucky Department of Education, 2004a.

*May be easily modified to address High School Practical Living Core Content PL-H-3.1.4. Methods and techniques of advertising exert an influence on consumer choices for products and services.

Greg also decided to ask Ms. Loria, the Spanish teacher, how she approached the goal of keeping the class in the target language. She pointed out that, in her experience, keeping the languages separate results in more proficiency achievement than mixing them or translating them. She said that she gives simple instructions in Spanish for classroom activities and does not translate them into English. If her students know that she will supply the English after the Spanish instructions, they stop listening to the Spanish. Ms. Loria also said that if she knows she is not going to use English, she puts more thought into making the input comprehensible.

Read the learning scenario entitled "It's McLicious! (C'est McLicieux! Es McLicioso! Es ist McLecker!)" and the guiding questions that follow it. Add your own suggestions on how Greg can find ways to promote and maintain target language usage in his class.

Ask yourself these questions:

1. What aspects of the learning scenario will appeal to middle level learners?
2. Where do you see the Cultures standards targeted in the scenario? How are products, practices, and perspectives highlighted for teaching? What activities and teaching practices are used to engage learners with culture?
3. Where do you see the Comparisons standards targeted in the scenario? How do you see students making linguistic comparisons? How do they make cultural comparisons? What activities and teaching practices are used to engage learners in this goal area?
4. What interdisciplinary aspects do you see in the scenario?

To prepare the case:

1. In Chapter 3, you learned about the importance of target language use and IRE/IRF classroom talk. To add to that knowledge, read pp. 34–37 of Curtain and Dahlberg (2004), "How do we keep the classroom in the target language?" Make a note of the techniques that the authors suggest and share with your classmates how you plan to implement them.
2. Recall your own school experience and a favorite teacher you had when you were eleven to thirteen and a half. Try to answer these questions: What did you like best about your teacher? What were some of the things you did in that teacher's class that you especially liked and especially didn't like? Relate these characteristics to the goal of keeping the class in the target language.
3. Interview a middle school student to find out what he or she likes about the way his/her favorite teachers teach. Ask the same questions you asked yourself above. Then read the article by Ralph (1994), "Middle and Secondary L2 Teachers Meeting Classroom Management Challenges Via Effective Teaching Research." Relate these characteristics to the goal of maximum use of the target language.

To prepare for class discussion:

1. Although this scenario is intended for middle level learners, the designers stated that it is easily adapted for high school learners. Create an adaptation of this scenario for high school learners.

REFERENCES

Abrams, Z. I. (2002). Surfing to cross-cultural awareness. *Foreign Language Annals, 35,* 141–160.

Adair-Hauck, B. (1992). Foreign languages in the middle schools: A curricular challenge. *Pennsylvania Language Forum, 64,* 12–18.

Allen, L. Q. (2000). Designing curriculum for standards-based culture/language learning. *NECTFL Review, 47,* 14–21.

Andis, M. F. (1981). Early adolescence. Skills essential to learning television project. Working paper. Bloomington, IN: Agency for Instructional Television.

Aurbach & Assoc., Inc. (1998). Grady Portfolio Assessment. Retrieved February 4, 2004, from http://www.aurbach.com.

Bateman, B. E. (2002). Promoting openness toward culture learning: Ethnographic interviews for students of Spanish. *The Modern Language Journal, 86,* 318–331.

Beane, J. A. (1986). A human school in the middle. *Clearing House, 60,* 14–17.

Brooks, N. (1975). The analysis of language and familiar cultures. In R. C. Lafayette (Ed.), *The cultural revolution* (pp. 19–31). Reports of the Central States Conference on Foreign Language Education. Lincolnwood, IL: NTC/Contemporary Publishing Group.

Caine, R. N., & Caine, G. (1997). *Education on the edge of possibility.* Alexandria, VA: Association for Supervision and Curriculum Development.

Caskey, M. M., & Ruben, B. (2003). Research for awakening adolescent learning. *Education Digest, 69*(4), 36–38.

Clark, S., & Clark, D. (1994). *Restructuring the middle level school: Implications for school leaders.* Albany, NY: State University of New York Press.

Coblin, M. P., Huss, D., Kirk, B., Lonneman, M., & Melville, C. (1998). *A standards-based thematic unit: "Crictor."* Ames, IA: M. H. Rosenbusch & E. Lorenz (Eds.), National K–12 Foreign Language Resource Center.

Council of Europe. (2000). European Language Portfolio. Retrieved May 11, 2004, from http://www.culture2.coe.int/portfolio.

Council for Basic Education. (2004). *Academic atrophy: The condition of the liberal arts in America's public schools.* Washington, DC: Author.

Curtain, H. A., & Dahlberg, C. A. (2004). *Languages and children—Making the match* (3rd ed.). Boston: Pearson Education.

Diamond, M., & Hopson, J. (1998). *Magic trees of the mind: How to nurture your child's intelligence, creativity, and healthy emotions from birth through adolescence.* New York: Penguin Putnam.

DiRocco, M. D. (1998–1999). How an alternating-day schedule empowers teachers [at Lewisburg Area Middle School, PA.]. *Educational Leadership, 56*(4), 82–84.

Donald, J. (1997). *Improving the environment for learning.* San Francisco: Jossey-Bass Publishers.

Egan, K. (1979). *Educational development.* New York: Oxford University Press.

Egan, K. (1986). *Teaching as story telling.* Chicago: The University of Chicago Press.

Eichhorn, D. H. (1966). *The middle school.* New York: Center for Applied Research.

Epstein, H. T., & Toepfer, C. F., Jr. (1978). A neuroscience basis for reorganizing middle school education. *Educational Leadership, 36,* 656–660.

Fantini, A. E. (Ed.). (1997). *New ways in teaching culture.* Arlington, VA: Teachers of English to Speakers of Other Languages.

Galloway, V. B. (1985). *A design for the improvement of the teaching of culture in foreign language classrooms.* ACTFL project proposal. Yonkers, NY: American Council on the Teaching of Foreign Languages.

Gardner, H. (1993). *Frames of mind: The theory of multiple intelligences.* New York: Basic Books.

Hadley, A. O. (2001). *Teaching language in context* (3rd ed.). Boston: Heinle & Heinle.

Jensen, E. (1998). *Teaching with the brain in mind.* Alexandria, VA: Association for Supervision and Curriculum Development.

Jensen, E. (2000). Brain-Based Learning. San Diego, CA: The Brain Store.

Johnston, J. H. (1984). A synthesis of research findings on middle level education. In J. H. Lounsbury (Ed.), *Perspectives: Middle school education, 1964–1984* (pp. 134–156). Columbus, OH: Middle School Association.

Johnston, J. H., & Markle, G. (1979). What research says to the middle level practitioner, Columbus, OH: National Middle School Association.

Kaplan, I. (1997). Activities to integrate culture into the classroom. Paper presented at the American Association of Teachers of Spanish and Portuguese Pedagogy Summit, Breckinridge, CO.

Kelley, C., & Meyers, J. (1995). *Cross-cultural adaptability inventory.* Minneapolis: MN. National Computer Systems. Retrieved February 24, 2004, from http://www.ncspearsonassessment.com.

Kennedy, D. F., & DeLorenzo, W. E. (1994). The case for exploratory programs in middle/junior high school. *Foreign Language Annals, 27,* 69–73.

Kennedy, D. F., & DeLorenzo, W. E. (1985). *Complete guide to exploratory foreign language programs.* Lincolnwood, IL: NTC/Contemporary Publishing Group.

Kentucky Department of Education. (2004a). The Kentucky Framework for World Language Learning: It's McLicious! Retrieved January 31, 2004, from http://www.education.ky.gov/KDE/Instructional+Resources/High+School/Language+Learning/Other+World+Languages/Kentucky+Framework+for+World+Language+Learning.htm

Kentucky Department of Education. (2004b). The Kentucky Framework for World Language Learning: Kentucky Multiple Entry Point Charts. Retrieved March 8, 2004, from http://www.education.ky.gov/KDE/Instructional+Resources/High+School/Language+Learning/Other+World+Languages/Kentucky+Framework+for+World+Language+Learning.htm.

Kluckhohn, F. R. (2004). The Florence R. Kluckhohn Center for the Study of Values: Retrieved February 28, 2004, from http://www.valuescenter.org/method.html.

Kluckhohn, F. R., & Strodtbeck, F. L. (1961). *Variations in value orientations.* Evanston, IL: Row, Peterson.

Knop, C. K., & Sandrock, P. (1994). The case for a sequential second language learning experience at the middle level. *Foreign Language Annals, 27,* 77–83.

Kohls, L. R., & Knight, J. M. (1994). *Developing intercultural awareness: A cross-cultural training handbook.* Yarmouth, ME: Intercultural Press.

Lange, D. L. (1999). Planning for and using the new national culture standards. In J. K. Phillips & R. M Terry (Eds.), *Foreign language standards: Linking research, theories, and practices* (pp. 57–135). Lincolnwood, IL: National Textbook Company.

Lipsitz, J. S. (1980). The age group. In M. Johnson (Ed.), *Toward adolescence: The middle school years* (pp. 7–31). Seventy-ninth Yearbook of the National Society for the Study of Education, Part. 1. Chicago: University of Chicago Press.

Martin, T. (1993). Turning points revisited: How effective middle-grades schools address developmental needs of young adolescent students. *Journal of Health Education,* Supplement, S-24–S-27.

Mead, M. (1965). Early adolescence in the United States. *Bulletin of the National Association of Secondary School Principals, 49,* 5–10.

Melton, G. E. (1984). The junior high school: Successes and failures. In J. H. Lounsbury (Ed.), *Perspectives: Middle school education, 1964–1984* (pp. 5–13). Columbus, OH: National Middle School Association.

Met, M. (1994). Current foreign language practices in middle schools. *Foreign Language Annals, 27,* 43–58.

Met, M. (1995). Foreign language instruction in the middle schools: A new view for the coming century. In R. Donato & R. M. Terry (Eds.), *Foreign language learning: The journey of a lifetime* (pp. 76–110). The ACTFL Foreign Language Education Series. Lincolnwood, IL: NTC/Contemporary Publishing Group.

National Middle School Association (NMSA). (2003). *This we believe: Developmentally responsive middle level schools.* Columbus, OH: Author. Retrieved February 28, 2004, from http://www.nmsa.org.

National Standards in Foreign Language Education Project (NSFLEP). (1999). *National standards for foreign language learning: Preparing for the 21st century.* Lawrence, KS: Allen Press.

Nerenz, A. G. (1990). The exploratory years: Foreign languages in the middle level curriculum. In S. Magnan (Ed.), *Shifting the instructional focus to the learner* (pp. 93–126). Northeast Conference Reports. Middlebury, VT: Northeast Conference on the Teaching of Foreign Languages.

Ortuño, M. M. (1991). Cross-cultural awareness in the foreign language class: The Kluckhohn Model. *The Modern Language Journal, 75,* 449–459.

Poplin, M. S., & Stone, S. (1992). Paradigm shifts in instructional strategies: From reductionism to holistic/constructivism. In W. Stainback & S. Stainback (Eds.), *Controversial issues confronting special education.* Boston: Allyn & Bacon.

Ralph, E. G. (1994). Middle and secondary L2 teachers meeting classroom management challenges via effective teaching research. *Foreign Language Annals, 27,* 89–103.

Redmond, M. L., & Lorenz, E. (1999). *Teacher to teacher: Model lessons for K–8 foreign language.* Lincolnwood, IL: National Textbook Company.

Roberts, C., Byram, M., Barro, A., Jordan, S., & Street, B. (2001). *Language learners as ethnographers.* Clevedon, UK: Multilingual Matters.

Robinson, G. (1981). *Issues in second language and cross-cultural education: The forest through the trees.* Boston: Heinle & Heinle.

Sandrock, P., & Webb, E. (2003). *Learning Languages in Middle School: Position paper.* Retrieved February 26, 2004, from http://www.ncssfl.org.

Savignon, S. J., & Sysoyev, P. (2002). Sociocultural strategies for a dialogue of cultures. *The Modern Language Journal, 86,* 508–524.

Shirts, G. R. (2001a). *Bafá Bafá.* Del Mar, CA: Simulation Training Systems. Retrieved March 8, 2004, from http://www.stsintl.com.

Shirts, G. R. (2001b). *Rafá Rafá.* Del Mar, CA: Simulation Training Systems. Retrieved March 8, 2004, from http://www.stsintl.com.

Shrenko, L. (1994). *Structuring a learner-centered school.* Palatine, IL: IRI/Skylight Publishing.

Shrum, J. L. (1991). Testing in context: A lesson from foreign language learning. *Vision, 1*(3), 7–8.

Stowell, L. P., & McDaniel, J.E. (1997). The changing face of assessment. In J. L. Irvin (Ed.), *What current research says to the middle level practitioner.* Columbus, OH: National Middle School Association.

Thiagarajan, S. (1994). *Barnga: A simulation game on culture clashes.* Yarmouth, ME: Intercultural Press. Retrieved March 2, 2004, from http://www.interculturalpress.com.

Ungerer, T. (1980). *Crictor.* Paris, France: L'École des Loisirs.

VanHouten, J. B., & Fulkerson, G. (2004). LinguaFolio Kentucky! Retrieved May 11, 2004, from http://www.education.ky.gov/KDE/Instructional+Resources/High+School/Language+Learning/Other+World+Languages/LinguaFolio+Kentucky.htm.

Verkler, K. W. (1994). Middle school philosophy and second language acquisition theory: Working together for enhanced proficiency. *Foreign Language Annals, 27,* 19–42.

Wing, B. H. (1996). Starting early: Foreign languages in the elementary and middle schools. In B. H. Wing (Ed.), *Foreign languages for all: Challenges and choices* (pp. 21–55). Northeast Conference Reports. Lincolnwood, IL: NTC/Contemporary Publishing Group.

Wiseman, D. G., Hunt, G. H., & Bedwell, L. E. (1986). Teaching for critical thinking. Paper presented at the Annual Meeting of the Association of Teacher Educators, Atlanta, GA.

Wolfe, P., & Brandt, R. (1998). What do we know from brain research? *Educational Leadership, 56*(3), 8–13.

Wright, D. A. (2000). Culture as information and culture as affective process: A comparative study. *Foreign Language Annals, 33,* 330–341.

Wright, D. A. (2003). Fostering cross-cultural adaptability through foreign language study. *NECTFL Review, 52,* 36–39.

NOTES

1. The National Middle School Association (NMSA) advocates the elimination of the following practices in middle schools: curriculum consisting of separate subjects and skills taught and tested in isolation from one another; content judged to be more important than the process by which it is learned; the excessive use of lecturing, rote learning, and drills; and the domination of textbooks and worksheets (Sandrock & Webb, 2003, p. 3).

2. See Wing (1996) for examples of middle school exploratory, sequential, and immersion programs. See Curtain & Dahlberg (2004, pp. 437–464) for a guide to program planning and articulation, detailing how to build a middle school program.

3. For a comprehensive discussion about exploratory language programs, see Kennedy and DeLorenzo (1985).

4. See Curtain & Dahlberg (2004) for tips about what materials to have available in your middle school classroom (pp. 299–326) and how to best teach from a mobile cart (pp. 219–223).

5. For example, in early times, an expected practice at mealtime was for those seated at the table to keep their hands on the table where they could be seen. The perspective underlying this practice was one of guarding one's safety and making sure that dinner guests did not conceal weapons under the table. This perspective is no longer operational in most contemporary cultures.

6. Note that German I students in Wright's (2000) study were asked to complete the culture portfolio in English.

However, we encourage teachers to integrate the target language and culture and guide students in using the target language as much as possible.

7. On the Doing/Being orientation, a midpoint, called "Being-in-Becoming," is often included (Ortuño, 1991).

8. The standardized survey and method created by Dr. Kluckhohn consisted of four dimensions, not including "Human Nature." Use of the survey by social science researchers resulted in the inclusion of this fifth orientation in the survey. Also, the "method" is sometimes called a "model." Kohls and Knight (1994, pp. 33–38) provide additional tools for using the Kluckhohn model in workshops.

9. For information on the Cross-Cultural Adaptability Inventory and workshops and simulations to increase cultural awareness, see the *Teacher's Handbook* Web site.

10. See Savignon & Sysoyev (2002) for discussion of additional conversations for each of the strategies outlined.

11. For another middle school lesson (grade 8) on French cities, see View and Reflect, Activity B on the *Teacher's Handbook* Web site.

12. *Realia* (cultural products) are real items or objects from the target culture, such as menus, train tickets, newspaper articles, party invitations, eating utensils, and toys.

13. See the *Teacher's Handbook* Web site for information on the Grady Profile CD-ROM and its use in ESL and second language teaching.

thandbook.heinle.com

CHAPTER 6

Using an Interactive Approach to Develop Interpretive Communication

In this chapter, you will learn about:

- the three modes of communication
- the interpretive mode for teaching listening, reading, and viewing
- the processes involved in listening and reading
- reader-/listener-based and text-based factors in comprehension and interpretation

- integration of authentic texts
- exploration of literary texts
- acquisition of new vocabulary through text exploration
- the interactive model for developing listening, reading, and viewing

Teach and Reflect: Using the Interactive Model to Explore an Authentic Printed Text; Using the Interactive Model to Explore an Authentic Audio/Video Segment; Teaching Literature at the Post-Secondary Level

Discuss and Reflect: Developing Interpretive Listening: Scripts or No Scripts?; Reading Aloud

CONCEPTUAL ORIENTATION

Historically, communicative ability in a foreign language has been described in terms of the four skills of listening, speaking, reading, and writing. As you learned in Chapter 2, instructional methods such as the Audiolingual Method (ALM) even fostered the teaching of the four skills separately and in a prescribed sequence (Chastain, 1988). Communication in the world, however, occurs as skills are used in concert, not in isolation, and it is shaped by specific cultural contexts. Listening and reading are often catalysts for speaking and/or writing; discussion often leads to written communication; and all of these aspects of communication occur within a specific set of cultural perspectives that govern patterns of interaction among individuals and interpretations of the message. Therefore, comprehension and interpretation involve both cognitive processes, for the integration of all skills, and social processes, such as discussing the possible meanings of texts with others. For example, you may have approached the task of reading this chapter by taking some notes about and/or discussing your background knowledge of the information you hope to learn. You might take notes as you read the chapter. After reading you will probably discuss the information with your classmates. You will have used all skills both cognitively and socioculturally as you explore the new information presented in the chapter.

In this chapter, we will explore the nature of interpretive communication and strategies for developing it in the classroom. *Teacher's Handbook* advocates the integration of interpretive communication with the other two modes of communication—interpersonal and presentational—and offers ideas in this chapter for how to accomplish this.

 The three modes of communication are interpersonal, interpretive, and presentational.

Framework of Communicative Modes

The standards define communication by means of the three communicative modes that emphasize the context and purpose of the communication and thus depict the four skills as working in an integrated fashion. The framework is based on the model proposed by Brecht and Walton (1995), the purpose of which is to illustrate how one participates in "cultural discourses," or within culturally defined contexts. Figure 6.1 illustrates the framework.

The Interpersonal Mode

This mode features active negotiation of meaning among individuals, regardless of skill modality. Since participants observe and monitor one another, they can make clarifications and adjustments in their communication. Communication can be realized through face-to-face conversation and written correspondence—all four skills of listening, speaking, reading, and writing can be involved in the interpersonal mode. This mode will be explored further in Chapters 7 and 8.

 The interpersonal mode features two-way oral or written communication and negotiation of meaning.

The Interpretive Mode

This mode focuses on the interpretation of meaning in oral and printed texts when there is no possibility of negotiation of meaning with the writer or speaker. This interpretation of meaning takes into account the cultural context in which the text is situated. Interpretation can occur in activities such as listening to an authentic news broadcast, reading a novel, or viewing a film. Clarification of meaning is not possible as the creator of the text is absent or not accessible. Since the interpretive mode does not provide for active negotiation between the reader and writer or the listener and speaker, it may also require a deeper knowledge of culture in order to gain a cultural interpretation of a text.

The interpretive mode encompasses listening, reading, and viewing skills. It involves not only literal comprehension of a text but also the interpretation of it, including cultural perspectives, personal opinions, and points of view. It is important to note that interpretation goes beyond the traditional idea of "comprehension," since interpretation includes the reader's/listener's ability to "read (or listen) between the lines" and bring his or her own background knowledge and ideas to the task (NSFLEP, 1999, pp. 36–37).

This ability to interpret is based largely on one's ability to engage in *inferencing,* "a thinking process that involves reasoning a step beyond the text, using generalization, synthesis, and/or explanation" (Hammadou, 2002, p. 219). For example, when reading

"My brother fell off the ladder and has to stay in bed for three days," the reader typically reasons beyond the text and infers what might have happened to the brother when he fell and why he might have to stay in bed.

To draw inferences, the reader/listener uses generalizations of typical events and explanatory reasoning of how those events might pertain to the text being explored (Hammadou, 2002). While typical comprehension questions that follow a text assess understanding of factual information, they may not engage the listener or reader in interpreting the text and drawing inferences, i.e., going beyond the literal level to bring in personal points of view and cultural perspectives that pertain to the text. It is important to note, additionally, that comprehension and interpretation of a text are *not* the same as translation of the text, since assigning meaning to a text involves much more than matching surface-level equivalencies from one language to another or only understanding the factual information in the text.

Interpretation of a text (use of inferencing) is not a skill that is reserved for advanced-level high school students, but rather should be fostered in language instruction in the early grades. In their native language, children engage in inferencing routinely when they read stories or see movies—they give their opinions and explain why they liked or didn't like the story/movie, describe the qualities of the characters, predict how the story will end, describe the moral of the story, and compare the story to others with which they are familiar. Foreign language teachers at the elementary and middle school levels can capitalize on students' L1 interpretation abilities and engage them in interpreting stories and fables in L2. High school language teachers can then build on these interpretive skills and focus on higher level interpretation that may involve aspects such as author's intent, tone of the text, and L2 cultural perspectives.

In foreign language learning and teaching, the interpretive mode refers to both (1) a component of daily communication that enables one to make sense of and interpret oral, printed, and video texts, and (2) a vehicle for language acquisition (i.e., interpreting input and texts facilitates language acquisition and development). As you read this chapter, you will notice that the interpretive mode is explored with both of these purposes in mind.

 The interpretive mode refers to both (1) a component of daily communication that enables one to make sense of and interpret oral, printed, and video texts, and (2) a vehicle for language acquisition. ▪

 Comprehension and interpretation of a text are *not* the same as translation of the text. ▪

The Presentational Mode

This mode features formal, one-way communication to an audience of listeners or readers. Speaking and/or writing skills are involved, but no direct opportunity exists for active negotiation of meaning between the presenter and audience. Examples include giving a speech or oral report, preparing a paper or story, and producing a newscast. Substantial knowledge of the language and culture is necessary on the part of the speaker and of the audience, to some extent, since the goal is to ensure that the audience will be able to interpret the message (NSFLEP, 1999). This mode will be explored further in Chapter 9.

 The presentational mode features formal, one-way communication to an audience of listeners or readers. ▪

As shown in Figure 6.1, successful communication in all three modes requires knowledge of cultural products, practices, and perspectives so that understanding of the appropriate patterns of social interaction and encoding of meaning can occur.

FIGURE 6.1 Framework for the Communicative Modes

	INTERPERSONAL	**INTERPRETIVE**	**PRESENTATIONAL**
Definitions	Direct oral communication (e.g., face-to-face or telephonic) between individuals who are in personal contact Direct written communication between individuals who come into personal contact	Receptive communication of oral or written messages Mediated communication via print and non-print materials Listener, viewer, reader works with visual or recorded materials whose creator is absent	Productive communication using oral or written language Spoken or written communication for people (an audience) with whom there is no immediate personal contact or which takes place in a one-to-many mode Author or creator of visual or recorded material not known personally to listener
Paths	Productive abilities: speaking, writing Receptive abilities: listening, reading	Primarily receptive abilities: listening, reading, viewing	Primarily productive abilities: speaking, writing, showing
Cultural knowledge	Knowledge of cultural perspectives governing interactions between individuals of different ages, statuses, backgrounds Ability to recognize that languages use different practices to communicate Ability to recognize that cultures use different patterns of interaction	Knowledge of how cultural perspectives are embedded in products (literary and artistic) Knowledge of how meaning is encoded in products Ability to analyze content, compare it to information available in own language and assess linguistic and cultural differences Ability to analyze and compare content in one culture to interpret U.S. culture	Knowledge of cultural perspectives governing interactions between a speaker and his/her audience and a writer and his/her reader Ability to present cross-cultural information based on background of the audience Ability to recognize that cultures use different patterns of interaction
KNOWLEDGE OF THE LINGUISTIC SYSTEM			
The use of grammatical, lexical, phonological, semantic, pragmatic, and discourse features necessary for participation in the Communicative Modes.			

Source: NSFLEP, 1999, p. 37.

STANDARDS HIGHLIGHT: Exploring the Interpretive Mode Through Listening, Reading, Viewing

Few would dispute the claim that comprehension is necessary in order for language acquisition to occur. To communicate successfully in the target language, learners depend upon their ability to comprehend the spoken and written word. As explored in Chapters 1, 2, and 3, current research in second language acquisition (SLA) and approaches to foreign language teaching acknowledge the role of input in the acquisition process. Integration of authentic oral and printed texts into language teaching serves to merge culture and context with language, provide engaging topics for learners to explore, stimulate learners' interest in language study, and offer a means for engaging learners in more challenging, higher order thinking tasks. Historically, however, interpretive skills have received less attention in language teaching than have interpersonal skills. Due in part to a lack of knowledge about interpretive processes, teachers often assumed that comprehension would occur on its own or that translation would lead to comprehension and interpretation. However, as you have already seen, merely exposing learners to oral or printed input is not sufficient, since they also must be equipped to make meaning of this input through avenues such as comprehension strategies and interaction with others.

Interpretive Communication: Listening and Reading Processes

How Comprehension Processing Occurs

Listening and reading comprehension involve both cognitive and social processes. Listening and reading are active cognitive processes that require an interplay between various types of knowledge. Listeners and readers draw upon the following as they attempt to interpret a text:

- their knowledge of the target language, e.g., vocabulary, syntax;
- their background knowledge and experiences in the world;
- their knowledge of how various types of discourse, such as magazine articles, literary texts, radio broadcasts, and talk shows, are organized, i.e., use of cohesive devices such as pronouns, conjunctions, and transitional phrases to link meaning across sentences, as well as the use of coherence to maintain the message's unity;
- their ability to hold information in short-term memory as they attend to the text; and
- their ability to use a variety of strategies to help them bring meaning to the comprehension task.

Listeners and readers rely upon the types of knowledge and abilities described above as they perform a variety of tasks in the comprehension process. Some tasks or subskills reflect *bottom-up processing* (see Chapter 2), in which meaning is understood through analysis of language parts. Simply put, the listener or reader processes language in a sequential manner, combining sounds or letters to form words, then combining words to form phrases, clauses, and sentences of the text (Goodman, 1967). Bottom-up subskills include discriminating between different sounds and letters, recognizing word-order patterns, recognizing intonation cues, analyzing sentence structure, translating individual words, and examining word endings. Bottom-up models that seek to explain reading comprehension are *text-driven* and portray the reader as someone who "approaches the text by concentrating exclusively on the combination of letters and words in a purely linear manner" (Martinez-Lage, 1995, p. 70).

Other comprehension tasks or subskills reflect *top-down processing* (see Chapter 2), in which meaning is derived through the use of contextual clues and activation of personal background knowledge about the content of the text. These subskills include identifying key ideas and guessing meaning through a process that Goodman (1967) calls a "psycholinguistic guessing game." In his description of a top-down approach to reading, Goodman states that "Efficient reading does not result from precise perception and identification of all elements, but from skill in selecting the fewest, most productive cues necessary to produce guesses which are right the first time" (cf. Chastain, 1988, p. 223). Top-down models of comprehension are *reader-driven* and focus on what the reader/listener brings to the text in terms of knowledge of the world (Lally, 1998).

The current view of the interpretive skills is that the listener/reader arrives at meaning by using *both* bottom-up and top-down processing, in concert (Bernhardt, 1991a; Swaffar, Arens, & Byrnes, 1991). According to Scarcella and Oxford (1992), "Listening can best be understood as a highly complex, interactive operation in which bottom-up processing is interspersed with top-down processing, the latter involving guessing" (p. 142). Similarly, in their discussion of the reading process, Swaffar, Arens, and Byrnes state that reading comprehension "results from interactive variables that operate simultaneously rather than sequentially" (1991, p. 21). Furthermore, they maintain that the message of the text interacts with reader perceptions and that these interactions have the following components:

Top-down factors: reader
   1. reader background (semantic knowledge)
   2. reader perspective (reading strategies)

Top-down factors: text
   3. text schema (topic)
   4. text structure (organizational pattern of the information)
   5. episodic sequence (scripts or story grammar)

Bottom-up factors: text and reader
   6. illustrative detail (micropropositions)
   7. the surface language features of the text in letters, words, and individual sentences
   8. reader language proficiency (p. 24)

There is evidence to suggest that learners perceive top-down strategies to be the more immediate strategies needed for comprehension and bottom-up strategies to be necessary in "repairing" comprehension in the face of difficulty (Vogely, 1995). This finding is supported by Eskey's (1986) interactive reading model, which proposes that readers use both (1) lower-level "identification" skills through which they recognize words and structures necessary for decoding; and (2) higher level "interpretive" skills through which they reconstruct meaning of whole parts of the text. Both of these skill types are interactive in that they blend into one as the reader or listener interprets a text and makes it a part of what he or she knows (Eskey, 1986).

In addition to the cognitive processes described earlier, listening and reading comprehension also involve a "social" process. In her sociocognitive view of second-language reading, Bernhardt (1991a) proposes that readers interact with the features of a text, select the features that they feel are important for processing the information, and then use the selected features to reconstruct the text and interpret the message.[1] This process involves a different concept of "text," one that includes not only linguistic elements, but also the text's pragmatic nature, its intentionality, its content, and its topic (Bernhardt, 1991a).

Furthermore, a great deal of comprehension and interpretation is based on the experiences the learner brings to the text. The learner gains new insights about the meaning of a text as a result of text-based discussions he or she has with others. This social view of comprehension reflects the sociocultural view of language learning and instruction posited in Chapter 1, in which learners and the teacher interact in the ZPD in order to co-construct meaning and interpretation of a text. This type of mediation mirrors the way in which comprehension is constructed socioculturally in the world outside the classroom.

 Top-down and bottom-up processes are used together in comprehension. ■

The Relationship of L1 and L2 Interpretive Processes

Much of the research in L2 listening and reading cognition is based on studies conducted in L1 (Fecteau, 1999; Brown, 1998; Rubin, 1994; Joiner, 1986; Bernhardt, 1986).[2] Many studies have examined the relationship between L1 and L2 comprehension. Bernhardt and Kamil (1995) found that both L1 reading skills and L2 linguistic knowledge contribute to one's L2 reading comprehension. They maintain that linguistic knowledge contributes more at lower proficiency levels, while L1 reading skills play a greater role in reading at higher levels. In other words, the reading ability of novice L2 learners might be predicted more on the basis of the level of their linguistic knowledge, while the reading ability of advanced L2 learners might be related more closely to their L1 reading skills. Fecteau's (1999) study of U.S. college students enrolled in an introductory French literature course also revealed that L1 and L2 reading skills are more interrelated among more proficient language learners, in which case L1 reading skills contribute more to L2 comprehension than does L2 proficiency. This study also showed that organization of the text and level of background knowledge are important factors that impact comprehension in both L1 and L2 reading tasks; the "story-like" organization of the text and activated background knowledge of readers led to greater comprehension.

Similar studies have compared L1 and L2 listening comprehension, particularly around the issue of *discourse signaling cues*, metalinguistic devices that function as directional guides to signal how readers and listeners should interpret the incoming information (Tyler, 1994). Examples of signaling cues are previews (e.g., *There are four stages of this culture shock*), summarizers (*To sum up so far*), emphasis markers (e.g., *This is the key*), and logical connectives (e.g., *and, or, first,* and *second*) (Jung, 2003, p. 563). Many studies confirm that the beneficial effects of signaling cues found in L1 reading research can also be found in L1 listening comprehension. Listeners who attended to signaled texts in their native language recalled significantly more main ideas and performed better on open-ended questions when tested (Richards, Fajen, Sullivan, & Gillespie, 1997; Hron, Kurbjuhn, Mandl, & Schnotz, 1985).

Jung (2003) conducted a study to determine whether the positive effects of signaling cues in L1 listening could also be applied to L2 listening. Results of her study revealed that students who listened to lectures in the target language that contained signaling cues recalled significantly more information (i.e., both main ideas and supporting details) than did their nonsignalled counterparts. These results corroborated the findings of several previous studies that examined the effect of signaling cues on L2 listening (Chung, 2000; Flowerdew & Tauroza, 1995). In these and other studies, as in the case of the L2 reading research presented earlier, text type was found to be important since certain text types make use of particular signaling cues or use them more or less frequently. For example, in texts that feature a "comparison-and-contrast" organization, signaling cues might not play a critical role in making the text comprehensible since the text structure in already evident to the listener (Jung, 2003; Dunkel & Davis, 1994). Similarly, students might not rely as much on signaling cues in certain text types where the chronological order might be more familiar to students, such as narratives, as compared to expository text types, which often present a more complex set of relationships among ideas and whose meaning could be clarified through signaling cues (Barry & Lazarte, 1998; Horiba, 2000).

Differences Between Listening and Reading

In the previous sections, you have seen that listening and reading are similar—both draw upon knowledge of the language, background knowledge, contextual clues, cognitive processing skills, and the use of comprehension strategies. However, there are also important differences between the two. Written texts, particularly those that are presentational and intended for an audience, are typically organized in grammatical sentences arranged in coherent paragraphs (Richards, 1983). Spoken texts, on the other hand, can include ungrammatical or reduced forms; are often marked by pauses, hesitations, and fillers; and may feature topics that shift as the conversation is co-constructed. Another difference deals with the "accessibility" of the text (Stevick, 1984). In the reading comprehension task, the reader can reread what was read before and can look ahead to anticipate what is coming. In listening comprehension, the listener may be forced to comprehend with only one opportunity to hear the oral segment; any inattention to what is being said at the moment may cause him or her to lose part of the message (Hadley, 2001). Lund (1991) found that presenting a text twice, either in listening or reading, can be beneficial to students. If students do not have multiple opportunities to hear an oral segment, there is a risk of depending too heavily on short-term memory, thus confusing comprehension with memory recall.

The Viewing Process

The interpretive mode relates not only to listening to an oral message and reading a written text, but also to viewing videos, movies, plays, and television programs. The viewing medium provides a unique way of bringing the target culture into the classroom and making learning more meaningful and stimulating. Through video, for example, learners can "witness the dynamics of interaction as they observe native speakers in authentic settings speaking and using different accents, registers, and paralinguistic cues (e.g., posture, gestures)" (Secules, Herron, & Tomasello, 1992, p. 480). Although multimedia research in second-language learning is still in its infancy, an increasing number of studies have verified the effectiveness of video instruction in the classroom (Hanley, Herron, & Cole, 1995; Herron, Cole, York, & Linden, 1999; Price, 1990; Secules, Herron, & Tomasello, 1992; Weyers, 1999). Students who view videos demonstrate greater listening comprehension than do students who do not view them (Price, 1990; Secules, Herron, & Tomasello, 1992; Weyers, 1999). Videos have also been found to have a positive effect on learning grammar in the foreign language (Ramsay, 1991), the development of advanced level proficiency skills (Rifkin, 2000), and learning cultural information (Herron, Corrie, Cole, & Dubreil, 1999). In addition, studies have indicated that videos that are shown as advance organizers prior to the reading of a passage facilitate the retention of cultural information in the written text (Herron & Hanley, 1992) and are more effective advance organizers than are pictures used with teacher narratives (Hanley, Herron, & Cole, 1995). Furthermore, one study indicated that, in addition to gains made in listening comprehension, students who viewed an authentic Spanish-language *telenovela* (soap opera) video showed greater confidence in generating output and greater scope and breadth of discourse (Weyers, 1999).

Videos that feature definite storylines and clearly drawn main characters are good texts for viewing (Joiner, 1990; Voller & Widdows, 1993). Studies show that videos that contain advance organizers and captions are most effective in facilitating comprehension (Chung, 1999; Herron, Cole, York, & Linden, 1998; Markham, 1999; Markham, Peter, & McCarthy, 2001). Swaffar and Vlatten (1997) propose that the viewing process should begin with silent viewing, during which students explore the possible messages and cultural perspectives implied by the visual images. Then, as students are exposed to sound, they verify whether their visual comprehension matches their understanding of what they hear. They engage in comprehension tasks and use the new information they learn through the viewing as the basis for discussion, role playing, and creative writing (Swaffar & Vlatten, 1997). Thus the viewing process involves predicting and anticipating the meaning of the visual images and then comparing these predictions to what is understood in the oral message.

Research on the Variables Involved in Comprehension and Interpretation

Research documents a number of variables that affect comprehension and interpretation of a text, be it oral or printed. These variables relate to (1) reader- and listener-based factors, such as familiarity with the topic, use of memory, use of strategies, purpose for listening/reading/viewing, and level of anxiety; and (2) text-based factors, such as text length, text organization, content and interest of the text, and vocabulary (Knutson, 1997).

Reader- and Listener-Based Factors

Topic Familiarity.   The first reader- and listener-based variable is the key role that *topic familiarity*, or background knowledge, plays in facilitating comprehension, regardless of the learner's proficiency level (Hammadou, 2000; Schmidt-Rinehart, 1994). This variable has already been explored in Chapter 2 in terms of the importance of context and background knowledge in understanding input. The degree to which the reader or listener is able to actually merge input with previously acquired knowledge structures, or schemata, determines how successful he or she will be in comprehending (Minsky, 1982). This linking of new and existing knowledge helps the listener or reader make sense of the text more quickly. The key role of topic/context and background knowledge has been verified by many studies on listening (Chiang & Dunkel, 1992; Bransford & Johnson, 1972) and reading (Hammadou, 2000; Hauptman, 2000; Hanley, Herron, & Cole, 1995; Herron & Hanley, 1992; Nunan, 1985; Lee, 1986a; Mueller, 1980; Omaggio, 1979). These experiments have shown that language learners who are provided with prior contextual assistance, such as pictures, video segments, or pertinent cultural information, comprehend more accurately than they do in the absence of such support. The use of contextual and background information aids understanding by limiting the number of possible text interpretations. Furthermore, Hammadou (2000, 2002) found prior knowledge of the topic to be a key factor in enabling students to recall what they read and to make more logical inferences (e.g., those that have direct support from the text). Even beginning language learners can engage in inferencing if they have background knowledge of the topic (Hammadou, 1991).

Teachers are cautioned to not confuse learners' background knowledge with their level of interest in a text topic. For example, Carrell and Wise (1998) found in their research that background knowledge and interest in a text topic may be essentially uncorrelated. Though on the surface this finding may seem to be counterintuitive, according to Baldwin, Peleg-Bruckner, and McClintock (1985), "It should not be surprising then to find that a group of above average students could be fairly knowledgeable about space exploration and American Indians, for example, without having any real enthusiasm for those subjects" (p. 502). Conversely, it is possible to encounter a learner who is very interested in space exploration and American Indians but may be very weak in background knowledge of the topics (Baldwin, Peleg-Bruckner, & McClintock, 1985). Therefore, teachers should realize that even if students have prior knowledge of a text topic, they may or may not have interest in exploring the text. You will read more about interest level later in this section.

Short-term or Working Memory.   A second reader- and listener-based variable is the ability of the reader or listener to hold information in his/her *short-term* or *working memory* during comprehension processing. According to Just and Carpenter (1992), the working memory stores words, phrases, meaning, and grammatical or thematic structures for later retrieval, in addition to performing language processing, such as accessing word meaning while syntactically processing a phrase. They suggest that listeners and readers with a small working memory span may have difficulty maintaining syntactic information (e.g., phrases and sentences from the text) while attending to nonsyntactic information (e.g., use of context and background knowledge). A larger working memory span may be necessary in order to allow for interaction between syntactic and nonsyntactic information, ". . . which is necessary for developing multiple interpretations, using context, making inferences, or integrating information over large distances in a text" (Brown, 1998, p. 195). Although much more research is needed in this area, the role of memory may be one factor that accounts for individual differences in comprehension. Teachers can limit the load on memory during a comprehension task by preparing students for the oral/printed segment, showing students the task or activity before they attend to the segment so that they know the purpose of what they are about to listen to/read/view, allowing students to have the printed text available to them during the reading comprehension process, and permitting students to listen to or view a segment multiple times.

Strategies in Comprehending and Interpreting.   A third variable is the degree to which the reader or listener uses *strategies* in comprehending and interpreting a text. In both listening and reading, prediction of forthcoming input, or the "activation of correct expectancies," is one characteristic of native listener and reader processing (Oller, 1983, p. 10). Many studies support the claim that learners who interact with the text through strategies such as predicting, skimming, scanning, and using background knowledge comprehend much better than learners who fail to use these strategies (Vandergrift, 1997; Bacon, 1992a; Barnett, 1988a; Carrell, 1985; Palinscar & Brown, 1984). In her study examining how beginning-level Spanish students use strategies to comprehend authentic radio broadcasts, Bacon (1992b) found significant differences in strategy use between upper and lower achievers. Figure 6.2 summarizes the characteristics of successful versus less successful listeners, as reflected in Bacon's study.

Vandergrift (1997) examined the types of reception strategies that students at the novice and intermediate levels of oral proficiency used in their interactive listening with target language speakers. Figure 6.3 presents and defines these strategies and provides examples. Vandergrift's study revealed that the novice conversational partners demonstrated a higher use of kinesics (e.g., body language); global reprises (e.g., requests for repetition, rephrasing, simplification); and hypothesis testing in English to clarify meaning or ask for additional input than did their intermediate-level counterparts. Intermediate-level conversational partners used global reprises and hypothesis testing in the target language,

FIGURE 6.2 Summary of Characteristics of Successful Versus Less Successful Listeners

Successful Listeners
1. Showed greater flexibility: Greater number and range.
2. Not reluctant to rely on English when other strategies failed.
3. Could verbalize their strategies for controlling input.
4. Showed interest in understanding and learning.
5. Able to summarize and add detail.
6. Effectively used personal, world, or discourse knowledge.
7. Controlled comprehension process.
8. Used monitor marginally more successfully to help revise a hypothesis or choose between alternative interpretations. More realistic in evaluation of comprehension.
9. Were conscious of losing attention to meaning and could refocus.

Less Successful Listeners
1. Showed less flexibility: Tended to stick with one or two strategies.
2. Unlikely to mention using English as a comprehension strategy.
3. Expressed frustration with input.
4. Seemed to lose interest easily.
5. Unable to summarize, or seemed satisfied with little information.
6. Overdependent on previous knowledge.
7. Distracted by unknown vocabulary or extraneous factors.
8. Used monitor, but not particularly successfully. Easily discouraged or overconfident of comprehension.
9. When they lost their attention to meaning, had trouble refocusing.

Source: Bacon, 1992b, p. 327.

but the use of kinesics was less obvious; their use of uptake reflected their higher level of linguistic knowledge and ease in interacting in the target language. Recall that an example of uptake is repairing errors in speech; see Chapter 8 for more about error repair.

Evidence suggests that students benefit from direct strategy training in listening (Bacon, 1992b; Rost & Ross, 1991), reading (Kitajima, 1997; Barnett, 1988b; Carrell, 1989; Hosenfeld, 1984), and language learning in general (Oxford, 1990). For example, in Rusciolelli's (1995) study, Spanish students received training in using the following strategies in reading: prereading activities, skimming, scanning, identifying unknown words, contextualized guessing (relating words by analyzing parts of speech and by linking them to the context), looking up words in the dictionary, and writing a summary. This research revealed that after the strategy training, students demonstrated an increased use of guessing unknown words by analyzing the part of speech and by relating words to the context, and a decreased use of accessing the dictionary. Furthermore, students used two additional strategies more often than they did prior to training: skimming for main ideas and using illustrations and titles as clues to meaning (Rusciolelli, 1995). Thompson and Rubin (1993) conducted a study on listening in which they taught students learning Russian to choose from among a set of strategies when viewing a video segment. Their research revealed that strategy training improves listening comprehension and that students can be taught to choose their own strategies effectively.

Similarly, a recent study in listening suggests that learners benefit from training in using nonverbal communication cues (e.g., body language and gestures) that accompany spoken messages and texts to interpret meaning (Harris, 2003). Some illustrative gestures may complement the spoken word by visually reinforcing meaning, such as twisting a

FIGURE 6.3 Reception Strategies Used in Interactive Listening: Definitions and Examples

TYPOLOGY OF LISTENER FEEDBACK MOVES AND LIKELY SPEAKER RESPONSE(S)			
Strategy	**Stage**	**Definition**	**Speaker Response**
Global Reprise	I	Listener asks for repetition, rephrasing, simplification, or simply states that nothing was understood.	Repeat or rephrase entire utterance or segment.
Continuation Signal	I	Listener requests no elaboration or repetition and indicates current status of understanding with an overt statement or a nonverbal gesture.	Continue.
Lexical Reprise	II	Listener asks a question about a specific word; may include repetition of word with questioning intonation.	Repeat or rephrase entire utterance or segment.
Fragment Reprise	II	Listener asks a question about a specific part of the previous discourse; may include repetition.	Repeat or rephrase specific part of utterance.
Lexical Gap	II	Listener asks a question about a specific word or term, often requesting a repeat for the word.	Same response as above.
Positional Reprise	II	Listener refers to a position in the previous utterance that was not understood.	Same response as above.
Hypothesis Testing	III	Listener asks specific questions to verify what was heard and indicates a prepositional understanding (or misunderstanding) of the utterance.	Confirm if hypothesis check is true or plausible. Provide other information if listener's hypothesis is false.
Forward Inference	III	The listener overtly indicates current understanding by asking a question using established information given by the interlocutor.	Answer question, confirm assumption if consistent with story/conversation, modify assumption or add information to clarify misunderstanding.

Source: Vandergrift, 1997, p. 497.

finger while saying the word *spiral*. Other gestures supply or extend meaning that is not present in the spoken word, such as actions that imply how someone feels or his/her attitude in a situation (Harris, 2003). Of interest is the claim that while the research has suggested that visual support is more useful for beginning language learners, strategy training in using gestures to interpret meaning seems to be equally helpful for learners at higher proficiency levels, especially when the gestures are used to *extend* the meaning of the spoken word. A recent study by Frantzen (2003) corroborated these findings that highlight the value of strategy training in interpreting texts and argues that it is not only beneficial but it may also be necessary in order to maximize success in comprehension. See more about this study in the discussion below pertaining to the treatment of new vocabulary. See Appendix 6.1 (on the Web site) for "rate-building" exercises that teach students the strategy of reading rapidly for global meaning.

thandbook.heinle.com

Purpose for Listening/Reading/Viewing.   A fourth reader- and listener-based variable that affects comprehension and interpretation is the *purpose* for listening/reading/viewing—that is, the nature of the task. Reading (and also listening and viewing) with a purpose means "approaching texts with a specific perspective or goal" (Knutson, 1997, p. 51). Munby (1979) identifies two kinds of reading that involve different goals and skills. *Extensive reading*, usually for pleasure, requires the ability to understand main ideas, find specific information, and read quickly. *Intensive reading*, most often for information, requires the ability to read for details, understand implications, and follow relationships of thought throughout a text. Knutson (1997) suggests strategies such as the following for providing learners with specific purposes for reading: asking learners to read from a particular point of view (e.g., that of a detective, child, etc.); providing a reason for reading that reflects a real-world situation (e.g., looking through movie listings to find an appealing movie); giving groups of students a task to complete based on reading (e.g., students plan a trip after reading brochures, timetables, and maps and listening to weather and traffic reports); guiding students in text analysis of rhetorical devices such as register and audience; developing language literacy by engaging students in reading and discussing literature; and providing opportunities for learners to learn new information and pursue their own interests and enjoyment through interpretive tasks (pp. 51–55).

Anxiety.   The fifth and final reader- and listener-based variable refers to the level of *anxiety* that the listener/reader brings to the comprehension task. In Chapter 1, you learned about how learners' anxiety can have negative effects on language learning. The issue of anxiety has been examined specifically in the contexts of reading and listening comprehension. In her study of university Spanish students, Sellers (2000) found that learners with higher levels of foreign language anxiety tended to have higher levels of foreign language reading anxiety and vice versa, recalled overall less passage content than students who claimed to experience only minimal anxiety, recalled fewer important ideas, and tended to experience more off-task, interfering thoughts. These results are similar to those obtained by Saito, Garza, and Horwitz (1999), whose work also showed that foreign language reading anxiety is distinguishable from general foreign language anxiety and that learners who perceive reading in their target language as relatively difficult have significantly higher levels of reading anxiety than learners who perceive it as somewhat difficult or as relatively easy. In addition, in this study, when reading, English-speaking learners of Japanese were the most anxious, followed by French learners, with Russian learners exhibiting the lowest anxiety; the researchers hypothesize that this difference may be due to the unfamiliar and non-Roman writing system and foreign cultural content in the texts. Other findings in this study reveal that students experience anxiety when (1) they encounter unfamiliar words and structures, because they feel a need to understand everything, and (2) they have to read about cultural topics with which they are unfamiliar. Although the curricula of the students in this study offered instruction on how to approach the reading task, many students reported using word-for-word translation when reading in their foreign language, and they reported a sense of anxiety when asked by their teachers to read aloud in class.

Similar studies have examined anxiety in L2 listening tasks. According to Scarcella and Oxford (1992), students experience listening anxiety when they feel they must perform a task that is too difficult or unfamiliar to them. In Vogely's (1998) study examining L2 listening anxiety, beginning-level Spanish students reported four primary sources of anxiety: (1) oral input was too fast, poorly enunciated, and featured different accents; (2) listening comprehension exercises contained unfamiliar topics and vocabulary and complicated syntax; (3) there was a lack of visual support to help them with contextual guessing; and (4) they were only permitted to listen to oral segments once.

Reader- and listener-based factors include topic familiarity, memory capacity, comprehension strategies, the purpose of the task, and anxiety level.

Text-Based Factors

Length of Text. A sixth, text-based, variable relates to the *length of text* presented for comprehension and interpretation. In beginning-level classes, students are typically given shorter, edited texts to listen to or read. Learners who process shorter texts are more likely to use word-for-word processing strategies since the demands on memory permit greater attention to detail (Kintsch & van Dijk, 1978; Swaffar, Arens, & Byrnes, 1991). Recent studies suggest that longer texts may actually be easier for students to comprehend because they are more cohesive and provide more of a context from which meaning may be derived (Gascoigne, 2002a; Maxim, 2002). According to Swaffar and Bacon (1993), longer text length encourages students to use cognitive strategies that they are already familiar with in L1. For example, in reading a longer text, students derive meaning by making connections between segments, episodes, and events in the text, rather than focusing their attention to meaning at the word and sentence levels. A longer text may provide students with the information necessary to compensate for their limited L2 proficiency (Maxim, 2002; Hammadou, 1991). Swaffar, Arens, & Byrnes (1991) have suggested that texts of more than 500 words are effective for activating the use of different reading strategies and recall. However, in her examination of beginning college French textbooks, Gascoigne (2002b) found that readings averaged 247 words in length, indicating a reluctance of textbook authors to give introductory students longer texts to read, despite support for this in the research.

Teachers are advised to select longer texts with great care and to develop strategies for guiding students through them, since longer texts may intimidate novice learners. Texts should be appropriate to the age and instructional level of students. Longer texts accompanied by visuals are much less daunting to students than multiple-page texts with dense prose. Also, the goal of reading longer texts should never be to comprehend every word; students may be expected to identify the main ideas and key details of a longer text on the first pass and perhaps later be asked to read more carefully for other details. Teachers should remember to *edit the task* to the level of students' interpretive abilities.

 Teachers should remember to *edit the task* to the level of students' interpretive abilities.

Organization of the Oral or Printed Text. A seventh, text-based, variable in the comprehension/interpretation process pertains to the *organization of the oral or printed text* presented. Traditionally, the difficulty of texts has been judged on the basis of the simplicity of grammatical structures and the familiarity of the vocabulary. According to Lee (1987), this may be due to the fact that we have often tested comprehension itself on the basis of grammar and vocabulary recognition rather than on the reader's/listener's interaction with the text's message. However, empirical studies have shown that exposure to texts with unfamiliar grammar and vocabulary does not significantly affect comprehension (Lee, 1987). Other factors, such as the quality of the text itself in terms of factual consistency and coherence, as well as the background knowledge and motivation of learners, may be more important considerations for teachers when selecting texts (Swaffar, Arens, & Byrnes, 1991).

A great deal of research has revealed that text structure is an important factor in comprehension (Barry & Lazarte, 1998; Fecteau, 1999; Horiba, 2000; Riley, 1993; Roller, 1990). Several studies have found that texts that are organized according to a "story" format (those that have a beginning event, introduction of a conflict, development or attempt to resolve the conflict, outcome, and ending) have a positive effect on L2 readers' ability to recall the text (Fecteau, 1999; Riley, 1993).

Another aspect of text structure found to play a key role in comprehension is the use of signaling cues or features. Earlier in the chapter you read about the use of discourse signaling cues in the L2 listening process. Linguistic and nonlinguistic signaling features are also important in a printed text—they increase the redundancy for the reader and often provide helpful clues to content and structure of the text (Hauptman, 2000). Linguistic signaling in a printed text is similar to that of a spoken message and serves to indicate connections, transitions, and summaries of ideas, e.g., *in addition to, on the other hand, in summary*. Nonlinguistic signaling features in a printed text include graphic organizers, such as charts, graphs, pictures, diagrams, and maps, as well as structural organizers, such as titles, subtitles, numbering of sections, boldfacing, underlining, margin notes, indentation, and outline form. The presence of these types of signaling features may contribute to a text's "low linguistic load"; that is, these cues enable learners to rely less on the language of the text (e.g., vocabulary) in interpreting it (Hauptman, 2000, p. 626).

The effect of text structure, however, may also be contingent on the language level of the learner, since in Riley's (1993) study, text structure made the biggest difference in comprehension for Level 2 students. Riley attributes this to the findings of Roller (1990), which suggest that structure is most important in comprehending "moderately difficult texts"; that is, texts in which the ideas are fairly unfamiliar and require the reader to depend upon text structure (signaling features) to determine which ideas are more important than others. If the language of the text is too difficult for the reader, then structure may not be utilized; if the language is simple, text structure may also be less important (Roller, 1990). This finding has been corroborated by more recent studies that examined the degree to which discourse signaling cues aid comprehension, as described earlier (Jung, 2003; Barry & Lazarte, 1998; Horiba, 2000).

 How does the "story" format discussed here relate to Oller's Episode Hypothesis, presented in Chapter 3?

Content and Interest Level of the Text. An eighth, text-based, variable relates to the *content and interest level of the text*. Is the content interesting, and relevant to students' interests and instructional objectives? Does the content provoke a topic to be discussed and ideas to be shared? Or does the content relate to the subject areas of the school curriculum (see Chapter 3 for discussion of content-based instruction)? The quality of the content will affect how successfully students will be engaged in exploring the text. In a study by Dristas & Grisenti (1995), students read one L2 text that reflected an area of interest for them but was judged to be more linguistically challenging and another L2 text that was not of interest to them but was judged to be less linguistically challenging. Students' ability to comprehend and interpret was greater with the L2 text that was more interesting to them, and they were able to say more about the information presented in the text, despite its linguistic challenge. This finding points to a possible relationship between interest level and content of a text and students' ability to interpret.

New Vocabulary. A ninth, text-based, variable involves the treatment of *new vocabulary*. The use of vocabulary lists with definitions does little to help the reader build vocabulary or comprehend more effectively while reading (Bensoussan, Sim, & Weiss, 1984; Johnson, 1982). A more effective teacher strategy is to present new words in terms of their thematic and discourse relationship to the text and link text information to the readers' background knowledge. According to Swaffar, Arens, & Byrnes (1991); readers should be encouraged to build their own vocabulary banks, since not all students need to learn the same words (e.g., word banks organized thematically). In-class vocabulary practice can provide opportunities for students to "find additional words that relate to the same semantic category . . . ; identify how the same words are redefined by different contexts . . . ; increase awareness of pronounceability; and identify affixes, suffixes, or parts of speech" (p. 68).

In a recent study that examined how learners use context to derive meaning, learners reported that, when faced with unknown words as they read, they (1) used the context to determine meaning, (2) identified cognates, and (3) used their previous knowledge of the meaning of the words (Frantzen, 2003). This finding corroborates many previous studies, which revealed that the use of context is the primary strategy used by learners in both L1 and L2 when they encounter unknown words as they read (e.g., Fraser, 1999; Lee & Wolf, 1997; Paribakht & Wesche, 1999). However, the context in which a word appears does not always lead a language learner to an accurate interpretation of its meaning.

Many studies provide evidence that the use of contextual cues is often an insufficient way to narrow in on a word's meaning, and furthermore, that contextual guessing alone seldom allows the reader to arrive at the correct meaning (Frantzen, 2003; Paribakht & Wesche, 1999; Stein, 1993; Kelly, 1990). Accurate contextual guessing seems to depend in part on the type of context in which unknown words are found; vague and ambiguous contexts, contexts in which the text is too difficult and inaccessible to the learner, and contexts that are dense in unknown words yield little in terms of figuring out meaning. Similarly, context can dissuade learners from words they already know (i.e., cause them to change their minds from correct to incorrect meanings of words), and glossing of words can sometimes lead to misunderstanding of meaning (e.g., glosses for phrases instead of for individual words and supplying incorrect synonyms) (Frantzen, 2003).

Inaccurate guessing may also stem from four types of ineffective learner behaviors:

1. the inattentive use of contextual cues (not paying sufficient attention to the context);
2. "oblivious certainty," a term used by Frantzen (2003) to refer to learners' attitude that they already know certain words despite what the context may suggest;
3. overuse of the "just-get-the-gist" method of reading, which can lead to a contentment with a superficial understanding of the text, even when it isn't sufficient given the comprehension task at hand; and
4. the use of misplaced guesses based upon memory of the story in the text (Frantzen, 2003, pp. 175–184).

Nagy (1997) warns that "although deliberate use of context to infer meanings of new words is an essential reading strategy, any instruction in such a strategy should be based on recognition of the fact that natural context is relatively uninformative" (p. 83; cf. Frantzen, 2003, p. 185). To assist learners in using contextual guessing more successfully, teachers might encourage them to re-evaluate their initial guesses by checking them against the context, since contexts can suggest a variety of meanings (Frantzen, 2003; Nagy, 1997; Haynes, 1984). Rather than overemphasizing the value of using "morpheme analysis" (i.e., using the meanings of parts of words such as prefixes and suffixes as well as word families), a strategy that often results in misunderstanding, teachers might encourage its use to verify a guess *after* the context and grammar have been analyzed (Clarke & Nation, 1980; Haynes, 1984). Teachers might also provide opportunities for students to read or listen for more than just the global meaning, particularly at advanced levels, so that they learn how to refine their understanding when they explore texts (Frantzen, 2003).

 Text-based factors include the length of text, organization of text, content/interest level of text, and treatment of new vocabulary.

According to the research presented throughout this section, we should take into consideration the following variables when we provide opportunities for students to comprehend and interpret oral, printed, and video texts: (1) topic familiarity and background knowledge of the learner, (2) the ability of the reader or listener to hold information in his/her short-term memory during comprehension processing, (3) strategies that learners use in the comprehension task, (4) the purpose for listening/reading/viewing, (5) the level of anxiety that the listener/reader brings to the comprehension task, (6) length of text, (7) organization of text, (8) content and interest level of text, and (9) treatment of new vocabulary.

Integration of Authentic Texts

What was the definition of *authentic texts* given in Chapter 3?

Chapter 3 introduced the concept of using authentic materials in order to establish a meaningful context and reflect target-language cultures. Empirical studies have confirmed the positive results gained by listeners and readers who are given opportunities to interact with authentic oral or written texts. It has been well documented that students who listen to authentic oral segments, such as radio broadcasts, demonstrate significantly greater listening comprehension than do students who do not interact with authentic segments (Herron & Seay, 1991; Bacon, 1992b).

Several recent studies have examined the effect of introducing authentic readings early in language study. Maxim (2002) found that college students in their first semester of German were able to successfully read a full-length authentic novel in German while at the same time continuing to progress in their language development at the same level as their counterparts who were not exposed to such reading. The success of these readers can be attributed to several factors: (1) students experienced a guided approach as they explored the reading, progressing from identification to summarization, synthesis, and eventual analysis, while working collaboratively with classmates to construct meaning; (2) students experienced less anxiety because the cultural context of the romance novel was familiar to them and the length of the novel provided recurring situations, characters, and words, which seemed to facilitate comprehension; and 3) students received training in the use of effective reading strategies, such as identifying key information and focusing on major events in the story and their consequences (Maxim, 2002). The results of Maxim's investigation in German were corroborated by Gascoigne's (2002a) study of beginning French students who successfully read authentic French texts of several hundred words in length within the first twelve hours of class meetings.

The benefits of exploring authentic texts seem to go beyond that of improving comprehension, as students in several studies have also experienced improvement in oral and written language performance as a result (Vigil, 1987; Weyers, 1999). The reading success of these beginning students would seem to dispute claims often made by teachers that reading in language programs adversely affects the beginning language learner's second language development. In fact, Maxim (2002) suggests that allowing time for extensive reading on a regular basis may contribute to the development of grammatical and communicative competence, and Gascoigne (2002a) encourages teachers to incorporate authentic reading into the L2 classroom from the very first weeks of instruction. These and other studies confirm the advantage of presenting unedited, authentic texts to students as early as possible in language study.

Many teachers feel a need to "simplify" or "edit" authentic texts in order to make texts easier for students in early levels of language study to understand. However, the research has verified that the opposite is true; that is, learners demonstrate a significantly higher level of comprehension on texts that are read in their unedited, authentic forms as opposed to versions simplified through lexical changes (Young, 1999, 1993; Vigil, 1987). Two implications of these studies merit attention. First, teachers in Young's (1999) study who were asked to simplify authentic texts did so primarily by (1) changing words, i.e., they substituted words or phrases that were less common with those that students would be more apt to recognize, (2) changing passive voice to active voice, and (3) deleting verbiage that was thought to be redundant or superfluous (pp. 364–366). These types of changes indicate that teachers believe that making lexical adjustments and shortening the text facilitate comprehension, and that they may also be convinced that students process texts by relying heavily on a word-for-word approach (Young, 1999). Evidence points to the possibility that language teachers may underestimate not only the abilities of their students to interact with authentic texts, but also the effect of a guided approach in greatly facilitating the comprehension process (Allen, Bernhardt, Berry, & Demel, 1988).

Simplifying an authentic text may actually be counterproductive, since the redundancy and richness of the context contributes to comprehension. This is important for language teachers to realize, since many textbooks still feature unauthentic oral and printed texts that carefully control for length and vocabulary, which may actually prove to be much more difficult for students to comprehend. The results of studies indicate that authentic texts should be used more extensively given their positive effects on comprehension and interpretation and on their overall second language development (see, for example, Bacon, 1989; Epstein, 2002; Lacorte & Thurston-Griswold, 2001; & Weissenrieder, 1987). However, teachers should remember to choose authentic texts that are age- and level-appropriate, and to *edit the task, not the text*.

 Choose authentic texts that are age- and level-appropriate, and *edit the task, not the text*.

Use of Literary Texts

While authentic materials are often primarily thought of as newspaper and magazine articles or news broadcasts, many other types of oral and written texts appropriate to specific age groups can be used effectively, including literary texts. Shook (1996) defines literature as "more than just informational in nature, but rather . . . compelling; that is, it makes the reader reflect inwardly, personally" (p. 202). Christensen (1990) suggests the use of authentic teenage adventure novels because of their potential for sustaining interest by means of suspense, intrigue, fast action, and cliff-hanging chapter endings.[3] Earlier chapters of this text have explored various possibilities for using folktales, stories, and legends. *Teacher's Handbook* advocates a prominent role for exploration of literary texts as a way to develop students' target culture and language competence, and to provide opportunities for students to use their cognitive skills and interact with one another through sharing of ideas.

In Chapter 5, you learned about a constructivist approach to engaging students in learning about culture and acquiring cultural perspectives (Wright, 2000), and the role of affective learning in helping students to become sensitive to cultural differences (Lange, 1999). Inspired by the approaches of Wright and Lange, Scott & Huntington (2002) conducted a study to explore the relationship between the study of a foreign language literary text and the development of competence in a second culture. Their study compared the attitudes and reactions of introductory-level university French students who read a fact sheet about the Ivory Coast with the attitudes and reactions of students who read a poem written by a poet from the Ivory Coast. After reading their respective texts, both groups of students were asked to present the most interesting element in the passage and discuss it with their classmates. The responses by the "fact sheet group" were brief, factual, very similar, and did not reveal much about how students processed the information they read. On the other hand, students who read the poem were able to generalize more personalized reactions to cultural themes, such as language and ethnicity, than were their counterparts who read the fact sheet. Their reactions revealed an ability to establish cross-cultural links between their own cultures and the culture of the Ivory Coast, to relate to the emotions presented in the poem, and to relate the poem to their own lives and experiences in unique ways. The findings of this study corroborate those of Wright, as they illustrate how an approach to teaching culture that relies only on the presentation of facts is very limiting. The authors conclude that exploration of literary texts can play a pivotal role in developing students' (1) affective awareness, i.e., awareness of feelings and attitudes, sensitivity to dimensions of emotion, empathy for others, and (2) cognitive flexibility, i.e., acknowledgement of multiple views, tolerance of ambiguity, nonjudgmental evaluation of others (Scott & Huntington, 2002, pp. 623–624). Their findings lend support for the claim that literary texts should be used, even at the earliest stages of language learning, as a basis for developing C2 competence and addressing the culture standards of the *SFLL*.[4]

In addition to serving as a useful context for developing cross-cultural perspectives, literature can also be used as the basis for developing language proficiency (Donato & Brooks, 2004). Students' language use should be monitored for its targeted level of proficiency, discourse features, and sociolinguistic appropriateness (Bernhardt, 2002). Recent findings, however, indicate that language teachers may not always take advantage of the opportunity to develop their students' language proficiency while exploring literary texts (Donato & Brooks, 2004). See Chapter 8 for a full discussion of the discourse of literature classes.

Foreign language teachers often express a concern that literary texts are too challenging for typical language students and restrict their use, if they use them at all, to the advanced level, particularly Advanced Placement classes. Many leading scholars who conduct L2 reading research warn that this perceived difficulty is a faulty one (Allen, Bernhardt, Berry, & Demel, 1988; Fecteau, 1999). Frantzen (2003) notes that one factor that contributes to the perceived difficulty of literature selections is that authors of works of literature do not write for L2 learners, but rather their fellow citizens, who most likely share the cultural and historical knowledge necessary to understand their work. Therefore, one of the principal reasons that students at all levels may find the literature difficult is because they often do not have this type of background knowledge. To compound the problem, in the absence of effective strategies for helping guide students through literary texts, language teachers often expect learners to understand the entirety of a text, which means that students either use word-for-word translation to attempt to comprehend the text and/or teachers resort to an explanation and discussion of the text in English.

In selecting texts for beginning foreign language learner-readers, Shook (1996) suggests that teachers choose literary texts that express the basic, shared cultural beliefs of the target culture. The texts do not have to be direct descriptions of values but can indirectly reflect or hint at values. The teacher should select subsequent literary texts that build upon the knowledge of the native and target cultures already explored by the readers' interaction with previous texts (Shook, 1996). Building on students' background knowledge also facilitates their ability to formulate inferences about what they read, as suggested earlier (Hammadou, 1991, 2000). Galloway (1992) suggests that as students explore literary texts, they need frequent comprehension checks, and guidance in sorting information, assigning meaning, formulating and testing hypotheses, and integrating new ideas. Reading tasks that build strategies will help students to overcome grammatical, lexical, and cultural difficulties and enable them to acquire new information and perspectives (Shook, 1996).

In a recent study, Wolfe (2004) explored ways in which adolescent ESL readers developed the ability to read literary texts in more "adult-like" ways and learned to identify and understand abstract literary concepts. Wolfe tape recorded study sessions in which fifteen ESL students discussed a novel with their teacher. Through an analytic tool called "chains of signification," the researcher studied how the meanings of words changed, and ultimately how abstract ideas evolved, through the study sessions, e.g., in the story, the word *owl* initially was used to discuss the animal, then to signify a messenger, then a symbol, and finally to refer to a more complex idea of a dichotomy in the novel. Wolfe (2004) attributes students' abilities to interpret the novel at an abstract level to the strategies used by the teacher in his role as a facilitator and guide. She guided students to more abstract interpretations of the text as a result of rechaining of words and concepts—i.e., redefining lexical items with a new accepted definition, such as redefining *owl* from *animal* to *symbol*. Rechaining was accomplished by four key teacher strategies:

1. validating the value of student contributions and not judging any contributions as "off task";
2. restating student comments in more adult-like ways while giving the student credit as the contributor of the idea, thus legitimizing the student's interpretation and sometimes repairing the utterance;
3. tying complex ideas of symbolism and theme to more concrete examples from students' lives and other texts; and
4. taking advantage of opportunities to offer his own literary interpretations of the text, thereby enabling students to rechain lexical items constantly (p. 411).

Wolfe's study suggests that teachers must have a metacognitive awareness of how to "lift the level" of the literary discussion, which is best accomplished through small, consistent shifts toward more complex interpretations (Edelsky, Draper, & Smith, 1983).

 How do these teacher strategies relate to the concept of the ZPD as an interactive activity, discussed in Chapter 1?

Implications for Teaching Listening, Reading, Viewing

If we adopt the definition of reading as proposed by Swaffar, Arens, and Byrnes (1991) and extend it to listening and viewing, then reading, listening, and viewing comprehension in L2 are functions of "cognitive development, the ability to think within the framework of the second language" (p. 63). According to their framework and the results of the studies described earlier, research points to the following implications for teaching the interpretive skills:

1. Students need prereading, prelistening, and pre-viewing activities that prepare them for the comprehension/interpretation task.
2. Students should be taught to interact with the text through the use of both bottom-up and top-down processes.
3. The information gained through interpreting a text can be used as the basis for interpersonal and presentational communication.

4. Students' comprehension will increase if they are trained to use strategies such as activation of background knowledge, contextual guessing, and use of nonverbal cues, which will also serve to lessen their anxiety.

5. In practicing contextual guessing, students should be encouraged to check their initial guesses against the context and revise them as necessary.

6. Students will have greater success if the texts selected deal with topics with which they are familiar and if they are encouraged to establish a purpose for exploring these texts.

7. Students (even in beginning levels of language study) can be engaged in drawing inferences from a text being explored if they have sufficient familiarity with the topic of the text and are provided with prompts and/or tasks that encourage them to do so.

8. Teachers should be aware of the load on memory that students may experience during the comprehension task, and they should plan to control for this by allowing students to have the printed text available while completing a reading comprehension task and allowing students to listen to an oral text or view a video text multiple times.

9. Factors to consider when selecting texts include the degree of contextual support (i.e., longer may be better), the organization of the text (i.e., story-like features and signaling features are helpful), and level of interest to students.

10. Effective strategies for helping students to deal with new vocabulary found in a text include helping them to explore new words in terms of their thematic and discourse relationship to the text; linking new words to their background knowledge; identifying words in similar semantic categories; identifying affixes, parts of speech, or word families; and building their individual vocabulary banks.

11. Teachers should encourage students to self-report periodically while listening, reading, and viewing so that teachers will be informed about the comprehension strategies their students are using.

12. Authentic texts provide an effective means for presenting real language, integrating culture, heightening comprehension, and stimulating interest in language learning.

13. Literary texts should be used from beginning levels of language instruction to develop affective awareness and cognitive flexibility, both of which will facilitate C2 competence.

14. Teachers should remember to *edit the task, not the text*.

The Role of the Interpretive Mode Across Instructional Levels

In Chapters 4 and 5, you learned about the key role that interpretive listening plays in teaching foreign language to elementary and middle school students. Listening is used as the vehicle for language acquisition and serves as a springboard for integrating the other modes and content. Elementary and middle school teachers use many techniques for improving interpretive listening, such as gestures, TPR, exploration of visuals and realia, and hands-on student participation.

For elementary school children, the transition from interpretive listening and interpersonal speaking to interpretive reading is made through the use of the language experience chart approach, as described in Chapter 4. At both the elementary and middle school levels, culturally appropriate stories, myths, folktales, science fiction, and adventure stories can be presented to combine cultural understanding and the teaching of interpretive reading. Chapter 5 presented an approach for using an oral or a printed text as the context for a thematic unit while integrating the practice of all three modes of Communication and Cultures.

At the middle/junior high school and high school levels and beyond, listening should also play a prominent role if students are to acquire language. Learners need to attend to large amounts of comprehensible input in the target language, and they benefit from training in strategy development. Authentic input provides the context and meaning stage for the story-based approach to grammar instruction that is presented in Chapter 7. The various types of authentic oral or printed texts, as described in earlier chapters, can be presented to students at all levels of instruction. Beginning language learners benefit from experience in top-down processing or listening/reading/viewing for the main idea, since this activity discourages the word-for-word decoding that often occurs in early language learning.

The research discussed earlier in this chapter refutes the notion of consistently matching text length and text type to particular levels of instruction or to students' proficiency levels. For example, beginning-level students should not just be given short texts dealing with concrete information, such as menus and advertisements. Instead, students should be given the opportunity to use the information in the text, grammar, vocabulary, and discourse markers that connect ideas and help with comprehension. In addition, by listening/reading/viewing from various perspectives, students can also gain additional insights about the text and the author's intent. Thus this type of interactive listening, reading, and viewing not only develops interpretive abilities but can also enable students to learn new ideas and improve global language competence.

Acquisition of New Vocabulary Through Reading/Listening/Viewing

A related issue concerning new vocabulary in a text concerns the difference between recognizing or correctly identifying the meaning of new words and learning their meaning. Many studies have pointed out that words that are correctly guessed or inferred in a text are not necessarily learned and/or remembered, perhaps because once the immediate comprehension need is met, further processing may not be seen as needed (Pressley, Levin, & McDaniel, 1987; Wesche & Paribakht, 2000). Research suggests that learning vocabulary through incidental exposure (i.e., reading and listening) is most effective when students know how to attend to new language—by being aware of word families and affixes for analyzing words into parts, by knowing how to use contextual cues, and by knowing when and how to use a dictionary effectively (Fraser, 1999).

Several researchers have suggested that for learning of new vocabulary, the degree of processing that occurs as meaning is figured out determines whether and to what degree a word will be learned (Paribakht & Wesche, 1999; Mondria & Wit-deBoer, 1991). On the one hand, if the word appears in a rich context that makes the meaning of a word obvious, the word will likely not be acquired (Mondria & Wit-deBoer, 1991; Nation & Coady, 1988). On the other hand, if the context is too difficult and reveals little about the word's meaning, then the word will not be inferred *or* learned, because the struggle in processing is too great (Paribakht & Wesche, 1999). It seems, then, that a "moderate" amount of struggling might lead to correct inference of a word's meaning and a greater likelihood that the word will be acquired (Frantzen, 2003).

A series of studies examined how (1) reading a text, versus (2) reading a text along with completing reading-based vocabulary exercises affects the acquisition of new vocabulary. Since learning a new word requires ongoing exploration and use of the word, several studies have examined the use of reading/vocabulary exercises that learners complete after or while reading a text (Wesche & Paribakht, 2000; Paribakht & Wesche, 1996, 1997). These exercises engage readers in tasks such as locating selected words in the text, matching definitions to the new words, producing derivatives of words to create other parts of speech in word families, replacing underlined words in new sentences with similar words from the text, and arranging words into sentences (Wesche & Paribakht, 2000). The use of these exercises along with a reading seems to make more L2 words more salient, or noticeable, to readers; guide readers' attention to different aspects of L2 word knowledge; and encourage them to explore some words on their own (Wesche & Paribakht, 2000). Thus, while reading, listening, and viewing provide effective contexts and activities for acquiring new knowledge and language, learners require opportunities to do focused work on the use of new vocabulary within a text if they are to acquire and retain new vocabulary and use it productively. Clearly this is an area ripe for further investigation.

An Interactive Model for Integrating the Three Modes of Communication

Here we present a model for developing students' communicative skills, using integration of the three modes of communication as the framework. The modes and skills are integrated as students are engaged in interaction with oral, printed, and video texts and with one another. This model is called *interactive* because it accounts for ways in which the message of the text interacts with reader/listener perceptions in both top-down and bottom-up ways, as described by Swaffar, Arens, and Byrnes (1991) earlier in this chapter. In other words, an interactive approach involves actively constructing meaning between the text and personal experience and/or background knowledge. Figure 6.4 illustrates the integrative aspects of the three modes in this model: (1) through the interpretive mode, students comprehend and interpret a text, acquiring new information and cultural perspectives; (2) through the interpersonal mode, students share information, inferences, and reactions with one another; and (3) through the presentational mode, students use their new knowledge and perspectives as they create a summary and/or an oral or written product.

As depicted in Figure 6.4, interaction in this model can begin with any of the three modes; for example, a story might be the springboard for discussion and for an oral presentation on a particular topic; a two-way discussion might prompt the viewing of a video text and lead to further sharing of ideas; a letter to the editor of a newspaper might serve as the basis for discussion and for listening to a news broadcast. Thus the communicative skills and strategies students might use are reiterative and nonlinear in nature. In addition, they reflect both cognitive and social processes.

Figure 6.5 presents the Interactive Model for Integrating the Three Modes of Communication according to the class activities, purpose, and discourse format for each mode. This model engages students in interaction with the text, helps them build

FIGURE 6.4 Integrating the Three Modes of Communication

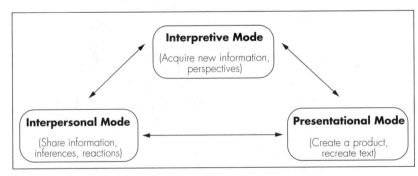

Source: Adapted from NSFLEP, 1999.

FIGURE 6.5 An Interactive Model for Integrating the Three Modes of Communication

MODE	CLASS ACTIVITIES	PURPOSE	DISCOURSE FORMAT
Interpretive	PREPARATION PHASE: Students preview the text, establish a purpose, predict meaning, activate background knowledge, preview unfamiliar content, anticipate new vocabulary and text language.	Prepare students for the task. Pique student interest.	Authentic text—printed, video, audio, live broadcast Story about real or imagined experience
	COMPREHENSION PHASE: Students skim for the gist, scan for specific information. Students create a list of main ideas and match them to sections of text. Students match main ideas to key details.	Identify main ideas and details. Connect main ideas and details. Identify key discourse markers (word order, transitional words, parts of speech) and/or specific linguistic features. Acquire new information.	Class story about common experience Current events Interdisciplinary content[5]
Interpretive + Interpersonal	INTERPRETATION PHASE: Students read/listen/view "between the lines." Students collaborate to identify the cultural products, practices, and perspectives found in the text. Students ask each other questions about the content, inferences, and author intent/perspectives of the text. Students share their opinions of and reactions to the text.	Interpret the text. Discuss cultural products, practices, perspectives. Interpret inferences and share reactions.	Pair/small group discussion Interviewing
Presentational	APPLICATION PHASE: Students create a written summary of text and/or design an oral/video presentation. Students create a follow-up product such as a letter, advertisement, new beginning or ending for text, and/or visuals.	Use new information to write a summary, complete a task, or create a product.	Written/oral summary of text Product (visual, oral, written)
Interpretive (revisited)	EXTENSION PHASE: Students analyze features of two texts and compare content and organization.	Compare text to another text (discourse, organization).	Authentic text—printed, video, audio, live broadcast

Source: Shrum & Glisan, original material; 1994; modified 2005.

strategies for comprehending and interpreting a text, and provides ways for them to use their newly acquired knowledge and skills in meaningful tasks. The model is interactive and procedural in nature, guiding the learner as he or she interacts with the text by using both bottom-up and top-down processes. It is also integrative, since it provides opportunities for students to combine skills from the three modes and cultural perspectives as they derive meaning from the text, recreate the text, and react to the text in a personal way. Note that students are guided through the text by means of five phases of interaction:

 I. Preparation
 II. Comprehension
 III. Interpretation
 IV. Application
 V. Extension

Although Figure 6.5 begins with the interpretive mode to illustrate the process, communication can begin with any of the three modes, as illustrated in Figure 6.4. Also, the interactive model outlined in Figure 6.5 can be implemented with any type of oral or printed text. See Chapter 12 for a web-based module using the interactive model. The amount of time spent on each mode will depend on the length and nature of the text as well as on the instructional objectives. Appendix 6.2 presents an example of how an authentic reading in Spanish can be used as the impetus for communication in all three modes, and Appendix 6.3 (see the Web site) provides an example of how the model can be used with a semiscripted audio segment in English.

thandbook.heinle.com

Teachers should spend sufficient time in the preparation phase so that students have the necessary skills, background knowledge, and motivation for the comprehension and interpretation tasks. This phase should include activation of prior knowledge about the content of the text, setting a purpose for exploring the text, opportunities for learners to predict and anticipate events in the text, and opportunities for learners to explore and predict new vocabulary (see the earlier section in this chapter dealing with the treatment of new vocabulary). In the comprehension phase, learners demonstrate that they have understood the main ideas and important details and that they can link these aspects to the text. In the interpretation phase, they interpret inferences and the author's intent as they exchange ideas and opinions with one another orally. It is important to note that students may draw inferences on their own as they assign meaning to the text, even before being asked to do so. The application phase provides the opportunity for learners to use knowledge and reactions gained in exploring the text to create a product. The extension phrase brings the model full circle as learners compare two texts in terms of content and organization.

The Interactive Model can be used effectively to explore literary texts; it addresses potential comprehension difficulties noted in the research. For example, Bernhardt (1990) notes that an initial misunderstanding of how the main idea of a story relates to its details can distort a reader's entire comprehension and interpretation of it. Swaffar (2001) suggests that teachers avoid telling students how to reconstruct and interpret the text, but instead guide students in finding global patterns in the text (e.g., specific literary features, such as repetition and use of striking language) and in identifying details that support those patterns. Students work best with literary texts by gleaning information collaboratively in stages and by applying a heavy dose of top-down reading strategies. During the initial stages of reading, students focus on what the text says as they identify the "who, what, where," clarifying the difference between what the text says and what they think it says. Only after students have an accurate understanding of the main ideas and details of the text does the teacher lead them in making inferences and exploring the "how and why" of the story. Swaffar (2001) suggests: "After a systematic and careful reading of any literary work, readers have earned the privilege of deciding what those patterns say to them, of drawing inferences and articulating implications. As long as their questions are text-based and their answers intelligible, student insights at this stage should be honored" (p. 146).

What role can the ZPD play as the teacher guides students through a text, using the Interactive Model?

One issue that teachers confront when teaching listening and reading is how much of the native language to use when checking students' comprehension of texts. Several studies have shown that learners receive higher comprehension scores when they are tested in their native language (Davis, Glass, & Coady, 1998; Godev, Martínez-Gibson, & Toris, 2002; Wolf, 1993). In a study by Davis, Glass, and Coady (1998), undergraduate and graduate students of Spanish demonstrated significantly higher recall of a written text when tested in their native language. The results of their investigation led these researchers to conclude that the language of recall affects FL readers' performance in terms of (1) the amount of textual information recalled accurately and (2) the number of inferences, elaborations, and metacognitive statements produced. These findings support Lee's earlier conclusion that "assessing comprehension with a target language task may limit learners' ability to demonstrate what they [have] comprehended" (1986a, p. 353). Another factor in using L2 for checking comprehension is that the wording of a question may reveal the answer by making it easy for the student to use the wording of the comprehension questions to look back to the passage and make a match. Consequently, students might identify a sentence from the text that correctly answers the question, but they may have no idea of what either the question or the answer means. This strategy reflects what Lee and VanPatten (1995) call the "look-back-and-lift-off approach" to reading and is problematic, since these readers rarely end up reading the entire passage and their comprehension consists of unconnected fragments of information (p. 189). When the native language is used to check for comprehension and recall, comprehension skill is not confused with productive use of the target language (Lee, 1986b; Swaffar, Arens, & Byrnes, 1991).

In the "look-back-and-lift-off approach" to reading, students' comprehension consists of unconnected fragments of information. ∎

It might be beneficial to conduct prelistening and prereading activities in the native language, particularly if students require new background information prior to the listening or reading task. Clearly, the decision to use either the native or target language for each phase of the interactive model presented here must be made by the teacher after considering the level of students' proficiency and the task to be accomplished. Godev, Martínez-Gibson, and Toris (2002) suggest that if teachers decide to use an all-L2 comprehension format, especially for testing purposes, this format should have "(1) questions that circumvent the potential problem of not being understood, (2) questions that preclude the possibility of answering correctly without understanding, and (3) a device that would prevent the mistaking of limited writing skills for limited reading comprehension" (p. 213). In sum, it is advantageous to use the target language to the maximum extent possible, while realizing that occasional use of the native language may be both necessary and helpful in guiding students in strategy use and in checking their comprehension.

This chapter presented the overall framework of the communicative modes together with a model for developing communication by integrating the modes. The focus here was on the interpretive mode as the processes underlying reading, listening, and viewing were discussed and implications for instruction were explored. Each of the next three chapters will examine a particular aspect of the other two modes—interpersonal and presentational—in an effort to explore specific issues relating to grammar, speaking, and writing. These modes and skills are analyzed somewhat separately in order to help the reader focus on particular issues one at a time. However, keep in mind that the approach advocated by *Teacher's Handbook* is to teach the modes and skills in an integrative manner, using the model presented in this chapter as well as other strategies.

Note: You may want to review the characteristics of authentic texts, presented in Chapter 3, before completing the following tasks.

NCATE
STANDARDS
4.b., 4.c.

EPISODE ONE
Using the Interactive Model to Explore an Authentic Printed Text

For this activity, you will need to select a targeted level of instruction: elementary school, middle/junior high school, high school, or beyond.

Option 1: Select an authentic magazine or newspaper article of at least 750 words.

Option 2: Select an authentic literary text (folktale, story, novel excerpt, poem, etc.).

Check the text for the characteristics of good episodic organization and organizational cues. First, decide how this text might be used in a particular thematic unit in order to address short- and long-range objectives. Second, design a plan for teaching the text by using the interactive model presented in this chapter. Begin with the interpretive mode and then integrate interpersonal and presentational communication. Remember that you may need to devote a portion of several class periods to this activity in order to complete your work on the text. For each day you plan to spend on the reading, describe what students will do in all stages of the procedure. Your instructor may ask you to present an element of your plan to the class.

NCATE
STANDARDS
4.b., 4.c.

EPISODE TWO
Using the Interactive Model to Explore an Authentic Audio/Video Segment

For this activity, you will again need to select a targeted level of instruction: elementary school, middle/junior high school, high school, or beyond.

Option 1: Select an authentic segment on audiotape/CD or videotape, an authentic live broadcast, or an authentic audio segment from the Internet (e.g., conversation, commercial, news report, talk show, song).

Option 2: Semiscript your own recorded conversation: Give two native speakers a particular situation or subject to discuss (for example, ask them to pretend that they are two students who meet for the first time while standing in the registration line); ask the speakers to talk spontaneously for two to three minutes. Do not prepare a written script, since the conversation should be as natural as possible.

Decide how this segment might be used in a particular thematic unit in order to address short- and long-range objectives. Then design a plan for teaching the segment by using the interactive approach presented in this chapter. Begin with the interpretive mode and then integrate interpersonal and presentational communication. Describe what students will do in each stage of the procedure. Your instructor may ask you to present your taped segment and an element of your lesson to the class.

NCATE
STANDARDS
3.a., 3.b.,
4.b., 4.c.

EPISODE THREE
Teaching Literature at the Post-Secondary Level

If you are preparing to or already teach at the post-secondary level, this task is designed to engage you in reflecting upon the teaching of literature in undergraduate language and literature classes.

Read Chapter 10 in *SLA and the Literature Classroom: Fostering Dialogue* (Bernhardt, 2002).

Research into the teaching of literature in a second language: What it says and how to communicate it to graduate students. Then complete the following tasks:

1. Describe the impact of the student's knowledge base when reading L2 literary texts.
2. Explain the significance of the "lang-lit split" that Bernhardt describes as it pertains to the nature of the teaching of literature.
3. Name three misconceptions that graduate students have about teaching literature to undergraduates.
4. Explain the principles of literature learning that deal with:
   - time on task
   - appropriate feedback
   - situated learning
   - release of control
5. Explain two ways in which a literature instructor could tap a student's conceptualization of a literary text.

thandbook.heinle.com

See Appendix 6.4 (on the Web site) for a description of a framework for teaching literature to the undergraduate foreign language major (Barnes-Karol, 2003).

DISCUSS AND REFLECT

CASE STUDY ONE
Developing Interpretive Listening: Scripts or No Scripts?

NCATE
STANDARDS
3.a., 3.b.,
4.b., 4.c,
6.a.

Ms. McAlister is a German teacher at Warrington High School, which is located in an urban, multicultural school district in the eastern section of a large city. She has been teaching German I–III for the past eight years. Ms. McAlister has kept abreast of changes in the field of foreign language teaching, having attended workshops on the implementation of standards and the three modes of communication. Although she believes in the value of using authentic audio, video, and printed texts, she also struggles with how to help students understand them, particularly beginning-level classes.

Due to budgetary constraints, Ms. McAlister's school district is using German textbooks that are ten years old, which makes it more difficult to integrate materials that support newer approaches to instruction. Nevertheless, Ms. McAlister tries her best to align her teaching practices with current trends in the field as much as possible. For example, she used to have students use the dialogues that appear at the beginning of each textbook chapter for reading practice and to learn new vocabulary. Since attending recent workshops on the three modes of communication, however, she has now begun to play the audio tapes of the dialogues that accompany the textbook so that students can hear the conversations instead of just reading them.

Today Ms. McAlister is being observed by the district's foreign language supervisor, Dr. Richard Cosgrove. She decides to integrate some listening comprehension work into her German II lesson, as she wants to show what she has learned as a result of recent in-service workshops. Since the new unit deals with making and accepting invitations and leisure-time activities, Ms. McAlister is using a semiscripted audio segment that accompanies a conversation textbook, which presents a phone conversation in which one friend calls another and invites her to the movies. The teacher's lesson procedures are:

1. She shows visuals of leisure-time activities and asks students to identify them in German.
2. She asks students to look at the list of ways to make and accept invitations in German, which are presented in the textbook. They take turns reading aloud some examples.

3. She prepares students for the listening task by telling them that they will hear a phone conversation between two friends, who make plans to see a movie. She gives students a list of ten new words and expressions in German with their English translations so that students will not be frustrated when they hear them.

4. She gives the class a written script of the conversation and asks them to follow along while they listen.

5. After hearing the conversation one time and following along with the script, students answer her oral questions about the main ideas and key details of the conversation.

6. For homework, students are asked to create a new ending for the conversation. The script will help them to recall what the conversation was about.

In their post-observation conference, one of the areas that Dr. Cosgrove and Ms. McAlister discuss is the use of scripts with listening comprehension activities. Dr. Cosgrove suggests that Ms. McAlister consider not using scripts since, in order to develop listening skills, students should rely only on what they hear. Ms. McAlister explains that she saw the use of the scripts as a way to minimize students' listening anxiety.

Ask yourself these questions:

1. Which strategies used by Ms. McAlister in this lesson reflect some of the research and/or suggestions described in this chapter with respect to developing interpretive listening?

2. What research supports Dr. Cosgrove's suggestion about not using scripts?

3. What are some other strategies that Ms. McAlister might use in order to lessen students' anxiety about listening and to help them experience success in listening tasks?

4. What other aspects of this lesson might be improved, based on research findings that you read about in this chapter?

5. What are some ways in which Dr. Cosgrove and Ms. McAlister might collaborate to inform other teachers of what they have come to understand?

To prepare the case:

1. Read Berne (1998) for a discussion of the gap between L2 listening research and classroom practice.

2. Read Rubin (1994) and Glisan (1995) for a review of second-language listening comprehension research.

3. Interview an experienced high school foreign language teacher to find out how he or she teaches interpretive listening.

To prepare for class discussion:

1. Revise Ms. McAlister's listening lesson, incorporating the ideas you explored while answering the questions above.

2. As a result of information gleaned from surveys completed by language instructors, Berne (1996, 1998) discovered a gap between L2 listening research and classroom practice. Imagine that you are Ms. McAlister and want to begin to work on closing the gap between listening research and your own teaching. You decide to develop a professional development plan in order to learn more about teaching interpretive listening and reflect new ideas in your classroom practice. Access some of the professional organizations to which you belong or in which you have an interest in joining (see Preliminary Chapter) to find professional development opportunities that may assist you. You might also investigate regional conferences and other resources described in the Preliminary Chapter as sources of possible assistance. Write a paragraph that outlines your professional development plan. You might include efforts you could make in the short-term (e.g., reading articles, trying new strategies in your classes) as well as endeavors that will entail long-term work (e.g., finding authentic texts, observing colleagues' classes, attending workshops).

CASE STUDY TWO
Reading Aloud

For twelve years, Ms. Dayton has been teaching French at Big Sky High School in a rural midwestern town. One of the first things she noticed about her students when she began teaching was the transference of students' regional English accent to their French pronunciation. She began to ask her students to read aloud in French to help them practice their pronunciation. Generally, her procedure is to introduce the activity by telling students that it's time to practice pronunciation. Sometimes she puts them through some practice exercises, repeating words that have a particularly troublesome sound. She then models for the students a short sentence that embodies the sound and asks for whole-class repetition. Finally, she asks individuals to read aloud subsequent sentences that also contain the troublesome sound.

Ms. Lilly teaches Spanish in the same school as Ms. Dayton and has roughly the same amount of teaching experience. Ms. Lilly also uses reading aloud in her Spanish classes, but for a different reason. She believes that reading aloud focuses students' attention on the text so that they can comprehend the language and then discuss what it means; the students listening to the oral reader also use the oral reading to figure out meaning. Earlier this week, for example, students in Ms. Lilly's Spanish III class read aloud a passage from *Mosén Millán*, after which they discussed what they had understood from it.

Today is a teachers' in-service day, and Ms. Dayton and Ms. Lilly's foreign language department is fortunate to have a workshop that focuses on a current topic in their subject area. Dr. Janet Farwell, a well-known specialist in second language reading comprehension, is scheduled to talk about "Strategies for Developing Interpretive Communication in the Foreign Language Classroom." Dr. Farwell begins the workshop by presenting teachers with an interactive hands-on activity, in which they are asked to give their opinions on a series of statements concerning the development of reading and listening comprehension. One of the statements prompts a lively discussion and some debate among the teachers: "Reading aloud isn't really reading."

Ask yourself these questions:

1. Why do you think that the teachers in this workshop engaged in a "lively discussion and some debate" concerning the statement, given by the workshop presenter, about reading aloud?
2. What are some possible metacognitive strategies that Ms. Dayton's students use during oral reading? How about Ms. Lilly's students?
3. What issues or factors related to the reading process presented in the chapter can you relate to the two approaches to reading aloud used by these teachers?
4. Do you agree with Ms. Lilly's belief that her students' comprehension is enhanced by listening to their classmates read aloud? Explain.

To prepare the case:

1. Read Bacon (1992b) for information about the metacognitive strategies learners use while listening.
2. Interview a beginning and an advanced language student to find out what they think about while they are reading aloud.
3. Interview a beginning and an advanced language student to find out what they think about while someone else is reading aloud.

To prepare for class discussion:

1. Conduct your own mini-experiment. Ask a student to read a paragraph aloud; ask two other students to listen and then to answer the following questions. Summarize your findings.

   ■ What was the first thing you did to make sense of this paragraph?

- Did you do anything else to help yourself understand the text at any point during the listening?
- Did you change your mind regarding what this passage was about or what to listen for at any point during the listening?
- What can you remember hearing?
- Can you remember anything else that you heard? Any new information?
- Did you learn anything new? Any new information?
- Do you remember anything else?
- Do you remember any new words?
- On a scale of one to ten, how confident are you that you understood this passage?
- On a scale of one to ten, how much did you already know about this topic? (adapted from Bacon, 1992a)

2. Write a description of the effectiveness or ineffectiveness of using reading aloud as a strategy in your foreign language classroom.

REFERENCES

Allen, E., Bernhardt, E. B., Berry, M. T., & Demel, M. (1988). Comprehension and text genre: An analysis of secondary foreign language readers. *The Modern Language Journal, 72,* 63–72.

Bacon, S. M. (1989). Listening for real in the foreign-language classroom. *Foreign Language Annals, 22,* 543–551.

Bacon, S. M. (1992a). Phases of listening to authentic input in Spanish: A descriptive study. *Foreign Language Annals, 25,* 317–334.

Bacon, S. M. (1992b). The relationship between gender, comprehension, processing strategies, and cognitive and affective response in foreign language listening. *The Modern Language Journal, 76,* 160–178.

Baldwin, R. S., Peleg-Bruckner, Z., & McClintock, A. H. (1985). Effects of topic interest and prior knowledge on reading comprehension. *Reading Research Quarterly, 20,* 497–504.

Barnes-Karol, G. (2000). Revising a Spanish novel class in the light of *Standards for Foreign Language Learning. ADFL Bulletin, 31,* 44–48.

Barnes-Karol, G. (2003). Teaching literature to the undergraduate foreign language major: A framework for a methods course. *ADFL Bulletin, 34,* 20–27.

Barnett, M. (1988a). Reading through context. *The Modern Language Journal, 72,* 150–159.

Barnett, M. (1988b). Teaching reading strategies: How methodology affects language course articulation. *Foreign Language Annals, 21,* 109–119.

Barry, S., & Lazarte, A. (1998). Evidence for mental models: How do prior knowledge, syntactic complexity, and reading topic affect inference generation in a recall task for nonnative readers of Spanish? *The Modern Language Journal, 82,* 176–193.

Bensoussan, M., Sim, D., & Weiss, R. (1984). The effect of dictionary usage on EFL test performance compared with student and teacher attitudes and expectations. *Reading in a Foreign Language, 2,* 262–276.

Berne, J. E. (1996). Current trends in L2 listening comprehension research: Are researchers and language instructors on the same wavelength? *Minnesota Language Review, 24,* 6–10.

Berne, J. E. (1998). Examining the relationship between L2 listening research, pedagogical theory, and practice. *Foreign Language Annals, 31,* 169–189.

Bernhardt, E. B. (1986). Reading in the foreign language. In B. H. Wing (Ed.), *Listening, reading, writing: Analysis and application* (pp. 93–115). Northeast Conference Reports. Middlebury, VT: Northeast Conference on the Teaching of Foreign Languages.

Bernhardt, E. B. (1990). A model of L2 text reconstruction: The recall of literary text by learners of German. In A. Labarca & L. M. Bailey (Eds.), *Issues in L2: Theory as practice/practice as theory* (pp. 21–43). Norwood, NJ: Ablex.

Bernhardt, E. B. (1991a). A psycholinguistic perspective on second language literacy. *Association Internationale de la Linguistique Apliquée Review, 8,* 31–44.

Bernhardt, E. B. (1991b). *Reading development in a second language: Theoretical, empirical, and research perspectives.* Norwood, NJ: Ablex.

Bernhardt, E. B. (2002). Research into the teaching of literature in a second language: What it says and how to communicate it to graduate students. In V. Scott & H. Tucker (Eds.), *SLA and the literature classroom: fostering dialogues* (pp. 195–210). Boston: Heinle & Heinle.

Bernhardt, E. B., & Kamil, M. L. (1995). Interpreting relationships between L1 and L2 reading: Consolidating the linguistic threshold and the linguistic interdependence hypotheses. *Applied Linguistics, 16,* 15–34.

Bransford, J. D., & Johnson, M. K. (1972). Contextual pre-requisites for understanding: Some investigations of comprehension and recall. *Journal of Verbal Learning and Verbal Behavior, 11,* 717–726.

Brecht, R. D., & Walton, A. R. (1995). The future shape of language learning in the new world of global communication: Consequences for higher education and beyond. In R. Donato & R. M. Terry (Eds.), *Foreign language learning: The journey of a lifetime* (pp. 110–152). The ACTFL Foreign Language Education Series Lincolnwood, IL: NTC/Contemporary Publishing Group.

Brown, C. (1998). L2 reading: An update on relevant L1 research. *Foreign Language Annals, 31,* 191–202.

Carrell, P. (1985). Facilitating ESL reading by teaching text structure. *TESOL Quarterly, 19,* 727–752.

Carrell, P. (1989). Metacognitive awareness and second language reading. *The Modern Language Journal, 73,* 121–134.

Carrell, P. L., & Wise, T. E. (1998). The relationship between prior knowledge and topic interest in second language reading. *Studies in Second Language Acquisition, 20,* 285–309.

Chastain, K. (1988). *Developing second language skills: Theory and practice.* San Diego, CA: Harcourt Brace Jovanovich.

Chiang, C. S., & Dunkel, P. (1992). The effect of speech modification, prior knowledge, and listening proficiency on EFL lecture learning. *TESOL Quarterly, 26,* 345–374.

Christensen, B. (1990). Teenage novels of adventure as a source of authentic material. *Foreign Language Annals, 23,* 531–537.

Chung, J.-M. (1999). The effects of using video texts supported with advance organizers and captions on Chinese college students' listening comprehension: An empirical study. *Foreign Language Annals, 32,* 295–308.

Chung, J. S. (2000). Signals and reading comprehension: Theory and practice. *System, 28,* 247–259.

Clarke, D. F., & Nation, I. S. P. (1980). Guessing the meanings of words from context: Strategy and techniques. *System, 8,* 211–220.

Davis, J. N., Glass, W. R., & Coady, J. (1998). Use of the target language versus the native language to assess foreign/second language reading comprehension: Still an issue? Unpublished manuscript.

Donato, R., & Brooks, F. B. (2004). Literary discussions and advanced speaking functions: Researching the (dis)connection. *Foreign Language Annals, 37,* 183–199.

Dristas, V. M., & Grisenti, G. (1995). Motivation: Does interest influence reading and speaking proficiency in second language acquisition? Unpublished manuscript.

Dunkel, P.A., & Davis, J. N. (1994). The effects of rhetorical signaling cues on the recall of English lecture information by speakers of English as a native and second language. In J. Flowerdew (Ed.), *Academic listening:*

Research perspectives (pp. 55–74). New York: Cambridge University Press.

Edelsky, C., Draper, K., & Smith, K. (1983). Hookin' 'em in at the start of school in a "whole language" classroom. *Anthropology and Education Quarterly, 14,* 257–281.

Epstein, S. (2002). The news as a textbook in the Spanish classroom: A language/social studies approach to teaching. *NECTFL Review, 51,* 27–31.

Eskey, D. E. (1986). Theoretical foundations. In F. Dubin, D. E. Eskey, & W. Grabe (Eds.), *Teaching second language reading for academic purposes* (pp. 3–23). Reading, MA: Addison-Wesley.

Fecteau, M. L. (1999). First- and second-language reading comprehension of literary texts. *The Modern Language Journal, 83,* 475–493.

Flowerdew, J., & Tauroza, S. (1995). The effect of discourse markers on second language lecture comprehension. *Studies in Second Language Acquisition, 17,* 435–458.

Frantzen, D. (2003). Factors affecting how second language Spanish students derive meaning from context. *The Modern Language Journal, 87,* 168–199.

Fraser, C. (1999). Lexical processing strategy use and vocabulary learning through reading. *Studies in Second Language Acquisition, 21,* 225–241.

Galloway, V. (1992). Toward a cultural reading of authentic texts. In H. Byrnes (Ed.), *Languages for a multicultural world in transition* (pp. 87–121). Northeast Conference Reports. Lincolnwood, IL: NTC/Contemporary Publishing Group.

Gascoigne, C. (2002a). Documenting the initial second language reading experience: The readers speak. *Foreign Language Annals, 35,* 554–560.

Gascoigne, C. (2002b). Reviewing reading: Recommendations versus reality. *Foreign Language Annals, 35,* 343–348.

Glisan, E. W. (1995). Listening. In V. Galloway & C. Herron (Eds.), *Research within reach II* (pp. 61–83). Southern Conference on Language Teaching. Valdosta, GA: Valdosta State University.

Godev, C. B., Martínez-Gibson, E. A., & Toris, C. C. M. (2002). Foreign language reading comprehension test: L1 versus L2 in open-ended questions. *Foreign Language Annals, 35,* 202–221.

Goodman, K. S. (1967). Reading: A psycholinguistic guessing game. *Journal of the Reading Specialist, 6,* 126–135.

Hadley, A. O. (2001). *Teaching language in context* (3rd ed.). Boston: Heinle & Heinle.

Hammadou, J. A. (1991). Interrelationships among prior knowledge, inference, and language proficiency in foreign language reading. *The Modern Language Journal, 75,* 27–38.

Hammadou, J. A. (2000). The impact of analogy and content knowledge on reading comprehension: What helps, what hurts. *The Modern Language Journal, 75,* 27–38.

Hammadou, J. A. (2002). Advanced foreign language readers' inferencing. In J. A. Hammadou Sullivan (Ed.), *Literacy and the second language learner* (pp. 217–238). Greenwich, CT: Information Age Publishing.

Hanley, J. E. B., Herron, C. A., & Cole, S. P. (1995). Using video as an advance organizer to a written passage in the FLES classroom. *The Modern Language Journal, 79,* 57–66.

Harris, T. (2003). Listening with your eyes: The importance of speech-related gestures in the language classroom. *Foreign Language Annals, 36,* 180–187.

Hauptman, P. C. (2000). Some hypotheses on the nature of difficulty and ease in second language reading: An application of schema theory. *Foreign Language Annals, 33,* 622–631.

Haynes, M. (1984). Patterns and perils of guessing in second language reading. In J. Handscombe, R. A. Orem, & B. P. Taylor (Eds.), *On TESOL '83: The question of control* (pp. 163–176). Washington, DC: Teachers of English to Speakers of Other Languages.

Herron, C., Cole, S. P., York, H., & Linden, P. (1998). A comparison study of student retention of foreign language video: Declarative versus interrogative advance organizer. *Foreign Language Annals, 82,* 237–247.

Herron, C., Corrie, C., Cole, S. P., & Dubreil, S. (1999). The effectiveness of a video-based curriculum in teaching culture. *The Modern Language Journal, 83,* 518–533.

Herron, C., & Hanley, J. (1992). Using video to introduce children to a foreign culture. *Foreign Language Annals, 25,* 419–426.

Herron, C. A., & Seay, I. (1991). The effect of authentic oral texts on student listening comprehension in the foreign language classroom. *Foreign Language Annals, 24,* 487–495.

Horiba, Y. (2000). Reader control in reading: Effects of language competence, text type, and task. *Discourse Processes, 29,* 223–267.

Hosenfeld, C. (1984). Case studies of ninth grade readers. In J. C. Alderson & A. H. Urquhart (Eds.), *Reading in a foreign language* (pp. 231–249). London, UK: Longman.

Hron, A., Kurbjuhn, I., Mandl, H., & Schnotz, W. L. (1985). Structural inferences in reading and listening. In G. Richheit & H. Strohner (Eds.), *Inferences in text processing* (pp. 221–245). Amsterdam, The Netherlands: North-Holland.

Johnson, P. (1982). Effects on comprehension of building background knowledge. *TESOL Quarterly, 16,* 503–516.

Joiner, E. G. (1986). Listening in the foreign language. In H. S. Lepke (Ed.), *Listening, reading, writing: Analysis and application* (pp. 43–70). Northeast Conference Reports. Middlebury, VT: Northeast Conference on the Teaching of Foreign Languages.

Joiner, E. G. (1990). Choosing and using videotexts. *Foreign Language Annals, 23,* 53–64.

Jung, E. H. (2003). The role of discourse signaling cues in second language listening comprehension. *The Modern Language Journal, 87,* 562–577.

Just, M., & Carpenter, P. A. (1992). A capacity theory of comprehension: Individual differences in working memory. *Psychological Review, 99,* 122–149.

Kelly, P. (1990). Guessing: No substitute for systematic learning of lexis. *System, 18,* 199–207.

Kintsch, W., & van Dijk, T. A. (1978). Towards a model of discourse comprehension and production. *Psychological Review, 85,* 363–394.

Kitajima, R. (1997). Referential strategy training for second language reading comprehension of Japanese texts. *Foreign Language Annals, 30,* 84–97.

Knutson, E. M. (1997). Reading with a purpose: Communicative reading tasks for the foreign language classroom. *Foreign Language Annals, 30,* 49–57.

Lacorte, M., & Thurston-Griswold, H. (2001). Music in the foreign language classroom: Developing linguistic and cultural proficiency. *NECTFL Review, 49,* 40, 49–53.

Lally, C. (1998). The application of first language reading models to second language study: A recent historical perspective. *Reading Horizons, 38,* 267–277.

Lange, D. L. (1999). Planning for and using the new national culture standards. In J. K. Phillips & R. M Terry (Eds.), *Foreign language standards: Linking research, theories, and practices* (pp. 57–135). Lincolnwood, IL: National Textbook Company.

Lee, J. F. (1986a). Background knowledge and L2 reading. *The Modern Language Journal, 70,* 350–354.

Lee, J. F. (1986b). On the use of the recall task to measure L2 reading comprehension. *Studies in Second Language Acquisition, 8,* 83–93.

Lee, J. F. (1987). Comprehending the Spanish subjunctive: An information processing perspective. *The Modern Language Journal, 71,* 51–57.

Lee, J. F., & VanPatten, B. (1995). *Making communicative language teaching happen* (2nd ed.). New York: McGraw-Hill.

Lee, J. F., & VanPatten, B. (2003). *Making communicative language teaching happen* (3rd ed.). New York: McGraw-Hill.

Lee, J. F., & Wolf, D. F. (1997). A quantitative and qualitative analysis of the word-meaning inferencing strategies of L1 and L2 readers. *Spanish Applied Linguistics, 1,* 24–64.

Lund, R. J. (1991). A comparison of second language listening and reading comprehension. *The Modern Language Journal, 75,* 196–204.

Markham, P. (1999). Captioned videotapes and second-language listening word recognition. *Foreign Language Annals, 32,* 321–328.

Markham, P., Peter, L. A., & McCarthy, T. J. (2001). The effects of native language versus target language captions on foreign language students' DVD video comprehension. *Foreign Language Annals, 34,* 439–445.

Martinez-Lage, A. (1995). Benefits of keeping a reading journal in the development of second language reading ability. *Dimension,* 65–79.

Maxim, H. H., II. (2002). A study into the feasibility and effects of reading extended authentic discourse in the beginning German language classroom. *The Modern Language Journal, 86,* 20–35.

Minsky, M. (1982). A framework for representing knowledge. In J. Haugeland (Ed.), *Mind design* (pp. 95–128). Cambridge, MA: MIT Press.

Mondria, J., & Wit-DeBoer, M. (1991). The effects of contextual richness on the guessability and the retention of words in a foreign language. *Applied Linguistics, 12,* 249–267.

Mueller, G. A. (1980). Visual contextual cues and listening comprehension: An experiment. *The Modern Language Journal, 64,* 335–340.

Munby, J. (1979). Teaching intensive reading skills. In R. Mackay, B. Barkenson, & R. Jordan (Eds.), *Reading in a second language* (pp. 142–158). Rowley, MA: Newbury House.

Nagy, W. (1997). On the role of context in first- and second-language vocabulary learning. In N. Schmitt & M. McCarthy (Eds.), *Vocabulary: Description, acquisition, and pedagogy* (pp. 64–83). Cambridge, UK: Cambridge University Press.

Nation, P., & Coady, J. (1988). Vocabulary and reading. In R. Carter & M. McCarthy (Eds.), *Vocabulary and language teaching* (pp. 97–110). New York: Longman.

National Standards in Foreign Language Education Project (NSFLEP). (1999). *Standards for foreign language learning in the 21st century.* Lawrence, KS: Allen Press.

Nunan, D. (1985). Content familiarity and the perception of textual relationships in second language reading. *RELC Journal, 16,* 43–51.

Oller, J. W. (1983). Some working ideas for language teaching. In J. W. Oller & P. A. Richard-Amato (Eds.), *Methods that work* (pp. 3–19). Rowley, MA: Newbury House.

Omaggio, A. C. (1979). Pictures and second language comprehension: Do they help? *Foreign Language Annals, 12,* 107–116.

Oxford, R. (1990). *Language learning strategies: What every teacher should know.* Boston: Heinle & Heinle.

Palinscar, A., & Brown, A. (1984). Reciprocal teaching of comprehension-fostering and comprehension-monitoring activities. *Cognition and Instruction, 1,* 117–175.

Paribakht, T. S., & Wesche, M. (1996). Enhancing vocabulary acquisition through reading: A hierarchy of text-related exercise types. *Canadian Modern Language Review, 52,* 250–273.

Paribakht, T. S., & Wesche, M. (1997). Vocabulary enhancement activities and reading for meaning in second language vocabulary development. In J. Coady & T. Huckin (Eds.), *Second language vocabulary acquisition: A rationale for pedagogy* (pp. 174–200). New York: Cambridge University Press.

Paribakht, T. S., & Wesche, M. (1999). Reading and "incidental" L2 vocabulary acquisition. *Studies in Second Language Acquisition, 21,* 195–224.

Pressley, M., Levin, J. R., & McDaniel, M. A. (1987). Remembering versus inferring what a word means: Mnemonic and contextual approaches. In M. G. McKeown & M. E. Curtis (Eds.), *The nature of vocabulary acquisition* (pp. 107–127). Hillsdale, NJ: Lawrence Erlbaum Associates.

Price, J. (1990). Improving foreign language listening comprehension. In J. A. Alatis (Ed.), *Georgetown University Roundtable on Languages and Linguistics 1990: Linguistics, language teaching, and language acquisition: The interdependence of theory, practice, and research* (pp. 309–316). Washington, DC: Georgetown University.

Ramsay, R. (1991). French in action and the grammar question. *French Review, 65,* 255–266.

Richards, J. C. (1983). Listening comprehension: Approach, design, procedure. *TESOL Quarterly, 17,* 219–240.

Richards, J. P., Fajen, B. R., Sullivan, J. F., & Gillespie, G. (1997). Signaling, notetaking, and field independence-dependence in text comprehension and recall. *Journal of Educational Psychology, 89,* 508–517.

Rifkin, B. (2000). Video in the proficiency-based advanced conversation class: An example from the Russian-language curriculum. *Foreign Language Annals, 33,* 63–70.

Riley, G. L. (1993). A story structure approach to narrative text comprehension. *The Modern Language Journal, 77,* 417–432.

Roller, C. M. (1990). The interaction between knowledge and structure variables in the processing of expository prose. *Reading Research Quarterly, 25,* 79–89.

Rost, M., & Ross, S. (1991). Learner use of strategies in interaction: Typology and teachability. *Language Learning, 41,* 235–273.

Rubin, J. (1994). A review of second language listening comprehension research. *The Modern Language Journal, 78,* 199–221.

Rusciolelli, J. (1995). Student responses to reading strategies instruction. *Foreign Language Annals, 28,* 262–273.

Saito, Y., Garza, T. J., & Horwitz, E. K. (1999). Foreign language reading anxiety. *The Modern Language Journal, 83,* 202–218.

Scarcella, R. C., & Oxford, R. L. (1992). *The tapestry of language learning.* Boston: Heinle & Heinle.

Schmidt-Rinehart, B. C. (1994). The effects of topic familiarity on second language listening comprehension. *The Modern Language Journal, 78,* 179–189.

Scott, V. M., & Huntington, J. A. (2002). Reading culture: Using literature to develop C2 competence. *Foreign Language Annals, 35,* 622–631.

Secules, T., Herron, C., & Tomasello, M. (1992). The effect of video context on foreign language learning. *The Modern Language Journal, 76,* 480–490.

Sellers, V. D. (2000). Anxiety and reading comprehension in Spanish as a foreign language. *Foreign Language Annals, 33,* 512–521.

Shook, D. J. (1996). Foreign language literature and the beginning learner-reader. *Foreign Language Annals, 29,* 201–216.

Shrum, J. L., & Glisan, E. W. (1994). *Teacher's handbook: Contextualized language instruction.* Boston: Heinle & Heinle.

Stein, M. (1993). The healthy inadequacy of contextual definition. In T. Huckin, M. Haynes, & J. Coady (Eds.),

Second language reading and vocabulary learning (pp. 203–212). Norwood, NJ: Ablex.

Stevick, E. (1984). Similarities and differences between oral and written comprehension: An imagist view. *Foreign Language Annals, 17,* 281–283.

Swaffar, J. (2001). Reading the patterns of literary works: Strategies and teaching techniques. In V. M. Scott & H. Tucker (Eds.), *SLA and the literature classroom: Fostering dialogues* (pp. 131–154). Boston: Heinle & Heinle.

Swaffar, J., Arens, K., & Byrnes, H. (1991). *Reading for meaning.* Englewood Cliffs, NJ: Prentice Hall.

Swaffar, J., & Bacon, S. (1993). Reading and listening comprehension: Perspectives on research and implications for practice. In A. Omaggio-Hadley (Ed.), *Research in language learning: Principles, processes, and prospects* (pp. 124–155). Lincolnwood, IL: National Textbook Company.

Swaffar, J., & Vlatten, A. (1997). A sequential model for video viewing in the foreign language curriculum. *The Modern Language Journal, 81,* 175–188.

Thompson, I., & Rubin, J. (1993). Improving listening comprehension in Russian. Report submitted to U.S. Department of Education, International Research and Studies Program. Grant #PO17A00032.

Tyler, A. (1994). The role of syntactic structure in discourse structure: Signaling logical and prominence relations. *Applied Linguistics, 15,* 243–262.

Vandergrift, L. (1997). The Cinderella of communication strategies: Reception strategies in interactive listening. *The Modern Language Journal, 81,* 494–505.

Vigil, V. D. (1987). Authentic text in the college-level Spanish I class as the primary vehicle of instruction. Unpublished doctoral dissertation. University of Texas, Austin.

Vogely, A. J. (1995). Perceived strategy use during performance on three authentic listening comprehension tasks. *The Modern Language Journal, 79,* 41–56.

Vogely, A. J. (1998). Listening comprehension anxiety: Students' reported scores and solutions. *Foreign Language Annals, 31,* 67–80.

Voller, P., & Widdows, S. (1993). Feature films as text: A framework for classroom use. *ELT Journal, 47,* 342–349.

Weissenrieder, M. (1987). Listening to the news in Spanish. *Foreign Language Annals, 71,* 18–27.

Wesche, M. B., & Paribakht, T. S. (2000). Reading-based exercises in second language vocabulary learning: An introspective study. *The Modern Language Journal, 84,* 196–213.

Weyers, J. R. (1999). The effect of authentic video on communicative competence. *The Modern Language Journal, 83,* 339–340.

Wolf, D. F. (1993). A comparison of assessment tasks used to measure FL reading comprehension. *The Modern Language Journal, 77,* 473–489.

Wolfe, P. (2004). "The owl cried": Reading abstract literary concepts with adolescent ESL students. *Journal of Adolescent and Adult Literacy, 47,* 402–413.

Wright, D. A. (2000). Culture as information and culture as affective process: A comparative study. *Foreign Language Annals, 33,* 330–341.

Young, D. J. (1993). Processing strategies of foreign language readers: Authentic and edited input. *Foreign Language Annals, 26,* 451–468.

Young, D. J. (1999). Linguistic simplification of SL reading material: Effective instructional practice? *The Modern Language Journal, 83,* 350–366.

NOTES

1. See Bernhardt (1991) for detailed information regarding the process of second-language reading.

2. For a review of L2 reading research based on L1 reading research, see Brown (1998); for a review of L2 listening, see Rubin (1994).

3. For excellent series of authentic French and Spanish magazines for children and adolescents, contact Bayard Presse, 9709 Sotweed Drive, Potomac, MD 20854; (301)/299–5920.

4. For an interesting description of how a college-level instructor revised a Spanish novel class in order to address the *SFLL,* see Barnes-Karol (2000).

5. Thanks to June K. Phillips for ideas on story formats for the interpretive mode.

CHAPTER 7

Using a Story-Based Approach to Teach Grammar

By Bonnie Adair-Hauck, Ph.D. (University of Pittsburgh), Richard Donato, Ph.D. (University of Pittsburgh) and Philomena Cumo-Johanssen (World Languages Educational Consultant, Pittsburgh, Pennsylvania)[1]

In this chapter, you will learn about:

- explicit/implicit grammar explanations
- focus on form
- reformulating grammar instruction
- a story-based approach to language instruction

- foreshadowing grammar explanations
- guided participation for grammar explanations
- The PACE Model: Presentation, Attention, Co-Construction, Extension

Teach and Reflect: Examining Grammar Presentations in Textbooks; Designing a Story-Based Language Lesson; Developing a PACE Lesson for the Post-Secondary Level

Discuss and Reflect: Using a Story-Based Approach to Teach Reflexive Verbs; Contrasting Explanations of Form

CONCEPTUAL ORIENTATION

In this chapter, you will explore a story-based approach to the teaching of grammar in a standards-based foreign language curriculum. The Standards for Foreign Language Learning in the 21st Century (*SFLL*) (NSFLEP, 1999) emphasize that communication is at the core of second-language learning. *Communication* has been defined as the personal expression, interpretation, and negotiation of meaning where information, feelings, and ideas are exchanged in talk, gesture, and writing (Lee & VanPatten, 2003). Communication also involves the development of relationships between individuals as they use language to create social bonds, show sympathy and understanding, and support each other. This type of communication contrasts sharply with communication that is aimed primarily at exchanging information in verbal transactions. Furthermore, communication involves private talk, or "communication with the self," to plan, organize, and evaluate one's thinking and doing (Brooks & Donato, 1994; Brooks, Donato, & McGlone, 1997), as discussed in the section on private speech in Chapter 1.

As you learned in Chapter 6, the standards further refine these definitions by organizing our language-using activities into the interpersonal, interpretive, and presentational modes of communication. Each mode specifies how language is used in the process of

189

communication. In the past, traditional grammar instruction emphasized explicit knowledge of language rules without providing occasions for learners to communicate in the ways currently being defined and understood by psycholinguists, applied linguists, and the language teaching profession. Unfortunately, as a result, many learners who spent years learning the formal properties of the language (the sound system, verb conjugations, rules of syntax, vocabulary, etc.) were not able to exchange information, participate in target language cultures, or develop and nurture a social relationship in a second language (Adair-Hauck & Cumo-Johanssen, 1997; Barnes, 1992; Hall, 1995, 1999).

Cooper underscores the important role of communication when he states that "It is through communication that we are able to improve our world, to prosper and enjoy it" (1993, p. 43). Communicating, in Cooper's broad sense of the word, involves more than Chomsky's (1965) notion of linguistic or grammatical competence; indeed, communication requires both communicative and interactional competence (Mehan, 1979; see Chapter 1) and the ability to use language in a variety of ways and for a variety of purposes. The *SFLL* capture these notions by stressing the need to "know how, when, and why to say what to whom" (NSFLEP, 1999, p. 11).

To realize the Communication goal area, learners may need opportunities to reflect on the language system they are learning at particular times during instruction. Teachers committed to providing communicative and interactive language learning experiences for their learners often find it a challenge to integrate grammar into their teaching. The standards stress that knowledge of the language system, including grammar, vocabulary, phonology, and pragmatic and discourse features, contributes to the accuracy of communication. Researchers agree that "focus on form" (i.e., reflecting on aspects of the language at times when those aspects are relevant to the communication task) can be beneficial to learners and is critical to making progress as language users (Adair-Hauck & Donato, 1994; Ellis, 1988; Herron & Tomasello, 1992; Hinkel & Fotos, 2002; Larsen-Freeman, 2003; Lightbown & Spada, 1990; Long, 1991; Salaberry, 1997). This treatment of grammar largely depends on what learners need for communicative purposes rather than on a predetermined grammatical syllabus. Liskin-Gasparro (1999) illustrates what teachers attempt to do when they focus students' attention on form for purposes of communication. She states that teachers are "supplying information about how the language works when one or more students experience what we might call communicative urgency, a need to say something and, thus, a desire for grammatical information."

 "Focus on form" largely depends on what learners need for communication purposes raher than on a predetermined grammatical syllabus.

The rationale for teaching grammar is multifaceted. The first reason is theoretically motivated. As the Variable Competence Model (Bialystok, 1982; Ellis, 1988; Tarone, 1983) states (see the *Variability in Performance* section of Chapter 1), depending on the social and communicative context, a learner draws on both their automatic (nonanalyzed) and controlled (analyzed) language knowledge. Ellis suggests that analyzed knowledge of grammar can become automatic as learners are placed into interactional situations that call for a two-way negotiation of meaning. The second reason for the teaching of grammar relates to the dynamics of classroom practice and, particularly, to the background knowledge of the learners. Learners in middle school and high school already have some knowledge of language and can reflect on and analyze how language forms are used to make meaning (Celce-Murcia, 1991; Swain & Lapkin, 2002).

Grammar instruction can also be beneficial because it raises learners' consciousness concerning the differences and similarities of L1 and L2 (Rutherford, 1988) and thus can directly address the Comparisons goal of the *SFLL*. In this respect, knowledge of a language can be used as a map with road signs to assist learners as they explore the landscape of the new language.

However, we need to remember that understanding grammatical structures apart from their use and function is pointless unless one wants to be a linguist or describe a language systematically without becoming a communicatively competent user of that language (Larsen-Freeman, 2003). Like road signs, grammatical structures take on meaning only if they are situated, within a context, within people, and within connected discourse. They become internalized only if the learners are placed in a situation in which they need to use the structures for communicative purposes (Adair-Hauck & Donato, 2002; DeKeyser & Sokalski, 1996; Fotos & Ellis, 1991; Salaberry, 1997; Shaffer, 1989; VanPatten & Cadierno, 1993). Thus, an important role of the language teacher is to create learning situations in which students perceive how grammar is used to make meanings and the need to make use of the grammar to comprehend and communicate in the target language.

 Grammatical structures will become internalized only if the learners are placed in a situation in which they need to use the structures for communicative purposes. ∎

The Explicit/Implicit Controversy

Although many researchers agree on the benefits of some grammar instruction, how to teach grammar is an issue of little agreement. Furthermore, research on focus on form is often conducted in highly controlled laboratory settings and rarely tested against the realities of the language classroom with real teachers and learners and all that this implies (Ellis, 1998). The controversy has become particularly acute in the framework of communicative language teaching, which has consistently underscored the importance of stressing meaning over form.

For several years, second language acquisition researchers and theorists have been grappling with polarized views concerning the teaching of grammar within a communicative framework. On the one side of the dichotomy is the *explicit* approach to grammar instruction that involves teacher explanations of rules followed by related manipulative exercises intended to practice the new structure.[2] Many language learners have experienced this method of grammar instruction. Most textbooks still present grammar explanations in this fashion, followed by manipulative drills that are cast in shallow and artificial contexts unrelated to the real concerns of learners (Aski, 2003). Thus, these practice opportunities are often meaningless to learners and are not capable of engaging their language problem-solving skills and their desire to communicate using the forms they are learning (Brooks & Donato, 1994). It is common for teachers to observe that these mechanical, repetitive drills often result in unmotivated and lethargic responses in learners, no matter how much context is given in the directions or how much personalization is provided.

Another potential problem with explicit grammar instruction is that it implies a direct instructional and authoritative role on the part of the teacher, who takes all of the responsibility for understanding and constructing grammatical knowledge. Conversely, explicit explanation of grammar assigns a passive role to the learners. Learner interaction takes place, if it occurs at all, only after the teacher's grammatical explanations and several practice exercises that may consist of disconnected sentences unrelated to an overall theme.

Approaches to grammar found in many textbooks and adhered to by many language teachers sequence the learning of grammar from mechanical practice to communicative language use. This practice has the disadvantage of requiring learners to focus on a grammatical form before experiencing its meaning and function in a communicative encounter (Larsen-Freeman, 2003). This linear model of teaching a form before using a form has distinct disadvantages and does not support learning grammatical knowledge. When learners are presented with ready-made explanations of grammar by the teacher, they are denied the opportunity to explore and construct for themselves an understanding of the form; predictably, they do not perceive a valid reason for learning the particular grammar point.

 What is explicit grammar instruction? Why does it appeal to some educators? What are its disadvantages? ■

On the other side of the instructional dichotomy is the *implicit* grammar approach. This approach, as presented by Krashen (1985), Terrell (1977), & Dulay & Burt (1973), rejects the need for any explicit focus on form. These researchers argue that learners can acquire language naturally if they are provided with sufficient comprehensible input from the teacher. Furthermore, the approach maintains that grammatical development follows its own natural internal syllabus; thus, any explicit teaching of form is pointless and not worth the instructional time and effort of the teacher and the students. If learners are exposed to a sufficient amount of language that interests them and is globally understandable to them, they will eventually be able to induce how the structures of the language work. As the theory goes, learners should be able to perform hypothesizing and language analysis on their own as comprehensible input becomes intake.

However, research has shown that some learners do not attend to or "induce" the teacher's grammatical agenda in these implicit, inductive lessons. One reason for this may be that the implicit approach clearly places little importance on direct instruction, reducing the teacher to a provider of input rather than explanation, the opposite of the explicit approach. Herron and Tomasello (1992) also state that the inductive method cannot guarantee that the learner will discover the underlying concepts or that the induced concepts will actually be correct. In the research of Adair-Hauck (1993), it was found that when learners were asked about their emerging understandings and "noticings" about form, they often had inaccurate or partial understandings of the grammatical concept. Additionally, some students failed to perceive the grammatical pattern the teacher presented even when the structure was embedded in a meaningful context. The implicit/inductive approach can frustrate adolescent or adult learners, many of whom have already become analytical with regard to the rules that govern their native languages. These learners often want to hasten the learning process by consciously comparing and contrasting their own native language rules to the rules that govern the new target language.

 What is the implicit grammar instructional approach? What are its advantages? What are some disadvantages? ■

Reformulating Grammar Instruction

Although explicit and implicit grammar instruction are clearly opposite approaches to teaching and learning grammar, they share some notable deficiencies. Neither approach acknowledges the critical role of the teacher in negotiating and constructing explanations of how the new language works, and neither acknowledges the contributions and backgrounds that the learners bring to the instructional setting for collaborating with the teacher on constructing an explanation (Donato & Adair-Hauck, 1992). Moreover, neither

FIGURE 7.1 Story-Based and Guided Participation: An Alternative Approach to Grammar Instruction

IMPLICIT EXPLANATIONS	GUIDED PARTICIPATION	EXPLICIT EXPLANATIONS
Learners analyze the grammar explanation for themselves.	Teachers and learners collaborate on and co-construct the grammar explanation.	Teacher provides explanation for learners.

Source: Adair-Hauck, 1993, p. 6.

approach recognizes how learning takes place among people in the world, outside of the classroom. A Vygotskyan approach to instruction (see Chapter 1) indicates that learning is an emerging, social, and interactive process situated in cultural contexts, such as schools and classrooms, and assisted through tools, the most notable being language.[3] Therefore, theory and research have provided two dichotomous approaches to learning and processing grammatical information, both of which fail to take into account the collaborative and social aspects of learning (Adair-Hauck, 1993; Adair-Hauck & Donato, 2002, 1994; Donato 2004). Neither approach recognizes the mutually responsive interactions that are fundamental to learning as it occurs naturally between humans in everyday life (Adair-Hauck, 1993; Adair-Hauck & Donato, 1994; Donato, 2004; Forman, Minnick, & Stone, 1993; John-Steiner, 2000; Lave & Wenger, 1991; Rogoff, 1990; Wenger, 1998).

We believe it is time to begin a serious reappraisal of the teaching of grammar and to formulate a new vision that goes beyond dichotomies. In this chapter, we are advocating a story-based and guided participatory approach (Adair-Hauck, 1993; Rogoff, 1990) that contrasts with both the traditional explicit approach and the implicit approach to learning.[4] In many ways, this alternative approach can reconcile the explicit/implicit polarized views, as shown in Figure 7.1. For a number of reasons that will be discussed later in this chapter, we believe that a story-based and guided participatory approach might hold the key to dramatic improvements in teaching grammar.

Basic Principles of Story-Based Language Teaching

Before discussing some practical applications of this approach, we present the principles of story-based and guided participatory teaching. Many specialists in first-language literacy development have explored the implications of story-based teaching and narrative ways of knowing for quite some time. Likewise, research in sociocultural theory has turned attention to guided participation and the importance of collaborative interaction in several academic disciplines. In an effort to situate grammar instruction in sociocultural theory, we will discuss the principles of a story-based approach to grammar instruction, and then present how to use guided and collaborative problem solving in a story-based lesson to enhance the learning and use of grammar.

Goodman (1986) states that "language is language only when it is whole" (cf. Fountas & Hannigan, 1989, p. 134).[5] According to Goodman, the whole is always viewed as being greater than the sum of its parts, and it is the whole that gives meaning to the parts. In terms of grammar instruction, words, phrases, or sentences are not linguistic islands unto themselves. On the contrary, these linguistic elements gain meaning and function— for example, giving advice on good eating habits to a friend using the subjunctive in

French, Spanish, or Italian—only when they are placed in context and in a whole text. Goodman's belief is that once learners experience the whole, they are then better prepared to deal with the analyses of the parts (Fountas & Hannigan, 1989). In our above example, the use of the subjunctive takes on meaning and is used for a function in the whole context of giving advice. Compare this to simply giving students an explicit explanation of the subjunctive, which does not situate its use and fails to illustrate how the form is used to make meaning in the language, resulting in a decontextualized academic exercise in language analysis rather than language use.

We should acknowledge that Goodman is primarily addressing the needs of first-language learners. However, research in first-language acquisition has often acted as a catalyst for theoretical advancement in second-language acquisition, including the development of language literacy skills. For example, concepts such as the importance of comprehensible input, the role of interaction, and the notion of scaffolding in caretaker speech are all derived from theories of first-language development (Ellis, 1988; Hatch, 1983; Hawkins, 1988). Furthermore, many second-language specialists (Celce-Murcia, 1991; Hinkel & Fotos, 2002; Hughes & McCarthy, 1998; Kramsch, 1993; Larsen-Freeman, 2003; Nunan, 1991) emphasize the importance of content-based instruction, authentic texts for listening and reading comprehension, and the need for thematically organized conversations and extended discourse. These approaches all share the common feature of using whole texts rather than fragmented phrase-level and sentence-level examples to illustrate and teach the foreign language.

Conceptually, then, we need to reappraise our orientation to grammar instruction. Teaching approaches have all too often focused on fragmented discourse and artificial, mechanical exercises. Many language programs stress a bottom-up or transmission approach by emphasizing the "bits and pieces" of language (e.g., word lists, verb conjugations, or isolated linguistic elements). A transmission, or language differentiation approach, usually results in what Goodman calls "non-language," which can be characterized as unnatural, cognitively undemanding, and dull (Cummins, 1984). Moreover, words, phrases, or sentences do not take on meaning when viewed in isolation from each other; on the contrary, these linguistic elements gain meaning only when used in connected discourse forming a coherent whole. Therefore, learners will need to experience "whole" contextualized language (e.g., stories, legends, poems, listening selections, cartoons, songs, recipes) with an emphasis on meaning-making and sense-making before a focus on form can be a productive instructional activity (Long, 1991). In this way, a story-based language approach stresses natural discourse and encourages learners to comprehend meaningful and longer samples of discourse from the very beginning of the lesson. Once learners map meaning onto the whole text, they are better able to focus on and understand the importance of the parts to the meaning of the text (Adair-Hauck & Cumo-Johanssen, 1997; Adair-Hauck & Donato, 1994; Fountas & Hannigan, 1989; Freeman & Freeman, 1992; Hughes & McCarthy, 1998).

A story-based language approach stresses natural discourse and encourages learners to comprehend meaningful and longer samples of discourse from the very beginning of the lesson.

By introducing a lesson with a whole text, the teacher *foreshadows* the grammar explanation through the use of integrated discourse that will highlight and make obvious the grammar structure to be taught. Galloway & Labarca (1990) explain how foreshadowing of new language elements is beneficial: It provides "learners with a 'feel' for what is to come and can help learners cast forward a familiarity net by which aspects of language prompt initial recognition and later, gradually, are pulled into the learner's productive repertoire" (p. 136). In this way, the story or text highlights the functional significance of the grammatical structure before the learners' attention is focused on the specific form.

This approach is also in agreement with Ausubel, Novak, and Hanesian's (1968) idea of using advance organizers to assist learners, providing an "anchoring framework" for the new concepts to be learned; in this approach, the story "anchors" the new structure.

Unlike many classroom textbooks, which may offer a group of disconnected sentences or a "contextualized" drill (Walz, 1989), a story-based approach invites the learner to comprehend and experience the meaning and function of grammar through integrated discourse in the form of a story. The process of understanding a story in a foreign language also creates a Zone of Proximal Development (ZPD) (see Chapter 1) where, through interest in understanding the narrative, the need to learn emerges and responsive assistance is provided. As a result, from the very beginning of the lesson, the teacher and learners are engaged in authentic use of language through joint problem-solving activities and interactions to render the story comprehensible. By using simplified language, pictures, and gestures, the teacher scaffolds (see Chapter 1) and guides learners to comprehend the story or other text types. Once comprehension is achieved, the teacher can then productively turn the learners' attention to various linguistic elements previously encountered and anchored in the narrative.

 Foreshadowing of new language elements provides learners with a "feel" for what is to come.

Storytelling is particularly adaptable to second-language instruction, since it is natural to tell stories orally, interpret their contents, and extend the story in various ways (e.g., talk about favorite parts, speculate on why an event occurred, express personal opinions about a character). Oller (1983) states that the episodic organization represented in stories aids comprehension and retention. Since individuals have prior knowledge concerning how stories are structured and expectancies about what should take place in stories, their comprehension is facilitated and meaning is established. Furthermore, using "multiple passes" and recycling the storyline through picture displays, Total Physical Response (TPR) activities, and role-playing scenarios deepen comprehension. The framework of the story provides a flow of mental images that help the learners to assign meaning and functions to the forms they hear. Again, after these initial activities and interactions have helped learners to understand the meaning of the discourse, the teacher turns the learners' attention to specific language forms or structure. This approach is in agreement with Celce-Murcia's suggestion concerning grammar instruction for ESL learners, that "one of the best times for them [the learners] to attend to form is after comprehension has been achieved and in conjunction with their production of meaningful discourse" (1985, p. 301).

 "One of the best times for them [the learners] to attend to form is after comprehension has been achieved and in conjunction with their production of meaningful discourse."

 Which elements of the story-based approach make it appealing?

A Model for Integrating Form in a Story-Based Language Approach

Focus on form has recently become the topic of intense research and has been shown to be an important design feature of language teaching (Ellis, 1998; Fotos, 1994; Kowal & Swain, 1994; Long, 1991; Spada & Lightbown, 1993; Swain, 1995, 1998; VanPatten & Cadierno, 1993; Wong & VanPatten, 2003). The theory of learning espoused in *Teacher's Handbook* emphasizes the importance of creating a ZPD with the learner so that the need to learn emerges and the help provided will enable the learner to become an independent language user at a later time. Grammar instruction and learning can also be viewed in this way and is an equally interactive process between expert and novice, similar to any other aspect of developing communicative ability in learners. Learners can be guided to reflect on language to create their own meanings.

Learners can be guided to reflect on language to create their own meanings. ▪

What is the Zone of Proximal Development (Chapter 1)? ▪

Language teaching should never be driven by grammar instruction alone, nor should grammar instruction be literally interpreted to mean instruction on morphology (e.g., adjective or subject-verb agreement, rules for pluralization, etc.) or meaningless, decontextualized manipulation of forms. When the teacher or students focus on form, attention is drawn to the formal properties of the language, which include its sound system, word formation, syntax, discourse markers, and devices for relating one sentence to another, to name a few; our colleagues who teach reading in the elementary schools call this form of instruction "Language Arts." Classes that focus on language form for the purpose of increasing comprehension and meaning making have been shown to result in greater language gains than classes in which no focus on form is available or in which forms are learned as meaningless structures (see Wong & Van Patten, 2003; Lightbown & Spada, 1990). Therefore, the issue is not whether a teacher should focus on form; instead, the issue is how, when, and where to focus on form in a lesson.

The following four sections present PACE, a model for contextualizing interactions with learners about the forms of language. *PACE* (Donato & Adair-Hauck, 1994) is an acronym for the four steps we have developed for integrating focus on form in the context of a story-based language lesson. The model allows for learners to construct understandings of form in collaboration with the teacher and each other. This process contrasts sharply with explicit teacher explanation of grammar and implicit approaches that assume that all structures can be analyzed equally well by students on their own, solely on the basis of the input they hear.

P: PRESENTATION of Meaningful Language

This first step of PACE represents the "whole" language being presented in a thematic way. It can be an interesting story (folktales and legends work well), a TPR lesson, an authentic listening segment, an authentic document, or a demonstration of a real-life, authentic task, such as playing a sport, making a sandwich, or conducting a science experiment. Even materials from a textbook chapter (narratives, dialogues, stories) may be used if they are found to be interesting and episodically organized. Episodically organized stories include stageable actions and events that are well suited for presentation, since the meanings of these texts can be made transparent and comprehensible through dramatization, actions, or TPR storytelling.

In the Presentation phase, the teacher presents the story orally, which facilitates aural comprehension and the acquisition of meaning and form; students do not see the written script of the story in this phase. This strategy parallels what occurs in natural language acquisition. The Presentation does not consist of isolated, disconnected sentences illustrating the target form in question; instead, it is thematic, contextualized, story-based language intended to capture learner interest and provide opportunities for the teacher to create comprehension through negotiation of meaning (see Chapter 1). Care should also be taken to ensure that the presentation adequately illustrates the structure in question and that the story and target structure are appropriate to the learners' potential level of development, as instruction in the ZPD suggests. The structure should appear often enough during the Presentation to be salient to learners, without making the language sound unnatural or stilted (see suggestions on creating a storytelling lesson below). Authentic stories, documents, or listening segments can guarantee naturalness and often contain *naturally occurring repetitions*; for example, think of the story of Goldilocks and the Three Bears.

The Presentation should also be interactive. By scaffolding participation in the activity, teachers can guide learners through the new element of the language to be learned. This scaffolded participation during the presentation of the text may take the form of learner repetitions of key phrases cued by the teacher during a storytelling session, the use of student actors to portray the events of the story as it is told, cloze exercises based on listening segments, K-W-L activities,[6] or discussions that anticipate the content of a reading. The goal here is to enable learners to stretch their language abilities by comprehending new elements of the target language in meaningful texts, through the help and mediation of the teacher and the while-listening tasks presented during storytelling.

The Presentation phase may last for part of a class, an entire class session, or even several class sessions, depending on the story selected and the sequencing of its presentation. For example, a storytelling lesson may contain prestorytelling activities focusing on prior knowledge, content, cultural references, language, dramatization, pair-work comprehension checks, or story-retelling exercises. The length of time required ultimately depends on the nature of the story, its length, and the amount of negotiation work required to establish meaning.

A: ATTENTION

This second PACE step focuses learners' attention on some aspect of the language used during the Presentation. In the Presentation phase, language is transparent and students may not notice important aspects of the language that will help them progress in proficiency. Thus, in this phase, the teacher highlights some regularity of the language. Highlighting can be achieved in several ways. Teachers can ask questions about patterns found in the text or about words and phrases repeated in a story. Overhead transparencies of example sentences from the Presentation story can be prepared, with important words and phrases circled or underlined. The point of this step is to help learners to focus attention on the target form without needless elaboration or wasted time.

Another purpose of this step is to ensure that learners are indeed focused on the grammatical element chosen for discussion which is, after all, the original purpose of following the PACE model. Recall that research has shown that learners do not always process or attend to input in ways that we expect (Herron & Tomasello, 1992). As an example of this, Adair-Hauck (1993) found that when learners were presented with contextualized sentences (examples taken from the "Le lion et la souris" story with sentences both in the present and in the past using the new past-tense verb form) and were asked by the teacher what they noticed about these sentences, the learners were unable to answer. Instead, they responded with puzzled looks. However, when the teacher provided responsive and graduated assistance and included the words *aujourd'hui* (today) and *hier* (yesterday), which are semantic, not syntactic, clues, learners were able to articulate the differences in the meanings of the sentences. After paying attention to the *semantic clues* (focus on meaning), the learners were able to attend to the *syntactic clues* (focus on form). This classroom-based observation highlights the important role of the teacher in guiding and assisting the learners in *attending to* the lesson objective.

It should also be pointed out that learners might reveal certain learning needs at this point in the lesson or show curiosity about certain aspects of the language. The teacher should allow the grammatical agenda to be set by students when this curiosity emerges, if the teacher is indeed working within the ZPD as Vygotsky (1978) outlined it. By assessing whether attention was drawn to a particular structure and what structures students seem to want to understand, the teacher can determine aspects of the language that were not transparent and need clarification, the function of the next phase.

C: CO-CONSTRUCT an Explanation

Learners and teacher should be co-constructors of grammatical explanations. After learners focus attention on the target form, the teacher assists them in raising their awareness about the target structure and enables them to contrast the structure with what they know about their own language. This phase directly addresses the Comparisons goal area, at a time when language comparisons are appropriate and can be discussed in a meaningful context. This third step of PACE features *guided participation*; learners are guided to hypothesize, guess, make predictions, and come to generalizations about the target form, all higher order thinking skills requiring observation, evaluation, analysis, and synthesis. Co-constructing an explanation requires teacher questions that are well chosen, clear, and direct.

Questions are powerful tools in the hands of teachers who can adjust their questioning "in flight" to meet the emergent understandings of their learners. For example, asking learners questions such as "What words do you hear or see repeated in the text, and what could they mean?," "What pattern do you see in this group of words?," and "How do certain words change as their meanings change?" is a way to help learners draw insights from the language they hear and understand. These assisting questions help learners discover regular grammatical patterns, sound systems, word order, unique cultural meanings of words, or language functions. Additionally, questions cannot be predicted in advance and need to be contingent upon learner contributions. Learners should also be encouraged to ask the teacher and each other questions if the explanation is to be truly co-constructed and negotiated. As learners hypothesize and generalize about the target form, teachers build upon and extend learners' knowledge without overwhelming them with superfluous grammatical detail. Hypothesis testing can also be conducted, with teachers leading learners in trying out their new knowledge by applying their generalizations to new situations. Teachers need to be aware that the help they provide is graduated and may range from brief hints about the target form to explicit instruction if needed (Aljaafreh, 1992; Aljaafreh & Lantolf, 1994).

It is important to note that, unlike guided induction techniques, which rely primarily on teacher questioning, a co-constructed explanation is not an inquisition; instead, co-constructed explanations recognize that learners may not be able to perceive the formal properties of language on the basis of the teacher's questions alone. What is obvious to an expert language user is often a mystery to the novice. A co-constructed explanation is as participatory for the teacher as it is for the learners; that is, teachers need to assess the abilities of their learners and assist them by providing and eliciting information when necessary. Teachers can be conversation partners and offer suggestions and observations, thereby modeling for the students the process of reflecting on language forms. As Tharp and Gallimore (1988) point out, teaching is responsive assistance and cannot be reduced to series of actions to be performed in the same order in every instructional circumstance. By listening closely to learner contributions during this step, teachers can assess how much help is needed to attain the concept. Over time, learners will develop the ability to reflect on language and some learners may be able to work in small groups on grammar problems and report back to the class about their discoveries (Fotos & Ellis, 1991).

The use of English for co-construction of grammatical knowledge may be necessary, depending on the level of the class and the structure under investigation. Indeed, it is hard to imagine that beginning language students can analyze language and arrive at generalizations in the target language. It is common to observe, however, that when students reflect on language form they do so in their native language (Swain & Lapkin 2002; Brooks, Donato, & McGlone, 1997; Brooks & Donato, 1994). However, if the grammatical conversation can be simplified—and this simplification would be largely determined on the basis if the structure being discussed and the level of the class—then the use of the target language may be possible and useful. As students progress, the teacher should be attentive to changes in students' language and observational abilities and determine if the co-construction can take place in the target language.

E: EXTENSION Activities

Focus on form is only useful if it can be pressed into service by the learners in a new way at a later time. In story-based language teaching, the teacher never loses sight of the "whole." Therefore, the Extension activity phase of PACE provides learners with the opportunity to use their new grammar skill in creative and interesting ways while at the same time integrating it into existing knowledge. Extension activities should be interesting, be related to the theme of the lesson in some way, and, most importantly, allow for creative self-expression. Extension activities are not worksheets on which learners use the target form to fill in blanks of disconnected sentences; instead, they can be information-gap activities, role-play situations, dramatizations, games, authentic writing projects, paired interviews, class surveys, out-of-class projects, or simulations of real-life situations (see Chapter 8). The possibilities are endless, as long as the learners have the chance to try to use the target form in ways that they see as useful, meaningful, and connected to the overarching theme of the lesson. Moreover, the Extension phase of the lesson allows the teacher to address other goal areas of the standards, such as Cultures, Communities, and Connections: The Extension activities can address cultural perspectives embodied in the story (West & Donato, 1995), bring learners into contact with target-language members of the community for further investigations of the story's country of origin, or link the story's theme to an academic subject area.

The Extension activity phase closes the circle of the PACE lesson and puts the "whole" back into story-based language teaching (see Figure 7.2). As is the case in the Presentation phase, the Extension phase can take several days as students are engaged in multiple communicative and interpersonal activities.

Elements of Story-Based Language Learning

Figure 7.3 summarizes the differences between a story-based language approach and the traditional explicit approach to teaching grammar. The earlier discussion should have led you to the conclusion that language learning is a thinking process or, from the learners' viewpoint, a challenging and intellectual guessing game. Teachers need to design cognitively demanding activities that will encourage learners to hypothesize, predict, take risks, make errors, and self-correct (Fountas & Hannigan, 1989). By doing so, learners become active participants in the learning process. All the story-based and guided participatory activities described later in this chapter have a common denominator—they all encourage learners to be active thinkers and hypothesizers as they collaborate in language-learning activities with the teacher or with their peers.

FIGURE 7.2 PACE: A Story-Based/Guided Participatory Approach
to Language Instruction

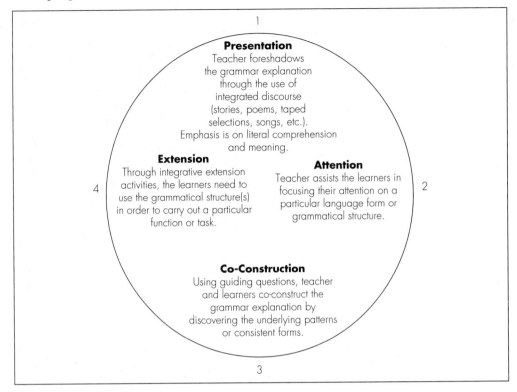

Source: Donato & Adair-Hauck, 1994.

Whether listening to a storytelling activity, co-constructing a grammar explanation, or collaborating with peers during an extension activity, learners are actively discovering and hypothesizing about the target language. This approach reflects the framework of the Communication goal area of *SFLL*, which advocates that learners be engaged in cognitively challenging activities that encourage them to use communication strategies, such as guessing intelligently, deriving meaning from context, asking for and providing clarification, making and checking hypotheses, and making inferences, predictions, and generalizations. Moreover, all of the classroom activities described encourage functional and interactional use of language by giving learners opportunities to share information, ask questions, and solve problems collaboratively.

Finally, a distinguishing theme of a story-based and guided participatory approach to grammar instruction is that learning needs to be integrated, contextualized, and meaning-centered (Pearson, 1989). In Appendix 7.1.0, we have included a sample story-based language lesson to teach the past definite in French with *avoir* (story suggested and edited by Terry [1986] and based on a well-known Aesop's fable). The lesson begins with a story, "The Lion and the Mouse" ("Le lion et la souris"), which foreshadows the functional significance of the grammar point. All of the subsequent classroom activities—for example, role-playing, paired activities to retell the story, and team activities using graphic organizers—are contextualized and relate to the theme of "The Lion and the Mouse." In this way, the unit is contextualized and integrated, which enables the instructional events to flow naturally. As noted earlier, integrated and meaning-centered activities facilitate comprehension and retention on the part of learners. Furthermore, the extension activities encourage learners to integrate meaning, form, and function while experiencing language in context.

FIGURE 7.3 Teaching Grammar: Story-Based/Guided Participation vs. Traditional Approach

STORY-BASED/GUIDED PARTICIPATION	TRADITIONAL/EXPLICIT APPROACH
1. Use of higher skills and language before moving to procedural skills	1. Sequencing of tasks from simple to complex
2. Instructional interaction between Teacher ("expert") and Learners ("novices")	2. Little teacher/learner interaction; teacher-directed explanation
3. Richly implicit explanation (guided participation)	3. Explicit explanation of grammar
4. Encourages performance before competence (approximations encouraged)	4. Learner must master each step before going to next step (competence before performance).
5. Learners participate in problem-solving process and higher-order thinking skills (opportunity for learners' actions to be made meaningful).	5. Learners are passive and rarely participate in constructing the explanation.
6. Language and especially questions must be suitably turned to a level at which performance requires assistance.	6. Few questions—mainly rhetorical
7 Lesson operationalizes functional significance of grammatical structure before mechanical procedures take place.	7. The functional significance of a grammatical point often does not emerge until end of lesson.

Source: Donato & Adair-Hauck, 1994, p. 20.

It should be mentioned that creating integrated and meaning-centered activities is probably one of the most difficult aspects of story-based language teaching, since many textbooks still stress context-reduced practice and fragmented materials. The following activities will provide you with suggestions on how to incorporate integrated and story-based language activities into your classroom. See the *Teacher's Handbook* Web site for a video of a sample PACE lesson.

thandbook.heinle.com

What is guided participation and how does it lead to language learning?

Designing a Contextualized Story-Based Language Lesson

Selecting an Appropriate Text.   One of the first steps in designing a story-based lesson is selecting an appropriate text for learners and for your instructional purposes. Text selection is not an easy task, given the many texts that exist, their contents, and their complexity. Interactive storytelling, rather than "story-reading," is an excellent way to make use of the myriad of stories that exist in the target-language cultures. Through storytelling, natural simplifications can occur, and teachers can shape the story to be within learners' ZPDs. The following are guiding principles for selecting a good text for a PACE lesson:

1. Do you like the text and find it appealing?
2. Will the learners enjoy the story you selected? Is it an age-appropriate story dealing with issues, experiences, and themes that reflect the lives of your learners? Does the story incite imagination or reflection?

3. Does the story lend itself to "stageable actions"?
4. Does the story suggest connections to academic content?
5. Does the story represent some aspect of the target culture that you will address?
6. Does the story present stereotypes or reasonable and fair depictions of the target language culture?
7. Is the language accessible or can it be made accessible through storytelling simplifications to the learners' current stage of linguistic development?
8. Is the theme of the story one that can be expanded upon and extended into various activities?
9. Does the story adequately represent a grammatical structure on which you will later focus?
10. Does the story lend itself to addressing some of the goal areas of the *SFLL*?

As a comprehension check, the teacher might play the "I Have: Who Has" game with students (Polette, 1991). This is an attentive listening comprehension game. The game can be constructed from any story and can be played as a whole-class activity or in groups. The teacher constructs a number of questions concerning the setting, character, major events, and final outcome of the story. Each student receives a card with one question and one answer to a different question written on it. The learner who has the starred card reads the first question. For "Le lion et la souris," the first question is "Where does the story take place?" The learner holding the card with the answer reads it and then provides the next question. By listening carefully, the learners should be able to respond correctly and thereby retell the story.

Creating Extension Activities. Creative extension activities are critical, for they afford the learners plenty of opportunities to develop interpersonal communication. In a constructivist approach, learners need to have opportunities to create and construct their own thoughts in the second language. Extension activities also encourage learners to collaborate and cooperate in meaningful, interpersonal contexts. Although these activities may be challenging for learners, students will be able to express their own thoughts with more confidence, and their interpretive, interpersonal, and presentational (both oral and written) communication will improve (Adair-Hauck, 1993).

Creative extension activities are critical, for they afford learners plenty of opportunities to develop interpersonal communication.

Extension activities often incorporate graphic organizers (such as story mapping, character mapping, or discussion webbing) to serve as anchoring devices to help learners organize their thoughts and ideas concerning the story. Vygotsky (1978) would argue that these graphic organizers may be viewed as mediating devices as well as psychological tools to organize the learners' higher psychological processes, such as perception, attention, and memory. *Story mapping* and *character mapping* can be accomplished in pairs or in groups. During story-mapping activities, learners work together to construct the principal elements of the story. The story map encourages learners to focus on the principal characters, problems, major events, and solutions to the problem. In character-mapping activities, learners focus on a number of elements, such as the character's physical and intrinsic traits, and the character's good and bad actions. For sample PACE lessons and accompanying story-based activities in French, German, Japanese, and Spanish, see Appendices 7.1.19–7.1.23 (on the Web site).

thandbook.heinle.com

At some point, the teacher will want to move the lesson from mere comprehension activities to activities that stimulate the learners' critical thinking skills. These activities encourage learners to analyze the events of the story and then to draw conclusions about the story. Alvermann (1991) suggests that critical thinking activities should be carried out collaboratively and cooperatively since "some of the best thinking results in a group's collaborative efforts" (p. 92).

Discussion webbing (Alvermann, 1991) is a critical thinking activity that can be developed for any story. Discussion webbing moves learners from what happened in the story to why it happened. For example, using "Le lion et la souris," the teacher can develop a discussion-webbing activity around the question "Should the mouse help the lion?" Discussion webbing encourages groups of learners to think about an even number of yes/no answers. Learners try to form a consensus on the best reason WHY the mouse should or should not help the lion. This encourages learners to look at both sides of an issue. Later, the groups can share their results from the discussion-webbing activity in a class discussion. For sample discussion-webbing activities, see Appendix 7.1.13 (on the Web site).

Discussion webbing moves learners from what happened in the story to why it happened. ■

Finally, the teacher may want to integrate an *intertextual* activity as a way to encourage learners to move beyond the mere recalling of events to higher critical thinking skills. During intertextual activities, learners working in pairs or groups analyze the components of stories by juxtapositioning two different texts or stories. Intertextual links can be made at various levels, by juxtaposing characters, content, plot development, style, and so on (Bloome & Egan-Robertson, 1993). A Venn diagram is often used as a graphic organizer (Christenbury & Kelly, 1983; Edwards, 1989; Redmond, 1994) to help learners analyze their thoughts (see Chapter 4). Note again that learners are encouraged to work in participatory groups during these intertextual activities, since a story-based approach emphasizes meaning-making and the *interpersonal* nature of language and literacy. For sample intertextual activities, see Appendix 7.1.1 (on the Web site) and the PACE lessons on the *Teacher's Handbook* Web site.

thandbook.heinle.com

Many teachers might wonder how learners with limited L2 resources will be able to participate in some of the more challenging story-based activities. Discussion-webbing and intertextual activities tap into learners' higher critical thinking skills; therefore, during these activities learners use their cognitive processes to concentrate on comparing and contrasting, analyzing, and synthesizing new information gleaned from the story with their prior background knowledge. In order to participate in these immersion-type activities, learners exploit a variety of compensation strategies to communicate their ideas in L2. As a result, their productive use of L2 varies. For example, some learners feel comfortable mixing L1 and L2, other learners seek assistance from the teacher or a more capable peer, and other learners feel more comfortable consulting a resource such as a dictionary (Adair-Hauck, 1996). The teacher creates a "social context" that assists and supports learners in activities that they would be unable to do alone or unassisted. According to Vygotsky (1986), instruction (assisted performance) leads to development (unassisted performance): "Therefore the only good kind of instruction marches ahead of development and leads it. It must be aimed not so much at the ripe, but at the ripening functions" (p. 188).

To illustrate this point, one foreign language teacher who uses a story-based approach encourages her learners to negotiate meaning in L2 using discourse strategies such as comprehension checks and clarification requests. To do so, she decorates her room with large, colored, laminated signs highlighting discourse facilitators, such as: "Répétez, s'il vous plaît"; "Comment?"; "Je n'ai pas saisi ça"; "Comment dit-on ___ en français?";

"Comment dirai-je ____?", and so on. She explained that in this way she is providing assistance to her learners and, at the same time, is decorating her classroom with the "curriculum." ACTFL's standards-based assessment research project (Glisan, Adair-Hauck, & Gadbois, 2000) has revealed that many learners are not aware of and cannot use discourse compensation strategies, which, in turn, deters their performance on standards-based interpersonal tasks. Therefore, we need to be integrating these discourse facilitators and compensation strategies into a standards-based curriculum early in the language learning sequence.

PACE and the Accuracy Issue.　Elementary/intermediate level learners certainly will make some grammatical errors while participating in extension activities. As learners work in groups, the teacher needs to serve as a participant observer for the various groups by providing assistance (e.g., requisite vocabulary, verb tense, etc.) when necessary. But in many instances learners will be capable of expressing their opinions regarding the events/ outcomes of the story, even if those opinions are at times not grammatically perfect. Frustration on the part of the teacher and/or learners will be reduced if the teacher places an emphasis on *meaning-making* or *sense-making* as learners try to create and construct meaning during these interpersonal and socially mediated activities.

As a debriefing activity, the teacher may want to focus attention on some common or frequently made errors. It is important to note that in a natural second language setting, error correction tends to be limited to errors regarding meaning, including vocabulary choice, rather than on pronunciation and grammar. Errors that do not interfere with meaning tend to be overlooked by native speakers (Lightbown & Spada, 2003). Unfortunately, in many formal second language classroom settings, accuracy has precedence over meaningful communication, and, therefore, errors are frequently corrected. Too much error correction can stifle learner motivation (Hadley, 2001), but, on the other hand, a teacher has the responsibility to bring to the learners' attention commonly made or persistent errors (Lalande, 1984).

A collaborative approach to error correction is advantageous, since it includes the learners in the learning process. For example, during the debriefing session, the teacher can remind learners that errors are a natural part of language development (Lightbown & Spada, 2003). In the natural second-language setting, errors regarding *meaning* would prompt a native speaker to correct or to ask for clarification. For purposes of instruction, the teacher may want to identify errors that interfere with meaning as *strong errors*; for example, a student might say *Il a travaillé en Europe* (He worked in Europe), when the learner really wants to say *Il a voyagé en Europe* (He traveled in Europe). This error involving vocabulary choice would negatively affect meaning and therefore would require a correction, or at least a clarification request, from a native speaker. Also, depending on the second language in question, certain grammar or pronunciation errors may interfere with meaning, such as *Elle veut aller à la boîte* instead of *Elles veulent aller à la boîte*. In this example, the pronunciation error of the verb changes the meaning from "She wants to go to the disco" to "They want to go to the disco," thus interfering with meaning.

By contrast, a *weak error* includes poor grammar usage or pronunciation but does not affect meaning; for example, *Il a resté toute la journée* instead of *Il est resté toute la journée*. This is a weak error since it does not interfere with meaning and probably would not be corrected by a native.

Learners enjoy collaborating with the teacher and investigating which of their mistakes are strong or weak errors (Adair-Hauck, 1995; Vavra, 1996). Using an overhead projector, the teacher can show learners examples of contextualized mistakes, errors in meaningful exchanges with longer stretches of discourse. Rather than identifying discrete-point errors, learners can work in peer groups to investigate whether the errors are strong or weak mistakes and why. They can then use problem-solving techniques to correct the errors.

Another strategy that encourages learners to pay attention to accuracy is to show elementary- or intermediate-level students a sample intermediate-level Oral Proficiency Interview (OPI) of a young adult in English (Adair-Hauck, 1996). Before playing the OPI, the teacher briefly discusses the *ACTFL Proficiency Guidelines—Speaking* (1999) for novice-, intermediate-, advanced-, and superior-level speakers. This explanation may have to be conducted in L1, depending on the level of the learners. Then the learners view the OPI and discuss with their teacher why the interviewee is at the intermediate or advanced level and which accuracy structures the interviewee needs to work on in order to receive a higher rating. Furthermore, the class can discuss what language functions or tasks the interviewee was able to carry out during the interview. In this way, the teacher crystallizes the importance of the functions and grammatical structures embedded in the curriculum. As Christenbury (1996) succinctly explains, "Grammar and usage cannot be taught effectively if students see no real need for it and if teachers cannot persuade them to see the need" (p. 12).

Moving to Independent Practice

At some point, the teacher will want learners to practice the target language independently. Ideally, group activities or working together on an interpersonal level will have prepared learners to function independently (Vygotsky, 1978). As an independent extension activity, the teacher may ask learners to create a different ending to the story. Learners may also use the story-mapping technique to create their own stories. A number of foreign language teachers have reported that learners enjoy creating humorous stories or "spoofs" related to the story in class. As a final presentational activity, learners can share their stories either with their class or with other members of the community (e.g., younger learners in the district, target culture student exchange groups).

Voices of the Learners

Before concluding, one should acknowledge the thoughts and opinions of learners regarding story-based language learning activities for foreign language learners. Adair-Hauck (1993) conducted a three-month, classroom-based research project using a story-based approach to teach intermediate-level French to a class of twenty learners ranging from fifteen to sixteen years of age. At the end of the project, learners' responses were overwhelmingly positive. For example, when asked, "Was it easier to learn French by listening to stories?" 90% of the learners answered "yes," one learner answered "no," and one learner answered "yes" and "no." Learners' qualitative responses to the question "What did you like most about the storytelling activities?" were particularly enlightening. One perceptive learner commented, "I liked learning with pictures and props. That way, if there was something I didn't understand, then I knew what it was." Another learner responded, "I liked the storytelling activities because they had a good effect. You seem to remember things better if you have something to do with the words you are learning." Finally, one learner made this comment regarding a positive, affective climate: "I liked the fact that it gets the class into the story and it makes it more fun. I think I learn better when I enjoy the class."

thandbook.heinle.com

TEACH AND REFLECT

NCATE____
STANDARDS
3.a., 3.b.,
4.c.

EPISODE ONE
Examining Grammar Presentations in Textbooks

Examine at least two textbooks in the target language. Decide whether the textbooks use an explicit or implicit approach to grammar explanation. To do so, answer the following questions for each textbook:

1. Does the textbook offer some form of grammatical analysis? If so, is the textbook advocating direct and explicit or indirect and implicit grammar explanations?
2. When is the teacher supposed to focus the learners' attention on form or on grammatical structures—at the beginning of the chapter, the middle, the end, or not at all?
3. Analyze the role assigned to the learner regarding grammar explanations. Is the learner a passive listener during the explanation? Is the learner supposed to be an active hypothesizer? Is the learner supposed to hypothesize alone or in collaboration with others?
4. Now identify a particular language function, such as asking and giving directions, making purchases, or describing people or things. (Turn to the chapter that focuses on your selected language function.) How does the chapter relate language function to form? Hint: Are students asked to do mechanical practice before communicative practice?
5. Examine the chapter to see if the learners are exposed to meaningful, integrated discourse. If so, how—through stories, poems, songs, videotapes, or drama? And when—at the beginning, the middle, or the end of the chapter?
6. In your opinion, how well does the chapter integrate (1) meaning—the thoughts and ideas of the message being conveyed; (2) form—the various linguistic and grammatical elements; and (3) function—the way to carry out a particular task by exploiting the appropriate grammatical structures?
7. In your estimation, is one particular dimension—meaning, form, or function—emphasized more than the others? If so, which one? Can you offer an explanation of why one dimension might be emphasized at the expense of the others?

NCATE____
STANDARDS
2.b., 3.a.,
3.b., 4.b.,
4.c.

EPISODE TWO
Designing a Story-Based Language Lesson

You are now going to design a lesson that emphasizes a story-based language approach to grammar instruction. First, you need to identify a particular linguistic function—for example, asking questions, making purchases, or describing people or things. Think of an appropriate context in which you would need to use this function. Then decide which structures should be incorporated into the lesson so that learners are capable of carrying out the function. Using the following steps as guidelines, decide how you are going to PACE the story-based language lesson.

1. Identify an integrated discourse sample that foreshadows the selected linguistic function, context, and accuracy structures. Remember that the "text" can be in the form of a story, poem, taped listening selection, advertisement, videotaped interview, and so on. Consult the section on selecting a text in this chapter before beginning this step.
2. Decide what you need to do to help learners comprehend the meaning of the text. For example, will it help learners' comprehension if you use visuals, mime, gestures, and

props? Gather all necessary supplemental materials. This phase is critical to the success of the lesson. Be creative!

3. Demonstrate for your fellow classmates how you plan to introduce the story-based text. Even if your classmates do not know your target language, see if you can convey the general meaning or significance of the text. (Make use of those props!)

4. Discuss how you will use "multiple passes" to recycle the storyline. In other words, what kind of TPR activities, role-playing scenarios, or other activities would be appropriate to deepen the learners' comprehension? Remember that at this stage the learners will become more participatory.

5. Write a short description of how you will focus the learners' attention on form. What hints or helping questions are you going to ask? In other words, how do you plan to *co-construct* the explanation?

6. Now design at least three extension activities that relate to the selected context. (Note: Use the extension activities in Appendix 7.1, including 7.1.1 through 7.1.21 (on the Web site) as guidelines.) These activities should create a need for the learners to use the identified accuracy structures. In doing so, the learners will develop a fuller understanding of the function of the grammar structures.

thandbook.heinle.com

EPISODE THREE
Developing a PACE Lesson for the Post-Secondary Level[7]

NCATE____
STANDARDS
2.b., 3.a.,
3.b., 4.b.,
4.c.

If you are preparing to teach or are already teaching at the post-secondary level, this task is designed to engage you in developing a PACE lesson for a college- or university-level class that is working toward advanced-level speaking functions. You might find it helpful to read about advanced-level discourse on pages 246–247 in Chapter 8 before you begin this task. Design your lesson according to the following steps:

1. Select a new grammatical form that you would like to target for a PACE lesson, but be sure that it is one that is useful in developing advanced-level discourse, such as the use of the imperfect subjunctive and conditional for hypothesizing in Spanish or the use of cohesive devices such as conjunctions and connector words (e.g., *therefore, on the other hand, however*). Decide how the grammatical form will be used in a specific advanced-level function.

2. Select an authentic text, preferably one that is in story form.

3. Design a lesson using the four stages of the PACE model (see the steps in Episode Two). Remember to incorporate visuals and props to clarify meaning. In your extension phase, be sure to engage your students in interpersonal communication, using the new structure in context. Your instructor may ask you to present your lesson to your classmates.

DISCUSS AND REFLECT

CASE STUDY ONE
Using a Story-Based Language Approach to Teach Reflexive Verbs

NCATE____
STANDARDS
2.b., 3.a.,
3.b., 4.b.,
4.c.

Mr. West, a French teacher, has learned about a new way to incorporate grammar teaching into a story-based language lesson. He is anxious to try out this new approach since the textbook he uses, which serves as the basis of his district's curriculum, is grammar driven. He has not yet succeeded in doing more than presenting the "grammar rule of the day" and completing the textbook exercises with his classes.

Mr. West previews the chapter and sees that he will need to teach reflexive verbs. He picks a context for this new structure: the morning routine. For his presentation, Mr. West writes the French equivalent of the following sentences on the board:

I wash my son's face.	I wash myself.
I get my son up.	I get up.
I look at my son.	I look at myself in the mirror.
I brush my son's hair.	I brush my hair.

Mr. West reads the sentences aloud, hoping that the class will perceive the non-reflexive/reflexive contrast in the two columns. The learners seem bored, uninterested, and unchallenged. He then asks a question: "What do you see here?" The learners are bewildered and silent until Mr. West calls on Mike, who says, "French sentences beginning with *Je*."

"These learners are clueless about these sentences and completely confused," Mr. West thinks to himself. He decides to abandon the questioning and delivers a lesson in English on the formation and use of French reflexive verbs. Because of this experience, he thinks that learners are unable to think about the target language and that all that can be done to ensure "learning" is to lecture learners on the rules they need to know.

Ask yourself these questions:

1. Why are the learners bored and uninterested?
2. How would you evaluate Mr. West's presentation? Does it satisfy the requirements of a presentation in the PACE model? Why or why not?
3. What would you have done when Mike responded with "French sentences beginning with *Je*"?
4. How do you think the learners feel about Mr. West's lesson?

To prepare the case:

1. Review the PACE model presented in this chapter and on the Web site.
2. Examine one or more textbooks in the language you teach to see how reflexive verbs are presented.
3. Read Celce-Murcia (1985), Aski (2003), and Larsen-Freeman (2003) for further information about the role of grammar in contextualized teaching.

To prepare for class discussion:

1. What type of text would you choose for contextualizing a lesson on reflexive verbs to describe daily routines?
2. What type of presentation would you design?
3. What type of Extension activities would enable learners to use these verbs to communicate?

CASE STUDY TWO
Contrasting Explanations of Form

NCATE
STANDARDS
3.a., 3.b.,
4.b.

Below are two scenarios of teacher and student talk about grammar points (Antón, 1999). Study them—perhaps even act them out—and use the questions at the end of each to guide your discussion about them.

Scenario I: The French class has just finished reading some examples from the textbook.

1. T: So, *alors, qu'est-ce qui se passe ici? Quelle est la différence ici? Quelle différence est-ce que vous pouvez remarquer ici dans les trois exemples?*

thandbook.heinle.com

(So, what's happening here? What's the difference? What difference can you see in these three examples?)

2. S1: *Être.*
(To be.)

3. T: *Être, oui, on utilize le verbe être, n'est-ce pas? Pour former le passé composé, n'est-ce pas? Est-ce qu'il y a d'autres différences que vous pouvez remarquer?*
(To be, yes, we use the verb *to be*, right? In order to form the past, right? Any other difference you can see?)

4. S2: New verb.

5. T: *Oui,* rentrer *c'est nouveau, n'est-ce pas?* Rentrer *for the verb* to return, *right?* Rentrer. *D'autres, il y a d'autres différences que vous pouvez remarquer? ... Si non, c'est pas un problème. On va essayer la réponse à ces questions....*

   (Yes, *rentrer* is new, right? *Rentrer* for the verb *to return,* right? Any other, is there any other difference that you can see? . . . If not, no problem. We are going to practice the answers to these questions. . . . (p. 307)

   [Students and teacher orally practice some questions that include *être* in the past. Then the following dialogue occurs.]

6. S3: There is something new in the third form, they add an *s*.

7. T: That's good, that's good, the third one [reading] *Paul et Karine* . . .

8. S3: Because, because it's plural.

9. T: That's good.

10. S3: That's new.

11. T: Good, so she is seeing here *Paul et Karine,* right? Good, so *sortis,* notice, there is an *s* at the end of *sortis,* so they are showing agreement now. The end of your . . . right? Your past participle, now they show agreement, there is an *s* because she knows it's *Paul et Karine,* so it's plural, so we add an *s,* that's good, that's what's happening (p. 307).

Scenario II: In this scenario, an Italian instructor has presented some new vocabulary and read several times a dialogue that students have repeated chorally.

1. T: In this lesson, you are doing two important things. We are learning possessive adjectives and another past tense. You've already had the *Passato Prossimo.* They are both past tenses but they have different uses in Italian. Intricate for the speaker of English, not so intricate for speakers of other Romance languages. Let's talk about possessives first. What's the word for *book?*

2. Ss: *Libro.*

3. T: What's the word for *house?*

4. Ss: *Casa.*

5. T: OK. Let's get a masculine and singular. *The book?*

6. Ss: *Il libro.*

7. T: The house?

8. Ss: *La casa.*

9. T: That's correct. Now we have masculine and feminine. Masculine article *il,* feminine *la.* We've also learnt that adjectives agree with nouns they modify [louder]. An adjective agrees with the noun it modifies. That was important until now, but it becomes more important now in this lesson, so, the . . . *beautiful book, il bel libro, the beautiful house, la bella casa.* Now we are going to adjectives, possessive adjectives. Adjectives are words which describe other words, other nouns, pronouns, or other adjectives. In *the beautiful book, beautiful* is an adjective, the red book, *red* is an adjective modifying *book.* Possessives in English and Italian are also adjectives, possessive adjectives. *My house, my* is a possessive in Italian, it's next to the noun, it is also an adjective. Now, what did we just say? Adjectives agree with the thing modified. *My book, il mio libro. This book is red, il mio*

libro è rosso. My house is white, la mia casa, adjectives agree with the noun they modify [louder]. So, when you are saying *my book* and *my house,* adjectives agree with the noun they modify. Okay, that goes for all of them: *my things, your things, his or her things, our things, your things,* and *their things.* [Writing the paradigm on the board] *Il mio libro, il tuo libro, il suo libro, la mia casa, la tua casa, la sua casa.* (My book, your book, *i miei, i miei libri, i tuoi libri, i suoi libri, le mie case, le tue case.* (pp. 308–309).

Guide your discussion of the preceding scenarios with the following questions:

1. Identify the "expert" and the "novice" players in each scenario.
2. How does the expert draw novices' attention to the forms in each scenario?
3. How do the novices show their attention to forms?
4. How does the role of the teacher in Scenario 1 differ from that of the teacher in Scenario 2?
5. Which scenario illustrates guided assistance, scaffolding, and development through the ZPD? Cite specific examples of each from the scenario.
6. Describe the role of interaction and collaboration in each of these scenarios.
7. What do you think would be the result of student learning in each of these scenarios?
8. How might students react as learners engaged in each of these scenarios?

To prepare the case:

1. Consult the following sources dealing with student interaction, and classroom talk: Antón, 1999; Brooks & Donato, 1994; Brooks, Donato, & McGlone, 1997; Donato, 2004; Hall, 1999; Johnson & Johnson, 1987; Platt & Brooks, 2002.
2. Observe a language lesson in which students are interacting with one another and identify how they bring their sociocultural identities to bear on their group tasks.

To prepare for class discussion:

1. Imagine that you are a student in the French class in scenario I. Write an entry in your journal reflecting on what you learned in the scenario above.
2. Imagine that you are a student in the Italian class in scenario II. Write a journal entry reflecting on what you learned in that scenario.
3. Using these two scenarios as examples, write a brief description comparing a traditional implicit approach to teaching grammar and an approach that is based upon guided participation and collaboration of teacher and learners.

REFERENCES

American Council on the Teaching of Foreign Languages. (1999). *ACTFL Proficiency Guidelines—Speaking.* Yonkers, NY: Author.

Adair-Hauck, B. (1993). *A descriptive analysis of a whole language/guided participatory versus explicit teaching strategies in foreign language instruction.* Unpublished doctoral dissertation. University of Pittsburgh, PA.

Adair-Hauck, B. (1995). Are all grammar errors created equal? Seminar presented at Millersville University Summer Graduate Program in French. Millersville, PA.

Adair-Hauck, B. (1996). Practical whole language strategies for secondary and university level FL learners. *Foreign Language Annals, 29,* 253–270.

Adair-Hauck, B., & Cumo-Johanssen, P. (1997). Communication goal: Meaning making through a whole language approach. In J. Phillips (Ed.), *Collaborations: Meeting new goals, new realities* (pp. 35–96). Northeast Conference Reports. Lincolnwood, IL: NTC/Contemporary Publishing Group.

Adair-Hauck, B., & Donato, R. (1994). Foreign language explanations within the zone of proximal development. *Canadian Modern Language Review, 50,* 532–557.

Adair-Hauck, B., & Donato, R. (2002). The PACE Model: A story-based approach to meaning and form for standards-based language learning. *The French Review, 76,* 265–296.

Aljaafreh, A. (1992). *The role of implicit/explicit error correction and the learner's zone of proximal development.* Unpublished doctoral dissertation. University of Delaware, Newark.

Aljaafreh, A., & Lantolf, J. (1994). Negative feedback as regulation and second-language learning in the zone of proximal development. *The Modern Language Journal, 78,* 465–483.

Alvermann, D. (1991). The discussion web: A graphic aid for learning across the curriculum. *The Reading Teacher, 45,* 92–98.

Antón, M. (1999). The discourse of a learner-centered classroom: Sociocultural perspectives on teacher-learner interactions in the second-language classroom. *The Modern Language Journal, 83,* 303–318.

Aski, J. M. (2003). Foreign language textbook activities: Keeping pace with second language acquisition research. *Foreign Language Annals, 36,* 57–65.

Ausubel, D., Novak, J., & Hanesian, H. (1968). *Educational psychology: A cognitive view.* New York: Holt, Rinehart & Winston.

Barnes, D. (1992). *From communication to curriculum.* Portsmouth, NH: Boynton/Cook.

Bialystok, E. (1982). On the relationship between knowing and using forms. *Applied Linguistics, 3,* 181–206.

Bloome, D., & Egan-Robertson, A. (1993). The social construction of intertextuality in classroom reading and writing lessons. *Reading Research Quarterly, 28,* 305–334.

Brooks, F., & Donato, R. (1994). Vygotskyan approaches to understanding foreign language learner discourse during communicative tasks. *Hispania, 77,* 262–274.

Brooks, F., Donato, R., & McGlone, J. (1997). When are they going to say it right? Understanding learner talk during pair-work activity. *Foreign Language Annals, 30,* 524–541.

Celce-Murcia, M. (1985). Making informed decisions about the role of grammar in language teaching. *Foreign Language Annals, 18,* 297–301.

Celce-Murcia, M. (1991). Grammar pedagogy in second and foreign language teaching. *TESOL Quarterly, 25,* 459–479.

Chomsky, N. (1965). *Aspects of the theory of syntax.* Cambridge, MA: MIT Press.

Christenbury, L. (1996). The great debate (again): Teaching grammar and usage. *English Journal, 85,* 11–12.

Christenbury, L., & Kelly, P. (1983). Questioning: A path to critical thinking. In *TRIP: Theory and research in practice.* Urbana, IL: National Council of Teaching of English. (Eric Document Reproduction Service No. ED226 372)

Cole, M. (1985). The zone of proximal development: Where culture and cognition create each other. In J. V. Wertsch (Ed.), *Culture, communication and cognition: Vygotskian perspective* (pp. 146–161). New York: Cambridge University Press.

Cooper, D. (1993). *Literacy: Helping children construct meaning.* Boston: Houghton Mifflin.

Cummins, J. (1984). *Language proficiency, bilingualism and academic achievement.* Bilingualism and Special Education: Issues in Assessment and Pedagogy. San Diego: College-Hill.

DeKeyser, R., & Sokalski, K. (1996). The differential role of comprehension and production practice. *Language Learning, 46,* 613–642.

Donato, R. (2004). Aspects of collaboration in pedagogical discourse. In M. McGroarty (Ed.), *Annual Review of Applied Linguistics (Vol. 24), Advances in language pedagogy* (pp. 284–302). West Nyack, NY: Cambridge University Press.

Donato, R., & Adair-Hauck, B. (1992). Discourse perspectives on formal instruction. *Language Awareness, 2,* 73–89.

Donato, R., & Adair-Hauck, B. (1994). PACE: A model to focus on form. Paper presented at the annual meeting of the American Council on the Teaching of Foreign Languages, San Antonio, TX.

Dulay, H., & Burt, M. (1973). Should we teach children syntax? *Language Learning, 23,* 245–258.

Edwards, A. (1989). Venn diagrams for many sets. *New Scientist, 121,* 51–56.

Ellis, R. (1988). *Classroom second-language development.* Englewood Cliffs, NJ: Prentice Hall.

Ellis, R. (1998). Teaching and research: Options in grammar teaching. *TESOL Quarterly, 32,* 39–60.

Forman, E., Minnick, N., & Stone, A. (1993). *Contexts for learning.* New York: Oxford University Press.

Fotos, S. (1994). Integrating grammar instruction and communicative language use through grammar consciousness-raising tasks. *TESOL Quarterly, 28,* 323–351.

Fotos, S., & Ellis, R. (1991). Communicating about grammar: A task-based approach. *TESOL Quarterly, 25,* 605–628.

Fountas, I., & Hannigan, I. (1989). Making sense of whole language: The pursuit of informed teaching. *Childhood Education, 65,* 133–137.

Freeman, Y., & Freeman, D. (1992). *Whole language for second-language learners.* Portsmouth, NH: Heineman Educational Books.

Galloway, V., & Labarca, A. (1990). From student to student: Style, process and strategy. In D. Birckbichler (Ed.), *New perspectives and new directions in foreign language education* (pp. 111–158). Lincolnwood, IL: NTC/Contemporary Publishing Group.

Glisan, E., Adair-Hauck, B., & Gadbois, N. (2000). *Designing standards-based assessment tasks: A pilot study.* Paper presented at the annual meeting of the American Council on the Teaching of Foreign Languages. Boston.

Goodman, K. (1986). *What's whole in whole language.* Portsmouth, NH: Heineman Educational Books.

Hadley, A. O. (2001). *Teaching language in context* (3rd ed.). Boston: Heinle & Heinle.

Hall, J. K. (1995). "Aw, man, where we goin'?" Classroom interaction and the development of L2 interactional competence. *Issues in Applied Linguistics, 6,* 37–62.

Hall, J. K. (1999). The communication standard. In J. Phillips (Ed.), *Foreign language standards: Linking research, theories, and practices* (pp. 15–56). Lincolnwood, IL: NTC/Contemporary Publishing Group.

Hatch, E. (1983). *Psycholinguistics: A second-language perspective*. Rowley, MA: Newbury House.

Hawkins, B. (1988). *Scaffolded classroom interaction and its relation to second-language acquisition for minority children*. Unpublished doctoral dissertation. University of California, Los Angeles.

Herron, C., & Tomasello, M. (1992). Acquiring grammatical structures by guided induction. *The French Review, 65,* 708–718.

Hinkel, E., & Fotos, S. (Eds.) (2002). *New perspectives on grammar teaching in second language classrooms*. Mahwah, NJ: Lawrence Erlbaum Associates.

Hughes, R., & McCarthy, M. (1998). From sentence to discourse: Discourse grammar and English language teaching. *TESOL Quarterly, 32,* 263–287.

John-Steiner, V. (2000). *Creative collaboration*. New York: Oxford University Press.

Johnson, D. D., & Johnson, R. T. (1987). *Learning together and alone: Cooperation, competition, and individualization*. Englewood Cliffs, NJ: Prentice Hall.

Kowal, M., & Swain, M. (1994). Using collaborative language production tasks to promote learners' language awareness. *Language Awareness, 3,* 73–93.

Kramsch, C. (1993). *Context and culture in language teaching*. Oxford: Oxford University Press.

Krashen, S. (1985). *The input hypothesis*. New York: Longman.

Lalande, J. (1984). Reducing composition errors: An experiment. *Foreign Language Annals, 17,* 109–117.

Larsen-Freeman, D. (1991). Teaching grammar. In M. Celce-Murcia (Ed.), *Teaching English as a second or foreign language* (pp. 279–295). Boston: Heinle & Heinle.

Larsen-Freeman, D. (2003). *Teaching language: From grammar to grammaring*. Boston: Thomson Heinle.

Lave, J. (1977). Cognitive consequences of traditional apprenticeship training in West Africa. *Anthropology and Education Quarterly, 8,* 177–180.

Lave, J., & Wenger, E. (1991). *Situated learning: Legitimate peripheral participation*. Cambridge, MA: Cambridge University Press.

Lee, J., & VanPatten, B. (2003). *Making communicative language teaching happen* (2nd ed.). New York: McGraw Hill.

Leontiev, A. (1981). The problem of activity in psychology. In J. V. Wertsch (Ed.), *The concept of activity in soviet psychology* (pp. 37–71). Armonk, NY: M. E. Sharpe.

Lightbown, P., & Spada, N. (1990). Focus on form and corrective feedback in communicative language teaching. *Studies in Second-language Acquisition, 12,* 429–448.

Lightbown P., & Spada, N. (2003). *How languages are learned* (2nd ed.). New York: Oxford University Press.

Liskin-Gasparro, J. (1999). Personal communication as reviewer of *Teacher's Handbook*.

Long, M. (1991). The least a second-language acquisition theory needs to explain. *TESOL Quarterly, 24,* 649–666.

Mehan, H. (1979). *Learning lessons*. Cambridge, MA: Harvard University Press.

National Standards in Foreign Language Education Project (NSFLEP). (1999). *Standards for foreign language learning in the 21st century*. Lawrence, KS: Allen Press.

Newman, D., Griffin, P., & Cole, M. (1989). *The construction zone: Working for cognitive change in school*. New York: Cambridge University Press.

Nunan, D. (1991). *Language teaching methodology*. New York: Prentice Hall.

Oller, J., Jr. (1983). Some working ideas for language teaching. In J. Oller, Jr. and P. Richard Amato (Eds.), *Methods that work* (pp. 3–19). Rowley, MA: Newbury House.

Pearson, D. (1989). Reading the whole-language movement. *Elementary School Journal, 90,* 231–241.

Platt, E., & Brooks, F. B. (2002). Task engagement: A turning point in foreign language development. *Language Learning, 52,* 365–400.

Polette, N. (1991). *Literature-based reading*. O'Fallon, MO: Book Lures.

Redmond, M. L. (1994). The whole language approach in the FLES classroom: Adapting strategies to teach reading and writing. *Foreign Language Annals, 27,* 428–444.

Rogoff, B. (1990). *Apprenticeship in learning*. Oxford: Oxford University Press.

Rutherford, W. (1988). Grammatical consciousness raising in brief historical perspective. In W. Rutherford & M. Sharwood Smith (Eds.), *Grammar and second-language teaching* (pp. 15–18). New York: Harper.

Salaberry, R. (1997). The role of input and output practice in second-language acquisition. *Canadian Modern Language Review, 53,* 422–453.

Shaffer, C. (1989). A comparison of inductive and deductive approaches to teaching foreign languages. *The Modern Language Journal, 73,* 395–403.

Spada, N., & Lightbown, P. (1993). Instruction and the development of questions in L2 classrooms. *Studies in Second-Language Acquisition, 15,* 205–224.

Swain, M. (1995). Three functions of output in second-language learning. In G. Cook & B. Seidholfer (Eds.), *Principles and practices in applied linguistics* (pp. 125–144). Oxford, UK: Oxford University Press.

Swain, M. (1998). *The output hypothesis and beyond*. Unpublished manuscript. University of Toronto, OISE.

Swain, M. & Lapkin, S. (2002). Talking it through: Two French immersion learners' response to reformulation. *International Journal of Educational Research, 37,* 285–304.

Tarone, E. (1983). On the variability of interlanguage systems. *Applied Linguistics, 4,* 142–163.

Terrell, T. (1977). A natural approach to second-language acquisition and learning. *The Modern Language Journal, 61,* 325–337.

Terry, R. M. (1986). *Let Cinderella and Luke Skywalker help you teach the passé composé and the imparfait.* Hastings-on-Hudson, NY: ACTFL Materials Center.

Tharp, R., & Gallimore, R. (1988). *Rousing minds to life: Teaching, learning and schooling in social context.* New York: Cambridge University Press.

Tharp, R., & Gallimore, R. (1991). *The instructional conversation: Teaching and learning in social activity.* Washington, DC: National Center for Research on Cultural Diversity and Second-Language Learning.

VanPatten, B. & Cadierno, T. (1993). Explicit instruction and input processing. *Studies in Second-Language Acquisition, 15,* 225–241.

Vavra, E. (1996.) On not teaching grammar. *English Journal, 85,* 32–37.

Vygotsky, L. S. (1978). *Mind in society: The development of higher psychological processes.* Cambridge, MA: Harvard University Press.

Vygotsky, L. S. (1986). *Thought and Language.* Cambridge, MA: MIT Press.

Walz, J. (1989). Context and contextualized language practice in foreign language teaching. *The Modern Language Journal, 73,* 161–168.

Wenger, E. (1998). *Communities of practice.* New York: Cambridge University Press.

Wertsch, J. (1991). *Voices of the mind.* Cambridge, MA: Harvard University Press.

West, M., & Donato, R. (1995). Stories and stances: Cross-cultural encounters with African folktales. *Foreign Language Annals, 28,* 392–406.

Wong, W., & VanPatten, B (2003). The evidence is IN: Drills are OUT. *Foreign Language Annals, 36,* 403–423.

NOTES

1. These individuals were asked to co-author this chapter since their research in the teaching of grammar supports the premise of contextualized language instruction espoused in *Teacher's Handbook.*

2. For a discussion of the implicit/explicit dichotomy, see Adair-Hauck (1993) & Adair-Hauck & Donato (1994).

3. All work in this area is to some degree rooted in the research of theorists such as Vygotsky (1978) and Leontiev (1981). For examples of supporting research, see Cole (1985); Kowal & Swain (1994); Lave (1977); Newman, Griffin, & Cole (1989); Rogoff (1990); Swain (1995); Tharp & Gallimore (1988, 1991); Wertsch (1991).

4. The term *guided participation* was first coined by Rogoff (1990).

5. As early as the first quarter of this century, Vygotsky and Piaget, both constructionists of sorts, stressed that the whole is always greater than and gives meaning to its parts.

However, unlike Piaget, Vygotsky stressed that assisted performance in learning activities led to development rather than development being a prerequisite to learning.

6. K-W-L activities are a way to organize classroom tasks around learners' background knowledge and their goals for learning. From the learners' perspective, K stands for what I know already; W stands for what I want to know; and L stands for what I have learned. For instance, if the topic is grasshoppers, the K activities might include making a list on the board of everything learners know about grasshoppers; the W activities might include the creation of a list of questions students have about grasshoppers, (e.g., "How long do grasshoppers live?"); and the L activities might include a videotaped presentation of a skit students wrote about the life of a grasshopper.

7. Thanks to Dr. Bonnie Adair-Hauck for the inspiration for this activity.

Developing Oral and Written Interpersonal Communication

In this chapter, you will learn about:

- the ACTFL oral proficiency scale and speaking from a proficiency perspective
- implications of proficiency for instruction
- nature of interpersonal communication
- instructional conversations (ICs)
- strategies for helping students interact orally
- turn-taking and gestures
- student discourse in pair/group activities
- conversational repair
- task-based instruction

- cooperative learning and interactive activities
- information-gap and jigsaw activities
- use of imagination
- developing interpersonal speaking through the study of literature and culture
- teaching interpersonal writing
- dialogue journals
- key pal and pen pal letter exchanges and synchronous electronic interaction
- providing feedback in oral interpersonal contexts

Teach and Reflect: Creating Information-Gap Activities for Various Levels of Instruction; Integrating Speaking with Oral or Printed Texts; Integrating Advanced-Level Discourse at the Post-Secondary Level

Discuss and Reflect: Interpersonal Speaking? I Already Do That!; Friday Is Culture Day

CONCEPTUAL ORIENTATION

Few would dispute the claim that, since the early 1980s, the concept of proficiency has had a major impact on how we view communication in a foreign language and how we articulate the goals of language study. For over two decades, the profession made astounding progress in enabling students in foreign language classrooms across the country to use the target language to communicate with one another, thanks to an ever-increasing body of research in second language acquisition and experience in assessing oral proficiency. The publication of *Standards for Foreign Language Learning in the 21st Century (SFLL)* (NSFLEP, 1996, 1999) expanded our notion of oral and written interpersonal communication and emphasized the pivotal role that it plays in learning content, acquiring new information, gaining cultural understanding, and engaging in activities and inquiry within communities beyond the classroom.

Historically, interpersonal communication has been treated primarily within the context of speaking, and the literature on interpersonal writing is scant. In an attempt to treat the interpersonal mode in an inclusive manner, however, this chapter will explore interpersonal communication as it occurs in both oral and written forms. The theme of oral interpersonal communication dominates more of the chapter, due to the complexity of speaking in interpersonal contexts and the vast number of issues that are pertinent to the discussion. At times throughout the chapter, oral and written interpersonal communication is treated as one topic in light of similarities of speaking and writing in this mode. At other times, speaking and writing in the interpersonal mode are explored separately in order to focus on their unique aspects and implications for instruction.

The *ACTFL Proficiency Guidelines—Speaking* (American Council on the Teaching of Foreign Languages, 1999) and the *ACTFL Proficiency Guidelines—Writing* (ACTFL, 2001) are applicable to both the interpersonal and presentational modes of communication. However, since the *ACTFL Proficiency Guidelines—Speaking* have the most applicability to and impact on the interpersonal mode, we present them in this chapter for review and implications for teaching. The *ACTFL Proficiency Guidelines—Writing* are presented in Chapter 9 as they are more applicable to presentational writing.

Interpersonal Speaking from a Proficiency Perspective

At the writing of this text, the profession was in the process of commemorating the twentieth anniversary of the publication of the first version of the *ACTFL Oral Proficiency Guidelines* (ACTFL, 1982), and a special issue of *Foreign Language Annals* (Clifford, 2003) was devoted to discussion of issues concerning these guidelines and the Oral Proficiency Interview (OPI). The concept of proficiency, as developed and explored over the past two decades, generated more discussion concerning the role of speaking in the curriculum than perhaps any other topic in the history of foreign language teaching. In her recent analysis of the survival of the *ACTFL Proficiency Guidelines* and the OPI, Liskin-Gasparro (2003) discusses three areas in which both have had a major impact on the field:

1. They served as a catalyst for major changes in foreign language teaching at all levels of instruction as the profession moved from a focus on grammar to a focus on communication. Accordingly, they sparked a new generation of pedagogical materials that contained novel features, such as multiple presentations of key grammatical structures in the same textbook, student-to-student interviews, set-ups for role plays and skits, and strategy instruction. They promoted attention to performance-based outcomes that would bridge communicative language teaching and language assessment. Furthermore, the two decades of emphasis on proficiency placed the profession in an ideal position to develop the *SFLL*.
2. The wealth of speech samples from OPIs continue to provide rich data regarding the nature of the language that is produced in face-to-face oral tests, the nature of language acquisition during study abroad experiences, and discourse analyses. These data are a valuable resource to researchers as they investigate issues pertaining to the development of language acquisition and speaking proficiency.
3. The guidelines and OPI have also had an impact on classroom testing, both formative and summative, in significant ways, see Chapter 11 (pp. 486–488).

What can we expect students at each level of language study to be able to communicate orally in the foreign language? What classroom strategies might enable students to develop speaking proficiency? In the early years of proficiency, Liskin-Gasparro's (1987) statement, "If you can't use a language, you don't know a language" reflected the basic idea underlying proficiency, one that is still applicable today (p. 26). Therefore, the current concept of proficiency describes the competencies that enable us to define in more specific terms what it means to know a language. As explained in Chapter 2, proficiency is the ability to use language to perform global tasks or language functions within a variety of contexts/content areas, with a given degree of accuracy, and by means of specific text types. In Chapter 2, you learned about how the proficiency concept evolved; you may find it helpful to review the summary chart in Appendix 2.2 in order to understand more fully the development of the proficiency concept.

Proficiency is the ability to use language to perform global tasks or language functions within a variety of contexts/content areas, with a given degree of accuracy, and by means of specific text types.

What are the characteristics of speech at each of the major borders of the ACTFL proficiency scale?

thandbook.heinle.com

The *ACTFL Guidelines* (Appendix 2.3 on Web site) provide detailed information about the performance characterized for listening, speaking, reading, and writing at each major level (or border)—novice, intermediate, advanced, superior—and sublevel—low, mid, high. These criterion-referenced descriptions are experientially based, describing how speakers typically function at various levels of ability. Figure 8.1 illustrates the four major levels of the rating scale in the form of an inverted pyramid, demonstrating that language facility increases exponentially, rather than arithmetically; in other words, it takes progressively more language ability to climb from one level to the next. Figure 8.2 illustrates the assessment criteria for speaking at each major level in terms of global tasks and functions, context/content, accuracy, and text type.

At this point, you will find it beneficial to familiarize yourself with the major levels of the rating scale.

It is important to note the following with respect to the sublevels:

- Speakers at the "low" sublevel use their linguistic energy to sustain the requirements of the level. They show less fluency and accuracy, more lapses in vocabulary, and more self-correction than the "mid" speaker. The "low" speaker functions primarily within the level with little or no demonstrated ability on the next higher level.
- Speakers at the "mid" sublevel represent a number of speech profiles, based on their mix of quantity (how much they say) and/or quality (efficiency and effectiveness with which message is communicated) at level, and/or the degree to which they control language features from the next level.
- Speakers at the "high" sublevel communicate with confidence when performing the functions of their respective level. They are capable of functioning for at least half of the time at the next higher level but are unable to sustain their performance at that next higher level without difficulty or intermittent lapses. Therefore, the dynamic of the "high" level is best understood in a top-down representation of proficiency: the "high" represents a fall from the next higher level rather than a strong ability demonstrated at the general level (Swender, 1999, pp. 18–19).

Teachers who experience training in using the OPI to elicit speech samples and rate proficiency and those who work in proficiency-oriented programs are able to develop

FIGURE 8.1 Inverted Pyramid Showing Major Levels of the ACTFL Rating Scale

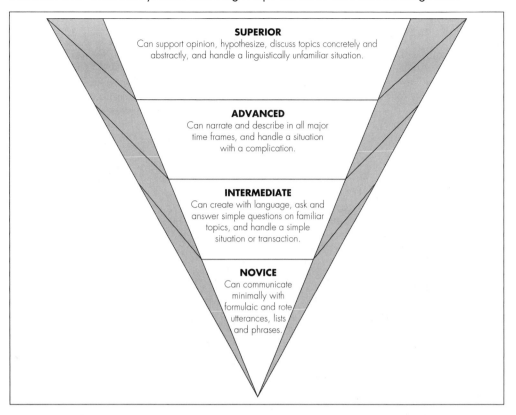

SUPERIOR
Can support opinion, hypothesize, discuss topics concretely and abstractly, and handle a linguistically unfamiliar situation.

ADVANCED
Can narrate and describe in all major time frames, and handle a situation with a complication.

INTERMEDIATE
Can create with language, ask and answer simple questions on familiar topics, and handle a simple situation or transaction.

NOVICE
Can communicate minimally with formulaic and rote utterances, lists and phrases.

Source: Swender, 1999, p. 9.

reasonably accurate intuitions and predictions about their students' levels of proficiency (Glisan & Foltz, 1998, p. 14). ACTFL conducts a rigorous training and practice program for those who wish to qualify as official oral proficiency testers and be certified to conduct interviews and accurately rate speaking skill (Swender, 1999). Chapter 11 discusses the interview procedure itself and its significance to classroom testing.

Figure 8.3 illustrates the relationship of the ACTFL rating scale to that of the original Interagency Language Roundtable (ILR) scale used by the government (see Chapter 2 for history). The ACTFL scale represents four of the six major levels of the ILR scale. The ACTFL Superior level rating corresponds to performance that comprises ILR levels 3–5 (Swender, 1999, p. 20).

Classroom Instruction and Oral Proficiency Levels

The emphasis on the development of proficiency over the past several decades continues to spark an interest in examining the extent to which classroom instruction and the language curriculum may influence students' abilities to reach specific levels of proficiency. The research in this area began with an analysis of how much time (i.e., years of classroom instruction) students spend in language study compared to what levels of oral proficiency they attain. More recently, however, the focus has turned to an examination of what happens in classrooms—that is, the degree to which learners are engaged in meaningful

FIGURE 8.2 Assessment Criteria—Speaking

PROFICIENCY LEVEL*	GLOBAL TASKS AND FUNCTIONS	CONTEXT/ CONTENT	ACCURACY	TEXT TYPE
Superior	Discuss topics extensively, support opinions, and hypothesize. Deal with a linguistically unfamiliar situation.	Most formal and informal settings/ *Wide range of general interest topics and some special fields of interest and expertise.*	No pattern of errors in basic structures. Errors virtually never interfere with communication or distract the native speaker from the message.	Extended discourse
Advanced	Narrate and describe in major time frames and deal effectively with an unanticipated complication.	Most informal and some formal settings/*Topics of personal and general interest.*	Understood without difficulty by speakers unaccustomed to dealing with non-native speakers.	Paragraphs
Intermediate	Create with language; initiate, maintain, and bring to a close simple conversations by asking and responding to simple questions.	Some informal settings and a limited number of transactional situations/ *Predictable, familiar topics related to daily activities.*	Understood, with some repetition, by speakers accustomed to dealing with non-native speakers.	Discrete sentences
Novice	Communicate minimally with formulaic and rote utterances, lists, and phrases.	Most common informal settings/ *Most common aspects of daily life.*	May be difficult to understand, even for speakers accustomed to dealing with non-native speakers.	Individual words and phrases

*A rating at any major level is arrived at by the sustained performance of the functions of the level, within the contexts and content areas for that level, with the degree of accuracy described for the level, and in the text type for the level. The performance must be sustained across ALL of the criteria for the level in order to be rated at that level.

Source: Swender, 1999, p. 31.

communication—and how instructional practice may have an effect on levels of oral proficiency that learners attain.

Several studies have examined the relationship between oral proficiency and length of language instruction, only a few of which have focused on the secondary level. Two studies (Glisan & Foltz, 1998; Huebner & Jensen, 1992) showed that, after two years of Spanish study, students' mean proficiency rating was Novice-High. After four years of study, however, results were mixed, with the mean rating for Level 4 students in the Glisan and Foltz study approaching Intermediate-Low, while in the Huebner & Jensen study the mean rating was Intermediate-Mid. An earlier study by Steinmeyer (1984)

FIGURE 8.3 Illustration Showing Relationship of ACTFL Scale to ILR Scale

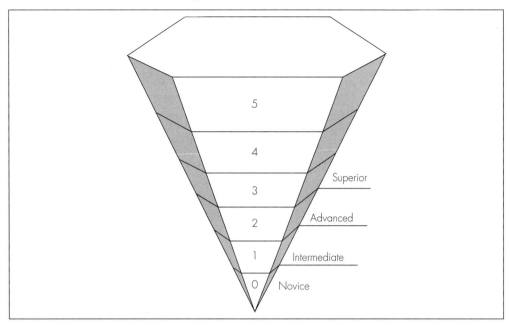

Source: Swender, 1999, p. 20.

reported similar findings in German: After two years of secondary school German instruction, the oral proficiency of students ranged from Novice-Mid to Novice-High, while after four years the mean rating was Intermediate-Mid. The Huebner and Jensen (1992) findings in French and German also revealed proficiency in the Novice range after two years of study, and proficiency in the Intermediate range after four years of study.[1] Figure 8.4 is adapted from Tschirner and Heilenman (1998) and depicts the results of the studies that have examined length of secondary school instruction in French, German, and Spanish with the oral proficiency levels attained.

Figure 8.5 illustrates the results of key studies that compared length of college-level instruction in French, German, and Russian and OPI ratings attained. Results of these studies generally revealed a mean rating of Intermediate-Mid range for students who completed two years of instruction, Intermediate High after three years, and Advanced-Low after four years. Among the studies that used certified testers to conduct and rate OPIs, Magnan's (1986) study of French students found a median of Intermediate-Mid after two years, Intermediate-High to Advanced after three years, and Advanced after four years. In German, Tschirner (1993) also reported a mean rating of Intermediate-Mid after two years of study. However, Tschirner and Heilenman (1998) found a mean rating of Intermediate-Low for students completing four semesters, or two years of study.[2] Thompson's (1996) study in Russian revealed similar results, although the ratings were somewhat lower: She found a median of Novice-High/Intermediate-Low after two years, Intermediate-Mid/High after three years, Intermediate-High/Advanced after four years, and Advanced/Advanced-High[3] after five years.

Rifkin (2004) reported on the results of testing students entering the Middlebury Russian School, who had formally studied Russian for various numbers of hours. His data revealed that "students entering at the Intermediate-Mid level alone represented a range of 180 to 600 hours of prior classroom instruction (with an average of 350 hours of classroom

FIGURE 8.4 Range of OPI Scores After 1, 2, 3, 4, and 5 Years of Secondary School Instruction in French, German, and Spanish

Study	1 Year	2 Years	3 Years	4 Years	5 Years
Steinmeyer (1984) German (N = 25)		NM – NH (NM)	NM – NH (NH)	NH – IH (IM)	IM – A (IH)
Moeller & Reschke (1993) German (N = 84)	NL – IM (NH)	NM – IM (NH)			
Huebner & Jensen (1992) German (N = 65)		NM – IM (NH)	NL – IH (IL)	NL – IH (IL)	
Huebner & Jensen (1992) French (N = 241)		NL – IH (NM)	NM – IH (IM)	IL – AH (IH)	IH – A (A)
Huebner & Jensen (1992) Spanish (N = 550)		NL – AH (NH)	NM – A (IL)	NH – AH (IM)	IH – A (A)
Glisan & Foltz (1998) Spanish (N = 59)		NL – IL (NH)		NM – IH (IL)	

Note: Median scores provided in parentheses. Median scores in Huebner & Jensen (1992) calculated from tabled data in original.

Source: Adapted from Tschirner & Heilenman, 1998, p. 149.

instruction)" (p. 583). This finding illustrates that perhaps time alone is not as critical a factor as was once thought in terms of its effect on growth in oral proficiency (more on this below).

Swender (2003) reported the proficiency levels of today's undergraduate foreign language majors using data collected from 501 official OPIs conducted through the ACTFL Testing Office between 1998 and 2002. The interviews were conducted face-to-face or telephonically and were double-rated and certified through the ACTFL Testing Office. The students assessed were foreign language majors in their junior or senior years, although the report did not correlate proficiency ratings to the specific number of semesters or years of study completed. Swender reports that the greatest concentration of ratings (55.8%) was in the Intermediate-High/Advanced-Low range (p. 523). According

FIGURE 8.5 Range of OPI Scores After 1, 2, 3, and 4 Years of College Instruction in French, German, and Russian

Study	1 Year	2 Years	3 Years	4 Years
Magnan (1986) French (N=40)	NM–IM/IH (IL/IM)	IL–A (IM)	IM/IH–A/AH (IH/A)	IM–AH (A)
Tschirner (1993) German (N=40)	NH–IM (IL)	IL–IM (IM)		
Thompson (1996) Russian (N=56)	NL/NM–IL/IM (NM)	NH/IL–IH/A (NH/IL)	IL/IM–AH/S (IM/IH)	IM–AH (IH/A)
Dugan (1988) French (N=?)	? (NH)	? (IL)		
Kaplan (1984) French (N=25)			NH–AH (IH/A)	? (A)
Freed (1987) French (N=206)		IL–A (IM)		
Tschirner (1992) German (N=549)	NH–IM (IM)	NM–A (IM)		

Note: Median scores provided in parentheses. Information not reported in original reports is represented by a question mark.

Source: Tschirner & Heilenman, 1998, p. 149

to the data analysis, slightly less than half (47%) of the foreign language majors tested were rated above the Advanced level border, and slightly more than half (53%) received ratings below Advanced. These statistics seem to lend support to the findings described above.

Perhaps the most significant finding revealed by these research studies is the range of oral proficiency levels attained by students *in* a given level of study. This is corroborated by Magnan's (1986) study, which found that proficiency levels form "bands" at each level of study and that the bands overlap from one level or year of study to the next. Magnan concludes that "this banding and overlapping reminds us that the process of language learning is a continuum on which learners progress at different rates, regardless of course boundaries" (p. 432). You may recall that in Chapter 4, you read about several studies that revealed a similar finding with elementary school students in a FLES program (Donato, Antonek, & Tucker, 1996; Montás, 2003). These studies are important because they indicate the extended sequence of instruction that most learners need to progress from one level of proficiency to the next and the variation of levels attained by learners who experience the same number of years of instruction. However, what this also indicates is that time is not the only factor in advancing in oral proficiency, given (1) the wide variance in proficiency levels among students who experience the same amount of instructional time (refer to the Magnan [1986] study) and (2) the similar range of proficiency levels among students who experience significantly different lengths of instruction (refer to the Rifkin [2003] study). Glisan & Donato (2004) suggest that what may be more critical than time itself is the type of classroom instruction that learners experience and the degree to which they are engaged in meaningful, goal-directed interaction with others in the target language. Study abroad and immersion programs that provide this type of experience and supportive assistance to students have a role to play in fostering growth in proficiency (Brecht, Davidson, & Ginsberg, 1993; DeKeyser, 2001; Wilkinson, 2002). However, in order to ensure maximum impact, these programs should be integrated with and be a natural extension of what occurs in secondary and post-secondary language classrooms.

 "Language learning is a continuum on which learners progress at different rates, regardless of course boundaries." ■

Implications of the OPI for Language Instruction

Research on the OPI and analysis of speech samples continue to shed light on features of spoken communication at each major proficiency border and what students need to be able to do in speaking in order to climb the scale. At the same time, an understanding of student performance at each level may help us to revision the types of instructional practices that may assist learners in developing their oral proficiency, keeping in mind that the *ACTFL Proficiency Guidelines* themselves do not represent a curricular outline, syllabus, sequence of instruction, or method of teaching (Hadley, 2001). Therefore, what implications for teaching does the proficiency concept offer teachers? First of all, teachers should become familiar with the *ACTFL Proficiency Guidelines* and the ILR rating scale. As discussed earlier, these rich descriptions of oral performance provide a clear picture regarding what students must be able to do at each level in terms of global tasks or functions, contexts/content areas, text types, and accuracy.

 What are some key factors in advancing oral proficiency in addition to time spent in foreign language study? ■

What types of practice do students need as they work toward proficiency at each of the major levels?:

- Novice: acquiring concrete vocabulary in context through activities such as TPR to acquire and retain it well; using contextualized vocabulary in short conversations and oral presentations; developing a personalized vocabulary
- Intermediate: engaging in spontaneous conversations on familiar topics related to self and personal environment, as well as work and/or school; asking questions; speaking in complex sentences (with dependent clauses); participating in simple survival situations (e.g., making invitations, asking for directions, ordering a meal); negotiating meaning in conversations; interpreting what a conversational partner says
- Advanced: conversing in a participatory manner; speaking in paragraphs using connector words such as adverbial expressions, subordinating conjunctions, and ordinal numbers (e.g., *therefore, although, before/after, first/second*, etc.); narrating and describing in present, past, future; participating in situations with unanticipated complications (e.g., losing one's luggage, reporting a car accident)

- Superior: discussing topics concretely and abstractly; supporting and defending an opinion through development of a logical argument, hypotheses, and extended discourse; circumlocuting in the absence of specific words/expressions (i.e., getting around unknown vocabulary by saying something in a different way); conversing in linguistically unfamiliar situations (Swender, 1999)

Appendix 8.1 (see the Web site) presents a detailed description of performance at each of the major borders according to the levels on the ILR scale, together with language learning activities that relate to each level of the scale (Herzog, 2003).

A second implication of the proficiency concept is that students must go beyond their traditional role as responder to the teacher's questions, and their interactions must take on the characteristics of typical conversations that occur between native and non-native speakers outside of the classroom (Rubio, 2003; Pica & Long, 1986). In Chapter 3, you learned that *discourse* refers to a back-and-forth communication of thought by means of a connected series of utterances shared through social interaction and collaboration. Ellis (1994) distinguishes between traditional instructional discourse and *natural discourse*, which fosters the development of oral proficiency:

> Instructional discourse arises when the teacher and the students act out institutional roles, the tasks are concerned with the transmission and reception of information and are controlled by the teacher, and there is a focus on knowledge as a product and on accuracy. Natural discourse is characterized by more fluid roles established through interaction, tasks that encourage equal participation in the negotiation of meaning, and a focus on the interactional process itself and on meaning (p. 580, cf. Rubio, 2003, p. 547).

Research on advanced-level speech indicates that learners who have had extensive exposure to natural native discourse have an advantage in terms of their fluency and use of evaluative devices in past narrations (Rubio, 2003; Lennon, 1990). *Evaluative devices* are those linguistic features that the narrator of a story uses to assign more weight or call more attention to certain parts of a story. For example, a narrator can use linguistic features to create anticipation or surprise the audience by changing the rhythm of the story, delaying the resolution, suspending the action, etc. (Rubio, 2003). To accomplish these effects, the narrator might incorporate evaluative devices such as *intensifiers* (e.g., repeat phrases in order to intensify ideas), *comparators* (e.g., make detailed comparisons), and *explicatives* (e.g., provide rich explanations or reasons).[4] In providing support for advanced-level language use, teachers should provide opportunities for students to hear ample amounts of authentic narrations that contain these types of devices and to practice using them in their own past narrations.

Fostering more natural conversations means that teachers must modify their traditional ways of interacting with students. Bragger (1985) describes typical teacher behaviors that should be modified in an attempt to provide a meaningful, interactive classroom environment. She bases her suggestions on the behaviors of trained testers in OPI situations and on their awareness of their own classroom behaviors as teachers. According to Bragger, teachers should

- attempt to take part in real conversation with students, without interrupting while they are speaking and without correcting while they are trying to communicate; teachers might keep track of repeated errors made by students, and, at the conclusion of the conversation or communicative activity, comment on the general patterns of errors made;
- listen to the content of what students are saying rather than listen exclusively to the structural accuracy;
- use an appropriate rate of speech when talking to students, use authentic language, and speak to students as naturally as they would to native speakers of the language.

Third, current research points to the third implication: the need to provide opportunities for students to hear a great deal of comprehensible and authentic language, to use the language in meaningful interaction with others, to negotiate meaning in cooperation with others, and to participate in an environment that encourages and motivates self-expression in a nonthreatening way (Gass & Selinker, 1994; Krashen, 1982; Lightbown & Spada, 2003; Long, 1983; Vygotsky, 1978). See Chapter 1.

STANDARDS HIGHLIGHT: Exploring the Interpersonal Mode Through Speaking and Writing

The Nature of Oral Interpersonal Communication

As you learned in Chapter 2, the interpersonal mode of communication refers to two-way interactive communication (NSFLEP, 1999). It is important to understand the characteristics of oral communication that make it interpersonal:

- Two or more speakers are engaged in conversation and exchange of information, either a face-to-face discussion or a phone conversation. Interpersonal communication is spontaneous; it is not scripted and read or performed as a memorized skit.
- Interpersonal communication is meaningful and has as its objective a communicative task or reason for communicating. Consequently, working in pairs to do mechanical grammar exercises out of the textbook does not constitute interpersonal communication.
- There is usually an "information gap"; that is, one speaker seeks to acquire information that the other speaker has, or at the very least, one speaker doesn't know what the other is going to say or how he or she will respond. Therefore, pair activities in which Student A and Student B know in advance how the other will respond do not reflect true interpersonal communication.
- Since interpersonal communication is spontaneous, conversational partners must listen to and interpret what the other speaker says.
- Conversational partners often find it necessary to negotiate meaning with one another in order to interpret meaning. Thus, the interpretive mode of communication is implied in interpersonal communication. Negotiating meaning involves asking for repetition, clarification, or confirmation, or indicating a lack of understanding. Natural conversations have pauses as speakers think of what they want to say and repetitions as they repeat, restate, or even correct their utterances.
- Conversational partners often find it necessary to use gestures to make their message clear and to circumlocute, or express a thought in an alternative way when specific words or expressions are unknown.

Interpersonal communication can also be written whenever a printed message, in the form of a letter, note, or e-mail exchange, is intended to prompt a response on the part of the recipient and/or engage two individuals in communication with each other. In this case, speaking and writing share similarities in the interpersonal mode. In written interpersonal communication, the reader must interpret the printed message and create a response.

Interpersonal communication stands in sharp contrast to the *presentational* mode of communication, which refers to one-way communication—one person produces language in oral or written form for an audience of listeners/viewers/readers. Although you will explore presentational communication fully in Chapter 9, it bears mentioning here that teachers have a tendency to include many opportunities for presentational communication and label them as interpersonal communication. It is important to distinguish between these two modes of communication in planning for instruction and to include a balance of both in language classrooms.

Strategies for Teaching Interpersonal Speaking

Below are sample techniques for interpersonal speaking that are based on the research findings presented in Chapter 1, as well as on the implications of proficiency introduced in this chapter. These activities may be adapted for use with elementary school, middle school, high school, and post-secondary classes. Note that, while these activities relate primarily to the interpersonal mode, speaking activities often address both the interpersonal and presentational modes of communication: Students interact with one another to perform a task (interpersonal mode) and then present this information to an audience (presentational mode). Furthermore, they are often based on or can lead to an interpretive task.

The reader is encouraged to review the information from Chapter 1 dealing with negotiation of meaning, which is a vital concept in developing interpersonal speaking. In the spirit of sociocultural theory, *Teacher's Handbook* advocates an approach to teaching interpersonal communication that actively engages learners in constructing and negotiating meaning.

Teacher Interaction with Students

The extent to which oral interpersonal communication is fostered in the classroom depends to a great extent on the types of interactions that the teacher has with learners. In Chapter 3, you learned about the importance of the following features of teacher talk and classroom interaction:

- The teacher provides maximum use of the target language that is both comprehensible and contributes to a larger topic or goal-directed agenda.
- The teacher uses a maximum amount of Initiation-Response-Feedback (IRF) activities to stimulate meaningful conversations and push learners to perform at higher levels.
- The teacher integrates authentic oral and printed texts that reflect natural language use and bring context and interest to the classroom.
- The teacher incorporates subject-matter content into the language learning experience in order to provide interesting context to explore and discuss.

Hall (1999) suggests the use of "instructional conversations" (ICs) as a way to facilitate a conversation with students on a topic or theme that is interesting to them and intellectually challenging, while providing them with assisted performance. Instructional conversations are defined as "discussion-based lessons geared toward creating opportunities for students' conceptual and linguistic development. They focus on an idea or a concept that has educational value and that has meaning and relevance for students" (Goldenberg, 1991, p. 1). According to Tharp and Gallimore (1988), the concept underlying ICs is also referred to as *responsive teaching*, the way that mothers teach their children language and letters, chat that accompanies action, and the natural conversational

FIGURE 8.6 Features of an Instructional Conversation

Instructional Features	Conversational Features
■ Thematic focus ■ Activation of background knowledge and schema ■ Direct teaching when necessary ■ Promotion of more complex language and expression ■ Promotion of bases for statements or positions	■ Few "known-answer" questions ■ Responsiveness to student contributions ■ Connected discourse ■ Challenging, but nonthreatening atmosphere ■ General participation, including self-selected turns

Source: Summarized from Tharp & Gallimore (1988) & Goldenberg (1991).

method of language instruction. ICs can also "wear the mask of a third-grade reading lesson or a graduate seminar" (p. 111). Figure 8.6 illustrates the features of an instructional conversation.

 Teachers use "instructional conversations" (ICs) as a way to facilitate a conversation with students on a topic or theme that is interesting to them and intellectually challenging, while providing them with assisted performance. ■

Tharp & Gallimore (1988) and their colleagues (Goldenberg, 1991; Rueda, Goldenberg, & Gallimore, 1992; Patthey-Chavez, Clare, & Gallimore, 1995) proposed ICs in order to foster assisted performance in ways reflected in Vygotsky's (1978) Zone of Proximal Development (ZPD) concept. In ICs, the teacher "acts as a discussion leader and facilitator, allowing students to initiate turns while making sure that all student voices are included in the discussion and, when necessary, drawing out and helping students to draw out their ideas" (Hall, 1999, p. 30). The teacher also assists students in connecting their background experiences to the discussion by making certain that responses are interconnected and build upon one another through extending previous turns. As described in Hall, in an IC, teachers assist performance by means of the following actions:

- Modeling: The teacher models his/her thinking on a particular task, giving students an example of how he or she connects given information to new information, how he or she constructs an argument to defend an opinion, or how he or she thinks through a problem. An example of an instructional strategy in which modeling plays a key role is "reciprocal teaching" (Palinscar, Brown, & Campione, 1993). The teacher models the use of effective reading comprehension strategies by "asking a question about a text," "summarizing," "clarifying a point," and predicting what is to happen (Hall, 1999, pp. 30–31). The teacher then guides students in performing these tasks, decreasing the amount of assistance as students are able to perform on their own.
- Feeding back: The teacher provides a clear model of expected performance, allows students the opportunity to compare their own performances with the model and self-correct, and tells students how they can improve their performance. Feedback should be framed in a positive way to foster students' positive perceptions of themselves and their performance.
- Contingency managing: The teacher rewards positive performance by students and closely connects rewards to feedback.

- Directing: The teacher focuses learners' attention on what is to be learned in a task or activity and directly teaches a skill or concept within a meaningful context.
- Questioning: The teacher assists learners' performance by asking questions that activate background knowledge, help students work through a task, or extend student discussion. Questioning can also be used to assess how much progress students have made in performing without assistance.
- Explaining: The teacher explicitly shows how information applies in new contexts and provides learners with frameworks for organizing new information.
- Task structuring: The teacher arranges tasks so that learners may perform them, moving from tasks they can do only with assistance to tasks they can do independently (pp. 30–32).

You may find it helpful to match the characteristics of ICs to the steps of the PACE model described in Chapter 7.

ICs help to foster interpersonal communication in ways that focus on the IRF pattern of teacher-to-learner interaction. Chapter 3 presented ideas on how to incorporate more interpersonal communication and IRF into classroom instruction. You may find it helpful to review this discussion. ICs can be used effectively as the teacher:

- engages students in "warm-up" discussions of a personalized topic of interest to students or a timely topic concerning the school community (e.g., a championship game, the prom);
- leads a discussion of an authentic oral, printed, or video text;
- sparks a discussion or the creation of a story based on a visual or cultural artifact
- elicits opinions about a topic of high interest to learners, e.g., mandatory drug testing for athletes;
- acquires new information with learners on a content-based or cultural theme;
- explores with learners the relationship among specific products, practices, and perspectives in C2 and makes comparisons with C1; and
- guides learners through the process of designing a presentation or creating a product for an audience.

While these specific types of strategies and activities are effective in promoting interpersonal communication, it is essential that the language classroom environment be one in which sharing opinions, offering a variety of possible responses, asking questions, and negotiating meaning are welcomed. Furthermore, the teacher should be sure to set up conversations so that:

1. students have opportunities to take multiple turns in a given conversational exchange;
2. students practice taking the floor in conversations;
3. students have sufficient time to respond as participants in conversations;
4. a variety of responses are accepted;
5. short answers are permitted where they would naturally occur (e.g., answers to yes-no questions);
6. students are encouraged and taught how to respond to statements made by their classmates in order to develop conversations that are connected and coherent; and
7. the teacher assumes the role of facilitator and guide, providing assistance and scaffolding as needed.

It is important to note that, in managing conversations, the teacher may find ideal opportunities to provide linguistic feedback, conversational repair, and explicit instruction on grammatical form when students require assistance in expressing themselves in the target language. It is the occurrence of these types of "teachable moments" when students benefit most from a focus on form that is directly applicable to the contextualized linguistic task at hand. You will learn more about providing feedback on form later in the chapter.

Teaching Strategies for Group Interaction

Turn-Taking

In conducting cooperative learning tasks, the teacher must often teach the interaction skills that are lacking or in need of improvement, such as taking turns at talking. Kramsch (1987) suggests that teachers use the following strategies for encouraging students to take control of turn-taking as they would in natural discourse:

- Tolerate silences; refrain from filling the gaps between turns. This will put pressure on students to initiate turns.
- Direct your gaze to any potential addressee of a student's utterance; do not assume that you are the next speaker and the student's exclusive addressee.
- Teach the students floor-taking gambits; do not grant the floor.
- Encourage students to sustain their speech beyond one or two sentences and to take longer turns; do not use a student's short utterance as a springboard for your own lengthy turn.
- Extend your exchanges with individual students to include clarification of the speaker's intentions and your understanding of them; do not cut off an exchange too soon to pass on the floor to another student (p. 22).

 The teacher must often teach the interaction skills that are lacking or in need of improvement. ■

Routines and Gambits

In order to interact spontaneously with others, students need to incorporate the use of what Yorio (1980) calls *routines*: words, phrases, or sentences that are predictable in a typical communicative situation by members of a speech community. The following are four types of routine formulae:

1. situation formulae, which are very culturally specific; for example, "You had to be there" when relating a humorous story;
2. stylistic formulae, which are normally used in written interpersonal communication; for example, "To whom it may concern";
3. ceremonial formulae for ritualistic interaction; for example, "Dearly beloved"; and
4. gambits, as described below (Yorio, 1980; cf. Taylor, 2002, p. 172).

The fourth category of routine formulae, *gambits,* are "devices that help the speaker maintain the smooth flow of conversation" (Taylor, 2002, p. 172). They function as (1) discourse organizers that introduce or frame what the speaker is about to say; (2) strategies to maintain the flow of conversations by signaling such actions as the desire to take a turn, offer an opinion, or express interest in the topic; and (3) pause fillers that buy time while the speaker thinks of a word or tries to hold a turn (Keller, 1981; cf. Taylor, 2002, p. 172).

Sample gambits are expressions used to interrupt to get the floor, such as *excuse me* and *wait a minute;* expressions used to buy time, such as *well, let's see,* and *as I was saying;* and expressions used to redirect the topic such as *by the way* and *on another topic.*

Taylor (2002) conducted a study of university-level students in a beginning Spanish conversation course to examine the effect of direct instruction on their use of gambits during discussions and role play situations. Students were divided into two groups (a discussion group and a role-enactment group) to assess their use of gambits before and after gambit training. In the instructional phase of the study, students from both groups received gambit instruction, during which they were given a list of gambits arranged in functional categories (adapted and translated from Kramsch, 1981). See Appendix 8.2 on the Web site for a list of the Spanish gambits used in this study. Students then viewed a video of an authentic Spanish language talk show, identified gambits they heard, and discussed the function of each, as an entire class. Next, students worked in pairs to react to statements made by the instructor using the appropriate gambits. Students then worked in pairs and gave their opinions on the topics they had previously been given, reacting to what their partners said by using appropriate gambits. As the last task on that day, students chose a topic that they would like to discuss, chose sides, and thought of arguments in support of their position.

On the second day of the study, students discussed the chosen topics with partners, agreeing or disagreeing by using appropriate gambits. Students then watched video clips of customer-clerk situations, after which they identified and discussed gambit use and role-played a situation that focused on a complaint and request for solution. After all of this training, the discussion group engaged in a discussion with a native Spanish speaker about cultural differences between the United States and Latin America. The native speaker played the role of a Latin American exchange student, having difficulty with cultural differences. The role-enactment group performed role plays with a native Spanish speaker in a customer-clerk situation in which students played the role of the customer (Taylor, 2002).

Results of Taylor's (2002) study indicated that gambit training resulted in gambit use by both groups in the follow-up tasks. These results confirmed earlier findings that illustrated the effect of direct gambit instruction on subsequent gambit use (Dörnyei, 1995; Wildner-Bassett, 1984). Gambit categories that showed the largest increase in use within the discussion group were those related to opinions, counterarguments, refining points, and buying time. Gambit categories with the largest increases within the role-enactment group were those related to politeness formulae, such as thanking, requesting, greeting, leave taking, and expressing assent.

Additionally, however, Taylor's (2002) study also revealed that the overall quality and variety of gambits increased significantly for the discussion group but not for the role-enactment group. This finding indicates that, while explicit instruction combined with practice can increase gambit use significantly, this may not occur in all contexts. Taylor hypothesizes that the production of gambits in the role-enactment situation may have been inhibited due to the stressful situation of the role play and the confrontational attitude of the native speaker partner, although additional research is needed to confirm this claim. The research on gambit use points to two implications for foreign language teachers:

1. Students incorporate gambits into their speech if they receive direct training and practice in gambit use.
2. Natural conversations (as exemplified earlier in ICs, for example) are an effective context for eliciting gambit use.

 Gambits are "devices that help the speaker maintain the smooth flow of conversation."

Gestures

Not all interpersonal communication is verbal. According to McCafferty (2002), gestures have a mediational function, not only in play and drama, but also in verbal interaction, and thus are a symbolic tool, i.e., they assist verbal performance. In his study of ESL students and an ESL instructor, McCafferty found that while students and the instructor used gestures to refer to lexical items (*iconic gestures*), not all gestures carried lexical meaning and some reflected cultural meaning. Students and teacher used gestures to illustrate concepts (*metaphoric gestures*), such as illustrating someone "thinking outside the box" by drawing a square in the air with one's fingers. They also used gestures to indicate images (*illustrators*), such as illustrating water being splashed by cupping both palms and "splashing" oneself by pumping one's arms up from a horizontal position on the lap inward toward oneself (p. 196). Finally, gestures were used to point out objects in the immediate environment and virtual or far-off contexts and thus indicate space and time (*deictic gestures*). Of interest is the fact that the students and the teacher imitated the gestures used by one another, scaffolded each other in their efforts to co-construct meaning, and created a shared history of signs, exemplifying the transformation of learner and instructor within the ZPD. McCafferty proposes that gestures play an important role in transforming teaching and learning in four ways, described by Wells (1999), in relation to the ZPD:

1. transformation of the learner's identity in relation to his or her capacity to participate in future actions;
2. the invention of new tools and practices or the modification of existing ones that lead to a transformation of the culture's repertoire for problem solving;
3. transformation of the activity setting brought about by the problem-solving action, which opens up further possibilities for action; and
4. transformation in the social organization of the way in which members relate to each other (McCafferty, 2002, pp. 200–201).

The implication of the research on the use of gestures for foreign language teachers is that L2 students exposed to natural contexts will benefit from becoming aware of the use of gestures as part of the process of making meaning. Thus the use of gestures should be encouraged. McCafferty (2002) suggests that, in order to do this, students first need the opportunity to examine the use of gestures in L2 by watching videotaped interactions and by explicitly discussing gestures when performing role plays and classroom scenarios. Awareness of gestures might help students both to comprehend the language and to express themselves more effectively.

 In what specific ways can gestures help language learners mediate between themselves and the world? See also Chapter 1. ■

Student Discourse in Pair/Group Activities

Several studies have revealed important findings regarding strategies and discourse that learners use when faced with interactive tasks and activities with their peers. A series of studies illuminates the ways students mediate their work on tasks in pairs and small groups over time (Donato & Brooks, 1994; Brooks, Donato, & McGlone, 1997; Liskin-Gasparro, 1996; Platt & Brooks, 1994). The following excerpt from a jigsaw activity illustrates the strategies students use when they participate in a problem-solving task of this kind for the first time:

249 J: uh well, now I'm even more confused

250 K: ha! ha!

251 J: see, I have um

okay let me try to do this in Spanish.

I'll at least put up the effort

253 En mi papel yo tengo muchos espacios algunos tienen películas otros están blancos [On my paper, I have many spaces, some have movies, others are blank.]

254 K: uh huh

255 J: y uh yo pienso que tú tienes un blancos donde yo tengo películas [And, uh, I think you have blanks where I have movies.]

256 K: uh huh

257 J: ¿entiendes? [Do you understand?]

258 K: uh sí

259 J: Y but that's not happening

. . .

264 J: I think um you're supposed to draw in what I have and I'm supposed to draw um um

(Brooks, Donato, & McGlone, 1997, pp. 524–525)

Through classroom speech samples such as the excerpt shown here, researchers identified four mediational strategies students use during pair-work activity: talk about talk, talk about task, the use of English, and whispering to self.

 Typical student language in pairs includes: talk about talk, talk about task, the use of English, and whispering to self. ■

When participants talk about their own talk, sometimes called *metatalk*, they use statements such as "¿*Cómo se dice* 'through'?" ("How do you say 'through'?"), or "That's a good word for that." (Brooks, Donato, & McGlone, 1997, p. 528). This talk about talk is also accompanied by *talk about task* when students say things like "I don't know if I'm right," or "¿*Tú quieres mi hablar mi hablo en español y tú oye oír?*" ("You want me to speak and you listen?") (p. 529).

As students think, act, and speak through a task, they mediate their work with the language that is available to them, most likely the native language. In the second language classroom this use of English is often distressing to teachers. Szostek (1994) points out that in her study insufficient time had been spent on preparing students for managing group dynamics, and they therefore resorted to English for exchanges. Brooks, Donato, & McGlone (1997) explain that use of English is normal and does not necessarily mean that target language use will not be achieved. They explain that students are learning to use the target language for such tasks, but they often start with the native language and move toward use of the target language as they resolve the problem of the task. Across time, English use diminishes dramatically as learners are provided with opportunities to complete similar tasks.

A final strategy identified by these researchers is *whispering to the self*. This mediation behavior appears early in L1 language acquisition, mostly when communication is difficult and thinking is verbal, and it is suppressed in adults except when under communicative duress. The subjects in these studies (Donato & Brooks, 1994; Brooks, Donato, & McGlone, 1997; Platt & Brooks, 1994) used this mediational tool in the native and the target language, and its use diminished over time as the tasks and how to resolve them became more familiar.

In sum, these studies indicate that if the purpose and function of learner language during problem-solving tasks is not clearly understood, learners might not be given the strategic opportunities that can lead to their successful performance of tasks using the target language; that is, they might have difficulty ever "saying it right" during such tasks (Brooks, Donato, & McGlone, 1997).

> **?** How does whispering to the self relate to the concepts of private speech and mental rehearsal discussed in Chapter 1?

Examining student discourse within the context of an oral proficiency interview, Liskin-Gasparro (1996) also found that students use a number of communicative strategies to manage discourse: asking for assistance, switching languages, transliteration (e.g., guessing that Spanish *ropa* must mean "rope" when it really means "clothing"), reconstructing the message, circumlocution or description, approximation (use of a near synonym), coining words, and abandoning the message (pp. 320–322). Advanced learners use more strategies that are based on the L2, abandoning those based on L1.

Another feature of student discourse characteristic of communication in pairs or groups is the use of *repair,* which is "a mechanism used to deal with trouble in speaking, hearing, or understanding" (Schegloff, Jefferson, & Sacks, 1977; cf. Liebscher & Dailey-O'Cain, 2003, p. 376). Repair has been discussed widely in SLA research (van Lier, 1988). It refers to more than just the replacement of an error with a correct utterance, since the presence of an identified error is not required for a repair process to be initiated. Repair has been found to consist of three components: the *trouble source* or *repairable*; the *repair initiation*, or the indication that there is trouble to be repaired; and the *outcome*, which is either the success or the failure of the repair attempt (Liebscher & Dailey-O'Cain, 2003). A repair operation might begin as words are being retrieved or turn-taking is being negotiated. It is "both a forward and a backward mechanism, acting on both vocalized and nonvocalized language" (Buckwalter, 2001, p. 381).

Repair can also be described in terms of who initiates the repair and who performs the repair. Buckwalter (2001) examined the use of repair by university-level Spanish students as they participated in communicative pair activities in their Spanish classes. She specifically examined the frequency of use of four repair strategies: self-initiated, self-repair; self-initiated, other-repair; other-initiated, self-repair; and other-initiated, other-repair. Findings indicated that learners overwhelmingly used self-initiated, self-repair, particularly as they attempted to deal with lexical and morphological difficulties. Self-initiated, other-repair, although used infrequently, was the second most-used strategy that occurred when learners recognized that their knowledge base was insufficient to carry out a repair action and sought help. Other-initiated repair strategies were rare in this study and were found primarily to signal non-understanding on the part of the listener.

The preference for self-repair mirrors L1 interaction and may be the result of attempts to maintain one's "public self-image" by not calling attention to or correcting problems in a partner's L2 production (Brown & Levinson, 1987). Another finding in this study is that the majority of repair work was "local"; that is, it focused on moving an utterance closer to the target language form as opposed to focusing on global features, such as message clarity. This finding supports earlier research indicating that, in the talk of language learners, repairs are mostly local, and as proficiency improves, repairs become increasingly more global and discourse related (Shonerd, 1994).

These studies on repair have the following important implications for language teachers:

1. Repair is possible only when students have opportunities for meaningful interaction in the classroom.
2. Communicative interaction in the classroom enables students to practice self-regulation (i.e., ability to function without assistance from others).
3. Long turns at talk provide many opportunities for use of self-initiated, self-repair strategies (Buckwalter, 2001).

Long turns at talk provide many opportunities for use of self-initiated, self repair strategies. ▪

Student Interaction

Task-Based Instruction

In Chapter 2, you explored the role of context in approaches to language teaching and in various types of activities and exercises used by instructors and characteristic of textbook programs. As you learned, mechanical types of drills and exercises have limited value in contributing to language acquisition and in developing communicative abilities (Wong & VanPatten, 2003; Brooks, 1990; Kinginger, 1990). Indeed, activities classified as "communicative" often consist of questions asked by the teacher and answers supplied by students (Lee, 1995). Studies dealing with the nature of classroom tasks confirm that when pair/group work entails discussion and negotiation of meaning, students perform a greater number of content clarifications, confirmation checks, and comprehension checks (Doughty & Pica, 1986; Porter, 1986) and use a greater number of conversational gambits (Taylor, 2002). According to Crookes and Gass (1993a, 1993b), the language students use in these types of interaction plays a vital role in language acquisition.

A strategy for restructuring the traditional question-answer type of class discussion is *task-based instruction*, which enables students to interact with others by using the target language as a means to an end (Lee, 1995). Through task-based instruction, learners use the language with a purpose so that language is not merely the object of manipulation or drill (Lee 1995; Richards, Platt, & Weber, 1985). A task-based approach to language teaching is based on two concepts that we have explored in previous chapters of *Teacher's Handbook* in great detail: communication and negotiation of meaning (Wilson-Duffy, 2003a). It emphasizes that communication (1) is the expression, interpretation, and negotiation of meaning; (2) requires two or more autonomous participants; and (3) should focus on the learners' use of the language, not the instructor's (Lee, 1995, p. 440).

Task-based instruction enables students to interact with others by using the target language as a means to an end. ▪

Wilson-Duffy (2003a) suggests that *pedagogical tasks* might be used as a technique for preparation and scaffolding prior to engaging students in the culminating *real-world task*. For example, in preparation for the real-world task of reporting items stolen in a hotel burglary, students might complete the pedagogical task of comparing two pictures of hotel rooms and describing differences between where objects are located (Wilson-Duffy, 2003a, p. 3). Wilson-Duffy (2003b) describes an online task-based activity in which students explore which movie they might like to see and convince their classmates to attend the movie they like. The activity consists of the following interrelated tasks, described below in terms of directions to the student:

1. Ask and answer questions regarding your schedule in order to decide on a day and time to see a movie, using audio or video chats to communicate.
2. Using a movie theater Web site in the target language, find a movie that you would like to see that fits into your schedule.
3. Convince your classmates to attend the movie you have chosen, using a written or oral chatroom (pp. 3, 6).

thandbook.heinle.com

In order to complete these tasks, students use computer-mediated communication, i.e., chatrooms and the Internet. See the *Teacher's Handbook* Web site for the link to the complete plan for this lesson.

One type of task-based activity is *task-based discussion*, which promotes self-expression, interpretation, and negotiation of meaning among learners (Lee, 1995). Figure 8.7 shows a sample task-based discussion activity that uses a discussion question as the springboard for communication. According to Lee, rather than starting the task with the discussion

FIGURE 8.7 Sample Task-Based Discussion Activity

ACTIVITY H. HOW HAVE TRADITIONAL ROLES CHANGED?

Step 1. Work in pairs or in groups of three. The instructor will assign one of the following to each pair or group:

    a. Prepare a list of actions, attitudes, and qualities that characterize the traditional role of the man in the family. Careful. What past tense will you need to do this?

    b. Prepare a list of the actions, attitudes, and qualities that characterize the contemporary role of the man in the family.

Step 2. Write your list on the board and compare it to those of your classmates. As you do, fill in the following chart with the ideas each group presents.

THE MAN'S ROLE	
In the past	**Today**

Step 3. Repeat Steps 1 and 2 but this time, focus on the role of a woman in traditional and contemporary families. That is, first make lists and then fill in the following chart.

THE WOMAN'S ROLE	
In the past	**Today**

Step 4. As a class, contrast the traditional roles men and women play in the family with their more contemporary roles. Have their roles changed? How? Why?

Step 5. Optional. Prepare a written summary of the class discussion using the information in the two tables.

Source: Lee, 1995, p. 444.

question, the teacher should lead up to it with a series of subtopics and scaffolding. He suggests the following steps for recasting questions into a task-based discussion format, as identified in Figure 8.7:

1. Identify a desired outcome: What information are students supposed to extract from the interaction? (Step 4 in Figure 8.7)
2. Break down the topic into subtopics: What are the relevant subcomponents of the topic? (Four subtopics: The man's role in the past and today, the woman's role in the past and today)
3. Create and sequence concrete tasks for learners to do, e.g., lists, charts, tables: What tasks can the learners carry out to explore the subcomponents? (Steps 1, 2, and 3)
4. Build in linguistic support, either lexical or grammatical or both: What linguistic support do the learners need? (Step 1: past tense; vocabulary for actions, attitudes, qualities) (p. 441).

It is important to note that the complexity of task-based discussions depends on the linguistic level of students. That is, the discussions that novices have are typically short and based on information collected in a task, whereas students at higher levels are able to exchange opinions and have more of an interactive discussion.

 What makes the discussion in Figure 8.7 "task-based"?

Cooperative Learning and Interactive Activities

In *cooperative learning*, students work in pairs or in small groups of four or five to help one another complete a given task, attain a goal, or learn subject matter. Each person in the group has a responsibility, and students depend on one another as they work to complete their task. Students learn to work together and respect their classmates. They are also encouraged to develop their own abilities and identities. The teacher may give points or some form of credit to the entire group for achieving the objectives and may also give individual students credit for their contributions.

Extensive research on cooperative learning by Johnson and Johnson (1987) suggests that this technique often produces higher achievement, increases retention, and develops interpersonal skills. Cooperative learning also has been shown to promote higher self-esteem and acceptance of differences, as well as to foster responsibility. Furthermore, it encourages creativity by giving students opportunities to observe the problem-solving approaches and cognitive processing strategies of others (Kohn, 1987). According to Johnson, Johnson, and Holubec (1988), cooperative learning provides the vehicle for teaching students to process skills that are needed to work effectively within a group. By using process observers and peer feedback on group processing skills, students begin to analyze and improve the group interaction. Of particular benefit to foreign language study, cooperative learning activities teach students how to ask questions, negotiate meaning, and interact in groups. Figure 8.8 is an example of a questionnaire designed to encourage students to think about the group process and their own participation (Scarcella & Oxford, 1992).

As discussed in earlier chapters, foreign language teachers should remember the importance of designing cooperative learning activities that are meaningful, contextualized, and engage students in offering diverse responses and opinions. You may find it helpful to consult Chapter 4 to review the considerations that elementary school teachers should make in planning for cooperative learning activities, as these considerations are also pertinent to the secondary and post-secondary levels of instruction.

FIGURE 8.8 Questionnaire: Conversational Skills

IN TODAY'S ACTIVITY	OFTEN	SOMETIMES	NEVER
1. I checked to make sure that everyone understood what I said.			
2. I gave explanations whenever I could.			
3. I asked specific questions about what I didn't understand.			
4. I paraphrased what others said to make sure that I understood.			
5. I encouraged others to speak by making such remarks as "I'd like to know what _____ thinks about that" and "I haven't heard from _____ yet" and "What do you think, _____?"			

Source: Scarcella & Oxford, 1992, p. 158.

In cooperative learning tasks, each person in the group has a responsibility, and students depend on one another as they work to complete their task. ■

Examples of Cooperative Learning Activities. Cooperative learning activities can range from the simple think-pair-share task described below (Kagan, 1989) to a more complex jigsaw activity. The following are only a few of the many types of cooperative learning activities:[5]

- *Peer tutoring* (Fotos & Ellis, 1991; Kagan, 1989): Teammates teach each other simple concepts in content areas such as math, science, or language arts. Richard-Amato (1988) suggests using this for a content-area class that includes ESL students.
- *Think-pair-share* (Kagan, 1989): Students use the following response cycle in answering questions: (1) they listen while the teacher poses a question; (2) they are given time to think of a response; (3) they are told to pair with a classmate and discuss their responses; and (4) they share their responses with the whole group.
- *Jigsaw* (Kagan, 1989): Each member of the group assumes responsibility for a given portion of the lesson. These members work with the members from the other groups who have the same assignment, thus forming "expert groups." Eventually, each member must learn the entire lesson by listening to and sharing information with others in the group. Figures 8.9A, B, and C depict a sample jigsaw activity, together with suggestions for how to form teams and expert groups. Notice that the expert groups refer to the first series of groups in which students become "experts" by learning their assigned content; each member of the group must have the knowledge for their group—learning is not divided into separate assignments. The

FIGURE 8.9A A Sample Jigsaw Activity

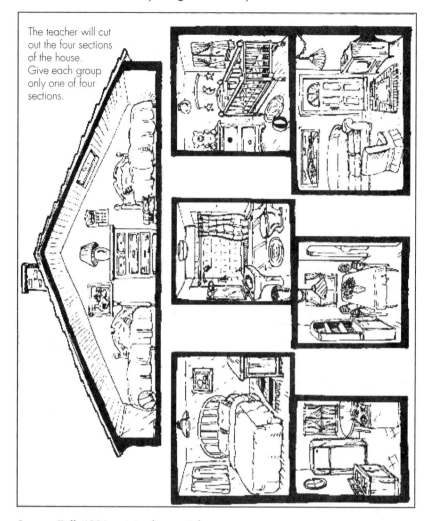

The teacher will cut out the four sections of the house. Give each group only one of four sections.

Source: Fall, 1991, original material.

"home groups" refer to the second set of groupings of students, each of which is comprised of an expert from each of the expert groups; each group has the collective knowledge of all of the expert groups. Once in home groups, students use their collective knowledge in order to complete a task, such as the one shown in Figure 8.9C. See also the videotape entitled "Happy New Year!" for an example of a jigsaw activity in action (Annenberg/CPB, & ACTFL, 2003).

■ *Information-gap activities (IGAs)* (Johnson, 1979; Walz, 1996): One student has information that another student does not have but needs. For example, pairs of students might be given the task of finding an hour that they both have free this week to play a game of tennis. Each student might have a copy of his/her schedule of activities for the week, and each has to ask questions in order to find out when the other person is free. As they share the information, the students eventually find a time slot that works for both of them. See Figure 8.10A & B "Where are my glasses?" for an example in English. On the Web site Appendices 8.3A & B

FIGURE 8.9B Jigsaw Activity for Four Groups of Students

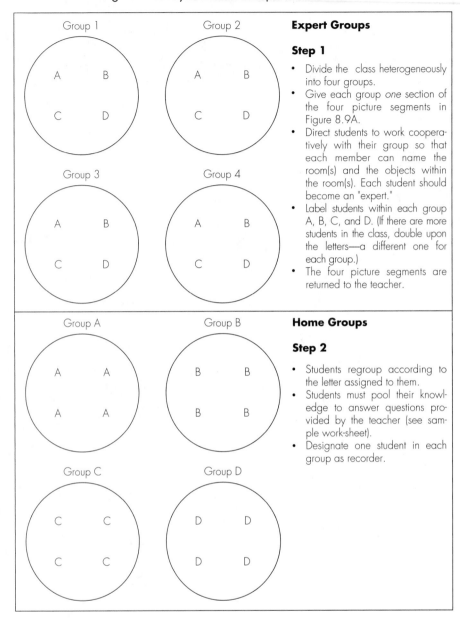

Expert Groups

Step 1

- Divide the class heterogeneously into four groups.
- Give each group *one* section of the four picture segments in Figure 8.9A.
- Direct students to work cooperatively with their group so that each member can name the room(s) and the objects within the room(s). Each student should become an "expert."
- Label students within each group A, B, C, and D. (If there are more students in the class, double upon the letters—a different one for each group.)
- The four picture segments are returned to the teacher.

Home Groups

Step 2

- Students regroup according to the letter assigned to them.
- Students must pool their knowledge to answer questions provided by the teacher (see sample work-sheet).
- Designate one student in each group as recorder.

Source: Fall, 1991, original material.

(Dreke & Lind, 2000), 8.4A & B (Freed & Bauer, 1989), 8.5A & B (Jansma & Kassen, 2004), and 8.6A & B (Hadfield, 1984; cf. Walz 1996) are sample information-gap activities in German, Spanish, French, and English, respectively. Note that Appendices 8.3A & B illustrate an IGA in German that is somewhat different from the other examples that follow in that it deals with storytelling.[6] Student B has a series of drawings arranged and numbered in the correct order to represent a story; he or she tells the story to Student A by describing the drawings. Student A asks questions as needed and numbers the drawings accordingly. This activity is repeated for a second story, but this time Student A tells the story as Student B numbers the drawings.

FIGURE 8.9C Jigsaw Activity Worksheet

Group _____

Names _____   _____

_____   _____

Each member of your group has seen one part of a house. You will need to work together to answer the following questions:

1. How many rooms are in the house?   _____
2. How many bathrooms are there?   _____
3. How many bedrooms are there?   _____
4. How many of the following did you see?

beds	_____	pictures	_____
tables	_____	sinks	_____
clocks	_____	doors	_____
chairs	_____	toys	_____
dressers	_____	pillows	_____
lamps	_____	bookshelves	_____
rugs	_____	waste baskets	_____
windows	_____		

5. How many children might live in this house?   _____
6. Do you think the children are older or younger?   _____

Variations: Selected readings may be given, or research assignments may be made, including biographies (each group studies one facet of the person's life) of cultural studies (each group studies one facet of a particular country or culture).

Target Language Use: To encourage use of the target language, give each student 5–10 bingo chips. Each time a student uses English, he or she must place a chip in a pile. Students receive bonus points dependng on the number of chips they still have at the end of the activity.

Process Objectives: Students will work cooperatively.
Students will engage in peer teaching.

Content Objectives: Students will communicate in the target language.
Students will recall and/or name vocabulary items or basic facts and information.

Source: Fall, 1991, original material.

At the end, students are asked to create a title for the stories and relate them to the class.

Teachers should recognize that, in order for jigsaw activities and IGAs to be most effective, students need preparation before they begin to do them. Teachers should guide students in activating background knowledge and in recalling/ reviewing key vocabulary and expressions that they will need in order to complete the task. If the activity includes visuals, students should have an opportunity to look at them to be sure that they understand what they are depicting and to brainstorm possible vocabulary. Furthermore, it is critical that students see a model of these activities before they engage in one themselves. Finally, students must be

FIGURE 8.10A Where Are My Glasses?: Student A

Source: Walz, 1996.

held accountable for these activities by being expected to perform a follow-up task, such as reporting back to the class. See a later section in this chapter on how to structure group tasks.

Brooks (1992) describes another type of information-gap activity: "There are two parts to a whole diagram or picture, Part A and Part B. When both parts are

FIGURE 8.10B Where Are My Glasses?: Student B

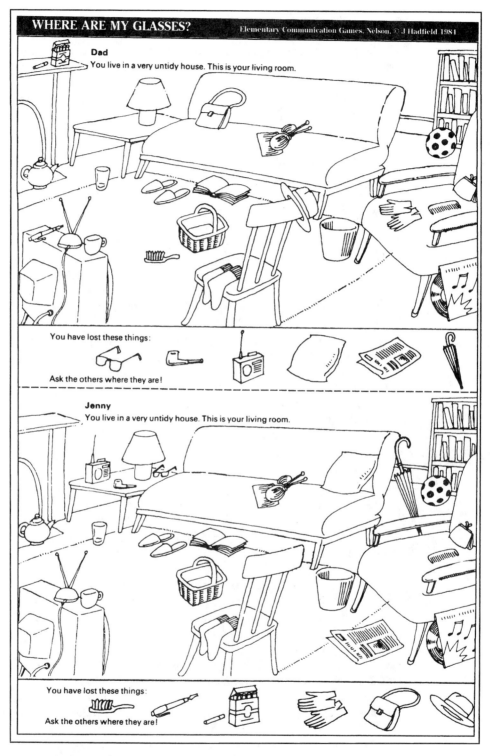

Source: Walz, 1996.

superimposed, they form a complete diagram. One student receives Part A, the other Part B. The teacher then asks the students to talk to one another in the foreign language to find out how their part of the diagram is both different from and similar to that of the partner and to draw in or add the missing information so that, by the end of their conversation, they both have replicas of the same master diagram" (p. 67). Appendix 8.6 (on the Web site) is an example of this type of IGA in which students draw the missing information from each drawing of the house so that, at the end of the activity, both students have the same drawing of the complete house. Appendix 8.6 also illustrates how the same jigsaw activity used in Figure 8.9 can be adapted for use as an information-gap activity of the kind described above.

When teachers use an information-gap activity for they first time, they must realize that students need sufficient opportunities to become comfortable with this type of task. If the teacher explains the task, models with another student what learners are to do, and then provides several similar but different tasks, students will find these tasks more productive and enjoyable than other kinds of practice, and the teacher will find that students begin to use the language more to exchange information. Also, the teacher might videotape students completing an information-gap activity and then show this video to students as an example of how this type of activity works. It is important to do several similar activities so that students can become comfortable managing intrapersonal communication—that is, figuring out in their own minds how they will sustain their involvement in the task (Brooks, Donato, & McGlone, 1997).

Information-gap activities provide a good opportunity for students to learn how to ask for clarification, how to request information, and how to negotiate when faced with misunderstandings. Teachers should realize, however, that not all IGAs are created equal. Some provide formulaic practice of language utterances and vocabulary, e.g., those that require students to give prices of items, while others, such as the ones included in this chapter, promote creativity and meaning-making.

 In information-gap activities, one student has information that another student does not have but needs.

- *Problem solving* (Long & Crookes, 1986): Group members must share information in order to solve a problem, such as how to find lost luggage at an airport.
- *Storytelling:* students recreate a familiar story, add more details, and change the ending. Students can also create a story with visuals.
- *Cooperative projects* (Kagan, 1989): Group members work together to complete a group project such as a presentation, composition, or art project. Oxford (1992) describes the "Heritage Project," a successful cooperative model for teaching culture in language classes, in which students design a culture-related project and have a large degree of freedom in topic choice, grouping, implementation, and time management.
- *Movement activities* (Bassano & Christison, 1987): Students get up from their seats and walk around the room in order to obtain information from classmates. For example, students might have a list of ten activities in the present tense and ask classmates whether or not they do each activity (wake up at 6:00 A.M., eat breakfast every morning, etc.); students share the information with the class afterward.
- *Paired interviews:* Students interview each other for specific information and share their findings with the class.
- *Role plays:* Students act out situations, such as a restaurant scene or a visit to a doctor. Beginning students can be given role-play cards with vocabulary/grammar

hints, intermediate-level students can practice role plays around survival situations, and advanced-level learners can present role plays around a problematic situation in which someone must solve a conflict or persuade someone else to do something within a culturally specific context (DiPietro, 1987; Hadley, 2001).

It is advantageous to present the situation card describing the role play in the native language so that students completely understand the task. However, when preparing role plays, students also benefit from well-organized instructions and guidance, such as a model situation and hints concerning vocabulary and grammar use. The extent to which the teacher offers specific suggestions will depend on the cognitive and linguistic levels of the students. Younger learners, for example, require more structured role-play directions in order to help them focus their ideas.

Richards (1985) describes the following procedure for using role plays with intermediate-level learners:

1. Learners participate in a preliminary activity in which the topic and situation are introduced.
2. They then work through a model dialogue on a related topic that provides examples of the type of language that will be required.
3. Assisted by situation cards, learners perform their assigned role play.
4. Learners listen to recordings of native speakers performing the role play with the role cards.
5. Follow-up activities exploit the native speaker performance.
6. The entire sequence is then repeated with a second transaction on the same topic. (pp. 85–88)

- *Open-ended free conversations:* Students are given a list of topics related to their lessons and told to select a topic and let the conversation flow from there. This is consistent with the *topicalization hypothesis*, according to which choice of topic allows for more natural flow of language (Ellis, 1990; Hatch, 1978; Kinginger, 1994; Long, 1983; Wells, 1985).
- *Sharing opinions, debating, narrating, describing, explaining:* These activities are particularly useful as students move into the advanced level of study, since they provide the impetus for self-expression, use of paragraph-length and extended discourse, and manipulation of more sophisticated vocabulary and grammatical structures.

Norman (1996) outlines a set of classroom activities designed to promote spontaneous oral interaction for students in an EFL classroom. The activities are based on the initial reading of texts such as diaries, newspaper articles, poems, and drama scenes (interpretive mode). Students work together to explore the texts and share reactions (interpersonal mode), after which they create a presentation or product, such as a drama activity or newscast (presentational mode) (pp. 598–602).

Conducting Cooperative Learning Activities

Grouping Students. Research in cooperative learning shows that the most effective way to configure small groups is to put together four students who represent a cross-section of the class in terms of level of past performance in the subject area, race or ethnicity, and sex (Slavin, 1986). Slavin suggests that "a four-person team in a class that is one half male, one half female, and three quarters white, one quarter minority might have two boys and two girls and three white students and one minority student. The team would also have a high performer, a low performer, and two average performers" (p. 16). Students should be assigned to groups or teams by the teacher, since they tend to choose partners who are like themselves.

When a class does not evenly divide up into groups, the extra students can be assigned the role of "floater." Floaters can have several functions, such as collecting information from each group (during paired interviews, for example), eavesdropping and reporting back to the class what he or she discovered, and serving as an observer of group processing. In this way, the extra students can contribute to the class at the end of the activity or during group reporting (R. Donato, personal communication, June 14, 1992).

Structuring Group Tasks.   The following are helpful guidelines for structuring co-operative learning and interactive activities:

1. Ensure that students do, in fact, need to cooperate in order to complete the task. They should not be able to complete it without interaction.
2. Keep the group size small; start with pair activities. Groups are most effective when they are no larger than five.
3. Set the stage; motivate the activity with drama, actions, or visuals.
4. Set clear goals; describe outcomes clearly for the students.
5. Make sure the students have the target language they need to accomplish the activity, that they know how to say what they will need to say.
6. Give exact directions for every step of the task. Model the sequence of the activity in precise steps.
7. Set a time limit to help students feel accountable and to make the best use of the time available. Use a kitchen timer with a loud bell or buzzer to provide a neutral time-keeper and a clear signal for the end of the activity.
8. Circulate among the students throughout the activity. This will enable you to monitor use of the target language, offer assistance, and check progress.
9. Establish a system for directing the attention of the students back to you, e.g., a hand signal such as a raised right hand, dimming the lights.
10. Elicit communicative feedback and process group effectiveness at the end of the activity (Curtain & Dahlberg, 2004, pp. 108–110).

 Define group tasks and set time and membership limits before the group begins. ▪

Detailed attention must be given to providing clear directions and examples before the task is begun (Johnson, Johnson, & Holubec, 1988). Modeling the task with students in front of the class and talking about the task while it is performed is another good way to provide support for the activity. While students are engaged in group activities, the teacher acts as both a process observer and a resource person. At the conclusion of the group activity, the groups report back to the whole class on their progress and on the process, thus helping the teacher to plan for future activities. Circulating around the room to monitor progress and making students responsible for reporting back to the class after the activity will encourage students to use the target language and may prevent them from reverting to the use of the native language. See Appendix 8.7 for a description of Donato's (1992) "Talk Scores," a technique for monitoring and evaluating group speaking activities.

Imaginative Activities

Sadow (1987) developed a number of *imaginative activities* for the language classroom in which students are asked to "solve a problem they would not normally have to face, concoct a plan they would never have dreamt of on their own, reconstruct the missing parts of stories, and act in outlandish ways" (p. 33). According to Sadow, imaginative activities have the following characteristics:

1. Students work from the known to the unknown.
2. The problem is deliberately ambiguous.
3. Any logical response to the problem is acceptable.
4. Role play is commonly used.
5. Listening skills are crucial at several points in the activity.
6. The teacher sets up the activity and then withdraws.
7. There is a summing up or debriefing following student discussion (pp. 33–34).

When students first begin to do imaginative work, Sadow (1987) suggests that they work with structured paired activities, such as rewriting conversations or dialogues to change the characters, perhaps by switching male and female or altering age and status. Beginning-level students might be engaged in activities such as designing a mask with unusual facial features, designing half-built houses, or inventing a job interviewer they would like to encounter. At the intermediate and advanced levels, challenging problem-solving activities can be presented that promote interaction and critical thinking through what Sadow (1994) terms *concoctions*. Students are presented with an unusual problem to solve creatively; for example, students might create a new animal, plan model cities, invent a heroine for a country that lacks one, and write plays with happy endings (p. 242).

The following is a sample concoction, the script of which is normally read by the teacher to the students in the target language: "After weeks of hiking through uninhabited, thick woodlands and open prairie; climbing steep mountainsides; boating down wild rivers and across quiet lakes, you have finally reached the long-sought coast. Your explorations have been a great success, and you expect to be heroes and heroines when you finally return home. But first you must draw a complete map of your travels. Draw your route as accurately as possible, pointing out places that are especially beautiful or especially difficult to cross. Be sure to invent names for all the places you've passed through" (Sadow, 1994, p. 242). Following the reading of the script, comprehension checks are conducted, and students work on the task in groups of three to five for fifteen to forty-five minutes; then each group presents its work to the entire class while designated secretaries record the reporting. Appropriate comments or questions in the whole-class format are then followed by writing activities or interrelated activities in subsequent classes (pp. 250–251).[7] As modeled by this sample concoction, imaginative activities can effectively integrate all three modes of communication.

Developing Interpersonal Speaking Through Study of Literature and Culture

In Chapters 6 and 7, you explored strategies for guiding students through oral and printed texts and using these texts as springboards for discussion and creative extension activities, including following the Interactive Model for Integrating the Three Modes of Communication. One of the advantages of this Model, presented in Chapter 6, is that it helps students understand a text and feel comfortable with it before being asked to engage in creative speaking. The difficulty students often experience when trying to discuss readings, particularly literary texts, is that they cannot communicate orally in the same style or at the same level as the text. The interactive model compensates for this difference in skill level by encouraging students to express their thoughts in their own words and at their own speaking level, while using parts of the text prose for additional support. Breiner-Sanders (1991) suggests that, when beginning to use reading as a basis for conversation, teachers select reading materials that are targeted more closely to students' speaking level, in order to help them gain confidence in discussing texts.

Sadow (1987) suggests the use of simulations or reenactment of scenes from a literary passage or historical event as a strategy for integrating interpersonal speaking with the study of literature and history. According to Cazden (1992), reenactments or performance activities stimulate discussion as groups plan and decide upon an interpretation of the text, and again later, in the post-performance discussion when the small groups' interpretive decisions are explained and compared. These activities provide opportunities for students to use the target language in preparing their reenactments while interacting with the text and assimilating text language into their linguistic repertoire.

Undoubtedly, students cannot be taught to engage in effective interpersonal communication without cultural understanding. *Teacher's Handbook* advocates the integration of culture and communication across the three modes. In Chapter 5, you learned about a *constructivist* approach to learning about culture, in which learners construct their views of culture through social interaction and interpersonal communication. In Chapters 6 and 7, you explored ways in which culture can be integrated in an oral, printed, or video text and used as the basis for communication.

In her reading process for using authentic texts to guide learners' cross-cultural discovery, Galloway (1992) suggests that students use speaking as they transfer and reflect on cultural information and insights acquired through exploration of a text. In oral interpersonal tasks, students might:

- role play a scenario using appropriate cultural and linguistic protocols, given the context;
- verbally support or refute a position from the point of view of a native from the target culture, using citations from an authentic text;
- debate an issue from the viewpoints of both the native and target cultures;
- analyze a possible target language utterance by determining the likelihood that it would have been said at all and identifying the type of speaker from whom it might have come; and
- respond to open-ended questions relating to cultural information they discovered in an authentic text (pp. 120–121).

thandbook.heinle.com

You may find it helpful to refer back to Viewing Activity B in Chapter 6 (see the Web site)—"Hearing Authentic Voices"—to see how this teacher engages students in viewing a video of Spanish-speaking youths who discuss their leisure activities as a prelude for the students' own discussions.

Another example of integrating interpersonal speaking and culture is the series of cross-level collaborative projects undertaken by the 1997 Northeast Conference on the Teaching of Foreign Languages to address the standards in classroom practice (Phillips, 1997). Two of the projects exemplify how interpersonal speaking and writing can be effectively integrated into exploration of cultures, comparisons of language and cultures, communication with native speakers, connections to other disciplines, and interaction with target language communities.

First, Haas and Reardon (1997) designed and taught an interdisciplinary unit on Chile to a seventh-grade Spanish class. Interpersonal speaking was integrated in various ways as students (1) discussed, in Spanish, slides and literary texts (including poetry) dealing with Chile; (2) interviewed a guest informant from Chile; and (3) as a culminating activity, visited a Chilean bakery in their local community and interacted with the store owners in Spanish, making purchases, asking questions about a food preparation demonstration, etc.

A key component of this project was that students also engaged in interpersonal writing by corresponding by e-mail with Chilean key pals (more on this in the next section). (See the Chapter 10 video segment on the *Teacher's Handbook* Web site for the bakery visit.)

Second, Schwartz and Kavanaugh (1997) taught a unit on immigration to a ninth-grade Spanish class through the study of conditions in Guatemala and the viewing of various video materials. Interpersonal speaking was incorporated by means of (1) discussion of video segments from the movie on video "El norte"; (2) role plays from video scenes; (3) interviewing a Guatemalan informant; and (4) debate on immigration to the United States.[8]

Using Literary Exploration to Develop Advanced-Level Discourse

One of the challenges of teaching interpersonal speaking is moving students' proficiency from the intermediate-low and -mid levels to the intermediate-high and advanced levels. This is difficult for several reasons, because at the advanced level:

- Students must move from sentences to connected paragraphs. In other words, according to the sociocultural framework, utterances and dialogue give way to discourse, which is used to clarify ideas, establish concepts, and relate opinions to others (Mantero, 2002; Wells, 1999). As you learned in Chapter 3, "discourse builds on understanding which has come to be over time and various situations with both the students and the teachers acting as speakers and listeners throughout communication" (Wells, 1999, p. 68; cf. Mantero, 2002, p. 440).
- Students must narrate and describe in present, past, and future time frames.
- Students must expand their discourse beyond their immediate worlds to topics of public interest.
- Students must deal with unanticipated complications.
- Students must be understood without difficulty by speakers unaccustomed to dealing with non-native speakers (Swender, 1999).

Advanced-level discourse competence requires attention to the use of cohesive devices, such as pronouns and conjunctions, which serve to illustrate a relation between one element or idea and another; e.g., conjunctions such as *therefore* and *however* connect the idea in one sentence with an idea in a subsequent sentence. Advanced-level discourse also has *coherence,* which refers to the organization of ideas within a text; i.e., the orderly presentation of ideas, consistency of facts and opinions, and completeness of the discussion (Canale, 1982). See Chapter 9 for a fuller discussion of cohesion and coherence as they deal with presentational writing.

Advanced-level discourse also requires interesting content to talk and learn about, beyond the scope of self, daily life, and weekend activities. In Chapters 5, 6, and 7, you explored ways in which *Teacher's Handbook* advocates a pivotal role of literature and culture in language instruction because they provide the means for more stimulating content, acquisition of interesting content, and extension of linguistic skills. Also, of course, upper-level classes at the secondary level and literature classes at the post-secondary level should offer the ideal environment for developing discourse into the advanced range of oral proficiency.

However, two recent studies have called into question the degree to which the discourse conditions of typical literature classes foster interactions that reflect advanced levels of language functioning. In their study of teacher-directed target language discussions of literary texts in a senior-level undergraduate Spanish literature course, Donato and Brooks (2004) examined discourse structure of the literary discussions, types of questions asked by the instructor, use of major time frames, and student uptake as indicators of advanced-level discourse. They found that (1) the discourse pattern established by the instructor inhibited students' elaboration of responses and prevented them from moving beyond word- and sentence-level utterances; (2) most of the teacher's questions were display questions, to which the instructor already knew the answer, and which provided an invitation to her to take the floor; (3) the range of time frames used in discussions was limited and the present tense was the predominant tense; and (4) students generally did not "uptake" speech modeled by the teacher (i.e., they did not show evidence of altering or correcting their language after instructor modeling or recasting, primarily due to the fact that the instructor accepted utterances that were incorrect and/or inappropriate in the context of the discussion). This study also revealed that both students and instructor were concerned about the lack of time to cover a large quantity of material in the literature class, that the teacher indicated as one of her goals that students would gain the ability to personalize literary works, and that students reported that the main impact of the class on their language was in the area of new vocabulary.

Findings of the Donato and Brooks (2004) study echo those of an earlier study that also examined the discourse of an undergraduate Spanish literature class. Mantero (2002) found that most text-centered classroom talk occurred at the level of dialogue and featured extensive use of IRE patterns, and that students' cognitive behavior focused on knowledge of specific pieces of information.

Donato and Brooks (2004) cite five implications of current research regarding the role of interpersonal speaking and advanced-level functions in literary discussions:

1. Discussions that take place in literature courses have the potential to incorporate advanced proficiency goals.
2. Literature classes need to include a variety of interaction patterns to provide for elaborated responses, one feature of an advanced speaker.
3. The potential of literary discussion to move students into advanced speaking tasks needs to be raised in the minds of instructors and students.
4. Literature instructors need to know the *ACTFL Proficiency Guidelines—Speaking,* the range of functions at each level of proficiency, and the modes of communication as described in the *SFLL*.
5. There is a critical need for more research into the literary discussion and its relationship to developing functional language abilities at the advanced level (pp. 195–196).

Teaching Interpersonal Writing

Two-way interpersonal communication can also be accomplished through written means, such as dialogue journals, letters, and e-mail projects.

Dialogue Journals

A *dialogue journal* is a written conversation in which students communicate individually with the teacher (Peyton, 1993; Peyton & Reed, 1990). It can also be used to engage students in interaction with one another or in small groups. Various studies have shown the effectiveness of using journal writing to help students create personal meaning and increase their motivation to write (Peyton, 1987, 1990; West & Donato, 1995). According to Hall and Robinson (1994), interactive journal writing can facilitate children's writing skills, aid in the transition from oral to written communication, and give students the chance to be an "author." Learning to write occurs when children are given a reason to write and a real audience to address (Jensen, 1993). Shohamy (1998) advocates the use of dialogue journals because they involve young learners in the learning process and provide the teacher with information about their perspectives on the language learning process.

The interactive dialogue journal is effective for learners of all ages and at all levels of language development. Curtain and Dahlberg (2004) suggest that, at very beginning stages of language learning in elementary school, students can write or copy the words they have learned and combine them with pictures, and then share this with the teacher for response. At more advanced stages, they suggest using the journal to engage in discussions of cultural issues or other content, as well as more personal feelings and opinions. It is important that the teacher respond to the content of each journal entry rather than using it as an opportunity to correct grammar, vocabulary, and spelling errors.

The dialogue journal can also be used as a tool to help students make sense of new content that they are learning in the language classroom. They might, for example, keep lists of new vocabulary, respond to questions posed by the teacher, or organize content through charts or outlines. Students might share their journal entries with the teacher or use them to engage in a private conversation with themselves in order to mediate learning. When the dialogue journal is shared with the teacher in this way, it also functions as a tool for alternative formative assessment since students continually provide feedback about what they understand in class as they progress with their language development, and this can enable the teacher to improve instruction (Peyton & Reed, 1990). Figure 8.11 shows

FIGURE 8.11 Types of Journal Writing Used to Foster Learning of Content Areas

Journal Type and Purpose	Science	Language Arts	Mathematics	Social Science
Dialogue/Buddy: to share with another	Explain to teacher or to friend what is happening in class and what is understood	Share with another about a story or poem being read; share other aspects of class	Let teacher or friend know how class or assignments are going	"Discuss" information pertaining to topics in class
Notebook: to take notes to assist memory	Write down information pertaining to an experiment in class	Take down conversations overheard for use in a story to be written	Keep notes about math concepts	Write down key information discussed in class
Learning logs: to discuss and process information from class	Write down notes about what one understands in the class and about what might seem unclear	Write down key concepts from class such as definitions of concepts: setting, theme, characterization	Try to explain math concepts for oneself or perhaps for another; clarify or try to apply a new concept	Take notes on causes of Civil War or other key ideas; ask self to identify and clarify ideas
Response journals: to respond openly and freely to any topic	Respond to feelings about scientific experimentation or use of animals as subjects of biogenetics	Make any comments on characters or conflicts presented in a story being read	Respond to math in an interesting way, such as ask questions about why people who would never admit to being illiterate will seemingly brag about their math ignorance	Respond to politicians' handling of peace after World War I or about attitudes of pilgrims toward Native Americans

Source: Peregoy & Boyle, 2001, p. 349.

the types of journal writing that might be used to foster student learning of content areas. A table such as this one helps the teacher monitor learning in the various subject areas by means of interpersonal written tasks. Although this table was developed to monitor learning in bilingual or immersion second language settings, it can also be used in foreign language classrooms that incorporate content-based instruction.

Borich (2001) reported on the use of the dialogue journal with a second-grade FLES class to assess learning related to the Cultures and Connections goal areas in a thematic unit on the Yucatan. Data obtained from the students' journal entries revealed their ability to identify cultural similarities and differences, identify cultural products and practices, and acquire new information related to other disciplines. Borich concluded that the journal enabled students to show what they had learned in a variety of ways, to use higher order thinking skills, and to provide their own perspectives on what had been taught. One disadvantage of the journal for teachers is the amount of time that it takes to read and respond. In a similar vein, some teachers in Borich's study expressed dissatisfaction with the amount of time taken out of the school day for students to write in their journals. However, as you will see in Chapter 11, taking time to integrate valuable assessment is justified, particularly since effective assessment informs and improves instruction and should be closely integrated with it.

At secondary and post-secondary levels, the interactive dialogue journal may be used through electronic mail. Wang (1994) observed that using e-mail to conduct dialogue journals in an intermediate ESL class had advantages over the paper-and-pencil journals: Students who used e-mail wrote more per writing session, asked more questions, used more language functions, and adopted a more conversational tone in their language than did their traditional counterparts. These findings were also reflected in a study of university Spanish students, whose electronic dialogue journals were found to have more language, a greater variety of topics and language functions, more student-initiated interactions, and more personal and expressive language use (González-Bueno, 1998).

Use of the electronic medium for interpersonal exchanges seems to facilitate participation by students who are reluctant to engage in face-to-face conversations, it allows time to process input and output, and it increases language production. Evidence suggests that the electronic dialogue journal improves students' attitudes toward language learning, promotes communicative and personalized interaction, increases the amount of language produced by students, and enables students and instructor to develop a positive rapport (González-Bueno, 1998; González-Bueno & Pérez, 2000; Warschauer, 1995; Warschauer & Healey, 1998). However, research results are mixed concerning whether or not the electronic format poses any significant advantage over the paper-and-pencil version in terms of improving lexical and grammatical accuracy (Florez-Estrada, 1995; González-Bueno & Pérez, 2000; Ittzes, 1997; Reichelt, 2001).

Key Pal and Pen Pal Letter Exchanges

Written interpersonal communication with members of the target culture not only provides a way to practice communication skills but is also an effective means of acquiring new information and cultural perspectives. A number of studies describe e-mail exchanges as an interpersonal communication activity that enhances student autonomy (Bernhardt & Kamil, 1998; Fischer, 1998; Van Handle & Corl, 1998). Fischer (1998) suggests that small talk in letter writing helps to form personal relationships and a sense of community. Van Handle and Corl (1998) suggest that students should be informed that their primary focus is on communication rather than linguistic accuracy and that they should write as much and as freely as they can. According to Kern (1998), e-mail correspondence stresses speed and conciseness of expression, while paper-and-pen writing is an intensive, recursive process that fosters development and elaboration of ideas (p. 75; cf. Yamada & Moeller, 2001, p. 32).

In an interdisciplinary unit on Chile that Haas and Reardon (1997) designed and taught to a seventh-grade Spanish class in New York, an integral component was the correspondence by e-mail with Chilean key pals. Over the course of the school year, three rounds of e-mail messages were sent back and forth to the students' peers in Chile. When students received their first set of letters from Chile, they noticed many concepts that they had learned about from class (e.g., numbers *do* go after street names, Chileans *do* often use their mothers' and fathers' names, the day *does* go before the month), they explored the metric system as they calculated how tall a Chilean friend was, they learned new descriptive adjectives, and they identified similarities between the Chilean students and themselves. With the arrival of the second letters, it was clear that students had begun to form friendships, as their questions were being answered and more were posed to them. The third set of letters, which arrived just as the school year was ending, described points of interest around the region and came with a package that contained pictures of the students and their school and information about Chile so that their U.S. counterparts would have a visual idea of who their key pals were and where they lived. The U.S. teacher assisted students' writing of the letters by helping them to brainstorm information they could use in their replies and questions they could ask their Chilean keypals. The key pal exchange proved to be a pivotal part of the unit, bringing the Chilean world into the Spanish classroom.

At the post-secondary level, Jogan, Heredia, and Aguilera (2001) report similar findings in their study of dialogue journals and key pals in a U.S. class of advanced Spanish conversation and composition and a Chilean class of advanced ESL. In addition to their asynchronous e-mail exchanges, U.S. students wrote reflections about the cultural knowledge they had gained, pointing out a lessening of stereotypes and an increase in understanding.

Yamada and Moeller (2001) report on a pen pal letter exchange conducted between students enrolled in a second-year Japanese class at a liberal arts college in the Midwest and a group of college students in Japan. Handwritten letters were electronically scanned and posted to a Web site, which enabled immediate access to the letters. Letters were exchanged three times during the semester; the entire process for one round of letter writing took three to four weeks and included the following steps: writing the draft, peer editing, writing the second draft, feedback from the instructor, writing the final draft, submission of the letter for grading and correcting, completion of the final letter and posting on the Web, reading the response letter from the pen pal, and bringing the letter to class when help was needed in interpreting it (p. 27). Results of the study indicated that students felt a sense of accomplishment by being able to engage in interpersonal communication with native Japanese speakers, they were motivated to write better as a result of peer editing, they became curious about the people of Japan and were prompted to make comparisons and contrasts, they improved their interpretive skills by reading pen pal letters, and they learned about age-appropriate cultural practices and perspectives. Similar results were reported by Hertel (2003), whose students reported greater understanding of the cultural practices of their Mexican keypals.

Synchronous Electronic Interaction

Modern technology has made it possible for learners to share ideas and receive responses immediately through real-life chats, or text-based instantaneous communication. Like face-to-face conversation, computer-mediated communication (CMC) takes place in real-time interaction in which language users negotiate meaning in written forms. A message is typed on a computer keyboard and is displayed immediately on the screen. During online negotiation, learners attend to input, feedback, and output similarly to the way they experience face-to-face spoken interaction (Lee, 2002). Research studies have revealed the positive effects of synchronous online discussion on teaching and learning as well as on fostering student interest and motivation for language learning (Beauvois, 1998; Lee, 1997; Pelletieri, 2000). The research indicates three benefits of CMC: (1) it offers opportunities for more equal participation than face-to-face interaction, (2) it allows the learner sufficient time to process input and monitor and edit output through a self-paced process, and (3) it increases language production and complexity (Lee, 2002, p. 17). Lee describes the use of an online chat room and task-based instruction to create a learning environment in which third-year college Spanish students used the target language to discuss, exchange, and debate issues related to real life. Students accessed online communication tools through *Blackboard* (an e-learning environment) and then completed task-based online activities, wrote online essays, and participated in online discussions on real-world topics of interest.[9] Lee proposes that "the combined use of online interaction and task-based instruction empowers students' communication skills by creating a lively environment in which they respond to real-time conversation about topics relevant to their interests" (p. 21). In Chapter 12, you will explore further the use of technology such as this to promote language acquisition.

In sum, strategies such as dialogue journals, pen pal/key pal letter exchanges, and synchronous electronic interaction are effective ways to engage students in written interpersonal communication while simultaneously addressing other goal areas.

Providing Feedback in Oral Interpersonal Contexts[10]

Language teachers have traditionally given students feedback in response to the correctness of language use. A "very good" awarded by the teacher undoubtedly means that the student used accurate grammar, vocabulary, and/or pronunciation, or used the designated linguistic pattern being practiced (see discussions of IRE in Chapter 3 and earlier in this chapter). Oral feedback given by the teacher in the classroom can generally be of two types: (1) error correction and (2) response to the content of the student's message, much as in natural conversation. In classrooms that focus on negotiation of meaning (as defined in Chapter 1), the teacher provides feedback that helps learners figure out meaning, make themselves understood, and develop strategies for interacting effectively in groups (Platt & Brooks, 1994).

 In Chapter 3, what did the discussion of IRE/IRF reveal about the nature of teacher feedback?

Summarizing the research from 1970 to the early 1990s, Mings (1993) draws these four conclusions about learner errors (1) different types of errors are made by learners; (2) they do not all produce identical consequences; (3) they originate from a variety of causes; and (4) they serve a very useful purpose in interlanguage development (p. 176). Terrell (1985) posits that correcting students' errors directly does not help them correct their mistakes in the future, may frustrate students, and may cause them to focus on language form rather than on meaning. Lightbown and Spada (1990) affirm that within a communicative contextual base, form-focus activities and correction in context are beneficial (p. 443).

In their hallmark study with French immersion students in grades four and five, Lyster and Ranta (1997) examined the effect of teacher correction strategies on student *uptake*—how the student incorporates teacher feedback into subsequent utterances. There are two types of student uptake: (a) uptake that results in "repair" of the error and (b) uptake that results in an utterance that is still in need of repair (p. 49). Students demonstrate uptake through repetition of the teacher's feedback that includes the correct form (provided by the teacher), incorporation of the correct form into a longer utterance, self-correction, and peer correction.

Lyster & Ranta (1997) believe that student-generated repairs may help learners to retrieve target language knowledge that already exists in some form and may help them to revise their hypotheses about the target language. (See discussion of conversational repair in pair and group interaction, presented earlier in this chapter.) Their study identified six types of teacher feedback:

1. *Explicit correction:* The teacher corrects the student, indicating clearly that what the student said was incorrect: "You should say . . . ".
2. *Recast:* The teacher reformulates all or part of a student's utterance minus the error. Recasts are implicit and are not introduced by "You should say . . . ". They may focus on one word, grammatical modification, or translation of the student's use of the native language: S: "I go not to the movies last night." T: "Oh, you didn't go to the movies last night."
3. *Clarification request:* The teacher identifies a problem in either comprehensibility or accuracy or both: "Pardon me?" or "What do you mean by X?"
4. *Metalinguistic feedback:* The teacher makes comments or asks questions about the form of the student's utterance without providing the correct form. These comments indicate that there is an error somewhere: "Can you find your error?" or "It isn't said in that way." This feedback includes some grammatical metalanguage that refers to the nature of the error: "It's masculine."
5. *Elicitation:* The teacher repeats part of the student's utterance and pauses to allow the student to complete the utterance at the place where the error occurred: S: "I had already went to the library." T: "I had already. . . ". The teacher can also use questions to elicit correct forms (e.g., "How do we say 'X' in French?"), or the teacher asks students to reformulate their utterance: "Try again, using the conditional."
6. *Repetition:* The teacher repeats the student's erroneous utterance, usually changing the intonation to highlight the error: S: ". . . many money." T: ". . . many money?" (pp. 46–48).

Figure 8.12 compares the percentage of times that a particular feedback strategy resulted in student uptake and repair and the percentage of time each strategy was used

FIGURE 8.12 Comparison of Teacher Feedback Strategies and Student Uptake in Lyster & Ranta's 1997 Study

Categories of Teacher Feedback Strategies	Percentage of Student Uptake	Percentage of Teacher Feedback Strategies
Elicitation	100%	14%
Clarification Requests	88%	11%
Metalinguistic Feedback	86%	8%
Repetition	78%	5%
Explicit Correction	50%	7%
Recasts	31%	55%

Source: Shrum & Glisan, 2005, original material.

Note: Data were gleaned from information in Lyster & Ranta (1997) article.

by teachers. The teachers in Lyster & Ranta's (1997) study used recasts more than any other strategy for correcting errors (55% of the time), with the other strategies occurring in the following order of decreasing frequency: elicitation (14%), clarification request (11%), metalinguistic feedback (8%), explicit correction (7%), and repetition (5%).

Interestingly, recast was the strategy that proved least likely to lead to uptake: Recast strategies led students to make attempts at repairing their utterances only 31% of the time. Explicit correction led to uptake only 50% of the time. Clarification requests, metalinguistic feedback, and repetition were effective strategies for eliciting uptake from students (88%, 86%, and 78%, respectively). The most effective strategy with respect to uptake was elicitation. In all cases, elicitation led to uptake. This finding confirms the claim made by Lightbown & Spada (2003) that feedback given in the form of "recasts" goes unnoticed by learners; that is, they don't recognize it as signaling an error in form but rather as the teacher's affirmation of the content of their message. Elicitation may be a more effective strategy, as illustrated in Lyster and Ranta's study, because it is a way for the teacher to signal to the student that there is a problem with form and consequently with meaning. Lightbown and Spada also suggest that, when teachers choose to reformulate a student's utterance, they use a method of signaling to the student, through a tone of voice, gesture, or facial expression, which says to the student, "I think I understand what you are saying and I'm telling you how you can say it better" (p. 167).

Some strategies, such as clarification requests, focus on the message while signaling to the student that there is a problem, most likely due to a grammatical or vocabulary error. The following is an example of an exchange between a Spanish teacher and a student where a clarification request is made by the teacher:

Estoy cansada hoy, clase. Trabajé hasta muy tarde anoche. ¿Qué hicieron Uds. anoche? Sí, Susana, ¿qué hiciste tú? [I'm very tired today, class. I worked until very late last night. What did all of you do last night? Yes, Susana, what did you do?]

Pues, tú no hiciste nada. [Well, you didn't do anything.]

¿Quién? ¿Yo? Sí, yo hice mucho anoche. [Who? Me? Yes, I did a lot last night.]

¡Oh! Yo no hice nada. [Oh! I didn't do anything.]

In this exchange, the focus on form happened in a meaningful context, as it resulted from a misunderstanding. It was not arbitrary or dependent on the teacher's hidden grammatical agenda. When errors are treated in this way, students must think about what went wrong in communication while they are developing strategies for negotiating meaning.

Another type of teacher feedback strategy that has been found to be effective in student uptake is *corrective confirmation checks*, in which the teacher provides learners with an appropriate L2 alternative in the form of a question, such as *"Did you mean, 'he goes?'"* (O'Relly, Flaitz, & Kromrey, 2001). These types of confirmation checks call attention to a linguistic problem in an unambiguous way. There are data to suggest that the use of feedback strategies such as clarification requests and corrective confirmation checks are most effective in reinforcing linguistic features that have already been introduced to and internalized by learners (O'Relly, Flaitz, & Kromrey), particularly since they have the knowledge necessary to make repairs.

Liebscher & Dailey-O'Cain (2003) recently compared conversational repair strategies in exchanges between teacher and advanced learners of German to repair strategies used in discourse outside the classroom. Their data revealed that repair initiation in classroom interaction differs from repair initiation in discourse outside the classroom. In the face of trouble in speaking, hearing, or understanding in a conversation, native speakers in naturally occurring discourse tend to use other-initiated strategies that are "less specific" at first (e.g., *Pardon?, Huh?, Hmm?*) (Schegloff, Jefferson, & Sacks, 1977). If these strategies are unsuccessful, they move on to "more specific" strategies as necessary, such as individual question words (e.g., *Who?, Where?, When?*), then to partial repeats of the trouble source, to partial repeats plus question words, to the most specific devices consisting of "you mean" plus a possible understanding of the prior turn (Liebscher & Dailey-O'Cain, 2003, pp. 376–377). The most specific devices to which they refer are the corrective confirmation checks described in the previous paragraph.

In the Liebscher & Dailey-O'Cain (2003) study, the teacher often used "less specific" repair initiations with students (i.e., those found in naturally occurring discourse). These repair initiations enabled students to effectively modify their output and thus make successful conversational repairs. This finding corroborates that of the Lyster & Ranta (1997) study that identified clarification requests to be an effective strategy for eliciting uptake from students. On the other hand, students in this study showed a marked preference for using more specific repair initiation techniques, i.e., those not found as prevalent in natural discourse, when they didn't understand what the teacher was saying, in an effort to avoid behaving in what might seem to be a confrontational manner, outside of the norms for student-to-teacher interaction. In initiating repairs themselves, students usually asked for specific vocabulary items, showing the teacher that they were trying to understand the vocabulary used and that they were following classroom discourse—thus enacting their designated roles as typical learners.

Liebscher & Dailey-O'Cain (2003) interpret the findings of their study to mean that (1) what keeps students from using certain types of repairs is an understanding of their roles in the classroom rather than an insufficient knowledge of L2; (2) the teaching of naturally occurring repair strategies must occur in classroom environments in which students are free to use such strategies and thus step out of their traditional learner roles; (3) students should be encouraged to use less specific repair initiations, especially in interactions with the teacher, because these are most effective in leading to modified output by the teacher and modified input for students; and (4) teachers should use repair strategies such as less specific repairs in order to facilitate modified output by students (p. 388).

In highly communicative or group activities, the teacher might do best to make mental notes of patterns of errors and use them as the focus for subsequent language activities. Kramsch suggests extensive use of natural feedback (i.e., IRF) rather than overpraising everything students say. Statements such as "Yes, that's interesting," "I can certainly understand that!" "That's incredible!" and "Hmm, that's right" show students that teachers are listening to what they're saying, and this strategy encourages students to focus more on meaning. When conversing with the class as a follow-up to group interaction, Kramsch also proposes that teachers give students explicit credit for their contributions by quoting them ("As X just said, . . ."). In this way, teachers are not taking credit for what students have said by using it to suggest their own ideas.

At more advanced levels of study, where one of the goals is to refine language use, students can be given increasingly greater responsibility for their accuracy. The following are a few ideas that merit further research:

- Peer editing of oral language samples: The teacher records role plays or situations that students enact in the classroom, after which pairs of students listen to the tapes in order to correct linguistic errors and identify ways to improve the content.
- Teacher feedback: At certain designated times throughout the year or semester, perhaps following speaking exams, the teacher gives helpful feedback to each student concerning progress made in speaking. This feedback can include patterns of errors that merit attention, with specific suggestions on how to improve accuracy.
- Error tracking system: As a class, students listen to tapes of themselves and, with the teacher's help, compile a listing of the kinds of errors they hear. They focus on eliminating certain errors over a specified period of time and agree on a system to check and reward their efforts.

Clearly, a great deal of research is still needed in order to understand more fully the role of feedback in interpersonal communication contexts. The research presented here points to the following implications regarding error correction and feedback in the classroom:

1. Students benefit most when the feedback they receive focuses on comprehensibility of the message itself, not just on accuracy of form.
2. The feedback strategies that lead to negotiation of form most effectively are elicitation, clarification requests, metalinguistic feedback, and repetition.
3. Learners may not recognize teacher response as corrective in nature unless the teacher has a strategy for signaling this to the learner.
4. Student-generated repairs may help learners to access target language forms and revise hypotheses about the target language.
5. The classroom environment should be one in which learners are encouraged to step out of their traditional learner roles when engaging in conversational repair.
6. Teachers should use less specific repair initiations with students and provide opportunities for students to use them as a strategy for facilitating uptake or modified input.
7. In order to focus on fluency and comprehensibility of speech, it is best to avoid trying to coerce correction of errors in speaking and to allow the interaction to develop as it would in natural discourse.
8. Teacher feedback should include comments that help the student to focus on negotiation of meaning.
9. Students should be made increasingly more responsible for their language accuracy so that their oral proficiency can improve.

This chapter presented many ideas for developing oral and written interpersonal communication. Continue to keep in mind that the approach of *Teacher's Handbook* is that all three modes of communication should be integrated closely, as described in the model presented in Chapter 6.

TEACH AND REFLECT

EPISODE ONE
Creating Information-Gap Activities for Various Levels of Instruction

NCATE
STANDARDS
3.a., 3.b.,
4.b., 4.c.

Create the following information-gap activities in the language you teach, according to the following instructions:

1. Elementary-school level: Design an information-gap activity that would be appropriate for elementary school children. You might create this for the content-based lesson you designed in the Teach and Reflect section of Chapter 4, or you could create it for practice within another context. Decide what the purpose of the activity is and how it relates to your unit objectives. Include specific directions for students and your procedure for grouping students (i.e., what you will do if you don't have an even number). Your instructor may ask you to present your activity to the class.
2. Secondary-school level: Create an information-gap activity to promote interpersonal speaking among your students. Decide what the purpose of the activity is and how it relates to your thematic unit objectives. What functions/contexts will students practice? What grammar and vocabulary are integrated? Include specific directions for students and your procedure for grouping students. Your instructor may ask you to present your activity to the class.

EPISODE TWO
Integrating Speaking with Oral or Printed Texts

NCATE
STANDARDS
3.a., 3.b.,
4.b., 4.c.

For this activity, work from the authentic reading or taped segment that you prepared in the Teach and Reflect section of Chapter 6, or work with a literary reading, such as a short story. Design the following three activities for integrating interpersonal speaking as a follow-up to exploration of the oral or written text:

1. an interactive activity, such as a movement activity, paired interview, or role play
2. an imaginative activity, such as changing the text or reenacting a part of the text
3. an open-ended discussion

Identify the objective of each activity. Include instructions to the students and your procedure for grouping students, if applicable. Your instructor may ask you to present one or more of these activities to the class.

EPISODE THREE
Integrating Advanced-Level Discourse at the Post-Secondary Level

NCATE
STANDARDS
3.a., 3.b.,
4.b., 4.c.

If you are preparing to teach or are already teaching at the post-secondary level, this task is designed to engage you in incorporating advanced-level discourse into your teaching. Select an authentic oral, printed, or video text for a course that you are teaching on culture, literature, conversation, or a content-based topic, in which students are working on using advanced-level functions. Use the interactive model for integrating the three modes of communication that you learned about in Chapter 6 to develop a lesson plan for guiding students through the text. Then develop three ideas for how you will build advanced-level discourse into your exploration of the content of the text.

DISCUSS AND REFLECT

CASE STUDY ONE
Interpersonal Speaking? I Already Do That!

NCATE
STANDARDS
3.a., 3.b.,
4.a., 4.b.,
4.c., 6.a.

Ms. Jacqueline Krause is a French teacher in a wealthy suburban school district in the eastern United States, where she has taught French for fifteen years and been chair of the Modern Languages Department for the past five years. She is a popular French teacher who usually attends at least one professional language conference each year and travels to France every other summer. Ms. Krause also mentors new teachers. This year her department has hired a new French teacher, Mr. Ray Polk, who comes to the district with three years of teaching experience in a midwestern state.

One of Mr. Polk's impressive qualifications is that he has recently completed course requirements for a Master of Arts in Teaching degree and only has his thesis left to write in order to finish the program. At the start of the school year, Mr. Polk and Ms. Krause are discussing Mr. Polk's area of interest for his thesis project. He tells her that he is exploring the idea of doing a project on the teaching of interpersonal speaking in the classroom. He has read a lot about it in recent professional literature and has attended several workshops on the topic. Furthermore, he feels that this is an area of his teaching that he needs to improve.

Ms. Krause is a bit surprised by Mr. Polk's choice of topic, and she tells him that most teachers, including herself, have "already been doing interpersonal communication" in their classrooms for many years before the standards came along. She explains that she can't see how there is "much new stuff" involved in interpersonal communication. After all, she uses these types of strategies in her class and students spend a lot of time speaking:

- She starts the class with a warm-up to engage students in speaking, by asking them questions about the weather, today's date, how they are feeling, what they did last night, and what plans they have for tomorrow. She tries to ask every student a question, although with larger classes, this isn't always possible.
- She puts students in pairs to review the homework assignment so that they have more opportunities to talk.
- She conducts several pair and small-group communicative activities, mostly from the department's new textbook, and afterwards she is sure to have students report back the information they learned as a result of talking to a classmate.
- At least twice a grading period, she has students create dialogues and present memorized versions of them to the class.
- At least once a grading period, she has students do oral presentations in front of the class on a topic of their choice, such as a holiday or French-speaking region.

Ms. Krause indicates that she would be interested in comparing her view of interpersonal speaking with that of Mr. Polk, especially in light of his ideas for a thesis project.

Ask yourself these questions:

1. Why does Ms. Krause feel that she has "already been doing interpersonal speaking" in her classroom?
2. How does Ms. Krause's description of interpersonal communication compare to that of the standards and the information you learned in this chapter? What aspects of interpersonal communication are absent from her teaching?
3. How might Mr. Polk illustrate for Ms. Krause "what's new" about interpersonal communication in a nonthreatening, professional manner?
4. After hearing Ms. Krause's description, what specific ideas might have occurred to Mr. Polk regarding the development of a thesis project?

To prepare the case:

1. Read Hall (1999) for more information about classroom discourse, instructional conversations, and supportive learning environments as they relate to the development of interpersonal communication in the classroom.
2. Read Taylor (2002) & McCafferty (2002) to understand more about the role of features of interpersonal communication, such as conversational gambits and gestures, and how to incorporate them into your teaching and classroom interaction.
3. Observe a class in the target language that you teach for the purpose of examining the degree to which interpersonal communication takes place.

To prepare for class discussion:

1. Comment on each of Ms. Krause's classroom strategies as they relate to interpersonal communication and offer a suggestion for how each strategy could be improved.
2. Design a professional development plan for Ms. Krause in order for her to gain the knowledge and expertise necessary for integrating interpersonal speaking into her teaching.
3. Design a proposal for a thesis project for Mr. Polk that deals with the integration of more effective oral interpersonal communication in his classroom.

NCATE_____
STANDARDS
2.a., 2.b.,
3.a., 3.b.,
4.a., 4.b.,
4.c.

CASE STUDY TWO
Friday Is Culture Day

Ms. Beecher has been teaching Spanish and social studies at Pelican High School for eight years. Her approach to teaching Spanish is essentially communicative in nature, as she involves her students in meaningful interaction with one another. She occasionally uses cooperative learning in her classes, although she is still experimenting with various techniques. Ms. Beecher travels to Hispanic countries frequently and brings back materials, such as slides, posters, magazines, and realia that she can use in her classes.

Today is Friday and a rather chaotic day, because students are having their individual and club pictures taken for the yearbook. Ms. Beecher realizes that she can accomplish very little today in terms of serious work, so she decides to pull out her slides from Peru and show them to her classes.

After her first-period Spanish II class enters her classroom, Ms. Beecher explains that she will be showing slides from Peru while describing them in Spanish. She asks students to take notes on the presentation, since she will be asking them questions later.

After a twenty-five minute slide presentation, Ms. Beecher begins asking questions about the slides she has presented. She is amazed and a little upset when she discovers that students have not taken notes as she instructed and can not answer most of her questions.

Ask yourself these questions:

1. What was Ms. Beecher's real objective in presenting the slide demonstration?
2. What might this lesson indicate about Ms. Beecher's approach to teaching culture?
3. Ms. Beecher thought that no serious work could be done today. What do you think she meant by "serious"? Was she justified in thinking this?
4. Why do you think the students failed to take notes during the slide presentation?
5. What are some possible student reactions to Ms. Beecher's activity?

To prepare the case:

1. Read Schwartz & Kavanaugh (1997) & Haas & Reardon (1997) for information on approaches to integrating Cultures and the other goal areas into language teaching.
2. Read Chapter 10 of Curtain & Dahlberg (2004), which deals with experiencing culture in the classroom.
3. Read Walz (1996) to find ways to incorporate information-gap activities with a cultural lesson.
4. Interview an experienced social studies teacher to learn about strategies he or she uses for teaching students about other cultures.

To prepare for class discussion:

1. If you were Ms. Beecher, how might you (1) integrate this slide presentation into classroom work on a given unit, and (2) use cooperative learning as a strategy for helping students understand and discuss the information given in the presentation?
2. What are some ways that Ms. Beecher might use her skill in teaching social studies as a vehicle for integrating culture into her Spanish curriculum?
3. What might you do with your classes on a day similar to Ms. Beecher's chaotic Friday?
4. Now choose a cultural concept and design one task that addresses the oral interpersonal mode and one task that addresses the written interpersonal mode of the Communication goal area.

REFERENCES

American Council on the Teaching of Foreign Languages. (1999). *ACTFL Proficiency Guidelines—Speaking.* Yonkers, NY: Author.

American Council on the Teaching of Foreign Languages. (2001). *ACTFL Proficiency Guidelines—Writing.* Yonkers, NY: Author.

American Council on the Teaching of Foreign Languages. (1982). *ACTFL Provisional Proficiency Guidelines.* Hastings-on-Hudson, NY: Author.

Annenberg/CPB, & American Council on the Teaching of Foreign Languages. (2003). *Teaching Foreign Language*

K–12: A library of classroom practices. Boston: WGBH Boston and ACTFL.

Bassano, S., & Christison, M. A. (1987). Developing successful conversation groups. In M. H. Long & J. C. Richards (Eds.), *Methodology in TESOL: A book of readings* (pp. 201–207). New York: Newbury House/Harper.

Beauvois, M. H. (1998). Write to speak: The effects of electronic communication on the oral achievement of fourth-semester French students. In J. A. Muyskens (Ed.), *New ways of learning and teaching: Focus on technology and foreign language education* (pp. 93–116). Boston: Heinle & Heinle.

Bernhardt, E., & Kamil, M. (1998). Enhancing foreign culture learning through electronic discussion. In J. A. Muyskens (Ed.), *New ways of learning and teaching: Focus on technology and foreign language education* (pp. 39–55). Boston: Heinle & Heinle.

Borich, J. M. B. (2001). Learning through dialogue journal writing: A cultural thematic unit. *Learning Languages, 6,* 4–19.

Bragger, J. (1985). The development of oral proficiency. In A. Omaggio (Ed.), *Proficiency, curriculum, articulation: The ties that bind* (pp. 41–75) Northeast Conference Reports. Middlebury, VT: Northeast Conference on the Teaching of Foreign Languages.

Brecht, R. D., Davidson, D., & Ginsberg, R. B. (1993). *Predictors of foreign language gain during study abroad.* Washington, DC: National Foreign Language Center.

Breiner-Sanders, K. E. (1991). Higher-level language abilities: The skills connection. In J. K. Phillips (Ed.), *Building Bridges and Making Connections* (pp. 57–88) Northeast Conference Reports. Middlebury, VT: Northeast Conference on the Teaching of Foreign Languages.

Brooks, F. B. (1990). Foreign language learning: A social interaction perspective. In B. VanPatten & J. F. Lee (Eds.), *Second language acquisition—Foreign language learning* (pp. 153–169). Clevedon, UK: Multilingual Matters.

Brooks, F. B. (1992). Can we talk? *Foreign Language Annals, 25,* 59–71.

Brooks, F. B., & Donato, R. (1994). Vygotskyan approaches to understanding foreign language learner discourse during communicative tasks. *Hispania, 77,* 262–274.

Brooks, F. B., Donato, R., & McGlone, V. (1997). When are they going to say "it" right? Understanding learner talk during pair-work activity. *Foreign Language Annals, 30,* 524–541.

Brown, P., & Levinson, S. C. (1987). *Politeness: Universals in language usage.* Cambridge, UK: Cambridge University Press.

Buckwalter, P. (2001). Repair sequences in Spanish L2 dyadic discourse: A descriptive study. *The Modern Language Journal, 85,* 380–397.

Canale, M. (1982). *Evaluating the coherence of student writing in L1 and L2.* Paper presented at annual Teachers of English to Speakers of Other Languages (TESOL) convention. Honolulu, HI.

Cazden, C. B. (1992). Performing expository texts in the foreign language classroom. In C. Kramsch & S. McConnell-Ginet (Eds.), *Text and context: Cross disciplinary perspectives on language study* (pp. 67–78). Lexington, MA: Heath.

Clifford, R. (Ed.) (2003). The OPI has everyone talking. *Foreign Language Annals, 36,* 481–482.

Cook, L. (1991). Cooperative learning: A successful college teaching strategy. *Innovative Higher Education, 16,* 27–38.

Crookes, G., & Gass, S. M. (Eds.). (1993a). *Tasks and language learning: Integrating theory and practice.* Clevedon, UK: Multilingual Matters.

Crookes, G., & Gass, S. M. (Eds) (1993b). *Tasks in a pedagogical context: Integrating theory and practice.* Clevedon, UK: Multilingual Matters.

Curtain, H. A., & Dahlberg, C. A. (2004). *Languages and children—Making the match* (3rd ed.). Boston: Pearson Education.

DeKeyser, R. M. (1991). Foreign language development during a semester abroad. In B. F. Freed (Ed.). *Foreign language acquisition research and the classroom* (pp. 104–119). Lexington, MA: D.C. Heath.

DiPietro, R. J. (1987). *Strategic interaction: Learning languages through scenarios.* New York: Cambridge University Press.

Donato, R., Antonek, J. L., & Tucker, G. R. (1996). Documenting a Japanese FLES program: Ambiance and achievement. *Language Learning, 46,* 497–528.

Donato, R., & Brooks, F. B. (1994). *Looking across collaborative tasks: Capturing L2 discourse development.* Paper presented at annual meeting of the American Association for Applied Linguistics. Baltimore, MD.

Donato, R., & Brooks, F. B. (2004). Literary discussions and advanced speaking functions: Researching the (dis)connection. *Foreign Language Annals, 37,* 183–199.

Dörnyei, Z. (1995). On the teachability of communication strategies. *TESOL Quarterly, 29,* 55–85.

Doughty, C., & Pica, T. (1986). Information gap tasks: Do they facilitate acquisition? *TESOL Quarterly, 20,* 315–326.

Dreke, M., & Lind, W. (2000). *Wechselspiel.* New York: Langenscheidt.

Ellis, R. (1990). *Instructed second language acquisition.* Cambridge, MA: Blackwell.

Ellis, R. (1994). *The study of second language acquisition.* Oxford, UK: Oxford University Press.

Fischer, G. (1998). Toward the creation of virtual classrooms: Electronic mail and cross-cultural understanding. In A. Moeller (Ed.), *Celebrating diversity in the language classroom.* Lincolnwood, IL: National Textbook Company.

Florez-Estrada, N. (1995). *Some effects of native-nonnative communication via computer e-mail interaction on the development of foreign language proficiency.* Unpublished doctoral dissertation. University of Pittsburgh, PA.

Fotos, S., & Ellis, R. (1991). Communicating about grammar: A task-based approach. *TESOL Quarterly, 25,* 605–628.

Freed, B., & Bauer, B. W. (1989). *Contextos: Spanish for communication*. New York: Newbury House.

Galloway, V. (1992). Toward a cultural reading of authentic texts. In H. Byrnes (Ed.), *Languages for a multicultural world in transition,* Northeast Conference Reports (pp. 87–121). Lincolnwood, IL: NTC/Contemporary Publishing Group.

Gass, S., & Selinker, L. (1994). *Second language acquisition*. Hillsdale, NJ: Lawrence Erlbaum.

Glisan, E. W., & Donato, R. (2004). It's not just a matter of "time:" A response to Rifkin. *Foreign Language Annals, 37,* 465–471.

Glisan, E. W., & Foltz, D. A. (1998). Assessing students' oral proficiency in an outcome-based curriculum: Student performance and teacher intuitions. *The Modern Language Journal, 82,* 1–18.

Goldenberg, C. (1991). *Instructional conversations and their classroom implication*. Washington, DC: The National Center for Research on Cultural Diversity and Second Language Learning. (ERIC Document Reproduction Service No. 341-253).

González-Bueno, M. (1998). The effect of electronic mail on Spanish L2 discourse. *Language Learning and Technology, 1*(2), 55–70. Retrieved March 17, 2004, from http://www.polyglot.cal.msu/llt/num1vol2/article3.

González Bueno, M., & Pérez, L. C. (2000). Electronic mail in foreign language writing: A study of grammatical and lexical accuracy, and quantity of language. *Foreign Language Annals, 33,* 189–198.

Haas, M., & Reardon, M. (1997). Communities of learners: From New York to Chile. In J. K. Phillips (Ed.), *Collaborations: Meeting new goals, new realities* (pp. 213–241) Northeast Conference Reports. Lincolnwood, IL: NTC/Contemporary Publishing Group.

Hadfield, J. (1984). *Elementary communication games: A collection of games and activities for elementary students of English*. Walton-on-Thames, UK: Thomas Nelson.

Hadley, A. O. (2001). *Teaching language in context* (3rd ed.). Boston: Heinle & Heinle.

Hall, J. K. (1999). The communication standards. In J. K. Phillips & R. M. Terry (Eds.), *Foreign language standards: Linking research, theories, and practices* (pp. 15–56). ACTFL Foreign Language Education Series. Lincolnwood, IL: NTC/Contemporary Publishing Group.

Hall, N., & Robinson, A. (Eds.). (1994). Keeping in touch: Using interactive writing with young children. *ERIC Database:* ERIC Document Reproduction Service No. ED 367–996.

Hatch, E. (1978). Discourse analysis and second language acquisition. In *Second language acquisition* (pp. 401–435). Rowley, MA: Newbury House.

Hertel, T. J. (2003). Using en e-mail exchange to promote cultural learning. *Foreign Language Annals, 36,* 386–396.

Herzog, M. (2003). Impact of the proficiency scale and the oral proficiency interview on the foreign language program at the Defense Language Institute Foreign Language Center. *Foreign Language Annals, 36,* 566–571.

Huebner, T., & Jensen, A. (1992). A study of foreign language proficiency-based testing in secondary schools. *Foreign Language Annals, 25,* 105–115.

Ittzes, Z. (1997). *Written conversation: Investigating communicative foreign language use in written form in computer conference writing and group journals*. Unpublished doctoral dissertation, The University of Arizona, Tucson.

Jansma, K., & Kassen, M. A. (2004). *Motifs*. Boston: Heinle.

Jensen, J. M. (1993). What do we know about the writing of elementary school children? *Language Arts, 70,* 290–294.

Jogan, M. K., Heredia, A. H., & Aguilera, G. M. (2001). Cross-cultural e-mail: Providing cultural input for the advanced foreign language student. *Foreign Language Annals, 34,* 341–346.

Johnson, D. D., & Johnson, R. T. (1987). *Learning together and alone: Cooperation, competition, and individualization*. Englewood Cliffs, NJ: Prentice Hall.

Johnson, D. D., Johnson, R. T., & Holubec, E. J. (1988). *Cooperation in the classroom*. Edina, MN: Interaction Book Company.

Johnson, K. (1979). Communicative approaches and communicative processes. In C. J. Brumfit & K. Johnson (Eds.), *The communicative approach to language teaching* (pp. 192–205). Oxford: Oxford University Press.

Kagan, S. (1989). *Cooperative learning: Resources for teachers*. San Juan Capistrano, CA: Resources for Teachers.

Keller, E. (1981). Gambits: Conversational strategy signals. In F. Coulmas (Ed), *Conversational routine*. The Hague: Mouton.

Kern, R. (1998). Technology, social interaction, and foreign language literacy. In J. A. Muyskens (Ed.), *New ways of learning and teaching: Focus on technology and foreign language education* (pp. 57–92). Boston: Heinle & Heinle.

Kinginger, C. (1990). *Task variation and classroom learner discourse*. Unpublished doctoral dissertation. University of Illinois, Urbana-Champaign.

Kinginger, C. (1994). Learner initiative in conversation management: An application of van Lier's pilot coding scheme. *The Modern Language Journal, 78,* 29–40.

Kohn, A. (1987). It's hard to get out of a pair: Profile: David & Roger Johnson. *Psychology Today,* (October): 53–57.

Kramsch, C. (1981). Teaching discussion skills: A pragmatic approach. *Foreign Language Annals, 14,* 93–104.

Kramsch, C. (1987). Interactive discourse in small and large groups. In W. Rivers (Ed.), *Interactive language teaching* (pp. 17–30). Cambridge, UK: Cambridge University Press.

Krashen, S. (1982). *Principles and practice in second language acquisition*. New York: Pergamon Press.

Lee, J. (1995). Using task-based instruction to restructure class discussions. *Foreign Language Annals, 28,* 437–446.

Lee, L. (1997). Using Internet tools as an enhancement of L2 cultural teaching and learning. *Foreign Language Annals, 30,* 410–427.

Lee, L. (2002). Enhancing learners' communication skills through synchronous electronic interaction and task-based instruction. *Foreign Language Annals, 35,* 16–24.

Lennon, P. (1990). Investigating fluency in EFL: A quantitative approach. *Language Learning, 40,* 387–417.

Liebscher, G., & Dailey-O'Cain, J. (2003). Conversational repair as a role-defining mechanism in classroom interaction. *The Modern Language Journal, 87,* 375–390.

Lightbown, P. M., & Spada, N. (1990). Focus on form and corrective feedback in communicative language teaching. *Studies in Second Language Acquisition, 12,* 429–448.

Lightbown, P. M., & Spada, N. (2003). *How languages are learned.* Oxford, UK: Oxford University Press.

Liskin-Gasparro, J. E. (1987). If you can't use a language, you don't know a language. *Middlebury Magazine,* (Winter): 26–27.

Liskin-Gasparro, J. E. (1996). Circumlocution, communication strategies, and the ACTFL proficiency guidelines: An analysis of student discourse. *Foreign Language Annals, 29,* 317–330.

Liskin-Gasparro, J. E. (2003). The ACTFL Proficiency Guidelines and the Oral Proficiency Interview: A brief history and analysis of their survival. *Foreign Language Annals, 36,* 483–490.

Long, M. H. (1983). Native speaker/non-native speaker conversation in the second language classroom. In M. A. Clarke & J. Handscomb (Eds.), *On TESOL '82: Pacific perspectives on language learning and teaching* (pp. 207–205). Washington, DC: TESOL.

Long, M. H., & Crookes, G. (1986). Intervention points in second language classroom processes. Paper presented at Regional Language Center seminar. Singapore.

Lyster, R., & Ranta, L. (1997). Corrective feedback and learner uptake. *Studies in Second Language Acquisition, 19,* 37–61.

Magnan, S. S. (1986). Assessing speaking proficiency in the undergraduate curriculum: Data from French. *Foreign Language Annals, 19,* 429–438.

Mantero, M. (2002). Bridging the gap: Discourse in text-based foreign language classrooms. *Foreign Language Annals, 35,* 437–455.

McCafferty, S. G. (2002). Gestures and creating zones of proximal development for second language learning. *The Modern Language Journal, 86,* 192–203.

Mings, R. C. (1993). Changing perspectives on the utility of error correction in second language acquisition. *Foreign Language Annals, 26,* 171–179.

Moeller, A., & Reschke, C. (1993). A second look at grading and classroom performance: Report of a research study. *The Modern Language Journal, 77,* 163–169.

Montás, M. (2003). Observing progress and achievement of beginning students in a fourth-grade Spanish FLES program. *Learning Languages, 9,* 8–20.

National Standards in Foreign Language Education Project (NSLEP). (1996). *National standards for foreign language learning: Preparing for the 21st century.* Lawrence, KS: Allen Press.

National Standards in Foreign Language Education Project (NSFLEP). (1999). *Standards for foreign language learning in the 21st century.* Lawrence, KS: Allen Press.

Norman, U. (1996). Promoting spontaneous speech in the EFL class. *Foreign Language Annals, 29,* 597–604.

O'Relly, L. V., Flaitz, J., & Kromrey, J. (2001). Two modes of correcting communicative tasks: Recent findings. *Foreign Language Annals, 34,* 246–257.

Oxford, R. L. (1992). Encouraging initiative and interest through the cooperative "Heritage Project." *Northeast Conference on the Teaching of Foreign Languages Newsletter, 32,* 13–16.

Palinscar, A. S., Brown, A., & Campione, J. (1993). First-grade dialogues for knowledge acquisition and use. In E. Forman, N. Minick, & C. A. Stone (Eds.), *Contexts for learning: Sociocultural dynamics in children's development* (pp. 43–57). New York: Oxford University Press.

Patthey-Chavez, G. G., Clare, L., & Gallimore, R. (1995). *Creating a community of scholarship with instructional conversations in a transitional bilingual classroom.* Washington, DC: The National Center for Research on Cultural Diversity and Second Language Learning.

Pelletieri, J. (2000). Negotiation in cyberspace: The role of chatting in the development of grammatical competence. In M. Warschauer & R. Kern (Eds.), *Network-based language teaching: Concepts and practice* (pp. 59–86). Cambridge, UK: Cambridge University Press.

Peregoy, S. F., & Boyle, O. F. (2001). *Reading, writing and learning in ESL: A resource book for K-12 teachers* (3rd ed.). New York: Addison-Wesley Longman.

Peyton, J. K. (1987). Dialogue journal writing with limited English proficient students. Washington, DC: Center for Applied Linguistics.

Peyton, J. K. (1990). *Students and teachers writing together: Perspectives on journal writing.* Alexandria, VA: TESOL.

Peyton, J. K. (1993). Dialogue journals: Interactive writing to develop language and literacy. *ERIC Digest.* Retrieved February 28, 2004, from http://www.cal.org/ericcll/ digest/peyton01.html.

Peyton, J. K., & Reed, L. (1990). *Dialogue journal writing with non-native English speakers: A handbook for teachers.* Alexandria, VA: TESOL.

Phillips, J. K. (Ed.). (1997). *Collaborations: Meeting new goals, new realities.* Northeast Conference Reports. Lincolnwood, IL: NTC/Contemporary Publishing Group.

Pica, T., & Long, M. H. (1986). The linguistic and conversational performance of experienced and inexperienced teachers. In R. R. Day (Ed.), *Talking to learn: Conversation in second language acquisition* (pp. 85–98). Rowley, MA: Newbury House.

Platt, E., & Brooks, F. B. (1994). The acquisition-rich environment revisited. *The Modern Language Journal, 78,* 497–511.

Porter, P. A. (1986). How learners talk to each other: Input and interaction in task-centered discussions. In R. R. Day (Ed.), *Talking to learn: Conversation in second language acquisition* (pp. 200–224). Rowley, MA: Newbury House.

Reichelt, M. (2001). A critical review of foreign language writing research on pedagogical approaches. *The Modern Language Journal, 85,* 578–598.

Richard-Amato, P. A. (1988). *Making it happen: Interaction in the second language classroom.* New York: Longman.

Richards, J. (1985). The context of language teaching. Cambridge, UK: Cambridge University Press.

Richards, J., Platt, J., & Weber, H. (1985). *Longman dictionary of applied linguistics.* New York: Longman.

Rifkin, B. (2003). Oral proficiency learning outcomes and curricular design. *Foreign Language Annals, 36,* 582–588.

Rubio, F. (2003). Structure and complexity of oral narratives in advanced-level Spanish: A comparison of three learning backgrounds. *Foreign Language Annals, 36,* 546–554.

Rueda, R., Goldenberg, C. & Gallimore, R. (1992). *Rating instructional conversations: A guide.* Washington, DC: The National Center for Research on Cultural Diversity and Language Learning.

Sadow, S. A. (1982). *Idea bank: Creative activities for the language class.* Rowley, MA: Newbury House.

Sadow, S. A. (1987). Speaking and listening: Imaginative activities for the language class. In W. M. Rivers (Ed.), *Interactive language teaching* (pp. 33–43). Cambridge, UK: Cambridge University Press.

Sadow, S. A. (1994). "Concoctions": Intrinsic motivation, creative thinking, frame theory, and structured interactions in the language class. *Foreign Language Annals, 27,* 241–251.

Scarcella, R. C., & Oxford, R. L. (1992). *The tapestry of language learning.* Boston: Heinle & Heinle.

Schegloff, E. A., Jefferson, G., & Sacks, H. (1977). The preference for self-correction in the organization of repair in conversation. *Language, 53,* 361–382.

Schwartz, A. M., & Kavanaugh, M. S. (1997). Addressing the culture goal with authentic video. In J. K. Phillips (Ed.), *Collaborations: Meeting new goals, new realities* (pp. 97–139). Northeast Conference Reports. Lincolnwood, IL: NTC/Contemporary Publishing Group.

Shohamy, E. (1998). Assessing foreign language abilities of early language learners: A reaction. In M. Met (Ed.), *Critical issues in early second language learning: Building for our children's future* (pp. 185–191). Glenview, IL: Scott Foresman-Addison Wesley.

Shonerd, H. (1994). Repair in spontaneous speech: A window on second language development. In V. John-Stiner, C. P. Panofsky, & L. W. Smith (Eds.), *Sociocultural approaches to language and literacy* (pp. 82–108). Cambridge, UK: Cambridge University Press.

Slavin, R. E. (1986). *Using student team learning.* Baltimore, MD: Johns Hopkins University Press.

Steinmeyer, G. (1984). Oral proficiency interviews at Amherst Regional High School: Report of a pilot project. *Unterrichtspraxis, 17,* 330–334.

Swender, E. (1999). *ACTFL oral proficiency interview tester training manual.* Yonkers, NY: ACTFL.

Swender, E. (2003). Oral proficiency testing in the real world: Answers to frequently asked questions. *Foreign Language Annals, 36,* 520–526.

Szostek, C. (1994). Assessing the effects of cooperative learning in an honors foreign language classroom. *Foreign Language Annals, 27,* 252–261.

Taylor, G. (2002). Teaching gambits: The effect of instruction and task variation on the use of conversation strategies by intermediate Spanish students. *Foreign Language Annals, 35,* 171–189.

Terrell, T. (1985). The natural approach to language teaching: An update. *The Canadian Modern Language Review, 41,* 461–479.

Tharp, R. G., & Gallimore, R. (1988). *Rousing minds to life: Teaching, learning, and schooling in social context.* New York: Cambridge University Press.

Thompson, I. (1996). Assessing foreign language skills: Data from Russian. *The Modern Language Journal, 80,* 47–65.

Tschirner, E. (1993). *Developing grammars: Acquired grammatical systems of beginning and intermediate students.* Paper presented at the annual meeting of the American Association of Teachers of German, San Antonio, TX.

Tschirner, E., & Heilenman, L. K. (1998). Reasonable expectations: Oral proficiency goals for intermediate-level students of German. *The Modern Language Journal, 82,* 147–158.

Ur, P. (1981). Discussions that work: Task-centred fluency practice. Cambridge, UK: Cambridge University Press.

Van Handle, D. C., & Corl, K. A. (1998). Extending the dialogue: Using electronic mail and the Internet to promote conversation and writing in intermediate level German language courses. *CALICO Journal, 15,* 129–143.

van Lier, L. (1988). *The classroom and the language learner.* London: Longman.

Vygotsky, L. (1978). *Mind in society: The development of higher psychological processes.* Cambridge, MA: Harvard University Press.

Walz, J. (1996). The classroom dynamics of information-gap activities. *Foreign Language Annals, 29,* 481–494.

Wang, Y. (1998). Email dialogue journaling in an English as a Second Language (ESL) Reading and Writing Classroom. *International Journal of Educational Telecommunications 4(2),* 263–287. Retrieved August 27, 2004, from http://dl.aace.org/9244.

Warschauer, M. (1995). *E-mail for English teaching.* Alexandria, VA: TESOL.

Warschauer, M., & Healey, D. (1998). Computers and language learning. *Foreign Language Annals, 31,* 51–72.

Wells, G. (1985). Language development in the pre-school years. Cambridge, UK: Cambridge University Press.

Wells, G. (1999). *Dialogic inquiry: Toward a sociocultural practice and theory of education.* Cambridge, UK: Cambridge University Press.

West, M. J., & Donato, R. (1995). Stories and stances: Cross-cultural encounters with African folktales. *Foreign Language Annals, 28,* 392–406.

Wildner-Bassett, M. (1984). *Improving pragmatic aspects of learner's interlanguage.* Tubingen: Narr.

Wilkinson, S. (2002). The omnipresent classroom during summer study abroad: American students in conversation with their French hosts. *The Modern Language Journal, 86,* 157–173.

Wilson-Duffy, C. (2003a). Creating online language activities: Putting task-based language teaching to use (Part 1). *CLEAR News, 7*(1), 1, 3–4.

Wilson-Duffy, C. (2003b). Creating online language activities: Putting task-based language teaching to use (Part 2). *CLEAR News, 7*(2), 1, 3, 6–7.

Wong, W., & VanPatten, B. (2003). The evidence is IN: Drills are OUT. *Foreign Language Annals, 36,* 403–423.

Yamada, Y., & Moeller, A. J. (2001). Weaving curricular standards into the language classroom: An action research study. *Foreign Language Annals, 34,* 26–33.

Yorio, C. (1980). Conventionalized language forms and the development of communicative competence. *TESOL Quarterly, 14,* 433–442.

NOTES

1. It should be noted that uncertified testers were used in the Huebner & Jensen (1992) & Steinmeyer (1984) studies.

2. Their study also provides an extensive and helpful review of recent studies that report average OPI levels of high school and college students.

3. Thompson's study occurred before the introduction of the new Advanced-Mid level.

4. See Rubio (2003) for detailed explanations and examples of external and internal evaluation devices.

5. For a review of many research-based activities that use cooperative learning in the college classroom, refer to Cook (1991).

6. Many thanks to Dr. Thekla Fall for her translation of the German in this IGA.

7. For a wealth of activities designed to promote divergent thinking and language production, consult Sadow (1982).

8. In both the Schwartz and Kavanaugh and the Haas and Reardon projects, students also designed and presented oral presentations on related cultural topics that they had researched.

9. For more information, consult http://www.blackboard.com and Lee (2002).

10. Providing feedback for written work is discussed in Chapter 9.

Developing Oral and Written Presentational Communication

In this chapter, you will learn about:

- presentational communication in speaking and writing
- the nature and purposes of oral and written presentational communication
- a problem-solving model of the L1 writing process
- teaching presentational writing and speaking as a process
- the importance of audience
- formats for presentational communication at the elementary, middle, and high school levels

- reading-to-write
- writing as product: *ACTFL Proficiency Guidelines—Writing*
- technologically enhanced presentations
- responding to writing
- peer revision
- scoring methods for evaluating writing
- evaluating oral and multimedia presentations

Teach and Reflect: Designing a Presentational Process-Oriented Writing Activity for Secondary Levels or Beyond; Finding the Oral and Written Presentational Elements in Prepared Project Units

Discuss and Reflect: A Play for My "Buddies"; Integrating Peer Revision into the Presentational Writing Process

CONCEPTUAL ORIENTATION

In this chapter we will explore presentational communication as it occurs in both speaking and writing. In this mode of communication, speakers and writers behave in similar ways. Although the following quote from Atwell (1985, p. 150) summarizes what writers need, it could also logically be applied to the needs of speakers:

> Writers need time—to think, write, confer, write, read, write, change our minds, and write some more. Writers need regular time that we can count on, so that even when we aren't writing we're anticipating the time we will be. And we need lots of time—to grow, to see what we think, to shape what we know, to get help where and when we need it. . . . When we allow time, conferences, and responsibility, we create contexts in which writers write and get good at writing (cf. Kauffmann, 1996, p. 400).

Since the concept of presentational communication was introduced only recently with the publication of *Standards for Foreign Language Learning in the 21st Century* (*SFLL*) (NSFLEP, 1999), research on this mode is scant at best. Historically, presentational communication has been explored by means of the development and evaluation of writing skills. In fact, this chapter in the second edition of *Teacher's Handbook* focused exclusively on written communication. Few ideas exist in the literature regarding ways to guide students in the creation of oral or multimedia presentations in the foreign language, yet these are important components of the presentational mode. In this edition, we attempt to treat presentational communication in a more inclusive manner by discussing not only writing but also presentational communication that is accomplished by means of speaking and projects such as those supported by multimedia. However, a great deal of our attention will still be devoted to writing, since it is the vehicle for much of the presentational communication that is currently the focus in language classes and because the bulk of the research deals with important issues involved in teaching and acquiring writing abilities. Throughout the chapter, where appropriate, we will explore oral and written presentational communication as one topic, while at other times we will focus on them separately in order to discuss their unique aspects and pedagogical implications for each. Finally, on several occasions, in the absence of research on oral presentational communication, we will glean implications from writing research and explore their applicability to speaking.

 ## STANDARDS HIGHLIGHT: Exploring the Presentational Mode Through Speaking and Writing

The Nature of Oral and Written Presentational Communication

In the *presentational mode* of communication, one person produces a message in oral or written form for an audience of listeners, viewers, or readers. Communication is one-way; unlike interpersonal communication, no opportunity exists for the negotiation of meaning to occur between the presenter and those who read, listen to, or view what is presented (NSFLEP, 1999, pp. 37–38). The presentation is in the form of one-to-many; that is, one person speaks or writes to an audience of many people. The creator of the message may be present, but he or she is not personally known or accessible to the audience. In learning how to communicate in this mode, students primarily use the productive skills of speaking and writing. In order to successfully communicate with an audience, speakers and writers need to know the cultural perspectives, backgrounds, and expectations of their listeners/readers.

Characteristics of presentational communication are:

- A presenter gives an oral or multimedia presentation to an audience of listeners/viewers, or prepares a written message, text, or product for an audience of readers.
- Oral, multimedia, and written presentations are prepared in advance and may require research on a given topic.
- Presenters may conduct an oral/multimedia presentation while reading from a script, they may use notes periodically during the presentation, or they may deliver a pre-planned talk spontaneously.

Presentational communication (oral and written), requires knowledge of how to communicate with audiences and an ability to present cross-cultural information based on the background of the audience. The purposes of oral and written presentational communication can be categorized into five major types: descriptive, narrative, demonstrative, explanatory, and transformative (O'Hair, Friedrich, Wienmann, & Wienmann, 1995). In *descriptive* presentations, we describe something or someone, e.g., our experiences, our feelings, physical objects, places, people, or events. In *narratives,* we tell a story or describe an event. *Demonstrations* allow us to show our understanding of how something works or offer instructions on how to do something. In *explanatory* presentations, we seek to create an understanding of a concept by providing evidence or justifying why something is so. We use *transformative* presentations to persuade an audience to adopt our point of view or rethink an idea (O'Hair, Friedrich, Wienmann, & Wienmann, 1995; cf. Hall, 1999, p. 42).

In writing in the presentational mode, often called *writing for publication*, learners produce written language for an audience of readers. This involves the creation of texts through which writers display what they know and explore what they do not know.

 Presentational communication, oral and written, requires knowledge of how to communicate with audiences and an ability to present cross-cultural information based on the background of the audience.

Presentational Writing and Speaking: Product vs Process

Traditionally, presentational communication focused on the skill of writing and had a rather narrow focus: (1) writing to practice grammar and vocabulary and (2) writing to produce a written product, such as compositions. In other words, the emphasis on presentational writing historically had been on the development of a product that illustrated grammatical and syntactic accuracy (Kern & Schultz, 1992). Research in the 1980s and 1990s however, began to focus on writing in order to communicate meaningful messages and on the writing *process*—the steps involved in producing a written text—as well as the writing *product*—the written text created by the writer (Barnett, 1989; Kern & Schultz, 1992; Scott, 1996).

Viewing writing as a process enabled researchers and teachers to understand how good writers write, and how and when to intervene as novice writers learn to write. In recent years, second language writing research has begun to explore the social aspects of writing. Trimbur (1994) refers to the "social turn" in writing research that views writing as a cultural activity in which writers position and reposition themselves in relation to their own and others' subjectivities, discourses, practices, and institutions (p. 109). Kent (1999) pointed out that writing is presentational when he characterized writing as "public," "interactive," and "situated" (cf. Matsuda, 2003, p. 74).[1] This view of writing as process is easily applied to presentational communication in speaking as well, as learners go through various steps in preparing a talk, demonstration, or multimedia presentation.

In this chapter, you will explore in greater detail the thought processes involved in creating presentational communication; later, you will learn how to implement a process-oriented approach to help learners communicate in the presentational mode in various task formats. First, however, we turn our attention to how learners go about engaging in presentational communication in L1 and how we can use this information to better understand how to help learners develop presentational writing and speaking in L2.

Presentational Communication: L1 vs. L2

Much of what we know about presentational communication stems from research in L1, particularly as it occurs in writing. In 1981, Flower and Hayes proposed a comprehensive problem-solving model of the L1 writing process, which has since become the most frequently cited model in connection with L2 writing instruction (Lee & VanPatten, 1995). Their model, depicted in Figure 9.1, attempts to explain the diverse set of thought processes in which writers engage while writing, and it is organized around three components: (1) the task environment, (2) the writer's long-term memory, and (3) writing processes (Flower & Hayes, 1981). *The task environment* refers to the rhetorical problem and the written text that is developing and providing direction for what comes next. The *rhetorical problem* is the writing situation, topic, audience, and writer's goals. The term *exigency*, listed in the model as an element in the rhetorical problem, refers to the situation that sparks a need to write. The second element in the model, the writer's long-term memory, contains stored knowledge, not only of the topic, but also of the audience and of various writing plans. The third element contains the writing processes described below, which are under the control of a "Monitor" that functions as a metacognitive editor or writing strategist and determines when the writer moves from one process to the next:

- Planning: Writers form an internal, abstract representation of the knowledge that will be used in writing. This involves subprocesses such as generating ideas, organizing thoughts, and setting goals for writing. Generating ideas includes retrieving information from long-term memory, grouping ideas, and forming new concepts. Organization of thoughts is often guided by the setting of goals. Goal setting may involve content (e.g., "I have to get a definition of _____ worked into this essay") as well as procedures (e.g., "Should I start with a definition and then give an example, or provide an example and then logically extract a definition?") (Lee & VanPatten, 2003, p. 248). The nature of the goal is very important and affects the quality of the written product. If a writer's goal is to write a certain number of words rather than to appeal to the interest of the reader, for instance, the quality of the product might be different. Goal setting may account for some of the differences between more successful and less successful writers (Lee & VanPatten, 2003).
- Translating: Writers put ideas into language. It is important to note that, in this context, the term translation does not mean translation of L1 utterances to L2. Instead, it is used to describe the process that L1 writers go through as they convert ideas into written language. Teachers of second languages need to be aware that there is an important difference in L1 and L2 process writing. In L1, writers begin by organizing their ideas and putting them into suitable language. They decide which aspects they will consciously attend to—for example, grammar, spelling, and organization. This process differs from the process typically used by L2 writers, which is to collect and organize words and phrases they will need to express ideas; for L2 writers, more time is spent in creating a word inventory and putting phrases and sentences together in the L2 with the help of some thinking in L1. In addition, research shows that students often use L1 during the L2 planning process to facilitate organization and coherence (Cohen & Brooks-Carson, 2001; Friedlander, 1990) and that use of L1 during prewriting activities does not alter the quality of compositions (Lally, 2000; Qi & Lapkin, 2001). Learners often use L1 in the L2 writing process to compensate for difficulties they have in using the second language, e.g., searching for vocabulary (Jones & Tetroe, 1987); to shape ideas and assess their use of linguistic form (Cumming, 1990; Qi, 1998); and to check on their restructuring processes once they realize that their plan needs to be revised (Roca de Larios, Murphy, & Manchón, 1999).

FIGURE 9.1 Cognitive Process of Writing (L1)

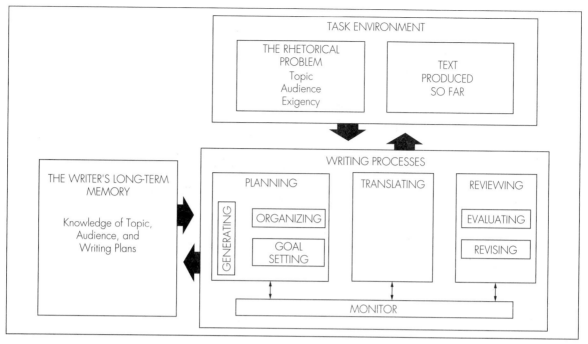

Source: Flower and Hayes, 1981, p. 370.

- Reviewing: Writers revise and evaluate their writing by reading, examining, changing, and correcting the text. They make surface changes that do not alter the meaning of the text, such as spelling, punctuation, verb tenses; and they make meaning or content changes that alter the meaning, such as additions, deletions, substitutions. Inexperienced writers tend to make more surface changes and fewer global meaning changes than do more expert writers (Scott, 1996). Revising and evaluating may occur at any time during the writing process and are usually repeated many times.

As depicted in Figure 9.1—and in subsequent L2 writing research—the overall writing process is not viewed as a linear sequence of stages, but rather a set of thought processes that do not occur in a specific order and that influence each other:

> Writing processes may be viewed as the writer's tool kit. In using the tools, the writer is not constrained to use them in a fixed order or in stages. And using any tool may create the need to use another. Generating ideas may require evaluation, as may writing sentences. And evaluation may force the writer to think up new ideas (Flower & Hayes, 1981, p. 376).

In Figure 9.1, note how the arrows indicate that information flows from one box or process to another; knowledge about the writing task or knowledge from memory can be transferred or used in the planning process, and information from planning can flow back the other way. According to Flower and Hayes (1981), "What the arrows *do not mean* is that such information flows in a predictable left to right circuit, from one box to another as if the diagram were a one-way flow chart. This distinction is crucial because such a flow chart implies the very kind of stage model against which we wish to argue" (p. 387). One of the key concepts of this cognitive process theory, therefore, is that writers are constantly orchestrating a set of cognitive processes as they integrate planning, remembering, writing, and rereading.

Although Flower & Hayes' (1981) model deals with the process of writing, the same process may be used in planning an oral presentation. Speakers often prepare their presentations in written form before they convert them to an oral format. Note that, in the case of oral presentations, the process may include planning for using visuals and/or multimedia support and reviewing by rehearsing the presentation.

The overall writing process is not viewed as a linear sequence of stages, but rather a set of thought processes that do not occur in a specific order and that influence each other. ■

Successful vs. Unsuccessful Writers and Speakers

In order to understand how to help learners communicate in the presentational mode, it is helpful to know about the ways in which they typically engage in presentational communication. Current research focuses on how written presentational communication occurs. Process-oriented writing research in ESL has shown that writing competence is not language-specific. The assumptions that students have about writing in their native language provide the foundation for making new hypotheses about writing in the foreign language (Edelsky, 1982). Similarly, both good and poor writing strategies transfer from L1 to L2 (Friedlander, 1990; Zamel, 1983). Successful writers, regardless of the language, spend time planning for writing, and they use a recursive, nonlinear approach; that is, they review and revise their written work as they compose. Good writers are also reader-centered because they keep the audience and the meaning of the message in focus.

Unsuccessful writers, however, are more likely to devote little time to planning and to use a linear approach to composing, writing in a step-by-step fashion without going back to review what was written. Poor writers focus more on their own goals for the task rather than on the audience, and they use revisions primarily to correct form errors and mechanics (Lapp, 1984; Magnan, 1985; Richards, 1990; Zamel, 1982). Kaldieh (2000) studied the learning strategies (Oxford, 1990) used by more and less proficient writers of upper intermediate/advanced Arabic as a foreign language. Both groups of writers used a variety of learning strategies, especially the cognitive strategies, but the proficient writers used them more actively and with more control. For instance, the proficient writers had more control over the language structure and vocabulary, knew how to generate well-formed sentences, and connected structure and meaning. They addressed the writing task directly, and used feedback from peers and the teacher. (The writers' comments as they used learning strategies appear in Appendix 9.1; see the Web site.) As pointed out by Rinnert and Kobayashi (2001), good versus poor writing can also be a matter of experience versus inexperience, with more experienced writers attending to clarity, logical connections, and organization while inexperienced writers are more concerned with content, balance, and redundancy.

thandbook.heinle.com

Although currently there are no research studies that examine the nature of oral presentational communication, there are implications of presentational writing that we can glean and apply to presentational speaking. Using the research presented above, one could predict that successful speakers also use a process that allows for generation of ideas, revision of multiple drafts, and attention to impact of the message on the audience. In addition, successful speakers, whether in L1 or L2, have the following characteristics:

■ They know the content of what they are presenting and have done the necessary background reading, writing, and other preparation necessary to produce the presentational product.

- They know when they should speak spontaneously and only refer to notes periodically so as to be more engaged with the audience, and when it would be appropriate to read from a script. For example, in an oral demonstration of how to prepare a typical dish from the target culture, presenters would find it more effective to speak spontaneously so that they are free to work with the food, whereas in a television news skit it would be more authentic to read news stories from a script.
- They maintain eye contact with the audience, whether they are speaking spontaneously or from a script.
- They use multimedia (including visuals, pictures, and props) to facilitate understanding of the presentation and to enhance the impact of the message.
- As part of the process, they practice their presentations prior to presenting before the targeted audience.
- They know how to alter the presentation as needed, given the reaction of the audience. For example, if it appears that members of the audience do not understand the message, the presenter knows how to expand extemporaneously on certain points, talk more slowly, repeat, etc.
- When possible and appropriate, they offer the audience an opportunity to ask questions.

Research on Teaching Presentational Writing

You have learned about how writers and speakers communicate in the presentational mode. In this section, we explore the research on teaching writing for presentational communication. We focus on writing here because there are so many related factors that are important when presentational communication is taught. There are no studies that focus on speaking specifically in the presentational mode, and research on interpersonal speaking was previously presented in Chapter 8.

Research on second language presentational writing has its roots in applied linguistics, L1 composition studies, and ESL/EFL studies. The connections with L1 composition studies have shown that learners transfer writing skills from one language to another, as discussed in the previous section (Silva & Leki, 2004). The connection with ESL/EFL research has been useful because learners share many commonalities of processing in planning, organizing, drafting, and revising written texts. However, ESL/EFL learners often have opportunities to use English with real purposes and with real audiences, while the L2 learner must consciously work to find real purposes and audiences apart from those in the classroom.

Since research in foreign language writing is a relatively young field, researchers have designed studies that examine many different aspects of writing, making it difficult to construct comparisons across studies or even draw many conclusions about the foreign language writing process. Research designs have also typically contained flaws that have made interpretation of results difficult. To date, findings are often inconclusive, but informative. For instance, Reichelt (2001) conducted a thorough review of thirty-two research articles on foreign language writing, from which the following points were gleaned:[2]

1. Explicit grammar instruction seems to have little to no effect on the grammatical accuracy of the written product (Frantzen, 1995; Manley & Calk, 1997).
2. There is some evidence to indicate that practice with sentence combining at the sentence, paragraph, and essay level improves the syntactic complexity of student writing.

Studies by Cooper & Morain (1980) & Cooper (1981) show that sentence-combining practice is more effective than "traditional writing practice" offered by workbook exercises in terms of helping students to write with greater syntactical complexity.

3. The use of the computer in tasks that engage students in interactive communication, such as e-mail and synchronous computer conferencing, may have little effect on gains they make in writing proficiency, particularly as evidenced by the quality of their writing in traditional compositions (Herrmann, 1990; Leh, 1997; McGuire, 1997). This finding confirms the fact that writing for interpersonal purposes is different from writing for presentational communication and that the goal of writing in FL classrooms must be clarified: If the goal is to prepare students to write traditional compositions, then interactive computer writing may not be appropriate to achieve that goal (Reichelt, 2001). However, the use of the computer for word processing *has* been shown to result in greater fluency in writing (based on word count) when compared to the use of handwriting—for some students, using a computer to create written products will prompt them to write more (Nirenberg, 1989). See the later discussion in this chapter on technologically-enhanced presentations.

4. Different writing tasks lead students to produce texts with differing characteristics. For example, dialogue journals (see Chapter 8) and other writing tasks that are free from focus on form or free from a final grade tend to result in greater quantity of writing; furthermore, they are syntactically as complex and grammatically more accurate than writing in which form is emphasized (Chastain, 1990; Martinez-Lage, 1992). In light of this finding, Reichelt (2001) suggests that FL teachers consider decreasing the emphasis on form in the instructions for tests of FL writing. McKee (1980) found that when students write in their own voices, their writing is more syntactically complex than in writing where they take on the role of another person.

   In addition, the mode of discourse elicited in writing tasks can also result in varying kinds of writing samples. Several studies point to the likelihood that *descriptive* tasks (e.g., describing oneself, others, places, things) seem to be easier for students than are *narrative* tasks (e.g., providing an account of a typical day or series of events), in terms of quantity of writing, syntactic complexity, and accuracy (Koda, 1993; Way, Joiner, & Seaman, 2000). *Expository* tasks, such as those in which students are asked to explain an issue and offer a point of view, are more challenging than descriptive and narrative tasks, and result in fewer number of words written, less accuracy, and less syntactical complexity (Way, Joiner, & Seaman, 2000).

5. The type of writing prompt also has an effect on the quality of students' writing. Way, Joiner, & Seaman (2000) compared the use of three kinds of writing prompts on writing samples produced by high school French students: a bare prompt, a vocabulary prompt, and a prose model prompt. Each prompt was presented in the context of a reply to Marie, a teenage pen pal from France. The *bare prompt* was a simple explanation of the task, presented in English only. The *vocabulary prompt* contained the same explanation along with a list of words and expressions in French with English definitions. The *prose model prompt,* advocated by researchers such as Terry (1989) & Dvorak (1986), contained the wording from the bare prompt plus a sample of a pen pal letter; i.e., a letter from a potential pen pal, with all the necessary kinds of content and grammatical structures used in context. Students were told to "write a letter back to Marie describing yourself, your family, your pets, your classes, your pastimes, and your likes and dislikes" (Way, Joiner & Seaman, 2000, p. 183). Of the three types of prompts, the prose model prompt produced writing samples with the best overall quality, the greatest fluency, the greatest syntactic complexity, and the highest accuracy, while the vocabulary prompt produced better results than did the bare prompt. This research indicates that students benefit from reading TL examples of written products that they are expected to create.

6. Aziz (1995) found that training in strategy use can have an effect on writing. In Aziz's study, undergraduate students of French were divided into two groups, a cognitive training group and a metacognitive/cognitive training group. The cognitive training group was trained in strategies such as note-taking during dictation, reconstruction of the dictated passage, and error analysis. The metacognitive/cognitive training group was trained in the same cognitive strategies, as well as in the metacognitive strategies of self-monitoring and self-evaluating while writing. Comparison of pre- and post-training essay tests indicated that the cognitive training group improved in grammatical agreement but not in ratings of overall writing (including sentence structure, text structure and coherence, idiomatic expressions, vocabulary, and mechanics). In contrast, students in the metacognitive/cognitive group outperformed the other group by showing improvement in both grammatical agreement and overall writing. This finding illustrates the importance of helping students to self-monitor and reflect on their writing while they write.

7. Process approaches to writing instruction have been shown to prompt students to write more and generate better organized written products (Gallego de Blibeche, 1993). Kern & Schultz (1992) reported on the positive results of teaching writing as a process in upper-level French classes, targeting especially the text-based argumentative essay. They found that poor writers benefited most from instruction that focused on thesis statement development, planning, and development of paragraphs; proficient writers benefited most from instruction that focused on refining interpretive analyses and developing a personal voice in their writing. An important implication of this study is that teachers should have realistic expectations concerning the level of sophistication with which students can write, given their L2 abilities.

 How can the type of writing task and type of writing prompt affect the written product that students create? ■

All of the studies reviewed above were carried out at secondary and post-secondary levels. As you learned in Chapter 4, there are few studies of foreign language literacy at the elementary school level. Since students benefit from the discovery that occurs as they read and compose using the target language, future research is needed to clarify findings and assist teachers in effectively integrating writing and literacy into language instruction right from the beginning of instruction (Blanton, 1998; Matsuda, 2001; Scott, 1995).

Research-Based Implications for Instructional Practices

The research summarized above points to the following suggestions for teachers as they incorporate presentational writing into the foreign language classroom (adapted from Scott, 1996). Where appropriate, suggestions are also applied to the teaching of oral and multimedia presentations.

thandbook.heinle.com

1. *Discuss the L1 writing process.* Make learners aware of the processes they use to write in L1 by having them identify both their own L1 writing strategies and strategies that may be unique to the L2 writing process. Scott (1996) suggests a writing process questionnaire such as the one that appears in Appendix 9.2 (see the Web site) to help learners analyze what strategies they use as they write in their native language. The written product created by means of the writing process is often used as the basis for an oral or multimedia presentation.

2. *Teach about the FL writing process.* Ask learners to reflect on strategies that they use when they write in L2. A writing process should include *prewriting*, usually led by the teacher in whole-class groups; *drafting*, done alone or in small groups; *sharing and responding* to writing with partners or in small groups; *revision*, done alone or in small groups; *editing,* with partners or in small groups; and *publishing* a final version (Curtain & Dahlberg, 2004, p. 82). Appendix 9.3 (see the Web site) illustrates a FL writing process questionnaire that might be used to direct learners' attention to effective and ineffective strategies for writing in the target language (Scott, 1996) and Appendix 9.4 on the Web site illustrates a teacher's checksheet for preparing the writing task.

thandbook.heinle.com

According to Scott (1992), generating ideas is the most challenging feature of the FL writing process because learners tend to use L1 idea generation strategies and then try to transfer or translate their ideas from the native language to the target language. Thinking and planning in the native language is useful, but since L2 students may possess a limited amount of vocabulary and grammatical knowledge, their translated ideas often lack comprehensibility. Teachers can help students generate ideas by (1) providing topics that are familiar and personal to them, (2) encouraging them to recall words and expressions in the TL associated with the topic, and (3) providing enough direction to help them focus on the TL while generating ideas (Scott & Terry, 1992). Figure 9.2 illustrates a sample worksheet for helping learners to generate ideas at the word level in the target language (Scott, 1996). This type of worksheet might include or be a springboard for vocabulary exercises that provide linguistic "scaffolding" for a given writing task (Koda, 1993). In this way, the writing process can be approached as an activity that stimulates new ideas and discovery instead of the tedious task of translating (Scott, 1996).

FIGURE 9.2 Sample Worksheet for Generating Ideas

SAMPLE WORKSHEET FOR GENERATING IDEAS
(Designed for use in the target language)

Topic: Describe your personality.

Underline the adjectives that describe you best:

intellectual	realistic	athletic	quiet
naïve	pessimistic	boring	loud
lazy	enthusiastic	anxious	active
serious	intelligent	calm	adventuresome
crazy	dull	depressed	loving
optimistic	hopeful	diligent	perfectionistic

Use the dictionary to find five more adjectives that describe you.

Use the some of the following expressions as you describe yourself:

intellectual	realistic	athletic	quiet
always	rarely	often	when I'm tired
occasionally	never	regularly	when it's rainy
in the morning	during the day	at night	when it's sunny
with my friends	with my parents	on a date	at a party
on a trip	when I meet someone		

Source: Scott, 1996, p. 53.

Help learners to generate ideas on a topic, recall words and expressions in the TL, and focus on the TL while generating ideas.

3. *Teach students to self-monitor and self-reflect.* Since another challenging aspect of the FL writing process is reviewing, learners must be taught to reread frequently while writing. Raimes (1987) suggests that students read their texts aloud, either to themselves or to a classmate, as this will help them edit what is on the page and generate new ideas. Similarly, students need to be taught to revise throughout the writing process and to make content changes as well as surface changes. Students should reread their written text for content and organization as a separate activity from rereading for linguistic accuracy (Scott, 1996). Changes in content often require direct suggestions from the teacher and can be incorporated in later drafts (Scott, 1995, p. 119). When it is time to reread for linguistic accuracy, students need explicit instructions on what types of errors to look for (e.g., subject-verb agreement, tense usage, noun-adjective agreement). Teachers can also model self-monitoring by sharing with students a draft of their own writing, for example, and thinking aloud as they contemplate revisions; they can also write a paragraph of self-reflection on the draft and share it with students. For oral presentations, students can tape record their talks and engage in self-monitoring and self-reflecting while they listen to them.

4. *Provide focused practice on syntax.* We have seen earlier that practice in sentence combining improves the syntactic complexity of student writing (Cooper, 1981; Cooper & Morain, 1980). Similarly, since syntactic complexity is an important aspect of good writing, Schultz (1994) suggests that learners be engaged in reformulation activities, through which they (1) analyze a poorly written text consisting of only three or four sentences, (2) work individually or in groups to rewrite the text, and (3) compare their rewritten version to one rewritten by a native speaker. This technique enables learners to integrate their knowledge of grammar, vocabulary, and syntax and make interpretive choices about the content of the text (Schultz, p. 176).[3]

   When students' writing is difficult to understand, teachers should be careful not to interpret what students are trying to say and reformulate their writing without discussing with students what their intended message was supposed to be (Krueger, 2001). Individual writing conferences can be helpful in this regard, as they provide an opportunity for discussion between teacher and student about specific areas of difficulty, progress being made, and strategies for improvement of writing. See related discussion later in this section.

5. *Distinguish between writing for communication and writing as an academic exercise.* Learners need to know the difference between using writing as a tool for communicating messages to others (e.g., notes, letters, e-mail messages) and using writing as an academic exercise in order to learn content (e.g., writing an essay about cultural comparisons). In writing to learn, students must use critical thinking skills such as analyzing, synthesizing, and decision making (Scott, 1996).

6. *Combine reading and writing.* There are at least two ways to combine reading and writing that result in the creation of presentational products. One way is to give learners authentic examples of written discourse as models to follow as they write. The use of writing prompts in the Way, Joiner, & Seaman (2000) research study was an interpersonal example of this method. A presentational example would be to provide students with a biographical poster and a photo of one of the athletes in their school's sports program. Students would then be asked to: "Create your own poster for another athlete in your school. Be sure to describe the athlete's birthplace and date, his or her likes and dislikes about playing this sport, how he or she got started in it, whom he or

she admires in the sport, and what he or she hopes to accomplish in this season or in his/her career."

A second strategy is to combine the interpretive and presentational modes of communication in a "reading-to-write" approach (Ruiz-Funes, 2001). The interactive model presented in Chapter 6 illustrates this approach—students first interpret a text and then use the information learned as a basis for the completion of a task or the creation of an oral or written product. There are, however, considerations to keep in mind when conducting these types of tasks. In her study of upper-level undergraduate French students, Ruiz-Funes found that (1) students interpreted the same reading-to-write task in different ways and therefore produced different types of products, and (2) their ability to write syntactically complex sentences and/or with grammatical accuracy did not result in cognitively sophisticated writing. She concluded that "the ability to read insightfully and write critically in a FL is linked to other, more-complex thinking and cognitive processes—rather than to the language skills of the student" (p. 233). It is therefore essential that, when teaching presentational communication and integrating the interpretive mode, teachers should emphasize the process rather than the product and engage learners in metacognitive training to help them to become conscious of their own thinking, through self-monitoring and self-reflecting, discussed above.

7. *Design writing tasks carefully*. Assign some writing tasks that are ungraded in order to prompt students to write more. Have realistic expectations for how well students will be able to write, given their levels of language proficiency. For example, if students struggle to write paragraphs, they can't be expected to demonstrate much of a personal voice in their writing. Recognize that certain types of writing may be more challenging for students, e.g., expository writing, and provide guidance and examples that will facilitate these types of writing. The same suggestion is applicable to oral presentational tasks: Remember that students need guidance and time to transform what they may have prepared first in written form to an oral product.

8. *Redefine "creative" writing*. Teach learners that one goal of FL writing is to create personal meaning with the TL. According to Scott (1996), students sometimes have the mistaken idea that in order to write creatively, they must possess the inspiration of a poet or novelist. When they don't feel inspired in this way, they often experience frustration with writing. Learners will be more likely to succeed if teachers can "remove the burden of creativity and teach the art of discovery" (Scott, 1996, p. 49). Various studies have shown the effectiveness of using journal writing in helping students create personal meaning and in increasing their motivation to write (Peyton, 1987, 1990; West & Donato, 1995). For example, in an interactive dialogue journal, which is effective at all age levels, the teacher and the student carry on a written conversation. Learners write about topics of interest to them, and the teacher participates in the dialogue by writing back with responses, comments, and observations. Since the learner and the teacher are focused on meaning, errors in language form are not corrected except by the teacher's use of correct modeling.

9. *Integrate a writing conference into your instructional approach*. The writing conference can occur at some point within the course or year, after students have done some writing and would benefit from discussion about their progress and ways in which they might improve. Effective conferences are those that engage students in talking about their writing process and in analyzing their written work. Teachers should avoid using the conference as an opportunity for a one-way lecture. Teachers may also conduct conferences with students in order to discuss their progress in creating and conducting oral and multimedia presentations.

You will find many of these instructional implications embedded in the instructional applications that follow.

Teaching Presentational Writing and Speaking as a Process

Teacher's Handbook recommends the use of a process-oriented approach in teaching presentational writing and speaking—here, the problem-solving model of the L1 writing process posited by Flower and Hayes (1981), explored earlier in the chapter, which can also easily be applied to presentational speaking.

In both native and foreign language writing instruction, the shift away from a focus on writing as *product* toward a focus on writing as *process* has resulted in an emphasis on the steps that learners complete in order to create a written product (Barnett, 1989; Dvorak, 1986; Silva, 1990). A process-oriented approach calls for a "positive, encouraging, and collaborative workshop environment within which students, with ample time and minimal interference, can work through their composing processes" (Silva, 1990, p. 15). The teacher's role, according to Silva, is to assist students in developing strategies (1) for beginning to write, e.g., finding topics, generating ideas, focusing, planning; etc.; (2) for drafting, e.g., revising by adding, deleting, modifying; and (3) for editing, e.g., attending to grammar, vocabulary, sentence structure, mechanics.

In the Flower and Hayes (1981) model, two key elements of the writing process that are important for teachers of ESL to consider are (1) the *rhetorical problem,* which refers to the writing situation, audience, topic, and the writer's goals; and (2) knowledge of the topic. A third issue for language teachers is the vocabulary, grammar, and syntax that students must use in order to write effectively. We will now turn our attention to a discussion of each of these three elements.

Addressing the Rhetorical Problem: Goals and Audience

The rhetorical problem involves the writer's goals or purposes for completing a presentational task, as well as the targeted audience. According to Lee and VanPatten (2003), the nature of writing assignments in foreign language classrooms often and unfortunately leads students to have only one purpose for doing them: "getting the assignment done" (p. 247). Since their writing goal in this case becomes meeting what they think is the teacher's desired outcome, students' writing processes of planning and reviewing are minimized. Lee and VanPatten suggest an approach to engaging learners in writing that involves a series of "thoughtful processes" and that uses the basis of the Flower and Hayes (1981) model. You may find it helpful to refer back to Figure 9.1 presented earlier. Figure 9.3 is an example of this approach applied to a typical presentational writing task given to a beginning foreign language class. Note that this writing task could easily be adapted for a presentational speaking task by having students present a talk instead of a composition. In oral and multimedia presentations, the process should include opportunities for students to conduct research (if applicable), practice the oral presentations, conduct the presentations, and participate in critiquing and assessing the presentations.

 Which elements of the Flower and Hayes' cognitive process model can you identify in the task in Figure 9.3?

 What specific parts of this activity would need to be adapted if this task reflected presentational speaking?

It is the consideration of *audience* that makes presentational writing and speaking communicative acts rather than activities to practice language forms. Historically, the audience for such presentations has been the teacher. Recent experimental studies (Roca de

FIGURE 9.3 Writing Process Applied to a Task

A. Generating Content

Step 1. To each group of three or four students, the instructor will assign one of the following topics:
- **a.** Family life at the turn of the century
- **b.** Family life today

Each group will have ten minutes to make a list of as many ideas as possible relating its topic to each of the following:
1. Family size
2. Economic opportunities
3. Educational opportunities
4. Male and female roles
5. Society

Step 2. Report to the rest of the class the ideas your group has generated. Create a master list on the board of the ideas generated on each topic. Are there any other ideas you can think of to add to the lists?

Step 3. Each member of the class should copy the lists from the board to use later in writing.

B. Selecting An Audience and Purpose

Step 1. Keeping in mind the ideas the class generated in the Activity A, think about an audience for your writing. Select an audience from the following list or propose one yourself:
- **a.** High school students you are addressing as part of a college recruitment program
- **b.** Readers of the school newspaper
- **c.** Members of a businesswomen's organization
- **d.** Members of a church council
- **e.** Panhellenic council that governs fraternities and sororities on campus
- **f.** Other suggestions _____

Step 2. Select one of the two topics. Then form groups of three with others working on the same topic and list your audience's characteristics. Report your list to the rest of the class. Try to help other groups by proposing characteristics they may not have considered. Take down any suggestions your classmates offer you.

C. Planning and Organizing

Step 1. Now that you have an audience, what will you say to them? Working in the same groups as in Activity B, examine the lists of ideas you prepared for Activity A, and indicate what information you might include in your composition.

Step 2. Working individually, prepare an outline of the composition. Once each of you has an outline, present it to each other. Have your partners thought of some things you didn't?

Step 3. (*Option*) Present your outline to someone who selected a different audience, and listen to his/her presentation. Can you offer any ideas or suggestions?

D. Composing

Step 1. Take your outline and list of ideas and keep them handy as you write a composition directed at the audience you selected. *Suggestion:* Write a draft of the work and let it sit for two days. Do not think about it or read it. At the end of the two days, pick it up and read it. As you do, answer the following questions:
- **a.** Content: Are these still the ideas you want to include?
- **b.** Organization: Does the order in which the ideas are presented help you get your message across to the audience?

If you answer "no" to either question, rewrite some of your composition.

Step 2. Once you think your composition is good enough to hand in, review the language you used:
- **a.** Verbs: Are the forms, spelling, and accents correct?
- **b.** Adjectives: What noun do they go with? Do the adjectives agree?
- **c.** [*Other elements of the language on which you want learners to focus*]

Source: Adapted from Lee & VanPatten, 2003, pp. 252–253.

Larios, Murphy, & Manchón, 1999; Zimmerman, 1996) focusing on how writers actually write for an audience of readers have elaborated on the processes of formulating text, generating ideas, restructuring and reformulating text. Unlike their counterparts in ESL classes, students in foreign language classes are rarely required to write or speak in the L2 outside of class. Greenia (1992) calls for instructional practices and textbook materials for L2 classes that do not overlook the importance of the purpose of L2 writing, audiences that can be realistically accessed, and assignments that allow students to take ownership over their writing. Teachers should make every effort to find other audiences for students' presentations so that students learn how to design presentations with various audiences in mind. Audiences can include students in other classes, students in specific clubs or organizations, parents, other faculty and administrators, and members of the local community, including native speakers of the target language.

Audiences should be matched to the students' level of linguistic competence and interests. Reichelt and Waltner (2001) describe an assignment for a group of L2 students learning German in which the intended audience was inappropriate. The students were instructed to write essays about everyday life in the United States for inclusion in a travel brochure for German visitors. The instructor saw this task as a chance for creative use of language, in which students would address a real audience, using topics familiar to novice-level writers. Results were disappointing, however, as students attempted to address this audience of educated native speakers. They relied excessively on the dictionary, misused words and compounds, and used L1 cues and catch-words instead of explaining or elaborating.

In contrast, Reichelt and Waltner describe an assignment involving a more realistic audience, consistent with the L2 learners' expressive capabilities: writing a children's story. This assignment enabled the L2 German students to first understand the literary genre of the fairy tale, create a story line showing understanding of plot development, build scaffolded versions of the story and the grammar and syntax in its narration, and receive feedback and peer revision on grammatical points and textual features. When the students read their stories to children in a local elementary school, their work represented a narrative voice that was their own, socioculturally developed within their roles as students and shared within a similar discourse community.

Acquiring Knowledge for Presentational Communication

Students need content knowledge about the topics on which they are to present, whether it be an oral or written product. A process-oriented approach involves learners in developing their own experiences and interests as possible sources of knowledge for writing. Reading other texts on the topic of their interests, conducting library and Internet research, and interviewing experts are other ways in which learners can acquire knowledge about a topic.

Reading to write. Some research proposes that reading may facilitate writing and that a well-read person has more knowledge about the conventions and features of writing (Scott, 1996). Reading can help learners to gain an understanding of patterns of discourse and connections between language and culture. Kern and Schultz (1992) found that composition instruction that is integrated with the reading of texts and that focuses on the writing process as well as on the final product helps learners improve their writing performance. In their study, undergraduate French students enrolled in an intermediate-level composition course read and discussed a series of texts, analyzed the texts as models of good writing, received sequenced lessons on how to write based on the readings, and created in-class essays based on various topics. Over the course of a year, students made significant progress in terms of the syntactic complexity and overall quality of their writing.

 A well-read person has more knowledge about the conventions and features of writing than a person who reads little. ■

Particularly in an academic setting, writing or speaking on a topic using knowledge from a source text such as a literary text, an online newspaper article, or a scholarly article involves the processes of planning, writing, revising, and editing, as one might expect. In a study of the presentational writings of skilled Spanish-as-a-second-language learners writing about a source text drama, Ruiz-Funes (1994, 1999) found that four processes were involved in reading-to-write text production in addition to planning, translating, and reviewing: (1) synthesizing served to design a framework or plan; (2) monitoring served to check for accuracy of information and to collect relevant information from the literary text; (3) structuring served to select relevant information from the literary text and structure it according to the writer's intent; (4) elaborating served to generate new ideas and evaluate and judge existing ideas (p. 520).

Writing about literature can be employed at all levels of language learning, as pointed out in Chapters 4 and 5. Employing reading-to-write strategies with students at the secondary and post-secondary level, Debevec Henning (1992) outlined a proficiency-oriented scale of students' ability to analyze literature in the target language. Believing that literature is suitable input for novice learners as well as advanced learners, she suggests that a teacher might ask a novice student to write a composition that recognizes main themes in a literary work and separates them from minor subthemes. A real audience for this might be program notes for the production of the literary work if it's a play, or jacket notes for the cover of the work if it's a novel. For advanced students, a teacher might ask for a description of the historical, sociopolitical, and sociocultural significance of the author's work. This description could be read at a local ceremony for international week, as a way to paying homage to the author.

For presentational assignments that require reading to acquire new information, foreign language teachers need to assist students in finding appropriate sources to read and in using effective interpretive strategies as they engage with these texts (see Chapter 6). These types of presentational tasks also provide an opportunity for the teacher to learn content along with students.

Using Vocabulary, Grammar, and Syntax in Presentational Communication

In a process approach to writing in L1, students elaborate ideas as a beginning step. L1 learners already have the vocabulary they need to explore ideas; L2 learners often need to create a word inventory. Use of appropriate vocabulary enhances the effectiveness of the learner's presentational writing and speaking. Morin and Goebel's (2001) research study revealed the effectiveness of *semantic mapping* (see Chapter 4) and *semantic clustering* as strategies that help learners recall and organize L2 vocabulary. Although their study dealt with vocabulary acquisition, their findings have applicability to use of vocabulary in presentational writing and speaking. *Semantic mapping* or thematic clustering refers to grouping words of any number of parts of speech around a thematic topic, e.g. *frog, green, pond, hopping, swim, slippery. Semantic clustering*, on the other hand, refers to words of a similar syntactical or semantic nature being grouped together, e.g. *apricot, peach, plum, nectarine, pear*. As students generate content for a presentational task, teachers might engage them in brainstorming vocabulary by using mapping or clustering strategies.

Another consideration pertaining to vocabulary is the use of varied vocabulary. The degree to which students need to use diverse vocabulary depends on the type of task; for example, descriptive tasks may require more varied vocabulary in order to produce greater imagery. In fact, Koda (1993) found that overall quality of descriptive writing was judged on the basis of diversity of vocabulary and topical depth, e.g., how extensively the topic was described. For other types of tasks, such as narrative writing, the diversity of vocabulary may not be as critical as features such as topical progression, which will help the reader follow the linear progression of the text.

Although knowledge of grammatical rules correlates more with written skills than oral skills (Dykstra-Pruim, 2003), knowledge of grammar does not guarantee writing competence (Schultz, 1991). Writers' skill in using language structures to communicate successfully seems to develop independently of their knowledge and use of grammatical rules (Coombs, 1986). The degree to which writing contains the use of particular grammatical structures or is grammatically complex depends on the nature of the writing task. For example, writing a postcard does not require grammatically complex sentences; on the contrary, more appropriate writing in this type of task would be to create short sentences and phrases. In comparison, narrative writing does require the appropriate use of tense and aspect. As teachers design tasks, they should determine ahead of time whether students have the grammatical structures necessary to complete the tasks. Furthermore, rather than designing tasks around a specific grammatical structure—which often results in disguised grammatical practice—teachers should design tasks that address their thematic unit or lesson objectives and then identify grammatical structures that might be necessary to engage in the tasks.

Schultz (1994) found that syntactic complexity is also an indicator of the quality of writing. Hence, the more equipped students are to produce complex sentences (i.e., sentences with subordinate clauses and connector words), the better able they will be to write compositions of high quality. You have seen earlier the suggestion to engage students in sentence combining as a way to improve their skill in writing by using more complex sentences. Nonetheless, it is important to note that presentational communication is more than a list of isolated sentences. Communicating in the presentational mode requires that students write cohesively and coherently. Cohesive devices indicate "a semantic relation between an element in a text and some other element that is crucial to the interpretation of it" (Halliday & Hasan, 1976, p. 8; cf. Scarcella & Oxford, 1992, p. 118). Halliday and Hasan cite five categories of cohesive devices: (1) reference, e.g., use of pronouns such as *he* or *it* to refer back to previously mentioned nouns; (2) substitution, e.g., use of pronouns such as *ones* that substitute for a noun referent when it is known, as in "There are big cookies and little cookies; I prefer the little ones"; (3) ellipsis or deletion of repeated words when the referent is known (e.g., "Yes, I will" for "Yes, I will come with you"); (4) conjunction, e.g., use of words that connect ideas across sentences such as *therefore, however*; and (5) lexical cohesion/repetition of the same word or use of a synonym to clarify the referent, e.g., "Jim finally got a job. It was the perfect job" (p. 119).

Appropriate use of cohesive devices contributes to the overall coherence of a text (Scarcella & Oxford, 1992). *Coherence* refers to the organization of ideas within a text. According to Canale (1982), the conditions of coherence are:

- Development: Presentation of ideas must be orderly and convey a sense of direction.
- Continuity: There must be consistency of facts, opinions, and writer/speaker perspective, as well as reference to previously mentioned ideas; newly introduced ideas must be relevant.
- Balance: A relative emphasis (main or supportive) must be accorded each idea.
- Completeness: The ideas presented must provide a sufficiently thorough discussion (cf. Scarcella & Oxford, 1992, p. 120).

Teachers should be aware that they need to address cohesion and coherence as they help students to communicate in the presentational mode. For example, teachers can engage students in analyzing printed texts to identify the use of cohesion and coherence, developing presentational topics with cohesion and coherence in mind, analyzing their writing and revising based on specific features of cohesion and coherence, and conferencing with the teacher on these features of their writing.

In sum, you have now seen how a process-oriented approach might be used to engage students in written and oral presentational communication and in using the cognitive processes presented in the Flower and Hayes (1981) model introduced earlier in the chapter.

Presentational Writing as Product: ACTFL Proficiency Guidelines for Writing

Thus far we have examined presentational writing and speaking from the standpoint of process. Of course, another aspect of presentational communication is the type of *product* that is created. This section examines the nature of presentational written *products* as reflected through the lens of the *ACTFL Proficiency Guidelines—Writing*.

In 2001, the *ACTFL Proficiency Guidelines—Writing* were revised to present the levels in a top-down fashion, from Superior to Novice, and were written to stress what students *can do* rather than what they cannot do. Furthermore, in response to criticism (e.g., Valdés, Haro, & Echevarriarza, 1992) that the *Guidelines* as published in 1982 and 1986 did not capture the manner in which writing skills develop, the 2001 revision addresses the reflective nature of more advanced tasks, the increased awareness of audience, and the difference between written products that have been created in a *spontaneous* manner versus writing that has been created in a *reflective* way. Spontaneous writing does not allow the writer time for revision, rewriting, clarification, or elaboration. In contrast, reflective writing provides the writer with time to plan and be involved in the writing process by rereading, revising, and rewriting; this method results in a written presentation that accounts for audience and reception of the written product (Breiner-Sanders, Swender, & Terry, 2001). The guidelines serve to evaluate both types of writing since it is not the type of writing but the product that is being evaluated. In spontaneous as well as reflective writing, learners may not always begin FL writing at the novice level since they may transfer their writing competence from L1 to L2 (Henry, 1996; Valdés, Haro, & Echevarriarza, 1992).

The revised guidelines also indicate that as tasks shift upward on the scale, writing becomes more reflective in order to satisfy the demands of the higher levels. Writers become more aware of audience and the purposes of their writing. At higher proficiency levels, writers use a variety of tools for monitoring and revising their work—for example, proofreading, editing, dictionary, and spell checks. Upper-level writers edit their own work in order to enhance the content, style, and impact of their text (See the *Teacher's Handbook* Web site for a link to the revised ACTFL writing standards.)

thandbook.heinle.com

The *ACTFL Proficiency Guidelines—Writing* provide a framework for assessing writing proficiency. Figure 9.4 summarizes the performance of writers across proficiency levels as stated by the guidelines. In terms of classroom instruction, teachers may find it useful to refer to the guidelines as they design presentational writing activities that address specific functions, contexts/content areas, text types, and levels of accuracy. For example, novices might produce posters that are labeled with words and phrases in L2 and that deal with familiar topics such as self, school, and activities; intermediate-level learners might write descriptions of famous people from the target culture; advanced-level learners might create narratives or stories in the past time frame. The guidelines can

FIGURE 9.4 Summary Highlights of the ACTFL Proficiency Guidelines—Writing

SUPERIOR	ADVANCED	INTERMEDIATE	NOVICE
Superior-level writers are characterized by the ability to	Advanced-level writers are characterized by the ability to	Intermediate-level writers are characterized by the ability to	Novice-level writers are characterized by the ability to
■ express themselves effectively in most informal and formal writing on practical, social, and professional topics treated both abstractly as well as concretely. ■ present well developed ideas, opinions, arguments, and hypotheses through extended discourse. ■ control structures, both general and specialized/professional vocabulary, spelling or symbol production, punctuation, diacritical marks, cohesive devices, and other aspects of written form and organization with no pattern of error to distract the reader.	■ write routine informal and some formal correspondence, narratives, descriptions, and summaries of a factual nature. ■ narrate and describe in major time frames, using paraphrase and elaboration to provide clarity, in connected discourse of paragraph length. ■ express meaning that is comprehensible to those unaccustomed to the writing of nonnatives, primarily through generic vocabulary, with good control of the most frequently used structures.	■ meet practical writing needs—e.g., simple messages and letters, requests for information, notes—and ask and respond to questions. ■ create with the language and communicate simple facts and ideas in a loosely connected series of sentences on topics of personal interest and social needs, primarily in the present. ■ express meaning through vocabulary and basic structures that is comprehensible to those accustomed to the writing of nonnatives.	■ produce lists and notes and limited formulaic information on simple forms and documents. ■ recombine practiced material supplying isolated words or phrases to convey simple messages, transcribe familiar words or phrases, copy letters of the alphabet or syllables of a syllabary, or reproduce basic characters with someaccuracy. ■ communicate basic information

Source: ACTFL, 2001, p. 7.

provide information that can be used to set long-term proficiency goals and to develop summative assessments.[4]

Formats for Presentational Communication in the Classroom

In this section, you will find ideas for formats that can be used to teach oral and written presentational communication. The formats suggested also address sample progress indicators of *SFLL* across grade levels. You will find examples that include all of the categories mentioned by Hall (1995), described on page 267:

- descriptive activities
- narratives
- demonstrations
- explanatory presentations
- transformative presentations

It is important to note that teachers should present these tasks within a process-oriented approach, as explored earlier in the chapter.

Formats for Presentational Communication in the Elementary and Middle School

In Chapters 4 and 5, you learned about some ideas for presentational communication appropriate for foreign language classes at the elementary and middle school levels. *Descriptive* presentational writing activities for elementary and middle school learners include materials "for publication" to a wider and public audience beyond their classroom and/or school. Presentational writing for young learners should offer scaffolding and provide for freedom and creativity of expression within guided frameworks. Beginning at the word level, elementary and middle school learners can create "concrete poetry" to connect meaning with visual representation, as shown in Figure 9.5. Writing is based on a clear pattern, and students contribute their own content to the pre-existing pattern, as in this poem frame taken from a second-grade classroom (Curtain & Dahlberg, 2004, p. 76):

Snow
Snow is as _____ as _____
Snow is as _____ as _____
Snow is as _____ as _____
Snow is as _____ as _____
by _____

Creative presentational writing activities for beginning learners include simple forms of poetry, such as fixed-form poetry and diamantes, through which learners can begin to play

FIGURE 9.5 Concrete poetry

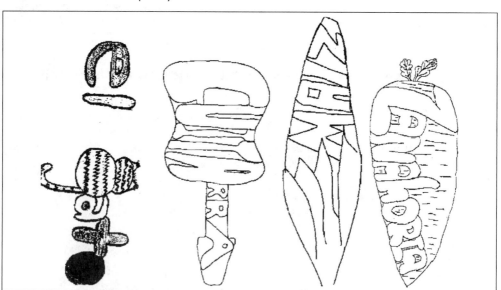

Source: Curtain & Dahlberg, 2004, p. 75.

with language. Laidlaw (1989) suggests the use of fixed-form poetry to tap the creative processes of young learners while enabling them to synthesize information. A sample integrative activity, perhaps from a social studies lesson and resulting writing assignment, is the following fixed-form poem:

Monument Poem

Line 1: Name of the monument

Line 2: Four adjectives describing the monument

Line 3: Constructed in (date, century)

Line 4: Constructed by _____

Line 5: Which is (on the right bank, left bank, in Paris, . . .)

Line 6: Which is near (another monument or landmark)

Line 7: Don't miss (the monument name) because _____

(cf. Nerenz 1990, pp. 120–121)

The following are directions for a diamante, a poem in the shape of a diamond, accompanied by an example in English (Curtain & Dahlberg, 2004, p. 79):

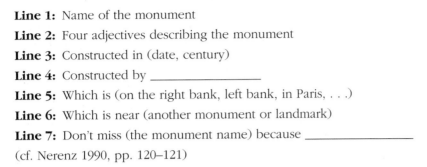

1	WORD	noun	Cats
2	WORDS	adjective describing noun	soft, warm
3	WORDS	participles (or verbs)	playing, leaping, purring
4	WORDS	nouns related to subject	tails, tongues, paws, whiskers
3	WORDS	participles (or verbs)	biting, licking, teasing
2	WORDS	adjectives	elegant, rough
1	WORD	synonym for first word	Siamese

Descriptive presentational activities for speaking at this level include:

■ short speeches advertising the attractions of a city or a famous landmark in one of the countries in which the target language is spoken;

■ PowerPoint or other types of media presentations to share the information gained through research into a topic drawn from a thematic unit;

■ production of video essays about the students' school and school life to send to a partner class or partner school in a country where the target language is spoken (Curtain & Dahlberg, 2004, pp. 72–73).

Now reconsider the language experience chart approach you learned about in Chapter 4 as you examine *narrative* and *demonstration* types of oral and written presentational activities. The *SFLL* suggest that narrating and retelling stories creates a connection between the interpretive mode and the presentational mode that helps young learners make sense of what they read and experience by *narrating* and retelling stories. In the following scenario from the *SFLL*, the teacher of a fourth-grade class presented La Fountaine's fable "Le cigale et la fourmi" ("The Grasshopper and the Ant") to her students. She uses pictures, gestures, and TPR activities to be sure that the students had interpreted the story well. Then the students begin the presentational phase by dividing up into pairs. The teacher again narrates the story while the students speak and act the roles, each student playing the role of the ant or the grasshopper and then switching roles. The class then develops a short play that they videotape and share with parents and other French classes (NSFLEP, 1999, p. 233). Aspects of presentational speaking include their narrative of the tale by demonstration of the actions of the grasshopper and the ant, and their

FIGURE 9.6 Thematic Web for Unit on Trees

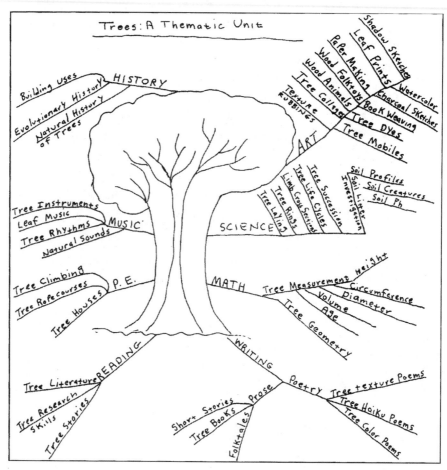

Source: Peregoy & Boyle, 2001, p. 82.

depiction of French culture to others in their school and community through dramatization of the fable.

Additional narrative presentational activities for speaking include:

- plays in which every student takes a role
- small group presentations of scenes from an authentic story that accompanies a thematic unit
- student-created skits that tie together the language and information from a thematic unit
- puppet plays, written by students and presented before an audience (Curtain & Dahlberg, 2004, p. 72)

For oral *demonstrations*, students might produce a videotape production of "how-to" shows, such as how to prepare a recipe or the steps in a craft project, taken from the target culture (Curtain & Dahlberg, 2004, p. 72). They might also demonstrate how to play a game or sport.

For *explanatory* and *transformative* oral and written communication, consider the example of the thematic web for a unit on trees in Figure 9.6. In one NSFLEP activity the goal for a selected group of foreign language students in the Pacific Northwest is to publish a brochure in French and English that explains the importance of maintaining hardwood and redwood forests. The students perform oral presentations on the value of forests on local radio and television stations. The unit is interdisciplinary in nature, as shown in Figure 9.6, involving subject area activities (history, art, music, physical education, math) and oral and written activities in the presentational mode (Peregoy & Boyle, 2001). Students might begin by using the foreign language as a support tool for filling out visitor identification forms (Hadley, 2001) like those found at national forest centers; they might also create partial sentences that might later become key logos for the brochure and make posters of them. Additionally, they might explain in French and English to a bilingual immersion class the importance of maintaining proper pH of soil for the preservation and long life of trees.

Formats for Presentational Communication at the Secondary and Post-Secondary Levels

In a standards-based approach, presentational communication can develop naturally as a result of work in the interpretive mode. In Chapter 6, you learned how the interpretive mode serves as the basis for speaking or writing in the presentational mode. For example, the *SFLL* sample progress indicators for grade 12 in the interpretive mode state, "Students analyze the main plot, subplot, and characters, and their descriptions, roles, and significance in authentic literary texts" (NSFLEP, 1999, p. 44). For the presentational mode, the sample progress indicator says, "Students select and analyze expressive products of the culture, from literary genres or the fine arts" (p. 46). These analyses can be mapped (see semantic maps in Chapters 4 and 5) and used as a prewriting stage for an assignment in which learners summarize a text or create their own similar type of text. Working in small groups, learners might construct written texts for an audience using the presentational mode, working toward the following sample progress indicator for grade 12: "Students create stories and poems, short plays, or skits based on personal experiences and exposure to themes, ideas, and perspectives from the target culture" (p. 46).

The NSFLEP (1999) Barber of Seville project is one in which all of the types of oral and written presentational texts can be incorporated to meet the above sample progress indicator. A group of third-year Italian students read, listen to, and view Web-based, print, and video material on the components of opera, how the libretto of the work results in the actual performance, the theatrical traditions of comedy in Italian opera, the visual representation of scenery and sets in opera, and the history of the period when *Il Barbiere di Siviglia* was written. As a *descriptive* oral or written presentation, students might write summaries of the historical period in which the opera was written, and present them as PowerPoints to members of the music class. Presenting in Italian could be understood by the music class members if the PowerPoint presentation is sufficiently graphic to convey meaning. As *narrative*s, the Italian students might then read the libretto and write presentational posters summarizing the main points of the plot. As *demonstrations,* the students might enact the roles of each of the characters of the *Commedia dell'arte*, wearing their traditional masks, in front of parents, other students, and school board members. An *explanation* of the history, plot, and characters of the play could be a part of the program handed out when parents visit the presentation of the opera put on by the students. Finally, related *transformational* oral or written presentations might be created to convince the school board to provide additional funds for the school's language programs (adapted from NSFLEP, 1999, p. 306).

Task-Oriented Presentational Writing

In Chapter 8, you learned about task-based instruction as a strategy for engaging students in interpersonal communication. Task-based activities can also be used for developing oral and written presentational communication skills. Scott & Terry (1992) have suggested a task-oriented approach to teaching writing, which is based on the principle that learners need explicit guidelines in order to complete a writing assignment. They propose that the assignment include (1) a general situation and (2) a series of tasks that specify the language functions, vocabulary, and grammar structures necessary for completing the activity. Figure 9.7 illustrates a task-oriented writing activity.

Using this task-based approach, Scott (1992) proposes a developmental writing program designed to initiate writing practice at the earliest levels of language instruction. In each writing assignment, the situation might remain the same while the tasks are changed to progress from simple to more complex language structures and functions. Figure 9.8 exemplifies one situation with tasks for first, second, and third years of study. Note that this particular activity also integrates the Communication, Cultures, and Comparisons goal areas of *SFLL*. It could also combine the three modes of communication if students were to read a text that pertains to the situation featured in the task (interpretive), discuss their findings and opinions with classmates (interpersonal), and complete the written task (presentational). Appendix 9.4 (see the Web site) presents a checklist that might be used by teachers as they prepare the writing task.

Variations on the tasks suggested above that could apply to different audiences and perspectives include those suggested by Krueger (2001). For instance, instead of asking students to describe themselves for the new student files, they could be given this prompt: Describe yourself from the point of view of someone who does not know you, but sees you reading in the library, the student union, or a café (p. 22).

Technologically Enhanced Presentations

In Chapter 8, you also explored the use of synchronous computer-mediated interaction, e.g., e-mail, online tasks, communication with key pals, etc., and its effectiveness in increasing the quantity of interpersonal communication and in improving students' attitudes toward language learning. As learners make use of more recent iterations of word processors in general, as well as target language word processors, the recursive and interactive aspects of

FIGURE 9.7 Task-Oriented Writing Activity

> **Situation: You have been asked to write a complete description of yourself for the new student files.**
>
> **Tasks:**
> 1. Describe yourself physically.
>   Function: Describing people
>   Grammar: Adjective position and agreement
>   Vocabulary: Hair color, body, face
> 2. Describe your personality, indicating positive as well as negative traits.
>   Grammar: Negation
>   Vocabulary: Personality
> 3. Conclude with a statement about how you feel about your school.
>   Function: Expressing an opinion

Source: Modified from Scott & Terry, 1992, p. 25.

FIGURE 9.8 Task-Oriented Writing Activity

Situation: You have heard that American and French students are different. In order to promote cultural understanding, you are writing an article for a French magazine about American students.

First-year tasks:
1. Begin with a general remark about American students.
2. Describe the way a female student might look.
3. Describe the way a male student might look.
4. Indicate three things that some American students like to do.
5. Conclude with a personal opinion about American students.

Second-year tasks:
1. Begin with a general remark about American students.
2. Describe the way students, both male and female, might look.
3. Indicate at least five things that some American students like to do, and three things that they don't like to do.
4. Conclude with several personal opinions about the individuality or conformity of American students.

Third-year tasks:
1. You will argue either for or against the idea that all American students are alike. Begin with a thesis statement.
2. Describe American students.
3. Define the term "stereotype" as it relates to American students.
4. Conclude by showing how the argument supports the thesis statement.

Source: Modified from Scott, 1992, pp. 7–8.

the writing process model described by Flower and Hayes (1981) have become even more evident. Planning, writing, and revising can now occur simultaneously and in an ongoing fashion. Learners can access resources and reference materials without leaving the screen that contains their essay. Use of word processors can also help learners in the creation of a more polished, revised presentational product (K. Hyland, 2003). Pennington (1996) identifies five principal benefits of computer-assisted writing:

1. quality of written work, shown by higher holistic and analytic ratings;
2. quantity of writing, shown by longer compositions or more time spent on writing;
3. writing processes, shown by writers' use of more experimentation with language, and more flexible use of writing process;
4. revision behavior, shown by more revisions and more meaning-based revisions; and
5. affective/social outcomes, e.g. less apprehension and better attitude toward writing (cf. Chikamatsu, 2003, p. 122).

Although there is currently insufficient evidence to point to clear conclusions, in general the research supports the use of the computer in producing more accurate written products because word processing can help students to think about and focus on form. The majority of studies done in this area have pointed out positive effects of using the computer by L2 learners of English and European languages (Pennington, 1996; Scott & New, 1994; Warschauer, 1995). Chikamatsu (2003) analyzed the effects of using the computer on writing efficiency and quality among intermediate undergraduate learners of Japanese. Results of this study revealed that (1) learners took more time to write using the computer, probably due in part to the time required to convert segments to *kanji* characters; (2) computer use improved word-level accuracy, but not the quality of sentence-level grammar or syntactic complexity; and (3) students whose ability in Japanese was low gained less advantage from computer writing; i.e., if a Japanese learner does not have sufficient knowledge of *kanji*, using a computer does not significantly increase *kanji* usage. In sum, studies indicate that use of word processing may produce different results depending on the foreign language being studied, the level of students' language abilities, and the goals of writing.

Two specific technology tools that can be useful in presentational writing are (1) word-processing tools such as *Système-D* and *Atajo* and (2) presentational tools such as Microsoft PowerPoint or Keynote. The unique *Système-D* (Noblitt, 2005) software enables students to develop their creative reading and writing skills in French. Also available in Spanish as *Atajo* (Domínguez & Noblitt, 2005), this program integrates its features into the standard word-processing programs, Microsoft Word and WordPerfect. Students express themselves using idiomatic expressions, accessing an 80,000-word dictionary, listening to pronunciation of individual words and phrases in complete sentences spoken by a variety of native speakers, checking usage, and referring to grammar rules as they compose written texts. In addition, the program features a keystroke tracking device that can inform the teacher about how long the learner spent formulating each phrase, and which resources were consulted. New (1999) used this tracking device in *Système-D* and found that both good and poor writers used the software's revising tools, and that they made more surface-level than content changes. New therefore recommends teacher guidance in reviewing and reworking written texts so that learners create and shape their work, using the software as an aid. Thorson (2000) also recommends the use of computerized tracking programs such as this to study learners' writing and revising processes.

The challenging nature of creative writing opportunities offered by *Système-D* was confirmed in Scott's studies (1990, 1992). She suggests that teachers create a series of interesting real-life situations paired with tasks that students need to complete in order to respond to each situation in writing. The tasks direct students to consult the grammar, vocabulary, and phrase indexes in *Système-D*. According to Scott, "Students who are encouraged to access the unique linguistic features of the software should, over time, increase their general competence in preparation for autonomous written expression without depending upon the software" (1990, p. 64). Although further research is needed to confirm the long-term benefits of using *Système-D*, the program provides an exciting and challenging tool for teaching creative writing in French.[5]

The Web has been found to be widely useful in developing presentational products. When students prepare Web pages of their own, they engage in presentational writing since the audience is not present and the communication is one-way, at least initially. In writing for the Web, learners have an authentic audience, a real purpose, and an opportunity to express their personal voice. Lam (2000) and Warschauer (1999) point out the importance of the role of identity in Web-based writing, and learners can develop their sense of membership in a discourse community or culture and expand it to a world-wide audience. Warschauer (2000) points out that high student engagement in writing for the Web can be accomplished if students (1) understand the purpose of the activity; (2) view the purpose as socially and/or culturally relevant; (3) find the electronic medium advantageous for fulfilling the purpose; and (4) are encouraged and enabled to use the medium-appropriate rhetorical features to fulfill the purpose. The Internet offers new tools for researchers and teachers alike as writing shifts to real audiences outside the classroom. The challenge for teachers will be to bring real-world writing *into* the classroom and enable learners to produce presentational products for use *outside* the classroom.

Al-Jarf (2003) found that Web-based tools were effective for struggling EFL students; their writing became more complex, and sentences were longer and more accurate. This researcher also suggests a variety of Web-based writing assistant programs, including Nicenet and the Online Writing Collaboration project.

Presentational Software (PS) are tools teachers and students can use to prepare presentational communication. These programs help students organize ideas and prepare logically sequenced visual representations. They allow users to adjust a presentation for different audiences, provide an interesting visual break from regular classroom activities, and combine several multimedia resources, such as the Internet, audio, and video (Nemtchinova, 2004). The formatting of the program normally leads the user to conceptualize and organize thoughts and ideas, thus supporting the use of higher level thinking skills. Some of the more highly recommended presentational software solutions include Microsoft PowerPoint (2003) & Keynote (2003).

Some guidelines for use of PS include:

■ Use a uniform background, bullets, and animation.
■ Limit the number of images on a slide.
■ Ask someone for feedback on a presentation before delivering it.
■ Don't overdo it—you don't have to use all of the feature of the PS in one presentation.
■ Have a technology-free presentation on hand in case the technology fails you (adapted from Nemtchinova, 2004, p. 22).

Additional information about using these technologies in the foreign language classroom can be find in Chapter 12.

You have now seen various formats that are possible for developing written and oral presentational communication. All of the suggested formats may be adapted for use at different levels of instruction and with students of different age groups. Teachers should keep in mind that engaging students in using a process-oriented approach with these types of presentational tasks will enable them to be more successful in communicating in the presentational mode and will result in more effective written and oral products. In the next two sections, we will turn our attention to ways in which we might respond to and provide feedback on students' presentational writing and speaking.

Responding to Presentational Writing

Traditionally, responding to presentational writing simply meant that the teacher corrected students' errors in grammar, vocabulary, and mechanics. However, in a process-oriented approach, feedback becomes part of the writing process as learners use feedback from peers and the teacher as they revise their work. The research indicates that learners want feedback on their writing (Leki, 1991; Schulz, 1996, 2001; Zhang, 1995), but they do not often find their teachers' comments useful because they are too short and uninformative (Cohen, 1987; Cohen & Cavalcanti, 1990). In a study of comments, reactions, and markings that university-level ESL instructors made on their students' compositions, Zamel (1985) found that instructors make comments about abstract rules and principles that are difficult for learners to interpret; they tend to give conflicting signals about what to improve; when providing suggestions, they respond to some problems but not others; and they tend not to revisit their own initial feedback when reviewing a revised composition (cf. Lee & VanPatten, 2003).

Students typically handle teacher feedback by making a mental note or wanting additional teacher explanation (Cohen & Cavalcanti, 1990). In addition, in an extensive study of over 200 college students learning foreign and second languages, Cohen (1987) found a difference between learners self-assessed as "good learners" and those self-assessed as "poor learners" with respect to their use of feedback. Learners who felt they were "good" at language learning paid greater attention to comments dealing with vocabulary, grammar, and mechanics than did those learners who reported being "poor language learners".

Effective error correction—that which is selective, prioritized, and clear—can and does help at least some student writers (Ferris, 1999; Ferris & Hedgcock, 1998; Reid 1998).

In this section, we will explain what kinds of feedback teachers and peers offer on student writing, how students respond to feedback, and some formats for teacher/student writing conferences, as well as ways to evaluate final written products. Keep in mind that students often first create a written draft of an oral or multimedia presentation and can benefit from feedback on the draft as they then adapt it for a live presentation. A discussion of feedback for oral and multimedia presentations follows in a subsequent section of this chapter. We will attempt to answer these questions:

- When should feedback focus on form (e.g., grammar, vocabulary, and mechanics) and when should it focus on content (e.g., organization and amount of detail)?
- What types of teacher feedback do learners report being most helpful to them in improving their writing?
- How can teachers best help learners to edit and revise their own writing and that of their peers?
- What are effective methods of assessing and scoring final written products?

You will see in Chapter 11 that an effective practice in instruction and assessment is to provide students with criteria for how they will be assessed on a particular task prior to having them begin the task. You will also learn how to accomplish this through the use of rubrics and work samples so that students have a clear idea of what the task expectations are, what they must consider to create their final product, and on what criteria their work will be evaluated. Although a full treatment of rubrics is given in Chapter 11, we will provide a definition of this term here since the use of rubrics is suggested at this point: a *rubric* is a set of scoring guidelines for evaluating student work (Wiggins, 1998, p. 154); rubrics provide the criteria by which performance should be judged and describe a range in the quality of performance. As you read this section, you may find it helpful to consult the part of Chapter 11 that deals with rubrics and/or examine the sample set of rubrics for presentational communication found in Appendix 11.7 (see the Web site).

thandbook.heinle.com

Learners want feedback on their writing, but they do not often find their teachers' comments useful because they are too short and uninformative.   ■

Types of Feedback Based on Goals for Writing

As pointed out previously in this chapter, the goal for writing often determines how students and their teachers carry out the process of writing. At the early stages of the writing process, the goal may be for students to produce large amounts of writing as they generate ideas, and the research indicates that at this phase feedback should comment encouragingly on content rather than form. If the goal is to produce written or spoken language that is accurate in terms of syntax, semantics and grammar, then feedback should focus on the details of the language forms as well as the format of the presentation.

The following sections describe how various approaches to feedback, which appear to be contradictory, can be reconciled by keeping the above two goals in mind. For instance, in *quickwriting* (Cohen, 1994), a strategy often used to generate ideas, students write as much as they can for a specified amount of time, e.g. five minutes, about a given topic. This kind of task places the emphasis on speed of writing, quantity of language produced, and creative use of language. Initial feedback on such a writing product should help the writer use the processes highlighted by Ruiz-Funes (1994, 1999) of synthesizing and structuring the content, and elaborating ideas. The feedback should not yet focus on the accuracy of form, or the correctness of syntactical or grammatical elements. Once the ideas are formed and placed in a structure that enables the writer to communicate well with an audience, focus-on-form feedback can help polish the work, using the process of monitoring suggested by Ruiz-Funes.

No Feedback.   Before discussing the benefits of certain kinds of feedback, let us first consider the condition of no feedback. Sometimes no feedback means that a teacher simply looks at student work to verify its completion, but does not comment on it or offer suggestions. Sometimes it means that the learner puts early drafts of work into a portfolio, planning to revise it with feedback later and develop a final version. Not every product of student work requires feedback. Graham (1983) found that students made no fewer errors when they got feedback on every third assignment than when they got feedback on every assignment. Fathman and Whalley (1990) reported that students significantly improved the content and length of their compositions when they did revisions in the absence of teacher feedback, which suggests that the mere act of rewriting is valuable and that teacher feedback may not always be necessary. Chastain (1990) found that there may be some relationship between the quality of learner compositions and whether or not a grade is being given by the teacher. His study showed that (1) periodic grades on compositions may motivate learners to work harder to increase the length of the written text and complexity of its sentences, and (2) including ungraded written work in language classes enables learners to work on developing their writing skills without constant preoccupation with grades.

The portfolio approach has been suggested as an alternative to grading every individual writing assignment. In this approach, learners set goals for what they hope to accomplish in their writing, compare drafts of how they revised and reformulated their writing, and write reflections on how their work has improved. The portfolio provides a record over time of how their writing has changed. From this record, the entire portfolio can be evaluated for a grade (Leki, 1990; Moore, 1994; Tierney, Carter, & Desai, 1991).

Figure 9.9 shows a diagram of the kinds of writing selections that might be included in a portfolio. A glance at the categories in this figure shows that these are presentational forms of writing, and hence entirely appropriate for the portfolio, which is presented in a one-to-many format with little opportunity for negotiation of meaning. Learners select items for inclusion, and may include multiple ungraded drafts of these samples of writing in order to show progress over time. Presentational speaking might also be included in a portfolio—learners could prepare a news broadcast or a videotape of a skit that they have created, accompanied by reactions of a preliminary audience, followed by a final revised version of the skit. See Chapter 11 for additional information about portfolio assessment.

Focus on Content.   Much of the literature on correcting written errors supports the claim that learners' writing skills may improve with teacher responses that focus on content rather than on form (Donovan & McClelland, 1980; Kepner, 1991; Semke, 1984; Zamel, 1983). Semke's (1984) study researched the effects of four types of feedback on students' freewriting journal assignments: (1) comments only, (2) corrections only, (3) corrections with comments, and (4) errors signaled with a correction code for students to self-correct. The results indicated that there was no significant difference among the groups in terms of effect on writing accuracy, but that the group receiving comments wrote significantly more than the other groups and made more progress in general language ability. Similarly, Kepner (1991) compared the effects of sentence-level error correction and message-related comments. She found that sentence-level correction did not help students avoid surface errors and that responding to a message was more effective in helping learners improve the quality of their written ideas and grammatical accuracy.

Providing content-focused feedback is sometimes difficult for teachers whose attention is often drawn to grammatical or syntactical errors because of the expectations of the environment in which they teach. Despite their wishes to provide content-focused feedback,

FIGURE 9.9 Writing That Might Be Included in a Portfolio

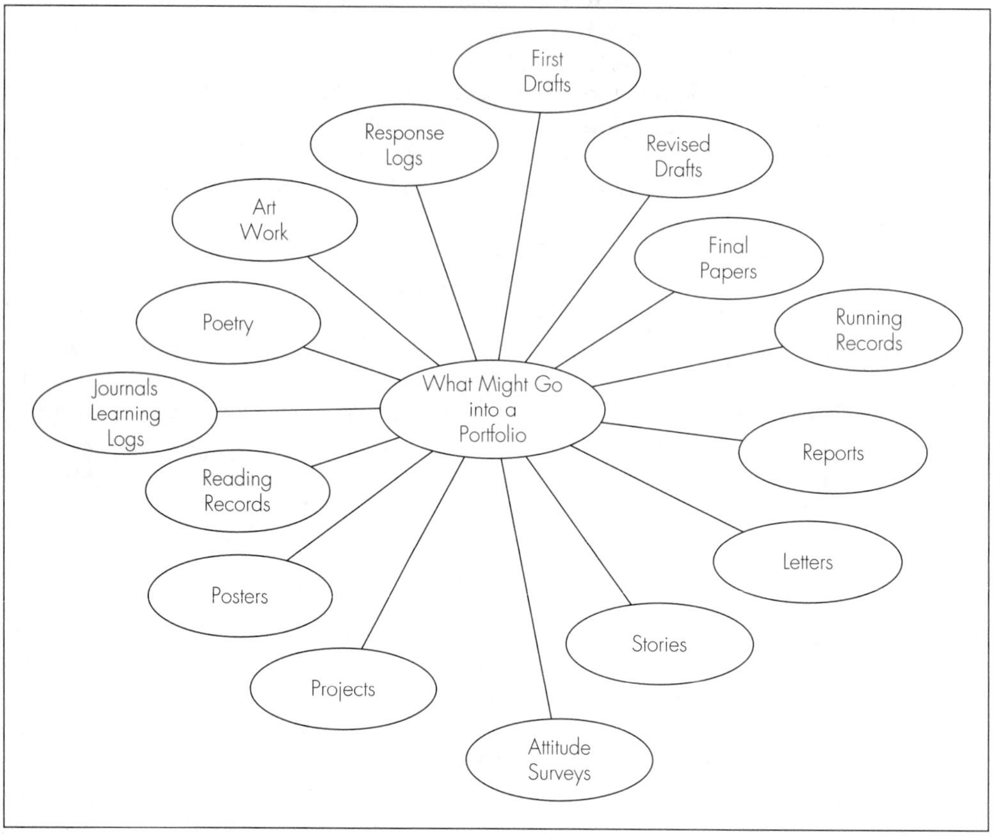

Source: Peregoy & Boyle, 2001, p. 365.

F. Hyland (2003) reports that grammatical accuracy and focus on form accounted for 58–75% of the feedback given by teachers of ESL in her study in Hong Kong. Ashwell (2000) found that content feedback had only a moderate effect on the revisions that students made, indicating that perhaps providing useful content-focused feedback is more difficult than it seems. K. Hyland (2003) suggests that teachers who provide feedback that focuses on content should draw from statements of praise, criticism, and suggestions, as shown in these examples:

- Praise: You have dealt with this topic well. There is a good flow of ideas and a very clear plan.
- Criticism: There is no statement of intention in the essay—what is the purpose of your essay and how are you going to deal with it? You are not giving me [as reader] any direction.
- Suggestion: This conclusion is all a bit vague. I think it would be better to clearly state your conclusions with the brief reasons for them (pp. 187–189).

Focus on form.   Much of the research examining the effect of correction of form errors provides little support for overt correction, i.e., giving the correct forms (Ashwell, 2000; Hendrickson, 1978; Lee, 1997; Truscott, 1996, 1999). Furthermore, Robb, Ross and Shortreed (1986) point out that even the most systematic attention to grammar correction produces insignificant improvement in subsequent writing tasks.

Focus-on-form feedback seems to produce surface-level improvements. Fathman and Whalley (1990) found that writing accuracy increases when teacher feedback gives the location of grammar errors and that grammar and content feedback, whether given alone or simultaneously, positively affect rewriting. In a study by F. Hyland (2003), students successfully revised 88–100% of the focus-on-form suggestions, perhaps because teachers usually expect form errors to be corrected. Some evidence also points to the likelihood that those learners who appreciate grammatical information may also be those who are able to identify gaps in their own grammatical knowledge (Manley & Calk, 1997). Also, students may benefit more from teacher feedback when the feedback is focused on two or three patterns of error rather than all errors at once (Ferris, 2002).

Ferris (1999) points out that students can be successfully taught to identify their own errors, describe their own work, and self-edit and revise their own texts if they are "focused on the importance of editing, trained to identify and correct patterns of frequent and serious errors, and given explicit teaching as needed about the rules governing those patterns of errors" (p. 5). Qi and Lapkin (2001) confirm students' ability to analyze their own work but point out that it is the more proficient learner who is better able to explain why a reformulated version of his composition is better. Although the use of error codes is somewhat productive, not all learners are sophisticated enough to understand and apply them, and some students may need explicit instructions about the underlying rules of the error codes.

An example of a focus-on-form error correction feedback system is Lalande's (1982, 1984) Essay Correction Code (ECCO), used for marking errors, and his Error Awareness Sheet (EASE), used for tracking errors. In his studies, the number of errors was reduced when teachers marked the errors with ECCO, used EASE to track errors, and required students to interpret the codes, correct their own mistakes, and rewrite their essays. See Appendix 9.5 (on the Web site) for an adapted version of ECCO and Appendix 9.6 (also on the Web site) for an adapted version of EASE.

thandbook.heinle.com

If the goal is that students produce large amounts of writing, the research indicates that feedback should comment encouragingly on content rather than form. If the goal is to produce written or spoken language that is accurate in terms of syntax, semantics and grammar, then feedback should focus on the details of the language forms as well as the format of the presentation.

Writing Workshop Conferences. Writing conferences, whether one-on-one or in small groups, are often touted as the preferred mode of giving feedback to learners. In a writing conference, the learner can ask the experts, the teacher or another content-area experts, for information about where writing might be weak. Teachers and experts can provide input that is focused on what the learner was trying to say. The environment of the writing conference is low-anxiety and generally perceived as helpful and productive.

Among ESL learners, Goldstein and Conrad (1990) and Patthey-Chavez and Ferris (1997) found differences in individual learners' responses to the conferences, but more importantly, they found that even the weaker students attempted to incorporate the changes suggested during the conferences into their subsequent drafts.

To prepare for writing conferences, teachers should be certain that students know the purpose of the activity, perhaps by explicitly instructing learners on what to do and say during the session, modeling, role-playing, and explicitly teaching language to be used to facilitate interaction during the session. Figure 9.10 shows a sample worksheet that can be used to prepare for a writer's conference.

How can a ZPD be created during a writing conference?

FIGURE 9.10 Writing Conference Preparation Worksheet

Initial Conference (about a topic)

1. Topic for my essay ....
2. Intended purpose of my essay ....
3. Intended audience for my essay ....
4. Prewriting about my topic ....

Essay Draft Conference

Statements 1–3 above plus
1. In group work my peers asked the following question about my topic ....
2. In group work my peers made the following suggestions ....
3. The problem(s) I'm having with this draft are ....

Revision Planning Conference

1. I thought the best part of my essay was ....
2. I thought the weakest part of my essay was ....
3. According to the teacher's comments, the strengths and problems in the draft are:

    Strengths   Problems

    (a) ....   (a) ....
    (b) ....   (b) ....
    (c) ....   (c) ....

4. Based on the feedback, here is my plan for revising the essay (list specific steps you intend to take and specific paragraphs you intend to revise):

    (a) ....
    (b) ....
    (c) ....

    Three questions I want to ask you (the instructor) are:

    (a) ....
    (b) ....
    (c) ....

Source: Reid, 1993, pp. 222–223; cf. K. Hyland, 2003, p. 196.

There are various ways in which teachers may respond to student writing, and each has a specific purpose given the goal of the writing activity. Teachers will undoubtedly use a variety of strategies to provide feedback to students, but they should be sure to match the feedback type to the goal of the writing task.

 Why is it necessary to match feedback to the goals for writing?

Student Responses to Feedback

Another way to consider the usefulness of feedback is to explore the kinds of changes students make following teacher or peer feedback. Providing feedback is a time-consuming activity for teachers, who are often unconvinced that students make use of it in subsequent drafts (Lee, 1997). Chandler's 2003 study offers support for a way to provide feedback while requiring students to make corrections themselves. She studied four kinds of teacher feedback/error correction over ten weeks in ESL classes: direct correction, underline and describe, describe, underline. She found that direct correction produced the most accurate revisions because students simply copied the changes that the teacher indicated, and not surprisingly, students thought it was the fastest and easiest way to make revisions. However, this approach did not encourage students to take responsibility for learning how to improve their writing, and they admitted that they learned more from self-correction when teachers used simple underlining on first drafts. However, this technique should not be used in isolation as the only form of feedback because studies show that students tend to make surface-level changes when working on their own, but they make mostly meaning-level changes when working with peer or teacher feedback (Paulus, 1999).

Hedgcock and Lefkowitz (1996) interviewed FL and ESL writers about the types of responses they would like to have in order to improve their writing. They gave the following suggestions for teachers:

- more practice in writing and more systematic opportunities to revise, e.g., through the use of quickwriting, other short activities, and multiple drafts;
- more personalized and explicit written feedback from expert readers, e.g., experts in the topic content or the language, other than the teacher, e.g., writing conferences;
- grammatical and rhetorical feedback geared more specifically to writer's level of proficiency and degree of readiness, e.g., too much feedback or too much detail is overwhelming; students should be guided to work on selected aspects of their writing;
- individualized writing conferences with instructors, other expert readers, or both (Beach, 1989); see below for an example;
- more peer interaction and response, e.g., see the description of peer revision below;
- more student control over the nature and extent of instructor/expert feedback; e.g., students need to be able to ask for targeted help from experts in the areas they feel they are weak;
- more extensive reading of L2 texts, particularly models that students are asked to imitate, e.g., reading more expository texts as models before being asked to write one (adapted from Hedgcock & Lefkowitz, 1996, p. 299).

Feedback from the teacher is one avenue for helping students to improve their writing. Another avenue for providing feedback comes from peers. The following section describes the process and benefits of peer review.

Peer Review

Having students engage in peer revision can help them edit and revise their written texts while providing them with an audience other than the teacher and encouraging them to work with others during the writing process (Scott, 1996). Research indicates that peer revision is successful because it allows students opportunities to take active roles in their own learning; reconceptualize their ideas, gain confidence, and reduce anxiety by seeing peers' strengths and weaknesses in writing; gain feedback from multiple sources; and build the critical skills needed for revision by responding to peers (Ferris, 2003).

According to the research, peer revision can be a positive experience if peer reviewers are given clear guidelines so that they know what to look for and what kinds of feedback will be most helpful (Amores, 1997; Hedgcock & Lefkowitz, 1996; Jacobs, Curtis, Braine & Huang, 1998; Stanley, 1992). In fact, peer assistance might be just as useful as feedback provided by the teacher (Hedgcock & Lefkowitz, 1996).

The first step in conducting a peer review session is to introduce the concept of peer editing. K. Hyland (2003) suggests the following description to introduce students to the session:

FIGURE 9.11 What Is Peer Editing?

> ### What is Peer Editing?
>
> Peer editing means responding with appreciation and positive criticism to your classmates' writing. It is an important part of this course because it can:
> - Help you become more aware of your reader when writing and revising
> - Help you become more sensitive to problems in your writing and more confident in correcting them
>
> Rules for Peer responding:
> - Be respectful of your classmate's work
> - Be conscientious—read carefully and think about what the writer is trying to say
> - Be tidy and legible in your comments
> - Be encouraging and make suggestions
> - Be specific with comments
>
> Remember: You do not need to be an expert at grammar. Your best help is as a reader and that you know when you have been interested, entertained, persuaded, or confused.

Source: K. Hyland, 2003, p. 202.

Hyland (2003) also suggests that learners think about how they want peer reviewers to respond to their writing. The following is suggested as a sample:

FIGURE 9.12 Peer Response Sheet

> ### Peer Response Sheet: Argument
>
> Author's Name ....   Title of Draft ....
> Write three questions you would like your responder to answer.
> 1.
> 2.
> 3.
> Responder's Name ....
> Read the questions above. Listen to the author read his/her draft aloud. Read the paper again if you want to. Then write a response for the author.
>
> ### Author's Reflection
> Read the response you have received carefully. Reflect on it and write what you have learned and what you intend to do next below.

Source: K. Hyland, 2003, p. 206.

Hedgcock and Lefkowitz (1996) suggest that teachers use the following stages to conduct peer reviews, after they have introduced the purpose of peer review:

Stage 1: Student writer distributes photocopies of the composition to peer reviewers and then reads the text aloud while the others listen and note their reactions. Peer reviewers are directed to ignore the grammatical aspects of the text and to focus on the content and clarity of the message.

Stage 2: Student writer distributes photocopies of the revised composition to peer reviewers and the same process is repeated, followed by a final reading aloud by the student writer during which peer reviewers identify grammatical errors (cf. Scott, 1996, p. 111).

 Peer revision can be successful if peer reviewers are given clear guidelines so that they know what to look for and what kinds of feedback will be most helpful.

As students progress through the stages, they will benefit from guidance on how to plan, what to look for, and how to revise their and their peers' work in ways consistent with sociocultural theory advocated in Chapters 1 and 7 of this book.

Villamil and DeGuerrero (1996) studied the recorded interactions of 40 pairs of students during peer review and found it to be a "total communicative experience in which students not only wrote and read but also spoke and listened" (p. 66). They found that the sociocognitive behaviors these students engaged in were reading, assessing, dealing with trouble sources, composing, writing comments, copying, and discussing task procedures (p. 57). The mediating strategies they found included using symbols and external resources, using L1, providing scaffolding, resorting to interlanguage knowledge, and vocalizing private speech (p. 61). Significant aspects of social behavior found were management of control as an author (i.e., giving it up, taking it over, respecting/not respecting it, struggling for and maintaining it), collaboration, affectivity, and adopting reader/writer roles (p. 64).

These same researchers also highlighted the complexity of student relationships during peer review sessions, and showed how students are first controlled by their written drafts and do not wish to respond to directions from a peer. Then, as they become more accustomed to the process, students accept peer guidance. Finally, when the process has been helpful, students anticipate peer guidance and respond quickly and efficiently to suggestions from a peer (DeGuerrero & Villamil, 1994; Villamil & DeGuerrero, 1996). Roebuck (2001) provides a worksheet that appears in Appendix 9.7 for peer and self-analysis based on the sociocultural approach advocated in *Teacher's Handbook*.

Initially, students may be reluctant to participate in peer review processes. Mangelsdorf & Schlumberger (1992) found that peer reviewers adopted one of three perspectives: (1) prescriptive, i.e., focused on form and on a predetermined notion of what the text should be; (2) interpretive, i.e., imposed their own ideas about the topic onto the text; and (3) collaborative, i.e., viewed the text from the author's perspective, made suggestions, and did not focus exclusively on form. Nearly half of the peer reviewers adopted a prescriptive approach, which the researchers attribute to the fact that they received the same kind of feedback from teachers in the past.

Amores (1997) cautions, however, that students often seem to be more concerned with the personal, social, and emotional aspects of peer editing. She therefore recommends that teachers (1) structure peer editing sessions so that students review texts that were not written by members of the editing group; (2) clearly define both the role of the students and the role of the teacher during the peer revision process; and (3) carefully group students into peer revision groups so that they are able to collaborate effectively.

 What are the benefits of peer revision?

Summary of Research on and Implications of Responses to Writing

In this section, you have learned about the important research that deals with the effects of various types of responses to student writing. In addition, implications were drawn from this research and suggestions were made to guide the foreign language teacher in responding to writing. The following are the key points to remember from the review of the research and implications:

- The goal for writing determines the type of feedback that is most effective.
- Feedback on content encourages students to produce more language and to use it creatively. Learners' writing improves most when students receive feedback dealing with the content of the message.
- Feedback that focuses on form will lead to greater accuracy in terms of syntax, semantics, and grammar, if it focuses on only a few patterns of error at once and allows students to self correct.
- Feedback should be given by teachers and by peers.
- Students should be given the responsibility for revisions and correction of errors.
- Intermittent evaluation and simple underlining of errors are effective and provide some relief to the teacher overburdened with grading papers.
- Peer revision can be successful if learners are given explicit guidelines for how to review others' writing.

Ferris (2003) also suggests that teachers should recognize that, at the lower levels of proficiency, feedback should be targeted and brief, focusing on a couple of points, whether related to content or form, at a time. Teachers should examine their feedback to be certain that it is clear and helpful, and model the kinds of helpful feedback in peer editing settings (p. 134).

Scoring Methods for Evaluating Writing

The following are four methods for scoring and assigning a grade to compositions. Teachers will find it beneficial to use these types of scoring systems throughout the year with different writing assignments, depending on the nature and purpose of each task:

thandbook.heinle.com

- Holistic (also called integrative or global): The rater gives one grade as an overall impression of the entire text, based on a combination of aspects such as clarity, effectiveness of message, control of language, and so forth. According to Terry (1989), the holistic scoring instrument used by the Educational Testing Service for evaluating the Advanced Placement Evaluation in foreign languages, as shown in Appendix 9.8 on the Web site, can be adapted to fit the level of students and the focus of instruction. The holistic method of scoring is most reliable when raters are trained to establish common standards based on practice rating the types of writing samples they will be evaluating (Cooper, 1977).
- Analytic: The rater scores various components of the composition separately and gives specific responses to the learner; scored components may include content, organization, vocabulary, language use, and mechanics. See Appendix 9.9 on the Web site for the ESL Composition Profile Scale, an example of an analytic scoring tool. See Amores (1999, p. 457) for another scoring profile. The advantage of an analytic scoring method is that it offers feedback to show the quality of students' work in each of the criteria specified, thereby informing students of the specific areas in which they need to improve. See Appendix 11.7 on the Web site for a sample set of presentational rubrics that are analytic in nature.
- Primary trait: The rater assigns a holistic score to one particular feature of writing that has been identified in the writing assignment, such as grammatical accuracy or vocabulary usage. Lloyd-Jones (1977) suggests using primary trait scoring to evaluate the quality of a particular mode of discourse such as explanatory, persuasive, or expressive, as shown in Appendix 9.10 on the Web site.

■ Multiple trait: The rater assigns a score on several qualities of writing that are important in a particular context or task, and allows the rater to score these qualities relative to each other. Hamp-Lyons (2003) points out that this scoring approach allows the rater to score some qualities higher than others, particularly within a specified context. See Appendix 9.11 on the Web site.

In this section, you have explored ways to provide feedback to learners on their writing, incorporate peer revision, and assess final written products. We will now ponder additional considerations when providing feedback on oral and multimedia presentations.

Responding to Oral and Multimedia Presentations

Given that our current framework for describing communication within the three modes is still a relatively new concept, little research exists on ways to provide feedback on presentational communication, particularly that which occurs orally or with multimedia. Many of the suggestions offered in the previous section for giving feedback on presentational writing, together with implications regarding feedback in interpersonal communication (refer back to Chapter 8), can also be appropriately applied to presentational speaking:

1. Students benefit from seeing models of presentations and receiving grading criteria before they begin work on their presentations.
2. Students benefit from feedback that focuses on comprehensibility of the message itself, not only on accuracy of form. Feedback on content encourages students to produce more language, and to use it creatively, with reduced anxiety.
3. Students should be made increasingly more responsible for their language accuracy so that their effectiveness in presentational communication can improve.
4. Peer feedback can be successful if learners are given explicit guidelines for how to review others' oral presentations.
5. Students want more personalized feedback from teachers (and by extension, their audiences), opportunities to ask for specific expert help, and more opportunities to revise.
6. Individual conferences with students can be effective in providing personalized feedback and in setting goals for improvement.

Criteria Specific to Oral Presentations

As with presentational writing, responding to oral presentations includes giving feedback on accuracy of language, e.g., grammar and vocabulary. In presentational speaking, accuracy of grammar usually includes the criterion of formal language use appropriate for a presentation to an audience, e.g., use of the formal "you" when addressing the audience and avoidance of slang. However, there are other characteristics unique to oral presentations to be considered as well, which are illustrated in the sample oral presentation evaluation form that appears in Figure 9.13. In this evaluation instrument, note that the term *delivery* refers to the manner in which the student presents the message to the audience and includes features such as maintaining eye contact, projecting one's voice and articulating clearly, and using effective body language and gestures. In Chapter 11, you will learn about a standards-based performance assessment in which the term *impact* is used as a criterion referring to an aspect of delivery: the degree to which the message maintains the attention of the audience.

Also key to effective delivery is the use of notes, if any are used. Traditionally, students gave oral presentations by standing up and reading their written scripts word for word while the rest of the class often paid little attention to what was being said. Presentations

FIGURE 9.13 Sample Oral Presentation Evaluation Form

Sample Language Related Activities:

Giving Effective Presentations: Learners should consider the following evaluation rubric when preparing and delivering their presentations. The instructor and classmates can use this rubric to evaluate the presentations.

Sample Presentation Evaluation Form

Speaker:

Delivery

_____ Maintained eye contact with listeners in all parts of the room
_____ Spoke loudly and clearly
_____ Spoke in a natural, conversational manner
_____ Used effective posture, movement, and gestures
_____ Used notes effectively (if applicable)

Communicative Ability

_____ Pronunciation was clear
_____ Spoke fluently, without too much hesitation or repetition
_____ Grammar and vocabulary choices were reasonably accurate

Content

_____ Met time limit
_____ Developed topic with sufficient reasons, examples, and detail
_____ Chose a topic that was appropriate for the audience
_____ Organization
_____ Effective introduction
_____ Logical development of ideas
_____ Clear transitions
_____ Effective conclusion

Additional Comments:

Source: Espinosa-Dulanto, 2003, p. 7.

that have *impact* are not read from a script, but rather are presented in a more extemporaneous form where the presenter uses notes periodically as a guide in remembering the order of ideas to be discussed. This frees the presenter to interact more with the audience, show visuals, or operate the computer in cases of multimedia presentations. Presentations that are totally memorized and read like the evening news scripts on television are lacking in impact and are often difficult for students in the class to comprehend because they lack natural pauses and other features of more extemporaneous speech that facilitate comprehension. Students need ample practice in doing presentations and receiving informal feedback before they are assessed on more formal presentations.

As depicted in Figure 9.13, the criterion of *communicative ability* includes pronunciation that makes the message comprehensible, fluency (not having too much hesitation or repetition), and grammar and vocabulary that have the expected level of accuracy given students' levels of language development. Finally, the criterion of *content* deals with the meaning of the message itself and completion of the assignment according to the instructions provided at the beginning. This criterion addresses specifically the depth with which the topic was developed, how the information was organized, the quality of the introduction and conclusion, the logical development of ideas, and the use of transitions. If the presentation required research on the part of the student, the quality of the research could be another element that is included here. Appendix 9.12 (see the Web site) contains an example of a rubric that can be used to assess oral presentations.

Criteria Specific to Multimedia Presentations

When students use multimedia to enhance their oral presentations, teachers should assess their use of media in addition to the other criteria discussed above that deal with language and content. Media might include visuals, paintings, cultural artifacts and other realia, video, audio, and music CDs, as well as Web-based connections and presentational software such as PowerPoint. Appendix 9.13 illustrates a rubric that might be used in assessing a multimedia presentation. Note the specific criteria that pertain to the use of media:

- selection of media type as an avenue for presenting the content;
- degree to which media elements accent the information being presented;
- way in which media are manipulated during the presentation.

For presentations that use a presentational software program such as PowerPoint, the following are some questions that might be used to assess this aspect of the presentation:

- Does the visual component support and/or enhance the content of the presentation?
- Is the number of slides appropriate given the length of the presentation, e.g., between five to six slides in a 15-minute presentation?
- Is the layout of the slides visually appealing (e.g., color, design scheme, amount of text on each slide, font)?
- Are the backgrounds and design appropriate, i.e., colors don't clash, design not too "busy"?
- Is animation appropriate, e.g., movement and timing of figures, graphics, and text?
- Are the appearance and sound of transition effects appealing, e.g., not too loud?

When Web-based connections are used as part of the presentation, the teacher might also assess the appropriateness of these connections to the content of the presentation.

Although it is important to assess the multimedia aspects of presentations, teachers are cautioned to keep in mind that the most important characteristics of presentations are those that deal with language use and content of the presentation.

Feedback from Audiences

With oral and multimedia presentations, feedback may come from not only the teacher, but also from "real" audiences, including peers, other teachers and administrators, parents, and other invited guests, such as native speakers of the target language who live in the local community. It is a good idea for students to provide feedback to their peers because (1) this feedback is usually meaningful to students and (2) this activity engages the rest of the class in listening and learning content from the presentations. Figure 9.14 illustrates a sample peer evaluation form for a group oral presentation. You will notice that in addition to providing evaluative comments, students are also held accountable for what they have learned as a result of having been the audience by describing what they learned, liked, and disliked about the presentation. Another format for holding students accountable as the audience is to have them write a brief summary of what they learned in the foreign language and then have them write one or two questions that they would like to ask the presenter.

FIGURE 9.14 Sample Peer Evaluation Form for Oral Presentations

Project:	*"13 Jahre Deutsche Vereinigung"*						
Group:	Sub-Topic of the group						
Speaker:	_____						

	−				++
SPEAKER:					
The speaker is comprehensible	1	2	3	4	5
The presentation was well-organized (beginning, middle, end)	1	2	3	4	5
The speaker provided enough vocabulary to help me understand	1	2	3	4	5
The speaker used aids (OHP etc.) to help me understand	1	2	3	4	5
The speaker presented interesting and valuable information	1	2	3	4	5
GROUP:					
The group presentation reflected team effort	1	2	3	4	5

I:
What I learned from the presentation?
What I liked in this presentation?
What I disliked in this presentation?

Source: Appel, 2003, p. 4.

Other types of audiences, such as parents and other teachers, might be invited to provide comments about the content of the presentation rather than an assessment of it. They could be given 3 x 5 note cards on which to place their comments; if they speak the target language, comments could be given in that language. Or they might write their comments on the bulletin board or other space dedicated to audience feedback. See Appendix 9.14 on the Web site for a set of scoring rubrics for a language contest in Spanish.

Teachers will find it helpful to provide feedback throughout the process of creating the presentation as well as at the end. For group presentations or projects, teachers are encouraged to provide both individual grades and group grades so that students' individual and collaborative efforts are recognized and rewarded.

In conclusion, in this chapter you have learned about a process-oriented approach to oral and written presentational communication, as well as formats for presentational tasks across levels of instruction and strategies for assessing presentational speaking and writing. It is important to note that, in the spirit of integrating the three modes of communication, presentational communication can be the culmination of work done in the other two modes. It can also be used as the catalyst for interpersonal discussion or acquisition of content through interpretive listening, reading, and/or viewing.

TEACH AND REFLECT

NCATE
STANDARDS
4.b., 5.b.,
5.c.

EPISODE ONE
Designing a Presentational Process-Oriented Writing Activity for Secondary Levels or Beyond

For this activity, use a thematic unit for the target language you teach, as approved by your instructor. Develop a presentational process-oriented writing activity that you might assign as part of your work on this unit. Use the criteria provided in the teacher checklist in Appendix 9.4

(see the Web site) as you prepare the task. Develop the assignment by using the process-oriented model applied to a task that is presented in Figure 9.3. Describe what students will do in each phase of their writing, how many days the activity might take, and how you will provide feedback and include peer review as well. Choose a scoring method from among those described in this chapter, and explain how you will assign a grade to the final product.

EPISODE TWO
Finding the Oral and Written Presentational Elements in Prepared Project Units

NCATE
STANDARDS
3.a., 4.b.,
4.c., 5.b.,
5.c.

On the *Teacher's Handbook* Web site, Appendices 9.15, 9.16, and 9.17 are a set of "project units" from The Pennsylvania State University Center for Advanced Language Proficiency Education and Research (CALPER). These units are the result of Project Work, through which students engage in substantial inquiry over a period of time on a particular topic as the basis for designing an oral or written presentation; they analyze and evaluate their own learning, work collaboratively with others, and receive guidance and direction from the teacher. Project Work offers a constructivist perspective on language learning and enables students to develop the ability to become more self-directed while creating a product that is realistic and meaningful. The project units are designed for high intermediate or advanced students, grades 7–12, or undergraduate students.

Go to the Web site and select one of the German, Spanish, or ESL projects:

- "13 Jahre Deutsch Vereinigung" (Appel, 2003)
- "Evocando y paso a paso avanzando" (Espinosa-Dulanto, 2003)
- "Let's Make a Deal" (Johnson, 2003)

Now complete the tasks below.

1. Analyze the project you selected for the following elements:
   a. real audiences
   b. opportunities to use a valid voice
   c. reading to write from source materials
   d. process approach to presenting (formulating/generating ideas, planning, writing, revising, restructuring, presenting)
   e. use of reference tools and source materials
   f. evaluation and critique possibilities
2. Describe how the final presentation for the particular project you read about is assessed. How does the assessment relate to the information presented in this chapter?

DISCUSS AND REFLECT

CASE STUDY ONE
A Play for My "Buddies"[6]

NCATE
STANDARDS
2.b., 3.a,
3.b, 4.a.,
4.b., 4.c,
6.a.

Ari teaches ESL to young children in a mid-sized southeastern city where 30% of the K–8 school-age population speaks a language other than English as a first language. Students in Ari's class are all between the ages of 5 and 9 years and their spoken and written English skills vary as well. Ari has read about a practice called *cross-age tutoring,* in which older students tutor younger students. He has also read about a teacher in Morocco who set up a *buddy system,* pairing her third graders with her kindergarten students to help develop literacy skills in reading and writing for both groups. Ari decides to combine what he knows about both cross-age tutoring and the buddy system and use it in his classroom. His first step is to have his third-grade learners brainstorm a list of the activities they would like to accomplish with their kindergarten "buddies" over the year. Some of the activities the students say they want to do are: "write our own book and read it to our buddy's" (sic); "write book reviews about the books we plan to read to whet our buddy's appetite"; "write a pamphlet encouraging parents to read to their children at home"; "help our buddy draw or paint pictures to accompany a story"; "work with our buddy to create puppets and then have the buddy retell a story with the puppets"; "make story figures out of clay"; "listen to our buddy tell a story which we write it (sic) down and then read to our buddy."

Ari next pairs each of the third graders, called "Turbo readers," with a buddy and asks them to read aloud from story books to the less experienced learners. Their favorite books are those that deal with animals, such as *Yertle the Turtle* (Geisel 1950) and *Clifford, the Big Red Dog* (Bridwell, 1985).

Ari reads that having his students keep a dialogue journal about their buddies in which he and the third-grade "Turbo readers" can exchange comments is a good idea. Here are three entries from Hamza's journal about his buddy, Ghali. Entry "a" relates to the reading of *Clifford the Big Red Dog,* and entries b and c relate to the reading of *The Principal's New Clothes* (Calmenson, 1989). Mr. Randolph is the school principal. (Note: The errors that appear are the result of students' interlanguage.)

   a. 3/28/95. My buddy liked the book because he tould me, "I like it." I asked him what is this or what is that. Like the dog[.] I tould him what is it. I think I would not read again Henry and Mudge.
   b. May 6, 1995. My buddy learned the polines [?]. I have learned to be pacions [patient] with little kids. Yesterday was the best one because we made a carde for Mr. Randolph it was realy fun.
   c. May 6, 1995.

Dear Hamza,
You two were so cute giving that card to Mr. Randolph. I think Ghali greatly enjoyed that. You have worked so well with Ghali this year. You're extremely patient with him and the activities you plan are interesting. Keep up the good work!

Ari now wants to provide more writing practice for his third graders. In an attempt to combine presentational writing and speaking, he asks them to write and present a play to their kindergarten buddies. Since the kindergarteners like lions, the third graders decide to create the following play about lions:

Narrator:	There once were two lions called Mufasa and Simba. Mufasa was Simba's father. Once Simba was attacked by Shenzi, Benzia and Ed.
Simba:	Help! Help!
Mufasa:	I'm coming Simba!
Shenzi, Benzai, and Ed:	I'm scared. Let's go!
Narrator:	When Shenzi, Benzai and Ed ran away, Simba said "Dad can you play hide and seek with me?"
Mufasa:	Yes, Simba.
Narrator:	When Mufasa was playing with Simba[,] Shenzi, Benzai and Ed came and said "1-2-3 go! Rrrrrrr.
Benzai:	That was it!
Shenzi:	Ha! Ha! Ha!
Ed:	H, H, H.

By Hamza, Karima, and Yassine (Blanton, 1998, p. 166)

Ask yourself these questions:

1. What examples of presentational communication are illustrated in this lesson?
2. What benefits of cross-age tutoring do you see for developing literacy and presentational communication skills?
3. How did the third graders take their audience into account as they designed activities?
4. What do the journal comments of the third graders reveal about their reactions to the "buddy system" project?

To prepare the case:

1. Review Chapters 4 and 5 for story experience approaches to be used with young children.
2. Read Chapter 6, "I know because I'm big: Children becoming writers and readers," and Chapter 7, "The Buddy System," in Blanton (1998).
3. Talk with elementary and middle school ESL teachers of about how they help learners read and write.

To prepare for class discussion:

1. Describe how students and teachers worked together as a community of learners in this example of cross-age tutoring.
2. Describe how oral and written presentational communication can be developed through cross-age tutoring.

CASE STUDY TWO
Integrating Peer Revision into the Presentational Writing Process

NCATE
STANDARDS
5.a., 5.b.,
6.a.

Ms. Reynolds has been teaching Spanish and German at Yuristown High School for three years. She has a heavy teaching schedule of seven classes, and one of her Spanish classes includes both Level 3 and Level 4 learners. Ms. Reynolds believes in teaching language for proficiency, and she provides many opportunities for her learners to use the language in meaningful contexts. Because of time constraints, and her own training and teaching experience, she tends to focus more on interpersonal speaking and writing in her classroom.

Recently she spoke to Ms. Savage, who has been teaching English at Yuristown for seven years, about the issue of doing more presentational activities in her language classes. Ms. Reynolds assigns periodic written presentational tasks and even used a process-oriented approach to some degree as she guided learners' writing. However, she is frustrated that learners do not seem to care much about correcting their errors, and she ends up practically rewriting their compositions for them. Ms. Savage suggests that Ms. Reynolds try peer revision, a technique that English teachers have been using for some time. She explains that learners work in pairs (usually with one weaker learner and one stronger) to help each other correct their mistakes. Ms. Savage also suggests the use of some type of correction code and the use of the Error Awareness Sheet to help learners keep track of their errors.

Ask yourself these questions:

1. At what stage of the presentational communication process would the peer revision be done?
2. What difficulties can Ms. Reynolds anticipate when introducing the peer revision technique to her classes?
3. What type of guidance will Ms. Reynolds need to give her learners so that they can use peer revision successfully?
4. How might peer revision be used effectively in oral or multimedia presentational activities?

thandbook.heinle.com

To prepare the case:

1. Review the portions of this chapter that show how to set up peer revision sessions.
2. Consult Byrd (2003) for practical suggestions on successful peer revision processes.
3. Consult Appendices 9.5 and 9.6 for versions of ECCO and EASE scoring guides.
4. Consult Chapter 8 of Scarcella and Oxford (1992) for sample peer review and writer response sheets.
5. Read Chandler (2003) for verification of the value of simply underlining errors.

To prepare for class discussion:

1. Imagine that you are Ms. Reynolds. Develop your own instruction sheet similar to those found in Figures 9.11 and 9.12 and Appendix 9.7 to help learners use peer editing.
2. As Ms. Reynolds, remember that you have one class with both Level 3 and 4 Spanish learners. Describe how you might use this situation to your advantage for the purposes of peer editing.
3. Describe how you can incorporate underlining of errors into the peer editing process.

REFERENCES

Al-Jarf, R. S. (2003). The effects of web-based learning on struggling EFL college writers. *Foreign Language Annals, 37,* 49–57.

American Council on the Teaching of Foreign Languages. *ACTFL proficiency guidelines—Writing.* (2001). Yonkers, NY: Author.

Amores, M. J. (1997). A new perspective on peer-editing. *Foreign Language Annals, 30,* 513–522.

Amores, M. J. (1999). Preparing graduate teaching assistants: An investment in excellence. *Foreign Language Annals, 32,* 441–468.

Appel, G. (2003). 13 Jahre Deutsche Vereinigung: A sample project for advanced learners of German. *CALPER Pedagogical Materials: Project Work, No. 2.* The Pennsylvania State University: Center for Advanced Language Proficiency Education and Research.

Ashwell, T. (2000). Patterns of teacher response to student writing in a multiple-draft composition classroom: Is content feedback followed by form feedback the best method? *Journal of Second Language Writing, 9,* 227–257.

Atwell, N. (1985). Writing and reading from the inside out. In J. Hansen, T. Newkirk, & D. Graves (Eds.), *Breaking ground: Teachers relate reading and writing in the elementary school* (pp. 147–165). Portsmouth, NH: Heinemann.

Aziz, L. (1995). *A model of paired cognitive and metacognitive strategies: Its effect on second language grammar and writing performance.* Unpublished doctoral dissertation, University of San Francisco, CA.

Barnett, M. A. (1989). Writing as a process. *The French Review, 63,* 39–41.

Beach, R. (1989). Showing students how to assess: Demonstrating techniques for response in the writing conference. In C. Anson (Ed.), *Writing and Response* (pp. 127–48). Urbana, IL: National Council of Teachers of English.

Blanton, L. L. (1998). *Varied voices: On language and literacy learning.* Boston: Heinle & Heinle.

Breiner-Sanders, K. E., Swender, E., & Terry, R. M. (2001). Introduction to *The ACTFL Proficiency Guidelines—Writing.* Yonkers, NY: ACTFL.

Bridwell, N. (1985). *Clifford, the big red dog.* New York: Scholastic.

Buckley, M. H., & Boyle, O.F. (1981). *Mapping the writing journey.* Berkeley: University of California/Bay Area Writing Project.

Byrd, D. R. (2003). Practical tips for implementing peer editing tasks in the foreign language classroom. *Foreign Language Annals, 36,* 434–441.

Calmenson, S. (1989). *The principal's new clothes.* New York: Scholastic.

Canale, M. (1982). Evaluating the coherence of student writing in L1 and L2. Paper presented at the annual TESOL convention. Honolulu, HI.

Chandler, J. (2003). The efficacy of various kinds of error feedback for improvement in the accuracy and fluency of L2 student writing. *Journal of Second Language Writing, 12,* 267–296.

Chastain, K. B. (1990). Characteristics of graded and ungraded compositions. *The Modern Language Journal, 74,* 10–14.

Chikamatsu, N. (2003). The effects of computer use on L2 Japanese writing. *Foreign Language Annals, 36,* 114–127.

Cohen, A. D. (1987). Student processing of feedback on their compositions. In A. Wenden & J. Rubin (Eds.), *Learner strategies in language learning* (pp. 57–68). Englewood Cliffs, NJ: Prentice Hall.

Cohen, A. D. (1994). *Assessing language ability in the classroom.* Boston: Heinle & Heinle.

Cohen, A. D., & Brooks-Carson, A. (2001). Research on direct versus translated writing: Students' strategies and their results. *The Modern Language Journal, 85,* 169–188.

Cohen, A. D., & Cavalcanti, M. C. (1990). Feedback on compositions: Teacher and student verbal reports. In B. Kroll (Ed.), *Second language writing: Research insights for the classroom* (pp. 155–177). Cambridge, UK: Cambridge University Press.

Coombs, V. M. (1986). Syntax and communicative strategies in intermediate German composition. *The Modern Language Journal, 70,* 114–124.

Cooper, C. R. (1977). Holistic evaluation of writing. In C. R. Cooper & L. Odell (Eds.), *Evaluating writing* (pp. 3–31). Urbana, IL: National Council of Teachers of English.

Cooper, T. (1981). Sentence combining: An experiment in teaching writing. *The Modern Language Journal, 65,* 158–165.

Cooper, T., & Morain, G. (1980). A study of sentence-combining techniques for developing written and oral fluency in French. *French Review, 53,* 411–423.

Cumming, A. (1990). Expertise in evaluating second language compositions. *Language Testing, 7,* 31–51.

Curtain, H., & Dahlberg, C. (2004). *Languages and children— Making the match* (3rd ed.). Reading, MA: Addison-Wesley.

Debevec Henning, S. (1992). Assessing literary interpretation skills. *Foreign Language Annals, 25,* 339–355.

DeGuerrero, M. C. M., & Villamil, O. S. (1994). Social-cognitive dimensions of interaction in L2 peer revision. *The Modern Language Journal, 78,* 484–496.

Domínguez, F., & Noblitt, J. (2005). Atajo 4.0. [Computer software] Boston: Heinle & Heinle.

Donovan, T. R., & McClelland, B. W. (1980). *Eight approaches to teaching composition.* Urbana, IL: National Council of Teachers of English.

Dvorak, T. (1986). Writing in the foreign language. In B. H. Wing (Ed.), *Listening, reading, writing: Analysis and application* (pp. 145–167). Northeast Conference Reports. Middlebury, VT: Northeast Conference on the Teaching of Foreign Languages.

Dykstra-Pruim, P. (2003). Speaking, writing, and explicit-rule knowledge: Toward an understanding of how they interrelate. *Foreign Language Annals, 35,* 66–76.

Edelsky, C. (1982). Writing in a bilingual program: The relation of L1 and L2 texts. *TESOL Quarterly, 16,* 211–228.

Espinosa-Dulanto, M. (2003). Evocando y paso a paso avanzando: A creative writing project for Spanish. *CALPER Pedagogical Materials: Project Work, No. 3.* The Pennsylvania State University: Center for Advanced Language Proficiency Education and Research.

Fathman, A. K., & Whalley, E. (1990). Teacher response to student writing. In B. Kroll (Ed.), *Second language writing: Research insights for the classroom* (pp. 178–190). New York: Cambridge University Press.

Ferris, D. (1999). The case for grammar correction in L2 writing classes: A response to Truscott (1996). *Journal of Second Language Writing, 8,* 1–11.

Ferris, D. R. (2002). *Treatment of error in second language student writing.* Ann Arbor, MI: University of Michigan Press.

Ferris, D. R. (2003). Responding to writing. In B. Kroll (Ed.), *Exploring the dynamics of second language writing* (pp. 119–140). Cambridge, UK: Cambridge University Press.

Ferris, D. R., & Hedgcock. (1998). *Teaching ESL composition: Purpose, process, and practice.* Mahwah, NJ: Erlbaum Associates.

Flower, L., & Hayes, J. R. (1981). A cognitive process theory of writing. *College Composition and Communication, 32,* 365–387.

Frantzen, D. (1995). The effects of grammar supplementation on written accuracy in an intermediate Spanish course. *The Modern Language Journal, 79,* 324–344.

Friedlander, A. (1990). Composing in English: Effects of a first language on writing in English as a second language. In B. Kroll (Ed.), *Second language writing: Research insights for the classroom* (pp. 109–125). New York: Cambridge University Press.

Gallego de Blibeche, O. (1993). *A comparative study of the process versus product approach to the instruction of writing in Spanish as a foreign language.* Unpublished doctoral dissertation. The Pennsylvania State University, University Park.

Geisel, T. (1950). *Yertle, the turtle.* New York: Random House.

Goldstein, L., & Conrad, S. (1990). Student input and negotiation of meaning in ESL writing conferences. *TESOL Quarterly, 24,* 443–460.

Graham, M. F. (1983). *The effect of teacher feedback on the reduction of usage errors in junior college freshmen's writing.* Unpublished doctoral dissertation, University of Southern Mississippi, Hattiesburg.

Greenia, G. (1992). Why Johnny can't *escribir:* Composition and the foreign language curriculum. *ADFL Bulletin, 24,* 30–37.

Hadley, A. C. (2001). *Teaching language in context* (3rd ed.). Boston: Heinle. & Heinle.

Hall, J. K. (1995). "'Aw, man, where we goin'?": Classroom interaction and the development of L2 interactional competence. *Issues in Applied Linguistics, 6*(2), 37–62.

Hall, J. K. (1999). The communication standards. In J. K. Phillips & R. M. Terry (Eds.), *Foreign language standards: Linking research, theories, and practices* (pp. 15–56). Lincolnwood, IL: National Textbook Company.

Halliday, M. A. K., & Hasan, R. (1976). *Cohesion in English.* London: Longman.

Hamp-Lyons, L. (2003). Writing teachers as assessors of writing. In B. Kroll (Ed.), *Exploring the dynamics of second language writing* (pp. 162–189). Cambridge, UK: Cambridge University Press.

Hedgcock, J., & Lefkowitz, N. (1996). Some input on input: Two analyses of student response to expert feedback in L2 writing. *The Modern Language Journal, 80,* 287–308.

Hendrickson, J. M. (1978). Error correction in foreign language teaching: Recent theory, research, and practice. *The Modern Language Journal, 62,* 387–398.

Henry, K. (1996). Early L2 writing development: A study of autobiographical essays by university-level students of Russian. *The Modern Language Journal, 80,* 309–326.

Herrmann, F. (1990). *Instrumental and agentive uses of the computer: Their role in learning French as a foreign language.* Unpublished doctoral dissertation, Stanford University.

Hyland, F. (2003). Focusing on form: Student engagement with teacher feedback. *System, 31,* 217–230.

Hyland, K. (2003). *Second language writing.* Cambridge, UK: Cambridge University Press.

Jacobs, G. M., Curtis, A., Braine, G., & Huang, S-Y. (1998). Feedback on student writing: Taking the middle path. *Journal of Second Language Writing, 7,* 307–317.

Johnson, K. E. (2003). Let's make a deal: A sample project for advanced ESL learners. *CALPER Pedagogical Materials: Project Work, No.1.* The Pennsylvania State University: Center for Advanced Language Proficiency Education and Research.

Jones, S., & Tetroe J. (1987). Composing in a second language. In A. Matsuhashi (Ed.), *Writing in real time: Modeling production processes* (pp. 34–57). Toronto: Ablex.

Kaldieh, S. A. (2000). Learning strategies and writing processes of proficient vs. less-proficient learners of Arabic. *Foreign Language Annals, 33,* 522–534.

Kauffmann, R. A. (1996). Writing to read and reading to write: Teaching literature in the foreign language classroom. *Foreign Language Annals, 29,* 396–402.

Kent, T. (1999). Introduction. In *Post-process theory: Beyond the writing-process paradigm* (pp. 1–6). Carbondale, IL: Southern Illinois University Press.

Kepner, C. G. (1991). An experiment in the relationship of types of written feedback to the development of second-language writing skills. *The Modern Language Journal, 75,* 305–313.

Kern, R. G., & Schultz, J. M. (1992). The effects of composition instruction on intermediate level French students' writing performance: Some preliminary findings. *The Modern Language Journal, 76,* 1–13.

Keynote [Computer software] (2003). Cupertino, CA: Apple Corporation.

Koda, K. (1993). Task-induced variability in foreign language composition: Language-specific perspectives. *Foreign Language Annals, 26,* 332–346.

Krueger, C. (2001). Form, content, and critical distance: The role of "creative personalization" in language content courses. *Foreign Language Annals, 34,* 18–25.

Laidlaw, A. (1989). Formula poetry fun. A presentation to the Washtenaw/Livingston Academic Alliance of Foreign Language Teachers. Ypsilanti, MI.

Lalande, J. F., II. (1982). Reducing composition errors: An experiment. *The Modern Language Journal, 66,* 140–149.

Lalande, J. F., II. (1984). Reducing composition errors: An experiment. *Foreign Language Annals, 17,* 109–117.

Lally, C. G. (2000). First language influences in second language composition: The effect of pre-writing. *Foreign Language Annals, 33,* 428–431.

Lam, Y. (2000). Technophila vs. technophobia: A preliminary look at why second-language teachers do or do not use technology in their classrooms. *Canadian Modern Language Review, 56,* 389–420.

Lapp, R. (1984). *The process approach to writing: Towards a curriculum for international students.* Unpublished Master's thesis. University of Hawaii.

Lee, I. (1997). ESL learners' performance in error correction in writing. *System, 25,* 465–477.

Lee, J. F., & VanPatten, B. (1995). *Making communicative language teaching happen* (2nd ed.). New York: McGraw-Hill.

Lee, J. F., & VanPatten, B. (2003). *Making communicative language teaching happen* (3rd ed.). New York: McGraw-Hill.

Leh, S. (1997). *Electronic mail in foreign language learning.* Unpublished doctoral dissertation, Arizona State University, Tempe.

Leki, I. (1990). Coaching from the margins: Issues in written response. In B. Kroll (Ed.). *Second language writing: Research insights for the classroom* (pp. 57–68). Cambridge, UK: Cambridge University Press.

Leki, I. (1991). The preferences of ESL students for error correction in college-level writing classes. *Foreign Language Annals, 24,* 203–318.

Lloyd-Jones, R. (1977). Primary trait scoring. In C. R. Cooper & L. Odell (Eds.), *Evaluating writing* (pp. 33–66). Urbana, IL: National Council of Teachers of English.

Magnan, S. (1985). Teaching and testing proficiency in writing: Skills to transcend the second-language classroom. In A. Omaggio (Ed.), *Proficiency, curriculum, articulation: The ties that bind* (pp. 109–136). Northeast Conference Reports. Middlebury, VT: Northeast Conference on the Teaching of Foreign Languages.

Mangelsdorf, K., & Schlumberger, A. (1992). ESL student response stances in a peer-review task. *Journal of Second Language Writing, 1,* 235–254.

Manley, J. H., & Calk, L. (1997). Grammar instruction for writing skills: Do students perceive grammar as useful? *Foreign Language Annals, 30,* 73–83.

Martinez-Lage, A. (September, 1992). Effect of grammar instruction on the development of accuracy and syntactic complexity of Spanish L2 written compositions. Paper presented at biennial meeting of the Northeast Regional American Association of Teachers of Spanish, Manchester, NH.

Matsuda, P. (2001). Voice in Japanese written discourse: Implications for second language writing. *Journal of Second Language Writing, 10,* 35–53.

Matsuda, P. (2003). Process and post-process: A discursive history. *Journal of Second Language Writing, 12,* 65–83.

McCullen, C. (1997). Presentation rubric. Retrieved May 15, 2004, from http://www.ncsu.edu/midlink/rub.pres.html.

McGuire, P. (1997). *The effects of interactive computer assignments on the writing skills and attitudes of fourth semester college students of Spanish*. Unpublished doctoral dissertation, University of South Carolina, Columbia.

McKee, E. (1980). *The effects of two types of simulations on measures of written performance in beginning college French*. Unpublished doctoral dissertation. The Ohio State University, Columbus.

Moore, Z. (1994). The portfolio and testing culture. In C. Hancock (Ed.), *Teaching, testing, and assessment: Making the connection* (pp. 163–82). Northeast Conference Reports. Lincolnwood, IL: NTC/Contemporary Publishing Group.

Morin, R., & Goebel, J. (2001). Teaching strategies or teaching words. *Foreign Language Annals, 34,* 8–17.

National Standards in Foreign Language Education Project (NSFLEP). (1999). *Standards for foreign language learning in the 21st century*. Lawrence, KS: Allen Press.

Nemtchinova, E. (2004). Creating original language teaching materials with presentational software. In Terry, R. M. (Series Ed.), & L. Lomicka, & J. Cooke-Plagwitz (Vol. Eds.), *The Heinle Professional Series in Language Instruction: Vol. 1 Teaching with technology* (pp. 19–25). Boston: Heinle & Heinle.

Nerenz, A. G. (1990). The exploratory years: Foreign languages in the middle-level curriculum. In S. Magnan (Ed.), *Shifting the instructional focus to the Learner* (pp. 93–126). Northeast Conference Reports. Middlebury, VT: Northeast Conference on the Teaching of Foreign Languages.

New, E. (1999). Computer-aided writing in French as a foreign language: A qualitative and quantitative look at the process of revision. *The Modern Language Journal, 83,* 80–97.

Nirenberg, E. (1989). *The effects of interactive writing assignments on the written language proficiency of first year students of Russian*. Unpublished doctoral dissertation, The University of California, Los Angeles.

Noblitt, J. S. (2005). Système-D 4.0. [Computer software]. Boston: Heinle & Heinle.

O'Hair, D., Friedrich, G., Wienmann, J., & Wienmann, M. (1995). *Competent communication*. New York: St. Martin's Press.

Oxford, R. (1990). *Language learning strategies: What every teacher should know*. NY: Newbury House/Harper & Row.

Patthey-Chavez, G., & Ferris, D. (1997). Writing conferences and the weaving of multi-voiced texts in college composition. *Research in the Teaching of English, 31,* 51–90.

Paulus, T. (1999). The effect of peer and teacher feedback on student writing. *Journal of Second Language Writing, 8,* 265–289.

Pennington, M. (1996). *The computer and the non-native writer: A natural partnership*. Cresskill, NJ: Hampton Press.

Peregoy, S. F., & Boyle, O. F. (2001). *Reading, writing and learning in ESL: A resource book for K–12 teachers* (3rd ed.). New York: Addison Wesley Longman.

Peyton, J. K. (1987). Dialogue journal writing with limited English proficient students. Washington, DC: Center for Applied Linguistics.

Peyton, J. K. (1990). *Students and teachers writing together: Perspectives on journal writing*. Alexandria, VA: Teachers of English to Speakers of Other Languages.

PowerPoint 2002 [Computer software]. (2003). Redmond, WA: Microsoft Corporation.

Qi, D. S. (1998). An inquiry into language-switching in second language composing. *Canadian Modern Language Review, 54,* 413–435.

Qi, D. S., & Lapkin, S. (2001). Exploring the role of noticing in a three-stage second language writing task. *Journal of Second Language Writing, 10,* 277–303.

Raimes, A. (1987). Language proficiency, writing ability, and composing strategies: A study of ESL college student writers. *Language Learning, 37,* 439–467.

Reichelt, M. (2001). A critical review of foreign language writing research in pedagogical practices. *The Modern Language Journal, 85,* 578–98.

Reichelt, M., & Waltner, K. B. (2001). Writing in a second year German class. *Foreign Language Annals, 34,* 235–244.

Reid, J. M. (1993). *Teaching ESL writing*. Englewood Cliffs, NJ: Regents/Prentice Hall.

Reid, J. M. (1998). "Eye" learners and "ear" learners: Identifying the language needs of international students and U.S. resident writers. In P. Byrd & J. M. Reid (Eds.), *Grammar in the composition classroom: Essays on teaching ESL for college-bound students* (pp. 3–17). Boston: Heinle, & Heinle.

Richards, J. (1990). *The language teaching matrix*. Cambridge: Cambridge University Press.

Rinnert, C., & Kobayashi, H. (2001). Differing perceptions of EFL writing among readers in Japan. *The Modern Language Journal, 85,* 189–209.

Robb, T., Ross, S., & Shortreed, I. (1986). Salience of feedback on error and its effect on EFL writing quality. *TESOL Quarterly, 20,* 83–93.

Roca de Larios, J., Murphy, L., & Manchón, R. (1999). The use of restructuring strategies in EFL Writing: A study of Spanish learners of English as a Foreign Language. *Journal of Second Language Writing, 8,* 13–44.

Roebuck, R. (2001). Teaching composition in the college level foreign language class: Insights and activities from sociocultural theory. *Foreign Language Annals, 34,* 206–215.

Ruiz-Funes, M. (1994). *An exploration of the process of reading-to-write used by skilled Spanish-as-a-foreign-language students*. Unpublished doctoral dissertation. Virginia Polytechnic Institute and State University, Blacksburg, VA.

Ruiz-Funes, M. (1999). Writing, reading, and reading-to-write in a foreign language: A critical review. *Foreign Language Annals, 32,* 514–526.

Ruiz-Funes, M. (2001). Task representation in foreign language reading-to-write. *Foreign Language Annals, 34,* 226–234.

Scarcella, R., & Oxford, R. (1992). *The tapestry of language learning.* Boston: Heinle & Heinle.

Schultz, J. M. (1991). Writing mode in the articulation of language and literature classes: Theory and practice. *The Modern Language Journal, 75,* 411–417.

Schultz, J. M. (1994). Stylistic reformulation: Theoretical premises and practical applications. *The Modern Language Journal, 78,* 169–178.

Schulz, R. A. (1996). Focus on form in the foreign language classroom: Students' and teachers' views on error correction and the role of grammar. *Foreign Language Annals, 29,* 343–364.

Schulz, R. A. (2001). Cultural differences in student and teacher perceptions concerning the role of grammar instruction and corrective feedback: U.S.A. Colombia. *The Modern Language Journal, 85,* 244–258.

Scott, R. S., & Rodgers, B. C. (1993). Assessing communication in writing: The development of a Spanish writing contest. *Foreign Language Annals, 26,* 383–392.

Scott, V. M. (1990). Task-oriented creative writing with *Système-D. CALICO Journal, 7*(3). 58–67.

Scott, V. M. (1992). Writing from the start: A task-oriented developmental writing program for foreign language students. In R. Terry (Ed.), *Dimension: Language '91* (pp. 1–15). Southern Conference on Language Teaching. Valdosta, GA: Valdosta State University.

Scott, V. M. (1995). Writing. In V. Galloway & C. Herron (Eds.), *Research within reach II* (pp. 115–127). Southern Conference on Language Teaching. Valdosta, GA: Valdosta State University.

Scott, V. M. (1996). *Rethinking foreign language writing.* Boston: Heinle & Heinle.

Scott, V. M., & New, E. (1994). Computer aided analysis of foreign language writing process. *Calico Journal, 11,* 5–18.

Scott, V. M., & Terry, R. M. (1992). *Système-D Teacher's Guide.* Boston: Heinle & Heinle.

Semke, H. D. (1984). Effects of the red pen. *Foreign Language Annals, 17,* 195–202.

Silva, T. (1990). Second language composition instruction: Developments, issues, and directions in ESL. In B. Kroll (Ed.), *Second language writing: Research insights for the classroom* (pp. 11–23). Cambridge, UK: Cambridge University Press.

Silva, T., & Leki, I. (2004). Family matters: The influence of applied linguistics and composition studies on second language writing studies-past, present, and future. *The Modern Language Journal, 88,* 1–13.

Stanley, J. (1992). Coaching student writers to be more effective peer evaluators. *Journal of Second Language Writing, 1,* 217–233.

Terry, R. M. (1989). Teaching and evaluating writing as a communicative skill. *Foreign Language Annals, 22,* 43–54.

Thorson, H. (2000). Using the computer to compare foreign and native language writing processes: A statistical and case study approach. *The Modern Language Journal, 84,* 155–170.

Tierney, R. J., Carter, M. A., & Desai, L.E. (1991). *Portfolio assessment in the reading-writing classroom.* Norwood, MA: Christopher-Gordon.

Trimbur, J. (1994). Taking the social turn: Teaching writing post-process. *College Composition and Communication, 45,* 108–118.

Truscott, J. (1996). The case against grammar correction in L2 writing classes. *Language Learning, 46,* 327–369.

Truscott, J. (1999). The case for "The case against grammar correction in L2 writing classes": A response to Ferris. *Journal of Second Language Writing, 8,* 111–122.

Valdés, G., Haro, P., & Echevarriarza, M. P. (1992). The development of writing abilities in a foreign language: Contributions toward a general theory of L2 writing. *The Modern Language Journal, 76,* 333–352.

Villamil, O., & de Guerrero, M. (1996). Peer revision in the L2 classroom: Social-cognitive activities, mediating strategies, and aspects of social behavior. *Journal of Second Language Writing, 5,* 51–75.

Warschauer, M. (1995). *E-mail for English teaching.* Alexandria, VA: TESOL.

Warschauer, M. (1999). Introductory chapter. *Electronic literacies: Language, culture, and power in online education.* Mahwah, NJ: Lawrence Erlbaum Associates.

Warschauer, M. (2000). Online learning in second language classrooms: An ethnographic study. In M. Warschauer & R. Kern (Eds.), *Network-based language teaching: Concepts and practice* (pp. 41–58). New York: Cambridge University Press.

Way, D. P., Joiner, E.G., & Seaman, M. A. (2000). Writing in the secondary foreign language classroom: The effects of prompts and tasks on novice learners of French. *The Modern Language Journal, 84,* 171–184.

West, M. J., & Donato, R. D. (1995). Stories and stances: Cross-cultural encounters with African folktales. *Foreign Language Annals, 28,* 392–406.

Wiggins, G. (1998). *Educative assessment.* San Francisco: Jossey-Bass.

Zamel, V. (1982). Writing: The process of discovering meaning. *TESOL Quarterly, 16,* 195–209.

Zamel, V. (1983). The composing processes of advanced ESL students: Six case studies. *TESOL Quarterly, 17,* 165–187.

Zamel, V. (1985). Responding to student writing. *TESOL Quarterly, 19,* 79–101.

Ziegler, R., & Ziegler, W. (2000). *Multimedia rubric.* Waco, NE: Learning for the Future.

Zhang, S. (1995). Reexamining the affective advantage of peer feedback in the ESL writing class. *Journal of Second Language Writing, 4,* 209–222.

Zimmerman, R. (1996). Formulating in L2 writing: Towards an empirical model. In A. Archibald and G. C. Jeffrey (Ed.), *Second language acquisition and writing: A multidisciplinary* approach (pp. 53–68). Southampton, UK: University of Southampton Press.

NOTES

1. According to Scott (1996), writing as a "process" means that "writing is a succession of actions undertaken to bring about some desired result" (p. 31). She also notes that the term *process* has never been clearly defined in the literature. Matsuda (2003) clarifies this notion and explains that process writing is a reaction to teacher-centered, product-oriented approaches to writing. The advocates of process pedagogy have changed the focus to a student-centered, process-oriented approach, with an emphasis on "the process of helping students discover their own voice, of recognizing that students have something important to say, of allowing students to choose their own topics, of providing teacher and peer feedback, of encouraging revision, and of using student writing as the primary text of the course." (p. 1)

2. See Reichelt (2001, pp. 594–598) for a comprehensive review of foreign language writing studies.

3. For a more detailed discussion of the use of stylistic reformulation to improve students' writing skills, see Schultz (1994).

4. See Scott and Rodgers (1993) for a description of a proficiency-oriented Spanish writing contest designed for secondary and undergraduate Spanish students. Appendix 9.14 (see the Web site) illustrates the contest specifications and set of rubrics for each level of writing. You may find it helpful to return to this set of rubrics when you study rubrics in Chapter 11.

5. See Scott (1990) for a detailed description of *Système-D* and her proposed framework for including task-oriented writing activities that engage students in the use of various writing strategies.

6. The buddy system procedure in this case study is adapted from Blanton (1998).

CHAPTER 10

Addressing Diverse Needs of Learners in the Language Classroom

In this chapter, you will learn about:

- diverse needs of students
- multiple intelligences
- learning styles and strategies
- students with physical and learning disabilities
- *at-risk* students

- gifted learners
- heritage language learners
- differentiated instruction
- community-based learning and service-learning
- the communities goal area

Teach and Reflect: Designing a Lesson Appropriate for Diverse Learning Styles; Working Within Communities

Discuss and Reflect: Preparing to Teach Special Education Spanish I and II Classes; Differentiating Instruction: Three Classrooms

As you prepare to read and discuss this chapter, you might want to take the following self-test as a way to examine some of your teaching practices and your beliefs about the diversity of students whom you will teach.

Do I (or Will I) . . .

- truly believe that all students can learn?
- have high expectations for all students?
- value and respect all students and cultures and model that respect in my classroom?
- go beyond school requirements for contacting parents?
- consult guidance counselors and ask why students have been taken out of my class or why a change in schedule has been made?
- share pertinent information with colleagues regarding learners with special needs and the strategies that promote student success?
- allow for differences in learning styles, amount of time needed to learn, and ways students most effectively demonstrate knowledge?
- try to teach to the strengths of each individual student?
- send home letters of commendation/appreciation?
- demand nonprejudicial conversations and/or comments in my classroom?

(Fairfax County Public Schools, 1992, p. 12)

"The United States must educate students who are equipped linguistically and culturally to communicate successfully in a pluralistic American society and abroad. This imperative envisions a future in which ALL students will develop and maintain proficiency in English and at least one other language, modern or classical. Children who come to school from non-English-speaking backgrounds should also have opportunities to develop further proficiencies in their first language" (NSFLEP, 1999, p. 7).

The inclusive orientation of the *Standards for Foreign Language Learning in the 21st Century* implies that in any given language classroom there may be students who differ from each other in various ways, including motivation, goals for learning, aptitude, Zone of Proximal Development (ZPD), ethnic or national origin, gender, socioeconomic status, and linguistic or cultural heritage.[1] Even in classes in which students appear to be relatively homogeneous in background and goals, they may differ along some other dimension. The challenge for the language teacher is to recognize and help learners appreciate these differences and similarities in the language classroom, and to design differentiated instruction so that each learner has opportunities to enhance thinking skills and learn how members of other cultures express themselves.

As the student population continues to grow in diversity, teachers will need to gain an understanding of the various needs that these learners bring to the foreign language classroom. Using Census 2000 data, the National Center for Education Statistics (NCES) reports that 39% of the school-age population are members of minority groups.[2] In the 2000 census, the largest minorities among students were Black and Hispanic, each representing 17% of the 39% minority (NCES, 2002). Interestingly, using 1990 census data, NCES projects that, by the year 2020, minority learners will constitute 50% of the public school population while only 15% of their teachers are members of minority groups (Yasin & Albert, 1999). The fact that many teachers may not belong to the minority groups represented by their students underscores the challenge the teachers may face in the classroom.

We often think of diverse populations of students in terms of gender, age, race, national origin, and ethnicity. However, diversity also includes the range of academic, linguistic, physical, and emotional characteristics that students bring to the classroom. Of particular interest to language teachers is linguistic diversity, one aspect of the changing complexity of U.S. schools. *Language minority* students are those who come from homes where a language other than English is actively used, who therefore have had an opportunity to develop some level of proficiency in a language other than English. A language minority student may be of limited English proficiency, bilingual, or essentially monolingual in English (August & Hakuta, 1997, p. 15). The presence of many language minority children in U.S. schools enriches the cultural and linguistic diversity of the classroom, and demands resources for those who speak English with difficulty. The number of school-age children (ages 5–24) increased by 6% between 1979 and 1999, and the number who spoke a language other than English at home increased by 118% (NCES, 2002). Among those who spoke a language other than English at home, 39% in grades 5–9 spoke English with difficulty, and 23% spoke English with difficulty in grades 10–12 (NCES, 2002).

In addition, learners are unique in the ways in which they approach language learning. The focus of this chapter is to explore the diverse needs of learners in language classrooms and to offer ideas to language teachers about how to address these needs so that language learning is facilitated for all learners. In this chapter, you will recognize that:

1. Learners approach language learning in a variety of ways.
2. Teachers can help learners to develop strategies that best use the teachers' teaching style and the learners' learning style.
3. In a standards-based approach, languages are for all learners but some may require special accommodations as illustrated by a parallel curriculum model.
4. Knowing about the special needs of disabled, gifted, and heritage learners will assist you in implementing a standards-based approach that benefits all learners.

As language teachers, it behooves us to provide a classroom atmosphere in which (1) all learners are respected and valued for the unique attributes and backgrounds that they bring to the learning experience, and (2) specific efforts are made to understand the various language learning needs of students and to accommodate those needs.

The Diverse Ways in Which Learners Approach Language Learning

This section will examine the ways in which multiple intelligences, learning strategies, and language learning strategies have an impact on language learning.

Multiple Intelligences

Gardner's (1993) explanation of multiple intelligences captured the attention of researchers and practitioners alike. He defined *intelligence* as "a biopsychological potential to process information in certain ways. Each intelligence can be activated in an appropriate cultural setting" (Von Károlyi, Ramos-Ford, & Gardner, 2003, p. 101). In his view, an *intelligence* is a set of brain functions that can be developed and expanded and that consists of skills for (1) resolving genuine problems or difficulties, and (2) finding or creating problems (Gardner, 1993, p. 61). Gardner's (1993, 1995) theory suggests eight intelligences with a ninth one—existential—identified and still being explored. Figure 10.1 categorizes the nine intelligences, and includes the characteristics of and sample foreign language classroom activities for each intelligence.

Diaz and Heining-Boynton (1995) point out four key elements to Gardner's theory:

1. Everyone possesses all nine intelligences, and others may exist, but this is a manageable list for educators.
2. Most of us have some of the intelligences highly developed; the other intelligences are either moderately developed or underdeveloped, but we can develop any of them to a moderate level.
3. The intelligences usually work in concert and not alone.
4. There are many ways to demonstrate intelligence within each category (adapted, p. 5).

These multiple intelligences can enable us to understand how a learner might more easily grasp a linguistic concept if it is presented in the form of a mathematical formula (logical/mathematical); how singing songs and doing TPR activities help learners who have trouble focusing attention on printed pages (musical/rhythmic, bodily/kinesthetic); how interacting in pairs helps learners acquire a new linguistic or cultural concept

FIGURE 10.1 Multiple Intelligences

CATEGORY OF INTELLIGENCE	CHARACTERISTICS	FL CLASSROOM ACTIVITIES
PERSONAL: Intrapersonal/Introspective	Self Smart: understanding oneself and taking responsibility for thinking on one's own	Goal setting; journals and personal reflection; problem-solving activities; independent assignments such as autobiographies and family heritage study; open-ended expression
Interpersonal/Social	People Smart: understanding others, getting along with others, interpreting individuals' moods, motivations, inhibitions	Cooperative tasks such as think-pair-share and jigsaws; creative group tasks such as collages and story books; interactive technology such as e-mail, CD-ROM, and Internet
ACADEMIC: Logical/Mathematical	Logic Smart: logical reasoning, categorizing facts, sequential thought	Graphic organizers that show patterns and relationships; problem-solving manipulatives; puzzles and games; challenge tasks
Verbal/Linguistic	Word Smart: communicating by listening, speaking, reading, and writing; using language to link new knowledge to prior experiences	Graphic organizers to promote brainstorming and generating ideas; list making; mnemonics; verbal games; speakers; interviews; peer teaching; personal expression (opinions, reactions); logs or journals
EXPRESSIVE: Bodily/Kinesthetic	Body Smart: skillfully controlling body motions; showing a keen sense of direction and timing in movement	TPR; creative dramatics and mime; creating things; role playing and interviews; projects, field trips, active learning
Visual/Spatial	Picture Smart: accurately comprehending the visual word; transforming mental images; seeing things in terms of pictures	Learning experiences using drawings, charts, props, posters, photographs; illustrations; demonstrations; use of overhead projector, chalkboard, video
Musical/Rhythmic	Music Smart: using pitch, rhythm, and so on, in enjoying and creating musical experiences; being attuned to rhythms, responding with actions	Songs, music, dance of the target culture; music mnemonics; jingles, raps, cheers; using movement or dance to illustrate ideas or concepts
EMERGING: Naturalist	Nature Smart: seeing deeply into the nature of living things; identifying and classifying things; problem solving	Data collection; demonstrations; research projects; logs; reports
Existential (unconfirmed intelligence)	Capturing and pondering the fundamental questions of existence; capacity to raise big questions about one's place in the cosmos	Reading literature or storytelling about life and living, such as the story of an immigrant or a member of a minority group

Source: Compiled from Gahala and Lange, 1997 (pp. 30–32); Gardner, 1993, 1995, 1999; Lange, 1999 (pp. 106–109); and Von Károlyi, Ramos-Ford, and Gardner, 2003, p. 102.

(interpersonal). Appendix 10.1 (see the Web site) provides an extensive list of multiple intelligences activities, classroom environments, and assessments.

thandbook.heinle.com

Haley (2001) reported the results of an action research pilot study in which she examined the effects of using instruction based on multiple intelligences with students in grades 8–12, Levels 1 through 3 of foreign language and ESL classes. She used the survey that appears in Appendix 10.2 (see the Web site) in order to raise student and teacher awareness of multiple intelligences. Students in the experimental group received instruction by means of content-based lessons that strengthened the multiple intelligences, while the control group was exposed to instruction that was primarily teacher-centered. Qualitative data included teachers' reflective journals, weekly activity logs, lesson plans, project descriptions, students' "exit slips" (the "minute paper" CAT from Chapter 11), and comments from participants at the end of the study. Quantitative data included student grades before and after the marking period. Results indicated that most students expressed positive feelings about teachers who used instructional and assessment strategies that addressed the multiple intelligences; teachers attributed this reaction to the "greater degree of flexibility, variety, and choice" that multiple intelligence strategies allow students (Haley, 2001, p. 359). Although student achievement in both groups improved, feedback affirmed that learner-centered instruction from the perspective of multiple intelligences can have an impact on students' strengths and weaknesses.

An intelligence is a "biopsychological potential to process information in certain ways. Each intelligence can be activated in an appropriate cultural setting."

Language Learning Styles

In language learning, a *learning style* is a general approach a learner uses to learn (Scarcella & Oxford, 1992, p. 61). In the previous section you saw how multiple intelligences allow us to understand how learners access and use information from a biopsychological perspective. Gardner points out similarities between multiple intelligences and learning styles, stating that the content discipline of a particular intelligence will drive the approach that the learner uses to acquire knowledge. For instance, musical intelligence, which is an ability to perceive and transform musical forms such as rhythm and pitch, probably is the intelligence used in the songs we sing to learn our ABCs (Díaz & Heining-Boynton, 1995)—the intelligence itself drives behaviors and actions. Learning styles are similar in that they represent another way learners process and perceive information. Proponents of learning styles attempt to describe an individual in terms of one learning style used across all content areas, whereas a learner may still select one of several multiple intelligences depending on the context.

Learning styles research has had particular influence on helping teachers identify ways in which learners differ in their approaches to language learning. Oxford (1990a) and Scarcella & Oxford (1992) identify five key dimensions of language learning styles:

1. *Analytic-global:* This dimension illustrates the difference between a detail-oriented individual and a holistic one. Analytic students concentrate on grammatical details and often do not participate well in communicative activities. They would rather find the meanings of words in a dictionary than guess in context. Global students like interactive tasks in which they use main ideas. They have difficulty dealing with grammatical details and are content to use guessing strategies.
2. *Sensory preferences:* This dimension highlights the physical, perceptual avenues for learning, such as visual, auditory, and hands-on (kinesthetic or movement-oriented

and tactile or touch-oriented). Visual students prefer to read and visualize information; they usually dislike having to process oral input in the absence of visual support. Auditory students enjoy conversations and other types of verbal interaction and often have difficulty with written work. Hands-on students do well with movement around the classroom and work easily with objects and realia.

3. *Intuitive/Random and Sensory/Sequential Learning:* This dimension deals with the type of organization students prefer in the presentation of material. Intuitive/random students think in an abstract, nonsequential, or random manner, making sense of the global picture. Sensory/sequential students prefer to learn new information by means of a step-by-step, ordered presentation. They perform tasks in a linear order and often have difficulty seeing the bigger picture. In the PACE model, presented in Chapter 7, for instance, intuitive/random students are often quite comfortable with language used in context during the Presentation phase and find the Co-Construction phase an interesting puzzle.

4. *Orientation to closure:* This dimension refers to the degree to which students need to reach conclusions and can tolerate ambiguity. Students oriented toward closure want all rules spelled out for them and use metacognitive skills such as planning, organizing, and self-evaluating. However, they often tend to analyze prematurely and experience difficulty dealing with abstract or subtle issues. Ehrman & Oxford (1989) show that the desire for closure might have a negative effect on a student's ability to participate in open-ended communication. Open learners, or those who have less need for closure, learn by osmosis rather than by conscientious effort and appear to use more effective language learning strategies than students who require quick closure (Scarcella & Oxford, 1992, p. 62). As an example, also drawn from the PACE model, learners who have little tolerance for ambiguity ask for the grammatical rule early in the process, and find co-constructing the rule a time-consuming and risky activity.

5. *Competition-cooperation:* This dimension illustrates the degree to which learners benefit from competing against or cooperating with others. Competitive learners are motivated by competition in which winning is of utmost importance. Cooperative individuals prefer working with others in a helpful, supportive situation. Studies show that the high degree of competitiveness in education may account for the fact that learners seldom report using cooperative, social strategies (Kohn, 1987; Reid, 1987). According to Bailey (1983), competition in language learning may result in feelings of anxiety, inadequacy, hostility, fear of failure, guilt, and too strong a desire for approval. As you learned in Chapter 8, cooperative learning provides an avenue for student interaction while increasing self-esteem, achievement, motivation, and the use of cognitive strategies (Kohn, 1987).

 A *learning style* is a general approach a learner uses to learn.

 What is your preferred learning style and why? Which intelligences do you use most often and in what contexts?

Teachers' Personality Types and Teaching Styles

Often teachers prefer certain instructional practices because they comfortably match their personalities. Research on personality types using the Myers-Briggs Type Indicator (Myers & McCaulley, 1985) has shown a high percentage of *feeling* types among foreign language teachers (Heining-Boynton & Heining-Boynton, 1994; Hunt, 1986; Lawrence, 1997, 1996; Myers, McCaulley, Quenk, & Hammer, 1998). Cooper (2001) adapted Lawrence's work on matching personality types with instructional preferences (see Appendix 10.3 on the Web site) and compared these instructional preferences with those of the beginning teachers in his methods class. He found a high percentage of feeling type personalities among the preservice teachers. As you can see in Appendix 10.3, teachers who are characterized as feeling types place importance on personal rapport with students, incorporate small-group work whenever possible, think people are more important than things or ideas, give personal meaning to an assignment, seek ways to give learners benefits from learning, and seek harmony when working with others (Cooper, 2001). However, even though teachers may have preferences for teaching practices, Lawrence (1996) points out that "A sign of a good teacher is the ability to flex one's teaching style to better fit the needs of those being taught" (p.74).

 "A sign of a good teacher is the ability to flex one's teaching style to better fit the needs of those being taught."

If teachers' preferences for certain instructional practices reflect their personalities and their own learning styles, how do the various learners' preferences match? Oxford and Lavine examined the mismatch between instructors' teaching styles and their students' learning styles. They claim that "Students whose learning processes resemble the teacher's are more likely to achieve good grades (and want to continue studying the language) than are students with opposing styles, who may drop the course or even discontinue studying the language" (Oxford & Lavine, 1992, p. 38). The researchers further assert that style wars between teachers and students are often disguised as poor language aptitudes, personality clashes, and bad learner attitudes (p. 42). They suggest six ways in which teachers can realistically deal with these teacher-student style conflicts:

1. Assess your style and students' styles and use this information to understand classroom dynamics. As teachers and students become aware of their major learning style preferences, they may be able to help one another understand diverse views and make an effort to compensate for any style mismatches. Instruments for assessing learning styles can be used, such as Oxford's (1990a) Strategy Inventory for Language Learning (SILL); the Swassing-Barbe Modality Index (Barbe, Swassing, & Milone, 1979); the Myers-Briggs Type Indicator (Myers & McCaulley, 1985); and the Learning Styles Inventory (Kolb, 1984; explained later in this chapter), among others.

2. Change your teaching behavior. Teachers can orient their teaching styles to meet their students' needs by providing a variety of multisensory, abstract, and concrete learning activities that appeal to different learning styles. A standards-based teaching approach that provides for a variety of activities, individual guidance, and an emphasis on meaning can enable students to experience many ways of learning. Learners who are analytic, sequential, or closure-oriented usually like questions and exercises requiring unambiguous information such as completions, definitions, true-false, slash sentences, cloze passages, and guided writing. Learners who are global, intuitive, or open often prefer open-ended activities, personalized questions, simulations and games, interviews, reading for the gist, and social conversation. Visual learners need visual stimuli such as transparencies, slides, video, charts, maps, magnetic or felt boards, posters, board games, and puppets. They benefit from written directions and from being shown, not told, what to do. Auditory learners prefer auditory input from radio, television, video, songs, interviews, oral reports, discussions, telephone conversations, and recordings. They need oral instructions and must be told, not shown, what to do. Hands-on learners require hands-on experiences, such as creating things, manipulating real cultural items, taking notes, doing TPR activities, and following directions. If these learners

"do not receive enough sensory stimuli, they might create their own movement activities unrelated to the learning task (such as tapping pencils, drawing, doodling, wiggling, or bouncing)" (Oxford & Lavine, 1992, p. 43).

3. **Change learners' behavior.** Language learners use their style preferences to their own advantage. Learners can benefit when teachers realize this and provide opportunities for students to move beyond their stylistic comfort zone through the use of strategies with which they might not initially feel comfortable (Scarcella & Oxford, 1992). For example, an analytic learner can benefit from an activity that involves understanding global meaning, while a global student similarly can benefit from specific linguistic analysis.

4. **Change the way students work in groups in your classroom.** Teachers can use the principles of cooperative learning when grouping students for interactive work. In certain tasks, students with similar learning styles might be grouped together, while in other activities, students might be grouped in a heterogeneous fashion so that members might practice stretching beyond their comfort zones.

5. **Change the curriculum.** Teachers can organize lessons as a series of activities or episodes, each with a different objective and style. New materials might be developed in learning-style modules. Multimedia materials can be integrated into the curriculum for classroom and individual use in order to guarantee the tapping of different sensory styles.

6. **Change the way style conflicts are viewed.** Teachers who encourage students to become aware of learning style preferences help promote flexibility and openness to the use of many styles.

 A standards-based teaching approach that provides for a variety of activities, individual guidance, and an emphasis on meaning can enable students to experience many ways of learning. ▪

Language Learning Strategies

Scarcella & Oxford (1992) define language learning strategies as "specific actions, behaviors, steps, or techniques—such as seeking out conversation partners, or giving oneself encouragement to tackle a difficult language task—used by students to enhance their own learning" (p. 63). According to MacIntyre & Noels (1996), almost any tactic or plan that the student believes will help in learning some part of the language or in managing the language learning process can be considered a strategy. Oxford's (1990b) Strategy Inventory for Language Learning (SILL) lists as many as eighty strategies.

Research shows that strategies are effective when used and that they can be taught, although not all strategies are useful for all people in all situations. Figure 10.2 depicts a list of language learning strategies categorized in terms of four stages in the learning process: (1) planning for learning, (2) regulating or facilitating one's learning, (3) problem solving, and (4) evaluating one's progress in learning (Alatis & Barnhardt, 1998).

 Language learning strategies are specific actions, behaviors, steps, or techniques used by students to enhance their own learning. ▪

Oxford (1990b) suggests that instructors teach students how to use strategies in order to help them in the language learning process. Earlier chapters of *Teacher's Handbook* presented ways to teach students effective strategies for using the three modes of communication. Strategy training can be integrated with language learning and communication activities and conducted through simulations, games, and other interactive tasks. Furthermore, MacIntyre & Noels (1996) add that strategy training can encourage the actual

FIGURE 10.2 Learning Strategies Model

PLAN		
Strategy name	Question student asks self	Definition
Goal setting	What is my personal objective? What strategies can help me?	Develop personal objectives, identify purpose of task, choose appropriate strategies
Directed attention	What distractions can I ignore? How can I focus my attention?	Decide in advance to focus on particular tasks and ignore distractions
Activate background knowledge	What do I already know about this topic/task?	Think about and use what you already know to help do the task
Predict/Brainstorm	What kinds of information can I predict for this task? What might I need to do?	Anticipate information to prepare and give yourself direction for the task
REGULATE		
Self-Monitor	Do I understand this? Am I making sense?	Check your understanding to keep track of how you're doing and to identify problems
Selective attention	What should I pay most attention to? Is the information important?	Focus on specific aspects of language or situational details
Deduction	Which rules can I apply to help complete the task?	Apply known rules
Visualize	Can I imagine a picture or situation that will help me understand?	Create an image to represent information to help you remember and check your understanding
Contextualize/ Personalize	How does this fit into the real world?	Think about how to use material in real life, relate information to background knowledge
Cooperate	How can I work with others to do this?	Work with others to help build confidence and to give and receive feedback
Self-talk	I can do this! What strategies can I use to help me?	Reduce anxiety by reminding self of progress, resources available, and goals
PROBLEM-SOLVE		
Inference/Substitute	Can I guess what this means? Is there another way to say/do this?	Make guesses based on previous knowledge
Question for clarification	What help do I need? Who/Where can I ask?	Ask for explanation and examples
Resource	What information do I need? Where can I find more information about this?	Use reference materials
EVALUATE		
Verify	Were my predictions and guesses right? Why or why not?	Check whether your predictions/guesses were right
Summarize	What is the gist/main idea of this?	Create a mental, oral, written summary

Source: Alatis and Barnhardt, 1998, p. 82.

use of the strategy by building assurance in learners that they know the strategies well, that the strategies will work, and that they are not difficult to use (1996, p. 383). Oxford (1990a) developed the following eight-step model for integrating strategy training into classroom activities:

1. Identify students' needs to determine what strategies they are currently using, how effective the strategies are, and how they can be improved.
2. Choose relevant strategies to be taught.
3. Determine how best to integrate strategy training into regular classroom activities.
4. Consider students' motivations and attitudes about themselves as learners and about learning new ways to learn.
5. Prepare materials and activities.
6. Conduct *completely informed* training, in which students learn and practice new strategies, learn why the strategies are important, learn to evaluate their use of the strategies, and learn how to apply the strategies in new situations (refer to Figure 10.2 for an example of this training model in action).
7. Evaluate the strategy training.
8. Revise the strategy training procedure for the next set of strategies to be taught (pp. 48–49).

An alternative to direct strategy instruction is suggested in a study in which Donato and McCormick (1994) helped students in a French conversation class to identify and create their own learning strategies by means of a portfolio assessment project. In this study, students were instructed to provide, in their portfolios, *evidence* of their learning. As they selected the evidence, they engaged in four cyclical steps: self-assessing, setting goals, using specific plans of action (strategies), and connecting to and reflecting upon past performance or evidence. For instance, a self-assessment statement such as "I can't speak quickly enough" could be turned into a goal such as "I'll speak more in class" (p. 459). This goal then became the strategy of talking with a friend in French twice a week on the telephone. Students demonstrated that they were connecting with their work and reflecting on past performance, saying, for example, "I listened to the recorded conversation I had with my friend and noticed I said '*Ah bon*' a lot and didn't attempt to paraphrase" (p. 461). Thus, the students engaged in a dialogue with themselves, their work, and their instructor, resulting in development and selection of strategies that facilitated their learning within the situated sociocultural framework of the classroom.

The use of appropriate learning strategies often results in increased language proficiency and greater self-confidence (Cohen, 1990; Oxford & Crookall, 1989). Research supports the idea that many learners are relatively unaware of the strategies they use and do not take advantage of the full range of available strategies. As you read about the learners with special needs described in the following section of this chapter, think about how you might help them use the learning strategies described above in a standards-based approach.

 The use of appropriate learning strategies often results in increased language proficiency and greater self-confidence. ▪

Addressing Diverse Learner Needs

In this section, we will explore two groups of learners who have special needs: (1) learners with special physical needs and (2) learners with special learning needs (learners with learning disabilities, at-risk learners, gifted learners, and heritage or home background learners). First, however, we will examine the definition of the term *disabilities* and explore how the federal government has ensured that students with disabilities are part of regular classrooms and receive special accommodations in those classrooms.

"Disabilities": Accommodating Learners Through Inclusion

Teaching foreign languages to all students, as specified in the *SFLL*, requires special attention to the needs of students with disabilities. A *disability* is a mental or physical impairment that limits a major life activity—for example, caring for oneself, performing a manual task, hearing, walking, speaking, thinking, and so forth. Disabilities include autism, deafness, deaf-blindness, hearing impairment, mental retardation, multiple disabilities, orthopedic impairment, other health impairments (such as limited strength due to asthma, heart condition, leukemia, etc.), serious emotional disturbance, a specific learning disability, speech or language impairment, traumatic brain injury, and visual impairment including blindness. Prior to 1975, students with these types of disabilities were placed together in classes often labeled "Special Education." In 1975, Public Law 94-142 (Education for All Handicapped Children Act of 1975) directed public schools to find, enroll, and educate all handicapped children. In addition, Public Law 101-476 (Individuals with Disabilities Education Act of 1990, sometimes called IDEA**)**, and Public Law 105-17 (Amendments to IDEA, 1997) ensure that persons with disabilities are not denied participation in or benefits from educational programs or activities, and that these persons do not face negative bias or stereotyping associated with a disability. Through a provision called *inclusion*, students who have physical, intellectual, or emotional impairments are now often part of regular classrooms and receive special accommodations in those classrooms (Good & Brophy, 1991).

In 2000–2001, more than six million school-age children in the United States received special support services to address their disabilities (NCES, 2002). School personnel work with families and learners to outline individualized education programs (IEPs) or individualized family service plans (IFSPs) to provide accommodations that must be offered to learners with disabilities or special needs. Roughly 13% of the school population has had an IEP developed by a team consisting of a counselor, principal, teacher, parent and sometimes the student (Hoffman, 2002). See Appendix 10.4 (on the Web site) for a definition of types of disabilities and the basis on which school-based committees in a large well-respected school division determine a student's eligibility to receive special education services.

thandbook.heinle.com

Through a provision called *inclusion*, students who have physical, intellectual, or emotional impairments are now often part of regular classrooms and receive special accommodations in those classrooms. ■

Teaching Foreign Languages to Learners with Special Physical Needs

Accommodating Learners' Physical Needs. Language teachers who work with students who have physical disabilities must make arrangements to ensure that these students have access to various areas in the classroom and that their special physical needs are met. Teachers need to be aware of how students' physical limitations will affect participation in certain types of hands-on activities, such as TPR, and how alternative activities might be provided to accomplish language learning goals. Students who have physical disabilities may require space for a wheelchair, crutches, or a walker. They may also need extra time to move through the halls to the next class and therefore might require early dismissal or a companion to help negotiate the hallways or carry books.

Accommodating Deaf and Hard-of-Hearing Learners. Deaf and hard-of-hearing students may come from a home where their family members are also deaf or hard-of-hearing, or they may come from a home where their family members are hearing. In either case, the students have the benefit of having learned American Sign Language (ASL)[3] or some other form of manual communication. Teachers should keep in mind that deaf and hard-of-hearing students come from a community of people who share or at least deeply understand their special needs in communication.

In a foreign language class, deaf students who have learned ASL and English in school could be learning a third or subsequent language (Strong, 1988). Spinelli (1989) describes an approach to language instruction for deaf students in which they are taught to use sign language in the foreign language through the use of videotapes showing target-culture signing. Using the target language signing system is a more effective system for communication than finger spelling the foreign language.

Foreign language teachers of deaf students must think visually about their teaching. Students might be given the scripts that often accompany audiocassette programs, and they should be permitted to refer to their textbooks or to other written material during oral presentations. Teachers may need to prepare written scripts of oral activities to assist students with comprehension, and a note taker may be required for discussions. The visual and written modalities might be stressed in combination with comparative study of the deaf culture as opposed to that of the hearing culture.

Students who have hearing impairments may also require preferred seating arrangements, face-to-face talk if they read lips, and perhaps interpreters. Students who are hearing impaired can often tell the teacher how they learn most effectively and can suggest ways for the teacher to aid their learning. Teachers should keep in mind that reading can be difficult and frustrating for a deaf person, depending on the degree of hearing loss. Since a great deal of reading ability is associated with phonological awareness and profoundly deaf children cannot make letter-sound correspondences, reading is a tedious process for most deaf children. The following are suggestions for teaching strategies:

- videotape classes;
- use visuals and audio materials together;
- summarize key points in an introduction and a conclusion;
- use a typed outline of the lesson;
- reduce the number of words in your directions (use key words);
- don't be afraid to repeat instructions (Moore & Moore, 1997).

Accommodating Visually Impaired Learners. In the case of students with visual impairments, large-type, braille, and auditory texts or other types of assistive technology are needed; oral examinations, reading services, preferred seating in the classroom, and perhaps space for a guide dog are other accommodations. Teachers can capitalize on oral skills and the use of discussion, especially since students' primary goal may be to develop interpersonal speaking abilities. In addition, students need extra class time to process material that they read in braille. Partnerships between class members can be arranged for TPR activities that involve manipulatives, which may result in greater use of the target language. For example, in practicing vocabulary dealing with clothing, a student with visual impairment tells a sighted student where he wants to place a specific item of clothing on a laminated paper doll (B. Kraft, personal communication, April 22, 1992). In exam situations, special considerations can be made, such as giving only oral exams for these students or having each student dictate his/her answers to another student who writes them down (Phillips de Herrera, 1984). Students may also be allowed to tape classes, or to put their responses to assignments on tape (Moore & Moore, 1997).

Teaching Foreign Language to Learners with Special Learning Needs

Schools deliver a variety of services to assist students who have special learning needs. Students who are considered *average* or *non-gifted* (the term *gifted* will be discussed later) may also have special cognitive needs. According to Fairfax County Public Schools (1992), some of these students have learning disabilities while others simply need some adjustments in their class schedules, testing or homework arrangements, or other educational services (see below). It is paramount that the foreign language teacher understand the characteristics of these groups in order to use specific teaching strategies that will enable them to experience success in the language classroom.

Accommodating Average or Non-Gifted Learners with Special Cognitive Needs. Average students with special cognitive needs are able to perform at expected levels, but they may perform at a lower level of expectation or ability because of emotional, motivational, cultural, or social difficulties; they may also have poor study skills. Specific strategies for the foreign language teacher include the following:

- Communicate specific expectations and monitor student progress constantly.
- Give specific explanations and instructions orally and visually, step by step.
- Provide a variety of activities, some of which require physical movement.
- Get students on task immediately and provide frequent changes of pace.
- Display student work as a form of reinforcement for work done well.
- Choose reading selections, writing assignments, and presentation topics related to student interests.
- Provide choices of activities and higher-level thinking activities as students seem ready.
- Have students repeat the homework assignment instructions and, if time allows, begin the assignment. This provides time to work with students needing assistance (Fairfax County Public Schools, 1992, p. 5).

Accommodating Students With Learning Disabilities. A second group of special needs students are those with learning disablilities. Public Law 94-142 defines a learning disability:

> A disorder in one or more of the basic psychological processes involved in understanding or in using language, spoken or written, which may manifest itself in an imperfect ability to listen, speak, read, write, spell, or do mathematical calculations. The term does not include children who have learning problems which are primarily the result of visual, hearing, or motor handicaps, or mental retardation, emotional disturbance, or environmental, cultural, or economic disadvantage (U.S. Department of Education; cf. Sparks, Ganschow, & Javorsky, 1995, p. 480).

A learning disorder interferes with a student's ability to store, process, or produce information. Learning disorders are intrinsic to the individual, are presumed to be due to central nervous system dysfunction, and may occur across the life span. Problems in self-regulatory behaviors, social perception, and social interaction may exist with learning disorders but do not by themselves constitute a learning disorder. Although learning disorders may occur concomitantly with other handicapping conditions (for example, sensory impairment, mental retardation, or serious emotional disturbance) or with extrinsic influences (such as cultural differences and insufficient or inappropriate instruction), they are not the result of those conditions or influences (Brinckerhoff, Shaw, & McGuire, 1993). An impairment can be quite subtle and may go undetected throughout life. Nevertheless, learning disorders create a gap between a person's true capacity and day-to-day productivity and performance (Levine, 1984).

The category of students labeled as having learning disabilities poses a challenge for teachers of all disciplines, partially because there is a lack of agreement among cognition experts concerning the specific criteria that determine whether or not a student has a learning disability, and partially because most of the related assessments are based on memory work, an area in which not all learners excel. State and local agencies have the responsibility to test and diagnose learning disabilities. Once diagnosed, the learners then have access to services provided by federal, state, and local agencies to help them achieve in the least restrictive educational environment. However, Lyon and Moats (1993) point out that these agencies use different testing measures and criteria in classifying learning disabled (LD) learners, and they are often influenced by the political/social agendas of community groups. For example, one criterion often used in diagnosing a learning disability is the discrepancy between the IQ score and the score on a measure of academic achievement.[4] In some states, a fifteen-point discrepancy would classify a student as being LD while in other states the discrepancy must be twenty-two points (Sparks & Javorsky, 1998).

Students are often categorized as learning disabled as a result of the type of instruction they receive and not necessarily because of verified learning disorders. For example, Bruck (1978) discovered that students with learning disabilities who learned French by means of a traditional approach actually acquired little knowledge of the language, because the method exploited the areas in which they had the most difficulties: memorization, learning language out of context, and understanding abstract rules. Learning disabilities, particularly in cases of students labeled *mildly disabled*, may be exacerbated by traditional classrooms that emphasize rules and bottom-up processing. Unfortunately, many learners are incorrectly classified as LD and carry that label with them throughout their educational experience, while other learners who may require special assistance are never diagnosed with a learning disability.

Although students labeled as LD may vary widely in their specific learning problems, Levine (1984) cites the following types of difficulties that are commonly exhibited:

- difficulties in keeping attention focused: tuning in and out, inconsistent performance, impulsive behavior, and a negative self-image;
- language processing difficulties;
- spatial orientation problems: words look different, and reversals in letters and in placement of letters and words are common;
- poor memory;
- difficulty in organizing work;
- sequencing problems: difficulty in putting a series of items in correct order, difficulty in following instructions, difficulty in organizing work (adapted from Levine; cf. Spinelli, 1996, pp. 74–75).

The initial research on learning disabilities and language learning was motivated by the practice of universities that waived the foreign language requirement for those students who had a documented learning disability. Several researchers in the field of special education noted that students who experience FL learning difficulties are likely to have phonological/syntactic problems in their native language (Sparks, Ganschow, &

Pohlman, 1989; Javorsky, Sparks, & Ganschow, 1992; Sparks, Ganschow, Javorsky, Pohlman, & Patton, 1992). Using research based on teaching methods that relied heavily on skill-based memory work, they initially posited the Linguistic Coding Deficit Hypothesis and later renamed it the Linguistic Coding Differences Hypothesis (LCDH) in an attempt to explain the differences between successful and unsuccessful FL learners in terms of their oral/written native language skills and FL aptitude (Sparks & Ganschow, 1995, 1996). They later found that no separate entity such as the Linguistic Coding Differences Hypothesis exists, but they proposed that skill in one's native language and aptitude for learning a foreign language may affect the learner's anxiety level (Sparks & Ganschow).

Continuing their work in studying learning disabilities among language learners, these researchers studied additional learning disability labels among language learners. They found that (1) students classified/not classified as LD who experienced FL difficulties did not demonstrate significant differences in cognitive achievement, FL aptitude, or FL grades; and (2) the majority of students receiving FL course substitutions failed to meet any LD legal/research criteria (Sparks, Artzer, Javorsky, Patton, Ganschow, Miller, & Hordubay, 1998; Sparks & Javorsky, 1998). The answer to the legal question of when, if ever, a university should be required to provide a waiver from the foreign language requirement came in a 1998 legal ruling in *Guckenberg* v. *Trustees of Boston University:* "Universities must provide accommodations, but are not legally required to provide course substitutions for the FL requirement, . . . if the university deems foreign language as an essential part of the curriculum" (cf. Sparks & Javorsky, 1998, p. 11). The implication of this ruling is that everyone can learn a language if appropriate accommodations are made.

More recently, the same team of researchers studied students who had difficulty in FL and were labeled as having a single learning disability, those who had difficulties in FL and were labeled as having a learning disability as well as the second disability of Attention Deficit Hyperactivity Disability (ADHD), and those who had difficulties in FL but were not labeled in either way. They found that presence of a second disability may not result in more severe FL learning problems, and that these students perform as well as students who are not labeled as having LD (Sparks, Phillips, & Javorsky, 2003). These findings seem to be consistent in supporting the notion that students labeled as having various types of learning disabilities can learn a language with appropriate accommodations.

The research conducted by Sparks, Javorsky, Ganshow, and colleagues has been criticized for not recognizing the ways in which the social context of learning and of the classroom can influence cognitive processes and language learning and the potential effects of affective variables when considering the relation between aptitude and achievement (Arries, 1999; Mabbott, 1995; MacIntyre, 1995). Key concepts that are current in the standards-based classroom of the 21st century should be considered in research on learning disabilities. Among these concepts and potential variables are proficiency and student-centered, standards-based, and socioculturally motivated instruction. Mabbott's (1994) study indicates that students with L1 difficulties were able to successfully acquire a second language. Arries (1999) suggests that teachers take a qualitative approach to analyzing how LD-classified students perform in their classes and make appropriate accommodations as suggested by the students through interviews and self-reports.

There are several implications from the LD foreign language research for the language teacher who has students manifesting learning difficulties:

1. In a proficiency-oriented, standards-based classroom, a learning disability may not have the confounding influence it might have in a more traditional memory/skills-based classroom.

2. Given the lack of consensus regarding the classification of LD, the language teacher should not assume that learners who are not labeled LD do not have learning disabilities.

3. The language teacher should not assume that students with learning disability labels cannot experience success in foreign language learning. Curtain (1986), Spinelli (1996), and Mabbott (1994) suggest that immersion programs may provide the best environment in which LD students can learn a foreign language, since students are involved in meaningful interaction and hands-on experiences.

4. A classroom environment that is rich in sociocultural learning (see Chapter 1) and includes content-based and story-based approaches (see Chapters 3, 4, 7) can provide the type of meaningful instructional support and learning experiences that facilitate language learning for students with learning disabilities.

5. The language teacher should carefully assess why an individual is having a problem in the class and should engage students in self-assessment and conferences (see Chapter 11). The teacher should be familiar with and use a variety of strategies for helping students with specific kinds of difficulties in learning the foreign language.

The following are some general strategies for helping students with learning disabilities in the foreign language classroom:

- Use a well-organized daily classroom routine, with frequent praise and repetition of ideas (McCabe, 1985; Moore & Moore, 1997).

- Develop a communicative-oriented rather than a grammar-oriented class, with as much personal interaction as possible (Mabbott, 1994).

- Use frequent review and repetition, and present small amounts of material at one time (Sparks, Ganschow, Javorsky, Pohlman, & Patton, 1992).

- When conducting listening and reading activities, give fewer instructions at one time, provide prelistening/prereading discussion, and give comprehension questions prior to and after the reading selection, spending more time focusing on a literal level first before moving to a figurative level (Barnett, 1985; Moore & Moore, 1997).

- Provide opportunities for students to learn through more than one modality, particularly through the tactile (touching, manipulating objects) or kinesthetic (use of movement, gestures) modalities (Spinelli, 1989). One such approach emphasizes the use of the tactile and kinesthetic modalities in teaching reading to dyslexic/learning disabled students (Gillingham & Stillman, 1969; Kennewig, 1986; Schneider, 1996; Sparks, Ganschow, Kenneweg & Miller, 1991). Sparks & Ganschow (1993) showed significant gains in teaching Spanish to learning disabled students using a multisensory, structured language approach for teaching phonological and syntactic elements of a foreign language.[5]

- Have realistic expectations of what students can do, and measure their progress in terms of their own abilities rather than in terms of what the entire class can attain.

- Provide ample opportunities for students to interact with other students in the class by means of cooperative learning activities. Emphasize how important it is for all students to understand, respect, and help one another in the learning process.

- Allow extra time, if needed, for students to complete assignments and tests.

- Make special provisions for testing. Allow students to take a test orally if they have trouble reading; allow students to take a test a second time if they did not do well the first time; give students additional time to complete tests; allow students to use grammar charts and dictionaries during tests. Realize that students with learning disabilities may not perform well on certain test formats such as spelling, memorizing dialogs, reading aloud, and taking notes (Mabbott, 1994). Consider integrating dynamic assessments by providing intervention between phases or part of an assessment in order to provide students with guided assistance, as in the IPA (see Chapter 11).

■ Provide time for more individualized work with special education students and offer continued feedback on their progress. During this time, work with them on developing effective learning strategies.

As you read through the lists of strategies presented here, you may have recognized that many of them have already been suggested throughout the *Teacher's Handbook* for use with all students. Research suggests that the instructional methods that are effective with students who have learning disabilities tend to be the same as those that are effective with other students, except that students with learning disabilities may need more attention (Larrivee, 1985). Students with physical or learning disabilities may need more individualized instruction and more one-to-one instruction from the teacher (Madden & Slavin, 1983), while students with behavior disorders may require closer supervision (Thompson, White, & Morgan, 1982).

Providing Effective Learning Experiences for At-Risk Students

As foreign language teachers face the challenge of teaching special needs students who have been mainstreamed into regular classes, they are also encountering more and more children labeled *at-risk* of educational failure. *At-risk* students are those who "are likely to fail—either in school or in life" (Frymier & Gansneder, 1989, p. 142) due to circumstances beyond their control (Spinelli, 1996, p. 72). In 2000, roughly 13% of the school population was considered at risk (NCES, 2002). These students have a high likelihood of dropping out of school, being low achievers, or even committing suicide. They are at risk because of a wide variety of circumstances they face outside of school: poverty, dysfunctional family life, neglect, abuse, or cultural/ethnic/racial background. The "three strongest social correlates of suicidal behavior in youth are family breakdown, a youth's unemployment, and decreasing religious observance among the young" (Garfinkel, interviewed by Frymier, 1989, p. 290). *At-riskness* has been described as "a function of what bad things happen to a child, how severe they are, how often they happen, and what else happens in the child's immediate environment" (Frymier & Gansneder, p. 142). At-risk students often display emotional and/or psychological symptoms such as depression, anxiety, difficulty in concentrating, and excessive anger, as well as physical symptoms such as respiratory problems, headaches, and muscle tension (Vanucci, 1991).

 At-risk students are those who are likely to fail due to circumstances beyond their control. ■

Socioeconomic status, educational level, and poverty are additional factors that may also put a student at risk of failure. Students who are at risk are often from low socioeconomic environments and single-parent families, and from certain heritage groups, such as African American, Hispanic, Asian, or Native American.[6] They frequently experience problems in school because of their loss of identity or ethnic roots, difficulty in integrating themselves into the majority culture, and other students' incorrect perceptions of them. The likelihood of attainment of educational milestones such as graduation from high school, enrollment in and graduation from a post-secondary institution is highest for some Asian heritage learners, and for whites. While the educational attainment of Hispanic and black students has increased in recent years, it is still lower than that of non-Black and non-Hispanic students (NCES, 2002).

In many cases, the difficulties that minority students face seem insurmountable when the students are placed in classrooms that stress total conformity to the majority culture. Educators have come a long way in the past twenty years in learning to address the needs of at-risk and minority students. Thirty-nine percent of the school systems in the US provide alternative schools for at-risk students (NCES, 2002). Students are sent to alternative schools if their performance indicates a risk of failure as revealed in possession, distribution, or use of alcohol or drugs; physical attacks or fights; chronic truancy; possession or use of a weapon other than a firearm; continual academic failure; disruptive verbal behavior; and possession or use of a firearm. Teen pregnancy/parenthood and mental health needs were least likely to be sole reasons for transfer (Kleiner, Porch, & Farris, 2002). Within alternative schools, the goal is to return students to a regular school as soon as possible, or to enable them to graduate by means of academic counseling, smaller class size than in regular schools, remedial instruction, opportunity for self-paced instruction, crisis/behavioral intervention, and career counseling.

Much of the research in multicultural education for teaching at-risk students has clear implications for classroom instruction. Heining-Boynton (1994) points out that frequent assessment and adaptation of instruction to learners' needs are beneficial for these learners, along with techniques that foreign language teachers have praised for years as good instruction. The following list illustrates possible strategies that foreign language teachers might use as they attempt to provide successful language learning for all students:

thandbook.heinle.com

1. Engage students in activities that encourage social interaction and promote the use of higher order thinking skills to challenge students' creativity (Kuykendall, 1989). See Appendix 10.5 (on the Web site) for a chart of strategies to extend student thinking.
2. Relate learning about another language and culture to students' own life experiences (Kuykendall, 1989).
3. Offer descriptive instead of evaluative feedback in an effort to encourage progress rather than cause frustration. Also, display each student's work at some time during the academic year (Kuykendall, 1989).
4. Maintain direct, sincere eye contact when communicating with individual students (Kuykendall, 1989).
5. Make every effort to give all students equal opportunities to participate.
6. Use heterogeneous and cooperative groupings for interactive tasks, as described in Chapter 8 (Kuykendall, 1989).
7. Make the language curriculum reflect the individual cultures of the students by including study of key historical/political figures from various cultures, inviting guest speakers from various cultures, engaging students in discussion in the target language about their own cultures, and discussing in the target language current events that involve the students' own cultures (Kuykendall, 1989).
8. If there are native speakers of the target language who are students in the language class, encourage their ethnic pride by engaging them in activities such as providing oral input in the target language, helping other students undertake culture projects, offering classmates additional cultural information, and sharing family photographs.
9. When presenting the cultures of the people who speak the target language, include people of different age groups, both male and female, and from as many geographical regions as possible.
10. When sharing opinions or discussing abstract topics, encourage students to express their own ideas concerning values, morals, and religious views, as shaped by their own cultures and religious convictions.
11. Use visuals that portray males and females of diverse racial and ethnic origins.

12. Hold the same achievement expectations for all students in the class, except in cases of physical or intellectual disabilities (Kuykendall, 1989).

13. Provide opportunities for students to help one another. Sullivan and McDonald (1990) found that cross-age peer tutoring is an effective strategy that enables students to exercise autonomy, gain self-esteem, achieve at a higher level than normal, and learn more about students who are different from themselves. In Sullivan and McDonald's (1990) study, high school Spanish III students in an urban school district taught Spanish to elementary school children. See Case Study I, "A Play for My 'Buddies,'" in Chapter 9 for an example of cross-age tutoring.

14. Maintain positive teacher-parent relationships by inviting parents to see students' work in the foreign language, such as special projects, exhibits, or drama presentations. Talk to parents about their children's individual talents and progress (Kuykendall, 1989).

Teaching Gifted Learners

Johnson and Johnson (1991) point out that a "concern of all educators is how to challenge the academic capabilities of all students and maximize their intellectual development" (p. 24). Gifted learners make up another category of special needs students. Challenging the academic capabilities of gifted learners is neither a more nor a less important charge than challenging the academic capabilities of slow learners.

Defining Giftedness. A specific definition of the term *gifted* was provided by Congress in P.L. 97-35 (1981), the Omnibus Education Reconciliation Act:

> Children who give evidence of high performance capability in areas such as intellectual, creative, artistic, leadership capacity, or specific academic fields, and who require services or activities not ordinarily provided by the school in order to fully develop such capabilities. (Sec. 582[3][A])

In their presentation of the work of twenty-nine researchers, Sternberg & Davidson (1986) conclude that giftedness is viewed most often in terms of cognitive processing capacities. Although identification of gifted learners has been a major focus of much of the literature in the area of gifted education, most measures are unsatisfactory. Researchers agree that multiple measures are preferred over any single achievement test and that efforts should be made to specify alternate types of giftedness (Feldhusen, 1989).

The National Council of State Supervisors of Foreign Languages describes linguistically gifted students as those who have an IQ, based on a standardized intelligence test, in the top three to five percent of the student population and scores of 500 to 600 on the verbal or math section of the SAT exam (Bartz, 1982). Although functional definitions generally refer to the upper two percent of the population as the *highly gifted* and the top five percent of the population as the *gifted,* to date there are no data to show what portion of the general population and what portion of the gifted population are linguistically gifted. Nor is there conclusive evidence to explain why certain students are gifted learners. Treffinger and Feldhusen (1996) propose identification and nurturing the talents of all students rather than identifying and serving a small percentage of the population. While practices in the past have been to identify a percentage of the population as gifted, current practice is to identify the giftedness within each learner.

Gifted education is often justified on the basis of generally accepted purposes: (1) to provide young people with opportunities for maximum cognitive growth and self-fulfillment through the development and expression of one or a combination of performance areas where superior potential may be present, and (2) to increase our society's reservoir of persons who will help to solve the problems of contemporary civilization by becoming producers of knowledge and creative works rather than mere consumers of existing information (Renzulli, 1999). Thus, programs for the gifted typically include challenging real-world tasks, instruction targeted to the learner's strengths, enabling students to observe and perform in ways consistent with what professionals in a given field might do; e.g., the study of science enables students to conduct experiments as a scientist would; the study of civics gives students practice in behaving as a delegate at a national political convention.

 Try to identify the giftedness in each learner. ■

Curricular and Instructional Modifications on Gifted Learners. Program models for gifted learners traditionally involved *acceleration*, which is instruction provided at a level and pace appropriate to the student's level of achievement or readiness (Feldhusen, 1989), and *enrichment*, which is in-depth study of broad topics involving higher level thinking processes (Renzulli, 1986; Renzulli & Reis, 1985). There is agreement among specialists in the field of gifted education that the best programs include acceleration as well as enrichment and other adjustments according to the learner's needs and abilities, often within, but not limited to, the regular classroom setting. All curricular models for the gifted call for use of varied modes and levels of thinking, grounded in learners' interests and capacities, in order to create meaningful products. Modifications to curriculum and instructional practices should be done so that all learners benefit, not just gifted learners (VanTassel-Baska, 2003). Successful models include the Integrated Curriculum Model (VanTassel-Baska, 2003), the Schoolwide Enrichment Model (Reis, Burns, & Renzulli, 1992; Renzulli & Reis, 2003), the Parallel Curriculum Model (Tomlinson, Kaplan, Renzulli, Purcell, Leppien, & Burns, 2002), and numerous others. The process of modifying curriculum and instructional practices to benefit specific groups of learners is called *differentiation*.

One technique used to modify instruction is *compacting*. According to Renzulli & Reis (2003), *curriculum compacting* is a way to "(1) adjust the levels of required learning so that all students are challenged, (2) increase the number of in-depth learning experiences, and (3) introduce various types of enrichment into regular curricular experiences" (pp. 190–191). As with all modifications, the first step is to define the goals and outcomes of a given unit, perhaps using *SFLL* or *ESL Standards,* pre- or post-tests for the unit, or standardized tests. The second step is to identify what the students already know and are able to do, noting what background knowledge they may already have about this unit and where they may be able to progress more quickly or where they may need further in-depth study.[7] In the final stage, students and teacher work together to gather materials to enrich their study, identify small flexible groups for skill instruction, or identify activities to replace others students already know.

Differentiated instruction is often a preferred means for matching a core curriculum to the abilities of learners, gifted or not. Differentiation requires that teachers deepen and widen fields of study, allow for accelerated progress through assigned material, minimize the extent of drill and practice activities, provide for in-depth study and use of critical-thinking skills, assess progress and then modify their instruction, and employ every possible strategy to ensure that instruction and practice are contextualized and meaningful. See further explanation and examples later in this chapter.

Cooperative learning, as described in Chapter 8, allows students to excel in social learning environments where their levels of expertise can be appreciated and used in task-oriented activities. With cooperative learning, as with differentiated instruction and curriculum compacting, educators should employ the program models and instructional strategies that suit the needs of learners, not restricting a particular model or practice to a select group of students.

There is concern among researchers and practitioners in gifted education that cultural, racial, and linguistic minorities are underrepresented in gifted programs and that they underachieve. Ford & Thomas (1997) cite studies showing that, on average, 50% of gifted minority students underachieve. Ogbu (1997) points out that neither the core curriculum movement nor the multicultural movement addresses the problem of minorities who could be gifted but do not do well in school. For the classroom teacher, specific challenges arise when attempting to help such learners. In Appendix 10.6 (see the Web site), Ford (2003) outlines useful techniques to enhance the achievement of gifted minority students.

thandbook.heinle.com

Strategies for Teaching Gifted Learners in the FL Classroom. The language teacher's task therefore is to organize instruction so that the linguistically gifted can benefit while other learners also benefit (Fenstermacher, 1982). Gifted learners need opportunities to use all of their abilities and to acquire new knowledge and skills. The following are strategies that might be used by the language teacher to teach gifted learners:

- Provide opportunities for students to study and research certain cultural topics in greater depth—for example, through projects in which they investigate the living patterns of the target language group.
- Present taped segments and readings that are appropriately challenging.
- Provide opportunities for students to use their critical thinking skills through debate of controversial societal issues and interpretation of literary works.
- Allow gifted students to choose the topic of their taped segments or readings from time to time, thereby encouraging work in areas of interest.
- Build in some time for gifted students to work with one another on assignments or projects, with you serving as facilitator.
- Allow some opportunities for gifted students to assume leadership roles through activities such as serving as group leaders/facilitators and providing peer help to students who missed class or need extra assistance.
- Involve gifted learners in interaction with other students in the class through cooperative learning tasks, such as those presented in Chapter 8. Research shows that cooperative learning for gifted students may result in (1) higher mastery and retention of material than that achieved in competitive or individual learning; (2) increased opportunities to use critical thinking and higher level reasoning strategies; (3) acquisition of cognitive restructuring, along with practice gained by explaining tasks and solutions to peers—in other words, learning through teaching; and (4) enhancement of social interaction and self-esteem (Fulghum, 1992; Johnson & Johnson, 1991).

Heritage Language Learners

Another growing group of students requiring specific types of attention in the classroom is the *heritage language learner* group. Heritage language learners, sometimes also called *home background learners*, have learned languages other than English at home in the United States, as a result of their cultural or ethnic backgrounds. The *SFLL* classifies students into four categories, depending on their home languages background: (1) those who have no home background other than English; (2) those who are second- and third-generation bilinguals schooled exclusively in English in the United States; (3) first-generation immigrant students schooled primarily in the United States; and (4) newly arrived immigrant students.

The issue of the heritage language learner is worldwide. According to Census 2000 figures, 17.9% of the U.S. population age five and over speaks a language other than English at home (NCES, 2002). Home background learners speak many languages in the United States, including Chinese, Spanish, Korean, Hmong, Greek, Armenian, and Ukrainian. In Canada, languages include Chinese, French, Italian, Japanese, Vietnamese, and Ukrainian. In Australia, fourteen languages ranging from Arabic to Vietnamese are listed as national priority languages (Gutiérrez, 1997; Ingram, 1994; Valdés, 1995).

Heritage learners are placed into foreign language classes at the K–12 level for a variety of reasons. Sometimes heritage learners take classes in their heritage language in order to acquire new content knowledge (e.g., culture or literature) and/or to improve their proficiency in the language. For example, as a teacher of Spanish, you may find heritage learners in your class who have fairly well-developed oral interpersonal communication skills in Spanish but limited reading ability and oral and written presentational skills. In other instances, heritage learners wish to study another language: As a teacher of French, you may have Asian or Hispanic heritage learners for whom French is their third language. Yet another scenario is the heritage learner of Chinese, whose grandparents speak Cantonese, and who has enrolled in your Mandarin Chinese class. Unfortunately, in some cases, school administrators may place heritage learners into foreign language classes where they already know the language, for reasons of convenience and in the absence of clearly defined goals for language study. In such cases, language teachers should work with these learners in order to develop goals and a plan for their learning.

Heritage or home background learners have learned languages other than English at home in the United States, as a result of their cultural or ethnic backgrounds.

The Constitution of the United States does not specify a national language (Thomas, 1996). In fact, documents written by the founding leaders of the Continental Congress as they were shaping the new country were circulated in French, German, and English. Researchers studying language changes among the multiethnic waves of immigrants who came to the United States found that the mother tongue was often displaced by monolingual English by the second, third, or fourth generation (Fishman, 1964, 1994; Veltman, 1983). While it is clear that learning to use English will result in greater access to education and employment opportunities (Valdés, 1999), preservation of the heritage language and culture helps foster understanding and diversity. Ethnic bilingualism is a mid-stage in the transition from the mother tongue to English monolingualism in the United States.

Valdés (1999) issues a strong challenge to language teachers, calling for awareness that "language maintenance efforts are as important a part of our profession as is the teaching of language to monolingual speakers of English." In the 1990s, a group called *U.S. English* attempted to establish English as the national language and later as the language of individual states. Fearing that English in the United States was threatened by immigrant populations, these groups ignored the facts of the United States 1990 census, in which the pattern of assimilation of immigrant groups outlined by Fishman in 1964 was affirmed (Valdés, 1999).

Schools have recognized, with the support of the National Association of Secondary School Principals, the American Association of Applied Linguistics, and other professional groups, that maintaining the heritage language while learning a new language enriches the academic and cultural experience of the learner and the society (Bucholtz, 1995). Simultaneously, the very presence of heritage learners can help schools and educators recognize the community "funds of knowledge" (Moll, 1992, p. 20) that exist in heritage language students' homes and communities. Just as there are multiple intelligences (Gardner, 1993, 1999), there are multiple dimensions and layers in literacy, identity, knowledge, and discourse in both the dominant and heritage languages and cultures. While students need to acquire the literacies of the dominant society, educators need to value the literacies that students possess (Wang & García, 2002).

FIGURE 10.3 Characteristics of Home Background Students

STUDENT CHARACTERISTICS	ENGLISH LANGUAGE DEVELOPMENT NEEDS	HERITAGE/HOME LANGUAGE DEVELOPMENT NEEDS
Second- and third-generation "bilinguals" schooled exclusively in English in the United States	Continued development of age-appropriate English language competencies	Maintenance, retrieval, and/or acquisition of language competencies (e.g., oral productive abilities) Transfer of literacy skills developed in English to the home language Continued development of age-appropriate competencies in both oral and written modes
First-generation immigrant students schooled primarily in the United States	Continued development of age-appropriate English language competencies	Development of literacy skills in first language Continued development of age-appropriate language competencies in oral mode
Newly arrived immigrant students	Acquisition of oral and written English	Continued development of age-appropriate competencies in both oral and written modes

Source: NSFLEP, 1999, p. 19.

Figure 10.3 shows the needs of each home background learner group in terms of the development in English and the heritage language. Home background learners sometimes use their home language and English, a practice that reflects their status as members of a speech community in which a single language does not meet all of their communicative needs (Gutiérrez, 1997). In further describing the language maintenance needs of home background or heritage learners, Valdés (1999) shows that these students already have highly developed interpersonal communicative abilities and perhaps need only to be able to learn ways to establish respect, distance, or friendliness and how to talk with adult strangers and in professional contexts. Heritage learners also require further assistance in developing interpretive skills and need to read a wide variety of authentic materials. Perhaps most essential is practice in oral and written presentational communication, since these learners often lack knowledge of formal language use appropriate for a presentation to an audience.

Goals and Strategies for Teaching Heritage Language Learners. Addressing Spanish in particular, Valdés (1995) outlines four goals of instruction for heritage speakers:

1. Spanish language maintenance: enabling learners to maintain their understanding and use of Spanish.
2. Acquisition of the prestige variety of Spanish: helping speakers of nonprestige varieties of Spanish to acquire the prestige or standard variety so that they are able to function in professional, more formal contexts.
3. Expansion of the bilingual range: helping speakers to expand the range of linguistic abilities and communicative strategies in both languages.
4. Transfer of literacy skills: enabling learners to carry over skills such as reading and writing efficiently and effectively into the other language (pp. 309–317).

In Chinese, a similar bilingual range of variation exists, as typified at Portland State University, where Chinese classes include a diverse mix of Chinese American students, young native English speakers, older native English speakers, native Japanese speakers, native Korean speakers, ethnic Chinese from Vietnam, ethnic Vietnamese, ethnic Chinese from Indonesia, and students from Hong Kong (Pease, 1996).

 Preservation of the heritage language and culture enriches the academic and cultural experience of the learner and the society. ■

thandbook.heinle.com

Valdés (1995) acknowledges that few theoretical advances have been made in teaching heritage language learners and no attempts have been made to analyze the theories underlying existing instruction. Recognizing the scarcity of research on heritage language learning, Webb and Miller (2000) collected data from experienced heritage language teachers and their students, which resulted in a statement of shared goals and fundamental beliefs that describe what teachers and learners themselves should do, what a successful heritage language learning environment looks like, and what is contained in an effective heritage language curriculum. The following are among the most salient of the shared beliefs (see Appendix 10.7 on the Web site for the full statement):

- Teachers of heritage languages should . . . enrich the lives of students by giving them options of variety in register so they can communicate with a variety of audiences in the heritage language (p. 83).
- Students of heritage languages should . . . be encouraged to teach their teachers as well as their peers the individual or unique characteristics of their heritage languages (p. 84).
- A successful heritage language environment is one in which . . . interaction among the school, the family unit, and the community is ongoing (p. 84).
- An effective heritage language curriculum is based on . . . recognized standards for both language arts and foreign language (p. 85).

Schools can play an important role in language maintenance and prevention of language loss by addressing the needs of heritage language learners in classrooms. Attitudes toward language learning and cultural diversity are more positive when students report a home language other than English, and when schools are located in ethnically and racially diverse settings (Cortés, 2002). So far, research on heritage language learners in schools has attempted to address the following issues from the perspective of the language learner:

- validation and appreciation of the language and culture of the language they speak;
- development of strategies to overcome embarrassment or anxiety about speaking their language;
- awareness of the existence of other varieties of the same language and the relative place of the variety they speak.

Validation and appreciation of their language was a motivating factor for the learners in the Webb & Miller (2000) study. Although they were initially reluctant to use the language in class or in social settings in school, their most successful teachers found ways to persist in showing the value of the language and ways in which it could be used effectively. Heritage learners may not use the language in foreign language class as often as teachers might expect (Webb & Miller, 2000). Potowski (2004) found only a 56% usage rate, with girls using more Spanish than boys; students used the language with the teacher 82% of the time but only used it 32% of the time to talk with peers; Spanish was used for on-task projects and English was used for more non-instructional, real-world communication.

Potowksi (2004) proposes that students' use or non-use of the heritage language could be due to the way they identify themselves with one of two or more cultural groups. Sometimes the failure of the school to address the needs of the learners can result in abandonment of the language by potential heritage learners. Kondo (1999), for example, found that heritage learners of Japanese wanted to improve their oral communication skills but were unmotivated beyond lower levels of language classes because undergraduate classes did not match their interests or needs.

Awareness of other varieties of the language they speak and the relative place of their variety in relation to others and to a standard variety is an important aspect of the knowledge needed by heritage learners. Pérez-Leroux & Glass (2000) found that teachers sometimes feel threatened by heritage learners when there is a mismatch between the standard dialect the teacher knows and the regional one the student knows. Salien (1998) emphasizes the value of students knowing a variant of French, but Auger and Valdman (1999) express cautions about the potential negative implications of learning a nonstandard variety of a language.

Despite the absence of a solid body of research on heritage language learning, instructors have reported success in using certain types of teaching strategies to help heritage learners adapt to and work with varieties of languages they speak. Figure 10.4 depicts sample instructional strategies that have been used at both the secondary and post-secondary levels as they address the four goals listed earlier (Valdés, 1995).

FIGURE 10.4 Heritage Language Learners: Instructional Goals and Frequently Used Pedagogies

INSTRUCTIONAL GOAL	FREQUENTLY USED PEDAGOGY	LESS FREQUENTLY USED PEDAGOGY
Transfer of literacy skills	Instruction in reading and writing Teaching of traditional grammar	
Acquisition of prestige variety	Teaching of prestige variety Teaching of traditional grammar Teaching of strategies helpful in monitoring use of contact features Teaching of strategies designed to monitor use of stigmatized features	Introduction to sociolinguistic principles of language variation and language use
Expansion of bilingual range	Teaching of vocabulary Reading of different types and kinds of texts	Structuring of classwork to provide participation in activities designed to expand linguistic, sociolinguistic, and pragmatic competence
Language maintenance	Instruction in reading and writing Teaching of vacubulary	Consciousness raising around issues of identity and language Reading of texts focusing on issues of race, class, gender, and other sociopolitical topics Carrying out ethnographic projects in language community

Source: Valdés, 1995, p. 309.

FIGURE 10.5 Sample Journal Writing Assignment for Home Background Students

EXPERIENCIAS ESCOLARES	SCHOOL EXPERIENCES
Instrucciones: Hable con dos o tres parientes (preferiblemente, su/s abuelos/as, si es posible) y pregúnteles sobre sus experiencias en la escuela. Pregunte sobre las materias, los maestros, la descripción de la escuela y de la sala de clase, los juegos de recreo, sus experiencias con la primera y segunda lengua, las aventuras después de clase, etcétera.	**Instructions:** Talk with two or three of your relatives (preferably your grandparents, if possible) and ask them about their experiences in school. Ask about subjects, teachers, the description of the school and the classroom, games during recess, their experiences with the first and second language, adventures after school, etc.
Escritura: En su diario compare sus propias experiencias con las de sus parientes. ¿En qué se parecen o difieren? ¿Cómo han cambiado las cosas/situaciones escolares? Mencione una o dos cosas del pasado que le hubiera gustado experimentar en la escuela.	**Writing:** In your journal, compare your own experiences with those of your relatives. How are they similar or how are they different? How have things and circumstances in school changed? Mention one or two aspects of the past that you would have liked to experience in your schooling.

Source: Rodríguez Pino, 1997, p. 72.

Rodríguez Pino (1977) suggests that home background language learners be engaged in the following types of classroom activities:

- ethnographic study of the community, such as tracing the genealogy of a family;
- vocabulary expansion activities to identify standardized synonyms and regional words beyond their current usage level;
- interactive diaries in which they write to each other and share ideas about sub-themes, such as the future, their culture, society, literature, vices and virtues, values, social relationships, and the arts; a typical assignment appears in Figure 10.5;
- sociolinguistic surveys; for instance, students might collect photos of six different kinds of flowers (or animals or tools or professions, etc.), all representing a specific category; students place them on a card and conduct a survey in their community asking native speakers to speak the words for the photographed items into a tape recorder, then they tabulate their results to make a linguistic map of their neighborhood;
- reading of the literature of the home background student, especially if it is not yet an integral part of the literary canon; for example, native speakers of Spanish in the southwestern United States might read Ricardo Aguilar's *Madreselvas en flor,* listen to the tape of the author reading aloud from his work, and complete the following sentences in Spanish:

1. When the author read about _____, I felt _____.

2. I like the way in which the author _____.

3. I didn't like _____.

4. I didn't understand _____.

5. The experiences of this author remind me of _____.
   (adapted from Rodríguez Pino, 1997, pp. 70–75)

Hancock (2002) also suggests the following activity that corresponds to the learning strategies described earlier in this chapter. Notice how it draws the learner's attention to developing strategies to use the language in class and other social settings.

> You are a high school student living in New York City with your parents, who are from Puerto Rico. They speak Spanish with you all the time, but you speak to them in English. You are getting ready to leave home to attend college, where you want to study advertising. You also want to study Spanish, because you realize that employers value bilingual employees. You want to practice reading and writing in Spanish before you leave for college. Which language learning strategies could you use to prepare yourself for college Spanish? (2002, p. 2)

In addition to the use of instructional strategies, program models specifically designed for heritage learners are vital. Such programs will provide data to help teachers determine whether heritage speakers maximize their potential when included in the regular language sequence, whether special courses or lines of study should be developed for them, and whether self-instructional models are helpful (see Mazzocco, 1996, for an example).

To summarize, you have seen that the diversity among learners in your classroom can be as varied as each of the individual students. You will find differences in intelligences, physical and mental abilities, learning styles, strategies, language background, home background, race, and ethnicity. Furthermore, as a teacher you bring your own particular style to the way you choose to teach.

We will now turn our attention to *differentiated instruction* as a strategy for enabling learners to take multiple, but equally valid, paths to reach a common learning goal.

Addressing Diverse Learner Needs Through Differentiated Instruction

Using the *SFLL*, which recognize learner diversity and the unique needs of learners, teachers can individualize learning to engage learners on the basis of their background knowledge, interests, needs, goals, and motivation. As explained earlier, *differentiated instruction* (Tomlinson, 1995, 1999a, 1999b; Tomlinson & Eidson, 2003) is a systematic approach to planning curriculum and instruction to address all of the individual learner variations discussed in this chapter as well as the learner variations pointed out in earlier chapters (e.g., variations in ZPD, background knowledge, educational goals, learning styles and modalities). This approach suggests that teachers concentrate on two classroom factors: the nature of the student and the essential meaning of the curriculum (Tomlinson & Eidson, 2003, p. 3). Flexibility in *how* we teach is more likely to result if we pay attention to *whom* we teach and *what* we teach them.

Instruction becomes differentiated if teachers vary five aspects of their teaching:

- content
- process
- products
- affective elements
- learning environment (Tomlinson & Eidson, 2003).

Of course, Tomlinson and Eidson (2003) also recommend that teachers keep these student characteristics in mind as they craft curriculum and instruction: what learners already know and are able to do, what they enjoy doing, and what their learning profiles look like with regard to learning style, intelligence preference, etc. as shown earlier in this chapter.

Differentiating content means varying what students will know and will be able to do as a result of instruction. Differentiating process means asking students to make sense of the content in varied ways, resulting in products that are also differentiated. Ways to differentiate affective elements in the classroom may include helping learners to feel safe and validated, and differentiated use of space could entail moving the classroom furniture into multiple configurations that facilitate whole-class, small-group, or individual work.[8] See Strickland (2003) for an example of a differentiated unit for French I.

Tomlinson (1999b) describes *undifferentiated, slightly differentiated,* and *fully differentiated* classrooms (see Case Study Two in this chapter for examples). Here we highlight the ways in which one teacher fully differentiates the content, process, product, affect, and classroom environment of a seventh grade social studies class or exploratory Latin class.

Ms. Cassell, the teacher of this fully differentiated class, focused her instruction around key questions for herself and for her students. First, she asked herself what she wanted students to know and be able to do upon completion of instruction, and she wrote these down in broad terms: why they should study ancient times, how cultures vary and share themes, etc. She began with learners' needs, and provided respectful tasks, flexible grouping, and ongoing assessment and adjustment. She asked students to assume the role of a member of Roman society and to conduct research to answer the core questions she provided. According to the students' interests, she adjusted **content** (e.g., whether they described a farmer's life or a soldier's), **process** (e.g., what kinds of skills they had in researching history), and **product** (e.g., whether they produced a first-person personal data sheet describing what their life in ancient Rome would have been like or developed a videotape describing what life would have been like).

Ms. Cassell also expected students to answer questions about their lives that were similar to the Roman culture questions they had just answered. The questions were consistent with student interests and appealed to their **affective** involvement in the class and in their communities: e.g., How is what you eat shaped by the economics of your family and by your location? What is your level of education and how is that affected by your status in society?

Ms. Cassell adjusted the learning environment by creating opportunities for the students to work in whole class or in small groups coupled with individual work. As students worked alone or in groups to conduct their research, the above questions led to other questions that were also differentiated based on:

- their readiness to build on what they knew already (e.g., small or large groupings, reading or writing goals with specific kinds of materials at varied levels of complexity and difficulty);
- their interests (e.g., What games did Roman children play? What was the practice of science like then? What was the purpose and style of art?);
- their learning profiles (e.g., whether students used a diary journal, or a monologue).

Ms. Cassell's differentiated instruction culminated in a final, complex question, tailored to the students' accomplishments in the lesson: "Now that you have seen how the lives and language of several generations of Romans varied, how will your life differ from that of the previous generation in your family, and how will your grandchildren's lives compare with yours?" This question's complexity lies in its requirement that the learner compare and contrast multiple aspects of the lives of members of two generations. By contrast, a less complex question might be "How will language change from the generation before you to two generations after you, and why will those changes take place?" (Tomlinson, 1999b). This question requires only that the learner process knowledge about the changes in languages and project what is likely to happen.

As you read this example provided by Tomlinson (1999b), you probably thought about how similar this lesson is to those you have been designing throughout *Teacher's Handbook.*

Indeed, this lesson is an example of the kind of standards-based, learner-centered instruction you have been studying. By contrast, the other two examples described by Tomlinson (1999b) and elaborated in Case Study Two are teacher-fronted: in one, the teacher explains and tests facts; in the other, the teacher offers multiple assignments for students to choose from, but does not facilitate engagement with her academic discipline. Although more work is needed in this area, differentiated instruction offers an effective and interesting way for teachers to address the varied needs of learners in the language classroom.

Another way to address the various needs of learners and to recognize and validate their diverse backgrounds is to engage them in using the foreign language to interact in TL communities. The *SFLL* Communities goal area (NSFLEP, 1999) offers an avenue for bringing students together with the common goal of exploring TL communities and interacting with members of these communities.

STANDARDS HIGHLIGHT: Bringing Diverse Student Groups Together Through Participation in Multilingual COMMUNITIES

The Communities Goal Area

As you read through the previous sections of this chapter, you probably noticed that lists of strategies for teaching diverse learners are often similar, and you may have wondered how these can be pulled together in a unifying way. The Communities goal area can be a vehicle for engaging diverse groups of learners in using the language both within and beyond the school setting. The Communities standards, which combine elements from each of the other goal areas, integrate meaningful language use; application of cultural practices, products, and perspectives; connections to other discipline areas; and development of insights into one's own language and culture. The two Communities standards are:

- Students use the language both within and beyond the school setting.
- Students show evidence of becoming life-long learners by using the language for personal enjoyment and enrichment (NSFLEP, 1999, pp. 64, 66).

The first standard focuses on language as a tool for communication with speakers in a variety of communities: the classroom, the school, the local community, target language communities within the United States, and target language communities abroad (NSFLEP, 1999). The second standard relates to the use of the target language for continued learning and for personal entertainment and enjoyment. As students gain confidence in the second language, they might use the language to access various entertainment and information sources, read a novel, travel abroad, or participate in a service-learning experience. Be sure to watch the video clip in the View and Reflect section (Activity A) for this chapter on the *Teacher's Handbook* Web site for an example addressing this standard.

thandbook.heinle.com

VIEW AND REFLECT

The Communities goal area focuses on language use within and beyond the school setting and for personal enrichment and enjoyment. ▬

Linking Language Learning Experiences to Communities

Having read about diverse kinds of students who may be in your foreign language class, you may begin to see that developing communities among learners in the classroom can

FIGURE 10.6 Kolb's Model of Community-Based Learning

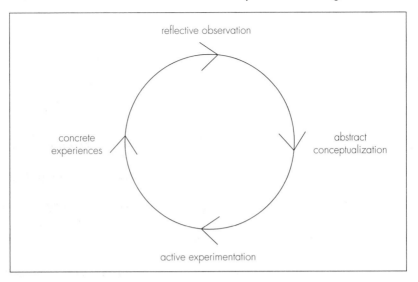

Source: Overfield, 1997, p. 486.

complement learners' work within the larger school community and in communities beyond the school. Over the past decade, colleges and universities have incorporated *community-based learning* (*CBL*) into their curricula in an attempt to engage students in responsible and challenging projects both inside and outside the classroom.

Kolb's (1984) model of CBL, shown in Figure 10.6, is a useful way to think about making learning real in communities. It is a student-centered model that uses learners' experiences as a basis for learning. Using concrete experiences with members of a community, the learner participates in guided reflection (e.g., class journal or group discussion), thinks about the hypotheses he or she formed prior to the experience, and formulates abstract concepts which are then put into practice in communicative situations outside the classroom (Overfield, 1997, p. 486).

Overfield (1997) describes an example of CBL in which students used language to connect with a community by responding to a call from a local agency to help refugees and recent immigrants learn about their new community (pp. 488–489). Spanish I students socialized with Cuban refugees through various activities, such as visiting an art gallery. The two groups learned about each other by asking and answering questions and comparing their cultures. Language learning was mediated through classroom reflection, written journal entries and portfolio documents, and generating comments like the following about the value of the learning experience:

> As an African American, I didn't think I'd have anything in common with these Cuban refugees. My Spanish isn't very good, and what do they know about my culture? When one asked me what I like to eat, I told her she wouldn't understand. She told me to tell her. So I tried to tell her what I eat, and I told her about Sunday dinners with my family. She said she does the same things with her family! We talked for an hour. On Saturday we [another student and herself] are going to the mall with her and her mother (p. 489).

This type of mediated learning is the result of "building bridges between classrooms and communities" (Cone & Harris, 1996, p. 39). As seen in Kolb's (1984) model, the abstract conceptualization of not having anything in common with the refugees was changed by active experimentation and concrete experiences, leading to reflective observation and more concrete experiences.

 How does the type of mediated learning described in this Communities project relate to the sociocultural theory of learning presented in Chapter 1?

Among the manifestations of CBL in recent years is a concept called *service-learning,* which involves an engagement in community action using knowledge gained in academic learning (Tilley-Lubbs, 2003, p. 42). Research has shown that service-learning increases civic responsibility and facilitates academic objectives (Roquemore & Schaffer, 2000). Among the benefits of service-learning experiences in communities are a reciprocity of understanding between learners and community members, the development of an "insider" perspective, the questioning of traditional stereotypes, and the improved use of the target language in real settings (Boyle-Baise & Kilbaine, 2000; Long, 2003; Tilley-Lubbs, 2003). In a study of 22,000 college students, using quantitative and qualitative measures, Astin, Vogelgesang, Ikeda and Yee (2000) found significant positive effects of service-learning on academic performance (e.g., GPA, writing skills, critical thinking skills), values (e.g., commitment to activism and to promoting racial understanding), self-efficacy, leadership (e.g., leadership activities, self-rated leadership ability, interpersonal skills), choice of a service career, and plans to participate in service after college.

An example of a service-learning project is the study conducted by Tilley-Lubbs (2003) in which post-secondary students learning Spanish were paired with members of the Hispanic community who had recently immigrated to the United States. The students helped the immigrants with getting a driver's license, renting an apartment, making doctor's appointments, etc. Collaborating with local high and middle school teachers, the post-secondary students and their Hispanic partners visited local schools to teach ESL and Spanish and to offer models of cross-cultural understanding.

The special emphasis of service-learning within CBL is the role played by academic learning. Students in the above study read more than fifty articles about multicultural education, educational theory, and immigration/migration issues. They then incorporated this academic knowledge into their reflections to understand their actions within the community. Results of the qualitative analysis of this project showed that students were transformed to become agents of change in the Hispanic families with which they worked and in their own families. Transformation was reciprocal for the immigrant families, as one group of students provided the legal and entrepreneurial expertise to enable the family to establish a Hispanic bakery. See Hellenbrandt, Arries, and Varona (2003) for other examples of service-learning projects; see the Haas and Reardon video segment (1997) on the *Teacher's Handbook* Web site for a description of a project in which students connected with the local Chilean community in New York by means of engaging in e-mail communications with key pals in Chile and interacting in Spanish in a local New York Chilean bakery.

thandbook.heinle.com

In sum, in this chapter you have reflected on the various types of needs that learners bring to the foreign language classroom. You have explored specific strategies for addressing those needs and for validating the diversity of learner backgrounds so that students experience success in their language learning. The chapter has presented ideas for differentiating instruction, all of which support the approach of *Teacher's Handbook* throughout the chapters. Finally, you have seen how the Communities goal area of *SFLL* offers ideas for developing communities among learners in the classroom and engaging them in interaction with members of TL communities.

TEACH AND REFLECT

NCATE_____
STANDARDS
3.a., 3.b.,
4.b., 4.c.,
5.a.

EPISODE ONE
Designing a Language Lesson Appropriate for Diverse Learning Styles

For this activity, use a lesson you created during earlier chapters of *Teacher's Handbook* or design a new one. Your lesson can focus on any of the elements previously discussed—for example, a presentation of grammar using the PACE model (Chapter 7) or work with an authentic listening or a reading appropriate for students at the elementary school, middle school, or high school level and beyond (Chapter 6). Within your lesson, design at least three activities that appeal to different learning styles. Refer to the elements of learning styles described earlier in this chapter (Oxford, 1990b; Scarcella & Oxford, 1992), and keep in mind the following suggestions (Gahala, 1993; Tomlinson, 1999a) on how to differentiate instruction:

1. Determine what you want students to know and be able to do at the end of the lesson. Identify major themes and essential questions that will serve as a compass to guide the lesson.
2. Provide basic instruction of vocabulary and structures by appealing to as many senses as possible.
3. Proceed through carefully sequenced in-class practice.
4. In interactive classroom activities, such as question-answer practice, allow sufficient wait time for students to process the questions, think of possible responses, formulate a response, and make the response.
5. Give clear instructions on all assignments and model process or desired outcomes with students before they begin the task. Use a more able student to assist in modeling the activity.
6. Regularly give a choice among two or three homework assignments. Instead of grading solely on accuracy, consider grading on any two of the following criteria: completion of task, comprehensibility, quality or appropriateness of information generated, individual improvement. Be sure to let students know the criteria in advance.
7. Regularly assess student progress in the tasks and adjust instruction accordingly. Involve students in the assessment processes.
8. Base assessment on a variety of procedures: taking short quizzes, participating in role plays, writing scenarios of oral activities, labeling pictures or visuals, creating personal flashcards or study devices, creating posters or cultural projects, actively participating in classroom interaction, describing a picture, creating a drawing from a description in the target language, writing a new study exercise, writing comprehension check questions for a reading or listening selection. See Chapter 11 for a discussion of rubrics.

EPISODE TWO
Working Within Communities

NCATE_____
STANDARDS
3.a., 3.b.,
4.a. 4.b.,
4.c.

Identify a community near your school where the target language is spoken at home or at work. Interview a selection of community members about how they learned the language and what it means to them. Identify a way in which students in your school can interact with members of the community in a focused project, perhaps by reading some poems, writing a play with native speakers, helping with child care, or helping teach literacy. Design the project so that it addresses the Communities goal area of *SFLL*. Read Hellenbrandt, Arries, and Varona

thandbook.heinle.com

(2003) for ideas on how to involve academic learning in communities. Read Overfield (1997) for insights into how she combined a model of communicative competence with Kolb's (1984) model of community-based learning and incorporate some of the aspects of her work into your project. See the Chapter 10 case study on the *Teacher's Handbook* Web site for a description of diversity in a small rural community. If your interest is in post-secondary instruction, see Overfield (2002) for similar insights.

DISCUSS AND REFLECT*

CASE STUDY ONE
Preparing to Teach Special Education Spanish I and II classes

NCATE____
STANDARDS
3.a., 3.b.,
4.a., 4.b.,
4.c.

Ms. Vella is a first-year Spanish teacher at Westtown High School, part of a small district in a farming community. She has been taught the latest research in language learning and teaching and is thoroughly prepared to teach Spanish for real communication. Ms. Vella has developed a repertoire of strategies for involving students in active language use, and she successfully used whole-language tasks and cooperative learning in her student teaching. She believes in using the target language as much as possible, integrating culture with her teaching, and providing opportunities for students to succeed with the language.

The principal at Westtown High School tells Ms. Vella that one of the classes she will be teaching is conversational Spanish. The class will consist of twelve special education students: eight in Spanish level I and four in Spanish Level II. The principal tells her that the goal for the class is "to make students aware of different cultures through the use of Spanish." Ms. Vella is a little perplexed by this assignment since these students will be in a separate class, rather than included with other students, and Levels I and II will be combined.[9]

Ask yourself these questions:

1. What expectations should Ms. Vella have for the students in this class?
2. What difficulties/successes might these students have in a language class?
3. What additional information will Ms. Vella need about her students as she plans for the class?
4. According to the principal, the goal for this class is "to make students aware of different cultures through the use of Spanish." What philosophy or attitude do you think motivates this goal? What other goals could there be?
5. What techniques might work well in teaching Spanish in this class?

To prepare the case:

1. Read Spinelli (1989, 1996) for more information on how to teach low-achieving learners.
2. Consult Appendix 10.1 (see the Web site) for strategies to incorporate multiple intelligences.
3. Interview an experienced special education teacher to discuss potential difficulties students might experience as well as how a language teacher might plan for these difficulties.
4. Talk to an experienced language teacher who has worked with mainstreamed and/or special education students to gain additional insights about implications for language teaching.

---

*See the *Teacher's Handbook* Web site for a third case study that deals with cultural diversity in a small rural community.

thandbook.heinle.com

5. If you will teach English as a Second Language, consult Appendix 10.8 (on the Web site) for a guide to teachers and parents on easing the differences felt as new students with special needs are welcomed to the regular elementary and middle school classroom (*Celebrate Diversity: A Handbook for Classroom Teachers of Limited English Proficiency Students*).

To prepare for class discussion:

1. Describe how you would approach Ms. Vella's conversational Spanish class. Include your expectations and the types of classroom activities you would provide.

2. Brainstorm and create a list of opportunities for working with learners with special needs on an individual basis.

CASE STUDY TWO
Differentiating Instruction: Three Classrooms

NCATE
STANDARDS
3.a., 3.b.,
4.a., 4.b.,
4.c.

As mentioned earlier in the chapter, Tomlinson (1999b) describes an undifferentiated, a moderately differentiated, and a fully differentiated classroom for a unit on Rome for seventh grade social studies; the topic is also appropriate for a Latin class at the same grade level.

The "just the facts" classroom.   In the undifferentiated classroom, Mr. Appleton teaches ancient Rome by having his students read the textbook in class and take notes on important details. Then they answer the questions at the end of the chapter. Students who don't finish must do so at home. The next day they answer the questions together in class.

Mr. Appleton likes to lecture on ancient Rome and works hard to prepare his lectures. He expects students to take notes. After his lecture, he gives a quiz on both the notes and the text. He gives students a study sheet before the test, clearly spelling out what will be on the test.

Mr. Appleton may have a sense of what he wants his students to know at the end of the lesson, but not about what his students should understand and be able to do. He teaches the facts of the content, but no key concepts, guiding principles, or essential questions.

The "students like it" classroom.   In the moderately differentiated classroom, Ms. Baker teaches about ancient Rome by giving her students graphic organizers to use as they read the textbook chapter; she later explains the organizers to the class so that anyone who missed details can fill them in. She brings in pictures of the art and the architecture of the period and tells students how important the Romans were in shaping our architecture, language, and laws. Among the class activities are a toga day and a Roman banquet day, a word-search puzzle of vocabulary words about Rome, a movie clip that shows gladiators and the Colosseum, and group study for the exam. The options for student projects include creating a poster that lists important Roman gods and goddesses, their roles, and their symbols; developing a travel brochure for ancient Rome that a Roman of the day might have used; writing a poem about life in Rome; dressing dolls like citizens of Rome or drawing the fashions of the time; building a model of an important ancient Roman building or a Roman villa; and making a map of the Holy Roman Empire. Students can also propose their own topic.

Although Ms. Baker's class is clearly more engaging and interesting than Mr. Appleton's, it still lacks definitive purpose. Without a clear vision of the meaning of her subject or of the nature of her discipline and what it adds to human understanding, there is little clarity about facts, concepts, guiding principles, or essential questions. "Because there is no instructional clarity, there is no basis for defensible differentiation" (Tomlinson, 1999a, p.16).

The differentiated classroom. As you saw earlier, in the fully differentiated classroom, Ms. Cassell introduces some major themes that will help her students understand why it's important for young people to study ancient times: varied cultures share common elements; cultures are shaped by beliefs and values, customs, geography, and resources; people are shaped by and shape their cultures; societies and cultures change for both internal and external reasons; and elements of a society and its cultures are interdependent. She groups facts and vocabulary terms around these themes and develops essential questions to intrigue her students and to cause them to engage with her in a quest for understanding.

Ms. Cassell continually assesses the way students are operating in their ZPDs, their interests, and their learning profiles; she involves them in goal setting and decision making about their learning, and she modifies her instructional framework and her instruction as needed. To answer the question "How would your life and culture be different if you lived in a different time and place?," one of the differentiated tasks her students engage in is to assume the role of someone from ancient Rome, such as a soldier, a teacher, a healer, a farmer, a slave, or a farmer's wife, basing their choice solely on their own interests. In this task, heritage learners might decide to take the role of the soldier who conquers new territories to understand political and cultural dominance and oppression; students with disabilities might select the role of the healer to explore medical issues of the time. Working alone and in groups, students investigate print, video, computer, and human resources to understand what their life in ancient Rome would have been like, and to create a first-person data sheet that provide accurate, interesting, and detailed information about daily schedule, food, clothing, home, and interactions with societal systems of the time.

Ms. Cassell plans for what students should know, understand, and be able to do at the end of a sequence of learning and, as they work through these tasks, she is able to differentiate the questions she poses to them, the kinds of research assignments she gives them, and the evaluation of their work in consultation with her (Tomlinson, 1999b).

Ask yourself these questions:

1. How does Mr. Appleton treat content, process, product, affect, and learning environment?
2. Tomlinson (1999b) says about Ms. Baker: "Without a clear vision of the meaning of her subject, of the nature of her discipline and what it adds to human understanding, . . . there is little clarity about facts, . . . concepts, guiding principles, or essential questions" (p. 16). What do you think this means? Do you agree that Ms. Baker lacks a clear vision of the meaning of her subject? If so, how could she add this vision?
3. What aspects of differentiated instruction do you see in Ms. Cassell's class?
4. What advantage is there to starting a new unit with a question? Use the examples in this case study to support your position.

To prepare the case:

1. Read Tomlinson (1995, 1999a, 1999b) or Tomlinson and Eidson (2003).
2. Review the videotaped lessons in Activities A and B in the View and Reflect section for this chapter on the *Teacher's Handbook* Web site. Make a list of the student behaviors you see that involve learning and how the teachers differentiate instruction to facilitate learning.

To prepare for class discussion:

1. Identify reasons why teachers might prefer an undifferentiated fact-based curriculum and develop a list of circumstances in which such an approach might suit special needs learners.
2. Identify alternative differentiated instructional practices that might benefit special needs learners.

thandbook.heinle.com

REFERENCES

Alatis, J., & Barnhardt, S. (Eds.). (1998). *Portfolio assessment in the modern language classroom*. Washington, DC: National Capital Language Resource Center.

Armstrong, T. (1993). *Multiple intelligences in the classroom*. Alexandria, VA: Association for Supervision and Curriculum Development.

Arries, J. F. (1999). Learning disabilities and foreign languages: A curriculum approach to the design of inclusive courses. *The Modern Language Journal, 83*, 98–110.

Astin, A. W., Vogelgesang, L. J., Ikeda, E. K., & Yee, J. A. (2000). *How service learning affects students. Executive summary*. Higher Education Research Institute, Los Angeles, UCLA Graduate School of Education & Information Studies. Retrieved April 5, 2004, from http://www.gseis.ucla.edu/slc/rhowas.html.

Auger, J., & Valdman, A. (1999). Letting French students hear the diverse voices of Francophony. *The Modern Language Journal, 83*, 402–412.

August, D., & Hakuta, K. (Eds.). (1997). *Improving schooling for language-minority children: A research agenda*. Washington, DC: National Academy Press.

Bailey, K. M. (1983). Competitiveness and anxiety in adult second language learning: Looking at and through the diary studies. In H. W. Seliger & M. H. Long (Eds.), *Classroom-oriented research in second language acquisition* (pp. 67–103). Rowley, MA: Newbury House.

Barbe, W. B., Swassing, R H., & Milone, M. N. (1979). *The Swassing-Barbe modality index in the Zaner-Bloser modality kit*. Columbus, OH: Zaner-Bloser.

Barnett, H. (1985). Foreign languages for the learning disabled: A reading teacher's perspective. *New York State Association of Foreign Language Teachers Bulletin, 36*, 7–9.

Bartz, W. (1982). The role of foreign language education for gifted and talented students. *Foreign Language Annals, 15*, 329–334.

Boyle-Baise, M., & Kilbaine, J. (2000). What really happens? A look inside service-learning for multicultural teacher education. *Michigan Journal of Community Service Learning, 7*, 54–64.

Brinckerhoff, L. C., Shaw, S. F., & McGuire, J. M. (1993). *Promoting postsecondary education for students with learning disabilities: A handbook for practitioners*. Austin, TX: Pro-ed.

Bruck, M. (1978). The suitability of early French immersion programs for the language disabled child. *Canadian Modern Language Review, 34*, 884–887.

Bucholtz, M. (1995). From Mulatta to Mestiza: Passing and the linguistic reshaping of ethnic identity. In K. Hall and M. Bucholtz (Eds.), *Gender articulated, language and the socially constructed self* (pp. 351–373). New York: Routledge.

Carroll, J.B., & Sapon, S. M. (1959). *Modern Language Aptitude Test*. San Antonio, TX: The Psychological Corporation.

Cassady, J. C., Neumeister, K. L. S., Adams, C. M., Cross, T. L., Dixon, F. A., & Pierce, R. L. (2004). On gifted students in school: The Differentiated Classroom Observation Scale. *Roeper Review, 26*, 139–146.

Cohen, A. D. (1990). *Language learning: Insights for learners, teachers, and researchers*. New York: Newbury House/Harper.

Cone, D., & Harris, S. (1996). Service-learning practice: Developing a theoretical framework. *Michigan Journal of Community Service Learning, 3*, 31–43.

Cooper, T. (2001). Foreign language teaching style and personality. *Foreign Language Annals, 34*, 301–317.

Cortés, K. H. (2002). Youth and the study of foreign language: An investigation of attitudes. *Foreign Language Annals, 35*, 320–332.

Curtain, H. A. (1986). The immersion approach: Principle and practice. In B. Snyder (Ed.), *Second language acquisition: Preparing for tomorrow* (pp. 1–14). Central States Conference Proceedings. Lincolnwood, IL: NTC/Contemporary Publishing Group.

Diaz, L., & Heining-Boynton, A. L. (1995). Multiple intelligences, multiculturalism, the teaching of culture. *International Journal of Educational Research, 23*, 607–617.

Donato, R., & McCormick, D. (1994). A sociocultural perspective on learning strategies: The role of mediation. *The Modern Language Journal, 78*, 453–464.

Education for All Handicapped Children Act, Public Law No. 94-142. 20 U.S.C. §§1400 et seq. (1975).

Ehrman, M. E., & Oxford, R. L. (1989). Effects of sex differences, career choice, and psychological type on adults' language learning strategies. *The Modern Language Journal, 73*, 1–13.

Fairfax County Public Schools. (1992). *Strategies for learners with special needs in the foreign language classroom: A teacher's guide*. Fairfax, VA: Fairfax County School Board.

Feldhusen, J. F. (1989). Synthesis of research on gifted youth. *Educational Leadership, 46(6)*, 6–11.

Fenstermacher, G. (1982). To be or not to be gifted: What is the question? *Elementary School Journal, 82*, 299–303.

Fishman, J. (1964). Language maintenance and language shift as a field of inquiry. *Linguistics, 9*, 32–70.

Fishman, J. (1994). Critiques of language planning: A minority languages perspective. *Journal of Multilingual and Multicultural Development, 15*, 91–99.

Ford, D. (2003). Equity and excellence: Culturally diverse students in gifted education. In N. Colangelo & G. A. Davis (Eds.), *Handbook on gifted education* (3rd ed.) (pp. 506–520). Boston: Pearson Education.

Ford, D. Y., & Thomas, A. (1997). Underachievement among gifted minority students: Problems and promises. Council for Exceptional Children. Retrieved October 29, 1998, from http://www.cec.sped.org/digests/e544.htm.

Frymier, J. (1989). Understanding and preventing teen suicide. *Phi Delta Kappan, 70,* 290–293.

Frymier, J., & Gansneder, B. (1989). The Phi Delta Kappa study of students at risk. *Phi Delta Kappan, 70,* 142–146.

Fulghum, R. (1992). A bag of possibles and other matters of the mind. *Newsweek, 88,* 90, 92.

Gahala, E. (1993). Differentiating instruction: Teaching all your students. *Foreign Language News/Notes 9,* 1–3.

Gahala, E., & Lange, D. L. (1997). Multiple intelligences: Multiple ways to help students learn foreign languages. *Northeast Conference Newsletter, 41,* 29–34.

Gardner, H. (1993). *Frames of mind: The theory of multiple intelligences.* New York: Basic Books.

Gardner, H. (1995). Reflections on multiple intelligences: Myths and messages. *Phi Delta Kappan, 77,* 200–202, 206–209.

Gardner, H. (1999). *Intelligence reframed: Multiple intelligences for the 21st century.* New York: Basic Books.

Gillingham, A., & Stillman, B. W. (1969). *Remedial training for children with specific disability in reading, spelling, and penmanship.* Cambridge, MA: Educators Publishing Service.

Good, T., & Brophy, J. (1991). *Looking in classrooms.* New York: Harper Collins.

Gutiérrez, J. R. (1997). Teaching Spanish as a heritage language: A case for language awareness. *ADFL Bulletin, 29,* 33–36.

Haas, M., & Reardon, M. (1997). Communities of learners: From New York to Chile. In J. Phillips (Ed.), Collaborations: Meeting new goals, new realities, *Northeast Conference Reports* (pp. 213–241). Lincolnwood, IL: NTC/Contemporary Publishing Group.

Haley, M. H. (2001). Understanding learner-centered instruction from the perspective of multiple intelligences. *Foreign Language Annals, 34,* 355–367.

Hancock, Z. (2002). Heritage Spanish speakers' language learning strategies. *ERIC Digest* EDO-FL-02-06. Washington, DC: Center for Applied Linguistics.

Heining-Boynton, A. (1994). The at-risk student in the foreign language classroom. In B. Wing (Ed.), Meeting new challenges in the foreign language classroom, *Northeast Conference Reports* (pp. 21–38). Lincolnwood, IL: NTC/Contemporary Publishing Group.

Heining-Boynton, A. L., & Heining-Boynton, D. B. (1994.) Learning styles, personality, and the foreign language teacher. In R. M. Terry (Ed.), *Dimension '94: Changing images in foreign languages* (pp. 53–65). Valdosta, GA: Southern Conference on Language Teaching.

Hellenbrandt, J., Arries, J., & Varona, L. (Eds.). (2003). *Juntos: Community Partnerships in Spanish and Portuguese: The AATSP professional development handbook series handbook, Vol. 5.* Boston: Heinle & Heinle.

Hoffman, L. (2002). Overview of public elementary and secondary schools and districts: School Year 2001–02. In National Center for Education Statistics, *Education Statistics Quarterly.* Retrieved April 8, 2004, from http://nces.ed.gov.

Hunt, M. (1986). Teachers: Foreign language in junior and senior high school. In G. P. Macdaid, N. G. McCaulley, & R. I. Kainz (Eds.), *Atlas of types tables* (p. 240). Gainesville, FL: Center for Application of Psychological Types.

Individuals with Disabilities Education Act, Public Law 105-17, 105-20, U.S.C. §§1400.

Ingram, D. E. (1994). Language policy in Australia in the 1990s. In R. D. Lambert (Ed.), *Language planning around the world: Contexts and systemic change* (pp. 69–109). Washington, DC: National Foreign Language Center.

Javorsky, J., Sparks, R. L., & Ganschow, L. (1992). Perceptions of college students with and without learning disabilities about foreign language courses. *Learning Disabilities: Research and Practice, 7,* 31–44.

Johnson, D. W., & Johnson, R T. (1991). What cooperative learning has to offer the gifted. *Cooperative Learning, 11,* 24–27.

Kennewig, S. (1986). Language disability students: Spanish is for you. Paper presented at the Fifth Conference on the Teaching of Spanish. Miami University, OH.

Kleiner, B., Porch, R., & Farris, E. (2002). Public alternative schools and programs for students at risk of education failure: 2000–01. In National Center for Education Statistics, *Education Statistics Quarterly.* Retrieved April 7, 2004, from http://nces.ed.gov.

Kohn, A. (1987). It's hard to get out of a pair: Profile: David & Roger Johnson. *Psychology Today,* (October):53–57.

Kolb, D. A. (1984). *Experiential learning: Experience as the source of learning and development.* Englewood Cliffs, NJ: Prentice Hall.

Kondo, K., (1999). Motivating bilingual and semibilingual university students of Japanese: An analysis of language learning persistence and intensity among students from immigrant backgrounds. *Foreign Language Annals, 32,* 77–88.

Kuykendall, C. (1989). *Improving Black student achievement by enhancing students' self image.* Washington, DC: Mid-Atlantic Equity Center.

Lange, D. (1999). Planning for and using the new national culture standards. In J. K. Phillips & R. M. Terry (Eds.), *Foreign language standards: Linking research, theories, and practices.* The ACTFL Foreign Language Education Series (pp. 57–135). Lincolnwood, IL: NTC/Contemporary Publishing Group.

Larrivee, B. (1985). *Effective teaching for successful mainstreaming.* New York: Longman.

Lawrence, G. (1996). *People types and tiger stripes.* Gainesville, FL: Center for Applications of Psychological Type.

Lawrence, G. (1997). *Looking at type and learning styles.* Gainesville, FL: Center for Applications of Psychological Type.

Levine, M. (1984). Learning abilities and disabilities. *The Harvard Medical School Health Letter: Medical Forum 9,* 1–3.

Long, D. R. (2003). Spanish in the community: Students reflect on Hispanic cultures in the United States. *Foreign Language Annals, 35,* 223–252.

Lyon, R., & Moats, L. C. (1993). An examination of research in learning disabilities: Past practices and future directions. In G. R. Lyon, D. Gray, J. Kavanagh, & N. Krasnegor (Eds.), *Better understanding of learning disabilities: New views from research and their implications for education and public policies* (pp. 1–15). Baltimore, MD: Brookes Publishing.

Mabbott, A. S. (1994). An exploration of reading comprehension, oral reading errors, and written errors by subjects labeled learning disabled. *Foreign Language Annals, 27,* 293–324.

Mabbott, A. S. (1995). Arguing for multiple perspectives on the issue of learning disabilities and foreign language acquisition: A response to Sparks, Ganschow, and Javorsky. *Foreign Language Annals, 28,* 488–494.

MacIntyre, P. (1995). How does anxiety affect second language learning? A reply to Sparks and Ganschow. *The Modern Language Journal, 79,* 90–99.

MacIntyre, P., & Noels, K. A. (1996). Using social-psychological variables to predict the use of language learning strategies. *Foreign Language Annals, 29,* 373–386.

Madden, N., & Slavin, R. (1983). Mainstreaming students with mild handicaps: Academic and social outcomes. *Review of Educational Research, 53,* 519–569.

Marks-Tarlow, T. (1996). *Creativity inside out: Learning through multiple intelligences.* New York: Addison-Wesley.

Mazzocco, E. H. D. (1996). The heritage versus the nonheritage language learner: The Five-Colleges' Self-Instructional Language Program's solutions to the problem of separation or unification. *ADFL Bulletin, 28,* 20–23.

McCabe, L. (1985). Teaching the slower student. *New York State Association of Foreign Language Teachers Bulletin, 36,* 5–6.

McCarthy, B. (1987). *The 4 MAT System.* Barrington, IL: Excel.

Moll, L. (1992). Bilingual classroom studies and community analyses: Some recent trends. *Educational Researcher, 21,* 20–24.

Moore, S., & Moore, F. X. (1997). Conference handouts. Retrieved April 6, 2004, from http://www.fln.vcu.edu/ld/conf.html.

Myers, I. B., & McCaulley, M. H. (1985). *A guide to the development and use of the Myers- Briggs Type Indicator.* Palo Alto, CA: Consulting Psychologists Press.

Myers, I. B., McCaulley, M. H., Quenk, N. L., & Hammer, A. L. (1998). *MBTI manual: A guide to the development and use of the Myers-Briggs type indicator* (3rd ed.). Palo Alto, CA: Consulting Psychologists Press.

National Center for Educational Statistics (NCES). (2002). *Digest of Educational Statistics.* Retrieved April 4, 2004, from http://nces.ed.gov/programs/digest/d02.

National Standards in Foreign Language Education Project (NSFLEP). (1999). *National standards for foreign language learning in the 21st century.* Lawrence, KS: Allen Press.

NCLB leaves behind liberal arts, according to study minority students most affected by curriculum changes. (2004). *Foreign Language Annals, 37,* 167.

Ogbu, J. U. (1997). Understanding cultural diversity and learning. *Journal for the Education of the Gifted, 17,* 355–83.

Omnibus Budget Reconciliation Act, Public Law 97-35, Congressional Information Services §8582 (1981).

Overfield, D. M. (1997). From the margins to the mainstream: Foreign language education and community-based learning. *Foreign Language Annals, 30,* 485–491.

Overfield, D. M. (2002). The foreign language learning community: Content and collaboration in the university. *NECTFL Review, 50,* 32–35.

Oxford, R. L. (1990a). *Language learning strategies: What every teacher should know.* Boston: Heinle & Heinle.

Oxford, R. L. (1990b). Language learning strategies and beyond: A look at strategies in the context of styles. In S. Magnan (Ed.), *Shifting the instructional focus to the learner* (pp. 35–55). *Northeast Conference Reports.* Lincolnwood, IL: NTC/Contemporary Publishing Group.

Oxford, R. L., & Crookall, D. (1989). Research on language learning strategies: Methods, findings and instructional issues. *The Modern Language Journal, 73,* 404–419.

Oxford, R. L., & Lavine, R. Z. (1992). Teacher-student style wars in the language classroom: Research insights and suggestions. *ADFL Bulletin, 23,* 38–45.

Pease, J. (1996). Teaching Chinese at an urban university. *ADFL Bulletin, 27(2),* 9–13.

Pérez-Leroux, A. T., & Glass, W. R. (2000). Linguistic diversity and inclusion in the foreign language classroom. *Foreign Language Annals, 33,* 58–62.

Phillips, J. (1997). Introduction. In J. Phillips (Ed.), *Collaborations: Meeting new goals, new realities, Northeast Conference Reports* (pp. xii–xviii). Lincolnwood, IL: NTC/Contemporary Publishing Group.

Phillips de Herrera, B. (1984). Teaching English as a foreign language to the visually handicapped. Paper presented at the annual convention of Teachers of English to Speakers of Other Languages, Houston, TX.

Potowski, K. (2004). Student Spanish use and investment in a dual immersion classroom: Implications for second language acquisition and heritage language maintenance. *The Modern Language Journal, 88,* 75–101.

Reid, J. M. (1987). The learning style preferences of ESL students. *TESOL Quarterly, 21,* 87–111.

Reis, S. M., Burns, D. E., & Renzulli, R. S. (1992). *Curriculum compacting*. Mansfield Center, CT: Creative Learning Press.

Renzulli, J. S. (1986). The three-ring conception of giftedness: A developmental model for creative productivity. In R. J. Sternberg & J. E. Davidson (Eds.), *Conceptions of giftedness* (pp. 53–92). New York: Cambridge University Press.

Renzulli, J. S. (1999). What is this thing called giftedness, and how do we develop it? A twenty-five year perspective. *Journal for the Education of the Gifted, 23*, 3–54.

Renzulli, J. S., & Reis, S. M. (1985). *The schoolwide enrichment model: A comprehensive plan for educational excellence.* Mansfield Center, CT: Creative Learning Press.

Renzulli, J. S., & Reis, S. M. (2003). The Schoolwide Enrichment Model: Developing creative & productive giftedness. In N. Colangelo & G. A. Davis (Eds.), *Handbook on Gifted Education* (3rd ed.) (pp. 184–203). Boston: Pearson Education.

Rodríguez Pino, C. (1997). La reconceptualización del programa español para hispanohablantes: Estrategias que reflejan la realidad sociolingüística de la clase. In M. C. Colombi & F. X. Alarcón (Eds.), *La enseñanza del español a hispanohablantes: Praxis y teoría* (pp. 65–82). Boston: Houghton Mifflin.

Roquemore, K. A., & Schaffer, R. H. (2000). Toward a theory of engagement: A cognitive mapping of service-learning experiences. *Michigan Journal of Community Service Learning, 7*, 14–24.

Salien, J. (1998). Quebec French: Attitudes and pedagogical perspectives. *The Modern Language Journal, 82*, 95–102.

Scarcella, R. C., & Oxford, R. L. (1992). *The tapestry of language learning.* Boston: Heinle & Heinle.

Schneider, E. (1996). Teaching foreign languages to at-risk learners. *ERIC Digest* EDO-FL-97-03. Washington, DC: Center for Applied Linguistics.

Sparks, R. L, Artzer, M. L., Javorksy, J., Patton, J., Ganschow, L., Miller, K., & Hordubay, D. (1998). Students classified as learning disabled and non-learning disabled: Two comparison studies of native language skill, foreign language aptitude, and foreign language proficiency. *Foreign Language Annals, 31*, 535–551.

Sparks, R. L., & Ganschow, L. (1993). The effects of a multisensory, structured language approach to teaching Spanish on the native language and foreign language aptitude skills of at-risk learners: A follow-up and replication study. *Annals of Dyslexia, 43*, 194–216.

Sparks, R. L., & Ganschow, L. (1995). A strong inference approach to causal factors in foreign language learning: A response to MacIntyre. *The Modern Language Journal, 79*, 235–244.

Sparks, R. L., & Ganschow, L. (1996). Anxiety about foreign language learning among high school women. *The Modern Language Journal, 80*, 199–212.

Sparks, R. L, Ganschow, L, & Javorsky, J. (1995). I know one when I see one (or I know one because I am one): A response to Mabbott. *Foreign Language Annals, 28*, 479–487.

Sparks, R. L, Ganschow, L., Javorsky, J., Pohlman, J., & Patton, J. (1992). Test comparisons among students identified as high-risk, low-risk, and learning disabled in high school foreign language courses. *The Modern Language Journal, 76*, 42–159.

Sparks, R. L., Ganschow, L., Kenneweg, S., & Miller, K. (1991). Use of an Orton-Gillingham approach to teach a foreign language to dyslexic/learning disabled students: Explicit teaching of phonology in a second language. *Annals of Dyslexia, 41*, 96–118.

Sparks, R. L., Ganschow, L., and Pohlman, J. (1989). Linguistic coding deficits in foreign language learners. *Annals of Dyslexia, 39*, 179–195.

Sparks, R. L., & Javorsky, J. (1998). Learning disabilities, foreign language learning, and the foreign language requirement. Paper presented at the annual meeting of American Council on the Teaching of Foreign Languages. Chicago, IL.

Sparks, R. L., Philips, L., & Javorsky, J. (2003). College students classified as having learning disabilities and attention deficit hyperactivity disorder and the foreign language requirement. *Foreign Language Annals, 36*, 325–338.

Spinelli, E. L. (1989). Beyond the traditional classroom. In H. S. Lepke (Ed.), *Shaping the future: Challenges and opportunities, Northeast Conference Reports* (pp. 139–158). Burlington, VT: Northeast Conference on the Teaching of Foreign Languages.

Spinelli, E. L. (1996). Meeting the challenges of the diverse secondary school population. In B. Wing (Ed.), *Foreign languages for all: Challenges and choices* (pp. 57–90). Northeast Conference Reports. Lincolnwood, IL: NTC/Contemporary Publishing Group.

Sternberg, R., & Davidson, J. (Eds.). (1986). *Conceptions of giftedness.* New York: Cambridge University Press.

Strong, M. (1988). *Language learning and deafness.* Cambridge, UK: Cambridge University Press.

Strickland, C. A. (2003). There's a pattern here folks! In C. A. Tomlinson & C. C. Eidson (Eds.). *Differentiation in practice: A resource guide for differentiating curriculum, grades 5-9.* Alexandria, VA: Association for Supervision and Curriculum Development.

Sullivan, V. J., & McDonald, W. E. (1990). Cross-age tutoring in Spanish: One motivating method. *The Pennsylvania State Modern Language Association Bulletin, 63(2)*, 13–17.

Thomas, L. (1996). Language as power: A linguistic critique of U. S. English. *The Modern Language Journal, 80*, 129–140.

Thompson, R. H., White, K. R., & Morgan, D. P. (1982). Teacher-student interaction patterns in classrooms with mainstreamed mildly handicapped students. *American Educational Research Journal, 19*, 220–236.

Tilley-Lubbs, G. A. (2003). *Crossing the border through service-learning: A study of cross-cultural relationships.* Unpublished doctoral dissertation. Virginia Polytechnic Institute and State University at Blacksburg, VA.

Tomlinson, C. A. (1995). *How to differentiate instruction in mixed-ability classrooms.* Alexandria, VA; Association for Supervision and Curriculum Development.

Tomlinson, C. A. (1999a). *The differentiated classroom: Responding to the needs of all learners.* Alexandria, VA: Association for Supervision and Curriculum Development.

Tomlinson, C. A. (1999b). Mapping a route toward differentiated instruction. *Educational Leadership,* 57(1), 12–16.

Tomlinson, C. A., & Eidson, C. C. (Eds.) (2003). *Differentiation in practice: A resource guide for differentiating curriculum, grades 5-9.* Alexandria, VA: Association for Supervision and Curriculum Development.

Tomlinson, C. A., Kaplan, S. N., Renzulli, J. S., Purcell, J., Leppien, J., & Burns, D. (2002). *The parallel curriculum.* Thousand Oaks, CA: Corwin Press.

Treffinger, D. J., & Feldhusen, J. F. (1996). Talent recognition and development: Successor to gifted education. *Journal for the Education of the Gifted,* 19, 181–193.

U.S. Department of Education. (1977). Assistance to states for education of handicapped children: Procedures for evaluating specific learning disabilities. *Federal Register, 42,* 65082–65085.

Valdés, G. (1995). The teaching of minority languages as academic subjects: Pedagogical and theoretical challenges. *The Modern Language Journal,* 79, 299–328.

Valdés, G. (1999). Introduction. In L. A. Sandstedt (Project Director), *The AATSP professional development handbook series for teachers: Spanish for native speakers,* Vol. 1. Greeley, CO: American Association of Teachers of Spanish and Portuguese.

VanTassle-Baska, J. (2003). What matters in curriculum for gifted learners: Reflections on theory, research, and practice. In N. Colangelo & G. A. Davis (Eds.). *Handbook on Gifted Education* (3rd ed.) (pp. 174–183). Boston: Pearson Education.

Vanucci, S. R. (1991). *Understanding dysfunctional systems.* Unpublished manuscript.

Veltman, C. (1983). *Language shift in the United States.* Berlin, Germany: Mouton de Gruyter.

Von Károlyi, C., Ramos-Ford, V., & Gardner, H. (2003). Multiple intelligences: A perspective on giftedness. In N. Colangelo & G. A. Davis (Eds.), *Handbook on Gifted Education* (3rd ed.) (pp. 100–112). Boston: Allyn & Bacon.

Wang, S., & García, M. I. (2002). Heritage language learners. White paper for the National Council of School Supervisors of Foreign Languages. Retrieved April 11, 2004, from http://www.ncssfl.org.

Webb, J. B., & Miller, B. L. (Eds.). (2000). *Teaching heritage language learners: Voices from the classroom.* ACTFL Foreign Language Education Series. Yonkers, NY: American Council on the Teaching of Foreign Languages.

Yasin, S., & Albert, B. (1999). *Minority Teacher Recruitment and Retention: A National Imperative.* Washington, DC: American Association of Colleges of Teacher Education.

NOTES

1. The Elementary and Secondary Education Act of 2001. P. L. 107-110, became known as "No Child Left Behind (NCLB)." See *Teacher's Handbook* Web site for links to this legislation and to a study critical of the effects of the law. This law shapes reform in education, placing emphasis on stronger accountability, more local freedom, proven methods, and more choices for parents. Each state sets challenging academic standards to be met by all students by 2013. Each state also decides which assessment measures it will use to determine whether or not student performance meets the goals, and sets a timeline by which it will accomplish its goals with Adequate Yearly Progress (AYP) reports. Furthermore, each state indicates what steps will be taken if the goals are not met. Federal funding is provided for state and local projects related to the law.

As of this writing, the assessments being emphasized are those for mathematics, science, and language arts (reading and writing in English). Assessment of foreign languages as a subject area is not specifically mentioned in NCLB. Of interest to language teachers are the following sections of the law related to academic assessment of students whose native languages are not English.

(6) LANGUAGE ASSESSMENTS—Each State plan shall identify the languages other than English that are present in the participating student population and indicate the languages for which yearly student academic assessments are not available and are needed. The State shall make every effort to develop such assessments and may request assistance from the Secretary if linguistically accessible academic assessment measures are needed. Upon request, the Secretary shall assist with the identification of appropriate academic assessment measures in the needed languages, but shall not mandate a specific academic assessment or mode of instruction.

(7) ACADEMIC ASSESSMENTS OF ENGLISH LANGUAGE PROFICIENCY—Each State plan shall demonstrate that local educational agencies in the State will, beginning not later than school year 2002–2003, provide for an annual assessment of English proficiency (measuring students' oral language, reading, and writing skills in English) of all students with limited English proficiency in the schools served by the State educational agency, except that the Secretary may provide the State 1 additional year if the State demonstrates that exceptional or uncontrollable circumstances, such as a

natural disaster or a precipitous and unforeseen decline in the financial resources of the State, prevented full implementation of this paragraph by that deadline and that the State will complete implementation within the additional 1-year period.

See the *Teacher's Handbook* Web site for a link to a recent study conducted by the Council for Basic Education concerning the effect of NCLB on instructional time in various subject areas.

2. It is important to note that the minority groups named in the census are defined in this way: American Indian includes Alaskan Native; Black includes African American; Pacific Islander includes Native Hawaiian; and Hispanic includes Latino. Race categories exclude Hispanic origin unless specified since Hispanic is generally viewed as a culture rather than a race.

3. In some states, instruction in American ASL for hearing students parallels the Five C's of the *SFLL*. For example, in the Virginia *Framework for Instruction in ASL (FASL)* a sample progress indicator for the Communication standard in the presentational mode for students in their third year of study of ASL is: "Students perform cultural arts events commonly enjoyed by members of the Deaf community; e.g., scenes from plays, poetry, excerpts from short stories" (1998, p. 8). See the *Teacher's Handbook* Web site for the Virginia ASL Frameworks.

4. In determining the discrepancy between an IQ score and a measure of achievement, the Modern Language Aptitude Test (MLAT) by Carroll and Sapon (1959) should not be used, as it is a measure of aptitude, not achievement. The test does, however, predict moderately well the likelihood of success in college-level foreign language classes (Sparks, Philips, & Javorsky, 2003).

5. Because of its emphasis on drills, this approach contradicts the position taken in *Teacher's Handbook*. It may nevertheless be effective for certain learners. Readers who would like more information on the approach should see Schneider (1996) or use the link on the *Teacher's Handbook* Web site to the Orton-Gillingham Academy Web site.

6. There is a larger percentage of students from African American, Hispanic, Asian, or Native American heritage groups within the at-risk population. The acronym to refer to these groups is AHANA. There are students, of course, within the heritage groups who excel as well.

7. See Renzulli & Reis (2003, p. 194) for a matrix called "The Compactor" that can be used to visually represent decisions made to compact curriculum.

8. To see what differentiation looks like in a classroom, refer to Cassady, Neumeister, Adams, Cross, Dixon, and Pierce (2004), who developed a Differentiated Classroom Observation Scale.

9. Thanks to a former student teacher for sharing with us this scenario of her first year of teaching.

thandbook.heinle.com

Assessing Standards-Based Language Performance in Context

In this chapter, you will learn about:

- the paradigm shift in assessment practices
- the washback effect of tests
- purposes of tests
- summative vs. formative assessments
- the continuum of test item types
- assessment formats: prochievement, performance-based, and PALS
- an interactive model for assessing interpretive communication
- authentic assessment and scoring rubrics

- standards-based Integrated Performance Assessments (IPAs)
- empowering students through assessment
- portfolios and self-assessments
- interactive homework
- classroom assessment techniques (CATs)
- implications of the OPI for oral interpersonal assessment

Teach and Reflect: Analyzing and Adapting a Traditional Test; Adding An Authentic Dimension to a Performance-Based Assessment Task; Designing a Summative Assessment for a Post-Secondary Class

Discuss and Reflect: Developing Authentic Assessment Tasks and Rubrics; Planning for Portfolio Assessment

CONCEPTUAL ORIENTATION

Assess: to gather information about and measure a learner's level of knowledge or skills

Test: a vehicle for determining a learner's level of knowledge or skills

Evaluate: to interpret and/or assign a value to information about a learner

Grade: to convert assessment information about a learner into a form that is understandable to the learner, such as a letter grade, points on a rubric, numerical score, or written feedback

All of the terms defined above are related to gathering information, interpreting it, and making decisions in a systematic way based on learners' performances of a given task, written or oral. In assessment, the results of the performance are reported to provide information; in evaluation, those results are given some subjective judgment by the interpreters of the results (Hammadou, 1998, p. 292). Educators typically associate the term *assessment* with describing and reporting a learner's performance and the term *evaluation* with assigning a value judgment to that performance.

We test, evaluate, and assess to make informed decisions. Sometimes we want to determine what a learner knows already, sometimes we want to sample a learner's knowledge about something that was taught, and sometimes we want to determine how to structure a lesson for a learner. The people who will make informed decisions are the "audience" for the test. Sometimes they are within the school, close to the instruction, such as teachers and learners. Sometimes they are parents, school board members, or administrative personnel. Sometimes the audience is outside the school and consists of legislators, college admissions officials, scholarship agencies, accreditation agencies, or funding agencies. Shohamy (2001) reminds us that tests can hold great power in the hands of bureaucrats who may use them to make predictions about the future, engage in decision-making that may impact a great of people, or even exercise power or control.

From the perspective of the learner and the teacher, the historical purpose of testing was to evaluate learner achievement and assign grades. In recent years, however, assessment has been given more prominence as a vehicle for providing feedback to learners, improving learner performance, and assessing and informing instruction. In fact, some of the current research centers around the concept of the benefits of "dynamic assessment," which gives the test examiner (i.e., the teacher) a greater role in intervening to help the test taker to improve test performance. This intervention is similar to how the classroom teacher interacts with learners in their individual Zones of Proximal Development, or ZPDs (see Chapter 1) (Poehner & Lantolf, 2003). Throughout this chapter, you will see the recurring theme of the value of assessment in assisting and improving learner performance and in therefore having a seamless connection to instruction.

Paradigm Shift in Assessment Practices

In Chapter 3, you explored a new paradigm for instructional planning that has occurred as a result of current SLA research, *SFLL*, and experiences in classrooms. This new way of envisioning planning and instruction has also affected the way we conceive of and conduct learner assessment. Figure 11.1 depicts the paradigm shift in assessment that has occurred in recent years. Planning begins with a consideration of what learners should be able to do by the end of a period of instruction and what assessments would best serve to assess achievement and track progress; you explored this type of "backward-design" planning process in Chapter 3, in which assessment plays a pivotal role.

An important concept in the new assessment paradigm is the emphasis on the use of multiple measures in assessing student progress in order to provide ongoing opportunities for students to show what they know and can do with the language. Furthermore, in order for broader program evaluation to occur, assessment should be done from the standpoint of multiple perspectives (Donato, Antonek, & Tucker, 1994). For example, you may recall that Chapter 4 reported a study by Donato, Antonek, and Tucker in which they assessed a Japanese FLES program through a multiple perspectives analysis that included oral interviews with learners, observations of classroom lessons, and questionnaires completed by learners, parents, foreign language teachers, and other teachers in the school. These types of assessment data provide the basis for a comprehensive assessment not only of learner progress but also of program effectiveness.

FIGURE 11.1 Paradigm Shift in Assessment Practices

	OLD PARADIGM	NEW PARADIGM
Purpose of Assessment	To evaluate learners and assign grades	To assess learner progress in proficiency and attainment of standards; to evaluate and inform instruction and program design; to make a seamless connection between instruction and assessment
Place of Assessment in Planning and Instruction	Assessment occurs at the end of instruction	Planning for instruction includes design of assessments so that targeted goals and performances guide classroom practices (backward design)
Types of Assessment	Focus on *either* formative or summative assessment; limited number of assessments; largely paper-and-pencil and textbook tests	Balance of formative and summative assessments; multiple measures; focus on performance in authentic tasks; integration of technology
Assessment Content and Formats	Testing of grammatical knowledge and vocabulary; contexts devoid of meaning; discrete-point items, often with one right answer	Integrated assessment of three modes of communication and goal areas of standards; meaningful contexts; open-ended formats, allowing for divergent responses and creativity; oral assessments, TPR, observation checklists
Role of Learner	Has limited opportunities to demonstrate knowledge and skills; must provide "right" answers; receives little feedback about how to improve performance; has few opportunities to learn as a result of assessment; has no role in assessment planning and decision-making	Has multiple opportunities to demonstrate knowledge and skills; encouraged to be creative in language use; receives rubrics before assessment; receives regular feedback on how to improve performance; learns as a result of assessment; participates in assessment planning and decision-making
Role of Teacher	Provides grades and corrective feedback	Describes targeted performance prior to administering assessments; reports on student progress; provides feedback for improvement; uses assessment results to improve program and teaching
Grading System/Feedback	Points/grades given for correct responses; corrective feedback	Rubrics to describe range of performance possible[1]; points/grades given for both accuracy and creativity in language use; rich feedback that describes how performance could improve

Source: Shrum and Glisan, 2005, original material.

The new vision for assessment highlights the need for both formative and summative measures (see Chapter 4), assessment within meaningful and authentic (i.e., real-world) contexts, and opportunities for students to exhibit creativity and divergent responses. In the new assessment paradigm, there is no place for decontextualized testing of discrete language elements such as translation of vocabulary words and fill-in-the-blank verb conjugations within disconnected sentences. In a standards-based language program, assessments feature a series of interrelated tasks that reflect the three modes of communication, more than one goal area, and technology. It is important to note that in the new paradigm, a *task* is a performance-based, communicative activity that reflects how we use language in the world outside of the classroom.

The new assessment paradigm also features expanded roles for both teacher and learners. Teachers inform students of how they will be assessed prior to an assessment, and they show students samples of performance that would meet and exceed expectations. Additionally, they provide rich feedback that describes how students could improve their performances. Learners have multiple opportunities to demonstrate growth in language development and progress in attaining the standards; they learn as a result of assessment; and they participate in the assessment planning process, through means such as portfolio development, in which they are empowered to make decisions about how they illustrate their own progress. Of course, the entire assessment process also serves to inform and improve classroom instruction and curricular development.

 In the new assessment paradigm, there is no place for decontextualized testing of discrete language elements such as translation of vocabulary words and fill-in-the-blank conjugations within disconnected sentences. ▪

Current research in assessment argues for "alternative approaches to assessment" that attempt to bring about a more direct connection between teaching and assessment (McNamara, 2001, p. 343). The same kinds of activities designed for classroom interaction can serve as valid assessment formats, with instruction and assessment more closely integrated. "Teaching to the test" is no longer viewed with disdain, but rather as a logical procedure that connects goal setting with goal accomplishment (Oller, 1991; Wiggins, 1989). Terry (1998) points out that "any material or technique that is effective for teaching a foreign language can also be used for testing" (p. 277). Thus as teachers and learners work toward standards-driven goals using authentic materials from real-world contexts, assessment also takes a more realistic form.

One of the ways in which assessment can be linked more closely to instruction is in the type of "washback effect" that it has on instruction; i.e., the impact of tests and assessment on the curriculum and on teaching and learning practices (Poehner & Lantolf, 2003; Shohamy, 2001; Swain, 1984). Tests have negative washback when they constrain teaching and learning practices, and positive washback when they promote learning that extends beyond the test (Messick, 1996). For example, preparing students for a high-stakes standardized test (i.e., a test upon which important decisions affecting a student's future may be based, such as entrance to a university, teacher certification, graduation) that consists largely of discrete point, multiple-choice grammatical items may have negative washback because it often forces the teacher to focus on decontextualized grammatical practice in place of meaningful communication. Additionally, these types of tests do not provide feedback to the test taker about his/her progress. On the contrary, preparing students for a performance-based or standards-based assessment is likely to have positive washback because instruction can include opportunities for language acquisition, exploration of authentic materials, and development of learning strategies.

Four basic principles that can guide foreign language teachers in the development of classroom tests are: (1) test what was taught; (2) test it in a manner that reflects the way in which it was taught; (3) focus the test on what students can do rather than what they cannot do; and (4) capture creative use of language by learners (Donato, Antonek, & Tucker, 1996). For example, if learners spend their class time developing oral interpersonal communication, then testing formats should include assessment of oral language output. Similarly, students who learn in class how to narrate in the past by writing paragraphs about events that occurred during their childhood should be tested by being asked to write paragraphs about past events in their lives. Walz (1989) reminds us that the same criticisms of foreign language textbooks, with respect to contextualization of activities, apply to classroom tests as well: Test items should be designed so that students must understand the meaning being conveyed in order to complete the tasks. Furthermore, since a large portion of classroom time is spent in learning language for communication in real-life contexts, testing should also reflect language used for communication within realistic contexts (Adair-Hauck, 1996; Harper, Lively, & Williams, 1998; Shrum, 1991).

Working Towards Standards-Based Authentic Assessment

Throughout this book you have explored ways to integrate *SFLL* into planning and instruction. The proof of the effectiveness of standards-based instruction is in the results of assessment of student learning. This edition of *Teacher's Handbook* proposes that teachers work toward designing and implementing authentic assessments that measure student progress in attaining the standards. Although the term *authentic assessment* will be explored in detail later in this chapter, we provide this explanation at this point. The term *authentic* has been used to describe the type of assessment that mirrors the tasks and challenges faced by individuals in the real world (Wiggins, 1998). As Ravitch (1993) has cautioned, "Standards will be meaningless if students continue to be tested without regard to them. Unless current tests change, the standards will wither and die" (p. 772). If student progress in attaining the standards is to be effectively assessed, teachers must adopt an approach to assessment that includes authentic assessment as one type of measure. Since implementation of authentic assessment is still a new endeavor for many teachers, a worthwhile goal is for teachers to work towards implementing more of these assessment tasks for both formative and summative purposes.

The reality of the classroom setting and instructional goals is that teachers make use of a wide variety of assessments, which may vary according to the degree to which they are authentic, given the definition provided above. In recognition of the value of multiple measures in assessing language performance, this chapter presents a variety of assessment formats that have a place in a standards-based curriculum. The latter part of the chapter deals with purely authentic and summative standards-based assessments and strategies for scoring or grading them. Although there are differences in the various test formats presented throughout the chapter in terms of their purpose, implementation, and the degree of authenticity that they reflect, they all share the following characteristics:

- They are contextualized, i.e., they are placed in interesting, meaningful contexts.
- They engage students in meaning-making and in meaningful communication with others.
- They elicit a performance of some type.
- They encourage divergent responses and creativity.
- They can be adapted to serve as either formative or summative assessments.
- They address at least one mode of communication.
- They can be used or adapted to address goal areas and standards.

 "Unless current tests change, the standards will wither and die." ■

Purposes of Tests: A Definition of Terms

Figure 11.2 categorizes key types of tests according to the purposes they serve. Administrative assessments often include *standardized tests* and *proficiency tests. Standardized tests,* also referred to as *norm-referenced* tests, measure learners' progress against that of other learners in a large population; examples are the SAT, the TOEFL, Advanced Placement Tests, and PRAXIS exams. Norm-referenced tests, for instance, might tell us that a student obtained a score that placed him or her in the top ten percent of students who took the test, or that he or she did better than sixty percent of those who took the test (Hughes, 2003). Standardized tests typically follow a uniform procedure for administration and scoring. On the other hand, *proficiency tests* are also called *criterion-referenced tests* because they measure learner performance against a criterion. For example, the ACTFL Oral Proficiency Interview uses the educated native speaker as the criterion against which to judge oral performance; one of the criteria used to judge speaking at the intermediate level is the ability to create with the language. Criterion-referenced tests, therefore, classify individuals according to whether or not they are able to perform a task or sets of tasks in a satisfactory manner (Hughes, 2003, p. 21). Proficiency tests might also be given for instructional purposes, in order to provide feedback regarding the learner's progress in reaching a specific proficiency level.

Instructional tests include *commercially prepared achievement tests,* such as textbook publishers' tests, which examine the extent to which students have learned a body of material taught, as well as *teacher-made classroom assessments,* which cover a wide range of strategies to assess achievement of instructional objectives and learner progress in attaining the standards and in meeting proficiency-based goals. In this chapter our focus is on instructional assessment—specifically, teacher-made classroom assessments—the purposes of which, as noted in Figure 11.2, are to diagnose learning difficulties, demonstrate evidence of learner progress, provide feedback to the learner, and use assessment results to evaluate teaching and the curriculum. As illustrated in Figure 11.2, tests may also be administered for *research* purposes, such as to learn more about language acquisition. Many of the empirical studies cited in this book used research-based tests.

Summative vs. Formative Assessments

All assessments have some characteristics in common, related to what learners can expect from them. Learners have the reasonable right to expect that their scores should be the same regardless of who is doing the scoring; that is, learners can expect that scorers will view the responses objectively. Furthermore, learners can expect that the test consistently measures whatever it measures. This is called *reliability* (Gay, 1987). Learners should also be able to expect that the test measures what it is supposed to measure and that this measurement is appropriate for this group of learners. This is referred to as *validity*. A test is considered to have *face validity* if it looks as if it measures what it is intended to measure, especially to the test taker (Hughes, 2003). For example, a multiple-choice grammar test that pretends to measure oral proficiency lacks face validity. As you will see later in the chapter, authentic and standards-based assessments are considered to have face validity because they mirror performance in the world.

As you learned in Chapter 4, assessments can be classified as either *summative* or *formative. Summative assessment* often occurs at the end of a course and is designed to

FIGURE 11.2 The Purpose of the Assessment

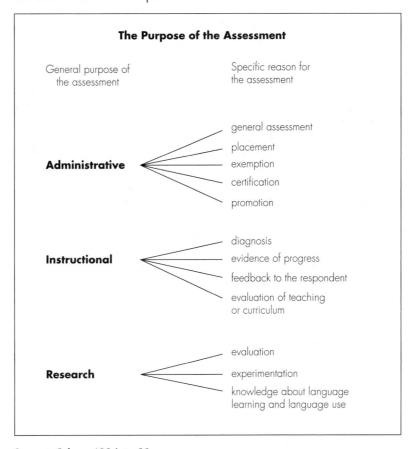

Source: Cohen, 1994, p. 23.

determine what the learner can do with the language at that point. Opportunities for further input or performance after the test is administered usually occur in the next language learning experience or course. The most common summative form of assessment is a final exam. *Formative assessments* are designed to help form or shape learners' ongoing understanding or skills while the teacher and learners still have opportunities to interact for the purposes of repair and improvement within the instructional setting. Specific types of summative and formative assessments will be presented later in the chapter.

Shohamy (1990) suggests that language teachers make extensive use of formative testing that is integrated into the teaching and learning process. Examples include quizzes of five to fifteen minutes' duration, class interaction activities such as paired interviews, and chapter or unit tests. A sufficient amount of formative testing must be done in the classroom in order to enable learners to revisit and review the material in a variety of ways, and formative feedback must enable the learner to improve without penalty. In this regard, teachers find it helpful to distinguish between ungraded assessment, which gives objective and formative information to the learner, and graded assessment or evaluation, which places value judgments on performance. In addition, programs should include summative assessment that focuses not only on achievement of unit and course objectives, but also addresses students' development of oral proficiency and progress in attaining standards-based goals.

Although summative and formative assessments differ in their purpose and in the nature of the evaluation designed for each, they also share similarities. Both types of assessments are systematic, planned, and connected to the curriculum. Also, many of the assessment tasks are similar. For example, a role-play situation may serve as both a formative assessment task designed to check learner progress within a unit and as a summative assessment at the end of the year or course to assess oral proficiency and learners' ability to perform global linguistic tasks. Consequently, planning a year-end summative assessment does not need to be overwhelming, since it should reflect the types of formative tasks that students have experienced throughout the instructional experience (Donato & Toddhunter, 2001).

Teachers should be advised that the results of summative assessments may be compared across grade levels, classes, and even schools; proficiency results are often used in this way. Additionally, the results of summative assessments may be used to justify the existence of programs and support advocacy, as in the case of early language programs (Donato & Toddhunter, 2001).

 Formative assessments are designed to help form or shape learners' ongoing understanding or skills while the teacher and learners still have opportunities to interact for the purposes of repair and improvement within the instructional setting. *Summative assessment* often occurs at the end of a course and is designed to determine what the learner can do with the language at that point. ■

Continuum of Test Item Types

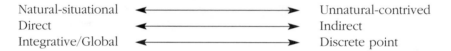

Natural-situational	⟷	Unnatural-contrived
Direct	⟷	Indirect
Integrative/Global	⟷	Discrete point

"Most language tests can be viewed as lying somewhere on a continuum from natural-situational to unnatural-contrived" (Henning, 1987). With this statement, Henning posited a continuum with the point on either end representing a specific type of test item.

Natural-situational assessments present tasks that learners might encounter in the world outside of the classroom, such as writing a response to a letter received from a pen pal or key pal from the target culture. In comparison, *unnatural-contrived assessments* feature traditional test items that often focus on isolated grammatical structures and vocabulary within contexts that do not reflect the world beyond the classroom, such as a fill-in-the-blank exercises for verb manipulation.

Cohen (1994) further explains the extreme points on this continuum by describing two types of contrasts: *direct* versus *indirect* assessments and *integrative/global* versus *discrete-point* test formats. *Direct assessments* are those that "incorporate the contexts, problems, and solution strategies that students would use in real life," while *indirect assessments* "'represent competence' by extracting knowledge and skills out of their real-life contexts" (Liskin-Gasparro, 1996, p. 171). For example, having students deliver a talk to an audience of their peers is a direct test of their ability to engage in oral presentational communication because it incorporates a context and communicative strategies found in real life; a multiple-choice grammar test is considered an indirect test of real grammar use because it is a contrived situation in which students are not demonstrating actual grammatical performance in typical contexts found outside the classroom.

Discrete-point assessments test one point at a time, such as a grammatical structure or one skill area, and include formats such as multiple-choice, true-false, matching, and completion; an example of this is a quiz on verb endings. Although discrete-point items are most often associated with assessment of one isolated grammar or vocabulary point, they can also be used to assess interpretive listening/reading/viewing or sociocultural knowledge, e.g., a multiple-choice item in which students read a brief description of a dinner invitation and must choose the appropriate form of refusal from among four options (Cohen, 1994).

Unlike discrete-point assessments, integrative or global assessments assess the learner's ability to use various components of the language at the same time, often requiring multiple modes or skills as well. For example, an integrative test might ask learners to listen to a taped segment, identify main ideas, and then use the information as the topic for discussion, as the theme of a composition, or to compare the segment to a reading on the same topic; learners could be graded on the basis of several criteria including their ability to interpret the text, interact interpersonally with a classmate, and produce a written product. Cohen (1994) describes the continuum of test items as featuring the most discrete-point items on one end, the most integrative items on the other end, and the majority of test items falling somewhere in between (pp. 161–162). Discrete-point and integrative test formats may be either direct or indirect assessments, depending on the degree to which the tasks address problems and strategies that learners would be likely to encounter in the world outside of the classroom.

What implications does the discussion of the continuum of test item types have for foreign language teachers? First, the selection of assessments and test types should always depend on the teacher's objectives and what is intended to be assessed. For example, if literal comprehension of a reading is being assessed, perhaps a discrete-point, multiple-choice test would be appropriate, while on the other hand, if interpersonal speaking is being assessed, an integrative assessment that engages students in real-life communication would be in order. Secondly, test types that directly address the knowledge, modes, or skills that they are intended to assess may be more valid measures than their indirect counterparts. Although at first students may seem to prefer "one-right-answer" types of tests because that is what they are most accustomed to, recent findings indicate that students may acquire a more positive attitude toward direct tests because they have face validity and allow them to show what they are able to do with the language in real-life contexts. Furthermore, students tend to be more enthusiastic about direct tests if they reflect the type of classroom instruction and practice that they have experienced. For example, in the Integrated Performance Assessment (IPA), about which you will learn later in this chapter, students overwhelmingly commented on how they were able to apply what they had learned to "real" tasks, how they had freedom to express themselves by using what they already knew, and how they felt a sense of accomplishment in being able to use what they had learned in real communicative tasks (Glisan, Adair-Hauck, Koda, Sandrock, & Swender, 2003). Thirdly, teachers should understand the limitations of discrete-point testing in terms of its role in assessing learner performance. As mentioned above, discrete-point items may be used appropriately to assess the interpretive mode of communication and sociocultural knowledge. However, when these items are used to assess grammar and vocabulary, teachers must understand that what is being assessed is recognition—not production or performance. To illustrate, if a learner accurately completes a fill-in-the-blank exercise that requires verb conjugation, the teacher cannot assume that the learner will be able to use these verbs appropriately and accurately in a real-life oral interpersonal task.

Assessment Formats: Definition of Terms

Figure 11.3 lists the key characteristics that are often used to describe attributes of foreign language assessments in the new assessment paradigm; you will see these terms in the descriptions of the assessment formats that follow in this chapter. You may notice that there is considerable overlap in the assessment formats and characteristics. For

FIGURE 11.3 Characteristics of Foreign Language Assessments

Proficiency-based/Prochievement	Learners perform tasks designed for a particular level of proficiency in order to determine their ability to perform specific language functions within contexts and content areas, using a particular text type and level of accuracy.
Performance-based	Learners use their repertoire of knowledge and skills to create a product or a response, either individually or collaboratively.
Interactive	Learners interact or are engaged in listening, reading, or viewing an authentic text, and they use that knowledge to communicate their opinions or to perform a related task.
Authentic	Learners perform tasks that mirror the tasks and challenges faced by individuals in the real world.
Standards-based	Learners perform tasks that require them to address one or more goal areas and standards in *SFLL*.

Source: Shrum and Glisan, 2005, original material.

example, all authentic tests are also performance-based and interactive; standards-based tests are performance-based and may also be proficiency-based.[2] All of these formats are also *integrative*, since learners attend to many linguistic elements, various types of knowledge, and/or more than one mode of communication at once.

Assessment Formats: Prochievement, Performance-Based, Interactive Model

This section presents several assessment formats that may be effectively implemented within a standards-based foreign language program. Although each format serves specific assessment purposes, they all feature contextualized test formats and focus on the creative use of the target language. Suggestions are provided for how each format can be adapted to assess learner progress in attaining specific standards of *SFLL*.

Prochievement Format: Assessing Achievement and Proficiency

Prochievement (**pro**ficiency + a**chievement**) tests are classroom tests designed to assess the degree to which students have achieved the objectives of a particular lesson or thematic unit while at the same time assessing their ability to function along a proficiency-based continuum (Gonzalez Pino, 1989). Prochievement tests, which may be oral or written, were born out of the desire to blend proficiency-based performance with grammatical structures and vocabulary being taught in classrooms and to enable learners to use the target language in life-like situations. Since the late 1980s, prochievement tests have offered foreign language teachers an appealing alternative to the classroom tests that traditionally had been mechanical and decontextualized. Formats include role plays,

FIGURE 11.4 Written Prochievement Test Item for Grammar/Vocabulary

Une description ennuyeuse. (A boring description.) Spice up this description a learner wrote in French about an evening on the town. Do so by adding at least one adjective to each underlined word. ATTENTION: Watch word order and agreement.

Nous partons à six personnes dans une <u>voiture</u>. Nous arrivons à un <u>restaurant</u>. Les <u>serveurs</u> qui y travaillent ont tous une <u>moustache</u>. A une table à <u>côté</u>, deux hommes bavardent. Ce sont le <u>propriétaire</u> et son <u>fils</u>. Un homme se plaint du restaurant à cause de ses <u>chaises</u> et son <u>service</u>. Lui et le propriétaire se disputent. Les <u>clients</u> quittent le restaurant. Nous, nous terminons cette <u>soirée</u> dans un bar où on a du Karioka.

N.B. You may use adjectives from this list or substitute those of your choice.

ancien	inconfortable	noir
dynamique	inefficace	nouveau
européen	jeune	petit
excellent	long	vrai
français	mémorable	???
gros	mécontent	

We leave, six people in one car. We arrive at a restaurant. The waiters who work there all have mustaches. At a nearby table, two men chat. They are the owner and his son. A man complains about the seating and the service. He and the owner argue. The customers leave the restaurant. As for us, we finish this evening in a Karioke bar.

old	uncomfortable	black
dynamic	inefficient	new
European	young	small
excellent	long	true
French	memorable	???
fat	mischievous	

Source: adapted from Phillips, 1996, original material.

paired interviews, picture descriptions, task-based discussions, and writing activities such as the one illustrated in Figure 11.4 that assesses grammar/vocabulary as well as intermediate-level writing proficiency. This test item could be adapted to address the written presentational mode of communication of *SFLL* (Standard 1.3) by adding a more authentic context and a potential audience of readers for the written product.

Figure 11.5 shows a sample oral prochievement task designed to assess use of reflexive verbs and intermediate-level speaking proficiency. This task could be adapted to reflect the oral interpersonal mode of communication (Standard 1.1) by making it a role play or interactive discussion in which students are required to ask questions, exchange information, and negotiate meaning.

Prochievement test items evaluate achievement of course content and assess performance along a proficiency continuum.

FIGURE 11.5 Oral Prochievement Task

Monologue. Describe your routine for a typical day during the school week. Tell what you do in the morning, during the day at school, and at home in the evening, and at what times. Then describe how this routine may be different on the weekend. Be sure to include interesting details!

Source: Shrum and Glisan, 2005, original material.

Performance-Based Format: Assessing Global Communication

Performance-based assessments require learners to use their repertoire of knowledge and skills to create a product or a response, either individually or collaboratively (Liskin-Gasparro, 1996). This format includes the use of prompts, which are complex questions or situations requiring the learner to make connections among concepts and develop a strategy for addressing the question or situation. There can be more than one right answer. In comparison to prochievement tests, which usually focus on a narrow area of knowledge and skills (e.g., a specific grammar point), performance-based tests require greater integration of accumulated knowledge and skills. The task-based instruction activities that you explored in Chapters 8 and 9 are performance-based strategies that could also be used for assessment. Figure 11.6 illustrates a sample performance-based test item for presentational speaking that addresses Standard 1.3. Figure 11.7 illustrates a sample performance-based test item for interpersonal writing that addresses several standards.

Which goal areas of *SFLL* are included in the performance task shown in Figure 11.7?

Performance-based assessments require learners to use their repertoire of knowledge and skills to create a product or a response, either individually or collaboratively.

PALS Project.   An effective example of performance-based assessment is the Performance Assessment for Language Students (PALS) project in Fairfax County, Virginia, the purpose of which is to design and implement performance tasks and evaluate the abilities of language learners (Tulou & Pettigrew, 1999). In order to design assessments that focus on what students know and can do in the foreign language, a task force of Fairfax County language

FIGURE 11.6 Sample Performance-Based Test Item (Presentational Speaking)

Task. Call your teacher on the phone and leave a message on his/her answering machine. (Administrative note: Have students call a number dedicated to this purpose or, if feasible, the teacher's or another person's number at a time when nobody will be there to answer the phone.) Your message should include the following information: your name, the day and time of your call, and your message, which can be anything that you wish to communicate to your teacher. Leave your message just as you would in English—do not write your message and then read or recite it from memory. Note that you will lose points if your message does not sound spontaneous.

Evaluation. Your performance will be evaluated on the basis of comprehensibility, inclusion of the three pieces of information requested, and spontaneity. See the evaluation scale below.

Descriptor	Points
Message is totally comprehensible and has all three elements.	10
Message is too brief or not complete and/or it is not completely comprehensible.	5
Message sounds as though it is being read or recited from memory.	3
Student did not leave a message.	0

Source: Liskin-Gasparro, 1996, p. 186.

FIGURE 11.7 Sample Performance-Based Test Item (Interpersonal Writing)

> **Task.** Your school is going to host an exchange student from Hamburg, Germany. The student's name is Hans Schmitter. Write Hans a letter in German welcoming him to your school and your community. In your letter, write about:
>
> ■ Your town or city: location, size, special features
>
> ■ Your school and typical daily activities
>
> ■ Your interests and hobbies
>
> ■ Two or three things that you expect Hans will find strange or different, given what you know about German high schools and how they are different from your school.

Source: Liskin-Gasparro, 1996, p. 179.

teachers created a variety of performance tasks that place students in real-life situations in which they need to use the language. The tasks, together with scoring criteria, were developed and used for both formative and summative assessment purposes. Tasks were designed so that they would "engage students in simulated real-world tasks; have more than one right answer; reward skill development, creativity, and linguistic accuracy; promote problem-solving skills and tap higher-level thinking skills (especially in upper levels); and let the students know how their performance will be evaluated before they perform the tasks" pp. 191–192). The decision was made to create assessments that would assess the presentational mode of communication (both speaking and writing) because teachers felt that this mode offered students the opportunity to perform to the best of their ability without relying on a peer's performance as is often the case in a face-to-face interpersonal task.

PALS tasks were designed for formative assessment according to the following template:

■ Theme and topic (as determined by the school curriculum)
■ A statement of the task objective
■ The task description
■ The minimal descriptions for completing the task
■ Suggestions
■ Directions (Tulou & Pettigrew, 1999, pp. 192–193)

Figure 11.8 illustrates a sample PALS writing task for Level 1 French/German/Spanish.[3]

The Fairfax County School District also used PALS to design summative assessment tasks to measure speaking and writing performance at the mid-year and end-year points. The purpose of these summative assessments was to chart the progress of each student on a proficiency continuum based on the *ACTFL Performance Guidelines for K-12 Learners* (1998). Figure 11.9 illustrates a series of end-of-year speaking tasks for Level 3; students respond spontaneously without prior preparation, and their responses are audiotaped.

See Appendix 11.1 on the Web site for an example of the end-of-year writing tasks for Level 3.

See the *Teacher's Handbook* Web site for a link to the Fairfax County School District site where you can find more information on the PALS project.

thandbook.heinle.com

An Interactive Model for Assessing Interpretive Communication

A strategy for assessing interpretive reading, listening, and viewing is the interactive format proposed by Swaffar, Arens, and Byrnes (1991). Their interactive model for testing reading parallels their approach to teaching reading, as well as that of the Interactive

FIGURE 11.8 PALS Writing Task for Level 1: French/German/Spanish

---

Figure 1. PALS Writing Task I
Level 1: French/German/Spanish

Theme: Student Life
Topic: School, Leisure Time
Task Objective: To write about your busiest day
Task Description: Your school is planning to create a web page on the Internet. On that page, the designers would like to let students of other countries know about the life of teenage students at your school.
Choose your busiest day and write a paragraph about what you do in the morning, afternoon, and evening.

Minimum requirements:
Write about:
a. one activity you do in the morning
b. two activities you do in the afternoon
c. two activities you do in the evening
Write 12 sentences (100 words or $\frac{1}{2}$ page).

Suggestions: You may use a graphic organizer such as a day planner, as given below; choose your busiest day and jot down your activities.

Directions: You may not use a dictionary.

Scoring Criteria: Level-1 writing rubric
Write as much as you can. Show what you can do.

* * *

Choose your busiest day . . .

day of the week: _____

morning	
afternoon	
evening	

Source: Tulou and Pettigrew, 1999, pp. 193–194.

Model for Integrating the Three Modes of Communication presented in Chapter 6, both of which consider the following key processing factors:

- informational background: the reader's context
- metacognition: How does the reader structure comprehension?
- intent: Why is the text being read?
- the learner's language ability

This test design, which can also be applied to the testing of interpretive listening and viewing, diagnoses not only text-based products, but also reader-based processing. An example of *text-based products* is finding factual answers to specific questions using information from the text; an example of *reader-based processing* is the ability to infer or

FIGURE 11.9 PALS End-of-Year Speaking Tasks for Level 3

Scenario: As part of a program to promote global understanding, you have entered a contest to win a free trip to France/Germany/Spain. For the application you must submit three speaking samples on tape to share some of your ideas and show your linguistic ability

Prompt #1 (60 seconds to prepare, 60 seconds to speak)
Describe the person you most admire and explain why. You may want to include a description of him/her and his/her influence on you.

Prompt #2 (60 seconds to prepare, 60 seconds to speak)
Describe your plans for the future. You may want to include summer, college, or career plans.

Prompt #3 (60 seconds to prepare, 60 seconds to speak)
Describe the best class you ever remember taking and tell why it was the best. You may want to include what you learned and how and why it affected you.

Source: Tulou and Pettigrew, 1999, p. 218.

formulate a main idea or to evaluate the text. Accordingly, the model features three components to verify whether the learner can:

1. account for a text's pragmatic as well as its informational and formal features (i.e., can the learner demonstrate literal comprehension and "read between the lines" to infer meaning?);
2. link comprehension of the text to L2 production or self-expression;
3. provide an individual interpretation of the text (Swaffar, Arens, & Byrnes, 1991, pp. 157–159).

Several aspects of this interactive testing format are similar to specific phases of the interactive model that you explored in Chapter 6—learners demonstrate literal comprehension of key information in the text, develop inferences, and share their personal points of view. This type of approach to testing interpretive communication is far different from the simple plot summaries or single factual questions that often appear on tests of reading or listening.

The design illustrated below is an adaptation of a five-step model proposed by Swaffar, Arens and Byrnes (1991). Sample items from their text are included to exemplify each step.

1. Students listen to, read, or view an authentic text.
2. *Focus on situational context:* Students identify main ideas by focusing on content or text schema.

Instructions: Identify and write down key words from the text that provide the following information about the main idea of the text:

Who: _____   What: _____

When: _____   Where: _____

Using these words, write a sentence expressing the main idea of the text.

3. *Focus on information:* Students identify details (vocabulary development).

> Instructions: Find synonyms or references from the text for the following words:

4. *Focus on grammatical competence:* Students use the grammatical structures in the text to further explore text ideas.

> Instructions: In the story, events and their timing are of major importance. Write two sentences about major events in the story. Use past tenses.

5. *Focus on intent of text:* Students develop their points of view.

> Instructions: What do you think would have happened if the story had continued? Write a three-to-five sentence description of another ending to the story. [This section could also attract learners' attention to particular cultural points.]

thandbook.heinle.com

As illustrated above, the interactive format can test learners on their interpretive listening/reading/viewing abilities; grammatical, lexical, and cultural knowledge; ability to interact with the text; and presentational writing, all within the framework of a real context. See Appendix 11.2 (on the Web site) for an example of a German reading used as a test within this framework.

What additional kinds of tasks does the Interactive Model for Integrating the Three Modes of Communication (Chapter 6) feature that are not found in this interactive testing format?

Authentic and Standards-Based Assessment

You have already explored several assessment formats that involve learners in using the target language for specific purposes within contextualized tasks, and you saw how these assessments could be adapted to address various goal areas of the standards. In this section, you will learn about new approaches to assessment: the *authentic* and *standards-based* approaches. You may recall the earlier suggestion that teachers should work towards developing authentic and standards-based assessments to include in their repertoire of assessments. An important issue concerning these types of assessments is how to score and grade them. To this end, you will also explore how to design and use scoring rubrics to be used with performance-based, authentic, and standards-based assessments.

Authentic Assessment

We have seen earlier that test results are often used by various groups of individuals in order to make decisions about instruction and about learners. Wiggins (1998) proposes that assessment also be educative in two ways: (1) It should be designed to teach by improving the performance of both teacher and learner, and (2) it should evoke exemplary pedagogy (p. 12). Educative tests must include credible tasks from which performance is assessed, reflecting a performance-based classroom and challenges learners will face in the real world.

As you learned earlier in this chapter, the term *authentic* is used to describe the type of assessment that mirrors the tasks and challenges faced by individuals in the real world (Wiggins, 1998). An assessment task, problem, or project is authentic if it:

- is realistic in that it tests the learner's knowledge and abilities in real-world situations;
- requires judgment and innovation;
- asks the student to "do" the [academic] subject rather than reciting information so that the student carries out a task using the language in a meaningful way;
- replicates or simulates the contexts in which adults are "tested" in the workplace, in civic life, and in personal life so that students address an actual audience, not just their teacher;
- assesses the student's ability to use a repertoire of knowledge and skill efficiently and effectively to negotiate a complex task; and
- allows appropriate opportunities to rehearse, practice, consult resources, and get feedback, and refine performances and products (pp. 22–23).

Authentic tasks, which may be used for either formative or summative purposes, engage learners in nonroutine and multistage tasks, real problems, or problems that require a repertoire of knowledge (Wiggins, 1994). They require learners to produce a quality product and/or performance. Authentic assessments involve "transparent or de-mystified criteria and standards" so that learners understand exactly what is expected of them and how their performance will be rated (see the next discussion on scoring rubrics). Furthermore, these assessments allow for thorough preparation, self-assessment, and clarifications and modifications through discussion with the assessor and/or one's peers (Wiggins, 1994, pp. 75–76).

Authentic assessments enable teachers to "assess what we value so that we value what we assess" (CLASS, 1998). Often learners are engaged in proficiency-based or standards-driven activities in the classroom but are then still tested on their knowledge of linguistic details by means of paper-and-pencil, discrete-point formats; in this case, there is a gap between the communication we value and the linguistic forms we assess. Authentic assessments provide a way to reduce this gap and they aim to improve performance. They involve challenges and roles that help students rehearse for complex tasks that face adults and professionals, while focusing on whether students can create polished, thorough, and justifiable responses, performances or products (Liskin-Gasparro, 1997; Wiggins, 1990). In this regard, authentic tests share the characteristics of performance-based tests except that they add the dimension of a real context and audience. For example, compare the performance-based task in Figure 11.6 with the authentic formative task shown in Figure 11.10. In Figure 11.6, the learner is performing with the language in a meaningful task, but the only audience is the classroom teacher. In Figure 11.10, the learner is also performing, but the audience is now a consumer who needs a particular service, which the learner will provide. (It is important to note that this task was designed so that students prepared a *real* itinerary for a *real* Spanish teacher, who is taking a *real* trip to Spain; this is not an imaginary situation.) The task will require multistaged research and interaction on the part of the learner, but the end result is meaningful use of language for real audiences.

In Case Study One in the Discuss and Reflect section of this chapter, you will find a Performance Task Template (CLASS, 1998) that includes the steps that might be followed in designing an authentic assessment task.

 Authentic tasks require learners to address an actual audience and mirror challenges faced by real individuals in real-world settings.

FIGURE 11.10 Authentic Assessment Task

Un viaje por España *(A Trip through Spain)*

You and your partner are Spanish travel agents who have decided to market your services to American school groups. You know there is intensive competition for this business. You have received a memo from Señorita Surprenant, one of New England's most traveled Spanish language teachers. She is heading back to Spain this spring with a group of her students. She is not committed to any specific regions, cities, or sights. She is looking for the following: a good price, great art museums, famous settings in literature, rare cultural opportunities (e.g., dance, sport, food), and all within a 7–10-day time frame.

You know Spain and its opportunities, but you are not really sure what will please Señorita Surprenant. You draw up a list of options that could be included in a trip and then call Señorita Surprenant. You talk with her about the options and use this chance to determine what will most convince her that you are the agency to handle the trip.

Using your knowledge and your impression of what Señorita Surprenant is looking for in the trip, you submit a written proposal, including an itinerary and your rationale for the itinerary, a map setting out the route to be followed, and a price list for students and chaperones.

Source: adapted from CLASS, 1998; contributed by J. Surprenant, teacher.

 The teacher is not the only audience in authentic tests. ▄

Evaluating Authentic and Performance-Based Tasks: Scoring Rubrics

Authentic and performance-based tasks can be assigned a grade with the use of a rubric,[4] a set of scoring guidelines for evaluating student work (Wiggins, 1998, p. 154). Rubrics answer the following questions:

- By what criteria should performance be judged?
- Where should we look and what should we look for to judge performance success?
- What does the range in the quality of performance look like?
- How do we determine what score should be given and what that score means?
- How should the different levels of quality be described and distinguished from one another? (Relearning by Design, Inc., 2000[5])

Rubrics provide the means for teachers to provide feedback to learners about their progress as well as to evaluate performance and even assign grades. Because rubrics contain rich descriptions of performance, teachers can use them effectively to provide feedback that focuses on the quality of learner performance and specifies how performance can be improved. However, perhaps of more importance, *rubrics show learners what good performance "looks like" even before they perform an assessment task.* Therefore, learners should see and discuss the rubrics for a particular assessment task *before* they begin the task.

Although rubrics can be created in a variety of formats, they all contain three common features:

1. They focus on measuring a stated **objective** (performance, behavior, or quality).
2. They use a **range** to rate performance.
3. They contain specific performance characteristics, arranged in levels indicating the **degree** to which a standard of performance has been met (San Diego State University, 2001a).

It is important to note that teachers sometimes use the term *rubric* to refer to any type of scoring guide. However, according to the strict definition of the term, *rubric* should only be used to describe a set of scoring criteria that reflect the three characteristics above and include a rich description of performance across a range of performance levels. Figure 11.11 illustrates a rubric that might be used to assess the authentic task in Figure 11.10. Examine Figure 11.11 as you continue to read about the features of rubrics.

A typical rubric:

1. Contains a *scale* of possible points to be assigned in scoring work, on a continuum of quality. High numbers are assigned to the best performances: Scales typically use 4, 5, or 6 as the top score, down to 1 or 0 for the lowest scores. Teachers often use an even number of total points (e.g., 4 or 6) to avoid the tendency to assign the middle score automatically.
2. Provides *descriptors* for each level of performance to enable more reliable and unbiased scoring.
3. Is either *holistic* or *analytic*. If holistic, a rubric has only one general descriptor for performance as a whole. If analytic, there are multiple rubrics corresponding to each independent criterion or dimension of performance being scored. Examples of criteria for interpersonal speaking might be "use of text type," "communication strategies," and "comprehensibility." (See Appendix 11.3 for ideas an generating performance dimensions for a rubric.)
4. Is *generic, genre specific*, or *task specific*. If generic, it can be used to judge a broad performance, such as communication or problem solving. If genre specific, it applies to a more specific type of performance within the broad performance category (e.g., essay, speech, narrative). A task specific rubric is unique to a single task.

Note that a rubric may be *longitudinal* when it measures progress over time toward mastery of educational objectives and enables us to assess developmental change. The ACTFL Proficiency Guidelines represent longitudinal, developmental rubrics (Relearning by Design, Inc., 2000).

 Rubrics show learners what good performance "looks like" even before they perform an assessment task. ■

According to Relearning by Design, Inc. (2000), there are different types of criteria that can be addressed in a rubric, and they relate to different aspects of performance:

"impact of performance"	the success of performance, given the purposes, goals, and desired results
"work quality and craftsmanship"	the overall polish, organization, and rigor of the work
"adequacy of methods and behaviors"	the quality of the procedures and manner of presentation, prior to and during performance
"validity of content"	the correctness of the ideas, skills, or materials used
"sophistication of knowledge employed"	the relative complexity or maturity of the knowledge employed

FIGURE 11.11 Sample Scoring Rubric for the Authentic Task in Figure 11.10

	EXCELLENT 4 POINTS	GOOD 3 POINTS	MINIMAL 2 POINTS	INADEQUATE 1 POINT
Quality of Research	Evidence of thorough research in preparation for proposal design; main facts and wealth of details about site, museums, culture	Evidence of effective research in preparation for proposal design; main facts with a few details about site, museums, culture	Evidence of some research; main facts with few or no details about sites, museums, culture	Little evidence of research; incomplete facts and details
Quality of Written Proposal	Well-written, clear, easy to understand; uses own words; few errors in grammar, vocabulary, spelling	Well-written, mostly clear with a few unclear parts or easy to understand except for a few places; uses primarily own words and some language from sources; some patterns of errors in grammar and/or vocabulary and/or spelling	Approximately half of writing is clear; quality of writing interferes with understanding in places; uses much language directly from sources; when using own language, patterns of errors in grammar, and/or vocabulary, and/or spelling	Poorly written; hard to understand; uses primarily language directly from sources; or if using own language, many patterns of errors in grammar, vocabulary, and spelling
Degree to Which Proposal Is Convincing	Very persuasive; addresses the requested information of client; convinces client to take the trip	Gives some reasons that are convincing: addresses most of the requested information of client; seriously persuades client to consider the trip	Gives only a partial rationale for taking the trip; addresses many though not all of the requested details and/or is not very convincing	Not persuasive; fails to address most of the client's requested information; language used does not convince client to take trip
Justification of Prices of Trip	Includes complete breakdown of prices with clear justification for costs	Includes some breakdown of prices and/or some justification for costs, although more clarity required	Either price breakdown or cost justification is incomplete: client still has questions	Incomplete breakdown of prices and incomplete justification of costs

Source: Glisan, 1998, original material. (Based on Task from CLASS [1998]).

Can you identify each of the criteria from the bottom of page 373 in the rubrics shown in Figure 11.11?

Many assessments make the mistake of overemphasizing content while underemphasizing impact of performance and adequacy of methods and performance (Relearning by Design, 2000). See Appendix 11.4 (on the Web site) for a fuller description of each of these criteria types.

thandbook.heinle.com

Designing Rubrics. How does a teacher design a rubric? To create a rubric for an authentic task, keep in mind that the audience is another individual in a real-world or simulated setting. What would an excellent performance look like if that person were the judge? Create a performance that such a person would judge as excellent. Then list the elements contained in that excellent performance and assign a range of points to each element (if you are designing an analytic rubric). Next, describe what unacceptable task completion would look like, then develop the levels in between. You will need to label the levels—for example, exemplary, accomplished, developing, beginning; or exceeds expectations, meets expectations, not there yet. Appendix 11.5 (see the Web site) illustrates a template for designing an analytic rubric across four levels of performance.

thandbook.heinle.com

Teachers should keep the following guidelines in mind as they design rubrics:

- The rubric must enable judges (and performers) to effectively discriminate between performances of different quality. The characteristic differences across levels of performance must be valid and salient, not arbitrary, and they must be reliable—the scores provided by the same judge at different times or different judges at the same time must be consistent.

- The descriptors should use language that is maximally descriptive of each level of performance and should reflect its most salient and defining characteristics. These descriptors should stem from an accurate analysis of many student work samples. Rubrics that rely on comparative or evaluative language will sacrifice validity. For example, overly comparative rubrics rely heavily on phrases such as "not as thorough as a 3" or "a more thorough argument." Teachers should avoid placing undue emphasis on the *quantity* of student work; they should be sure to reward students appropriately for the *quality* of their work. In addition, descriptors should be written in simple, concise terms that are understandable to learners.

- Since rubrics are meant to be criterion-referenced (not norm-referenced), the highest point on the scale should describe genuinely excellent performance, as derived from student samples of genuine excellence. The standards or performance criteria described in the rubrics are not the same as expectations: The scoring should alert students to their real levels of performance. Consequently, on a given task, it may happen that no one gets the highest score, and many students may get low scores. Therefore, scores do not automatically translate into letter grades, since letter grades tend to reflect "norms" instead of criteria or standards.

- The two most important points to establish on the scale are the top point and the "cut" point between passing and failing. Since the test is criterion-referenced, teachers cannot declare what constitutes a passing score prior to looking at student work samples. It does not follow, for example, that a 2 on a five-point scale is passing merely because of our custom of calling a D a passing grade on a five-point letter grade system, unless teachers judge actual 2-level work samples to be just passing and 1-level work to be not acceptable. (See the next section for more information on converting rubric scores to grades.)

- The descriptions of each point on the scale should represent a smooth continuum as much as possible.

- Teachers are faced with the decision of whether to create generic or task-specific rubrics. The more task specific the rubric, the more specific the performance descriptions, as shown in Figure 11.11, for example. However, teachers often design generic rubrics for issues of feasibility, i.e., they can be used to score multiple authentic tasks. You will see example of generic rubrics later in the chapter (CLASS, 1994, pp. 1–6).

- As teachers become familiar with learner performance, they should change rubrics as necessary in order to describe performance more effectively. In other words, rubrics should always be a work in progress.

See the *Teacher's Handbook* Web site for a link to Rubristar, a tool that teachers can use to develop rubrics when they do not wish to start from scratch.

Converting Rubric Scores to Grades.   An important issue when using rubrics is how to convert the rubric scores to gradebook scores. The Fairfax County Public School System has an excellent, detailed system for providing teachers with concrete ideas and mathematical formulas that they can use to convert scores easily. This system was developed for scoring the PALS tasks; see the *Teacher's Handbook* Web site for the rubrics and grading system. It is important to note that the Fairfax County system is based on a four-point range of performance: exceeds expectations, meets expectations, almost meets expectations, and does not meet expectations. Teachers should remember that the level that "meets expectations" is not the highest level attainable and does not receive the highest grade. A student who meets the expectations of the task receives a grade in the "B/B+" range. Therefore, the student who "exceeds expectations" merits an "A." The student who "almost meets expectations" earns a grade in the "C/C+" range, and one who "does not meet expectations" receives a grade in the "F/D+" range.

Different methods for making score conversions are used for holistic rubrics and for analytic rubrics. Holistic ratings using the four-point range of performance can be converted to percentages and letter grades in one of two ways:

1. Assign a specific percentage to each performance rating, using percentage ranges such as the following:

"Exceeds expectations"	A	=	95%			
"Meets expectations"	B	=	85%			
"Almost meets expectations"	C	=	75%			
"Does not meet expectations"	D	=	65%	or	F	= 55%

(depending on quality of performance)

2. Assign a range of percentages for each level on the rubric, as in the example below, which is used in the FairfaxCounty Public Schools (1999):

Exceeds expectations	93.5–100%
Meets expectations	84–93%
Almost meets expectations	74–83%
Does not meet expectations	54–73%

Then assign a letter grade, depending on where the student performed within the specific level. For example, the following percentage ranges for the performance levels were determined based on the grading scale of Fairfax County Public Schools (1999):

A	94–100%
B+	90–93%
B	84–89%
C+	80–83%
C	74–79%
D+	70–73%
D	64–69%
F	0–63%

For analytic scoring criteria, **it is important to remember not to convert the raw scores directly to percentages.** For example, if a student receives threes on each of the six criteria on the scoring rubric (meets expectations), he or she earns 18 out of 24. In percentages, this is 75%, which on the Fairfax County grading scale is a C. That conversion system, however, aligns the points earned with the school district's philosophy of a B for "meets expectations" (Fairfax County Public Schools, 1996). Therefore, points must be adjusted mathematically to convert rubric scores to grades. Appendix 11.6 (see the Web site) contains two conversion charts that provide helpful references for converting scores to grades. To convert raw rubric scores to percentage scores, teachers should consult the chart in Appendix 11.6.1 (on the Web site), which uses the following formula to calculate the percentages in the chart:

$$\frac{(\text{Student raw score}) \times 52}{(\text{Maximum raw score})} + 48 = \underline{\hspace{1cm}}\%$$

According to the Fairfax County Public Schools (1996), "This formula divides the span of percentage points between the highest possible A and the highest possible F. This span is then divided into equal increments to establish a percentage score for each student raw score" (p. 22). In this system, Fairfax County allows for a range of 52 points for scoring PALS tasks and 48 points as the lowest possible score if one could score a zero on PALS tasks, which is not possible. For example, if Student X earned a score of 18 out of a possible maximum of 24, then Student X earned:

$$\frac{18 \times 52}{24} + 48 = 87\% \text{ (a B on the Fairfax County grading scale)}$$

If Student Y earned a score of 11 out of a possible maximum of 24, then Student Y earned:

$$\frac{11 \times 52}{24} + 48 = 71.8\% \text{ (a D+ on the Fairfax County grading scale)[6]}$$

This grading system may feel unwieldy initially because the scoring criteria focus on what the students are actually able to do in the language and not on how many correct (or incorrect) answers they provide. While the scores at first appear to be "inflated," once they are converted to percentage grades, the grades will tend to follow a more normal distribution (Fairfax County Public Schools, 1996, 1999).

Teachers who use a point system of scoring instead of percentages should use the chart in Appendix 11.6.2 (see the Web site). (For more assistance, see the *Teacher's Handbook* Web site for the link to the Fairfax County PALS Web site.) In this case, the converted percentage score is multiplied by the total number of points the teacher assigns to the particular task and then divided by 100. For example, if a teacher gives an assignment a maximum gradebook score of 40 points and Student X earned a percentage score of 91.3%, the formula works as follows:

thandbook.heinle.com

Either: $\quad 91.3 \times \dfrac{40}{100} = 36.50$ out of a possible maximum of 40 points

Or: $\quad 91.3 \times .40 = 36.50$
(Fairfax County Public Schools, 1996)

Conceptual Orientation **377**

Many school districts are increasingly developing their own electronic programs for converting rubric scores to gradebook scores.

Standards-Based Integrated Performance Assessments (IPAs)

As you read earlier in the chapter, authentic assessments offer an exciting means of engaging students in tasks that reflect the challenges faced by individuals in the world beyond the classroom. Since a focus of *SFLL* is to weave foreign language more closely into the total educational experience and to enable learners to use L2 for a variety of real-life purposes, authentic assessments have a place in assessing student progress in attaining the standards. The *Integrated Performance Assessments (IPAs)* were recently designed by ACTFL to address a national need for measuring student progress in attaining the competencies described in both the national standards and the *ACTFL Performance Guidelines for K–12 Learners* (1998) within authentic contexts. The design of the IPA is based on the following principles regarding assessment, instruction, and the nature of guidance and feedback to learners:

- Performance is effectively assessed within tasks that test learners' knowledge and skills in real-world situations, i.e., in "authentic" contexts in which students use the language in their lives both within and outside of the classroom.
- Performance-based tasks require students to "do something with the language" (complete a task) and not merely recite from memory.
- Performance-based situations provide opportunities for students to use a repertoire of skills, areas of knowledge, and modes of communication in order to negotiate tasks; therefore the IPA features an integrated sequence of tasks reflecting the interpretive, interpersonal, and presentational modes of communication within a specific area of content (e.g., health).
- In order for students to be successful in performance assessment, they need to be aware of what their performance should look like; students should be given models of the standards we expect them to achieve.
- Performance-based assessment blends classroom instruction and experiences; it features a cyclical approach in which learners receive modeling, engage in practice, perform the assessment task, receive feedback from the teacher, engage in additional practice, perform another task, etc.
- Assessment can improve performance if students receive feedback in their attempts to complete tasks.
- Teacher feedback of high quality is that which provides learners with information regarding their performance as compared to model performance. Based on clearly defined criteria, teacher comments address whether the student performance "meets" the expectations for the level, "exceeds" the expectations, or "is not there yet." Comments do not consist of judgmental statements such as, "That was good" (Glisan, Adair-Hauck, Koda, Sandrock, & Swender, 2003, pp. 9–10).
- Performance-based assessment requires more time than traditional testing, but this time is justified since this type of assessment is linked closely to instruction and leads to improvement in student performance.

Reflecting the interconnected nature of communication as proposed in the standards, IPAs provide opportunities for students to demonstrate the ability to communicate within a specific content area across the three modes of communication. IPAs were developed to meet the need for valid and reliable assessments that "determine the level at which students comprehend and interpret authentic texts in the foreign language, interact with others in the target language in oral and written form, and present oral and written messages

FIGURE 11.12 Integrated Performance Assessment: A Cyclical Approach

I. Interpretive Communication Phase
Students listen to or read an authentic text (e.g., newspaper article, radio broadcast, etc.) and answer information as well as interpretive questions to assess comprehension. Teacher provides students with feedback on performance.

III. Presentational Communication Phase
Students engage in presentational communication by sharing their research/ideas/opinions. Sample presentational formats: speeches, drama skits, radio broadcasts, posters, brochures, essays, websites, etc.

II. Interpersonal Communication Phase
After receiving feedback regarding interpretive Phase, students engage in interpersonal oral communication about a particular topic which relates to the interpretive text. This phase should be either audio- or videotaped.

Source: Glisan, Adair-Hauck, Koda, Sandrock, and Swender, 2003, p. 18.

to audiences of listeners and readers" (Glisan, Adair-Hauck, Koda, Sandrock, & Swender, 2003, p. 8). The IPA prototype consists of a series of tasks at each of three levels—Novice Learner, Intermediate Learner, and Pre-Advanced Learner—as defined in the *ACTFL Performance Guidelines for K–12 Learners* (1998). As illustrated in Figure 11.12, the IPA series features three interrelated tasks, each of which reflects one of the three modes of communication, and integrates another goal area of the standards (e.g., Connections or Cultures). Each task provides the information and elicits the L2 interaction necessary for students to complete the subsequent task.

Figure 11.13 illustrates an overview of the Intermediate-Level task for the context "Famous Person."

 Which goal areas and standards are reflected in this IPA series of tasks? ▬

FIGURE 11.13 Overview of Intermediate-Level IPA Task for "Famous Person"

You are a member of the language club at your school. The club members have decided to name the club in honor of a famous person from the _____ culture. All members will vote soon in order to select a famous person in whose honor the club will be named. However, you all need to do some research in order to make a good decision! After locating some interesting descriptions of famous people from the _____ culture, you decide to read an article about _____, a famous _____, that has recently appeared in the popular magazine _____. After reading the article, you discuss this famous person as a possible candidate with a classmate, as well as discussing the classmate's choice from the article s/he has just read. Finally, you make a decision and write a letter of nomination for the famous person of your choice. Your letter must be convincing to the other members of the language club!

Source: Glisan, Adair-Hauck, Koda, Sandrock, and Swender, 2003, p. 22.

A unique feature of the IPA prototype is its cyclical approach to language instruction, which includes modeling, practicing, performing, and feedback phases (see Figure 11.14):

1. Modeling of expected student performance is an important feature of the IPA framework. Before students begin a task, teacher and students view samples of exemplary student work in the target language and discuss the criteria presented in the IPA rubrics that determine what constitutes performance at each level: exceeds expectations, meets expectations, does not meet expectations. The IPA rubrics for interpretive, interpersonal, and presentational communication for novice, intermediate, and pre-advanced levels appear in Appendix 11.7 on the Web site. It is important to note that these rubrics are analytic and generic across IPA tasks, and that they address the criteria for the various modes of communication described in the *ACTFL Performance Guidelines for K-12 Learners* (1998).

2. Teachers provide ample practice of the types of tasks that students will be asked to perform on the IPA. For example, classroom activities that take place during the year can be focused on students being able to interpret authentic texts and use L2 in meaningful contexts with one another.

3. Students begin the IPA by performing the interpretive task, and the teacher rates individual student performance using the interpretive rubrics. In the feedback phase, the teacher provides quality feedback by discussing with students why their interpretive skills are rated *exceeds, meets,* or *does not meet* expectations. Through the use of assisting questions and collaborative dialogue (in the ZPD), the teacher assists students in understanding the strengths and weaknesses of their performance as well as how to improve their performance. This feedback loop not only serves to inform students of their progress, but it also enables all learners to gain the same level of comprehension of the authentic text before they proceed to the interpersonal and presentational tasks. This is important because, if a learner is not able to interpret the authentic text successfully, this will prohibit him/her from performing the interpersonal and presentational tasks.

4. Students then perform the interpersonal task, which requires that they use the information they learned from the interpretive task to discuss a particular issue or question with a classmate.[7] The teacher uses the interpersonal rubrics to rate performance and provides feedback. It is critical to note that feedback in an IPA does not mean saying "Good job" but rather providing helpful comments about how to improve, such as "You are able to communicate autobiographical information. You are able to ask only one question. You have difficulty asking most questions. You need to work on the various types of asking questions in German" (Glisan, Adair-Hauck, Koda, Sandrock, & Swender, 2003, p. 35). Students use this specific type of feedback to focus on areas that need attention in order to improve future performances.

5. Finally, students perform the presentational task, and the teacher rates performance using the presentation rubrics. The feedback phase follows.

thandbook.heinle.com

See the *Teacher's Handbook* Web site for a link to the CARLA Virtual Assessment Center (VAC) of the Center for Advanced Research in Language Acquisition (CARLA) for ideas on developing performance assessments that are based on the "backward design" concept, integration of the three modes of communication, and the IPA framework.

It is interesting to note that an IPA can be used as either a formative or summative tool. As can be seen in the description of the cyclical process, it is clearly a formative assessment that directly informs instruction and improves learning and performance. The IPA can also be used as a summative tool in assessing student progress at the end of a course or sequence of instruction. In this case, however, teachers need to administer four

FIGURE 11.14 A Cyclical Approach to Second Language Learning and Development

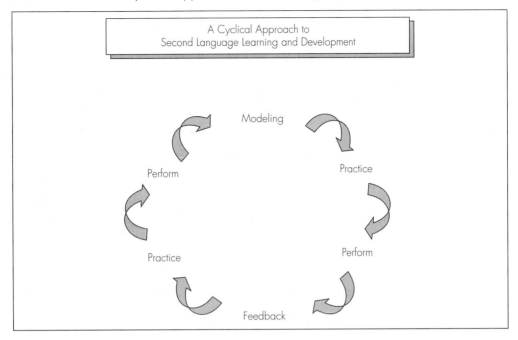

Source: Adapted from Wiggins, 1998.

or five IPAs in order to have enough data to confirm a learner's ability to function within the contexts of several goal areas of *SFLL* and his/her ability to perform at a given proficiency level.

 What is the role of the ZPD in the IPA feedback Phase? ■

 In what way does the IPA framework illustrate a seamless connection between instruction and assessment? ■

As illustrated in Figure 11.14, the IPA framework supports the seamless connection between instruction and assessment. Furthermore, the feedback loop distinguishes the IPA from other types of assessment—the teacher intervenes after each phase of the IPA to provide feedback, improve student performance, and equip the students with the background knowledge necessary to engage in the subsequent task. In this vein, the IPA model illustrates many aspects of a dynamic assessment, as advocated by Poehner and Lantolf (2003), since the teacher helps learners to perform better on the assessment as a result of intervention between phases (Sternberg, 2000). The IPA has the potential to serve as an effective research tool as the profession examines ways to assess progress in meeting the standards and proficiency-based goals. Currently, the IPA is the only standards-based model that assesses progress made in attaining the goal areas of *SFLL* plus progress along the proficiency continuum. In the IPA field testing that occurred in six pilot site school districts across the country, teachers strengthened their teaching as a result of integrating this type of assessment. For example, as a result of using an IPA, many teachers found that their students experienced difficulty in performing an oral interpersonal task because they needed strategies for negotiating meaning and practice in communicating spontaneously without having recourse to a printed script. In addition, a frequent student comment was that, during the IPA, it was "difficult to tell what was classroom practice and what was assessment"; this comment revealed the degree to which the IPA succeeded in making the connection between instruction and assessment seamless (Glisan, Adair-Hauck, Koda, Sandrock, & Swender, 2003).

thandbook.heinle.com

As more work is done in developing and refining the IPA, this assessment prototype has tremendous potential for helping the profession come to a better understanding of what standards-based assessment is and how such assessment can inform and improve classroom instruction.[8] (See Appendix 11.16 on the *Teacher's Handbook* Web site for a description of a national foreign language assessment currently being developed to assess performances across the three modes of communication and progress in the goal areas of *SFLL*.)

In sum, authentic assessment, the use of scoring rubrics, providing rich feedback to learners about their performance, and standards-based assessment such as the IPA provide exciting options for teachers as they work towards linking instruction more closely to assessment, improving learner performance, and assessing learner progress toward attaining the standards within tasks that they are likely to encounter in their lives outside the classroom.

Empowering Students Through Assessment

As you have seen in this chapter, current approaches to assessment emphasize the role of the learner in using L2 to accomplish a variety of communicative tasks, acquire information about C2 and other content areas through exploration of authentic texts, and create products and performances in L2. The discussion thus far in this chapter has echoed the pivotal role that modeling, feedback, and interaction play in guiding learners in language classrooms. In performance-based, authentic, and standards-based tasks, learners are given more responsibility for their learning than they were in the traditional assessment paradigm. In other words, they are able to interact with and help their peers, obtain feedback and guidance from the teacher, make decisions about how they will prove that they have acquired knowledge and skills, and formulate individual responses to open-ended questions, problems, and/or projects. In this regard, the new assessment paradigm has *empowered* learners to play more of an active role in the assessment and improvement of their learning. When students are empowered, they are better able to set personal goals for learning, self-assess accurately, seek out assistance when necessary, monitor their own progress, make improvements in their performances, and participate in learning communities.

Another way through which we empower learners is to give them responsibility for assessing their own progress, making decisions about which work samples best illustrate their progress in attaining the standards, using the foreign language outside of the classroom setting, and providing feedback to teachers about instruction. This section presents several assessment strategies that empower the learner in these ways. These strategies also enable the teacher to assess learners and instruction by means of multiple perspectives, as was discussed at the beginning of this chapter. In addition, each of these strategies may be used as an *informal* means of assessment, a way to obtain data and feedback concerning student progress and effectiveness of instruction without necessarily assigning formal grades.

Portfolio Assessment: Collection, Selection, Reflection

A *portfolio* is a "collection of evidence used by the teacher and learner to monitor the growth of the learner's knowledge of content, use of strategies, and attitudes toward the

FIGURE 11.15 Traditional Assessment vs. Portfolio Assessment

Traditional Assessment	Portfolio Assessment
Measures student's ability at one time	Measures student's ability over time
Done by teacher alone; student often unaware of criteria	Done by teacher and student; student aware of criteria
Conducted outside instruction	Embedded in instruction
Assigns student a grade	Involves student in own assessment
Does not capture the range of student's language ability	Captures many facets of language learning performance
Does not include the teacher's knowledge of student as a learner	Allows for expression of teacher's knowledge of student as learner
Does not give student responsibility	Student learns how to take responsibility

Source: NCLRC, 2004b.

accomplishment of goals in an organized and systematic way" (Tierney, Carter, & Desai, 1991, p. 41). For example, a portfolio may contain learner goal-setting worksheets, tape-recorded interpersonal tasks, journal entries, written responses to interpretive tasks, cultural investigations, self-assessments, etc. A portfolio documents the growth and development of students *over a period of time;* it is a rich description of a learner's work and offers perspectives that tests do not provide.

The portfolio collection must include "student participation in selecting contents, the criteria for selection, the criteria for judging merit, and evidence of student self-reflection" (Paulson, Paulson, & Meyer, 1991, p. 60). In a portfolio, learners have an opportunity to select evidence of their learning, reflect on it, and make it part of the assessment of their learning.[9] In this way, they become empowered to participate in their own assessment.

In a portfolio, learners have an opportunity to select evidence of their learning, reflect on it, and make it part of the assessment of their learning.

Figure 11.15 compares traditional assessment and portfolio assessment. The following are reasons for implementing portfolio assessment:

- Portfolios can include evidence of language development *at a specific time* and also evidence of language performance and progress *over time.*
- Since portfolio assessment is closely linked to instruction, teachers can be certain that they are measuring what they have taught, and they can give feedback on the effectiveness of instruction.
- Since portfolio assessment is incorporated fully into instruction, it does not require additional time spent specifically on assessment.
- Portfolios promote positive student involvement, which has a positive impact on students self-confidence, facilitates student use of learning strategies, and increases students' ability to assess and revise their work.
- Portfolios offer the teacher and student an in-depth knowledge of the student as a learner, which enables the teacher to individualize instruction for the student.
- Using portfolios introduces students to an assessment format with which they may need to become familiar—more and more schools and districts are adopting portfolio assessment for both students and teacher professional development.

FIGURE 11.16 Types of Portfolios

PORTFOLIO TYPE	DESIGNER/ DEVELOPER	TYPE OF ASSESSMENT	NUMBER OF ENTRIES; FREQUENCY	AUDIENCE
Show-case or best-works	Teacher designs according to a set of established goals; teacher selects documenta-tion of own per-formance	Self-evaluation	Few, over a career	Hiring bodies, parents, school administrators, legislators
Documentation	Teacher or super-visor designs; teacher or students compile it	Student self-evaluation as well as teacher evaluation	Many, over time	Parents at parent conferences, student
Evaluation	Outside agency or statewide group of teachers; students and teachers create a set of tasks	Everyone com-pletes the same tasks; standardi-zation of evalua-tion	Specified and limited number and format	Legislators, par-ents, educational agencies
Process	Student selects goals; student selects and nar-rates value of documents	Self-reflection of the learning process, usually not graded	Rough drafts, peer reviews; usually shortened intensive period of time or single task	Primarily the student for self-reflection; also teachers and parents

Source: Adapted from Hammadou, 1998, pp. 293–294.

- Using assessment portfolios gives teachers opportunities to involve parents in their children's language learning (NCLRC, 2004b).

There are various types of portfolios. Hammadou (1998) identifies several types of portfolios: showcase, documentation, evaluation, and process. Some portfolio character-istics are shown in Figure 11.16. Portfolios at the K–12 level are most often used for doc-umentation and process. Evaluation and showcase portfolios are frequently compiled by teachers and other school professionals in order to (1) demonstrate accountability to their students, parents, school administrators, and governmental agencies by showcasing their abilities and the performance of their students; and/or (2) demonstrate required skills nec-essary to achieve licensure or certification (i.e., National Board Certification).[10] Such a portfolio might include a teacher's certificate of rating on the Oral Proficiency Interview, a statement of philosophy about teaching, videotaped teaching scenarios, lesson plans addressing national standards with self-reflections on lessons taught, standards-based per-formance assessments, a professional development plan, and samples of student work.

Framework for Portfolio Process.   Barrett (2000) describes the following stages in the portfolio development process, which contribute to an approach to lifelong learning on the part of both teachers and students:

- Collection: Teacher and students learn to save artifacts that represent the successes (and "growth opportunities") in their day-to-day teaching and learning.

- Selection: Teacher and students review and evaluate the artifacts they have saved, and identify those that demonstrate achievement of specific standards.
- Reflection: Teacher and students become reflective practitioners, evaluating their own growth over time and their achievement of the standards, as well as the gaps in their development.
- Projection: Teacher and students compare their reflections to the standards and performance indicators, and set learning goals for the future. This is the stage that turns portfolio development into professional development and supports lifelong learning.
- Presentation: Teacher and students share their portfolios with their peers. This is the stage where appropriate "public" comments can be made to encourage collaboration and commitment to professional development and lifelong learning.

Barrett also suggests that a "Connection" stage can be added (either before or after the Projection stage), through which the portfolio is presented to the appropriate audience and discussed in meaningful conversation about teaching and/or learning. Often, the feedback received in these conversations can also encourage collaboration and commitment to professional development and lifelong learning and can lead to further goal setting.

Contents of the Portfolio.   The contents of the portfolio are generally determined by the two principal players in the creation of a portfolio. First is the portfolio designer, who sets the guidelines for what it should contain. This person is either the audience for the portfolio or knows what the audience will expect to see. The portfolio developer is the person whose work is featured in the portfolio. Usually this person selects items to be included as documents based on his/her judgment and the stipulations of the portfolio designer. The size and format of the portfolio are determined by decisions the designer or developer of the portfolio makes about the purpose of the portfolio, the selection of type and number of documents, and the type of self-reflective narrative that highlights the importance of the contents of the portfolio.

The items to be included in the portfolio are called *artifacts*. These include student products, student goals, and self-reflections: Student products document what students have learned, and the self-reflections and goals show how students are learning and how progress is being made (NCLRC, 2004b). In a standards-based program, learners must demonstrate their progress in each of the five goal areas of *SFLL*.

The self-reflections are usually prepared in the form of a narrative and justify why each piece of work was selected and what it means in the student's personal growth as a language learner. Sample artifacts include goal-setting worksheets; self-assessment records; tape-recorded oral proficiency interviews; video-taped interpersonal discussions and oral presentations/speeches; journal entries; letters to pen pals/key pals; compositions; written responses to interpretive tasks; analyses of cultural products, practices, perspectives; and ratings on performance assessments. Appendix 11.8 on the Web site features a sample portfolio template and Appendix 11.9 on the Web site presents a sample portfolio table of contents.

thandbook.heinle.com

Important features in the presentation of artifacts are the goal-setting and self-reflection components, which encourage students to be involved as active learners in their learning and self-assessment. Teachers should provide learners with the opportunity to set their own personal goals and thus reflect on their reasons for learning a second language. Goals can be short term (What do I want to be able to do by the end of this thematic unit?) or long term (What do I want to be able to do by the end of this year/semester?). Students need assistance in setting appropriate, reachable goals; a goal that would not be appropriate would be "I want to understand everything my French-speaking friends say." See the *Teacher's Handbook* Web site for a link to the NCLRC Web site that contains a sample lesson for setting reasonable goals for a middle school class and a student goals-setting worksheet. Appendix 11.10 (see the Web site) provides a goal-setting and self-assessment form.

In the self-reflection component, students describe why they selected each artifact for inclusion in the portfolio, what they learned from the artifact, and what the artifact illustrates about their performance. This is a pivotal feature of the portfolio because it holds students accountable for their selections and verifies the degree of learning that has taken place. Self-reflections should address the goals that students set initially and the learning objectives that they were attempting to achieve (i.e., standards-based objectives). The self-reflection could also address implications for future learning needed (Campbell, Melenyzer, Nettles, & Wyman, 2000). The following is an example of a self-reflection:

> I included this composition because it shows that I understand the perspectives behind the practice of the "Quinceañera" in Spanish-speaking countries. My goal in this unit was to understand why this custom is so important and whether we have anything like it in the US. I learned from our readings and my e-mail discussions with my Mexican key pal that there is a lot of religious importance connected to this custom and also a history of traditions. I was able to compare this custom to some customs that we have in the US such as "sweet sixteen" celebrations. This paper also shows how many new words I learned in Spanish for many products and practices associated with the Quinceañera. I still need to work on my use of transitions between paragraphs and indirect object, pronouns. In the future I would be interested in learning about other typical customs in the life of young Hispanics and what perspectives they represent.

Source: Shrum and Glisan, 2005, original material.

Portfolios may also include *attestations,* evidence of a student's progress that comes from teachers, peers, parents, or other adults; examples include records from a parent-teacher conference, teacher observation notes, and peer-assessment forms (NCLRC, 2004b).

 Portfolio artifacts include student products, student goals, and self-reflections.

Steps in Designing and Implementing Portfolio Assessment. The Portfolio Assessment Project, conducted through the National Capital Language Resource Center, identifies the following steps for designing and implementing foreign language portfolio assessment:

1. *Set assessment purpose:* Determine the purpose in order to have a focus and direction for the assessment. What aspect of language learning will the portfolio be used to assess? Who will use the portfolio? Why are you making the assessment?
2. *Identify instructional objectives:* Identify portfolio objectives or standards-based goals for students to work toward in the area specified by the assessment purpose. What exactly do you want students to achieve? Consider the goal areas of *SFLL*.
3. *Match tasks to objectives:* Identify language learning tasks that match the objectives and through which students will obtain artifacts to be used in the portfolios. What can students do to show evidence of their progress toward the objective? Plan

language tasks that will allow students to systematically practice and reflect on their learning.

4. *Describe student reflection:* Describe how students will reflect on their work. What self-assessment, goal-setting, and metacognitive tasks will you include?

5. *Set criteria:* Establish criteria by which the individual artifacts and the portfolio will be assessed. How will you determine the degree of student progress toward the goals?

6. *Determine organization and logistics:* Determine how the portfolio will be managed, considering the purpose of the assessment and the audience. Where will the portfolio be stored? How often will artifacts be submitted? Who will select the artifacts? Remember that it takes more than one artifact to reliably show progress toward a goal and that artifacts should be selected in a systematic manner. Will parents participate as an audience, and if so, how?

7. *Monitor progress:* Continually monitor the portfolio for validity and reliability and make adjustments as necessary. Is the portfolio assessing the specified areas consistently? Are you receiving useful information about your students to inform instruction?

8. *Evaluate the portfolio process:* After you have completed the portfolio semester or year, reflect on the entire process and evaluate your success with the portfolio. What worked well that you will include next time? What changes will you make for the next time? (NCLRC, 2004b)

Since the main purpose of a portfolio is to track progress and empower learners to assess their own learning, the issue of assigning grades to a portfolio can be a challenging one. Given the realities of the classroom and school policies, foreign language teachers may find it necessary to score or grade their students' portfolios. When teachers score classroom portfolios, the experience should be constructive and positive. Criteria for grading should include the degree to which the artifacts illustrate progress in attaining the various standards of *SFLL* and other learning objectives (i.e., proficiency development), quality of self-reflections, organization, presentation, etc. Appendix 11.11 on the Web site provides an example of a portfolio evaluation scoring sheet. Teachers are encouraged to develop rubrics for evaluating portfolios and to present these to students prior to beginning the portfolio process.

thandbook.heinle.com

Whether or not portfolios are graded, it is critical that teachers provide feedback to learners, as illustrated in Appendix 11.12 on the Web site, which contains a feedback sheet that could be used in a formative conference with students. In addition, students may be asked to present their portfolios formally to the teacher, peers, parents, or other outside audiences.[11]

Electronic Portfolio Formats. Recently, there has been much attention paid to electronic portfolios, which involve "the use of electronic technologies to enable students and teachers to collect and organize artifacts in various media types (texts, graphs, audio, video, etc.) and establish hypertext links to organize that material and connect it across artifacts as well as to appropriate standards, especially in the case of standards-based portfolios" (Egéa-Kuehne, 2004, pp. 21–22).[12] The advantages of electronic portfolios are that they:

- increase students' technological and multimedia skills and knowledge;
- provide hyperlinks to foreign language content standards and educational technology standards (see Chapter 12), thus enabling students to effectively show evidence of having met standards;
- use minimal storage space;
- are more portable;
- have a long shelf life;
- are more easily and widely accessible and distributed;

■ enable the projection of artifacts and performances anytime and anywhere. (Egéa-Kuehne; Kilbane & Milman, 2003)

The process of compiling an electronic portfolio is similar to that of a traditional paper portfolio except that students need to select and use appropriate technological tools and strategies in order to digitize images, audio recordings, video artifacts, etc., and to individualize their portfolios. It is important to remember that the primary goals of the electronic portfolio are the same as those of paper portfolios. In other words, teachers must be cautious to not allow the "glitz" of an electronic portfolio to become the focus. The primary focus should be the degree to which artifacts and self-reflections illustrate learner progress in attaining learner goals and standards. As Barrett (2000) reminds us, an electronic portfolio without goals, standards, and/or reflections is just a multimedia presentation, a fancy electronic resume, or a digital scrapbook.

Barrett (2000) suggests five stages in developing an electronic portfolio:

1. Defining the Portfolio Context:

   a. Identify the purpose and primary audience.
   b. Identify the standards or goals to be used in organizing the portfolio.
   c. Select the developmental software to be used and use this tool in Stage 1.

2. The Working Portfolio Stage:

   a. Collect digital portfolio artifacts that illustrate progress.
   b. Use graphics and the layout capability of the chosen software to interject your personality into the portfolio artifacts.

3. The Reflective Portfolio Stage:

   a. Select the artifacts that will compile the formal or presentation portfolio.
   b. Write reflective statements and identify learning goals for the future.

4. The Connected Portfolio Stage:

   a. Convert documents into a format that allows hypertext links.
   b. Navigate the portfolio using hypertext links.
   c. Insert multimedia artifacts into the portfolio.
   d. Share the portfolio with an audience and obtain feedback.

5. The Presentation Portfolio Stage:

   a. Record the portfolio to an appropriate presentation and storage medium.
   b. Present the portfolio before an audience (real or virtual).
   c. Evaluate the portfolio's effectiveness in light of its purpose and the assessment context.

thandbook.heinle.com

See the *Teacher's Handbook* Web site for a link to Barrett's detailed site that deals with how to develop electronic portfolios; this site contains information concerning the specific technology tools, details for each of the five stages presented above, and rubrics for evaluating electronic portfolios. Also, for assistance in managing the portfolio development process, see the links provided to The Grady Portfolio and The Open Source Portfolio Initiative.

Learner Self-Assessment

In addition to engaging students in selecting and reflecting on work samples that illustrate their progress, another strategy for empowering students is to have them perform self-assessments. These assessments might be done as part of a review for a test on a thematic unit, in order to prompt students to review and assess what they are able to do and what areas still need attention. For example, at the end of a "Making Social Plans" unit, students might be given a list with statements such as:

	YES	ALMOST	NOT YET
I can call and invite someone to go to a party.			
I can convince a friend to go out even if he or she doesn't want to.			
I can accept an invitation.			
I can decline an invitation and give a reason.			
I can write an e-mail message to a Spanish-speaking friend and discuss plans for the weekend.			
I can read the movie listings in an authentic Spanish newspaper and identify movies of interest and times they are playing.			
I can describe social events that a Hispanic teenager typically enjoys.			

Following this self-assessment, students would have the opportunity to collaborate with the teacher and/or peers to work on the objectives that had not yet been attained.

Self-assessments can also be implemented as a summative way to have students evaluate their progress. Figure 11.17 illustrates a summative self-assessment checklist for a third-grade Japanese class that experienced standards-based instruction. Note that, prior to completing the summative assessment, the student self-assesses using a checkmark placed in the appropriate column for each item. After the actual assessment, the teacher indicates with circles what the student was actually able to do on the assessment. This type of system enables the teacher and students to determine how accurate students' self-assessments are in terms of actual assessment results. A worthwhile goal would be for the teacher to help learners acquire more skill in self-assessing, and hence, in improving their learning and performances.

Interactive Homework

Another aspect of empowering students is providing them with interesting opportunities to use the foreign language outside of class and thereby to assess their learning at home. Despite inconclusive research on advantages and disadvantages of homework (Cooper, 1994), the U.S. Department of Education advocates its use as a way to promote learning, stating that student achievement rises when teachers regularly assign homework and students conscientiously do it (United States Department of Education, 1986).[13]

FIGURE 11.17 Summative Self-Assessment Checklist for Third-Grade Japanese Students

Name _____   December 3rd grade

Things I Can Do in Japanese

Think about what you can do in Japanese. Make a checkmark under the appropriate column for each sentence. After our testing, Jessica-sensei will write a red "O" in the correct column according to how you do on the test.

	Yes!	With help	Not yet
Communication Skills			
I can say whether I have something using "_ ga aru."	○	✓	
I can ask for things using "kudasai."	✓		
I can say "here you are" and "thank you."	✓		
I can count to 100 by tens.		○	✓
I can count to 1,000 by hundreds.	✓		○
I can read all the hiragana we learned so far (35).	All ✓	Many ○	Few ____
Culture Skills			
I can recognize three kinds of Japanese writing: Kanji, hiragana, and katakana.	✓	○	
I can recognize different Japanese coins.	✓		
I can play rock-paper-scissors in Japanese.	✓		
Connections to Other Subject Areas			
I can find Japan and the U.S. on a globe and a map. (geography)	✓		
If you give me a price, I can "draw" the correct amount of money I need using 1, 5, 10, 50, 100, and 500 yen coins. (math)		✓	
Comparisons (of language and culture)			
I know the difference between Japanese and American money and I can tell you about how much each Japanese coin is worth in American dollars.	✓		
Communities (Japanese Beyond the School)			
I have done at least two homeworks for Japanese so far this year.	Yes! ✓	No _____	
I have told someone outside of school about the things I learned in Japanese class.	Yes! ✓	No _____	

Source: Curtain and Dahlberg, 2004, p. 168; original material by Jessica Haxhi.

According to Antonek, Tucker, and Donato (1997), homework functions on three interrelated levels:

1. Homework communicates to the parent what and how well the child is learning in the classroom.
2. Homework facilitates classroom learning if it is linked to what the child can realistically perform without the assistance of the teacher and other students.
3. Homework mediates the relationship of school and home by serving as a public awareness tool that informs parents about the curriculum and encourages their support for programs (p. 65).

The principles of teaching language in context for meaningful communication found throughout *Teacher's Handbook* apply to homework tasks as well. Specifically, *Teacher's Handbook* suggests that foreign language homework assignments:

- consist of more than mechanical, decontextualized workbook exercises;
- be clear enough so that students can understand instructions at home;
- be related to activities done in class;
- provide the basis for activities to be done in class the next day (e.g., students might prepare interview questions that they will use the next day in a pair activity);
- be meaningful and interesting to students;
- evaluate the extent to which learners can use language independently (their actual level of development);
- if possible, engage students in interaction with others (peers, parents);
- enable students to self-assess their progress;
- provide the teacher with feedback regarding the effectiveness of instruction (e.g., if many students are experiencing difficulty with an assignment, it may point to specific work that needs to be done in class); and
- empower student learning.

The professional literature as revealed in research articles and methodology textbooks has failed to consider fully the role of homework. However, one study suggests the concept of "interactive foreign language homework" as a way to involve parents/caretakers in schoolwork. Antonek, Tucker, and Donato (1997) based their work on that done by the Center on Families, Communities, Schools, and Children's Learning at the Johns Hopkins University, where interactive homework in various subject areas was piloted. Through a process called Teachers Involve Parents in Schoolwork (TIPS), students talk about homework in the classroom, describe the types of homework they like best, explain how their parents help them with homework at home, and solicit parents' active involvement in completing assignment at home (Epstein, 1993).

 Interactive foreign language homework is a way to involve parents/caretakers in schoolwork. ■

In the study by Antonek, Tucker, and Donato (1997), interactive homework assignments were developed and piloted in a K–5 Japanese program in an effort to involve parents in helping students with Japanese vocabulary and cultural information. The majority of parents reported having enjoyed completing the assignments with their children and having the opportunity to learn more about the Japanese program. Figure 11.18 illustrates a sample interactive homework assignment, which consists of six parts:

1. title introducing the topic of the homework, a statement indicating the connection between the assignment and classwork, the date, and student signature;
2. a list of FL phrases with English translations;
3. instructions for students to carry out three to five language functions (e.g., expressing thanks and greeting someone);
4. instructions for students to teach their parents how to carry out language functions;
5. ways for students and parents to interact in the foreign language (e.g., exchange greetings and courtesy expressions);
6. cultural information relevant to the lesson.

Space is also provided for parents to sign and give feedback on the child's performance (Antonek, Tucker, & Donato, 1997, pp. 67–68).

FIGURE 11.18 Interactive Homework Assignment

Japanese: Greetings

Dear Family,
In Japanese class we have learned how to greet people. This activity will let me show you how I do it. This assignment is due _____

Sincerely, _____
Student's signature

In Japanese I am able to say and respond greetings and courtesy expression properly.

O.high.yo!	"Good morning!"
Cone.knee.chi.wa!	"Hello, Good afternoon!"
Cone.ban.wa!	"Good evening!"
Sa.yo.(o).na.ra!	"Good bye!"
Are.lee.ga.toe!	"Thank you!"
Dough.e.ta.she.ma.she.tay.	"You are welcome."
ao.men.na.sigh.	"I am sorry."
Ee.des.yo!	"It's OK!"

To your parent, how do you...
greet him or her in the morning? afternoon? evening?
greet him or her when you go apart?
thank him or her? or respond when he or she says "thank you"?
apologize? or respond when he or she says "I'm sorry"?

Teach your parent how to greet in Japanese!

With your parent, exchange greetings and courtesy expressions.

1. A.M.	2. early P.M.	3. Evening	4. Gift	5. Oops!	6. Bye!

The tradition of bowing in Japan is a common gesture used in introductions, greetings, partings, apologizing, and thanking.

Student's name _____ Class _____ Date _____
How well do you think your child performed this skill?
1. _____ Child seems to perform this skill well.
2. _____ Please check work. Child needs some help on this.
3. _____ Please note (other comments below):

_____
Parent's signature

Source: Antonek, Tucker, and Donato, 1997, p. 175.

The researchers suggest that ten-minute assignments work best and that they be kept to one page and be reproduced on colored paper for easy identification by parent and child. Although the example in Figure 11.18 focuses on verbal language, the assignments could also guide students and parents in producing a short written product, such as a note, letter, or creative paragraph. It is important to note that these assignments must be carefully designed since parents may not know the target language; parents become learners along with their children. Appendix 11.13 on the Web site contains a checklist for constructing an interactive homework assignment.

Spanish teachers in Pinellas County, Florida, designed a similar approach using tasks that elementary school students do at home with their parents (Kucerik, 2000). Through this

thandbook.heinle.com

endeavor, a home assessment system was developed that makes parents and classroom teachers partners in assessment. Parents are introduced to the program by way of a letter that explains the goals of the program and the role of the parent. This assessment process uses a pocket chart in each classroom; assessment cards (held in the pocket chart), which contain written language tasks reflecting the goals of the program; name cards for each student in the program; and a "profile sheet" for recording the long-range achievement of each student. The profile sheet is kept in the student's portfolio and is updated regularly. As the school year begins, each student receives the first assessment card (see Appendix 11.14 on the Web site), which contains ten tasks or "skills," written in the native language. Below each skill is also printed a place for the student's name, the date, and parent signature. Students are instructed to take the assessment card home and practice the skills with a family member until they feel ready to present them in class. The goals are consistent practice and increasing confidence in using the language, not rapid completion of the cards. Once a child is ready to return a card to school, he or she places it in the pocket chart in the classroom. The teacher uses the completed cards placed in the pocket chart to review and assess students. When a student demonstrates the ability to successfully complete the task, the teacher initials the card and records it on the student's profile sheet. Students receive the next level card once all of the skills on the previous card have been successfully demonstrated in class (Kucerik, 2000, pp. 4–5). The goals of this home assessment program "empower students to set learning objectives and direct their own achievement" (pp. 4–5).

thandbook.heinle.com

Designed in these innovative ways, homework assignments can play a new role in engaging learners in interesting language use outside of the classroom, in setting their own learning goals, and in directing their own achievement.

Classroom Assessment Techniques (CATs)

This final assessment strategy is different from those previously described in that its purpose is to engage learners in providing feedback on instruction, and indirectly, on their learning. *Classroom Assessment Techniques* (CATs) are informal, formative assessment strategies that are aimed at improving instruction, rather than assigning grades or points (Angelo & Cross, 1993). According to Angelo and Cross, the function of CATs is to "improve the quality of student learning, not to provide evidence for evaluating or grading students" (p. 6). The goal of these strategies is therefore to better understand students' learning and how to improve one's teaching. Consequently, CATs are both a set of assessment strategies and a teaching approach, based on the principle that the more teachers know about what and how their students are learning, the better equipped they are to improve their teaching.

CATs are largely simple, non-graded, anonymous, in-class activities that give both the teacher and learners useful feedback on the teaching-learning process (ACTFL/Weber State University, 2003). The following is an example of the Minute Paper CAT, which is one of the most commonly used strategies.[14] It should take a minute to do, usually at the end of a class period, and its purpose is to provide rapid feedback on whether the teacher's objective for the lesson matched what learners actually learned:

The Minute Paper

1. What are the two [three, four, five] most significant [central, useful, meaningful, surprising, disturbing] things you have learned during this class?

2. What question(s) remain uppermost in your mind?

Source: Southern Illinois University at Edwardsville Undergraduate Assessment and Program Review, 2004.

The questions posed can be made specific to the content of the foreign language class, as Carduner (2002) did in her third-year college Spanish composition course (see Appendix 11.15).

A sample CAT that addresses higher-level thinking skills is the RSQC2, an acronym for Recall, Summarize, Question, Comment, and Connect (Angelo & Cross, 1993, pp. 344–48). Students take two minutes to *recall* and list in rank order the most important ideas from a previous day's class. Then they take another two minutes to *summarize* those points in a single sentence in order to "chunk" the information. Next, students are asked to write one major *question* that they want answered. Finally, students identify a thread or theme to *connect* this material to the course's major goal. As an option, students may add a *comment* regarding their confidence in or areas of doubt concerning the specific course content being explored (Southern Illinois University at Edwardsville Undergraduate Assessment and Program Review, 2004). Spanos, Hansen, and Daines (2001) reported on their use of the RSQC2 CAT in an advanced-level German culture course, in which students posted their feedback anonymously through an online bulletin board. The German instructor found that several students were missing key ideas and connections on a particular topic, and she was able to modify instruction accordingly.

thandbook.heinle.com

The Southern Illinois University at Edwardsville Undergraduate Assessment and Program Review has a comprehensive Web site that features a list of sample CATs, a description of each, and a course example (see the *Teacher's Handbook* Web site for the link). You may also find it helpful to consult Angelo and Cross (1993) for additional examples.

The function of CATs is to "improve the quality of student learning, not to provide evidence for evaluating or grading students." ▪

A number of research studies have cited the merits of CATs (Angelo, 1991, 1998; Angelo & Cross, 1993; Carduner, 2002; Steadman, 1998), particularly in terms of affect. The most frequently cited advantage to using CATs reported by faculty in Steadman's study was "an increase in student satisfaction as a result of having a voice in their learning" (Carduner, 2002, p. 544). Faculty in multiple research studies indicated that the use of CATs served as a catalyst for (1) promoting a greater sense of the classroom as a learning community (Angelo & Cross, 1993); (2) encouraging reflective practice, and thus positive change, on the part of the instructor (Steadman, 1998); and (3) raising students' metacognitive awareness (Angelo & Cross, 1993; Carduner, 2002).

CATs have been used effectively in an electronic format for students in upper-level foreign language courses. Spanos, Hansen, and Daines (2001) found that having students engage in CATs by using an online bulletin board, portfolios, and online discussions instead of using the traditional paper-and-pencil format had unique advantages: students provided more reflective responses because they had more time to plan and submit their responses; the voices of more introverted students were heard more often since they had additional time to plan what they wanted to say; and students were actively engaged with the course material outside of class (p. 323).

In conclusion, for teachers, frequent use of CATs can (1) provide ongoing feedback about the day-to-day learning and teaching process at a point when it is still possible to make instructional changes, (2) provide useful information about student learning with a much lower investment of time compared to other means of formal assessment, (3) help to foster good rapport with students and increase the efficacy of teaching and learning, and 4) encourage the view that teaching is a formative process that evolves with time and feedback (ACTFL/Weber State University, 2003). For students, frequent use of CATs can (1) help them to become better monitors of their own learning, (2) point out the need to alter study skills, (3) provide concrete evidence that the instructor cares about learning, and (4) help them to feel that their opinions about instruction are valuable (ACTFL/Weber State University, 2003).

In sum, students can play a greater role and be more empowered in their learning through assessment strategies, such as portfolios, self-assessment, interactive homework, and classroom assessment techniques.

The Oral Proficiency Interview and Its Implications for Classroom Assessment

In Chapter 8, you learned about the impact that the ACTFL Oral Proficiency Interview (OPI) has had on language instruction over the past two decades. Here we revisit the OPI for the purpose of exploring its implications for classroom assessment, particularly as it relates to oral interpersonal communication.

As you learned in earlier chapters, the OPI is a standardized procedure for the global assessment of oral proficiency. It measures language production holistically by identifying patterns of strengths and weaknesses within the assessment criteria of global tasks or functions, contexts/content areas, accuracy, and text type. An official OPI is a face-to-face, tape-recorded interview lasting from five to thirty minutes and conducted by a certified proficiency tester. The following is a brief description of how the interview is conducted. As pointed out in Chapter 8, an understanding of the scale and/or the interview procedure does not imply an ability to rate oral speech samples. Furthermore, the OPI is not designed to be used as a classroom test. The ACTFL OPI Testing Program is administered by Language Testing International (LTI). For more information about the OPI or to schedule an OPI, see the link to LTI on the *Teacher's Handbook* Web site.

thandbook.heinle.com

The interview begins with a brief warm-up in order to help the interviewee feel comfortable and confident. Next, the interviewer moves the conversation forward through one or more level checks to establish the floor of performance or to determine at what level the interviewee can consistently perform the tasks for a given level. This phase demonstrates the tasks/contexts that the interviewee can perform with confidence and accuracy. Once the interviewer has determined that the speaker can handle the tasks and topics of a particular level, he or she raises the interview to the next major level by means of probes to establish the ceiling of the performance. The interaction in this phase illustrates the limitations of the interviewee's proficiency. The level check and probe phases may need to be repeated as each level is verified and the next level is examined. After the level checks and probes have been conducted and the interviewer believes that the evidence points to a particular level, the interviewee is asked to participate in a role play, which serves as a final level check or probe. The role play checks the functions that cannot easily be elicited by means of the conversation itself. Finally, the interview is brought to a close in the wind-down, at which time the discussion returns to a comfortable linguistic level for the interviewee and ends on a positive note (Swender, 1999).

A modified version of the OPI, called the Simulated Oral Proficiency Interview (SOPI), was developed at the Center for Applied Linguistics and uses taped responses as a cost-effective alternative to the face-to-face OPI (Stansfield & Kenyon, 1992, 1996). The SOPI consists of a master tape with test directions and questions, a printed booklet with pictures and other materials used in responding, and an audio tape for recording the interviewee's responses (Hadley, 2001, p. 438). Stansfield and Kenyon (1996) describe the SOPI as consisting of the following phases: (1) personalized questions simulating an initial encounter with a native speaker; (2) performance-based tasks such as those based on a visual to elicit questions, directions, descriptions, or narrations; and (3) topic- and

thandbook.heinle.com

situation-based tasks that elicit functions such as supporting an opinion, describing advantages and disadvantages, apologizing, or giving an information talk (p. 1; cf. Hadley, 2001, p. 438). Interviewees' oral responses are recorded individually and evaluated by a tester. Stansfield and Kenyon (1992) report high correlations between the proficiency ratings given in the OPI and those given in the SOPI. For more information on the SOPI, consult the Center for Applied Linguistics Web site (Link provided on the *Teacher's Handbook* Web site).

That the OPI has had an impact on assessment over the past two decades would be an understatement. The descriptions of performance that characterize each of the OPI levels now provide a common frame of reference to describe achievement in terms that have become meaningful to the vast majority of educators and students (e.g., *functions, text types*) (Liskin-Gasparro, 2003; North, 1993). As Liskin-Gasparro noted in her historical description of the OPI in celebration of its twentieth anniversary, testing formats such as prochievement tests and oral performance tests were inspired by the "emphasis in the OPI on formats and techniques that maximize student language production, along with its focus on tasks rather than linguistic accuracy alone" (p. 487).

The format of the OPI has provided many ideas for classroom assessment of oral interpersonal speaking:

1. The OPI has illustrated to teachers that they can use similar formats in assessing interactive speaking in the classroom: paired interviews, spontaneous role plays, individual interviews. Note that the OPI format has most applicability for assessing interpersonal communication that is two-way and interactive. As explained in Chapter 8, teachers should be careful not to confuse interpersonal and presentational communication. Formats for assessing oral presentational communication include oral presentations, skits, multimedia presentations, and demonstrations.

2. The structure of the OPI offers a guide for how individual interviews with students might be structured: a warm-up, tasks to check for the level, probes to push for language at a higher level, possibly additional level checks, and a wind-down.

3. OPI interviewers must leave their traditional teacher behaviors behind during the assessment (e.g., correction, repetition of interviewee's responses). This is also advisable during classroom assessment, since traditional teacher behavior—such as overt correction—will often undermine attempts to obtain a ratable speech sample (i.e., students will be too anxious to talk).

4. The role of questions asked during an OPI is pivotal. Yes/no questions should be reserved for finding topics of interest to discuss, making novice speakers confident about their performance, and obtaining permission to pursue a topic. In classroom oral interview situations, an abundance of yes/no questions will result in a lot of talking on the part of the teacher and little speech on the part of the student.

5. Listening and responding to the interviewee is essential in an OPI, and this principle should also be followed in classroom assessments. If active negotiation of meaning is the goal in an oral interview, then the teacher must listen to the content of the interviewee's message and respond accordingly.

6. In an OPI, interviewers generally stay with the same topic and spiral the function up to the next level. For example, if the topic is "work" and the discussion is occurring at the intermediate level, the interviewer might probe to the advanced level by asking how the interviewee obtained a job. It is more natural and less demanding on the interviewee to probe within the same topic rather than changing both the topic and the proficiency level. This same principle applies to individual classroom interviews in order to keep the natural flow of conversation and minimize anxiety on the part of the interviewee.

7. As in an OPI, interviewees need sufficient time to think in assessment situations, and teachers should not expect rapid-fire answers to questions. Pauses to think do not necessarily indicate a performance deficit.

The *ACTFL Proficiency Guidelines—Speaking* (1999) offer ideas for how to construct rubrics at the various proficiency levels. You might examine the IPA rubrics for the interpersonal mode of communication to see the proficiency-based criteria for rating performances: language function, text type, communication strategies (quality of engagement and interactivity and clarification strategies), comprehensibility, and language control.

As teachers prepare for assessing oral interpersonal communication, they will want to plan multiple opportunities for formative assessment, such as paired interviews, information-gap and jigsaw activities, and role plays. An effective means of grading these activities is using the "TALK Scores" (Donato, 2004), a method for monitoring and evaluating group speaking activities, presented in Appendix 8.7. Teachers should also plan for summative assessments to track students' progress in achieving proficiency levels; an OPI-like format for individual interviews would work well in this regard. Rubrics similar to those used for an IPA are effective in assessing the skills that are required for satisfactory performance at each level of proficiency.

Conducting oral assessment in the classroom poses feasibility challenges, particularly in cases of larger classes. In planning for oral assessment, the teacher might consider the following alternatives: (1) assess pairs of learners using audiotape; (2) assess groups of four or five learners using videotape; (3) manipulate the scheduling of the assessment—for example, assess only part of the class orally on each thematic unit, making sure that at the end of the grading period every learner has the same number of oral test grades, or conduct oral assessment over the course of several days so that part of the class is assessed each day; or (4) while a group of learners is being assessed orally, engage the rest of the class in an interesting reading or writing task.

Teachers should remember that, in a standards-based program, oral interpersonal and presentational communication do not occur in a vacuum, but rather are linked to communication in other modes (as in the IPA and the Interactive Model for Integrating the Three Modes of Communication), as well as to exploration of content in the other goal areas of *SFLL*. The OPI offers many effective ideas for assessing oral communication, and connecting these ideas to the broader issues of standards-based instruction and authentic assessment is likely to result in more effective assessment of learners and of instruction.

Planning for Classroom Assessment

The following are guiding principles that should assist foreign language teachers as they plan for assessment in a standards-based classroom.[15] Each principle is further exemplified by a listing of sample assessments that were presented in this chapter. This listing of principles and sample assessments also serves as a summary of the key points presented in this chapter.

1. Instruction and assessment should be mirror images of each other. (formative assessments, IPAs, CATs)
2. Assess learner progress by means of multiple measures that encompass both formative and summative assessments. (self-assessments, portfolios, IPAs)
3. All assessments must be contextualized and feature meaningful use of language. (IPAs, authentic assessments, performance-based assessments)
4. Performance-based assessment should have a central place in the assessment plan. (IPAs, authentic assessments, performance-based assessments)

5. Use the *ACTFL Proficiency Guidelines* and the *ACTFL Performance Guidelines for K-12 Learners* to frame descriptions of performance and set expectations. (IPAs)
6. Consider working towards more authentic and standards-based assessment formats. (IPAs)
7. Consider the value of rubrics to measure student performance when performance-based, authentic, and/or standards-based assessments are used. (IPAs, authentic assessments, performance-based assessments)
8. Consider the importance of empowering students in tracking their own progress, selecting and reflecting on their own work samples, making improvements in performance, and providing feedback about the instruction they are receiving. (self-assessments, portfolios, interactive homework, CATs) (adapted from Duncan, 2000).

TEACH AND REFLECT

NCATE_____
STANDARD
5.a.

EPISODE ONE
Analyzing and Adapting a Traditional Test

Task One: Analyze the following traditional test given to a French I class. Why is it considered "traditional"? Explain, using the following questions as a guide:

1. Is there a context? If there is none, what context could be applied?
2. What knowledge and/or skills are being evaluated?
3. How is the learner asked to use the target language?
4. Does the test address standards-based competencies? Explain.
5. Why is this test not considered performance-based, authentic, integrative, or interactive?
6. What might this test reflect concerning the classroom practices of the test designer?

Chapter 6 Test: French I
Name_____

I. Write the French equivalents for the following numbers:

1. 23 _____
2. 46 _____
3. 69 _____
4. 72 _____
5. 95 _____

II. Complete the following sentences with the present tense of the infinitives:

1. (descendre) Nous _____ en ville.
2. (attendre) La famille _____ un autobus.
3. (vendre) Un homme _____ des sandwiches.

III. Change the present-tense sentences below to the near future using aller + infinitive.

1. Nous arrivons de France. _____
2. Il va de Paris à Chicago. _____

IV. Give the French translations for the words and expressions below.

1. tomorrow _____   3. next week _____
2. next Wednesday _____   4. tonight _____

Task Two: Now, on a separate sheet of paper, adapt this test to make it contextualized and performance-based. Explain how each section will be scored.

EPISODE TWO
Adding an Authentic Dimension to a Performance-Based Assessment Task

NC**ATE**_____
STANDARD
5.a.

Analyze the following oral performance-based assessment task in which learners are asked to use the target language in order to communicate meaningful information. Make a list of the global functions, information, vocabulary, and grammatical points learners would have to use to complete the following task:

> Describe your routine for a typical day during the week. Tell what you do throughout the day and at what times. Include details such as with whom and where you do these activities.

Now adapt this task to make it authentic according to the criteria for task authenticity presented earlier in the chapter (Wiggins, 1998). Think of which elements you need to add to the task in order to make it reflect a real-world situation. You might start by asking yourself, "In what settings do people find themselves having to elaborate their daily schedules?"

EPISODE THREE
Designing a Summative Assessment for a Post-Secondary Class

NC**ATE**_____
STANDARD
5.a.

If you currently teach or are preparing to teach at the post-secondary level, complete the following task:

Design a *summative* assessment designed to assess what learners can do at the end of a particular language course (e.g., assessment on culture, literature, content, conversation). Decide first what knowledge, skills, and/or standards are being assessed. Then create a performance-based, standards-based assessment, complete with rubrics to score performance. Consider making the assessment authentic, if possible.

DISCUSS AND REFLECT

CASE STUDY ONE
Developing Authentic Assessment Tasks and Rubrics

NC**ATE**_____
STANDARD
5.a.

Mr. Alma teaches Spanish at Bustamante High School in La Plata City. This year he has three Spanish II classes and two Spanish III classes. A teacher for eight years, he has kept abreast of innovations in teaching foreign languages by reading journal articles and attending workshops and conferences. He is active in his local foreign language collaborative and the state foreign language association. Mr. Alma uses the principles of proficiency-oriented instruction when he plans and designs activities, and recently he has experimented with standards-based learning scenarios.

For the past year, Mr. Alma has been trying to develop more effective means of assessing learners' functional use of the language. Last week, he attended a full-day workshop on authentic assessment sponsored by the state foreign language association. Mr. Alma had been integrating performance-based testing into his assessment plan by designing situations in which learners would use the language orally in order to complete a communicative task successfully. However, as he learned at the workshop, while his performance-based tasks were effective in eliciting oral performance, they tended to measure speaking alone, with no integration of other skills; they were seldom designed to include more than two learners; and they did not address standards-based goals. With his new knowledge of and motivation for authentic assessment, Mr. Alma attempts the design of an authentic assessment task to evaluate learner performance in Unit 4 for Spanish II. He uses the authentic performance task template presented at the workshop (CLASS, 1998) in his task design (see Figure 11.19). Here is the task he designs:

Task: You are a writer for your school newspaper, and the editorial team is planning an issue of the paper for the Hispanic community nearest your school. You have been assigned a feature story dealing with a popular Hispanic singer, actor/actress, or sports figure. Your end product will be a magazine story describing the life of the person and will include some photographs. In order to write the story, you need to do the following:

1. Working with two cowriters (classmates), investigate popular magazines to find out who some popular Hispanic singers, actors/actresses, or sports figures are. Use the Internet to access this information quickly. Choose a Hispanic figure of interest to you and your co-writers. (Note: A variation on this assignment would be to have students interview a Hispanic individual who lives in the community and treat him/her as a "famous person.")

2. Find out everything you can about the Hispanic figure through research, using the Internet and other sources. Decide what information each cowriter will be responsible for finding.

3. Have a discussion with your cowriters in order to obtain the information that they found in their research. Decide what details you want to include in your story. Young readers will undoubtedly want to know how the person got started in his/her career and became so famous.

4. Together with your cowriters, write the newspaper story. Make it exciting enough to attract the attention of youth who will want to buy the issue just to read your article!

Mr. Alma's task is a multistage activity that requires various subtasks and opportunities for students to engage in discussion, research, and work together. On the next page is the template distributed during the workshop Mr. Alma attended. He plans to build his scoring rubrics from it.

Ask yourself these questions:

1. What makes this an authentic task according to the criteria set forth by Wiggins (1998)?
2. Were opportunities provided for students to practice carrying out a range of tasks likely to be necessary in the real world? Explain.
3. Was there concern for the development of linguistic accuracy? Explain.
4. How does this task address standards-based goals?

To prepare the case:

1. Read Wiggins (1989, 1998) for additional information about authentic tests.
2. Read Genesee and Upshur (1996) for additional ideas about classroom testing.
3. Read Liskin-Gasparro (1996) for additional examples of multistage projects that include multiple goals and standards.
4. Consult the Relearning by Design Web site (see the *Teacher's Handbook* Web site for link).

To prepare for class discussion:

1. Design a timeline for this task in order to project how much class time will be needed, which parts will be completed out of class, and which aspects will be done individually

thandbook.heinle.com

FIGURE 11.19 Authentic Performance Task Template

AUTHENTIC PERFORMANCE TASK TEMPLATE

Spanish II: Unit 4 (The World of Work), Grade 10

Achievement Target(s):

Performance Competencies: Discuss work and career: narrate and describe in the past; obtain information.
Content Standards: Communication (1.1, 1.2, 1.3); Cultures (2.1); Connections (3.2): Communities (5.1)

Criteria To Be Used in Assessing Performance:

Impact of Performance: Is the article informative and engaging?
Work Quality and Craftsmanship: Is the article well-designed, effectively written, clear?
Adequacy of Methods and Behavior: Was the student methodological in the process of producing the product? Did s/he conduct appropriate research and keep in mind the audience?
Validity of Content: Is the article accurate? Does it reflect correct information?

Mode(s) and Genre(s) of Performance:

Modes: oral, written, displayed (presentational)
Genres: oral interview, discussion; written interview questions, article; displayed article with photographs

---

Source: Adapted from CLASS, 1998.

and collaboratively. What will students submit to Mr. Alma in addition to the final magazine article?

2. Develop a scoring rubric to assess learner performance on this task. Remember to use the criteria on the template. Begin by developing the description of what exemplary task completion would look like for each criterion. Then describe what unacceptable or poor task completion would look like, and then develop the levels in between. Refer to the rubric presented in Figure 11.11 as an example.

3. Now design your own authentic task related to the same thematic unit that you designed in Episode One, Task C, of Teach and Reflect for Chapter 3. Be sure that the task reflects a real-world activity and has a real audience. You may find it helpful to examine the authentic task presented in Figure 11.10 and the one given in this case study. You may also wish to use the authentic performance task template presented in this case study in Figure 11.19. Design a scoring rubric similar to the one presented in Figure 11.11.

CASE STUDY TWO
Planning for Portfolio Assessment

NCATE
STANDARD
5.a.

Over the past year, the teachers in Las Palmas School District, a large urban district in a northeastern state, have been participating in professional development designed to help them to implement portfolio assessment. Portfolios are new to the majority of teachers in this district. Below are mini-scenarios of two foreign language teachers who are ready to implement portfolio assessment.

Scenario 1: Ms. Sylvie Dupois is a French teacher at one of the middle schools, where language instruction begins in seventh grade. She is also a native speaker of French from Montreal. School district administrators and language faculty have been considering moving language instruction down to grade 6. In order to obtain information to help them make a final decision, the school district decides to have Ms. Dupois offer a pilot language and culture course to interested sixth-grade students for the academic year. School administrators and faculty design the program with the primary purpose of exposing students to the language and culture of Quebec. They are realistic and acknowledge that a one-year class will not result in a high level of oral proficiency in French or extensive understanding of the culture of Quebec. However, they hope to have evidence of the level of students' interest in learning about language and culture in sixth grade and also information about what they are able to realistically accomplish after one year of study. In addition, their hope is that parents will also become interested in having their children learn a foreign language earlier in their middle school years. Ms. Dupois decides that portfolio assessment would provide the information that faculty, administrators, and parents need in order to determine the future design of the language program.

Scenario 2: Mr. Claude Maltz and Ms. Bernadette Smolkovich are high school German teachers who have worked diligently over the past three years to implement standards-based instruction in their German III, IV, and V classes. They decide to work collaboratively to conduct portfolio assessment in these classes in order to evaluate their students' progress in achieving the standards. Although students' abilities and level of interest in German are diverse, the majority of the learners are very technologically literate and have expressed an interest in "virtual" portfolios. The audience for the portfolios would be teachers and students. School administrators will receive recommendations for revising the curriculum based on the portfolio assessment project, but they will not see the portfolios themselves.

Note: These scenarios are adapted from scenarios provided by NCLRC (2004a).

Ask yourself these questions:

1. How do the purposes and audiences for each of these portfolio endeavors differ?
2. How will portfolio assessment provide needed information that traditional assessment would not supply?
3. What are some initial decisions that will need to be made by these teachers as they begin to implement portfolio assessment?
4. What are some sample artifacts that would be appropriate for portfolios in each of the scenarios?

To prepare the case:

thandbook.heinle.com

1. Consult the NCLRC Portfolio Assessment in the Foreign Language Classroom Web site for planning worksheets and other information about implementing portfolio assessment (see the *Teacher's Handbook* Web site for link).
2. Read Egéa-Kuehne (2004) and Barrett (2000) for information about electronic portfolio design.

To prepare for discussion:

1. Describe how Ms. Dupois would implement portfolio assessment, using the eight steps presented on pages 386–387.
2. Describe how Mr. Maltz and Ms. Smolkovich would implement electronic portfolio assessment, according to Barrett's (2000) five stages presented on page 388.
3. Choose one of these scenarios and describe how the portfolios will be assessed and how assessment results will be used to make programmatic decisions.

REFERENCES

American Council on the Teaching of Foreign Languages. (1998). *ACTFL performance guidelines for K–12 learners*. Yonkers, NY: Author.

American Council on the Teaching of Foreign Languages. (2001). *ACTFL proficiency guidelines—Speaking*. Yonkers, NY: Author.

American Council on the Teaching of Foreign Languages/ Weber State University. (2003). *Foreign Language Methods On-Line*. Ogden, UT. Funded by the U.S. Department of Education. Module 10, Theme 3.

Adair-Hauck, B. (1996). Authentic assessment in second language learning. *Pennsylvania Language Forum, 68*, 10–30.

Angelo, T. A. (Ed.). (1991). *Classroom research: Early lessons from success. New Directions for Teaching and Learning, No. 46*. San Francisco, CA: Jossey-Bass.

Angelo, T. A. (Ed.). (1998). *Classroom assessment and research: An update on uses, approaches, and research findings. New Directions for Teaching and Learning, No. 75*. San Francisco, CA: Jossey-Bass.

Angelo, T. A., & Cross, K. P. (1993). *Classroom assessment techniques: A handbook for college teachers* (2nd ed.). San Francisco, CA: Jossey-Bass.

Antonek, J. L., Tucker, G. R., & Donato, R. (1997). Interactive homework: Creating connections between home and school. In A. Mollica (Ed.), *Teaching languages—Selected readings from Mosaic* (pp. 169-184). Lewiston, NY: Soleil Publishing.

Barrett, H. C. (1999). *Electronic teaching portfolios*. Retrieved April 12, 2004, from http://www.electronicportfolios.com/portfolios/site2000.html.

Barrett, H. C. (2000). *The electronic portfolio development process*. Retrieved April 11, 2004, from http://www.electronicportfolios.com/portfolios/EPDevProcess.html#epdev.

Campbell, D. M., Melenyzer, B. J., Nettles, D.H., & Wyman, R. M. (2000). *Portfolio and performance assessment in teacher education*. Boston: Allyn & Bacon.

Carduner, J. (2002). Using classroom assessment techniques to improve foreign language composition courses. *Foreign Language Annals, 35*, 543–553.

CLASS (The Center on Learning, Assessment, and School Structure). (1994). *Rubrics and scoring criteria: Guidelines and examples*. Paper presented at the meeting of the ACTFL Beyond the OPI Assessment Group. Yonkers, NY: ACTFL.

CLASS (The Center on Learning, Assessment, and School Structure). (1998). *Developing authentic performance assessments*. Paper presented at meeting of the ACTFL Beyond the OPI Assessment Group. Yonkers, NY: ACTFL.

Cohen, A. D. (1994). *Assessing language ability in the classroom* (2nd ed.). Boston: Heinle & Heinle.

Cooper, H. (1994). *The battle over homework*. Thousand Oaks, CA: Corwin Press.

Curtain, H. A., & Dahlberg, C. A. (2004). *Languages and children—Making the match* (3rd ed.). Boston: Pearson Education.

Donato, R. (1995). Original unpublished material.

Donato, R., Antonek, J. L., & Tucker, G. R. (1994). A multiple perspectives analysis of a Japanese FLES program. *Foreign Language Annals, 27*, 365–378.

Donato, R., Antonek, J. L., & Tucker, G. R. (1996). Documenting a Japanese FLES program: Ambiance and achievement. *Language Learning, 46*, 497–528.

Donato, R., & Toddhunter, S. (2001). *Creating and conducting year-end assessment interviews in a Spanish FLES program*. Presentation at the IUP Spring Methodology conference. Indiana, PA.

Duncan, G. (2000). The standards-based classroom and assessment: The proof is in the pudding. In G. Guntermann (Ed.), *Teaching Spanish with the Five C's: A blueprint for success* (pp. 71–90). Fort Worth, TX: Harcourt College.

Egéa-Kuehne, D. (2004). Student electronic portfolio assessment. In C. Cherry & L. Bradley (Eds.), *Assessment practices in foreign language education* (pp. 19–28). Southern Conference on Language Teaching *Dimension 2004*. Valdosta, GA: Valdosta State University.

Epstein, J. (1993). School and family partnerships. *Instructor, 103*(2), 73–76.

Fairfax County Public Schools. (1996). *A.S.A.P. Alternative strategies for assessing performance. Foreign Language Program*. Fairfax County, VA.

Fairfax County Public Schools. (1999). *Scoring the level one speaking task. PALS: Performance Assessment for Language Students*. Retrieved April 27, 2004, from http://www.fcps.edu/DIS/OHSICS/forlang/PALS/rubrics/1spk_hol.htm.

Gay, L. R. (1987). *Educational research: Competencies for analysis and application*. Columbus, OH: Merrill Publishing.

Genesee, F., & Upshur, J. A. (1996). *Classroom-based evaluation in second language education*. Cambridge, UK: Cambridge University Press.

Glisan, E. W., Adair-Hauck, B., Koda, K., Sandrock, S. P., & Swender, E. (2003). *ACTFL integrated performance assessment*. Yonkers, NY: ACTFL.

Gonzalez Pino, B. (1989). Prochievement testing of speaking. *Foreign Language Annals, 22*, 487–496.

Hadley, A. O. (2001). *Teaching language in context* (3rd ed.). Boston: Heinle & Heinle.

Hammadou, J. A. (1998). A blueprint for teacher portfolios. In J. Harper, M. G. Lively, & M. K. Williams (Eds.), *The coming of age of the profession: Issues and emerging ideas for the teaching of foreign languages* (pp. 291–305). Boston: Heinle & Heinle.

Harper, J., Lively, M. G., & Williams, M. K. (1998). Testing the way we teach. In *The coming of age of the profession:*

Issues and emerging ideas for the teaching of foreign languages (pp. 263–276). Boston: Heinle & Heinle.

Henning, G. (1987). *A guide to language testing.* Rowley, MA: Newbury House.

Hughes, A. (2003). *Testing for language teachers.* Cambridge, UK: Cambridge University Press.

Kilbane, C. R., & Milman, N. B. (2003). *What every teacher should know about creating digital teaching portfolios.* Boston: Allyn & Bacon.

Kucerik, J. (2000). Let's assess: Connecting students, parents, and teachers. *Learning Languages, 5,* 4–9.

Liskin-Gasparro, J. E. (1996). Assessment: From content standards to student performance. In R. C. Lafayette (Ed.), *National standards: A catalyst for reform.* The ACTFL Foreign Language Education Series (pp. 169–196). Lincolnwood, IL: NTC/Contemporary Publishing Group.

Liskin-Gasparro, J. E. (1997, August). *Authentic assessment: Promises, possibilities and processes.* Presentation made at University of Wisconsin-Eau Claire.

Liskin-Gasparro, J. E. (2003). The ACTFL Proficiency Guidelines and the Oral Proficiency Interview: A brief history and analysis of their survival. *Foreign Language Annals, 36,* 483–490.

McNamara, T. (1997). 'Interaction' in second language performance assessment: Whose performance? *Applied Linguistics, 18,* 446–466.

McNamara, T. (2001). Language assessment as social practice: Challenges for research. *Language Testing, 18,* 334–399.

Messick, S. (1996). Validity and washback in language testing. *Language Testing, 13,* 241–257.

National Capital Language Resource Center (NCLRC). (2004a). *Portfolio assessment in the foreign language classroom.* Washington, DC: NCLRC.

National Capital Language Resource Center (NCLRC). (2004b). *Portfolio assessment in the foreign language classroom.* Washington, DC: NCLRC. Retrieved April 11, 2004, from: http://www.nclrc.org/portfolio/intro.html.

National Standards in Foreign Language Education Project (NSFLEP). (1999). *Standards for foreign language learning in the 21st century.* Lawrence, KS: Allen Press.

North, B. (1993). *The development of descriptors on scales of language proficiency.* Washington, DC: National Foreign Language Resource Center.

Oller, J. (1991). Foreign language testing: Its breadth (Part 1). *ADFL Bulletin, 22*(3), 33–38.

Paulson, F. L., Paulson, P. R., & Meyer, C. A. (1991). What makes a portfolio a portfolio? *Educational Leadership, 48,* 60–63.

Phillips, J. K. (1996). Original material.

Poehner, M. E., & Lantolf, J. P. (2003). Dynamic assessment of L2 development: Bringing the past into the future. CALPER Working Papers Series, No. 1. The Pennsylvania State University, Center for Advanced Language Proficiency, Education and Research.

Ravitch, D. (1993). Launching a revolution in standards and assessments. *Phi Delta Kappan, 74,* 767–772.

Relearning by Design, Inc. (2000). *Rubric sampler.* Retrieved April 5, 2004, from: http://www.relearning.org/resources/PDF/rubric_sampler.pdf.

San Diego State University. (2001a). *Rubrics for Web lessons.* Retrieved April 5, 2004, from: http://webquest.sdsu.edu/rubrics/weblessons.htm.

San Diego State University. (2001b). *Rubrics for Web lessons.* Retrieved April 5, 2004, from: http://edweb.sdsu.edu/triton/july/rubrics/Rubric_Template.html.

Shohamy, E. (1990). Language testing priorities: A different perspective. *Foreign Language Annals, 23,* 385–394.

Shohamy, E. (2001). *The power of tests.* London, England: Pearson Education Limited.

Shrum, J. L. (1991). Testing in context: A lesson from foreign language learning. *Vision,* 1, 3, 7–8.

Southern Illinois University at Edwardsville Undergraduate Assessment and Program Review (2004). *Classroom assessment techniques.* Retrieved April 6, 2004, from: http://www.siue.edu/~deder/assess/catmain.html.

Spanos, T., Hansen, C. M., & Daines, E. (2001). Integrating technology and classroom assessment. *Foreign Language Annals, 34,* 318–324.

Stansfield, C. W., & Kenyon, D. M. (1992). The development and validation of a simulated oral proficiency interview. *The Modern Language Journal, 76,* 129–41.

Stansfield, C. W., & Kenyon, D. M. (1996). Simulated oral proficiency interviews: An update. *ERIC Digest.* Washington, DC: Center for Applied Linguistics.

Steadman, M. (1998). Using classroom assessment to change both teaching and learning. In T. A. Angelo (Ed.), *Classroom assessment and research: An update on uses, approaches, and research findings* (pp. 23–35). New Directions for Teaching and Learning, No. 75. San Francisco, CA: Jossey-Bass.

Sternberg, R. J. (2000). Prologue to dynamic assessment: Prevailing models and applications. In C. Lidz & J. G. Elliott (Eds.), *Dynamic assessment: Prevailing models and applications.* Amsterdam: Elsevier.

Surprenant, J. (1998). Un viaje por España. Test item developed for a workshop with CLASS.

Swaffar, J., Arens, K., & Byrnes, H. (1991). *Reading for meaning.* Englewood Cliffs, NJ: Prentice Hall.

Swain, M. (1984). Large-scale communicative language testing: Case study. In S. J. Savignon & M. S. Berns (Eds.), *Initiatives in communicative language teaching: A book of readings.* Reading, MA: Addison-Wesley.

Swender, E. (1999). *The ACTFL oral proficiency interview tester training manual.* Yonkers, NY: ACTFL.

Terry, R. M. (1998). Authentic tasks and materials for testing in the foreign language classroom. In J. Harper, M. G. Lively, & M. K. Williams (Eds.), *The coming of age of the profession: Issues and emerging ideas for the teaching of foreign languages* (pp. 277–290). Boston: Heinle & Heinle.

Tierney, R. J., Carter, M. A., & Desai, L. E. (1991). *Portfolio assessment in the reading-writing classroom*. Norwood, MA: Christopher-Gordon.

Tulou, G., & Pettigrew, F. (1999). Performance assessment for language students. In M. A. Kassen (Ed.), *Language learners of tomorrow: Process and promise* (pp. 188–231). Lincolnwood, IL: National Textbook Company.

United States Department of Education. (1986). *What works: Research about teaching and learning*. Washington, DC: United States Department of Education.

Walberg, H.J., Paschal, R., & Weinstein, T. (1985). Homework's powerful effects on learning. *Educational Leadership, 42*, 76–79.

Wallinger, L. M. (1997). *Foreign language homework from beginning to end: A case study of homework practices in foreign language classes*. Unpublished manuscript. College of William and Mary, Williamsburg, VA.

Wallinger, L. M. (2000). The role of homework in foreign language learning. *Foreign Language Annals, 33,* 483–97.

Walz, J. (1989). Context and contextualized language practice in foreign language teaching. *The Modern Language Journal, 73,* 160–168.

Wiggins, G. (1989). Teaching to the (authentic) test. *Educational Leadership, 46,* 41–47.

Wiggins, G. (1990). The case for authentic assessment. Washington, DC: ERIC Clearinghouse on Tests, Measurement, and Evaluation.

Wiggins, G. (1994). Toward more authentic assessment of language performances. In C. Hancock (Ed.), *Teaching, testing, and assessment: Making the connection* (pp. 69–85). Lincolnwood, IL: National Textbook Company.

Wiggins, G. (1998). *Educative assessment*. San Francisco: Jossey-Bass.

NOTES

1. The term *rubrics* will be defined and described later in this chapter.

2. The term *alternative assessment* is also used to refer to assessment formats that focus on student-generated responses, on performance, and/or communicative language use in authentic contexts.

3. See Tulou and Pettigrew (1999) for models of student performance on the formative writing tasks in French, German, and Spanish. Detailed descriptions of the scoring criteria are included.

4. The word *rubric* comes from the Latin word *ruber* meaning "red." In medieval times, a rubric was a set of instructions or a commentary attached to a law or liturgical service and was usually written in red ink. Rubric came to mean a guideline or something that instructs people (Wiggins, 1998, p. 154).

5. Relearning by Design was formerly The Center on Learning, Assessment, and School Structure and was established in 1991 as a not-for-profit corporation in Rochester, New York. Relearning by Design moved to Geneseo, New York, in 1991 and to the Princeton, New Jersey, area in 1994.

6. Many thanks to Ghislaine Tulou from Fairfax County Public Schools, Virginia, for helping us to understand this score conversion system. See also Tulou and Pettigrew (1999) for an explanation of this score conversion system.

7. In the project conducted by ACTFL to develop and field test the IPA, teachers video taped the interpersonal phase in order to be able to analyze the interpersonal communication for rating purposes and to examine the strategies that students used to communicate with one another. We encourage teachers to videotape at least once or twice during the school year in order to have a record of student progress and to gather student work samples that can be used as exemplars.

8. ACTFL conducts IPA workshops that train teachers in how to design and implement IPAs. Also, individuals may purchase the *ACTFL Integrated Performance Assessment Manual,* available through ACTFL, which has a detailed explanation of the IPA and how to implement it.

9. The Center on Learning, Assessment, and School Structure (1998) has coined the term "anthology" to describe an "assessment portfolio" that contains a valid sample of student work, including performance on authentic performance tasks, traditional classroom test results, and scores from standardized testing. An anthology can be used "to base important decisions about student competence, promotion, and graduation on a collection of credible work . . ." (Wiggins, 1998, p. 197).

10. See Campbell, Melenyzer, Nettles, and Wyman (2000) and Barrett (1999) for ideas on how portfolios are used in teacher education programs to document growth in teaching.

11. For additional information about portfolio assessments and worksheets to guide in planning, compiling, and evaluating a portfolio, see *Portfolio Assessment in the Foreign Language Classroom,* available from the National Capital Language Resource Center (http://www.nclrc.org.).

12. Some researchers make a distinction between electronic and digital formats. Technically, *electronic portfolios* contain artifacts that may be displayed in analog form (e.g., videotapes) or computer-readable form (e.g., word processing document files). *Digital portfolios* contain artifacts that have been converted to computer-readable forms (e.g., scanned documents) (Egéa-Kuehne, 2004, p. 22). In *Teacher's Handbook,* the term *electronic portfolio* is used to refer to either type of digital integration.

13. The average American student spends four to five hours on all homework per week (Walberg, Paschal, & Weinstein, 1985). Wallinger (1997) reports that writing is the primary skill practiced in homework assignments, and that beginning-level assignments tend to be rote practice. Assignments requiring higher-order thinking and allowing for individual expression are reserved primarily for advanced learners. Wallinger (2000) also reports that, in her study of sixty-six schools offering French I in grade 9, students were expected to complete 1 to 1.25 hours of homework in French per week.

14. Other names used for the Minute Paper CAT are "Ticket Out the Door" and "Exit Slips."

15. See Appendix 11.16, National Assessment of Educational Progress (NAEP) in Foreign Languages, for a discussion of the measurement of educational progress in foreign languages.

thandbook.heinle.com

CHAPTER 12

Using Technology to Contextualize and Integrate Language Instruction

In this chapter, you will learn about:

- a standards-based approach to technology use in teaching languages
- Technology Enhanced Language Learning (TELL)
- types of technology
- multimedia centers
- use of video
- reading, listening, and writing assistant programs

- computerized simulations
- courseware (*Blackboard, WebCT*)
- Computer-mediated communication (CMC) (synchronous and asynchronous formats)
- WebQuests
- distance learning

Teach and Reflect: Are Your Students Technologically Literate? Helping Students Address the *National Educational Technology Standards;* Examining the Potential Use of a TELL Exercise, Creating a WebQuest

Discuss and Reflect: Incorporating Video into Language Instruction; Creating a Template for Web-Enhanced Materials

CONCEPTUAL ORIENTATION

Some teachers may wonder why they should use technology in their classrooms. Certainly there are mandates to do so. In 1998, President Clinton's Educational Technology Initiative outlined the Technology Literacy Challenge, identifying four key goals:

1. Modern computers and learning devices will be accessible to every student.
2. Classrooms will be connected to one another and to the world.
3. Educational software will be an integral part of the curriculum and as engaging as the best video game.
4. Teachers will be ready to use and teach with technology (United States Department of Education, 1998).

Despite the mandates and the ever-increasing presence of technology in everyday life, technology use in the language classroom should be embraced only if there are substantial benefits to learners. Martínez-Lage & Herren (1998) suggest that "technology is not the panacea for magically improved language learning" (p. 162). However, they also offer three benefits of planned and purposeful use of technology:

1. Better and more effective use of class time, i.e., some activities can be moved outside the classroom, thus extending contact time with the target language and reserving classroom time for interpersonal face-to-face interaction between teachers and learners;
2. Individualized learning, i.e., technology enables learners to work at their own pace and level;
3. Empowerment, i.e., teachers can provide more authentic, current, and culturally rich materials to the learners, and learners can gain new control over their own learning (adapted from Martínez-Lage & Herren, 1998).

In recognition of these benefits, recent standards movements have incorporated the use of technology. The *Standards for Foreign Language Learning in the 21st Century* (*SFLL*) (NSFLEP, 1999) include technology as one of the elements in the weave of foreign language learning, and the International Society for Technology Education (ISTE) provides standards for technologically literate students. Technology helps us reach our goals for teaching and learning languages in ways that we cannot do otherwise. It provides interesting and unique ways to connect language learners to the target language and culture, building communities of language learners around the world. It enables learners to establish interaction with peers who are learning the language and with experts and native speakers of the target language they are studying. It helps improve student motivation and enthusiasm for language learning. It brings the world into contact with the learner, transforming a teacher-centered classroom into a learner-centered one (Maxwell, 1998). As a professional, you will find technology useful if you apply the basic principles of good language instruction to the selection of technology tools and materials for your students.

In the related literature, you will see the term *Computer-Assisted Language Learning* (*CALL*) used to refer to the application of computers in teaching and learning languages. Although much of the use of technology in teaching and learning involves a computer, not all technological applications require a computer. We will use the term *Technology Enhanced Language Learning* (*TELL*) to refer to all uses of technology in language education. Subsumed within TELL, then, are the terms *CALL* and *Computer-Mediated Communication* (*CMC*).

 TELL is Technology-Enhanced Language Learning.   ▬

In previous chapters, you have seen some examples of the use of technology to help you guide your students in what they should know and be able to do. The technologies have been integrated into contextualized language instruction based on the *SFLL* as appropriate for the topic of each chapter. In this chapter we will explore the connections between the *SFLL* and the *National Educational Technology Standards* (*NETS*), which were developed by the International Society for Technology Education (ISTE). We will provide examples of successful integration of technology in second language classrooms, in most cases using more than one type of technology. We will also provide a template for a Web-enhanced unit, based on the integrative model described in Chapter 6. The *Teacher's Handbook* Web site provides additional resources and information.

thandbook.heinle.com

Technology Connects the Standards

Using technology in the language classroom provides a unique way to connect the goals for language learning as described in the *SFLL*. In earlier chapters of *Teacher's Handbook*, you learned about an important goal of language learning: to know how, when, and why to say what to whom. You also learned about the motivation that students may have for reaching this goal, and about how the five Cs represent the content goal areas in broad terms. You saw how sample performance indicators can measure learners' progress in what they know and are able to do with the target language.

Learning scenarios that accompany the standards show how teachers might address the *SFLL* in their instruction. These scenarios contain a broad richness of circumstances specific to each instructional setting that goes beyond the standards, and, indeed, forms a backdrop, or a fabric, on which the standards may operate. This fabric has been called the "weave" of curricular elements, and appears in Figure 2.3 (see Chapter 2) (NSFLEP, 1999, p. 33).

The elements of this weave are unique to each instructional setting, yet each setting contains all of them: the language system, cultural knowledge, communication strategies, critical-thinking skills, learning strategies, other subject areas, and technology. You saw how learners grapple with the forms of the language system. You also observed that learners bring to the language learning experience a set of cultural understandings, and that they take away new understandings of the target culture and their own culture as a result of language study. You saw that learners develop communication strategies, such as circumlocution or intelligent contextualized guessing, making inferences, and setting hypotheses as they study language. They use critical-thinking skills as they select information from what they already know and apply it to new situations or reflect on and evaluate their communication. They also develop learning strategies such as previewing, skimming, and reading for the main idea to enable them to build ways of approaching any new learning task. And you have seen how learners use their knowledge for cross-disciplinary study.

All of these elements of the weave can be brought together through the use of technology to thread rich curricular experiences through the language learning process.

Through the use of online chats and electronic pen pals ("key pals"), teachers can present students with living, vibrant people who use the target language for daily communication. Cultural elements, from daily table manners to world-famous paintings and literature, can be represented on the World Wide Web in authentic visual and print dimensions. Authentic audio to accompany the visual images can be delivered in person by the teacher, by classroom guests, or via technology with video/audio tape recordings, DVDs, CD-ROMs, and the Internet. Technology mediates language learning by forming a bridge between the authentic world and the language learner. Through the purposeful use of technology, teachers can connect all five of the goal areas for productive language learning experiences.

 Through the purposeful use of technology, teachers can connect all five of the goal areas for productive language learning experiences. ▪

 What is the role of mediation in language learning? Refer to Chapter 1. ▪

Using Technology to Support Standards-Based Instruction

As you saw in Chapter 1, learners use tools such as language and social interaction as mediation between themselves and their environments. Technological tools can also be used for mediation to help learners interact with the body of content knowledge and processes. For example, imagine a classroom in which French II students are seated in a circle, facing each other, interacting around a topic of discussion such as the question of resistance or collaboration that faced citizens of Europe during World War II. Prior to this session, students have studied in their textbooks and on the Internet the historical and cultural aspects of that period, and have described the choices individuals faced as they decided whether to resist or collaborate with invading military forces. Each student has either a handheld computer or a laptop, and all are online so that they can type their communication in a *chat room*, which is an electronic space where students can communicate. Students first type their comments and respond to each other in the online chat. Then they conduct the conversation orally face to face, while referring to the language on their screens. This process enables them to try out language first in written form, take the time to self-correct, and interact with each other in two ways. Reticent students can participate more fully, and are more motivated to interact because of the use of the technology. The teacher can monitor the online chat as well as the face-to-face interactions, providing direction and corrections when needed. In this example, technology is a mediational tool that enables learners to expand their oral expression, acquire new language, learn about cross-cultural perspectives, and interact with content knowledge.[1]

 Technology is a mediational tool that enables learners to expand their oral expression, acquire new language, learn about cross-cultural perspectives, and interact with content knowledge.

Research on TELL in Language Classrooms

Research on the use of technology in language classrooms has focused primarily on the potential for improved learning of language skills and the appeal technology holds for students. Products designed for language learning in the 1980s and early 1990s were of the drill/practice type, and language educators quickly moved beyond them to embrace more interactive approaches to technology in such programs as the Daedalus Integrated Writing Environment (1988–2002) and other software described in Chapters 8, 9, and later in this chapter. Use of the Internet, the World Wide Web, and other interactive programs captivated the attention of language teachers and researchers. Teachers felt assured that their students would not be disadvantaged by the use of technology in tandem with class activities, or even by replacement of some of their classroom time with technologically enhanced activities (Adair-Hauck, Youngs, & Willingham-McLain, 1998).

Researchers now study the ways in which technology can be used to help learners acquire aspects of language, such as vocabulary, or skills, such as reading or writing. Much of the research is analysis of specific software and its effectiveness for learners. However, studies have shown that technology in general has been used effectively to:

- facilitate the acquisition of vocabulary (Beauvois, 1997; Chun & Plass, 1996; Davis & Lyman-Hager, 1997; Grace, 1998; Jones & Plass, 2002; Pennington, 1996);
- support input-rich activities through use of reading assistant software, integrated video, and the Internet (Cononelos & Oliva, 1993; Davis & Lyman Hager, 1997; Garza, 1991);
- facilitate increased writing through use of writing assistant software, e-mail, and chatrooms (Chikamatsu, 2003; Oliva & Pollastrini, 1995; Suh, 2002);
- provide intelligent computer-mediated feedback (Cononelos & Oliva, 1993; Kern, 1995; Nagata, 1993, 1999; Nagata & Swisher, 1995);
- enhance listening comprehension and retention (Jones & Plass, 2002; Murphy & Youngs, 2004);

- facilitate exploration of authentic language use through e-mail or the Internet (Oliva & Pollastrini, 1995); and
- enhance student motivation (Borrás & Lafayette, 1994; González-Bueno & Pérez, 2000; Lee, 2002; Masters-Wicks, Postelwate, & Lewental, 1996) (adapted from Cubillos, 1998).

As teachers decide to deliver instruction with the assistance of a technological tool, such as a cassette recorder, an overhead projector, a video or DVD, or a computer-related technology, they use their knowledge of the five Cs and the weave of other curricular elements particular to their circumstances to select suitable technological products and techniques. These questions might be used as a guide when considering inclusion of technological tools in instruction:

1. How will the use of technology help students learn aspects of the language in meaningful contexts?
2. What can students presently do with the language in each of the five *SFLL* goal areas?
3. What standards within the goal areas will this tool help students address?
4. How will the tool help students use language in response to those standards?
5. What process will learners experience in using the technology and associated materials? What elements of the "weave" will be included?
6. What will this tool cost in terms of time, planning, supplies, and equipment? List costs.
7. What are the alternatives? Is there a high school, college, university, library, or other agency nearby that could help by providing services or resources?
8. Is this the best way to accomplish the objectives of instruction and to meet the needs of students?

Implementing Technology Standards in the Classroom

The International Society for Technology in Education (ISTE) developed the *National Educational Technology Standards* (*NETS*). The standards describe what students, teachers, and administrators should know and be able to do with technology in the service of instruction. According to Terry (2000) and ISTE (2002), approximately 90–92% of state education agencies have used the *NETS* to help teachers and students develop competency in using technology

thandbook.heinle.com

Regarding technology, what do students and teachers need to know and be able to do? The *NETS* begin with what students need to know about how to use technology as a foundation (see Appendix 12.1, on the Web site). These are sometimes referred to as the *National Educational Technology Standards–Students* (*NETS–S*). Standards for teachers (*NETS–T*) then build on the student standards, and standards for administrators and school technologists are derived from the teacher and student standards. In this chapter we focus our attention on technology standards as they relate to student performance. You may wish to consult the *Teacher's Handbook* Web site for the teacher standards (see Appendix 12.2, on the Web site).

To help us understand what good standards-based instruction using technology looks like, the student standards provide profiles of technologically literate students, along with scenarios for each grade level, pre-K through grade 12. A sample of a performance indicator for pre-K–2 appears in Appendix 12.3 on the *Teacher's Handbook* Web site, along with a sample of a learning scenario for those same grade levels in Appendix 12.4 (see the Web site). We will describe the learning scenario entitled "I lost my tooth" later in this chapter. The Web site also contains links to the performance indicators and learning scenarios for all other grade levels. In addition, the Web site contains a chart showing correlation of the technology standards with the INTASC standards for beginning teachers (Appendix 12.5), and a link to a correlation between *NETS–T* and the NCATE standards.

The *National Educational Technology Standards* consist of two standards that deal with basic operations and ethical issues of technology use, and four standards that deal with use of technological tools. The six standards state that students need to know how to use technology for these purposes:

1. basic operations and concepts
2. social, ethical, and human issues
3. technology productivity tools
4. technology communications tools
5. technology research tools
6. problem-solving and decision-making tools (ISTE/NETS, 2003a).

Implementation of the first standard means that students in a language classroom understand how to operate a computer or a VCR and the systems related to that equipment. For example, the profile for technologically literate students shows that the performance indicator for grades pre-K–2 is that students can use a keyboard, a mouse, or a remote control. The profile for language learners in grades 9–12 asks learners to show how they make informed choices among technology systems, resources, and services. For example, students at these grade levels might choose Web sites to find information on Chinese wedding customs; connect perspectives, products, and practices; and assist a Chinese American bride in creating a wedding that her grandparents might appreciate. They might seek information on the Web to show how the color red represents happiness (a perspective), and how the bride dresses in red (a practice), and in decorations found on the banquet table (products) at a Chinese wedding. They also might choose video conferencing as a way to enable the bride's grandparents in China to view the wedding ceremony in the United States.

The second standard requires that students understand the ethical, cultural, and societal issues related to technology and that they practice responsible use of technology systems, information, and software. For instance, they should understand the importance of copyright laws as related to use of materials on the Web, and they should appropriately cite the online sources that they use. In terms of language learning, students should make use of online dictionaries in the same way they use text dictionaries; that is, to find a definition, and to cite the source if they use a quotation directly. They should use translation services as a reference source; they should not use translation services to write their papers for them. Responsible and ethical behaviors of this sort will enable learners to develop positive attitudes toward technology, supporting lifelong learning, collaboration, personal pursuits, and productivity (*NETS*, 2003a).

In the application of this standard to language learning, students might create a report on the climactic conditions in Argentina in the months of June and July, contrasting these conditions with those of their hometown and elaborating on the kinds of activities they might engage in during those months in each location. Researching information on the Web and using the information in a poster in class would actually demonstrate the first and second technology standards, provided the student included a citation of the sources at the bottom of the poster.

The third standard requires that students use technology tools to enhance learning, increase productivity, and promote creativity. The standard refers to productivity as something students create by using technology, e.g., a *Linguafolio* or a culture portfolio such as those described in Chapter 5, or a PowerPoint presentation as described in Chapter 9 and later in this chapter. The standard also suggests that students use productivity tools to collaborate in constructing technology-enhanced models, e.g., computer models tracking changes in the number and types of restaurants that serve international foods, which might provide insights into changing demographics and language patterns in their community.

The fourth technology standard refers to student use of communication tools to interact with peers, experts, and other audiences; the fifth standard refers to use of research tools; and the sixth standard refers to the use of problem-solving and decision-making tools. These kinds of tools are often used together to enhance learning and address the third standard. Especially in language learning, we tend to think in terms of whole products that learners might produce using research, communication, and problem-solving tools in order to enhance their learning. In using technological research tools, students in a Russian class might use the U.S. Census data available on the Web to investigate the patterns of immigration from former Soviet bloc regions (fifth technology standard). They might then use a spreadsheet to present and analyze their data, and incorporate it into a PowerPoint presentation to be used with audiences of classmates, parents, or the school board (fourth technology standard). In so doing, they might highlight the need for more ESL teachers, who will be able to develop English-language literacy among the community's recent Russian immigrants (sixth technology standard). In this example, students have integrated the technology standards with the five Cs, specifically Communication (presentational mode), Connections, and Communities (NSFLEP, 1999).

thandbook.heinle.com

As an example of the implementation of the technology standards, we explore here Boehm's (1997) project on "I lost my tooth," reported as one of the sample scenarios of the technology standards in Appendix 12.4 (see the Web site). (This scenario of a first-grade class of native English-speaking learners can easily be recreated as a group of first-grade students in a language immersion class.) In the "I lost my tooth" project, students collaborated with other students around the world via e-mail. They recorded how many teeth they lost along with one special fact about their region or culture. Students shared tooth fairy traditions and other stories from their region. The stories were then used in storytelling strategies as explained in Chapters 4, 5, and 7. Using the information gathered from students around the world, teachers also developed activities including creative writing, graphing, art, and social studies. For instance, students used an interactive bulletin board on the Internet where they posted dates when teeth were lost, created a class letter about the project to post on the Internet, collected information from other children about tooth fairy stories, developed creative writing stories about their tooth experiences, and shared their stories with other children via a listserv.

To expand this scenario, students could incorporate their studies from social studies or mathematics by initiating electronic conversations about where other children live, using Internet maps to locate countries/cities, and addressing topics online with other children, such as weather, politics, clothing, and local heroes. Students might also use presentation and drawing software to illustrate the fairy stories and graph the tooth data. They then might write a letter explaining what the graph means and send it to key pals around the world, or prepare charts for a presentation to parents. In these projects, students demonstrate use of all of the modes of the Communication goal area, as well as the Connections, Comparisons, Cultures, and Communities goal areas of the *SFLL*.

The same scenario could be used to show how students demonstrate their ability to address the *ESL standards* (TESOL, 1997). For example, students could demonstrate their ability to use English for personal expression and enjoyment, and they could demonstrate the progress indicator of asking information questions for personal reasons as they corresponded via e-mail with their peers about teeth lost each month (Goal 1, Standard 2).

Finally, students also show in this scenario that they can address a number of the *NETS*. For instance, they address the first technology standard of being able to control basic operations by sending e-mail. They show that they can locate, evaluate, and collect information from a variety of sources by collecting data about how many teeth were lost among their peers and by using maps to locate where their key pals live, as well as by gathering information about local heroes (Standard 5). They show their facility with Standard 4 by collaborating and interacting with other students about stories and by publishing them. Additionally, they enhance their learning and promote creativity (Standard 3) by writing their own stories about tooth experiences.

Types of Technology at a Glance

Figure 12.1 provides an overview of various types of technology and their uses for communication in each of the three communicative modes. You will notice that this chart illustrates how each type of technology might be used to address one or more of the *SFLL* modes of communication. As you explore this chapter, you might also consider how each type of technology can also address the Cultures, Connections, Comparisons, and Communities *SFLL* goal areas.[2]

We have not made an attempt to include every possible technology or every possible use in this chapter. We have selected those technologies that offer the greatest potential for addressing standards-based goals in the foreign language classroom. As you use the chart in Figure 12.1 to organize your thinking about types of technology, consider also how teachers can use these technologies for the types of language learning purposes that you have explored in *Teacher's Handbook*, to encourage communication between students, between students and the teacher, and between students and expert speakers of the language in the classroom and beyond.

FIGURE 12.1 Types of Technology at a Glance

Technology	Interpretive Communication	Interpersonal Communication	Presentational Communication
Overhead projector	x		x
Multimedia center	x	x	x
Video	x		x
Reading assistant	x		
Listening assistant	x		
Writing assistant	x	x	x
Simulation	x	x	
Courseware (such as Blackboard and WebCT)	x	x	x
MOO/MUD	x	x	x
E-mail	x	x	
Listserv	x	x	
Usernet; bulletin board; blog	x	x	x
Chat room; threaded discussion	x	x	
Presentation Software			x
WebQuest	x		x
Distance learning	x	x	x

Source: Shrum and Glisan, 2005, original material.

Using Technology to Assist with Language Learning Processes

In the following sections of this chapter, we have identified some key technology that you may wish to incorporate into your classroom.

Overhead Projector

The overhead projector is an example of a low-level technology used by teachers to supplement or replace the chalkboard—with the important difference that it allows them to face the class. Transparencies can be prepared in advance of actual teaching and then manipulated during presentation by using masks made of opaque paper, or overlays containing additional coordinated material. Adding information during class discussion is easy: The teacher or student scribes can write directly onto the transparency with a permanent or water-soluble marker. For example, a set of interview questions printed on the transparency in permanent ink can be answered in class in water-soluble ink and then washed off between class periods, allowing the original interview transparency to be used again during the next class. See Appendix 12.6 (on the Web site) for additional tips on using the overhead projector.

thandbook.heinle.com

The next generation of overhead projectors, often incorporated into a language lab, is the touch-sensitive *smartboard* which can be used in this traditional way, as well as connected to a computer that projects materials from its hard drive or from a disk onto a screen, a television monitor, or a whiteboard. The smartboard materials also can be broadcast as part of a distance-learning class. Whether computer mediated or not, the overhead projector continues to be a tool with wide utility for teachers.

Multimedia Center

A *multimedia center* is a place where several types of technology are centrally located to allow students to use them in tandem or separately, as individual learners or in pairs or groups. Formerly called *language laboratories*, modern multimedia centers are flexible in their physical appearance and in the instructional tasks that students and teachers can perform. These centers may consist of four to eight computers grouped in a circular arrangement with workstation tables for each, so that students can work individually or in pairs at each computer. The computers are networked to each other and to a central computer or console controlled by the teacher or a laboratory assistant. Computers may be linked via a wiring system or they may be wireless, and the console may be mobile so that teachers can move it from classroom to classroom, or from place to place within a classroom. Wireless communication unleashes the possibilities of a multimedia center, freeing students and teacher from a central location, allowing them to become "satellites" that can access the central information from a handheld or laptop computer as in the example on page 410 earlier in this chapter.

Multimedia centers allow access to authentic speech and video recorded live in the target country, with follow-up tasks in which students engage in contextualized two- or three-way communication with other students, the teacher, or native speakers. These sophisticated multimedia systems offer students the opportunity to view video, graphics, or Internet-based programs focused around topics of their interest or their teacher's selection. Use of a multimedia center can assist in the development of auditory literacy through listening and using tapes; of visual literacy through pictures and use of presentational software (as described in Chapter 9) of verbal literacy through use of language; and of computer literacy through use of computers, VCRs, DVDs, and other equipment in the center. See the View and Reflect section for this chapter on the *Teacher's Handbook* Web site for three videos of a multimedia laboratory in operation.[3]

As an alternative to a lab, many teachers use one or more small cassette or CD players in their classrooms. One can be used for listening as a whole class, or several can be placed around the classroom as listening stations with individualized directions for singles, pairs, or small groups of learners. Students often have their own CD or portable cassette players and can practice at home. Many publishers package tapes and CD-ROMs with each textbook for use at home. See Chapter 6 for ways to use authentic taped materials to enhance listening practice for students, and Chapters 8, 9, and 11 for ideas about using these materials in written and/or oral form. The following sections of this chapter describe materials that can be incorporated into a multimedia center. You may also wish to consult Appendix 12.7 (see the Web site) for a rubric for evaluating multimedia projects (see also Chapter 9); in addition, Appendix 12.8 (see the Web site) contains a rubric for evaluating software.

thandbook.heinle.com

Video

Videotext as a contextualized segment can be in the form of film, videotapes, laserdiscs, CD-ROMs, or DVDs. These are texts in the sense that they present an authentic piece of language and culture that can be presented in written form as well as visual form. The videotext may contain elements of language use and cultural authenticity; it is possible to access all five Cs of language learning through videotext. As we elect to use videotext, we should apply the same criteria and careful judgment in selection and use as we apply to reading or listening texts. See Chapter 6 for a thorough treatment of the use of videotexts. Also, see Appendix 12.9 on the Web site for ways to use a videotext for language learning. Appendix 12.10 on the Web site provides clues to give students to help them comprehend as they watch a videotext.

Multimedia Technology in the Three Modes of Communication

Reading Assistant Technologies. Reading assistant software helps learners interpret communication by providing authentic reading selections, along with annotations or glosses that are Web-based or CD-ROM-based to assist with comprehension and interpretation. Among the types of glossed resources typically available in a reading assistant program are target language definitions for key vocabulary words, dictionary translations, audio pronunciation of the key words, grammatical explanations, explanations of relationships between grammatical elements, and in-context use or pictorial representations of the key words.

Several studies have examined the ways in which students use these annotations and their effect on the interpretive process. Davis and Lyman-Hager (1997) investigated the ways in which 42 intermediate-level undergraduate students of French interacted with a computerized L2 reading gloss while reading the authentic francophone novel *Une vie de boy*, by Oyono (1956). Students used a multimedia reading assistant that contained glosses with definitions in English and French, grammar explanations, pronunciation in French, cultural information, pictures, and information about relationships between grammatical features and among characters in the novel. Results of the study illustrated that the most frequently consulted category was English definitions (85% of the look-ups). The most pivotal finding in this study, however, was that, although students reported high levels of satisfaction with the use of reading assistant software, there was no evidence that the program had enhanced comprehension (Davis & Lyman-Hager, 1997). The researchers therefore suggest that foreign language teachers (1) do more explicit teaching of the reading process in class and prepare students to engage in a particular reading so that they do not rely on translation as a key strategy and (2) provide more instruction on how to use reading assistant software to ensure that students will access other informational categories, also important to comprehension, more often. These suggestions support those made in Chapter 6 with respect to preparing students to engage in interpreting a text.

In an attempt to understand why students access certain glosses and whether the glosses aid their comprehension, Lomicka (1998) conducted a study with native speakers of English in undergraduate-level French classes, in which they read a poem in French by a francophone writer while thinking aloud in English. Students were randomly assigned to one of three groups: (1) no access to glosses; (2) access to glosses of definitions in French and translations in English; (3) access to all glosses, e.g., definitions in French, images, references, questions, pronunciation, and translation in English. As they thought aloud in English, students generated 734 clauses, mostly explanations of their understanding as they worked through the poem. In this study, the ability to make causal inferences (see Chapter 6) was an indicator of comprehension. Students made such inferences when they had access to the widest variety of glosses, and particularly after consulting glosses that used questions to lead them through the poem. Research indicates that students understand readings and learn more vocabulary when they can choose from a variety of assistive annotations or glosses.

Nagata (1999), in a study of students learning Japanese, found similar results showing that providing learners with choices beyond that of single translations or definitions is most beneficial in leading to more effective comprehension. In this study, one group of students read a text with single glosses (English translations). The other group read the same text with multiple-choice glosses: Students were given two possible translations, and after making their selections, were provided feedback as to whether their choices were correct or not. Findings revealed that students who were offered multiple-choice glosses recalled more vocabulary and grammatical items than students who had glosses with a single translation or definition. Nagata attributes these findings to the notion that students in the multiple-choice group paid more attention to the TL items and made a greater effort to interpret them than did students in the single gloss group. An implication here, then, is that annotations and glosses may be most effective when they include feedback to and interactivity with language learners.

These studies support Mayer's (1997, 2001) premise of the Generative Theory of Multimedia Learning, based on Paivio's (1971, 1986) Dual Coding Theory, which proposes that, in order to understand a text, students must select relevant written and pictorial information from it, organize this information into mental representations, and then integrate these verbal and visual representations by building referential connections between them. Several other studies have illustrated how comprehension and vocabulary recall are enhanced when students have access to both pictorial and written annotations as they read a computer-based text (for example, see Chun & Plass, 1996; Plass, Chun, Mayer, & Leutner, 1998)

Listening Assistant Technologies.   In recent years, teachers and researchers have paid more attention to helping learners to develop interpretive listening skills. A number of products have appeared that incorporate listening into textbooks, CD-ROMs, and DVDs. Jones and Plass (2002) examined the effect of written and pictorial computerized annotations on the ability of 171 undergraduate students of second-semester beginning French to recall vocabulary and demonstrate comprehension of an authentic listening segment. In this study, students heard an oral narration of an authentic passage dealing with the interactions between Native Americans and French settlers in the Mississippi River Basin. Students were assigned to one of four treatment groups. The "none" group had no annotations for vocabulary words and could only select a loudspeaker icon to hear the pronunciation of the

FIGURE 12.2 Screen Shot of French Listening Comprehension Materials: Pictorial and Written Annotations Treatment

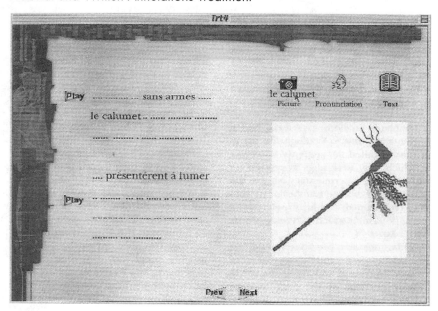

Source: Jones and Plass, 2002, p. 551.

words; they heard the pronunciation by dragging the word over the icon. A second group, called the "pictorial" group, had a camera icon and a loudspeaker icon; the camera icon enabled students to see a pictorial representation of the vocabulary word. A third group, called the "pictorial and written" group, had an open book icon, which enabled them to see a written translation of the word; they could also access the camera and see the picture of the key word. (See Figure 12.2 for a screen shot of the French listening comprehension materials that the students in the pictorial and written group saw.) Finally, a fourth group of students had access only to the open book icon, and could see only the written translation as an annotation.

Results of this study revealed that students who had access to both pictorial and written annotations in their multimedia environment recalled more vocabulary and demonstrated a higher level of comprehension (shown by the number of text propositions recalled) than did students with access to the other annotation options. An equally interesting finding is that vocabulary recall and text comprehension were higher for students who had access to pictorial annotations only than for those who had written annotations only (Jones & Plass, 2002). This finding confirms the results of the research discussed in Chapter 6 regarding the effect of advance organizers such as visuals on a learner's ability to interpret a text. The results of the Jones and Plass study support the Generative Theory of Multimedia Learning (Mayer, 1997, 2001) and illustrate the value of written as well as pictorial assistance in multimedia materials used to develop interpretive communication.

Teachers often find themselves creating their own materials using assistant or authoring programs to help learners develop interpretive communication. Murphy and Youngs (2004) describe a project that incorporated video with listening practice using software called *Listening Assistant.* Among the kinds of help that teachers can incorporate into their own materials following the guidelines in this listening assistant program are culture tips, a glossary, grammar and vocabulary tips in pictorial and written form, guided questions, key words, subtitles, a transcript, and a translation. There are also buttons the learner can use to control

thandbook.heinle.com

the video, e.g., to slow down the video, to repeat a section, or to rephrase the audio. See the *Teacher's Handbook* Web Site for a link to sample multimedia lessons in Russian, ESL, and Spanish, focusing on listening and viewing comprehension at the advanced level.

In sum, research indicates that as teachers use listening assistant software, they should be sure that students have a variety of glosses or annotations at their disposal and that they know how best to use them to enhance their interpretive abilities, as with reading assistant software. Teachers should also keep in mind that students appear to be concerned first with vocabulary and tend to consult native-language definition glosses first; then as they understand more they will consult target-language glosses, and glosses that assist them in thinking through meaning via questions will lead to comprehension. As discussed in Chapter 6, what is still of most benefit to learners is the preparation they receive in class before they engage with a text (for reading, listening, or viewing) and the variety of interpretive strategies that they have at their disposal as they work through a text.

Writing Assistant Software and Word Processing Technologies.　Writing assistant software can be used to help learners develop interpersonal and presentational communication. This software typically provides features similar to those found in word-processing programs in English but adapted for use in the target language. In addition, writing assistant software focuses student attention on the process of writing: prewriting, generation of ideas, organization, and revision/rewriting. Collaborative writing, using this type of software, results in substantial interaction that can involve negotiation of meaning and self-correction during a process approach to writing (Phinney, 1989; Warschauer & Healey, 1998). For examples of such programs and their effectiveness, see Chapter 9 for a description of *Atajo* (Domínguez & Noblitt, 2005) and *Système-D* (Noblitt, 2005). *Sin falta* (Guyer, Debrauwer, Carpenter, Ondich, & Beliahov, 2004), another recommended program, is available in French (Brulé, Caudron, Debrauwer, Carpenter, & Ondich, 2004), and in German (Carter-Smith, von Schwerin-High, Carpenter, Ondich, & Caudron, 2004).

Writing assistant programs such as those described above provide scaffolded help for learners that focuses on the writing process. Even though they do not focus on the writing process itself, word processing programs such as Corel WordPerfect and Microsoft Word provide ease of correction and revision that benefits students. In a comprehensive review of the literature on the effects of computer-assisted writing, mostly word processing, Pennington (1996) found overall positive effects of computer-aided writing in terms of four broad areas: (1) the quality of written work was higher as shown in scores on holistic and analytic ratings of compositions, and there was more thorough development of content; (2) more time was spent on compositions and the compositions were longer; (3) there was more experimentation with language and more flexible writing processes; and (4) affective/social outcomes showed reduced writing apprehension, improved attitudes toward writing, greater objectivity about one's own writing, and more active collaboration among student writers.

Recently, Rubio (2004) described the use of the comments feature in Microsoft Word to provide extended written or voice comments to students as they revised drafts. From the point of view of the instructor in the study, the software saved time and allowed for more extensive feedback, and it allowed the instructor and student to dialogue about the marked errors. Rubio reported that students praised the system as a better way to improve their writing skills, used the extended written and voice comments, and appreciated the chance to respond to them. See Appendix 12.11 (on the Web site) for a screen shot of the comments generated using this program.

Some interesting results can accrue in research on the use of word processing programs that may be attributable to the nature of the software. For example, Chikamatsu (2003) found that learners of Japanese using a word processing program wrote more accurately at the word level, though their writing speed was slower. He suspected that the students took longer to look up words because the software did not recognize approximations in *kanji* keystrokes, so students had to re-enter their word-level queries more than once.

In addition to writing assistant and word-processing technologies, teachers often incorporate the Internet to assist student writing. Suh (2002) reports that Korean students learning English as a foreign language found that the Internet and e-mail facilitated a process approach to writing. Use of writing assistant programs, word processing programs, and other technologies should be guided by the principles for teaching writing as outlined in *Teacher's Handbook*—that is, clear goals for writing tasks, use of writing process, authentic materials, and constructivist approaches to writing. Teachers who recognize the ways in which technology can address individual student needs will then guide their students in how to use and benefit from writing assistant software and other technologies, as predicted by Scott (1990) & Davis & Lyman-Hager (1997).

Ethical Use of Translation Technologies. Translation programs and online dictionaries are available for free and for purchase online. These programs can provide low-cost, nearly immediate translations of documents needed for personal use or for business. Translator programs operate by analyzing the structure of a sentence in the source language and then generating a sentence based on the rules of the target language. The difference between learning a language and using a translation is in the complexity of language and its ability to express human thought with precision. Translation programs are intended to provide the general idea, or "gist," of an article or document (Transparent Language, 2004). Students may use these programs inappropriately for their homework or their compositions. The translation may lack cultural knowledge and the application of higher level thinking that students would normally apply to creating their own expression. Students should be cautious in using a translation program because such programs do not help them learn how to interpret and communicate in the TL.

thandbook.heinle.com

Similarly, use of an online dictionary should be limited to consulting the meaning and proper use of a word, while also verifying that the correct meaning or connotation of the word is selected, e.g., "fly"—the insect or the verb. See the *Teacher's Handbook* Web site for suggested sources for online dictionaries.

Teachers should be aware of how students often use materials from Web pages without proper citation. Teachers can avoid these issues by teaching students proper citation format, making them aware of how to take notes and incorporate reference material, asking for an annotated bibliography, and structuring assignments so that students must apply their own higher level thinking skills as described in Bloom's taxonomy (see Chapter 3). See the *Teacher's Handbook* Web site for recommended Web sites on citation and strategies to avoid inappropriate use of information.

Simulations

As teachers help students to develop interpretive and interpersonal communication using computer software, they may find that the next step in creating presentational communication lies in the use of the scaffolding features built into simulations. In a simulation, the technology provides a "scaffold of a situation and enough information to function within it . . . participants make decisions and negotiate their way through the simulation as they might if it were real" (Levine & Morse, 2004, p. 139). Jones (1982) identifies the necessary elements of a simulation as (1) a simulated environment or a representation of the real world; (2) structure, created by rules of conversational interaction; and (3) reality of function or the learner's "reality" perspective of the event. Students are often familiar with simulations because many computer games are simulations.

In simulations, the computer provides a simulated environment by presenting an image on the screen. The structure of a simulation is created by rules concerning the learner task. The computer appears to understand language and produces it meaningfully, thus supporting the learner's "reality" perspective of their interactions with the simulation and others involved in the situation (Crookall & Oxford, 1990). For example, a murder is committed in a small town in the target country. Students see a map of the town with salient buildings and descriptions of key characters who knew the victim. Students are given roles to follow, such as reporter, detective, family members, and town citizens. As they participate in the investigation, students make decisions about whom to interview, what to say, and how to respond. The computer then incorporates their input, resulting in varied consequences and opportunities for further use of language to solve the murder.

Several programs have been developed that respond to selections and choices that students make as they solve daily problems; for example, renting an apartment in *A la rencontre de Philippe* (Furstenberg & Malone, 1993); setting up an Internet retail company in a simulation entitled *www.technomode.de* (Levine & Morse, 2004); moving about on site in foreign countries in *Montevidisco* (Larson & Bush, 1992); and relating target language literature to their own lives in *Ciberteca: Una carta a Dios* (Chun & Plass, 1999). Some simulation software packages integrate the Internet, e-mail, *Blackboard* or *WebCT* to enable students to practice a variety of language uses as they solve mysteries through the technology media. Some examples include *Un Muertre à Cinet* (Oliver & Nelson, 1998), *Un Misterio en Toluca* (Oliver & Nelson, 1997), and *Mord in Mainz Murder Mystery* (Goulding & Jorth, 2004). Discussion boards are also available through the publishers of the materials, on which possible theories about each murder mystery can be developed with students worldwide who are using the program.

Computer-Mediated Communication (CMC)

As you have seen, not all use of technology involves computers, though much of it does. *Computer-mediated instruction* is when the computer serves to facilitate or enhance communication between the learner and the source of authentic material, between learners, or between machines. A product of computer-mediated instruction is *computer-mediated communication* (*CMC*).

 Computer-mediated instruction is when the computer serves to facilitate or enhance communication between the learner and the source of authentic material, between learners, or between machines.

Computer-mediated communication involves use of all three modes of communication: interpretive, interpersonal, and presentational. Liu, Moore, Graham, and Lee (2002) report that CMC offers several widely acclaimed benefits:

1. more equal and increased participation than in regular face-to-face classroom-based activities (Blake, 2000; Bump, 1990; Cahill & Catanzaro, 1997; Chun, 1994; Kelm, 1992; Kern, 1995; Sullivan & Pratt, 1996; Warschauer, 1996);
2. positive attitudes (Beauvois, 1994);
3. greater student empowerment with decreased teacher control and dominance (Kern, 1995; Sullivan & Pratt, 1996); and
4. wider variety of discourse functions and interactional modifications (Chun, 1994; Sotillo, 2000) (cf. Liu, Moore, Graham & Lee, 2002, p. 258).

Two forms of computer-mediated communication have developed: synchronous and asynchronous. In *synchronous* CMC, people communicate with each other in real time, and simultaneously, e.g. *Instant Messenger*, online chatrooms. In contrast to synchronous CMC, *asynchronous* CMC is carried out by participants at different times, e.g. bulletin boards, forums, e-mail, threaded discussions. In the following sections, we will briefly discuss specific formats of synchronous CMC (a task-based project among native and nonnative speakers, and MOOs) and asynchronous CMC (e-mail; listservs; UserNets, newsgroups, bulletin boards, forums, and blogs or weblogs; chat rooms and threaded discussions).

 In *synchronous* communication, people communicate with each other in real time, and simultaneously. ■

 Asynchronous computer-mediated communication is carried out by participants at different times. ■

Synchronous CMC

Chun & Wade (2004) point out that synchronous CMC has been shown to be an effective tool for improving speaking and communication (Beauvois, 1998; Lee, 2002), for developing grammatical competence (Pellettieri, 2000), and for developing discourse competence (Chun, 1994). See Chapter 8 for a description of a synchronous CMC project using task-based instruction (Lee, 2002). In 2004, Lee described a study designed to explore the sociocultural aspects of synchronous communication. Well-designed online discussion activities were used by native-speaker and nonnative-speaker students at two U.S. universities. One of these discussions, conducted through a networked program called *Blackboard*, included these questions: (1) Do the new information technologies contribute to the creation of the famous "global village"?; (2) In what ways do the new technologies influence your professional life or the life of your classmates and families? And your personal life?; (3) Do the new information technologies allow the exchange of ideas in a more democratic way? Give examples for or against (p. 252). Through questionnaires, oral interviews, and analysis of the online discussions, Lee (2004) found that the online format provided a kind of ZPD through which native speakers and more capable peer students provided scaffolding that facilitated the use of correct forms, the negotiation of meaning, and the development of ideas.

 What benefits of synchronous electronic communication do you recall from Chapter 8? ■

thandbook.heinle.com

There is evidence to indicate that students who use synchronous CMC engage in negotiation of meaning in ways similar to that of oral interpersonal communication (Beauvois, 1997; Blake 2000; Warschauer, 1996). Smith (2003) studied the chatscripts of 14 nonnative students studying intensive English. The students used ChatNet Internet Relay Chat (IRC), a program that shows two windows on the screen, one for typing a message to send and one for reading a message the learner just received. Students were given two types of tasks, jigsaw (cleaning up a garage) and decision-making (shopping for a gift), and were expected to participate actively in solving the problems presented to them. On the *Teacher's Handbook* Web site, see Appendix 12.12, "Jigsaw Task: Messy Garage," and Appendix 12.13, "Decision-Making Task: Gift." Results showed that 34% of the turns taken by the participants were used to negotiate meaning, while the other turns were used to complete the various tasks the students had been given. Smith was able to map the CMC interaction in ways similar to those found in face-to-face communication. These tasks might be used for other classroom activities as well. Undoubtedly, the negotiation of meaning that takes place in CMC has the potential to help students in their spoken, face-to-face negotiations as well.

In addition to showing that students do negotiate meaning in CMC, some research has compared the quality of the increased output that students create in synchronous CMC versus asynchronous CMC. Abrams (2003) studied how students used synchronous and asynchronous CMC in preparation for subsequent face-to-face communication. Students who used synchronous CMC did produce more language, but there was no difference in the quality of the language as measured in richness of vocabulary and in the variety and complexity of sentences. Students who used asynchronous CMC produced the least amount of language, but Abrams attributes this to the nearly week-long time delay in responses, creating a lack of motivation and interest.

MOOs and MUDs. Examples of synchronous chat rooms that involve students in interpretive and interpersonal communication are *MOOs* (Multiple-User Object Oriented) and *MUDs* (Multiple User Domain). These are electronic, often password protected spaces accessible through the Internet, in which users can communicate around settings or tasks that are often incorporated with a CD-ROM. See the *Teacher's Handbook* Web site for links to examples of MOOs in French, German, and Spanish. In one of these MOOs, a community of native speakers of Spanish from around the world, teachers and learners of these languages, and computer programmers volunteer to create a virtual world in which learners can enter at a visual representation of the Puerto del Sol in the center of Madrid, for example, and have virtual *tapas* (snacks) and Web conversation in the *Café Ojalá*. According to Warschauer and Healey (1998), sentences produced in these spaces are generally shorter and simpler than those produced with writing assistant software. Some such technologies are available on CD-ROM, incorporated with textbooks, or maintained through a website, as in the case of *QUIA* (see the *Teacher's Handbook* Web site).

thandbook.heinle.com

MOOs are often considered so complex that most teachers typically purchase products that incorporate them, but Von der Emde, Schneider, and Kötter (2001) found that the creation of a MOO is no more trouble than learning any new software. They describe a MOO entitled "MOOssiggang" in which U.S. students of German worked with German students to define their learning goals and describe topics of interest. For example, they read Kafka's *Der Bau (The Burrow)*, which describes a mole's relationship to the living space in his burrow. They also read two other literary passages about homes and offices and wrote about the readings in German. Then they designed a room in the MOO, assigning space and features to it as they worked in the target language. Five benefits of the MOO were pointed out:

1. authentic communication and content as seen in the literary selections;
2. autonomous learning and peer teaching in a student-centered classroom: e.g., U.S. and German students negotiated how long to spend on each discussion and how to handle each other's corrections;
3. individualized learning, as shown in a student's comment: "I pick up on mistakes . . . and correct them; this is easier in the MOO because the text is right in front of us";
4. importance of experimentation and play, as shown when students make jokes or puns in the MOO;
5. students as researchers/the intellectual dimension, as shown when students consult reference materials and each other, e.g., to define the intellectual properties of concepts such as assimilation and integration, students sought authoritative definitions from a dictionary and then added those they found in *Der Bau,* as well as definitions from popular culture in their countries (pp. 213–220).

A recent study of the language produced by students in a MOO (Warner, 2004) reveals that students play with language online. Some of their play has to do with noticing the foreignness of words that sound funny, or making plays on words. For instance, the students in Warner's study created an online commercial for a cushion, playing on the German words for "cushion": *kissen* and *puffer*. The students engaged in language play in their online communication, and the result of the language play was reflected in their final ad product. Another type of communication online is that which substitutes for body language. For example, in a face-to-face conversation, participants may laugh, but to show this in an online conversation a participant whose pseudonym is "Freak" has to type "emote laughs," which is then seen by the other participants as "Freak laughs." While the laughter is spontaneous in face-to-face conversation, it is deliberate and strategic in online interaction, and may reveal that participants are playing with language at a conceptual level. Warner (2004) recommends that scholars expand their conception of interpersonal communication and interaction to explore these features of online discourse.

In sum, learners use synchronous CMC to communicate in a written interpersonal mode with others. Learners negotiate meaning and complete interactive tasks in ways similar to face-to-face communication, but they may require some additional steps to accommodate body language. As you read the next section on asynchronous CMC, keep in mind the elements of synchronous CMC.

 How does the important concept of negotiation of meaning function in synchronous and asynchronous computer-mediated communication?

Asynchronous CMC

E-mail. The first type of asynchronous CMC was e-mail, which has since evolved into various other forms. Chun and Wade (2004) report that e-mail is an effective means of promoting L2 linguistic development (González-Bueno, 1998; González-Bueno & Pérez, 2000), for promoting C2 learning (Cononelos & Oliva, 1993; Jogan, Heredia & Aguilera, 2001), and for exploring linguistic and cultural learning within constructivist and social contexts. The *SFLL* make numerous suggestions for use of e-mail; a sample progress indicator for grade 4 regarding presentational communication is: "Students give short oral notes and messages or write reports about people and things in their school environment and exchange the information with another language class either locally or via e-mail." (p. 45).

E-mail is a form of written interpersonal communication (see Chapter 8). The tone and register used is like that of spoken language, with the added advantages reported by students that they have time to look at their messages, to think about how their correspondence will be understood, and to make revisions. The rapid-fire turn taking of speaking face-to-face that intimidates slow or timid learners can be modified with a "window" on the screen in which learners can type their comments, taking the time to monitor them and make them as correct as possible.

E-mail can be incorporated into real tasks that teachers ask learners to perform. For example, to practice realistic communication, a student can write the instructor an e-mail message explaining an absence from school, justifying the seriousness of the excuse, requesting information about the assignment for the next class day, and apologizing for being absent. Many teachers report that students find that this mode of communication offers an accessible means of gaining the floor and making conversational gambits, thus creating more opportunities to practice the target language. See Chapters 4, 5, and 8 for descriptions of key pals and other uses of e-mail.

Listservs. An outgrowth of e-mail is the use of listservs, which enable teachers to communicate with a group, and allow the group members to communicate with each other to share information about assignments or class progress.

Many professional listservs are available to teachers as shown in the preliminary chapter. Two popular international listservs are FLTEACH, administered by LeLoup & Ponterio (2004)

thandbook.heinle.com

at SUNY Buffalo, and LLTI (Language Learning and Technology International), a listserv maintained at Dartmouth University. On these listservs, teachers exchange information about texts, materials, teaching techniques, learner difficulties and successes, and sources of new information. Some listservs allow members to receive a compilation of e-mail messages, called a *digest*, instead of receiving each message individually. See the *Teacher's Handbook* Web site for information on how to subscribe and access information from these listservs.

Usernets, Newsgroups, Electronic Bulletin Boards, and Weblogs (Blogs). These forms of communication are extensions of listservs that operate on the Internet and usually are established around a topic of common interest. An FLTEACH *newsgroup*, for instance, enables subscribers to read the e-mails for that listserv without having their e-mail account filled up by the 50–60 messages generated per day on the list. Caution should be exercised in accessing these kinds of sources because they may not be monitored. However, use of these resources can be effective when teachers monitor them, as reported by Cononelos & Oliva (1993), who successfully used Italian usernet groups and e-mail to enable learners to access Italian news broadcasts and write to each other via e-mail about the weather and news in their areas.

Blogs, originally called *weblogs*, are Web sites on which participants can post asynchronous comments that often take the form brief essays, or expository writing. The sites are usually maintained and monitored. Cooke-Plagwitz (2004) reports successful use of blogs in German. See the *Teacher's Handbook* Web site for links to information on how to set up a blog and to the *Raison d'Être Project*, which makes effective use of a monitored blog.

Chat Rooms and Threaded Discussions. Chat rooms and threaded discussions enable exciting uses of the computer's capacity for increasing learner communication. Chat rooms are sites on the Internet where various computer users can "talk" with each other electronically; threaded discussions are similar in that they follow a topic thread, tracking who responds to whom in a chronological order. Chun and Wade (2004) report a successful project based on a constructivist approach to the learning of culture that combined forums (threaded discussions) and e-mail, enabling students to reach deeper levels of intercultural understanding and to make more use of negotiation of meaning. The project, called InterCultural Exchange (ICE), involved students in two universities, one in the United States and one in Germany. First students answered online questionnaires about their word associations with topics presumed to be of interest to them, dating and cheating. Then they used an online forum to read and comment in writing on the results of the questionnaire responses. Next, they read and commented in writing on all of the responses in the forum, where they could see who responded in what way to whom. Students were able to negotiate meaning by learning how to ask for clarification, or by making polite requests for more information. They were also able to co-construct new knowledge by noticing that culture-laden terms like *date* and *grades* imply different schema in the two countries.

Similarly, Weasenforth, Biesenbach-Lucas and Meloni (2002) found that asynchronous CMC, such as "chatting," provided learners with the time and reflectivity to produce good language, and visual display enabled them to follow the content of the discussion. See the *Teacher's Handbook* Web site for additional projects that integrate chat and threaded discussions.

PowerPoint. The *SFLL* make specific mention of Microsoft PowerPoint as a tool by which students can demonstrate their oral and written presentational communication. See Chapter 9 for a description of its use as one of several presentational software (PS) programs. Nemtchinova (2004) points out that PS is (1) easy to learn and use; (2) allows the teacher to adjust a presentation to match learners' needs; (3) creates an emotional impact and taps student interest; and (4) efficiently manages text, sound, illustrations, and other technological tools, such as a VCR, a cassette player, or the Internet. Teachers can use PowerPoint, for example, to present new vocabulary in context in pictorial or auditory form. Once created, the presentation can be shared via the Internet for students who were absent, those who need additional reinforcement or practice, or students in another class. With storytelling, for example, student scribes can type the contributions of their classmates on a single slide, which can then be edited collaboratively by the class and shared with another audience, such as a lower-level class.

In sum, both synchronous and asynchronous CMC offer rich environments in which learners negotiate meaning and explore new ways to learn language. As technologies develop, learners and teachers are likely to continue to make effective use of them to develop interpersonal and presentational communication.

Empowering Learners Through Web-Enhanced Technologies

In this section, we will explore WebQuests, an example of an instructional strategy that uses the World Wide Web to assist learners. First, however, it is important to point out that, with increasing use of Web sites as sources of information, teachers and students need to carefully assess the accuracy of what is contained on those sites. These questions can act as guidelines in evaluating Web sites to be used in instruction:

1. Accuracy: How reliable and free from error is the information? Are there editors and fact checkers?
2. Authority: What are the author's qualifications for writing on the subject? How reputable is the publisher?
3. Objectivity: Is the information presented with a minimum of bias? To what extent is the information presented trying to sway the opinion of the audience?
4. Currency: Is the content of the work up-to-date? Is the publication date clearly indicated (date created, date posted, and date last revised)?
5. Coverage: What topics are included in the work? To what depth are topics explored? (Alexander & Tate, 1999)

WebQuests

Dodge (1997) defines a WebQuest as "an inquiry-oriented activity in which some or all of the information that learners interact with comes from resources on the Internet, optionally supplemented with videoconferencing" (p. 1). WebQuests are based on principles presented in earlier chapters of *Teacher's Handbook*. They use constructivist approaches to learning, cooperative learning activities, and scaffolding within a sociocultural learning environment. After completing a WebQuest, a learner will have deeply analyzed a body of knowledge, transformed it in some way, and demonstrated an understanding of the material by creating something that others can respond to, online or off-line (Dodge, 1997). There are six parts to a good WebQuest:

1. an *introduction* that sets the stage and provides some background information; it may also capture the learners' interest;
2. a *task* that is doable and interesting;
3. a set of *information sources* needed to accomplish the task;
4. a description of the *process* or strategies student should use to complete the task;

5. some *guidance* on how to organize the information acquired, e.g., guiding questions, concept maps, timelines, cause-and-effect diagrams, flow charts;

6. a *conclusion* that brings closure to the quest, reminds students of what they have learned, and encourages them to reflect on the experience and to extend it into other domains (adapted from Dodge, 1997).

Students typically respond well to WebQuests that assign them (1) a role to play, e.g., scientist, detective, reporter; (2) persons with whom to interact, e.g., classmates, key pals, fictitious personalities; and (3) a scenario in which to work, e.g., "You've been asked by the Roman Senate to brief them on the recent conquests of General Caesar" (adapted from Dodge, 1997). Students can be asked to synthesize conflicting opinions and put multiple sources of data together to discover the non-relevant and the relevant factual information, take a stance and defend it (Dodge, 1998). WebQuests may be short-term or long-term. A short-term WebQuest can be accomplished in one or two class periods, whereas a long-term WebQuest may last a month or two. You will find examples of WebQuests for all subject areas as well as help in designing then at http://webquest.org, a site managed by Bernie Dodge, originator of the concept.

thandbook.heinle.com

In this section, we will help you set up a WebQuest. See Figure 12.3 for the WebQuest Design Process in a flow chart, and visit http://www.ozline.com/webquests/design.html, where you can click on each box of the flow chart for additional guidance. On the *Teacher's Handbook* Web site, you will also find links to the "*Idea Machine*" to help generate ideas for a WebQuest, and "*WebQuest Taskonomy*" to generate tasks for inclusion in a WebQuest.

In the first phase of creating your WebQuest, you will *explore the possibilities* by brainstorming ideas for a topic and by drawing a web much like those you used in Chapters 4 and 5. Use March's (2004) "*Idea Machine*," and then chunk or cluster similar ideas together by looking for relationships among topics or people involved in the topics. Brainstorming about survival, for instance, produced the results found in Figure 12.4. Identify what your students may already know about this topic, and identify the learning gaps they need help in filling. Consult the *Teacher's Handbook* Web site and search on the Internet to see what other WebQuests, as well as what other information, are available. This is not necessarily a linear process and you need to return to Step 1 as you design the WebQuest. After you have found a topic, identified the learning gaps, and inventoried the resources, you are ready to uncover the questions. This box in the flow chart in Figure 12.3 is in a different shape because here you must decide whether or not you have enough information to create a WebQuest, and whether or not the topic lends itself to this strategy.

The second phase in creating your WebQuest is *designing for success*; you will shape, outline, and draft your WebQuest. Establish the learning outcomes and identify the transformations you want to happen as your students work with information they learn as input. The learner is transformed, the material is transformed, and perhaps you are transformed. Identify tasks that students will perform in the WebQuest by coordinating your goals in the *SFLL* or the *ESL Standards* with the "*WebQuest Taskonomy*" (see Dodge, 2004). For instance, in the "Survival" topic on Figure 12.4, students who investigate the social studies aspects of earthquakes might hypothesize that government has provided inadequate help to people dealing with the psychological stress of rebuilding. They could then write the hypothesis, along with their justification of it, in a short e-mail or videotape sent to an expert, asking for verification or feedback. Here they might use their skills in written or oral presentational communication, seeking real-world feedback.

In the second phase, you also determine the roles students will play. The roles should be real-world jobs that students can learn about from the links you give them so that they can speak and behave like a person who holds that job. For instance, in earthquake survival, one student role might be the public health officer who designs

FIGURE 12.3 The WebQuest Design Process

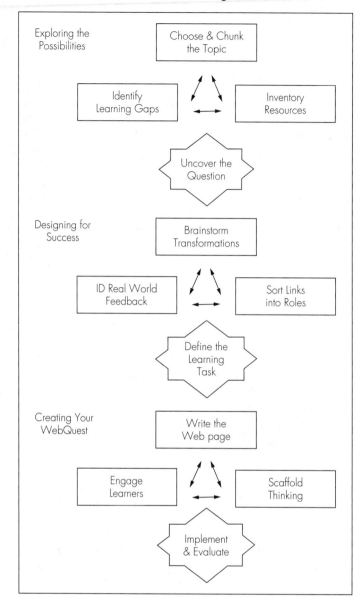

Source: March, 1998, http://www.ozline.com/webquests/design.html.

educational pamphlets or gives interviews with news media about dangers of disease after an earthquake. Another real-world role would be that of that of news reporter, in which students ask questions, probe, and summarize. In these roles, students use interpretive, interpersonal, and presentational communication. The WebQuest could even be designed to address the Communities standard by setting up a student role in which a public health worker brings warnings in the target language of impending earthquakes to members of a recently immigrated population.

Having worked through these aspects of the second phase, you are at another decision point: defining the learning task. Here you must ask yourself questions about whether the available resources on the Web address learning gaps and support the roles, whether you

FIGURE 12.4 Web for "Survival"

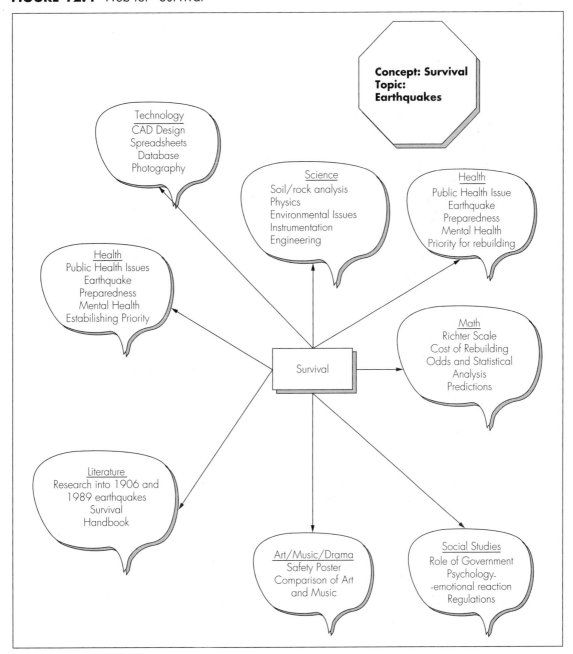

Source: March, 2004, http://www.ozline.com/learning/machine.html.

have identified the kinds of higher level thinking you want students to engage in, and whether the activities in the WebQuest mirror the real world.

In the third phase, you use all of the resources you have gathered to actually *create your WebQuest*. Here you create the WebQuest's main web page and write an introduction that "hooks" the students into the activities and sends them to the Web pages you have already found for them. You create activities for students to do using the target language, and they will create a final product or products to show what they have learned.

In creating a WebQuest, keep in mind the standards-based goals you have for student learning and provide appropriate grouping activities as well as motivational elements. Make sure that you provide supportive scaffolded instructions and write a conclusion that wraps up the WebQuest. Also be sure to include a measure of evaluation of students' performance (see Chapter 11) and an evaluation of or feedback on the WebQuest itself. See Teach and Reflect, Episode Three in this chapter for a WebQuest design assignment. Also see the *Teacher's Handbook* Web site for a listing of sample WebQuests in a variety of languages.

Distance Learning

The technological applications discussed previously in this chapter refer to settings in which teachers make use of the technology within their classrooms, or for assignments students can complete outside of class. *Distance learning* refers to classroom situations in which the teacher and the students are in different classrooms. Students could be learning foreign languages from a teacher in another school, town, state, or country via a computer network or a telephone system (NCSSFL, 2002). Distance learning offers a solution for the limited availability of foreign language teachers, especially for students in remote locations, for school districts wishing to expand their offerings to include elementary school programming or advanced placement/upper level offerings, and for school systems wishing to offer language classes with small enrollments.

Successful distance learning programs are based on development of proficiency, within standards-based approaches to language instruction. Decisions about use of distance learning technology generally do not rest with the classroom teacher, but rather with school boards, or institutions of higher education. Since the primary focus of *Teacher's Handbook* is to provide useful information for beginning and accomplished teachers relative to their daily work in classrooms, we do not provide an elaborated section on distance learning in this chapter. We have instead mentioned it throughout this chapter when its application seemed warranted, and we have described an elementary school distance language program in Chapter 4 (Glisan, Dudt, & Howe, 1998). Please see the *Teacher's Handbook* Web site for additional sources and for the link to the National Council on Secondary School Supervisors of Foreign Languages "Position Paper on Distance Learning in Foreign Languages," which approaches the impact of distance learning on students from the decision-maker's perspective.

What the Future of Technology Holds for Language Learning

Levy's seminal study on technology and foreign language learning (1997) suggests that there should be a fit between teachers' philosophies of language teaching and learning and what they see as the capabilities of technology to facilitate use of the technology in their classrooms. Throughout *Teacher's Handbook*, you have seen that the use of authentic texts helps students as they learn how to communicate, to make connections and comparisons, and to understand cultures and communities. As teachers shape language learning and cultural content around the five goal areas outlined in the *SFLL* and the goals of the *ESL Standards*, they often find that technology helps them make the target language and its texts more real and accessible to learners. Not only are students the receivers of the language and culture, but they are now capable of direct interaction with peers and experts who use the language daily. Teachers have at their fingertips the language learning standards to guide them and the technology to connect the real world to the classroom in ways never before possible. Technology has become more user friendly, and teachers have learned ways to make it work for their students and in their classrooms.

Among the technologies we might expect in the future are better speech-recognition programs that can understand what language learners say despite their imperfect use of language; additional user-friendly ways of merging text, video, and sound; and faster response times in computer-mediated communication. As we study the kinds of communication produced through technology, we will perhaps expand our understanding of virtual space and communication—for example, what it means to be the first person online in a chat room and how to use that time for learning purposes while waiting for others to be online, or how to signal and understand emotions in online communication (Warner, 2004).

Whatever the future may hold, two things are certain: Technology and technologists have much to offer language teachers, and language teachers are eager to find new ways to put technology to work in the service of instruction.

TEACH AND REFLECT

EPISODE ONE
Are Your Students Technologically Literate? Helping Students Address the *National Educational Technology Standards*

NCATE
STANDARDS
2.b., 3.a.,
3.b., 4.a.,
4.b., 4.c.,
5.a., 5.b.

thandbook.heinle.com

This episode is designed to enable you to showcase your technological skills in helping your students address the *National Educational Technology Standards*.

First, re-examine Appendices 12.1, 12.2 , 12.3, 12.4, and 12.5 to become more familiar with the *National Educational Technology Standards* for Students (NETS-S). Second, refer to the link to the technology standards on the *Teacher's Handbook* Web site to find profiles and learning scenarios for students at the grade level you teach. Third, compile a list of five Web sites written in the language you teach. The sites should focus on a topic of your choice and can serve as the basis for a lesson you might teach. Include the name of each site, its URL, and the reasons why you chose it. Fourth, apply the guidelines by Alexander & Tate (1999) in this chapter to evaluate the quality of the Web sites. Fifth, brainstorm a list of ways in which you might use each site in your lessons. Sixth, show which of the technology standards for students you will address with the sites you have selected and the ways in which you will use them.[4]

EPISODE TWO
Examining the Potential Use of a TELL Exercise

NCATE
STANDARDS
3.a., 3.b.,
4.a., 4.b.,
4.c.

Appendix 12.14 on the Web site is an example of a TELL meaning-enhancing communicative information-gap exercise presented by Chun & Brandl (1992, pp. 260–262). Using what you learned about information-gap activities in earlier chapters, analyze this activity for its communicative potential. Use Appendix 12.15 on the Web site to assist you in your analysis. Then answer the following questions:

1. How do you think students will communicate with the computer in this exercise?
2. At what point in a lesson would this exercise be used?
3. What kind of grouping circumstances do you envision when using this kind of exercise with a class?
4. How will students communicate in the three modes, as a result of using this exercise, when they communicate with peers?
5. How would you revise this activity for your language? Consult preview opportunities at the Web sites of various textbook publishers (such as the *QUIA* at http://heinle.com) to see examples of exercises or consult various textbooks or software packages, and apply Appendix 12.15 for guidance.

EPISODE THREE
Creating a WebQuest

NCATE_____
STANDARDS
3.b., 4.a.,
4.b., 4.c.,
5.a.

thandbook.heinle.com

Create your own WebQuest. Start by reviewing Figures 12.3 and 12.4 online at http://www.ozline.com/webquests/design.html, where you can click on the boxes of Figure 12.3 for additional guidance. See also Dodge's (1997) recommendations for the content of a WebQuest and view several sample WebQuests linked to from the *Teacher's Handbook* Web site. Next, use March's (2004) "*Idea Machine*" tool to brainstorm a planning web, and use Dodge's (2004) "*WebQuest Taskonomy*" to decide which tasks to include (again, see the Web site). Use Alexander & Tate's (1999) guidelines for evaluating the Web sites you select. Share your WebQuest with your classmates and use it with your students. Reflect on how you might improve it.

DISCUSS AND REFLECT

CASE STUDY ONE
Incorporating Video into Language Instruction

NCATE_____
STANDARDS
2.b., 3.a.,
3.b., 4.a.,
4.b., 4.c.

Ms. Silver has taught German at Ridge Runner High School in Carrollton for three years. She began her teaching career in Austria, teaching elementary school, but she changed to teaching high school German when her children grew up and left for college. She is a dynamic, energetic, and enthusiastic teacher who expects as much from her students as she gives in preparation and presentation. In class, Ms. Silver speaks German almost entirely and uses a wide variety of communicative activities. She spends several hours each day planning her lessons.

Over the past several months, Ms. Silver has been reading about the use of video in language teaching, and she attended a workshop on listening comprehension that offered some ideas about integrating video. She has become interested in experimenting with video in her German classes. She uses her many connections in her Austrian hometown to her advantage and asks a relative who works in a television station to seek permission for her to obtain a videotape of various television segments. The station sends Ms. Silver a video containing several segments from a television drama, some news broadcasts, a variety of commercials, and a talk show segment. The station also grants her permission to use the video for educational purposes. Ms. Silver now has the video and is planning how to integrate it into her teaching.

Ask yourself these questions:

1. What will Ms. Silver have to consider as she decides how to integrate the video segments into her teaching?
2. What functions, contexts, and standards goal areas might be addressed with the types of segments included in the video she received from the television station?
3. How might she apply Joiner's (1990) guide in Appendix 12.9 on the Web site to use videotexts as she plans her lessons?
4. How might she address the fact that the video contains authentic speech and has not been produced for use in teaching? What use might she make of Lonergan's (1984) tips for listening and viewing shown in Appendix 12.10 on the Web site?

To prepare the case:

1. Read the articles by Swaffar & Vlatten (1997) and by Joiner (1990) on how to select and use videotexts.
2. Reread Chapter 6 to refresh your understanding of the interactive model for developing listening, reading, and viewing.

3. Read Maxim's (1998) article on implementation of the Swaffar system if you are a German teacher.
4. Read Ito's (1996) article if you teach Japanese.
5. Read Herron's (1994) article for secondary/college teachers or Herron & Hanley's (1992) article for FLES teachers about the effectiveness of using video.
6. Read the section of Garrett's (1991) article that deals with using video in the classroom.
7. Interview a language teacher who has had some experience with video in language teaching to obtain some practical suggestions. See Appendices 12.9 and 12.10 for guidance.

To prepare for class discussion:

1. Describe how you would use the interactive model for developing listening, reading, and viewing that is presented in Chapter 6 to engage students as they watched the talk show segment of the video.
2. Identify the language learning standards and the technology standards your students would address as they viewed the newscast and the commercial announcements segments of the video.

CASE STUDY TWO
Creating a Template for Web-Enhanced Materials

NCATE
STANDARDS
2.b., 3.a.,
3.b., 4.a.,
4.b., 4.c.,
5.a.

thandbook.heinle.com

A group of Spanish teachers from Summerville High School met with a group of college Spanish instructors from State University to figure out some ways to increase student practice outside of class, including how to use what students have practiced in class for face-to-face communication. They discussed their students' abilities and interests, and their lesson materials. When they talked about their students' proficiency in Spanish, they realized that their students were mostly somewhere in the intermediate-mid range, regardless of whether they were in high school or college.

The teachers decided that they needed to use authentic materials, not just their textbooks, and that they wanted to engage their students in a process approach to language learning. They hoped that what they devised could be used as a template for future modules, to also be used by other teachers in other languages. They created a technology-enhanced module on the life and work of Frida Kahlo. The Kahlo module follows and is available as Appendix 12.16 (see the Web site) if you wish to download it as a template. Note that this module follows the steps of the Interactive Model for Integrating the Three Modes of Communication presented in Chapter 6.

Ask yourself these questions:

1. What principles of language learning have you learned in *Teacher's Handbook* that you also see embodied in this module?
2. What elements of the module appear especially workable to you? What elements appear to need more development?

To prepare the case:

1. Read March (1998, 2004) and Dodge (1997, 1998, 2004) for a description of another approach to Web-based learning, WebQuests.
2. Read Kern (1995) for summaries of student-to-student interactions in chat rooms.
3. Identify the elements of the curricular weave do you see in this module.
4. See http://SASinSchool.com for additional web inquiries about Spanish artists.

To prepare for class discussion:

1. Using a lesson you have prepared or a topic in the textbook from which you teach, find a Web site that uses authentic language and create a short module of your own, using the

A Module on Frida Kahlo

Student's name: _____

INTERPRETIVE MODE

Preparation Phase: In this module, you will learn about the life and works of Frida Kahlo, a famous Mexican painter. As you prepare to read texts about her that you find on the Internet, complete the following tasks.

1. Write three things you already know about Frida Kahlo.

_____; _____; _____

2. Using your Web browser, find three sites about Frida Kahlo and list them here.

http://www._____; http://www._____; http://www._____

3. Look at a photo of Frida Kahlo on one of the sites you found, and answer the following questions:

   a. What impression does her face/expression give you?

   _____

   b. What do you think her personality was like? Why?

   _____

   c. Write three adjectives that describe her clothing.

   _____

   d. Describe her hair. What does her pose suggest to you?

   _____

4. Why might you be interested in reading about Frida Kahlo?_____

5. Brainstorm some key words and expressions that you might encounter in the texts you read._____

Comprehension Phase: Main Ideas: Skim the text of the Web sites that you identified above. For each site, write one sentence in Spanish that summarizes the gist or main idea of the text.

Text 1, http://www._____

    Main idea: _____

Text 2, http://www._____

    Main idea:_____

Text 3, http://www._____

    Main idea:_____

Important Details. Write five details in Spanish to clarify each of the main ideas listed above.

Text 1: Five Details:

_____

_____

_____

_____

_____

Text 2: Five Details:

_____

_____

_____

_____

_____

Text 3: Five Details:

_____

_____

_____

_____

_____

Vocabulary Work: Write the Spanish equivalent for the following words that you may find important for describing Kahlo's life and painting.

monkey _____   spider web _____

obsessive love _____   matriarchal _____

domination _____   self-portrait _____

overcome _____   abortion _____

married people _____   spinal column _____

developed _____

Now list 5–8 new words that you learned in reading these texts, together with their English definitions.

_____; _____;

_____; _____;

_____; _____;

_____; _____;

INTERPRETIVE + INTERPERSONAL MODES

Interpretation Phase: Now imagine that you have to explain the life and work of Frida Kahlo to a student in another class. Write five sentences about these aspects of her life and work and post them in the chat room discussion dedicated for your class or send them by e-mail to a classmate.

Personal life: where she's from, her body, her marriage, her lovers

Art: reflection of her personality as a Mexican woman, as a European woman

Symbols: animals, hair, blood

Events in her life: abortion, marriage, separation

_____

_____

_____

Interpersonal Task: Chat room discussion: Now, in the chat room (which you can find listed on your instructor's homepage, _____), write five opinions of six lines each about what you have read and seen in the work of Frida Kahlo. Be sure that you give and justify your opinions on the role of men and women in society and as artists. Respond to the comments of your peers, and be sure to ask others for their opinions. Don't forget to narrate and describe in the past. Your chat room discussion will be assessed according to the following criteria:

- Reference to details about Kahlo's life and works
- Stating of opinions about men and women in society and as artists
- Responding to and asking for the opinions of others
- Accuracy of language forms: description and narration in the past

PRESENTATIONAL MODE

Application Phase: Now create a brochure to invite visitors to the Frida Kahlo Museum in Coyoacán, México, D.F. You must include descriptions of the artist's life and at least three of her paintings as well as a description of men and women in society and as artists in Mexico in the early twentieth century. Use the new vocabulary you have learned in this module, describe and narrate in the past, and incorporate the passive voice where appropriate. Make sure your brochure is appealing enough to draw visitors to the museum. As shown in Figure 12.5, your work will be assessed according to:

- Quality of description of Frida Kahlo's life
- Quality of summary of selected works of Frida Kahlo
- Language accuracy and use of passive voice
- Vocabulary
- Impact of brochure (appeal to audience)

INTERPRETIVE MODE (revisited)

thandbook.heinle.com

Extension Phase: (Exploring intertextuality):   Visit two other Web sites to acquire some additional information and perspectives about Frida Kahlo's life and works. Compare what you learned earlier in this module with the new information on these two Web sites. Write a paragraph of at least ten sentences.

Source: Shrum and Glisan, 2005, original material.

Interactive Model for Integrating the Three Modes of Communication presented in Chapter 6. A corresponding module template appears in Appendix 12.16 (see the Web site).

2. See Appendix 12.17 (on the Web site)[5] for some selections from chat transcripts among learners after completing the module. These comments were written in asynchronously Spanish, over several days. Identify the five Cs and the elements of the curricular weave in these comments. Identify discourse about the topic, about the computer mediation, about personal opinions, and about extended learning.

3. Ultimately, determine whether you think this tool has been useful for the learners.

4. Complete the partial rubric shown in Figure 12.6 for assessment of student performance in the chat room task.

FIGURE 12.5 Rubric for Frida Kahlo Module: Recreation of Text in a Brochure

Teacher Name: _____

Student Name: _____

CATEGORY	4	3	2	1
Quality of description of Frida Kahlo's life	A concise but complete description of her life; accurate facts; description illustrates effective research into her life.	Description is accurate and reflects effective research; is either too long containing extraneous details or lacks sufficient details.	Description contains mostly accurate information but is missing key details, making it difficult to understand fully.	An arbitrarily selected series of disconnected facts about her life; may be some inaccuracies in the facts presented.
Quality of summary of selected works of Frida Kahlo	An accurate summary of at least 3 works with an interpretation of each in terms of representation of key societal issues and/or views about the human condition.	An accurate summary of at least 3 works but interpretation lacking in sufficient detail.	Fewer than 3 works described. Superficial interpretation of works; interpretation may be lacking in accuracy.	Some information given about 1–3 works but no interpretation of them.
Language accuracy and use of passive voice	High degree of accuracy in verb tense, aspect, and agreement; no major patterns of errors. Past tenses used correctly and appropriately in context.	Some errors in either verb tense or aspect or agreement, but they do not interfere with comprehensibility; past tenses may either have some incorrect forms or may not always be used appropriately in context.	Some patterns of errors in verb tense, aspect, and agreement; past tenses may be used incorrectly or inappropriately in context.	Major patterns of errors in verb tense, aspect, and agreement that make writing hard to understand; past tenses either not used or used incorrectly or inappropriately in context.
Vocabulary	Varied vocabulary with wealth of new vocabulary used.	Several new vocabulary words used; some variety.	A few new vocabulary words but little variety overall.	Few new vocabulary words used; lack of variety in vocabulary.
IMPACT of brochure and appeal to audience	Attractive design; no spelling errors or typos; likely to convince reader to visit museum.	Several parts of brochure are appealing and would spark interest in visiting museum; may have a few typos and/or spelling errors.	One aspect of brochure seems most appealing but the rest is uninviting; several spelling errors and/or typos.	Little to no attention to appeal of brochure; unlikely to convince reader to visit museum; may have spelling errors and typos throughout.

Score: _____/20

Source: Shrum and Glisan, 2005, original material.

FIGURE 12.6 Rubric for Kahlo Chat Room Conversations

Teacher Name:_____

Student Name:_____

CATEGORY	4	3	2	1
Reference to details about Kahlo's life and works	Multiple references to life and work and the relationship between them.			
Stating of opinions about men and women in society and as artists			Opinions offered only on men and women in society or as artists; justification is weak.	
Responding to and asking for the opinions of others		Responses to opinions of others accompanied by queries inviting the opinions of others.		
Accuracy of language forms: description and narration in the past	Abundant description and narration in the past with few errors in contextualized use or forms.			

Score: _____/16

Source: Shrum and Glisan, 2005, original material.

REFERENCES

Abrams, Z. (2003). The effect of synchronous and asynchronous CMC on oral performance in German. *The Modern Language Journal, 87,* 157–167.

American Council on the Teaching of Foreign Languages (2002). *ACTFL/NCATE program standards for the preparation of foreign language teachers.* Yonkers, NY: ACTFL.

Adair-Hauck, B., Youngs, B. E., & Willingham-McLain, L. (1998). Assessing the integration of technology and second language learning. Paper presented at ACTFL. meeting, Chicago, IL.

Alexander, J., & Tate, M. A. (1999). *Evaluating Web resources.* Retrieved April 19, 2004, from http://www2.widener.edu/Wolfgram-Memorial-Library/webevaluation/webval.htm.

Aplevich, P. A., & Willment, J. A. (1998). Teaching and learning language through distance education: The challenges, expectations, and outcomes. In J. Harper, M. G. Lively, & M. K. Williams (Eds.), *The coming of age of the profession: Issues and emerging ideas for the teaching of foreign languages* (pp. 53–77). Boston: Heinle & Heinle.

Beauvois, M. H. (1992). Computer-assisted classroom discussion in the foreign language classroom: Conversation in slow motion. *Foreign Language Annals, 25,* 455–464.

Beauvois, M. H. (1994). F-talk: Attitudes and motivation in computer-assisted classroom discussion. *Computers and the Humanities, 28,* 177–190.

Beauvois, M. H. (1997). Computer-mediated communication (CMC): Technology for improving speaking and writing. In M. D. Bush & R. M Terry (Eds.), *Technology-enhanced language learning* (pp. 165–184). Lincolnwood, IL: NTC/Contemporary Publishing Group.

Beauvois, M. (1998). Write to speak: The effects of electronic communication on the oral achievement of fourth semester French students. In J. A. Muyskens (Ed.), *New ways of learning and teaching: Focus on technology and foreign language education* (pp. 165–183). Boston: Heinle & Heinle.

Blackboard 5 [Computer software]. (2001). Washington, DC: Blackboard.

Blake, R. (2000). Computer-mediated communication: A window on L2 Spanish interlanguage. *Language Learning & Technology, 4,* 120–136. Retrieved May 15, 2004, from http://llt.msu.edu/vol4num1/blake/default.html.

Boehm, D. (1997). I lost my tooth! *Learning and Leading with Technology, 24*(7), 17–19.

Borrás, I., & Lafayette, R. C. (1994). Effects of multimedia courseware subtitling on the speaking performance of college students of French. *The Modern Language Journal, 78,* 61–75.

Brulé, J-P., Caudron, P., Debrauwer, L., Carpenter, S., & Ondich, J. (2004). Sans faute [Computer software]. Boston: McGraw-Hill.

Bump, J. (1990). Radical changes in class discussion using networked computers. *Computers and the Humanities, 24,* 49–65.

Cahill, D., & Catanzaro, D. (1997). Teaching first-year Spanish online. *CALICO Journal, 14*(2–4), 97–114.

Carter-Smith, C., von Schwerin-High, F., Carpenter, S., Ondich, J., & Caudron, P. (2004). Ultralingua auf deutsch [Computer software]. Boston: McGraw-Hill.

Chikamatsu, N. (2003). The effects of computer use on L2 Japanese writing. *Foreign Language Annals, 36,* 114–127.

Chun, D. (1994). Using computer networking to facilitate the acquisition of interactive competence. *System, 22,* 17–31.

Chun, D. M., & Brandl, K. K. (1992). Beyond form-based drill and practice: Meaning-enhanced CALL on the Macintosh. *Foreign Language Annals, 25,* 255–267.

Chun, D., & Plass, J. (1996). Effects of multimedia annotations on vocabulary acquisition. *The Modern Language Journal, 80,* 183–98.

Chun, D., & Plass, J. (1999). Ciberteca: Una carta a Dios [Computer software]. New York: Nonce Publishing Consultants, Ltd.

Chun, D. M., & Wade, E. R. (2004). Collaborative cultural exchanges with asynchronous CMC. In R. M. Terry (Series Ed.), L. Lomicka, & J. Cooke-Plagwitz (Vol. Eds.), *The Heinle professional series in language instruction: Vol. 1. Teaching with technology* (pp. 220–247). Boston: Heinle & Heinle.

Cononelos, T., & Oliva, M. (1993). Using computer networks to enhance foreign language/culture education. *Foreign Language Annals, 26,* 527–534.

Cooke-Plagwitz, J. (2004). Using the Internet to train language teachers to use the Internet: A special topics course for teachers of German. In R. M. Terry (Series Ed.), L. Lomicka, & J. Cooke-Plagwitz (Vol. Eds.), *The Heinle professional series in language instruction: Vol. 1. Teaching with technology* (pp. 220–247). Boston: Heinle & Heinle.

Crookall, D., & Oxford, R. L. (1990). *Simulation, gaming, and language learning.* New York: Newbury House.

Cubillos, J. (1998). Technology: A step forward in the teaching of foreign languages. In J. Harper, M. G. Lively, & M. K. Williams (Eds.), *The coming of age of the profession* (pp. 37–52). Boston: Heinle & Heinle.

Daedalus Integrated Writing Environment [Computer software]. (2002). Austin, TX: The Daedalus Group.

Davis, J. N., & Lyman-Hager, M. A. (1997). Computers and L2 reading: Student performance, student attitudes. *Foreign Language Annals, 30,* 58–72.

Dodge, B., (1997). *Some thoughts about WebQuests.* Retrieved April 14, 2004, from http://edweb.sdsu.edu/courses/edtec596/about_webquests.html.

Dodge, B. (1998). WebQuests: A strategy for scaffolding higher level learning. Paper presented at National Educational Computing Conference. San Diego, CA. Retrieved April 15, 2004, from http://webquest.sdsu.edu/necc98.htm.

Dodge, B. (2004). WebQuest taskonomy: A taxonomy of tasks. Retrieved April 15, 2004, from http://webquest.sdsu.edu/taskonomy.html.

Domínguez, F., & Noblitt, J. (2005). Atajo 4.0 [Computer software]. Boston: Heinle & Heinle.

Furstenberg, G. (1999). Dans un quartier de Paris [Computer software]. New Haven: Yale University Press.

Furstenberg, G., & Malone, S. A. (1993). A la rencontre de Philippe [Computer software]. New Haven: Yale University Press.

Garrett, N. (1991). Technology in the service of language learning: Trends and issues. *The Modern Language Journal, 75,* 74–101.

Garza, T. J. (1991). Evaluating the use of captioned video material in advanced foreign language learning. *Foreign Language Annals, 24,* 239–258.

Glisan, E. W., Dudt, K. P., & Howe, M. S. (1998). Teaching Spanish through distance education: Implications of a pilot study. *Foreign Language Annals, 31,* 48–66.

González-Bueno, M. (1998). The effect of electronic mail on Spanish L2 discourse. *Language Learning and Technology, 1*(2), 55–70. Retrieved March 17, 2004, from http://www.polyglot.cal.msu/llt/num1vol2/article3.

González-Bueno, M., & Pérez, L. C. (2000). Electronic mail in foreign language writing: A study of grammatical and lexical accuracy, and quantity of language. *Foreign Language Annals, 33,* 189–198.

Goulding, C, & Jorth, C. (2004). *Mord in Mainz* murder mystery. [Computer software]. Boston: Heinle & Heinle.

Grace, C. A. (1998). Retention of word meanings inferred from context and sentence-level translations: Implications for the design of beginning-level CALL software. *The Modern Language Journal, 82,* 533–544.

Guyer, L., Debrauwer, L., Carpenter, S., Ondich, J., & Beliakov, S. (2004). Sin falta [Computer software]. Boston: McGraw-Hill.

Herron, C. (1994). An investigation of the effectiveness of using an advance organizer to introduce video in the foreign language classroom. *The Modern Language Journal, 78,* 190–198.

Herron, C. A., & Hanley, J. E. B. (1992). Using video to introduce children to culture. *Foreign Language Annals, 25,* 419–426.

International Society for Technology Education (ISTE)/National Educational Technology Standards (NETS) Project. (2002). *National Educational Technology Standards.* Retrieved April 15, 2004, from http://cnets.iste.org.

International Society for Technology Education/National Educational Technology Standards Project. (2003a). *National Educational Technology Standards for Students.* Retrieved April 15, 2004, from http://cnets.iste.org/students/s_stands.html.

International Society for Technology Education/National Educational Technology Standards Project. (2003b). *National Educational Technology Standards for Teachers.* Retrieved April 15, 2004, from http://cnets.iste.org/teachers/t_stands.html.

Ito, Y. (1996). Communication between high school and college Japanese language education: Implications from a survey on the use of video materials in the United States. *Foreign Language Annals, 29,* 463–479.

Jogan, M. K., Heredia, H. A., & Aguilera, M. G. (2001). Cross-cultural e-mail: Providing cultural input for the advanced foreign language students. *Foreign Language Annals, 34,* 341–346.

Joiner, E. G. (1990). Choosing and using videotext. *Foreign Language Annals, 23,* 53–64.

Jones, K. (1982). *Simulations in language teaching.* Cambridge, UK: Cambridge University Press.

Jones, L. C., & Plass, J. L. (2002). Supporting listening comprehension and vocabulary acquisition in French with multimedia annotations. *The Modern Language Journal, 86,* 546–561.

Kelm, O. R. (1992). The use of synchronous computer networks in second language instruction: A preliminary report. *Foreign Language Annals, 25,* 441–453.

Kern, R. G. (1995). Restructuring classroom interaction with networked computers: Effects on quantity and characteristics of language production. *The Modern Language Journal, 79,* 457–476.

Larson, J., & Bush, C. (1992). Montevidisco [Computer software]. Provo, UT: Brigham Young University.

Lee, L. (2002). Enhancing learners' communication skills through synchronous electronic interaction and task-based instruction. *Foreign Language Annals, 35,* 16–24.

Lee, L. (2004). Perspectives of nonnative speakers of Spanish on two types of online collaborative exchanges: Promises and challenges. In R. M. Terry (Series Ed.), L. Lomicka, & J. Cooke-Plagwitz (Vol. Eds.), *The Heinle professional series in language instruction: Vol. 1. Teaching with technology* (pp. 248–265). Boston: Heinle & Heinle.

LeLoup, J., & Ponterio, R. (2004). FLTEACH: On-line professional development for preservice and inservice foreign language teachers. In R. M. Terry (Series Ed.), L. Lomicka, & J. Cooke-Plagwitz (Vol. Eds.), *The heinle professional series in language instruction: Vol. 1. Teaching with technology* (pp. 26–44). Boston: Heinle & Heinle.

Levine, G., & Morse, S. (2004). Integrating diverse digital media in a global simulation German course. In R. M. Terry (Series Ed.), L. Lomicka, & J. Cooke-Plagwitz (Vol. Eds.), *The Heinle professional series in language instruction: Vol. 1. Teaching with technology* (pp. 248–265). Boston: Heinle & Heinle.

Levy, M. (1997). *Computer assisted language learning: Context and conceptualization.* Oxford, UK: Clarendon Press.

Liu, M., Moore, Z., Graham, L., & Lee, S. (2002). A look at the research on computer-based technology use in second language learning: A review of the literature from 1990–2000. *Journal of Research on Technology in Education, 34,* 250–273.

Lomicka, L. (1998). To gloss or not to gloss: An investigation of reading comprehension online. *Language Learning and Technology, 1*(2), 41–50.

Lonergan, J. (1984). *Using video in language teaching.* Cambridge, UK: Cambridge University Press.

Magnan, S., Farrell, M., Jan, M-F., Lee, J., Tsai, C-P., & Worth, R. (2004). In R. M. Terry (Series Ed.), L. Lomicka, & J. Cooke-Plagwitz (Vol. Eds.), *The Heinle professional series in language instruction: Vol. 1. Teaching with technology* (pp. 171–179). Boston: Heinle & Heinle.

March, T. (1998). *The WebQuest design process.* Retrieved April 15, 2004 from http://www.ozline.com/webquests/design.html.

March, T. (2004). *The idea machine.* Retrieved April 15, 2004 from http://www.ozline.com/learning/machine.html.

Martínez-Lage, A., & Herren, D. (1998). Challenges and opportunities: Curriculum pressures in the technological present. In J. Harper, M. Lively, & M. Williams (Eds.), *The coming of age of the profession: Issues and emerging ideas for the teaching of foreign languages* (pp. 141–167). Boston: Heinle & Heinle.

Masters-Wicks, K., Postlewate, L., & Lewental, M. (1996). Developing interactive instructional software for language acquisition. *Foreign Language Annals, 29,* 217–22.

Maxim, H. H. (1998). Authorizing the foreign language student. *Foreign Language Annals, 31,* 407–430.

Maxwell, D. (1998). *Technology and foreign language learning. A report to the Charles E. Culpeper Foundation.* Washington, DC: National Foreign Language Center.

Mayer, R. E. (1997). Multimedia learning: Are we asking the right questions? *Educational Psychologist, 32,* 1–19.

Mayer, R. E. (2001). *Multimedia learning*. Cambridge: Cambridge University Press.

Moore, M., & Thompson, M. (1997). The effects of distance learning 15. ACSDE Research Monograph. State College, PA: The Pennsylvania State University.

Murphy, D., & Youngs, B. (2004). From the classroom to the Web: Applying best practices from foreign language education in the development of Web-based listening materials. In R. M. Terry (Series Ed.), L. Lomicka, & J. Cooke-Plagwitz (Vol. Eds.), *The Heinle professional series in language instruction: Vol. 1. Teaching with technology* (pp. 121–128). Boston: Heinle & Heinle.

Nagata, N. (1993). Intelligent computer feedback for second language instruction. *The Modern Language Journal, 77,* 330–339.

Nagata, N. (1999). The effectiveness of computer-assisted interactive glosses. *Foreign Language Annals, 32,* 469–479.

Nagata, N., & Swisher, M. V. (1995) A study of consciousness-raising by computer: The effect of metalinguistic feedback on second language learning. *Foreign Language Annals, 28,* 337–347.

National Council of State Supervisors of Foreign Languages (NCSSFL). (2002). Position statement on distance learning in foreign languages. Retrieved April 21, 2004, from http://www.ncssfl.org/position.htm.

National Standards in Foreign Language Education Project. (NSFLEP). (1999). *National standards for foreign language learning in the the 21st century*. Lawrence, KS: Allen Press.

Nemtchinova, E. (2004). Creating original language teaching materials with presentational software. In R. M. Terry (Series Ed.), L. Lomicka, & J. Cooke-Plagwitz (Vol. Eds.), *The Heinle professional series in language instruction: Vol. 1. Teaching with technology* (pp. 19–25). Boston: Heinle & Heinle.

Noblitt, J. S. (2005). Système-D 4.0 [Computer software]. Boston: Heinle & Heinle.

Oliva, M., & Pollastrini, Y. (1995). Internet resources and second language acquisition: An evaluation of virtual immersion. *Foreign Language Annals, 28,* 551–563.

Oliver, W., & Nelson, T. (1997). Un Misterio en Toluca [Computer software]. Boston: Heinle & Heinle.

Oliver, W., & Nelson, T. (1998). Un Muertre à Cinet [Computer software]. Boston: Heinle & Heinle.

Oyono, F. (1956). *Une vie de boy*. Paris: Julliard.

Paivio, A. (1971). *Imagery and verbal processes*. New York: Holt, Rinehart & Winston.

Paivio, A. (1986). *Mental representations: A dual coding approach*. Oxford: Oxford University Press.

Pellettieri, J. (2000). Negotiation in cyberspace: The role of chatting in the development of grammatical competence. In M. Warschauer & R. Kern (Eds.), *Network-based language teaching: Concepts and practice* (pp. 59–86). Cambridge, UK: Cambridge University Press.

Pennington, M., (1996). *The computer and the non-native writer: A natural partnership*. Cresskill, NJ: Hampton Press.

Phinney, M. A. (1989). Computers, composition, and second language teaching. In M. C. Pennington (Ed.), *Teaching languages with computers: The state of the art* (pp. 81–96). La Jolla, CA: Athelstan.

Plass, J. L., Chun, D. M., Mayer, R. E., & Leutner, D. (1998). Supporting visual and verbal learning preferences in a second language multimedia learning environment. *Journal of Educational Psychology, 90*(1), 25–36.

QUIA. (1998–2004). Quia corporation. Retrieved April 15, 2004, http://www.quia. com/web.

Rubio, F. (2004). Online feedback in foreign language writing. In R. M. Terry (Series Ed.), L. Lomicka, & J. Cooke-Plagwitz (Vol. Eds.), *The Heinle professional series in language instruction: Vol. 1. Teaching with technology* (pp. 9–18). Boston: Heinle & Heinle.

Scott, V. (1990). Task-oriented creative writing with Système-D. *CALICO Journal, 7*(2), 58–67.

Smith, B. (2003). Computer-mediated negotiated interaction: An expanded model. *The Modern Language Journal, 87,* 38–57.

Sotillo, S. (2000). Discourse functions and syntactic complexity in synchronous and asynchronous communication. *Language Learning and Technology, 4*(1), 82–119. Retrieved May 26, 2004, from http://llt.msu.edu/vol4num1/sotillo/default.html.

Spartanburg School District III. *Creating a WebQuest: Survival*. Retrieved April 15, 2004, from http://www.spa3.k12.sc.us/survival.htm

Spodark, E. (2002). The Tek.Xam as a framework for pre-service foreign language teacher technology training. *Foreign Language Annals, 35,* 427–436.

Suh, J-S. (2002). Effectiveness of CALL Writing Instruction: The voices of Korean EFL learners. *Foreign Language Annals, 35,* 669–679.

Sullivan, N., & Pratt, E. (1996). A comparative study of two ESL writing environments: A computer-assisted classroom and a traditional oral classroom. *System, 24(4),* 491–501.

Swaffar, J., & Vlatten, A. (1997). A sequential model for video viewing in the foreign language curriculum. *The Modern Language Journal, 81,* 175–188.

Terry, R. M. (2000). *Technology competencies for teacher certification: A survey of the states*. Retrieved April 14, 2004 from http://oncampus.richmond.edu/~rterry/Survey/start.html

Teachers of English to Speakers of Other Languages (TESOL). (1997). *ESL standards for pre-K–12 students*. Alexandria, VA: Author.

Transparent language [Computer software]. (2004). Transparent Language, Inc. Retrieved May 25, 2004, from http://www.transparent.com.

United States Department of Education. (August 3, 1998). *The Technology Literacy Challenge*. Office of Educational Technology. Retrieved November 19, 1998, from http://www.ed.gov/Technology.

Von der Emde, S., Schneider, J. & Kötter, M. (2001). Technically speaking: Transforming language learning through virtual learning environments (MOOs). *The Modern Language Journal, 85,* 210–225.

Warner, C. (2004). It's just a game, right? Types of play in foreign language CMC. *Language Learning & Technology 8*(2), 69–87. Retrieved May 25, 2004, from http://llt.msu.edu/vol8num2/ warner/default.html.

Warschauer, M. (1996). Comparing face-to-face and electronic communication in the second language classroom. *CALICO Journal, 12,* 7–26.

Warschauer, M., & Healey, D. (1998). Computers and language learning: An overview. *Language Teaching, 31*(2), 57–71.

Weasenforth, D., Biesenbach-Lucas, S., & Meloni, C. (2002). Realizing constructivist objectives through collaborative technologies: Threaded discussions. *Language Learning & Technology, 6*(3), 58–86. Retrieved May 15, 2004, from http://llt.msu.edu/vol6num3/weasenforth/ default.html.

WebCT [Computer software]. (2001). Lynnfield, MA: WebCT.

NOTES

1. This example is based on an online chat discussion format described in Magnan, Farrell, Jan, Lee, Tsai and Worth (2004).

2. Keep in mind that teachers may adapt and apply technologies in tandem and for multiple purposes, and that those technologies listed in this chapter often require an infrastructure of several other technologies in order to operate in the form we have listed them. Furthermore, as teachers and students use technologies, new and modified versions continue to be released, which in turn offer new opportunities for creative uses. Remember also that in recent years teachers and students have increasingly used the types of technology that appear in Figure 12.1 in both their academic and everyday lives. For example, course management programs such as *Blackboard* and *WebCT* enable instructors to create their own course documents, communicate via e-mail, assess and tabulate grades, and monitor student progress. *QUIA* is a similar program that connects publishers' textbooks and workbooks to other course materials and processes the teacher designs. Students and teachers move freely between types of technology on the Internet and those networked in their institutions and provided on their computers. See the *Teacher's Handbook* Web site for links useful courseware and software.

3. There are a number of programs available for language learning that can be delivered online, downloaded, or installed via CD-ROM. These programs can be useful for professionals in business, for home schooling, for additional practice, or for adding less commonly taught languages to a curriculum. See the *Teacher's Handbook* Web site for the links to programs developed by Transparent Language, Rosetta Stone, and Berlitz. Each of these products has adopted an approach to language learning compatible with its products.

4. Spodark (2002) offers six modules for use in a methods of teaching class using the Tek.Xam, a national standard in literacy developed by the Virginia Foundation for Independent Colleges. See also http://www.cortland.edu/flteach/ methods/ for a technology module for teacher education.

5. Thanks to the students of SPAN 2984 (2114) Accelerated Intermediate Spanish, fall 1998, Virginia Tech., for their commentary on this chatroom.

thandbook.heinle.com

Appendices

APPENDIX 1.1 SOME TYPES OF LANGUAGE-PROMOTING ASSISTANCE

Teacher provides encouragement for students to talk by

- complimenting students;
- encouraging students to communicate;
- encouraging students to talk through nonverbal means such as smiling, nodding in approval.

Teacher helps students to understand the input by

- using caregiver talk (speaking slowly and clearly, rephrasing key ideas, repeating important words, explaining words, expanding utterances);
- checking for understanding by asking questions and asking students to point to things or perform actions;
- teaching students to ask questions when they don't understand;
- activating students' background knowledge and previewing material in order to prepare students for tasks; and
- illustrating words that students do not understand by using visuals, charts, and realia, and by acting out meaning.

Teacher helps students to remember key words and ideas by writing them on the board and asking questions about them.

Teacher helps students to interact by

- conducting confirmation checks ("Is this what you are saying?"), comprehension checks ("Do you understand what I am saying?"), and clarification requests ("What do you mean by that?");
- eliciting more language from students with questions, restatements, increased wait time, invitations to expand (such as "Tell me more about that");
- encouraging all students to participate in discussion and prompting students to negotiate a turn in speaking (i.e., without necessarily raising hands to receive a turn);
- asking questions that may have more than one answer; and
- modeling correct forms.

Teacher provides direct teaching of concepts, structures, functions; when students are having difficulty.
Teacher maintains the students' interest by

- personalizing instruction;
- focusing on thematically related topics of interest to students and encouraging students to choose their own topics of interest;
- focusing primarily on meaning rather than on linguistic forms; and
- highlighting and integrating the students' culture and the target language culture in the classroom.

Source: Adapted from Scarcella, R.C., & Oxford, R.L. (1992). *The Tapestry of Language Learning* (pp. 32–33). Boston, MA: Heinle & Heinle.

APPENDIX 2.1 THE CHRONOLOGICAL DEVELOPMENT OF LANGUAGE TEACHING

approach = a set of theoretical principles or basic assumptions that are the foundation of a method

method = a procedural plan for presenting and teaching language, based on the approach adopted

technique = a particular strategy—one of many—for implementing a method

(Anthony, 1963)

What is the role of context in each method described below?

ERA	TIME PERIOD	APPROACH	METHOD	TECHNIQUES	PROPONENT(S)
I. Influence of Teaching of Latin and Greek	until late 19th century	The mind needs to be trained by analysis of the language, memorization of rules, paradigms; application of these rules in translation exercises (Chastain, 1988).	Grammar-translation	translation; learning of grammar rules; memorization of bilingual word lists; little or no emphasis on oral skills	No one person; German scholar Karl Ploz (late 1800s) very influential
II. Reaction to Grammar-Translation Method	late 19th–early 20th century	Learners should acquire rules of grammar inductively through imitation, repetition, speaking, and reading. The best way to teach meaning is to use visual perception (Chastain, 1988).	Direct	exclusive use of L2; use of visuals; grammar rules taught through inductive teaching; emphasis on correct pronunciation	Comenius, Gouin, Jespersen, de Sauzé
III. Result of Structural Linguistics and Behavioral Psychology/ National Emphasis on Oral Skills	1940–1950	L2 should be taught without reference to L1. Students learn through stimulus-response (S-R) techniques. Pattern drills should precede any explanation of grammar. The natural sequence LSRW should be followed in learning the language (Chastain, 1988).	Audiolingual (ALM)	stimulus-response pattern drills; memorization of dialogues; correction a must; comparison of L1 and L2; exclusive use of L2; grammar rules learned through induction; skills learned in the sequence of listening, speaking, reading, writing; focus on culture	Fries, Skinner, Bloomfield, N. Brooks

Category	Date	Description	Method	Characteristics	Proponent
IV. Reaction to ALM	1960s	Learners must attain control over the rules of the target language so they can generate their own utterances. The teacher should move from known to new information. Creative use of the language should be promoted. Grammar should be explained so that students understand the rules. Language practice should always be meaningful (Chastain, 1988).	Cognitive (Code)	meaningful language use; deductive teaching of grammar in native language; grammar practice follows mechanical, meaningful, communicative sequence	Chomsky, Ausubel
V. Result of Studies in First Language Acquisition	1974	Comprehension must be developed before speaking. Speech will emerge naturally as students internalize language. Learners learn to understand best through physical movement in response to commands (Asher, Kusudo, & de la Torre, 1974).	Total Physical Response	listening and responding physically to oral commands for first ten hours of instruction; exclusive use of target language; creative language use	Asher
	late 1970s, early 1980s	Learners should acquire language before being forced to learn it. Affective factors merit much attention in language instruction. Communicative competence should be the goal in beginning language instruction. Learners need to acquire a great deal of vocabulary to understand and to speak (Terrell, 1982).	Natural (Approach)	creative, communicative practice; limited error correction; "foreigner talk"; acquisition activities: comprehension, early speech production, speech emergence; inductive teaching of grammar	Terrell
VI. Focus on Effective Development of Individual: Humanistic Methods	1972–1973	Teachers can help students most by allowing them to take more responsibility for their own learning. Learning is not relegated to imitation and drill. Learners learn from trial and error and are capable of making their own corrections (Gattegno, 1976).	Silent Way	use of Cuisenaire rods to denote words and structures; students more responsible for learning; self and peer correction; early writing practice	Gattegno

	1976	The teacher, in the role as "knower" or "counselor," should remain passive in order to reduce anxiety among students. Learners learn when working in community with others who are trying to achieve similar goals (Curran, 1976).	Community Language Learning	translation by teacher from native language to target language in early lessons; theme of each class determined by learners; analysis of group conversations from tape	Curran
	1978–1979	Relaxation techniques and concentration assist learners in releasing the subconscious and in retaining large amounts of language (Lozanov, 1978).	Suggestopedia	"suggestive" atmosphere (living room setting, soft lights, baroque music, dramatic techniques by teacher); dialogues accompanied by music in background; role-play and activities to "activate" the material in dialogues; grammatical explanations given in native language	Lozanov
VII. Effects of Drama on Language Teaching	1972–1980	The teacher must help learners to overcome their inhibitions so that they can live the language experience more fully. The teacher should be an actor and possess vitality in the classroom. The target language should be spoken exclusively, and all errors should be corrected. The language must come to life in the classroom (Rassias, 1983).	Dartmouth Intensive Language Model (DILM)	drama and action by teacher; immediate correction of grammar and pronunciation errors; skits and games; "micrologue" for teaching culture; master teacher and apprentice teachers (who conduct drill sessions); inductive teaching by master teacher	Rassias

VIII. Proficiency	1980s–1990s	Knowing a language means being able to use it in communication. Learners use the language to perform functions in a range of contexts and with a level of accuracy in grammar, vocabulary, pronunciation, fluency and pragmatic competence, and sociolinguistic competence.	No particular method	opportunities for self-expression and creativity; use of language in a variety of contexts; exposure to authentic texts; interaction with others; integration of culture and language	Proficiency Guidelines established by ACTFL/ETS
IX. Standards	1996–present	Foreign language has a central role in the learning experience of every learner. Competence in a language and culture enables the learner to communicate with others in a variety of settings, gain an understanding of self and other cultures, acquire new bodies of knowledge, develop insight into his or her own language and culture, and participate in the global community. Language and culture education enhances communication skills and higher order thinking skills.	No particular method	opportunities to use the language as a vehicle for learning content; integration of skills and culture; interaction with others by means of technology; exploration of cultural products and practices and their relationships to cultural perspectives	Standards developed by ACTFL (in collaboration with AATF, AATG, AATSP) and TESOL.

Source: Adapted from Shrum and Glisan (1994).

APPENDIX 2.2 THE CONCEPT OF PROFICIENCY: A HISTORICAL SUMMARY

Prior to World War II	Foreign language instruction centers on the development of literacy skills, reading, and writing.
World War II	Realization that Americans had difficulty communicating with foreigners; Army Language School (later to become the Defense Language Institute) in Monterey, California, begins teaching oral communication.
1950s	Foreign Service Institute (FSI) Language School begins to rate speaking ability of students and personnel using an interview-based evaluation procedure linked to a rating scale.
1960s	Educational Testing Service (ETS) staff are trained in the Oral Proficiency Interview (OPI) procedure and begin to test Peace Corps personnel.
1970s	Application of OPI to educational setting (as part of certification procedure for bilingual and ESL teachers, evaluating students and personnel). "Common Yardstick project" begins, bringing together ETS with the English Speaking Union of Great Britain, the British Council, the *Deutscher Volkschochschulerband,* representatives of the U.S. government, and various business and academic groups for the purpose of refining the FSI (currently called The Interagency Language Roundtable [ILR]) scale and interview procedure for academic use.
1978–1979	President's Commission on Foreign Language and International Studies formed to assess need for language specialists, recommend types of language programs needed, recommend how to call public attention to the importance of foreign language and international studies, and to identify legislative changes. Report of the Commission, *Strength Through Wisdom,* recommends that foreign language proficiency test be developed to assess foreign language teaching in the United States. MLA-ACLS (Modern Language Association-American Council on Language Studies) Language Task Force for the President's Commission makes similar recommendations.
1980	ILR scale expanded at Levels 0 and 1 and levels renamed. Under the sponsorship of two grants, ACTFL continues development of longer verbal descriptions of each level in the form of "guidelines" for the four skills and culture. ACTFL begins to conduct OPI tester training workshops.
1986	*ACTFL Provisional Proficiency Guidelines* published.
1986–87	*ACTFL Proficiency Guidelines* revised, no longer provisional. Features of less commonly taught languages are included. Culture guidelines are eliminated since it is recognized that language-specific work is needed. Teaching for proficiency workshops of various kinds are added to the ACTFL Professional Development Workshop list.
1990	First extensive research on comparability of the proficiency scales across languages and skills reported in Dandonoli and Henning (1990); reveals that speaking guidelines are solid in terms of validity. Projects are initiated to work on guidelines in other skills.
1992	OPI testing expanded to commercial sector. Language Testing International (LTI) is established to handle the volume of testing. Simulated Oral Proficiency Interview (SOPI) procedure is designed by the Center for Applied Linguistics as an adaptation of the OPI.

1994	The first tape-mediated proficiency test (Texas Oral Proficiency Test) is used as a competency examination for FL and bilingual teachers.
1998	*ACTFL Performance Guidelines for K-12 Learners* published.
1999	*ACTFL Proficiency Guidelines* in speaking revised.
2000	ACTFL OPI accepted by the American Council on Education (ACE) College Credit Recommendation Service as a measure through which college credit may be granted.
2001	*ACTFL Proficiency Guidelines* in writing revised.
2003	Twentieth anniversary of *ACTFL Proficiency Guidelines* commemorated with special issue of *Foreign Language Annals* dedicated to oral proficiency testing.

APPENDIX 3.1 EXCERPT FROM NEBRASKA K–12 FOREIGN LANGUAGE FRAMEWORKS

Goal One: COMMUNICATION
Progress Indicators

Goal One: *Standard 1.1*	**Communicate in Languages Other than English** *Students engage in conversations, provide and obtain information, express feelings and emotions, and exchange opinions.*		
Students are able to:	**Beginning**	**Developing**	**Expanding**
A	Express basic needs.	▶ Elaborate on needs. ▶ Interact in basic survival situations.	▶ Manage unforeseen circumstances and complicated situations.
B	Express basic courtesies.	▶ Incorporate appropriate gestures into conversations.	▶ Converse using language and behaviors that are appropriate to the setting.
C	Express state of being.	▶ Create simple descriptions within a context.	▶ Create detailed oral descriptions within a context.
D	Express likes and dislikes.	▶ Qualify likes and dislikes.	▶ Exchange personal feelings and ideas for the purpose of persuading others.
E	Express agreement and disagreement.	▶ Support opinions. ▶ Describe a problem. ▶ Make suggestions and recommendations.	▶ Express individual perspectives and defend opinions. ▶ Collaborate to develop and propose solutions to problems. ▶ Negotiate a compromise.

▶▶▶

Goal Two:	**Gain Knowledge and Understanding of Other Cultures**	
Standard 2.1	*Students demonstrate an understanding of the relationship between the perspectives and practices of cultures studied and use this knowledge to interact effectively in cultural contexts.*	

Students are able to:	**Beginning**	**Developing**	**Expanding**
A	Identify and react to cultural perspectives and practices in the culture studied.	▶ Describe and analyze cultural characteristics and behaviors of everyday life. ▶ Identify differences in cultural practices among same-language cultures.	▶ Analyze the development of different cultural practices. ▶ Compare and contrast cultural practices among same language cultures.
B	Recognize and interpret language and behaviors that are appropriate to the target culture.	▶ Produce language and behaviors that are appropriate to the target culture.	▶ Apply language and behaviors that are appropriate to the target culture in an authentic situation.
C	Identify some commonly-held generalizations about the culture studied.	▶ Analyze some commonly held generalizations about the culture studied.	▶ Evaluate some commonly held generalizations about the culture studied.
D	Identify social and geographic factors that affect cultural practices.	▶ Discuss social and geographic factors that affect cultural practices.	▶ Analyze social and geographic factors that affect cultural practices.
E	Identify common words, phrases, and idioms that reflect the culture.	▶ Interpret the cultural connotations of common words, phrases, and idioms.	▶ Integrate culturally embedded words, phrases, and idioms into everyday communication.

▲▲▲

Source: Nebraska Department of Education, 2004, http://www.nde.state.ne.us/FORLG/Frameworks/Frameworks.pdf, pp. 23–34.

APPENDIX 3.2 EXCERPT FROM NEBRASKA'S YEAR PLANNER FOR LEVEL ONE FOREIGN LANGUAGE

Goals	Goal 1: COMMUNICATION	Goal 2: CULTURES	Goal 3: CONNECTIONS	Goal 4: COMPARISONS	Goal 5: COMMUNITIES
Standards	1.1 Students engage in conversations	2.1 Students … perspectives and practices of cultures	3.1 Students reinforce … their knowledge through other disciplines	4.1 Students … use different patterns to communicate and apply to own language	5.1 Students apply language skills beyond school setting
Contexts/ Outcomes	Students engage in conversations about typical school situations	Students demonstrate an understanding of the relationship between the perspectives and practices of greetings and leave-takings in Germany	Students reinforce and further knowledge of art by studying German artists	Students recognize that the German language uses different sound patterns from English	Students apply language skills beyond the school setting by using the Internet to converse in German with German teenagers
Progress Indicators	1.1.A Express basic needs 1.1.B Express basic courtesies	2.1.A Identify and react to cultural perspectives and practices	3.1.B Identify information for use in other disciplines	4.1.A Identify sound patterns and compare to own language	5.1.A Identify the target language in daily lives
Essential Skills/ Knowledge	• Verbs—want, need • Vocabulary for school items, clothes, gift suggestions • Phrases for polite requests	• Descriptions of greetings • Leave-taking customs	• Accessing information from computer and library • Listing of resources for the information desired • Information on artists-their lives and times	• Vowel sounds • Consonant sounds	• How-to log-skills • Conversation skills • Writing skills
Assessments	• Situation cards—role-plays of losing school supplies and borrowing from friends • Quizzes • Letter to pen-pal on Internet	• Role-play greetings and leave-taking situations	• Student log/notes • Projects on various perspectives on relationships of art to society	• Listening identification • Pronunciation test	• Student logs of language use • Internet chat paper copies
Resources	• Chapter 2 • Chapter 9 • Video • Internet pen-pals	• Chapter 1 • Video	• Library • WWW	• Tapes • Videos	• Logbook • Computer-Internet account • Addresses for Internet

Source: Nebraska Department of Education, (2004), http://www.nde.state.ne.us/FORLG/Frameworks/FLFCurric.pdf, p. 212.

Unit: Shopping at the Market
A unit integrating the five Frameworks goals

Goals:
Goal 1: Communicate in Languages other than English
Goal 2: Gain Knowledge and Understanding of Other Cultures
Goal 3: Connect with Other Disciplines and Acquire Information
Goal 4: Develop Insight into the Nature of Language and Culture
Goal 5: Participate in Multilingual Communities at Home and Around the World

Standards: Students…

1.1 Engage in conversations…exchange opinions.
1.2 Understand…written and spoken language…
1.3 Convey information…
2.1 Demonstrate an understanding of the relationship between the perspectives and practices of cultures studied and use this knowledge to interact effectively in cultural contexts.
3.2 Acquire information and perspectives through authentic materials …within the cultures.
4.2 Recognize that cultures use different patterns of interaction and can apply this knowledge to their own culture.
5.1 Apply language skills and cultural knowledge within and beyond the school setting.

Contexts/Outcomes:

Students engage in conversation and convey information in a market using correct cultural practices.

Progress Indicators: *Students are able to…*

1.1.A Express basic needs.
1.1.C Create simple descriptions.
1.1.D Express likes and dislikes.
1.1.F Respond to one-on-one interactions.
1.1.G Ask and answer simple questions.
1.2.A Respond appropriately to directions.
1.2.E Identify aural, visual and context clues.
1.3.A Give directions.
1.3.B Give a description orally.

2.1.A Identify and react to cultural perspectives and practices in the culture studied.
2.1.B Recognize and interpret language and behaviors that are appropriate to the target culture.

3.2.A Extract information from sources intended for native speakers....

3.2.B Use authentic sources to identify the perspectives of the target culture.

4.2.A Identify similarities/differences between the target culture and the students own culture using evidence from authentic sources.

4.2.B Identify similar and different behavioral patterns between the target culture and the student's own culture.

5.1.B Locate connections with the target culture through the use of technology, media, and authentic sources.

Essential Skills/Knowledge:

- Vocabulary for foods and daily needs
- Common phrases for shopping
- Use of the verb *gustar*
- Question formation
- Simple commands
- Adjectives
- Cultural information for do's and don'ts of shopping at Mexican markets
- Use of the World Wide Web

Assessments:

- Quizzes on the vocabulary and simple commands
- Review quiz on gustar and adjective agreement
- Listening check from video
- Role play of shopping at the market (culminating assessment*)

Instructional Strategies:

- TPR for foods
- Video practice of market situations in Mexico
- Role-play situations
- Description of pictures of markets
- Interviews with native speakers
- Practice with commands

Resources:

- WWW search for Mexican markets
- Hyperstudio lesson on markets in Cuernavaca
- Photos of Mexican markets
- Textbook

*Performance task:

Students will role-play a shopping experience in a Mexican market using appropriate cultural behavior. The student will go to the market stall owner (the teacher) and, with a list of three items to purchase, will select the three items from the ones displayed and bargain for the best price for each.

Rubric.

	4 Exeeds expectations	3 Excellent	2 Good	1 Not yet
Expresses likes/dislikes	no errors	almost all correctly expressed	some errors, majority correctly stated	few or none correctly stated
Is comprehensible (pronunciation, structures, vocabulary usage) (x 2)	near-native pronunciation, use of structures beyond expected proficiency	easily understood, infrequent errors	comprehensible with noticeable errors in pronunciation, structures and/or vocabulary usage	nearly or completely incomprehensible
Asks and answers questions accurately	no errors	almost all correctly stated	some errors, majority correctly stated	few or none correctly stated
Demonstrates appropriate cultural practices	near-native use of practices	almost all demonstrated and appropriate	some demonstrated and appropriate	inappropriate or none demonstrated
Follows Instructions	bought more items than required	followed instruction completely	mostly followed instructions	little evidence of following instructions

Source: Nebraska Department of Education (2004). http://www.nde.state.ne.us/FORLG/Frameworks/FLFCurric.pdf, pp. 227–228.

APPENDIX 3.4 BLOOM'S TAXONOMY OF THINKING

Bloom's Taxonomy is a model that focuses on six levels of thinking. The six levels roughly form a two-tiered arrangement that represents levels of complexity in thinking. *Knowledge* and *comprehension* are the lower or more concrete levels of thinking. *Analysis, evaluation,* and *synthesis* represent higher or more complex levels of thinking. The *application* level, which falls between the lower and higher levels, can be very concrete or very complex depending on the task.

A variety of instructional strategies and products may be categorized for each level of thinking. Teachers who design a variety of learning activities that require different levels of thinking will provide appropriate opportunities for the diverse number of students whose thinking levels range throughout the spectrum.

Winebrenner's (1992) Figure F on the next page provides a model for instructional planning based on Bloom's taxonomy of thinking.

Figure F: **Planning Model using Bloom's Taxonomy (adapted from Winebrenner, 1992)**

Level		Definition	Instructional Strategies	Activities, Tasks, & Products
Lower, less complex, more concrete levels	**Knowledge**	Students recall information to recite or write.	• ask • define • describe • discover • identify • label • list • listen • locate • match • memorize • name • observe • recite • recognize • remember • research • select • state • tell	• book • diagrams • events • exams • facts in isolation • films • filmstrips • magazine articles • models • newspapers • people • plays • quiz • radio • recordings/ records • tapes • television shows • tests • text readings • vocabulary • workbook pages
	Comprehension	Students restate the information in their own words.	• ask • change • compare • convert • defend • discover • distinguish • edit • explain • express • extend • generalize • give examples • identify • illustrate • infer • interpret • listen • locate • match • observe • paraphrase • predict • relate • research • restate • rewrite • show symbols • summarize • transform • translate	• casual relationships • comparison of like/unlike items • conclusion/implication based on data • diagrams • drama • drawing • events • films • filmstrips • graph • magazines • models • newspapers • outline • own statement • people • photograph • radio • response to questions • revision • skit • speech • story • summary • tape recording • television
Level depends on complexity of task	**Application**	Students apply the information in one or more contexts.	• apply • build • change • choose • classify • construct • cook • demonstrate • discover • dramatize • experiment • interview • list • manipulate • modify • paint • prepare • produce • record • report • show • sketch • solve • stimulate • teach • use guides, charts, maps	• artwork • collection • crafts • demonstration • diagram • diorama • diary • drama • forecast • illustration • list • map • meeting • mobile • model • painting • paper which follows outline • photographs • project • puzzle • question • recipe • scrapbook • sculpture • shifting smoothly from one gear into another • solution • stichery

Level		Definition	Instructional Strategies	Activities, Tasks, & Products
Higher, more complex, more abstract levels	**Analysis**	Students understand component parts to be able compare and contrast or categorize information.	• advertise • analyze • categorize • classify • compare • contrast • differentiate • dissect • distinguish • infer • investigate • point out • select • separate • solve • subdivide • survey	• argument broken down • chart • commercial • conclusion checked • diagram • graph • parts of propaganda statement identified • plan • prospectus • questionnaire • report survey • report • solution • survey • syllogism broken down • word defined
	Synthesis	Students judge what they have analyzed and support their opinions.	• combine • compose • construct • create • design • estimate • forecast • hypothesize • imagine • infer • invent • predict • produce • rearrange parts • role-play • write	• advertisement • article • book • cartoon • experiment • formation of a hypothesis or question • game • invention • lesson plan • machine • magazine • new game • new product • new color, smell, taste • news article • pantomime • play • poem • puppet show • radio show • recipe • report • set of rules, principles or standards • song • speculate on or plan alternative courses of action • story • structure • television show
	Evaluation	Students create and/or gather pieces of information to form a novel thought, idea, product, or perspective.	• appraise • choose • compare • consider • criticize • critique • debate • decide • discuss • editorialize • evaluate • give opinion, viewpoint • judge • prioritize • recommend • relate • summarize • support • weigh	• conclusion • court trial • critique • debate • decision • defense/verdict • discussion • editorial • evaluation • group discussion • group • letter • news item • panel • rating/grades • recommendation • self-evaluation • standard compared • standard established • survey • valuing

APPENDIX 4.5 THEMATIC PLANNING WEB

Source: Curtain, H., & Pesola, C. A. B. *Languages and children—Making the match.* Copyright 1994, 1998 by Longman Publishing Group. Used by permission of Addison-Wesley Educational Publishers Inc., p. 203.

APPENDIX 4.6 IDENTIFYING IMMERSION LANGUAGE OBJECTIVES

Content-obligatory and content-compatible language objectives include the following kinds of language skills:

- Functions, such as: requesting/giving information, comparing, and describing
- Vocabulary
- Grammar, such as: question formation, adjective agreement, and comparatives.

Let's examine a grade 1 mathematics lesson. The objective is for students to learn to construct and interpret information from simple pictographs. Because you know students will need food vocabulary for an upcoming social studies unit, People Need Food, you have selected a variety of fruits for the introductory lesson on graphing. You have selected red, green, and yellow apples, green and yellow pears, bananas, and oranges. As you demonstrate to students how to graph the number of each type of fruit, you will find that you must use certain language so that students understand how to construct and interpret graphs (content-obligatory language objectives). Other language objectives, such as the names of the fruits selected, may be varied at your discretion (content-compatible language objectives). Review the content obligatory and content-compatible language objectives below that were identified by a veteran immersion teacher.

CONTENT-OBLIGATORY LANGUAGE OBJECTIVE

Functions	Vocabulary	Grammar
Understanding directions	Ordinal numbers 1–10	Singular and plural nouns
	Horizontal axis	Definite and indefinite
Understanding requests for information—How many red apples are there?	Vertical axis	articles
Describing—There are three green apples.		

CONTENT-COMPATIBLE LANGUAGE OBJECTIVE

Functions	Vocabulary	Grammar
Expressing preferences—I like red apples.	apples	Noun/adjective agreement
	pears	
Expressing dislikes—I don't like green apples.	bananas	
	oranges	

Source: Lorenz, E., & Met, M. (1989). *Planning for instruction in the immersion classroom.* Rockville, MD: Montgomery County Public Schools, pp. 28–29.

APPENDIX 4.7 SEMANTIC MAP

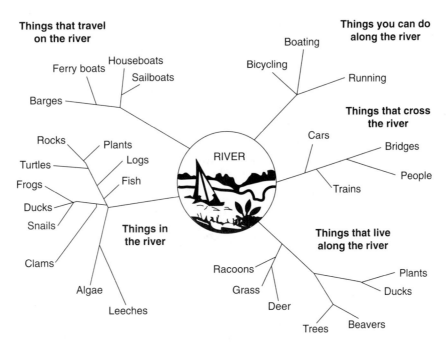

Source: Curtain, H., & Pesola, C. A. B. *Languages and children—Making the match.* Copyright 1994, 1998 by Longman Publishing Group. Used by permission of Addison-Wesley Educational Publishers Inc., p. 167.

APPENDIX 4.8 TREE MAP

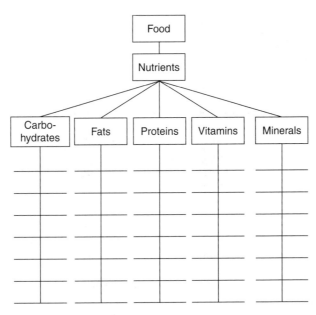

Source: Curtain, H., & Dahlberg, C. A. *Languages and children—Making the match.* Copyright 2004, 1994, 1988 by Pearson Education, Inc., p. 265.

APPENDIX 6.2 INTERACTIVE MODEL USED WITH AN AUTHENTIC SPANISH READING

Interpretive Mode:

Preparation Phase:

You will read a magazine article about a popular Hispanic singer, Shakira. In preparation for reading this article, explore the following questions.

1. What do you know about Shakira?
2. Have you listened to her music? Which songs? Do you like her music? Explain.
3. Glance at the article for 30 seconds. What type of information do you expect to find in this type of article?
4. Why might you be interested in reading this article?
5. Brainstorm some words and expressions you might encounter in this article.

Comprehension Phase:

Main Ideas. Skim the article for one minute and select the subtitle that would best describe it.

_____ **1.** Corazón y cerebro

_____ **2.** Sus preocupaciones

_____ **3.** Su nueva vida como actriz

   Important Details. Work with a classmate to find the following details from the article in Spanish.

1. Cómo aprendió inglés: _____
2. Lo que expresa en español: _____
3. Un premio que había ganado: _____
4. Cómo es ella, según ella misma: _____
5. El origen y significado de su nombre: _____
6. Dónde nació: _____
7. Lo que dice sobre Colombia: _____
8. Algún detalle sobre su familia: _____

   Optional vocabulary work: Review/learn key vocabulary words and/or expressions in the text.

1. Identify five words/expressions that deal with singing, song producing, and artist awards.
2. Identify five words/expressions that deal with faith and/or religion.
3. Identify five adjectives that describe people.
4. Identify two nationalities.
5. Identify three words/expressions that deal with careers/aspirations/dreams.

¡Qué caña!
famosos

Música, deporte, películas, libros, juegos para consola y ordenador, Internet...

Shakira

Sólo los chicos de Operación Triunfo han podido con ella en las listas de ventas. Y, por si fuera poco, su "Servicio de lavandería", su primer disco con canciones en inglés, ya está "centrifugando" a mil revoluciones en EE UU.

Érase una vez...: "Oré y le pedí a Dios que me enviara una buena canción, y recuerdo que, unas horas después, empecé a componer 'Objection', el primer tema de *Servicio de lavandería*".

"My taylor is rich": "Tenía que buscar una manera de expresar mis ideas y mis sentimientos, mis historias del día a día en inglés. Así que compré un par de diccionarios de rima, leí poesía y también a autores como Leonard Cohen y Walt Whitman".

Bilingüe: "Puedo hablar de negocios en inglés, pero lloro, grito y amo en español".

¡Ay, el amor!: "Es imposible no hablar del amor en mis canciones. Es el gran misterio de la vida. Hace que me haga nuevas preguntas todos los días".

Ritmo en el cuerpo: "Soy roquera, pero nadie me gana a bailar salsa, cumbia y valienato" (ritmos latinos muy populares en Colombia).

Un ritual: "Antes de un concierto, rezo el Salmo 91 de la *Biblia*, ese que habla de acogerse a la sombra del Todopoderoso y evitar al león, a la víbora, al cazador".

Se define como... "apasionada y obstinada, pero racional y analítica; o sea, una mujer con corazón, cerebro y coraje".

¡A sus órdenes!: "A mí nadie me obliga a hacer absolutamente nada con lo que no esté de acuerdo. Al menos, en este momento de mi vida...".

Tras el 11 de septiembre... "me preocupa que surjan brotes de xenofobia. Porque yo digo que no todos los árabes son musulmanes, y no todos los musulmanes árabes son terroristas, ni mucho menos. Por ejemplo, yo vengo de una familia libanesa católica, que no es terrorista".

Llanto por Colombia: "Somos una nación con gente pujante, creativa, trabajadora, soñadora, alegre. Sin embargo, cada día tenemos que enterrar a nuestros muertos y procurar mantener la esperanza".

Sueños cumplidos: "Llevo 11 años de carrera y he logrado muchos sueños. No me podía imaginar cuando empezaba, y era una cantante para adolescentes, que terminaría grabando un *MTV Unplugged* (disco acústico grabado en directo)".

¿Y mañana...? "El día que hacer música deje de producirme placer, pues dejaré de componer"

AQUELLOS MARAVILLOSOS AÑOS

1985: Empieza a componer sus primeras canciones. Poco después, con sólo 13 años, comienza a cantar profesionalmente.

1991: Firma su primer contrato con Sony Music y graba su primer álbum: *Magia*.

1993: Alcanza el tercer puesto en el Festival de Viña del Mar (Chile) con la canción "Eres".

1996: Su tercer disco, *Pies descalzos*, vende más de cuatro millones de copias y logra 25 discos de oro y 55 de platino.

1998: Su álbum *¿Dónde están los ladrones?* supera los diez millones de copias vendidas.

2000: Premio "Lo Nuestro" a la Mejor Artista Femenina; premio MTV, y dos Grammy Latino en las categorías de Mejor Interpretación Femenina de Pop y de Rock.

2001: Premio Grammy al Mejor Álbum Pop Latino, y dos premios "Lo Nuestro" en las categorías de Mejor Interpretación Rock y Mejor Álbum Rock. La revista británica Teen People la elige entre las 25 personas más bellas del mundo menores de 25 años.

2002: Su último disco, *Servicio de lavandería (Laundry Service)* vende más de medio millón de copias en España y supera ya los dos millones en Estados Unidos.

Okapi, mayo 2002
8

La foto del mes

okapi es más

DNI

Nombre: Shakira Isabel Mebarak Ripoll. Shakira, en árabe, significa "diosa de la luz".

Nacimiento: Barranquilla (Colombia), 2 de febrero de 1977.

"Grupo sanguíneo": Sangre libanesa, por parte de padre, y colombiana, por parte de madre.

Estado civil: Soltera con compromiso. Su novio, Antonio de la Rúa, de 26 años, es hijo del ex presidente de Argentina, Fernando de la Rúa.

Profesión: Artista, de toda la vida. A los cuatro años de edad ya bailaba la "danza del vientre", rezaba cantando y escribía poemas.

Discos: *Magia* (1991), *Peligro* (1993), *Pies descalzos* (1996), *The Remixes* (1997), *¿Dónde están los ladrones?* (1998), *Shakira MTV Unplugged* (2000) y *Servicio de lavandería* (2001, Columbia).

Interpretive + Interpersonal Modes:

Guessing Vocabulary in Context. Use the context of the article to guess the meaning of the following words. Check your guesses with a classmate and your teacher.

Page 8

Paragraph 3: negocios _____ lloro _____

grito _____

Paragraph 5: roquera _____

Paragraph 9: brotes de xenofobia _____

Paragraph 10: gente pujante _____ soñadora_____

Paragraph 11: he logrado muchos sueños _____

Page 9

grupo sanguíneo _____

Interpretation Phase. Use the following questions to interpret the article in more detail and share your reactions. Share your opinions with a small group of classmates.

1. ¿Qué tipo de persona es Shakira? Explique con ejemplos del artículo.
2. ¿De qué se preocupa en cuanto al 11 de septiembre?
3. Describa la etnicidad de Shakira.
4. En su opinión, ¿qué influencia ha tenido su origen hispano en su carrera y en el éxito que ha tenido?
5. ¿Qué otra información le gustaría saber sobre Shakira?

Interpersonal Task: Role Play

Student A: You are a reporter for a popular Hispanic teen magazine (your Spanish study has paid off!) and have pulled some strings to get an exclusive interview with Shakira! Ask her six questions (three might be questions taken from the article, but three should be new ones). Be sure to obtain information that would be of interest to your teenage readers!

Student B: You are Shakira's public relations manager. Shakira was scheduled to be interviewed by a Hispanic teen magazine today, but unfortunately she is sick. Shakira has asked you to participate in the interview in her place, since you also speak Spanish and know her so well. Give details that you think Shakira's teenage fans will enjoy!

Presentational Mode:

Application Phase:

Oral: Answering Machine Message. Leave a three-minute message in Spanish in which you tell your best friend about your exciting interview with Shakira. Share the most exciting information that you learned about her. Ask your friend to return the call so that you can tell him/her the rest of the story.

Written: Magazine Article. Using some information from the article you read and the additional information from your exclusive interview, write a feature article about Shakira for your Hispanic teen magazine. Pay attention to the layout of the article: Use subtitles and perhaps some photos. Write at least 200 words in Spanish and use five new words/expressions (that you learned in the original article). Ask a classmate to read your first draft and respond to the content and accuracy.

Interpretive Mode (*revisited*):

Extension Phase: (Exploring intertextuality)

Access the website http://www.mtv.es and find out more information about Shakira. You can also listen to some of her songs! Share additional details about Shakira and her life with a group of classmates.

> Source of lesson: Glisan, 2004, original material
> Source of reading:
> *Okapi es más.* Mayo 2002. Bayard Revistas. Madrid, España, pp. 8–9

APPENDIX 7.1.0 SAMPLE LESSON IN STORY-BASED LANGUAGE LEARNING: PACE MODEL

OBJECTIVES:
Functional: The learners will listen to and comprehend a narrative in the past tense. Learners will tell a story using past narration.

Performance:
Interpretive Mode: Learners listen to "Le lion et la souris" as the teacher uses puppets and other props to tell the story. Learners identify new vocabulary through puppets and pictures and read a text in past narration.
Interpretive Mode: Learners retell the story using puppets or pictures. Learners write events of the story using various graphic organizers and other learning activities.
Presentational Mode: Learners create an original poem and read it to the class.

Grammatical: Learners recognize forms of the *passé composé* and practice using it.

Vocabulary: Learners recognize nouns needed to comprehend the story by identifying puppets and pictures and later retelling the story using these props.

Cultural: Learners become familiar with the fable genre and the author, La Fontaine, when using "The Fox and the Crow" (Appendix 7.1.1, on the Web site). Learners recognize acceptable behavior through animal allegory.

MATERIALS:
Puppets, props, pictures, scrambled sentences, graphic organizers, transparencies, colored markers

PROCEDURES:
Day 1 Anticipatory set: Using pictures of unfamiliar nouns, students identify and learn vocabulary necessary to comprehend the story. They guess at the context (Appendix 7.1.2, on the Web site).

PRESENTATION:

Interpretive Mode: The teacher tells the story in the present tense using puppets, pictures, and gestures. The teacher verifies comprehension through comprehension checks (yes/no questions or signaling with thumbs up/thumbs down); some learners will participate in dramatizing the story. In groups, learners unscramble pictures from the story, putting the events in chronological order. The teacher distributes a copy of the story (Appendix 7.1.2, on the Web site) and the vocabulary reference (Appendix 7.1.3, on the Web site). If time, learners read the story, asking the teacher for help when necessary. Homework: Finish reading the story and make a list of all the -er verbs in the text.

Day 2: Presentation (continued): Interpretive Mode: Using pictures (Appendix 7.1.4, on the Web site) and props, as well as some learners acting as characters, the teacher retells the story (this time in the past tense). Also, this time the teacher leaves out certain key words that learners provide, thus letting the class participate in retelling the story.

See Appendices 7.1.15 through 7.1.21 for a continuation of this PACE lesson.

APPENDIX 8.7 "TALK SCORES": MONITORING AND EVALUATING GROUP SPEAKING ACTIVITIES

What: An uncomplicated way to assess student performance during small group activities.

When: As often as possible and as much as you can observe during a group activity.

Why: Often we have subjective impressions (often correct!!!) about a student's level of participation, cooperation, performance. The TALK SCORES allow you to compare your impressions with real classroom performance.

How: Each letter of the word *TALK* represents one PERFORMANCE OBJECTIVE to be observed during small group activity. During an activity, the teacher should select only ONE objective to observe. The goal should be that at the end of one or two weeks, students have been observed for ALL FOUR performance objectives (a "round)".

PERFORMANCE OBJECTIVES:

T = TALKING IN THE TARGET LANGUAGE
Is the student TALKING in the target language?
Is the student TRYING to communicate?
Is the talk TASK RELEVANT?

A = ACCURATE
Is the student performing at an ACCEPTABLE level of ACCURACY?
Does the student demonstrate the objective of the lesson that is being used in this activity (i.e., grammar focus, vocabulary, language function)?

NB Total accuracy is not to be expected but you should have a clear idea of what language elements you will observe. For example, in an activity that requires students to use "time," the teacher could observe how accurately students are constructing time expression (It's 2:30, 3:45, etc.).

L = LISTENING
Is the student ON TASK?
Does the student LISTEN to his/her partner or partners?
Does the student LISTEN to directions?

K = KIND
> Is the student KIND and COOPERATIVE?
> Does the student KILL the activity by his/her lack of cooperation?
> Does the student work with his/her group?

PROCEDURES:
During an activity, circulate around the room observing for ONE performance objective for each activity (T, A, L, or K). Record in your grade book the objective you are observing, the date, and the activity:

EXAMPLE:
Obj. – T
date – 9/18/2003
Act. – ex. c page 12—partner practice

In other words, on September 18, 2003, you decided that this activity was a good one to use for observations on TRYING TO TALK IN THE TARGET LANGUAGE.

You should try to cover all four objectives over a two-week period. Again, covering all four objectives is called a round. As your grade book fills up with scores for students, you *will begin to see* students who need more observation and students whom maybe you should observe less often. For example, if at the end of the week Mary Leech has been observed for three objectives while John Arnold has been observed for only one, that will indicate that John needs more of your attention. The goal is that when it is time to compute scores you have an equal number of rounds for each student (e.g., two T scores, two A scores, two L scores, two K scores).

SCORING:

For each objective, score with either a "+", "✓", or "–"

Example

T+	A–	L✓	K+

Plus ("+") scores are worth 2 points   ➜ EXCELLENT
Check ("✓") scores are worth 1 point   ➜ GOOD TO FAIR
Minus ("–") scores are worth 0 points   ➜ NEEDS WORK

For *one round of scoring* (one T, A, L, K) the following grade conversions can be use:

POINTS

7–8	=	A
5–6	=	B
3–4	=	C
1–2	=	D
0	=	F

At the end of a round you will have a PROFILE of a student's activity during pair or group work (See sample grade book page). You may want to experiment with observing more than one objective per activity or per student.

Class: Spanish 2003–2004						
	T	A	L	K		
NAMES					Round one	Grade
Jason	T✓	A−	L−	K+	3	C
Ann	T−	A−	L✓	K+	3	C
John	T+	A+	L+	K−	6	B+
Kelly	T+	A−	L+	K✓	5	B
Mark	T−	A−	L+	K+	4	C+
Kelly	T+	A+	L+	K+	8	A+
Jen	T✓	A+	L+	K+	7	A
Robert	T+	A−	L−	K✓	3	C
Sharon	T✓	A+	L+	K+	7	A
	ex. C p.12 partner practices	Time activity	info-gap activity	peer correction of HW assign.		

Source: Donato, 2004, original material.

APPENDIX 9.7 PEER AND SELF ANALYSIS WORKSHEET FOR PEER REVISION

Worksheet for Peer-Analysis

Your analysis should be one page long. You will need to hand in two copies, one for the writer and one for the instructor. You should clearly indicate at the top of the page the following information: your name, the name of the writer, the title of the composition, and the question being addressed.

Begin your analysis with a general paragraph stating the topic of the composition, its strong points, and any areas that need improvement. Remember to keep your language positive. This paragraph can only be written after you have answered the following questions.

(These questions should be answered and included in your peer analysis.)

1. What is the topic and purpose of this composition? Is it clear? Would you have known what the writer was talking about if you had not know what the question was?
2. Does this composition seem to be well organized? Does it have a clear beginning and end?

3. Is there logic to the argument? Is it well supported with examples or pertinent details? On the other hand, are there irrelevant details?
4. Is this composition interesting? If not, what might the author add to make it more interesting?
5. Are there areas that needed more information?
6. Is the title appropriate to the composition?
7. What are the strong points to this composition?
8. Make one or two concrete suggestions for improvement.

See the attachment for a sample composition and sample peer analysis.

Worksheet for Self-Analysis

There are three sections to this assignment. In the first, you will assess the structural and logical characteristics of your composition. In the second, you will reflect on the grammatical accuracy of the composition. In the third, you will summarize the results of the your analysis.

It is important for you to read the composition carefully and thoroughly in order to answer the following questions. Thus, you should begin the analysis at least 24 hours after having finished writing the composition. Additionally, you should take a break of at least 2 hours between the first two sections of this assignment.

After you have completed this assignment, you should make whatever corrections you feel are necessary to your composition. You will hand in your summary to the instructor along with your preliminary composition. (Remember also that you will hand in a copy of the preliminary composition to a classmate.)

I. Content analysis
1. What is the topic or purpose of your composition? Is it stated clearly in the first paragraph?
2. Does this composition seem to be well organized? Does it have a clear beginning and end?
3. Have you included enough details to support your argument? Any details you would leave out?
4. Do you think you would find this composition interesting as a reader?
5. Does the title reflect the content of the composition?
6. What do you like best about this composition?

II. Form analysis
1. Carefully check the gender and number of all nouns used in the composition. Make sure they agree with their articles and adjectives.
2. Carefully identity all verbs and their corresponding subjects in the composition. Make sure they agree in number and person.
3. If you have used *ser* or *estar,* double check to make sure you are using them correctly.
4. If you have used the past tense, make sure you have correctly distinguished between the imperfect and preterite.
5. If there is any vocabulary you are unsure of, try to verify your usage using two different sources (for example, a Spanish only dictionary, your instructor).

III. Summary
Briefly summarize (1-2 paragraphs) any changes you made to the composition based on the questions in I and II. Hand in this typed summary to your instructor.

Source: Roebuck, R. (2001). Teaching composition in the college level foreign language class: Insights and activities from sociocultural theory. *Foreign Language Annals, 34,* 206–215.

APPENDIX 9.13 MULTIMEDIA RUBRIC

Presenter _____   *Place a checkmark in the box that best describes each topic*   wziegler@stewireless.com   rziegler@esu8.org

Topic/Content	Learning	Progressing	Proficient	Excelling
Idea Development	Student selects a topic unrelated to the unit theme.	The student's topic related to the unit theme. Topic is too narrow or too broad for the level or time provided for the project.	Student selects topic or theme consistent with unit theme. There is a clear understanding of appropriate depth.	Student selects topic or theme consistent with unit theme and clearly identifies the theme to the reader.
Audience	Consideration for the audience appears to be missing.	The students develop the presentation without a theme or audience in mind.	The project is at the correct level of learning for this audience. The demonstration of learning is appropriate for the audience.	The information speaks clearly to the presentation audience. The presentation stretches the audiences' knowledge or imagination.
Organization	The information sequences appear to be out of order with details missing the beginning/middle and end. The presentation appears confused.	The information sequences and details have some order. The beginning/ middle and end of the presentation have some structure.	The information sequencing, details and summary encourage the viewer to continue learning from the presentation. There is clear development of beginning, middle and end.	The information sequence, introduction, summary, and closing invite the audience to continue learning through the presentation.
Content	The information is inaccurate and/or has no cited references as to source.	The information may be accurate; information sources may be referenced.	The content meets the learning goals. Accuracy is apparent in the presentation of the information. Sources cited identify location of the information used to develop the presentation.	The content presented meets the intended learning goals with the information clearly documented as to accuracy and source. Appropriate and consistent voice.
Media Selection	The media selected for the presentation interferes with learning about the topic.	The media selected limits learning about the topic.	The media selected helps the student share their information, knowledge or opinions in a pleasing, appropriate and purposeful manner.	The media selected enhances the content presented in the presentation.
Design	The media elements limit and/or confuse learning about the topic.	The media elements are more important than the content of the presentation.	The media elements (colors, balance, animation, font, graphics and/or special effects) contribute to the presentation of the content.	The media elements included in the presentation accent the media information presented.
Media Manipulation	The media takes center stage with little focus on the content. The media becomes a distraction.	The audience focuses on the media and the media transitions making focus on the content difficult.	The focus of the presentation centers on the content rather than on the media used to present the information.	The audience focuses on the content. The media is seamless and invisible, thus allowing the viewer to learn and enjoy the presentation.
Assessment	The learner missed the unit learning goals. The learner's understanding of their performance is missing.	The learner mastered few of the unit learning goals. The learner's understanding of their performance is beginning to develop.	The student demonstrates understanding, applies content and skills appropriately and measures the learning gained in this unit by using a rubric.	The learner's presentation meets the unit learning goals The learner can identify/ analyze and defend why their presentation received the ranking.

Source: Zeigler & Zeigler, 2000.

APPENDIX 11.3 GENERATING PERFORMANCE DIMENSIONS FOR A RUBRIC

If the Task has these elements . . .	then consider these as possible dimensions:
Oral Presentation	Voice projection Body language Grammar and pronunciation Organization
PowerPoint or HyperStudio Presentation	Technical quality Aesthetics Grammar and spelling
Written products	Grammar and spelling Organization Formatting
Creative products	Surprisingness, novelty Technical quality Adherence to conventions of the genre
Collaboration	Cooperation Taking responsibility Conflict resolution
Design	Solution effectiveness Solution creativity Justification of solution
Persuasion	Quality of argument Match of appeal to audience Organization & sequence
Analysis (Scientific or otherwise)	Data gathering and analysis Inferences made
Judgment	Adequacy of elements considered Articulation of ranking criteria
Compilation	Selection criteria Organization
Journalism	Accuracy Organization Completeness

Source: San Diego State University, 2001a. Retrieved on April 5, 2004, from http://webquest.sdsu.edu/rubrics/rubrics.html.

APPENDIX 11.15 CLASSROOM ASSESSMENT TECHNIQUE (CAT) USED IN SPANISH COMPOSITION

One-Minute Papers

Minute Paper (1): Proofreading and Using a Bilingual Dictionary

    A. About proofreading in Spanish, I have learned …
    B. About proofreading, I still don't understand …
    C. About using a bilingual dictionary, I have learned …
    D. About using a bilingual dictionary, I still don't understand …

Minute Paper (2): Accent Marks
    About accent marks (choose 1)
      ☐ I understood how to use them before the lesson.
      ☐ I understand them better now.
      ☐ I am still confused about …

Long Minute Paper (3): Survey on Nouns in Spanish
    1. About the gender of nouns I *already knew* how to predict the gender of nouns ending in …
      (circle all that apply)   -a -o -dad -tad -tud -ista -sión -ción -umbre.
    2. About the gender of nouns I have learned …
    3. I am still confused about nouns ending in …
    4. About animate nouns (nous that represent people and animals) I have learned …
    5. About animate nouns I am still confused by …
    6. *Before* the lesson on nouns I used my dictionary to find out the gender of a noun
      ☐ frequently   ☐ never   ☐ only when …
    7. In the future I will use my dictionary to look up nouns that …
    8. About making nouns plural I have learned …
    9. About making nouns plural I still don't understand …
    10. Other comments on your knowledge or the lesson …

Source: Carduner, J. (2002). Using classroom assessment techniques to improve foreign language composition courses. *Foreign Language Annals, 35,* 543–553.

Credits

This page constitutes an extension of the copyright page. We have made every effort to trace the ownership of all copyrighted material and to secure permission from copyright holders. In the event of any question arising as to the use of any material, we will be pleased to make the necessary corrections in future printings. Thanks are due to the following authors, publishers, and agents for permission to use the material indicated.

Chapter 1. 3: M. Celce-Murcia, Z. Dornyei, and S. Thurrell, "Communicative competence: A pedagogically motivated model with content specifications," *Issues in Applied Linguistics*, 6, 5-35, p. 20. Used by permission of the McGraw-Hill Companies. **12:** Bonnie Adair-Hauck, 1995, "Exploring language and cognitive development within the zone of proximal development." Paper presented at the University of Pittsburgh. Used by permission of the author.

Chapter 2. 45, 46, 48: *Standards for Foreign Language Learning in the 21st Century*, 1999. Used by permission of ACTFL.

Chapter 3. 67: *Standards for Foreign Language Learning in the 21st Century*, 1999, p. 28. Used by permission of ACTFL. **78:** M. Met, "Making Connections," in Phillips and Terry, eds., *Foreign Language Standards: Linking Research, Theories, and Practices*, p. 137-164. Used by permission of the McGraw-Hill Companies. **82, 83:** *Nebraska K-12 Foreign Language Frameworks*. Used by permission of the Nebraska Department of Education. **89:** *ACTFL Professional Issues Report*, 1996, p. 68. Used by permission of ACTFL.

Chapter 4. 101, 108, 109: H.A. Curtain and C.A. Dahlberg, *Languages and Children - Making the Match*, 3rd ed., 2004. Published by Allyn & Bacon, Boston, MA. Copyright © 2004 Pearson Education. Adapted by permission of the publisher.

Chapter 5. 135: H.A. Curtain and C.A. Dahlberg, *Languages and Children - Making the Match*, 3rd ed., 2004, p. 228. Reprinted by permission of Jessica Haxhi. **135:** *Standards for Foreign Language Learning in the 21st Century*, 1999, p. 47. Used by permission of ACTFL. **138:** I. Kaplan, "Activities to Integrate Culture into the Classroom," 1997. Paper presented at the American Association of Teachers of Spanish and Portuguese Pedagogy Summit. Used by permission. **140:** D.A. Wright, "Fostering cross-cultural adaptability through foreign language study," *NECTFL Review* 52, 36-39, p. 37. Used by permission of the *NECTFL Review*. **143, 149:** Kentucky Multiple Entry Points Charts, 2004. Used by permission of the Kentucky Department of Education. **144:** M.P. Coblin, et al., "A Standards-Based Thematic Unit: Crictor," 1998, p. 2. Used by permission of Marcia Harmon Rosenbusch, Director, National K-12 Foreign Language Resource Center, Iowa State University.

Chapter 6. 157, 176: *Standards for Foreign Language Learning in the 21st Century*, 1999. Used by permission of ACTFL. **164:** S.M. Bacon, "Phases of listening to authentic input in Spanish: A descriptive study," *Foreign Language Annals*, 25, 317-334, 1992, p. 327. Used by permission of ACTFL. **165:** L. Vandergrift, "The Cinderella of communication strategies: Reception strategies in interactive listening," *Modern Language Journal*, 81, 494-505, 1997, p. 497. Used by permission.

Chapter 7. 193: Bonnie Adair-Hauck, 1993, *A Descriptive Analysis of a Whole Language/Guided Participatory versus Explicit Teaching Strategies in Foreign Language Instruction*, p. 6. Used by permission of the author. **200, 201:** R. Donato and B. Adair-Hauck, "PACE: A model to focus on form," 1994. Paper presented at the annual meeting of the ACTFL. Used by permission of Bonnie Adair-Hauck.

Chapter 8. 217, 218, 219: E. Swender, *ACTFL Oral Proficiency Interview Tester Training Manual*, 1999. Used by permission of ACTFL. **220, 221:** E. Tschirner and L.K. Heilenman, "Reasonable expectations: Oral proficiency goals for intermediate-level students of German," *Modern Language Journal*, 82, 147-158, 1998. Used by permission of Blackwell Publishing. **234:** J. Lee, "Using task-based instruction to restructure class discussions," *Foreign Language Annals*, 28, 437-446, 1995, p. 444. Used by permission of ACTFL. **240, 241:** J. Walz, "The classroom dynamics of information-gap activities," *Foreign Language Annals*, 29, 481-494, 1996. Used by permission of ACTFL. **249:** S.F. Peregoy and O.F. Boyle, *Reading, Writing and Learning in ESL: A Resource Book for K-12 Teachers*, 3rd ed., 2001. Published by Allyn & Bacon, Boston, MA. Copyright © 2001 Pearson Education. Used by permission of the publisher.

Chapter 9. 269: L. Flower and J.R. Hayes, "A cognitive process theory of writing," *College Composition and Communication*, 32, 365-387, 1981, p. 370. Copyright © 1981 by the National Council of Teachers of English. Reprinted with permission. **278:** Adapted from J.F. Lee and B. VanPatten, *Making Communicative Language Teaching Happen*, 3rd ed., p. 252-253. Used by permission of the McGraw-Hill Companies. **283:** ACTFL Proficiency Guidelines, 2001, p. 7. Used by permission of ACTFL. **284:** H.A. Curtain and C.A. Dahlberg,

Languages and Children - Making the Match, 3rd ed., 2004, p. 75. Copyright © 2004 Pearson Education. Adapted by permission of the publisher. **286, 294:** S.F. Peregoy and O.F. Boyle, *Reading, Writing and Learning in ESL: A Resource Book for K-12 Teachers*, 3rd ed., 2001. Published by Allyn & Bacon, Boston, MA. Copyright © 2001 Pearson Education. Adapted by permission of the publisher. **296, 298:** K. Hyland, *Second Language Writing*, 2003. Reprinted with permission of Cambridge University Press. **302:** M. Espinosa-Dulanto, "Evocando y paso a paso avanzando: A creative writing project for Spanish," CALPER Pedagogical Materials: Project Work, No. 3, 2003, p. 7. Copyright © 2003 Center for Advanced Proficiency Education and Research (CALPER) The Pennsylvania State University, http://calper.la.psu.edu. Reprinted by permission. **304:** G. Appel, "13 Jahre Deutsche Vereinigung: A sample project for advanced learners of German," CALPER Pedagogical Materials: Project Work, No. 2, 2003, p. 4. Copyright © 2003 Center for Advanced Proficiency Education and Research (CALPER) The Pennsylvania State University, http://calper.la.psu.edu. Reprinted by permission.

Chapter 10. 322: J. Alatis and S. Barnhardt, eds., *Portfolio Assessment in the Modern Language Classroom*, 1998, National Capital Language Resource Center, Washington, D.C. Used by permission. **336:** *Standards for Foreign Language Learning in the 21st Century*, 1999, p. 19. Used by permission of ACTFL. **338:** G. Valdes, "The Teaching of Minority Languages as Academic Subjects: Pedagogical and Theoretical Challenges," *Modern Language Journal*, 79, 299-328, 1995, p. 309. Used by permission. **339:** C. Rodriquez Pino, "La reconceptualizacion del programa espanol para hispanohablantes: Estrategias que reflejan la realidad sociolinguistica de la clase." In Colombi and Alaracon, eds, *La Ensenanza del Espanol a Hispanohablantes: Praxis y Teoria*, p. 65-82, 1997, p. 72. Boston: Houghton-Mifflin. Used by permission. **343:** D.M. Overfield, "From the margins to the mainstream: Foreign language education and community-based learning," *Foreign Language Annals*, 30, 485-491, 1997, p. 486. Used by permission of ACTFL.

Chapter 11. 366, 367: J.E. Liskin-Gasparro, "Authentic Assessment: Promises, possibilities and processes," p. 1-15. Presentation at University of Wisconsin-EU Claire, August, 1997. Used by permission of the author. **368, 369:** G. Tulou and F. Pettigrew, "Performance assessment for language students." In M.A. Kassen, ed., *Language Learners of Tomorrow: Process and Promise*, p. 193-194, National Textbook Company, 1999. Used by permission of the McGraw-Hill Companies. **372, 374, 401:** Adapted from Center on Learning, Assessment, and School Structure, "Developing authentic performance assessments," 1998. Paper presented at meeting of ACTFL Beyond the OPI Assessment Group. Used with permission. **379:** Glisan, et al., *ACTFL Integrated Performance Assessment*, 2003. Used by permission of ACTFL. **381:** G. Wiggins, "Teaching to the (authentic) test," *Educational Leadership*, 46, 41-47, 1998. Used by permission of John Wiley and Sons. **383:** *Portfolio Assessment in the Foreign Language Classroom*, 2004, National Capital Language Resource Center, Washington, D.C. Used by permission. **390:** From H.A. Curtain and C.A. Dahlberg, *Languages and Children - Making the Match*, 3rd ed., 2004, p. 168. Reprinted by permission of Jessica Haxhi. **392:** Antonew, et al., "Interactive homework: Creating connections between home and school." In A. Mollica, ed., *Teaching Languages - Selected Readings from Mosaic*, p. 169-184, 1997, p. 175. Lewiston, NY: Soleil Publishing, Inc. Used by permission.

Chapter 12. 418: L.C. Jones and J.L. Plass, "Supporting listening comprehension and vocabulary acquisition in French with multimedia annotations," *Modern Language Journal*, 86, 546-561, 2002, p. 551. Used by permission of Blackwell Publishing. **428, 429:** From Tom March, 2004, http://www.ozline.com. Used by permission.

Appendices. 471: J. Carduner, "Using classroom assessment techniques to improve foreign language composition courses," *Foreign Language Annals* 35, 543-553. Used by permission of ACTFL. **470:** San Diego State University, http://webquest.sdsu.edu/rubrics/rubrics.html, April 5, 2004. Used by permission of Dr. Bernie Dodge. **449, 451, 452-454:** *Nebraska K-12 Foreign Language Frameworks*. Used by permission of the Nebraska Department of Education. **457, 459:** H.A. Curtain and C.A. Dahlberg, *Languages and Children - Making the Match*, 3rd ed., 2004. Published by Allyn & Bacon, Boston, MA. Copyright © 2004 Pearson Education. Adapted by permission of the publisher. **457:** Lorenz and Met, "Planning for instruction in the immersion classroom," Montgomery County Public Schools, Rockville, MD, 1989, pp. 28-29. Used by permission. **461:** From *Okapi es mas*, May 2002. Used with permission. **465:** R. Donato, B. Adair-Hauck, & P. Cumo-Johanssen, 2000, in Shrum & Glisan, *Teacher's Handbook*. Boston: Heinle & Heinle. Used by permission. **466:** Used by permission of Richard Donato. **469:** Used by permission of Ziegler and Ziegler, Learning for the Future. **468:** Adapted from J.F. Lalande, II, "Reducing Composition Errors: An Experiment," *Foreign Language Annals* 17, 109-117, 1984. Used by permission of ACTFL.

Index

AAAL (American Association for Applied Linguistics), 4
Acceleration, 333
Acquisition-Learning Hypothesis (Krashen), 14
ACTFL (American Council on the Teaching of Foreign Languages), 2
  performance guidelines, 47
  speaking proficiency guidelines, 43, 85, 215–216, 217. *See also* Oral Proficiency Interview (OPI)
  standards, 8
  writing proficiency guidelines, 282, 283
Actional competence, 14
Adair-Hauck, B., 192, 193
ADFL (Association of Departments of Foreign Languages), 2
Advance organizers, 85–86
Affect, role of, 28–30
Affective Filter Hypothesis (Dulay and Burt), 28
Affective Filter Hypothesis (Krashen), 15
Age, language acquisition and, 96–97
Alatis, J., 321
Alvermann, D., 203
American Association for Applied Linguistics (AAAL), 4
American Council on the Teaching of Foreign Languages. *See* ACTFL
American Sign Language Teachers Association (ASLTA), 4
Amores, M.J., 299
Analytic-global learning style, 318, 320
Analytic rating systems, 300
Antonek, J.L., 391, 392
Anxiety, in learners, 29, 166
Asher, J., 42, 111–112
ASLTA (American Sign Language Teachers Association), 4
Assessment(s)
  authentic. *See* Authentic assessment
  characteristics of, 364–365
  classroom, 393–395, 471
  direct, 362
  at elementary school level, 116–119
  formative, 360–362
  integrative-global, 362, 363
  interactive, 367–370
  by learner, 389, 390
  at middle school level, 145–146
  natural-situational, 362
  paradigm shift in, 356–359
  performance-based, 366–367. *See also* Authentic assessment
  planning for, 397–398
  of portfolios, 382–388, 401–402
  proachievement, 364–365
  purposes of, 360
  of speaking skills, 217–222
  standards-based, 359, 378–382
  student empowerment through, 382–394
  summative, 360–362

traditional vs. portfolio, 383
  See also Tests
Association of Departments of Foreign Languages (ADFL), 2
Astin, A.W., 344
At-risk students, 330–332
Atajo, 290
Atlas Complex, 68
Audiolingual Method, 41
Audiotapes, 180, 416
Auditory learning style, 319, 320
Ausubel, D., 85–86, 445
Authentic assessment
  converting rubric scores to grades in, 376–377
  defined, 359, 371
  developing tasks for, 399–401
  rubric design for, 374–376, 399–401, 470
  rubrics for scoring in, 372–374
  sample task, 372
Authentic materials
  defined, 73–74
  as language samples, 73–74
  for listening and reading, 73, 170–173, 180
  simplifying, 170–171
Automatic processes, 17, 18
Aziz, L., 273

Bacon, S.M., 163, 164
Ballman, T.L., 85
Barrett, H.C., 388
Bernhart, E.B., 160
Bialystok, E., 190
Binding, 15
Block schedules, 88–90
Blogs, 424
Bloom's Taxonomy of Thinking. *See* Taxonomy of Thinking (Bloom)
Borich, J.M.B., 249
Bottom-up approach, 51–52, 158–159
Bragger, J., 79, 223
Broner, M.A., 27
Brooks, F.B., 240–241
Buckwalter, P., 232–233
Burt, M., 28

CAL (Center for Applied Linguistics), 6
CALICO (Computer Assisted Language Instruction Consortium), 4
CALL (Computer-Assisted Language Learning), 408
  See also TELL
Canale, M., 281
Carduner, J., 471
Carrell, P.L., 73
CATs. *See* Classroom assessment techniques
CBI. *See* Content-based instruction
CCAI (Cross-Cultural Adaptability Inventory), 135, 140
Celce-Murcia, M., 13
Center for Applied Linguistics (CAL), 6
Chandler, J., 296–297

Character mapping, 202
Chat rooms, 251–252, 423–424, 425
Children's literature, in the target language, 113
Chomsky, N., 12–13, 41–42
Class schedules, lesson planning and, 88–90
Classroom assessment techniques (CATs), 393–395, 471
Classroom management, 133
Classroom talk, 70–71, 225–228, 252–256
Clément, R., 29
Closure, orientation to, 319
Cognitive approach, 41–42
Cognitive involvement, 109
Cognitive styles, role of, 29
Cohen, A.D., 291, 362, 363
Coherence, in presentational communications, 281–282
Cohesive devices, 281
Communication
  cognitive involvement in, 109
  defined, 189
  integrating modes of, 176–179, 460–464
  modes of, 154–158
  See also Interpersonal communication; Interpretive communication; Presentational communication
Communication Goal, of *SFLL,* 189–191
Communicative approach, 42
Communicative competence, 13–14
Communities Goal, of *SFLL,* 342–344
Community-based learning, 343–344, 345–346
Community Language Learning (Curran), 42, 446
Compacting, 333
Comparisons Goal, of *SFLL,* 137–141
Competence, 12–14, 27–28
Competition-cooperation, in learning, 319
Comprehension
  anxiety and, 166
  authentic texts and, 170–173
  listener-based variables in, 162–166
  "look-back-and-lift-off" approach, 179
  purpose and, 166
  reader-based variables in, 162–166
  short-term memory in, 163
  strategies for, 163–165
  technological assistance for, 417–419
  text-based factors in, 167–170
  topic familiarity in, 162–163
  See also Listening skills; Reading skills
Computer Assisted Language Instruction Consortium (CALICO), 4
Computer-Assisted Language Learning (CALL), 408
  See also TELL (Technology Enhanced Language Learning)
Computer-mediated communication
  asynchronous, 424–426. *See also* E-mail
  benefits of, 421
  forms of, 422
  synchronous, 251–252, 422–424

Student Oral Proficiency Assessment (SOPA), 118
Suggestopedia (Lozanov), 42, 446
Summative assessment, 117
Swaffar, J., 369–370
Swain, M., 20
Swender, E., 216, 222–223
Systéme-D, 290

Talk Scores technique (Donato), 466–467
Target language (TL), 12, 148–150
Task-based instruction, 233–235
Taxonomy of Thinking (Bloom), 84, 454–456
Taylor, B.P., 229
Teacher feedback
  content-focused, 293–294
  form-focused, 294–295
  on multimedia presentations, 303, 469
  on oral presentations, 301–304
  for presentational writing, 291–296
  student responses to, 296–297
  types of, 252–256, 443
  vs. evaluation, 70–73
Teacher-student style conflicts, 319–321
Teacher talk, 69–70
Teachers of English to Speakers of Other Languages (TESOL), 3–4, 8, 48–49
Teaching styles, 319–321
Technological tools
  future of, 430–431
  listening assistant, 417–419
  multimedia center, 415–416
  online dictionaries, 420–421
  overhead projectors, 415
  in presentational communication, 288–291, 303
  reading assistant, 416–417
  smartboard, 415
  translation programs, 420–421
  types of, 414
  video materials, 416
  Web-enhanced, 426–430, 433–437
  See also TELL
Technology Enhanced Language Learning. *See* TELL
Technology Literacy Challenge, 407
TELL (Technology Enhanced Language Learning), 408
  classroom implementation of, 411–413, 431
  classroom research on, 410–411
  See also NETS (National Educational Technology Standards)
Terrell, T.D., 15
TESOL (Teachers of English to Speakers of Other Languages), 3–4, 8, 48–49
Tests
  analyzing, 398–399
  authentic. *See* Authentic assessment
  discrete-point, 362–363
  impact on curriculum, 358
  integrative/global, 363
  interactive, 367–370
  item types on, 362–363
  performance-based, 366–367
  proachievement, 364–365
  purposes of, 360

types of, 360
washback effect of, 358
See also Assessment(s)
Text
  content and interest level of, 168
  length of, 167
  new vocabulary in, 168–169
  organization of, 167–168
  for story-based approach, 201–202
Textbooks
  contextualized exercises in, 59–60
  evaluating, 56, 59–60
  grammar presentations in, 206
  integrating into classroom, 73–77
  role of, 55–57
  Spanish, example of, 74–77
Tharp, R.G., 225–226
Thematic units, 107–108, 457
Think-pair-share, 236
Threaded discussions, 425
Three P's, 134–135, 146, 147
Tilley-Lubbs, G.A., 344
TL. *See* Target language (TL)
Tomlinson, C.A., 340–341
Top-down approach, 52–55
  ESL lesson using, 61–63
  to listening and reading, 158–160
Topic familiarity. *See* Context
Topicalization hypothesis, 243
Total Physical Response (TPR) Method (Asher), 42, 111–112, 445
Toth, P., 69–70
Transformation, 24–25
Translation programs, 420–421
Travel unit, 54
Turn-taking, 228

U-shaped behavior, 18
Units
  fantasy experience, 116
  global, 116
  sample plan for, 452–454
  thematic, 81–84, 452–454
  vacation and travel, 54
U.S. Department of Education, 6
U.S. English group, 335

Vacation unit, 54
Valdés, G., 336
Validity, 360
Values Orientation Method (Kluckhohn), 137
Vandergrift, L., 117, 163
VanPatten, B., 16–17, 68
Variable Competence Model (Bialystok), 190
Venn diagrams, 111
Video, 416
  authentic, 180
  effectiveness of, 161–162
  integrating into language instruction, 232–233
Viewing process, 161–162
Villamil, O., 299
Visual learning style, 319, 320
Visually impaired learners, 325–326
Vocabulary acquisition, 15–16, 168–169
  contextual cues in, 169

in elementary school learners, 111–112
for presentational communication, 280–281
through reading/listening/viewing, 175–176
Vogely, A.J., 166
Von der Emde, S., 422
Vygotsky, L.S., 21–27, 203

Walz, J., 55, 237–238, 240–241, 359
Washback effect, 358
Way, D.P., 272
Web logs, 425
Web sites
  evaluating, 426
  presentational writing skills and, 291
  template for classroom use, 433–437
  See also WebQuest
Webb, J.B., 337
WebQuest, 426–430, 432
Wells, G., 24
Whispering to self, 232–233
Whole language approach. *See* Story-based approach
Wiggins, G., 371
Wilson-Duffy, C., 233–234
Word processing, 289–290, 419–420
World Languages Other Than English Standards, 8
Writing
  cognitive processes in, 268–270
  as a process, 267, 273
  as a product, 267, 282
  prompts for, 273
  successful vs. unsuccessful, 270
Writing instruction
  conferences for, 295
  dialogue journals in, 248–250
  elementary level, 248–249
  grading methods for, 300–301
  key pal exchanges in, 250–251
  middle school level, 250–251
  pen pal letters in, 250–251
  post-secondary level, 251
  teacher feedback in, 291–295
  See also Interpersonal communication; Presentational communication
Writing skills
  ACTFL proficiency guidelines for, 282
  assessment of, 117–118
  assistant technologies for, 419–420
  presentational. *See* Presentational writing
  See also Interpersonal communication; Presentational communication

Yamada, Y., 251
Year planner, 451
Yorio, C., 264
Ziegler, R., 469
Zone of Proximal Development (ZPD) (Vygotsky), 21–27
  continuous cycle of assistance in, 22–23
  defined, 21
  instructional conversations and, 226
  mediation in, 25–27
  scaffolding in, 23, 443
  transformation in, 24–25
  vs. $i + 1$, 25